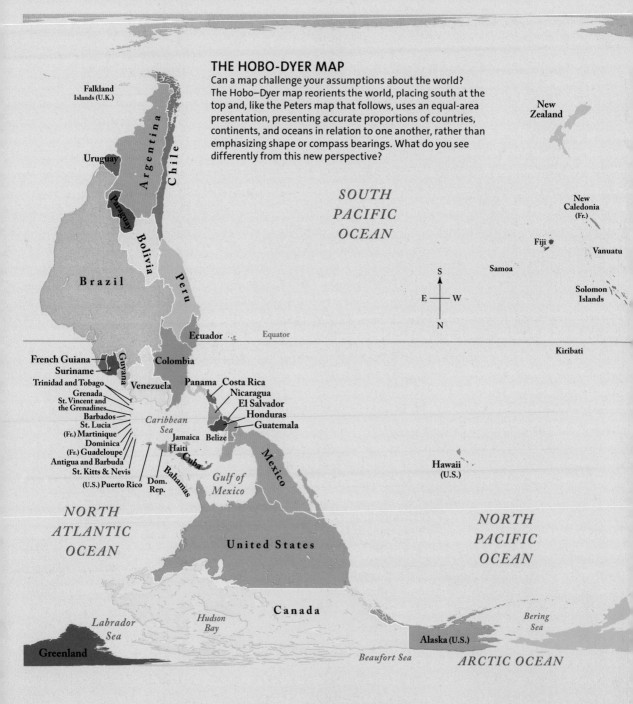

THE HOBO-DYER MAP

Can a map challenge your assumptions about the world?
The Hobo–Dyer map reorients the world, placing south at the
top and, like the Peters map that follows, uses an equal-area
presentation, presenting accurate proportions of countries,
continents, and oceans in relation to one another, rather than
emphasizing shape or compass bearings. What do you see
differently from this new perspective?

Falkland
Islands (U.K.)

Uruguay

Argentina

Chile

Paraguay

Bolivia

Brazil

Peru

Ecuador   Equator

French Guiana
Suriname
Guyana
Trinidad and Tobago
Grenada
St. Vincent and
the Grenadines
Barbados
St. Lucia
(Fr.) Martinique
Dominica
(Fr.) Guadeloupe
Antigua and Barbuda
St. Kitts & Nevis
(U.S.) Puerto Rico

Colombia

Venezuela

Panama   Costa Rica
Nicaragua
El Salvador
Honduras
Guatemala

Caribbean
Sea

Jamaica   Belize
Haiti
Cuba

Dom.
Rep.

Bahamas

Gulf of
Mexico

Mexico

NORTH
ATLANTIC
OCEAN

United States

SOUTH
PACIFIC
OCEAN

New
Zealand

New
Caledonia
(Fr.)

Fiji

Vanuatu

Samoa

S

E   W

N

Solomon
Islands

Kiribati

Hawaii
(U.S.)

NORTH
PACIFIC
OCEAN

Canada

Labrador
Sea

Hudson
Bay

Bering
Sea

Greenland

Alaska (U.S.)

Beaufort Sea   ARCTIC OCEAN

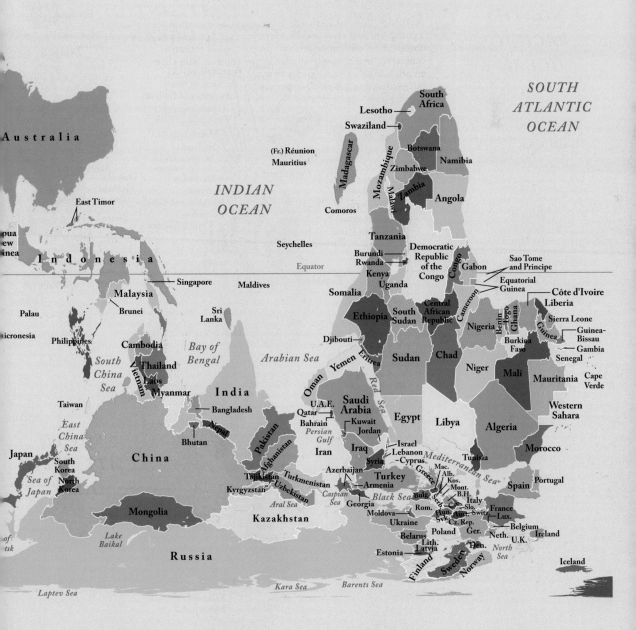

Antarctica

SOUTH
ATLANTIC
OCEAN

Australia

East Timor

Indonesia

Papua
New
Guinea

INDIAN
OCEAN

(Fr.) Réunion
Mauritius

Madagascar

Mozambique

Malawi

Zambia

Zimbabwe

Botswana

South
Africa

Lesotho

Swaziland

Namibia

Angola

Comoros

Equator

Singapore

Maldives

Seychelles

Tanzania

Burundi
Rwanda

Democratic
Republic
of the
Congo

Congo

Gabon

Sao Tome
and Principe

Malaysia

Brunei

Sri
Lanka

Kenya

Uganda

Somalia

South
Sudan

Central
African
Republic

Cameroon

Equatorial
Guinea

Côte d'Ivoire

Liberia

Palau

Micronesia

Philippines

Cambodia

South
China
Sea

Vietnam

Thailand

Laos

Myanmar

Bay of
Bengal

Arabian Sea

Ethiopia

Djibouti

Yemen

Eritrea

Sudan

Chad

Nigeria

Benin
Togo
Ghana

Burkina
Faso

Niger

Mali

Guinea

Sierra Leone

Guinea-
Bissau

Gambia

Senegal

Cape
Verde

Taiwan

East
China
Sea

Japan

South
Korea

North
Korea

Sea of
Japan

China

Mongolia

Lake
Baikal

Bhutan

Nepal

Pakistan

Afghanistan

India

Bangladesh

Oman

U.A.E.

Qatar

Bahrain

Kuwait

Jordan

Saudi
Arabia

Red Sea

Iran

Iraq

Israel

Lebanon

Cyprus

Syria

Egypt

Libya

Mediterranean Sea

Tunisia

Algeria

Morocco

Western
Sahara

Mauritania

Spain

Portugal

Azerbaijan

Armenia

Turkey

Greece

Mac.

Alb.

Kos.

Mont.

B.H.

Italy

Tajikistan

Kyrgyzstan

Uzbekistan

Turkmenistan

Caspian
Sea

Aral Sea

Georgia

Black Sea

Bulg.

Serb.

Rom.

Cro.

Hun.

Svk.

Cz. Rep.

Slo.

Aust.

Switz.

France

Lux.

Belgium

Neth.

U.K.

Ireland

Kazakhstan

Moldova

Ukraine

Poland

Ger.

Den.

North
Sea

Iceland

Russia

Belarus

Lith.

Latvia

Estonia

Finland

Sweden

Norway

Laptev Sea

Kara Sea

Barents Sea

Sea of
Okhotsk

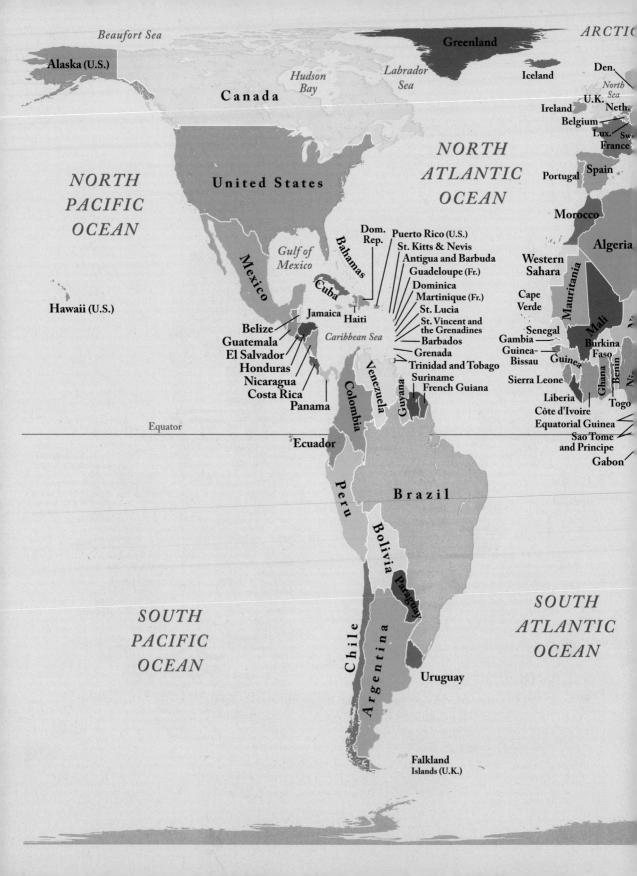

OCEAN
Barents Sea   Kara Sea   Laptev Sea

rway
den
Finland
Latvia — Estonia
Lith.
oland Belarus
ep.
Syk.
Hun. Ukraine
Rom. Moldova
Serb. Georgia
Bulg. Black Sea
Kos. Armenia
Greece Mac.
nt. Turkey
Alb.
Mediterranean Sea
Cyprus
Syria
Israel Lebanon
ya Jordan — Kuwait
Egypt Bahrain
Saudi Qatar
Arabia U.A.E.
Red Sea
Oman
Sudan Eritrea Yemen
Chad Djibouti
Central South
African Sudan Ethiopia Somalia
Republic
Dem. Uganda Kenya
Rep.
of the Rwanda
Congo Burundi
Tanzania
ngola
Zambia Malawi
Namibia Zimb. Mozambique
Botswana
Madagascar
South
Africa Lesotho
Swaziland

Russia
Lake
Baikal
Sea of
Okhotsk
Kazakhstan
Aral Sea
Uzbekistan Kyrgyzstan
Caspian Tajikistan
Sea Turkm.
Azerbaijan
Afghanistan
Pakistan
Nepal Bhutan
India Bangladesh
Myanmar
Laos
Thailand Vietnam
Bay of Cambodia
Bengal
Sri
Lanka
Maldives
Singapore

Mongolia
China
North Sea of
Korea Japan
South Japan
Korea
East
China
Sea
Taiwan
South
China
Sea
Micronesia
Philippines
Palau

Arabian
Sea

NORTH
PACIFIC
OCEAN

Equator   Kiribati

I n d o n e s i a   Papua Solomon
New Islands
Guinea
East Timor

INDIAN
OCEAN

Seychelles
Comoros

Samoa
Vanuatu Fiji

Mauritius
Réunion (Fr.)

N
W   E
S

New
Caledonia
(Fr.)

A u s t r a l i a

New
Zealand

THE PETERS WORLD MAP

How do maps shape the way you think about the world and its
people? The Earth is round. So every flat, rectangular map involves
distortions. But which distortions? The Peters world map is an
equal-area map, showing countries and continents in accurate
proportion with one another and reducing the visual dominance of
the Northern Hemisphere by shifting the equator to the middle of the
map, both in sharp contrast to the more familiar Mercator projection.

A n t a r c t i c a

WORLD · POLITICAL

NATIONAL BOUNDARIES

While humanity's impact is quite evident, and even striking, on many remotely sensed scenes, sometimes, as is the case with most political boundaries, it is invisible. State, provincial, and national boundaries may follow natural features, such as mountain ridges, rivers, or coastlines. Artificial constructs that possess no physical reality—for example, lines of latitude and longitude—can also determine political borders. This world political map represents humanity's imaginary lines as they slice and divide earth.

The National Geographic Society recognizes 193 independent states in the world as represented here. Of those nations, 192 are members of the United Nations.

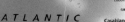
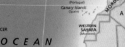

Essentials of Cultural Anthropology

Fourth Edition

Essentials of Cultural Anthropology

A Toolkit for a Global Age

Fourth Edition

Kenneth J. Guest

**Baruch College
The City University of New York**

W. W. NORTON & COMPANY
Celebrating a Century of Independent Publishing

W. W. Norton & Company has been independent since its founding in 1923, when William Warder Norton and Mary D. Herter Norton first published lectures delivered at the People's Institute, the adult education division of New York City's Cooper Union. The firm soon expanded its program beyond the Institute, publishing books by celebrated academics from America and abroad. By midcentury, the two major pillars of Norton's publishing program—trade books and college texts—were firmly established. In the 1950s, the Norton family transferred control of the company to its employees, and today—with a staff of four hundred and a comparable number of trade, college, and professional titles published each year—W. W. Norton & Company stands as the largest and oldest publishing house owned wholly by its employees.

Editor: Michael Moss

Senior Project Editor: Caitlin Moran

Assistant Editor: Allen Chen

Managing Editor, College: Marian Johnson

Managing Editor, College Digital Media: Kim Yi

Senior Production Manager: Stephen Sajdak

Media Editor: Eileen Connell

Associate Media Editor: Alex Park

Media Project Editor: Rachel Mayer

Media Editorial Assistant: Caleb Wertz

Marketing Manager, Cultural Anthropology: Julia Hall

Design Director: Rubina Yeh

Photo Editor: Thomas Persano

Director of College Permissions: Megan Schindel

Permissions Associate: Patricia Wong

Composition: Six Red Marbles

Manufacturing: Transcontinental Printing

ISBN: 978-0-393-88874-4

W. W. Norton & Company, Inc., 500 Fifth Avenue, New York, NY 10110-0017

wwnorton.com

W. W. Norton & Company Ltd., 15 Carlisle Street, London W1D 3BS

1 2 3 4 5 6 7 8 9 0

About the Author

Kenneth J. Guest is Professor of Anthropology at Baruch College, CUNY, and author of *God in Chinatown: Religion and Survival in New York's Evolving Immigrant Community*. His research focuses on immigration, religion, globalization, ethnicity, and entrepreneurialism.

Professor Guest's ethnographic research in China and the United States traces the immigration journey of recent Chinese immigrants from Fuzhou, southeast China, who, drawn by restaurant, garment shop, and construction jobs and facilitated by a vast human smuggling network, have revitalized New York's Chinatown. His writing explores the role of Fuzhounese religious communities in China and the United States; the religious revival sweeping coastal China; the Fuzhounese role in the rapidly expanding U.S. network of all-you-can-eat buffets and take-out restaurants; and the experiences of the Fuzhounese second generation.

A native of Florida, Professor Guest studied Chinese at Beijing University and Middlebury College. He received his B.A. from Columbia University (East Asian Languages and Cultures), an M.A. from Union Theological Seminary (Religious Studies), and an M.A., M.Phil., and Ph.D. from The City University of New York Graduate Center (Anthropology).

Brief Contents

Contents

Part 2: Unmasking the Structures of Power

Part 3: Change in the Modern World

Chapter 10: The Global Economy 280

Preface

Anthropology may be the most important course you take in college. That may seem like a bold statement. But here's what I mean.

CULTURAL ANTHROPOLOGY: A TOOLKIT

The world in the twenty-first century is changing at a remarkable pace. We are experiencing an interaction with people, ideas, and systems that is intensifying at breathtaking speed. Communication technologies link people instantaneously across the globe. Economic activities challenge national boundaries. People are on the move within countries and between them. As a result, today we increasingly encounter the diversity of humanity, not on the other side of the world but in our schools, workplaces, neighborhoods, religious communities, and families. How will we develop the skills and strategies we need to engage and navigate the complex, multicultural, global, and rapidly changing reality of the world around us?

Anthropology is the toolkit you are looking for. Cultural anthropology is the study of humans, particularly the many ways people around the world today and throughout human history have organized themselves to live together: to get along, to survive, to thrive, and to have meaningful lives. This fourth edition of *Essentials of Cultural Anthropology: A Toolkit for a Global Age* will introduce you to the fascinating work of anthropologists and the research strategies and analytical perspectives that anthropologists have developed—our tools of the trade—that can help you better understand and engage today's world as you move through it.

I teach Introduction to Cultural Anthropology to hundreds of students every year at Baruch College, a senior college of The City University of New York. Baruch has an incredibly diverse student body, with immigrants from over a hundred countries, speaking dozens of languages and thinking about culture, race, gender, and family in as many different ways. Some of my students will become anthropology majors. More will become anthropology minors. But at Baruch, in fact, most students will become business majors.

This book emerges from my efforts to make anthropology relevant to all of my students as they navigate their everyday lives, think about the world as it is and as it is becoming, and consider tackling the crucial issues of our times. On a practical level, we all employ the skills of anthropology on a daily basis. Every time you walk into a room and try to figure out how to fit into a new group of people—in your classroom, in a student club, at the office, at a party, in your religious community, when your new love interest takes you home to meet the family—how in the world do you deduce what the rules are? Where you fit in? What you're supposed to do? What the power dynamics are? What you can contribute to the group? *Essentials of Cultural Anthropology: A Toolkit for a Global Age* is designed to help you develop those skills—to think more deeply and analyze more carefully—and to prepare you to use them in diverse settings at home or around the world.

A TEXTBOOK THAT REFLECTS TODAY'S ANTHROPOLOGY

The world has changed dramatically in the past forty years and so has the field of anthropology. *Essentials of Cultural Anthropology: A Toolkit for a Global Age* presents the theoretical, methodological, and pedagogical innovations that are transforming anthropology and highlights both historical and contemporary research that can provide students with insights about how anthropologists are approaching the crucial challenges and questions of our times.

Globalization. As the world is changing, so too are the people anthropologists study. Even the way anthropologists conduct research is changing. In our contemporary period of rapid globalization, the movement, connection, and interrelatedness that have always been a part of human reality have intensified and become more explicit, reminding us that our actions have consequences for the whole world, not just for our own lives and those of our families and friends. This book integrates globalization into every chapter, analyzing its effects throughout the text rather than in a series of boxes, icons, or the occasional extra chapter so commonly seen in contemporary textbooks. The introductory chapter, "Anthropology in a Global Age," establishes an analytical framework of globalization that is developed in every succeeding chapter—whether the topic is fieldwork, language, ethnicity, economics, kinship, or art—and gives students tools they can use to understand the impact of globalization on people's lives as they encounter it in ethnographic examples throughout the book.

Reframing the Culture Concept. The concept of culture has been central to anthropological analysis since the beginning of our field. But anthropologists have significantly reframed our thinking about culture over the past sixty years. In the 1960s, Clifford Geertz synthesized anthropological thinking about culture as a system of meaning—shared norms, values, symbols, and categories. In the ensuing years, anthropologists have paid increasing attention to the relationship of power to culture, building on the work of Antonio Gramsci, Michel Foucault, and Eric Wolf to examine how cultural meanings are created, learned, taught, enforced, negotiated, and contested. *Essentials of Cultural Anthropology: A Toolkit for a Global Age* integrates this holistic and complex concept of culture into every chapter, exploring both meaning and power in human culture. Chapter 5, for example, is titled "Race and Racism," acknowledging not only that race is a social construction of ideas but also that ideas of race can be expressed and made real through cultural processes, institutions, and systems of power—racism—in ways that create patterns of stratification and inequality in U.S. culture and in cultures around the world.

Anthropology for the Twenty-First Century. *Essentials of Cultural Anthropology: A Toolkit for a Global Age* reflects the field of anthropology as it is developing in the twenty-first century. While carefully covering the foundational work of early anthropologists, every chapter has been designed to introduce the cutting-edge research and theory that make anthropology relevant to today's world. Chapters on classic anthropological topics such as language, religion, kinship, and art incorporate contemporary research and help students understand why anthropological thinking matters in day-to-day life. Chapters on sexuality, the global economy, and health, illness, and the body give students a sense of historical and contemporary research in the field and bring the presentation of anthropology fully into the twenty-first century.

Ethnography. Anthropologists conduct fascinating research about the lives of people all over the world. In many ways ethnography is at the heart of anthropology, reflecting our unique research strategies, our analytical methodologies, and our deep commitment to the project of cross-cultural understanding and engagement in our attempts to make the world a better place. But ethnographies often get lost in introductory textbooks. *Essentials of Cultural Anthropology: A Toolkit for a Global Age* introduces scores of ethnographic studies set in dozens of different countries, presenting both new research and classic studies in ways accessible to undergraduates so that the rich work of anthropologists comes alive over the course of the semester.

Relevance. *Essentials of Cultural Anthropology: A Toolkit for a Global Age* responds to my students' request for relevance in a textbook. Each chapter opens with a recent event that raises central questions about the workings of human culture. Key questions throughout the chapter guide students through an introduction to the anthropological strategies and analytical frameworks that can enable them to think more deeply about the chapter-opening event and the underlying issues they may confront in their own lives. "Thinking Like an Anthropologist" sections wrap up each chapter and challenge students to apply what they have learned.

What's New in the Fourth Edition

Reflecting the dynamic nature of the field, this new fourth edition of *Essentials of Cultural Anthropology: A Toolkit for a Global Age* includes revisions and updates to every chapter that introduce cutting-edge developments in the discipline, new theoretical frameworks, and new ethnographies. New chapter openers and examples continue the book's pedagogical approach to engage students in thinking like an anthropologist and provide them with an anthropological toolkit for analyzing and engaging the world around them.

EIGHT NEW CHAPTER-OPENING STORIES ON FAMILIAR TOPICS AND CURRENT EVENTS

Chapter 1 examines COVID-19 and its global impact in an increasingly interconnected world. specifically on the Filipino community pantry movement, a worker strike in France, and efforts to address food insecurity in the United States.

Chapter 2 analyzes cultural attitudes toward mask wearing and considers how face masks became a cultural battlefield for debates about individual liberties and public health concerns.

Chapter 5 connects the murder of George Floyd to the rise of the Black Lives Matter movement to end repeated and systemic police violence against Black Americans, calling attention to how race impacts the distribution of power, privileges and resources.

Chapter 7 explores the story of Sarah Rose Huckman, a student at the University of New Hampshire and transgender rights activist who advocates for transgender and gender nonconforming student athletes. Huckman's experience challenges the limits of a binary understanding of gender and sex.

Chapter 9 assesses the challenges of Zhang Alan, an unmarried single woman looking to have children in Beijing, where she is not allowed to access the nation's sperm banks. Zhang's story calls attention to the complicated cross-cultural frameworks for forming families and kinship, including the role of the state.

Chapter 12 investigates the connection between war and power through Russia's invasion of Ukraine, drawing on longtime Russian editor and journalist Marina Ovsyannikova's anti-war protest. Global repercussions of war are discussed, such as supply chain disruptions, increased food and fuel prices, and challenges to the nation-state.

Chapter 13 examines the role of religion in life through the work of Reverend Dr. William Barber II and the Poor People's Campaign to address long-term poverty in the United States by integrating theology, social analysis, and action.

Chapter 14 considers the relationship between health and gun violence in the United States through the elementary school shooting in Uvalde, Texas. The chapter explores health not only as access to adequate nutrition, housing, education, and health care, but also as the absence of poverty and violence.

OVER 15 NEW ETHNOGRAPHIES ADDED THROUGHOUT THE TEXT

Ethnographies are at the heart of anthropological inquiry. This edition introduces new ethnographies drawing on classic figures and the latest research in the field. Set across the world, these new ethnographies highlight research in the American South, Malawi, Afghanistan, and Tibet, among other places. New ethnographies by chapter are listed below.

- **Chapter 3:** Zora Neale Hurston's ethnography of southern Black folklore in *Mules and Men* and Yarimar Bonilla and Jonathan Rosa's digital ethnography of social media as political activism

- **Chapter 4:** Jonathan Rosa's book *Looking Like a Language, Sounding Like a Race*

- **Chapter 5:** Laurence Ralph's book *Renegade Dreams: Living Through Injury in Gangland Chicago* and Christopher Loperena's ethnographic research of the Garifuna people in Honduras

- **Chapter 6:** Ismael García-Colón's book *Colonial Migrants at the Heart of Empire: Puerto Rican Workers on U.S. Farms*

- **Chapter 7:** David Murray's book *Real Queer? Sexual Orientation and Gender Identity Refugees in the Canadian Refugee Apparatus*

- **Chapter 8:** Jennifer Hirsch and Shamus Khan's book *Sexual Citizens: A Landmark Study of Sex, Power, and Assault on Campus*

- **Chapter 9:** Cati Coe's books *The Scattered Family: Parenting, African Migrants, and Global Inequality* and *Changes in Care: Aging, Migration, and Social Class in West Africa* and Sibel Kusimba's book *Reimagining Money: Kenya in the Digital Finance Revolution*

- **Chapter 10:** Savannah Shange's book *Progressive Dystopia: Abolition, Antiblackness, + Schooling in San Francisco* and Sisel Kusimba's book *Reimagining Money: Kenya in the Digital Finance Revolution*

- **Chapter 11:** Carolyn Rouse's fieldwork in Ghana and Melissa Checker's books *The Sustainability Myth: Environmental Gentrification and the Politics of Justice* and *Polluted Promises: Environmental Racism and the Search for Justice in a Southern Town*

- **Chapter 12:** Omotayo Jolaosho's book *You Can't Go to War without Song*

- **Chapter 13:** David B. Edwards's book *Caravan of Martyrs: Sacrifice and Suicide Bombing in Afghanistan*

- **Chapter 14:** Natasha Iskander's research on migrant construction workers in Qatar

- **Chapter 15:** Aimee Cox's book *Shapeshifters: Black Girls and the Choreography of Citizenship*

These new ethnographies are set in places such as the American South; the internet; Chicago, Illinois; Honduras; Puerto Rico; Canada; Malawi; New York City; Brazil; Ghana; Kenya; Augusta, Georgia; Tibet; South Africa; Afghanistan; Qatar; Detroit, Michigan; and Jamaica, Topics covered include southern Black folklore, social media as political activism, raciolinguistic ideologies, community resilience to gun violence, the Garifuna people of Honduras and environmental racism, migrant agricultural labor, sexual orientation and refugee status, the Brazilian health care system, parenting in Ghana, aging in Ghana, digital finance in Kenya, sustainability in Ghana and New Jersey, environmental gentrification, environmental racism, war and memory in Tibet, public performance in political activism in contemporary South Africa, sacrifice and suicide bombings in Afghanistan, migrant construction workers in Qatar, Black girls and performance art, and informal commercial importers in Jamaica.

COVERAGE OF ENGAGING, CUTTING-EDGE TOPICS

- **The environment and climate change.** The book's focus on the environment includes ethnographies and explorations of current issues and events, including rising sea levels and small island nations like the Maldives; Native American language use and the environment; water crises in Flint, Michigan, and Mumbai, India; environment and health disparities in Harlem; deforestation in Malaysia; climate activists in Bangladesh, Paris, Sweden, and U.S. college campuses; environmental gentrification in New York and Georgia; landfills in the U.S. Midwest; and water temples in Bali.

- **The anthropology of the body.** Cross-cultural anthropological studies have challenged the notion of the body as isolated, natural, and universal and revealed a more complex picture of human bodies as products of specific environments, cultural experiences, and historical contexts.

- **The anthropology of food.** Always central to anthropological studies, food has received increased attention in recent years. The anthropology of food is explored throughout the book, including food production; food and colonialism; religious symbolism of food; water and inequality in Flint, Michigan, and Mumbai, India; the global trade in tuna; food and ethnic identity; and migration of Chinese restaurant workers.

- **Anthropology's biocultural perspective.** *Essentials of Cultural Anthropology* presents the latest thinking on human evolution, development, and adaptation as a continuous biocultural process in which biology, culture, and the environment are deeply intertwined in an ongoing interaction through which humans are continually evolving and changing, both on a species level and in our individual lifespans.

Additional Resources

Learn more at *wwnorton.com/instructors* and *digital.wwnorton.com/essculturalanthro4*.

CULTURAL ANTHROPOLOGY: A READER FOR A GLOBAL AGE

In *Cultural Anthropology: A Reader for a Global Age*, Ken Guest presents the essential readings and diverse voices that will help students understand and engage their rapidly globalizing world. This concise, affordable reader is designed to complement any introductory syllabus and is the perfect companion for *Essentials of Cultural Anthropology: A Toolkit for a Global Age*, Fourth Edition. Each chapter in the *Reader* includes two or three readings that supplement the chapters in *Essentials*. Selections focus on cutting-edge topics that students care about, like the environment, the body, income inequality, sexuality, race and racism, migration, and more. In addition, Guest's rich headnotes and smart discussion questions help students understand important contexts and apply what they learn in the readings to the world around them.

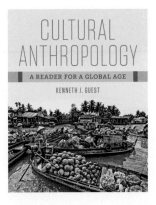

CULTURAL ANTHROPOLOGY FIELDWORK JOURNAL

Ethnographic fieldwork is one of the most fundamental (and for students sometimes daunting) tools for anthropological study. Ken Guest's *Cultural Anthropology Fieldwork Journal*, Fourth Edition, provides seventeen step-by-step exercises to help students apply the concepts they are learning in class while out in the real world. Designed to complement *Essentials of Cultural Anthropology: A Toolkit for a Global Age*, Fourth Edition, every activity in the *Fieldwork Journal* enhances students' understanding of the concepts covered in the parent textbook. Compact and easy to use, the *Fieldwork Journal* includes space to write notes and record data. The *Fieldwork Journal* can be packaged for free with *Essentials of Cultural Anthropology*, Fourth Edition.

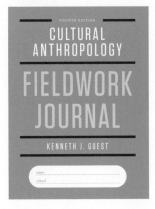

The media package for *Essentials of Cultural Anthropology: A Toolkit for a Global Age*, Fourth Edition provides additional pedagogical tools that inspire students to *do* anthropology and apply it to their own lives.

FOR STUDENTS
INQUIZITIVE

Available at *digital.wwnorton.com/esscuturalanthro4*.

InQuizitive, an adaptive learning tool, personalizes quiz questions in an engaging, game-like environment to help students master the learning goals outlined in each chapter of *Essentials of Cultural Anthropology*. Used as a pre-lecture tool, InQuizitive helps students improve their reading comprehension and critical thinking skills so that they come to class better prepared to think like anthropologists.

NEW NORTON ILLUMINE EBOOK CHECK YOUR UNDERSTANDING QUESTIONS

Available at *digital.wwnorton.com/esscuturalanthro4*.

Low-stakes Check Your Understanding questions with rich answer-specific feedback in the Norton Illumine Ebook motivate students and give them opportunities to practice their learning. Student engagement is tracked as they work toward completion through easy-to-use assignment tools and LMS integration.

PRACTICING ETHNOGRAPHY ONLINE ACTIVITIES

Available at *digital.wwnorton.com/esscuturalanthro4*.

Five practice activities strengthen essential skills such as taking fieldwork notes, conducting ethical research, perfecting ethnographic writing techniques, and reading ethnographic literature. They can be assigned both to reinforce the concepts introduced in Chapter 3 and to prepare students for the *Fieldwork Journal* activities. Each online activity is in the tutorial framework and includes InQuizitive-style questions that report to the instructor gradebook as well as short essay questions that can be graded as complete/incomplete in the system. These are graded 100 percent for completion, but instructors can adjust the grades if they want to do so.

NEW NORTON ILLUMINE EBOOK

Available at *digital.wwnorton.com/esscuturalanthro4*.

Cultural Anthropology is also available as Norton Illumine Ebook which provides students and instructors an enhanced reading experience at a fraction of the cost of a print textbook.

- **Easy to use.** The Norton Illumine Ebook works on all computers and mobile devices and includes intuitive highlighting, note taking, and bookmarking features that students who dog-ear their printed texts will love.

- **Enhances teaching and learning.** Note-sharing capability allows instructors to focus student reading by sharing notes with their classes, including embedded images and video. Reports on student and classwide access and time on task allow instructors to monitor student reading and engagement.

- **Integrates with other learning tools.** The Norton Illumine Ebook Reader can also be integrated into your campus learning management system. When integration is enabled, every time students click on a link to the ebook from their campus LMS, they'll be redirected immediately to their text without having to sign in.

- **Saves your students money.** Norton Illumine Ebooks are a fraction of the price of print textbooks. Learn more by contacting your local Norton representative. With a Norton Illumine Ebook, your students automatically have access to InQuizitive, Norton's informative, adaptive quizzing environment, to ensure they get the most out of their reading and study.

FOR INSTRUCTORS
LECTURE POWERPOINTS

Visually dynamic lecture PowerPoint slides include a suggested classroom lecture outline in the notes field that will be particularly helpful to first-time teachers.

ART POWERPOINTS AND JPEGS

All of the art from the book sized for classroom display.

VIDEO CLIPS

Available at *digital.wwnorton.com/esscuturalanthro4.*

Documentary and ethnographic film clips are ideal for initiating classroom discussion and showing students how anthropology is relevant to their lives. The book's LMS resources include questions for each clip that can be used for short-answer exercises or classroom discussion.

RESOURCES FOR YOUR LMS

Easily add high-quality Norton digital resources to your online, hybrid, or lecture course. All activities can be accessed right within your existing learning management system, and many components are customizable. Resources include the following:

- **InQuizitive**, Norton's adaptive learning tool, helps students learn and apply core concepts and ethnographic examples from the text.

- **Short answer quizzes** test on twenty-six streaming documentary and ethnographic video clips (clips are streaming on the DLP rather than in the coursepack for this edition).

- **Chapter learning objectives** ask students to consider the big questions in each chapter.
- **Flashcards** help students review key terms in each chapter and key term matching quizzes report to the LMS gradebook.

TEST BANK

The test bank for *Essentials of Cultural Anthropology* is designed to help instructors prepare exams. Each chapter contains sixty multiple choice questions and ten essay questions. All questions are tagged with difficulty level, Bloom's taxonomy, and a reference to a pertinent section in the chapter, making it easy to construct tests that are meaningful and diagnostic. The test bank is available on the Norton Testmaker website.

NORTON TEACHING TOOLS

The easy-to-navigate Norton Teaching Tools make lecture development easy with an array of teaching resources that can be searched and browsed according to a number of criteria. Resources include chapter outlines, learning objectives, lecture ideas, discussion questions, a short review quiz, various fieldwork activities, and a recommended videos list.

Acknowledgments

Writing a book of this scope is a humbling experience. I have been awed by the remarkable work of the anthropologists I have encountered, whether through written texts, films, or one-on-one conversations. And I have been inspired by the commitment of my fellow anthropologists to deep understanding of people and cultures, to the search for insights into how the world really works, and to engagement with the world and its people in ways that may help make the world a better place. I have learned a great deal, personally and professionally, on this journey. Along the way it has been my privilege to have the support and encouragement of a remarkable array of people.

First, I would like to thank all of the reviewers who shared comments on different stages of the manuscript and suggested ways to improve the book. I have adopted many of the recommendations that they made.

Abigail Adams, Indiana University of Pennsylvania

Kathleen Adams, Loyola University Chicago

Sabrina Adleman, Lansing Community College

Augustine Agwuele, Texas State University

Mark Allen, California State Polytechnic University, Pomona

Peter Allen, Rhode Island College

Hayder Al-Mohammad, University of Wisconsin–Madison

Deborah Altamirano, State University of New York, Plattsburgh

Myrdene Anderson, Purdue University

Tracy J. Andrews, Central Washington University

Iván Arenas, University of Illinois Chicago

Kristi Arford, Northern Essex Community College

James D. Armstrong, State University of New York, Plattsburgh

Elizabeth Arnold, Grand Valley State University

Christine B. Avenarius, East Carolina University

Bridget Balint, Indiana University

Data Barata, California State University, Sacramento

Jennifer Basquiat, College of Southern Nevada

Diane Baxter, University of Oregon

AnnMarie Beasley, Cosumnes River College

Sara Becker, York College of Pennsylvania

Monica Bellas, Cerritos College

O. Hugo Benavides, Fordham University

David Beriss, University of New Orleans

Victoria Bernal, University of California, Irvine

Ethan Bertrando, Cuesta College

Catherine Besteman, Colby College

Brad Biglow, Florida State College at Jacksonville

Krista Billingsley, University of Tennessee

Maggie Bodemer, California Polytechnic State University

Deborah A. Boehm, University of Nevada, Reno

Claudia Bosch, Southern Connecticut State University

Natalie Bourdon, Mercer University

Laurian Bowles, Davidson College

Rachel Brackett, Black Hawk College

Angela Bratton, Georgia Regents University

Elise Brenner, Bridgewater State University

Caroline B. Brettell, Southern Methodist University

Mary Jill Brody, Louisiana State University

Keri Brondo, University of Memphis

Boyd Brown III, Nichols College

Nina Brown, Community College of Baltimore County

Susan Brownell, University of Missouri, St. Louis

Margaret Bruchez, Blinn College-Bryan Campus

Ronda Brulotte, University of New Mexico

Jan Brunson, University of Hawai'i at Manoa

Kathleen Bubinas, University of Wisconsin–Madison, Waukesha

Pem Davidson Buck, Elizabethtown Community and Technical College

Liam Buckley, James Madison University

Andrew Buckser, State University of New York, Plattsburgh

Anne Buddenhagen, John Jay College of Criminal Justice

Jennie Burnet, University of Louisville

Noah Butler, Loyola University Chicago

Maria Leonor Cadena, Fullerton College

Josephine Caldwell-Ryan, Southern Methodist University

Walter Calgaro, Prairie State College

Jerome Camal, University of Wisconsin–Madison

Keri Canada, Colorado State University

Brandon Chapman, Rowan College

Jennifer Chase, University of North Texas

Leo Chavez, University of California, Irvine

Kristen Check, University of South Carolina

Melissa Checker, Queens College

Kun Chen, California State Polytechnic University, Pomona

Thomas Chivens, University of Michigan

Aldo Civico, Rutgers University

Paula Clarke, Columbia College

Kimberley Coles, University of Redlands

Elizabeth E. Cooper, University of Alabama

Carolyn Coulter, Atlantic Cape Community College

Susan Bibler Coutin, University of California, Irvine

Mark Cozin, Raritan Valley Community College

Mary Lou Curran, Mount Wachusett Community College

Sasha David, Los Angeles Harbor College

Joanna Davidson, Boston University

Christina Davis, Western Illinois University

Dona Davis, University of South Dakota

Allan Dawson, Drew University

Jeffrey Debies-Carl, University of New Haven

Jeanne de Grasse, Butler Community College

Teresa Delfin, Whittier College

Aaron Christopher Delgaty, University of North Carolina at Chapel Hill

Rene M. Descartes, State University of New York at Cobleskill

Rosemary Diaz, Southern Connecticut State University

William Doonan, Sacramento City College

Haley Duschinski, Ohio University

Whitney Easton, Emory University

Paulla Ebron, Stanford University

Terilee Edwards-Hewitt, Montgomery College

Kenneth Ehrensal, Kutztown University

Tracy Evans, Fullerton College

Susan Falls, Savannah College of Art and Design

Tessa Farmer, Whittier College

Jason Fancher, Mt. Hood Community College

Jay Fancher, Verto Education

Derick Fay, University of California, Riverside

Rick Feinberg, Kent State University

Doug Feldman, The College at Brockport, State University of New York

Janina Fenigsen, Northern Arizona University

Elena Filios, Charter Oak State College

Mike Folan, New Hampshire Technical Institute

Allison Foley, Indiana University South Bend

Ben Ford, Indiana University of Pennsylvania

Carla Freeman, Emory University

Todd French, DePauw University

Jonathan Friedman, University of California, San Diego

John Fritz, Salt Lake Community College

Cynthia Gabriel, Eastern Michigan University

Sue-Je Gage, Ithaca College

Ismael García Colón, College of Staten Island

Claudia García-Des Lauriers, California State Polytechnic University, Pomona

Carlos Garcia-Quijano, University of Rhode Island

Peter M. Gardner, University of Missouri

Vance Geiger, University of Central Florida

Christina Marisa Getrich, University of Maryland

Lesley Gill, Vanderbilt University

Laura Gonzalez, San Diego Miramar College

Daniel Goldstein, Rutgers University

Julie Goodman, California Baptist University

Henri Gooren, Oakland University

Mark Gordon, Pasadena City College

Thomas Gordon, Monroe College

Alexis Gray, Norco College

Peter B. Gray, University of Nevada, Las Vegas

Thomas Gregor, Vanderbilt University

Hugh Gusterson, George Washington University

George Haber, Vaughn College of Aeronautics and Technology

Joyce D. Hammond, Western Washington University

Diane Hardgrave, College of Southern Nevada

Jessica Hardin, Rochester Institute of Technology

Melissa D. Hargrove, University of North Florida

Amy Harper, Central Oregon Community College

Adam Harr, St. Lawrence University

Tina Harris, University of Amsterdam

K. David Harrison, Swarthmore College

Kimberly Hart, Buffalo State, State University of New York

Angelique Haugerud, Rutgers University

Bridget Hayden, University of Southern Mississippi, Hattiesburg

Gary Heidinger, Roane State Community College

Deanna Heikkinen, Los Angeles Valley College

Gilbert Herdt, San Francisco State University

Nicole Hess, Washington State University, Vancouver

Josiah Heyman, University of Texas at El Paso

David Hicks, Stonybrook University

Jude Higgins, Salt Lake Community College

Servando Z. Hinojosa, University of Texas Rio Grande Valley

Dorothy L. Hodgson, Rutgers University

David Hoffman, Mississippi State University

Jon Holtzman, Western Michigan University

Derek Honeyman, University of Arizona

Sherman Horn, Tulane University

Kendall House, Boise State University

Brian Howell, Wheaton College

Jayne Howell, California State University, Long Beach

Aimee Huard, Nashua Community College

Douglas William Hume, Northern Kentucky University

Arianne Ishaya, De Anza College

Alice James, Shippensburg University

Paul James, Western Washington University

William Jankowiak, University of Nevada, Las Vegas

Kiran Jayaram, University of South Florida

Alana Jolley, Saddleback College

Patricia Jolly, University of Northern Colorado

Barbara Jones, Brookdale Community College

Carla Jones, University of Colorado

Jessica Jones-Coggins, Madison Area Technical College

Hannah Jopling, Fordham University

Ingrid Jordt, University of Wisconsin–Milwaukee

Matthew Kalos, Brookdale Community College

Karen Kapusta-Pofahl, Washburn University

Peta Katz, University of North Carolina at Charlotte

Neal B. Keating, College at Brockport, State University of New York

Grace Keyes, St. Mary's University

Hareem Khan, California State University, San Bernardino

Ritu Khanduri, University of Texas at Arlington

Diane E. King, University of Kentucky

Melissa King, San Bernardino Valley College

Alice Kingsnorth, American River College

Ashley Kistler, Rollins College

Christine Kitchin, Ocean County College

Chhaya Kolavalli, University of Kentucky

Kathryn Kozaitis, Georgia State University

Kathy Koziol, University of Arkansas

Don Kulick, Uppsala University

Ruth Laird, Mission College

Clark Larsen, Ohio State University

Gabriel Lataianu, Bergen Community College

Ida Leggett, Middle Tennessee State University

Elinor Levy, Raritan Valley Community College

Ellen Lewin, University of Iowa

Pierre Liénard, University of Nevada, Las Vegas

Linda Light, California State University, Long Beach

Martha Lincoln, San Francisco State University

Pamela Lindell, Sacramento City College

David M. Lipset, University of Minnesota

Chris Loeffler, Irvine Valley College

Aurolyn Luykx, University of Texas at El Paso

Pamela Maack, San Jacinto College

Yvette Madison, Pennsylvania Highlands Community College

Kathe Managan, Louisiana State University

Teresa Mares, University of Vermont

Nadia Marín-Guadarrama, State University of New York at Albany

Lisa Markowitz, University of Louisville

Valentina Martinez, Florida Atlantic University

Scott Matter, University of Vermont

Michael Mauer, College of the Canyons

Kathryn Maurer, Foothill College

Siobhan McCollum, Buffalo State, State University of New York

Jack McCoy, Monmouth University

Felicidad McDonald, Florida Gulf Coast University

Jon Reece McGee, Texas State University

Bettie Kay McGowan, Eastern Michigan University

Melanie Medeiros, State University of New York at Geneseo

Karletty Medina, Northern Essex Community College

Arion Melidonis, Oxnard College

Seth Messinger, University of Maryland, Baltimore County

Jim Mielke, University of Kansas

Derek Miller, University of Richmond

Katherine Mitra, Suffolk County Community College

Mohsen Mobasher, University of Houston–Downtown

Angela Montague, Utah State University

Ryan Moore, Florida Atlantic University

Scotty Moore, Houston Community College

Juliet Morrow, Arkansas State University

Amy Mountcastle, State University of New York, Plattsburgh

Martin Muller, University of New Mexico

Joylin Namie, Utah Valley University

Chris Nelson, University of North Carolina at Chapel Hill

Sally Ann Ness, University of California, Riverside

Neil Nevins, New Hampshire Technical Institute

Rachel Newcomb, Rollins College

Andrew Newman, Wayne State University

Evelyn Newman Phillips, Central Connecticut State University

Carol Nickolai, Community College of Philadelphia

Worku Nida, University of California, Riverside

Jeremy Nienow, Inver Hills Community College

Jennifer Oksenhorn, Suffolk County Community College

Michael O'Neal, St. Louis Community College

Erik Ozolins, Mount San Jacinto College

Liana Padilla-Wilson, Los Medanos College

Eric Paison, Golden West College

Craig Palmer, University of Missouri

Anastasia Panagakos, Cosumnes River College

Faidra Papavasiliou, Georgia State University

Richard Parker, Columbia University

Amanda Paskey, Cosumnes River College

Phyllis Passariello, Centre College

Crystal Patil, University of Illinois Chicago

Mike Pavlik, Joliet Junior College

Linda Pelon, McLennan Community College

Ramona Pérez, San Diego State University

Dana Pertermann, Blinn College

Holly Peters-Golden, University of Michigan

Claudine Pied, University of Wisconsin–Plattville

Mieka Brand Polanco, James Madison University

Wayne Politsch, Lewis and Clark Community College

Dana Powell, Appalachian State University

Lin Poyer, University of Wyoming

Marla Prochnow, College of the Sequoias

Erica Prussing, University of Iowa

James Quesada, San Francisco State University

Sharon Rachele, California State Polytechnic University, Pomona

Michelle Raisor, Blinn College

Pilar Rau, Rutgers University, New Brunswick

Amanda Reinke, University of Tennessee, Knoxville

Angela Reyes, Hunter College

Michael Robertson, Los Angeles Harbor College

Daniel Robinson, University of Florida

Irene Louis Rolston, Oregon State University

Matthew Rosen, Ohio University

Monica Rothschild-Boros, Orange Coast College

Frances Rothstein, Montclair State University

Alissa Ruth, Arizona State University

Stephanie Sadre-Orafai, University of Cincinnati

Kristin Safi, Washington State University

Rita Sakitt, Suffolk County Community College

Maureen Salsitz, Cypress College

Bruce Sanchez, Lane Community College

Keri Sansevere, Monmouth University

Antonia Santangelo, York College, City University of New York

Richard Sattler, University of Montana

Naomi Schiller, Brooklyn College

Jennifer Schlegel, Kutztown University

Scott Schnell, University of Iowa

Kathy Seibold, The College of Idaho

Frank Shih, Suffolk County Community College

Gregory Simon, Pierce College

Suzanne Simon, University of North Florida

Michael Simonton, University of Cincinnati

Nancy Smith, South Plains College

Sarah Smith, Delta College

Genese Sodikoff, Rutgers University

Marisa Solomon, Baruch College

Brian Spooner, University of Pennsylvania

Amy Speier, University of Texas at Arlington

Amy Stambach, University of Wisconsin–Madison

Chelsea Starr, University of Phoenix

Erin E. Stiles, University of Nevada, Reno

Karen Stocker, California State University, Fullerton

Michelle Stokely, Indiana University Northwest

Richard Stuart, University of North Carolina at Greensboro

Circe Sturm, University of Texas at Austin

Noelle Sullivan, Northwestern University

Rania Sweis, University of Richmond

Patricia Taber, Ventura College

Orit Tamir, New Mexico Highlands University

Sabra Thorner, Florida State University

Milena Melo Tijerina, University of Texas Rio Grande Valley

Arthur Tolley, Indiana University East

Patricia Tovar, John Jay College of Criminal Justice

Mark Tracy, Minneapolis Community and Technical College

Susan Trencher, George Mason University

Monica Udvardy, University of Kentucky

Rebecca Upton, DePauw University

Lisa Valkenier, Merritt College

Jay VanderVeen, Indiana University South Bend

Emma Varley, Brandon University

Shelly Volsche, Boise State University

Katherine Wahlberg, Florida Gulf Coast University

Salena Wakim, Mount San Jacinto College

Renee Walker, State University of New York at Oneonta

Deana Weibel, Grand Valley State University

Nicole Weigel, State University of New York at Oneonta

Margaret Weinberger, Bowling Green State University

Jill Wenrick, California State Polytechnic University, Pomona

Cynthia Werner, Texas A&M University

Chelsi West, University of Texas at Austin

Paige West, Columbia University

Cassandra White, Georgia State University

Max White, Piedmont College

Jennifer Wies, Eastern Kentucky University

Rebecca Wiewel, University of Arkansas, Fort Smith

Laura Wilhelm, University of Nevada, Reno

Jeffrey Williams, Texas Tech University

Dorothy Wills, California State Polytechnic University, Pomona

Benjamin Wilreker, College of Southern Nevada

Scott Wilson, California State University, Long Beach

Jessica Winegar, Northwestern University

Paul C. Winther, Eastern Kentucky University

Sara Withers, University of New Hampshire

Katrina Worley, American River College

Aníbal Yáñez-Chávez, California State University, San Marcos

Laura Zeeman, Red Rocks Community College

I would also like to thank the editors and staff at W. W. Norton who took a chance on this project to rethink the way anthropology is learned and taught. Julia Reidhead years ago encouraged me to keep my lecture notes in case I might write a textbook someday. Peter Lesser originally embraced the vision of this book, brought me into the Norton fold, and, with associate editor Samantha Held, guided the creation of *Essentials*. Karl Bakeman intrepidly guided me through the writing and production process of the first edition. Thomas Persano insightfully identified photo options that challenge the reader to think. Caitlin Moran and Stephen Sajdak masterfully stitched the many pieces of this project—words, photos, graphs, maps, captions, and more—into whole cloth and managed to keep the countless pieces of the book moving through production. Norton's cultural anthropology marketing and sales team, Julia Hall, Erin Brown, Julie Sindel, and Annette Stewart, among many others, have advocated for the book with enthusiasm and boundless energy. Eileen Connell, Alex Park, and Caleb Wertz put together all of the media resources that accompany the textbook. When it comes to creating new digital resources to help anthropologists teach in the classroom or teach online, I couldn't ask for a better team of people. Michael Moss, my editor, and his assistant editor, Allen Chen, have brought vitality and energy, along with enormous patience, persistence, and generous collegiality, to the creation of this fourth edition. I am incredibly grateful. Thanks to you all.

Heartfelt thanks to my many colleagues who have helped me think more deeply about anthropology, including members of the Sociology and Anthropology Department at Baruch College, as well as Glenn Petersen, Jane Schneider, Louise Lennihan, Ida Susser, Peter Kwong, Leith Mullings, Angelique Haugerud, Carol Greenhouse, Sally Merry, Hugh Gusterson, Daniel Goldstein, Sam Martinez, Carole McGranahan, Shanti Parikh, Gina Ulysse, Shalini Shankar, Marc Edelman, Jackie Solway, Carolyn Rouse, Alisse Waterston, Alessandro Angelini, Melissa Checker, Paige West, Michael Blim, Jonathan Shannon, Christa Salamandra, Russell Sharman, Dana-Ain Davis, Jeff Maskovsky, Rudi Gaudio, George Gonzalez, and Zoë Sheehan Saldana. Susan Falls's invaluable advice continues to shape the Social Life of Things feature. Colleagues featured in "Anthropologists Engage the World" inspired me with their stories and their work. Members of the New York Academy of Sciences Anthropology Section helped me think more deeply about the relationship of culture and power. Leslie Aiello, Danilyn Rutherford, and the staff of the Wenner-Gren Foundation provided a vibrant venue to engage the cutting edges of anthropological research. The American Ethnological Society continues to introduce me to the rich ethnographic writing and deep theoretical engagements of emerging scholars in our field. My research assistants Chris Baum, Amanda Munroe, and Scott Erich have deepened my awareness of the richness of contemporary scholarship and creative strategies for teaching and learning. Thanks also to a wonderful group of friends and family who have supported and encouraged me during this fascinating and challenging journey: Marybeth, Vicki, Karen and David, Douglas, K and Charlene, Julia, Dayna, Ilene, Sallie and Steve, Marty, Brooke and the staff at Quinipet Retreat Center, the guys at the Metro Diner—Nick, Angelo, Marco, and Antonio—the SPSA community, Shari, the wonderful Colette, and especially Thomas Luke. This edition is offered in memory of Frances Helen Foley Guest (1925–2019) who taught me to see.

Finally, I would like to thank my students at Baruch College who every class ask to be introduced to an anthropology that is relevant to their daily lives, that tackles significant contemporary issues, and that provides them the tools of analysis and empowerment to live awake, conscious, and engaged. This book is dedicated to you and your potential to make the world a better place.

Essentials of Cultural Anthropology

Fourth Edition

Part 1

Anthropologists in the twenty-first century are engaging a world that is experiencing an unprecedented—and intensifying—interaction of people, ideas, images, and things. Communication technologies link people instantaneously across the globe. Economic activities challenge national boundaries. People are on the move between countries and within them. How can you use the tools of anthropology to engage this world on the move?

Anthropology for the 21st Century

Chapter 1
Anthropology in
a Global Age

Learning Objectives

- Define anthropology and its unique approach to studying people.

- Explain how the four fields of the discipline of anthropology form its comprehensive view of human cultures.

- Describe globalization and its four key dynamics.

- Analyze how the author's fieldwork exemplifies how globalization has changed anthropology.

On the morning of April 14, 2021, Ana Patricia Non, a twenty-six-year-old owner of a small furniture repair business in Manila, capital of the Philippines, filled a bamboo cart with rice, vegetables, vitamins, face masks, and canned goods and rolled it out by a street lamp near her home. On the lamppost, she hung a simple handmade cardboard sign: "Community Pantry: Give What You Can, Take What You Need." Her country's COVID-19 infections and deaths were surging again more than a year into the global pandemic. Nearly one-fifth of all Filipinos had lived below the poverty line before the pandemic, struggling to feed their families. Now, the situation was deteriorating rapidly.

In response to COVID-19, Ana Patricia Non created the Maginhawa community food pantry in Manila, Philippines, full of basic necessities like food, toiletries, and medicine. Tagalog for "relief," Maginhawa was aimed at assisting those in need.

Lines of cars at the San Antonio Food Bank in Texas, during the initial surge of the COVID-19 pandemic in April 2020.

Over the course of the day, hungry people began to line up for food. Other neighbors restocked the cart. That night, Non posted about her community pantry on Facebook. By morning, her project had gone viral on social media, inspiring hashtags like #FreeFoodForAll and #MassTestingNow. Over the following days, local fishermen brought their catch. Farmers donated baskets of produce. Within a week, hundreds of other community pantries spontaneously opened across the country as local Filipinos launched a nationwide mass movement to feed their fellow citizens.

The Filipino community pantry movement is one among many grassroots efforts that have arisen to address the effects of the global COVID-19 pandemic on local communities where the coronavirus has exposed long-standing patterns of inequality. In Marseille, France, where a local McDonald's had once provided rare job opportunities in a poor neighborhood, low-wage workers occupied the restaurant rather than allowing its owner to sell the store. When COVID-19 struck, the workers converted the building into a community food pantry for local residents, over 40 percent of whom had been living below the poverty line even before the arrival of the pandemic.

In Texas, weeks before Thanksgiving in 2020, churches, businesses, and individuals donated food to hundreds of thousands of people waiting in cars lined up for miles at emergency food banks, forced there by unemployment, illness, lack of insurance, and depleted savings. In Philadelphia, neighbors opened over twenty-five street-side community refrigerators stocked with free food to address food insecurity in the city. The level of food insecurity in the United States doubled to 23 percent of all households during the pandemic. Families with children were particularly hard-hit. Perhaps you or someone you know struggled with food insecurity before or during the pandemic.

MAP 1.1
Manila, Philippines

Never before has the world seen a disease spread across the globe as quickly, or as widely. Of course, never before has the world been so deeply interconnected. In today's global age, people, ideas, and things move along expansive transportation and communication routes at a speed and in numbers unimaginable only a few years ago. Humans have carried COVID-19 along these same elaborate pathways.

When the city of Wuhan, China, abruptly locked down in January 2020 to prevent the spread of the highly infectious and deadly coronavirus that causes COVID-19, few expected that within months, people in every part of the world would be confronting pandemic conditions. Local communities fought the disease with stay-at-home orders, school closings, travel bans, testing, contact tracing, quarantines, and vaccines. Individuals practiced physical distancing, mask wearing, and handwashing. Despite often heroic efforts over the ensuing years, millions of people had died of COVID-19–related illness and millions more continue to struggle with its long-term effects (World Health Organization 2021). Perhaps you or someone close to you has been affected.

Everywhere the coronavirus has spread, its effects have made visible the many common experiences that humans share in today's increasingly integrated global economy. Irrespective of country or region, the virus has taken root wherever vulnerable populations lack reliable access to health care, shelter, and food. Rates of illness and mortality have been consistently correlated with age, class, race, ethnicity, and other systems of inequality. Surging global hunger has also become a defining characteristic of the coronavirus pandemic. In 2020, 768 million people—10 percent of the world's population—were hungry, and 2.38 billion people—30 percent of the world's population—suffered food insecurity, lacking year-round access to adequate food (United Nations 2021). But in the face of these crises, local communities have mobilized to address the needs of their neighbors.

The stories of the Filipino community pantry movement, the worker uprising in France, and widespread food insecurity in the United States challenge us to think both globally and locally about the effects of the pandemic and, in the process, to consider how closely our lives connect with those of others around the world. The stories also present opportunities to think more deeply about the how the world really works, to understand one another more fully, and perhaps to explore new strategies for living together in this global age.

Today, we encounter and interact with people, ideas, systems, and even viruses around the world in ways that would have been almost unimaginable to previous generations. The iPhone, Facebook, Zoom, and other communication technologies link people instantaneously across the globe. Transnational corporations, international banking, cryptocurrencies, and other economic activities challenge national boundaries. Despite a global pandemic, business elites, low-wage

In the twenty-first century, people are experiencing unprecedented levels of interaction, encounter, movement, and exchange. Here, traders gather at the port of Mopti, Mali, the region's most important commercial center at the confluence of the Niger and Bani Rivers.

workers, and refugees are on the move within and between countries. Violence, terrorism, and cyberwarfare disrupt lives and political processes. Viruses like COVID-19 travel along elaborate air, rail, sea, and road transportation networks, easily moving within countries and across borders. Humans have had remarkable success at feeding much of a growing world population, yet extreme income inequality continues to increase—both among nations and within them. And increasing human diversity on our doorstep opens possibilities for both deeper understanding and greater misunderstanding. Clearly, the human community in the twenty-first century is being drawn even further into an intense global web of interaction.

For today's college student, every day can be a cross-cultural experience. This may manifest itself in the most familiar places: the news you see on television, the music you listen to, the foods and beverages you consume, the people you date, the classmates you study with, the religious communities you belong to. Today, you can realistically imagine contacting any of your 8 billion co-inhabitants on the planet. You can read their posts on Instagram and watch their videos on YouTube. You can visit them. You wear clothes that they make. You make movies that they see. You can learn from them. You can affect their lives. How do you meet this challenge of deepening interaction and interdependence?

Anthropology provides a unique set of tools, including strategies and perspectives, for understanding our rapidly changing, globalizing world. Most of you are already budding cultural anthropologists without realizing it. Wherever you may live or go to school, you are probably experiencing a deepening encounter with the world's diversity.

Whether our field is business or education, medicine or politics, we all need a skill set for analyzing and engaging our multicultural and increasingly interconnected world and workplaces. *Cultural Anthropology: A Toolkit for a Global Age* introduces the anthropologist's tools of the trade to help you better understand and engage the world as you move through it and, if you so choose, apply those strategies to the challenges confronting us and our neighbors around the world. To begin our exploration of anthropology, we'll consider four key questions:

- **What is anthropology?**
- **What lenses do anthropologists use to gain a comprehensive view of human cultures?**
- **What is globalization, and why is it important for anthropology?**
- **How is anthropology changing today?**

What Is Anthropology?

Define anthropology and its unique approach to studying people.

Anthropology is the study of the full scope of human diversity, past and present, and the application of that knowledge to help people of different backgrounds better understand one another. Anthropologists investigate both our human origins and how we live together in groups today. The study of the vast diversity of human cultures across geographic space and time allows us to glimpse the broad potential for human belief and behavior that stretches beyond what we may have imagined in our own cultural context.

anthropology

The study of the full scope of human diversity, past and present, and the application of that knowledge to help people of different backgrounds better understand one another.

BRIEF BACKGROUND

The roots of anthropology lie in the eighteenth and nineteenth centuries, when Europeans' economic and colonial expansion increased that continent's contact with people worldwide. The era's technological breakthroughs in transportation and communication—shipbuilding, the steam engine, railroads, the telegraph—rapidly transformed the long-distance movement of people, goods, and information in terms of both speed and quantity. As colonization, communication, trade, and travel expanded, groups of merchants, missionaries, and government officials traveled the world and returned to Europe with reports and artifacts of what seemed to them to be "exotic" people and practices. More than ever before, Europeans encountered the incredible diversity of human cultures and appearances. *Who are these people?* they asked themselves. *Where did they come from? Why do they appear so different from us?*

Since the field's inception in the mid-1800s, anthropologists have conducted research to answer specific questions confronting humanity. And they have applied their knowledge and insights to practical problems facing the world.

Franz Boas (1858–1942), one of the founders of American anthropology, became deeply involved in early twentieth-century debates on immigration, even serving for a term on a presidential commission examining U.S. immigration policies. In an era when many scholars and government officials considered the different people of Europe to be of biologically distinct races, U.S. immigration policies privileged immigrants from northern and western Europe over those from southern and eastern Europe. Boas worked to undermine these racialized views of immigrants. He conducted studies that showed the wide variation of physical forms within groups of the same national origin as well as the marked physical changes in the children and grandchildren of immigrants as they adapted to the environmental conditions in their new country (Baker 2004; Boas 1912).

Audrey Richards (1899–1984), who studied the Bemba people in the 1930s in what is now Zambia, focused on issues of health and nutrition among women and children, bringing food to the forefront of anthropology. Her ethnography *Chisungu* (1956) featured a rigorous and detailed study of the coming-of-age rituals of young Bemba women and established new standards for the conduct of anthropological research. Richards's research is often credited with opening a pathway for the study of women's and children's health as well as food and nutrition in anthropology.

Today's anthropologists, like Boas and Richards before them, apply their knowledge and research strategies to a wide range of social issues. More than half of anthropologists today work in *applied anthropology*—that is, they work outside of academic settings to apply anthropological strategies and insights directly to current world problems (American Anthropological Association 2019). Even many of us who work full time in a college or university are deeply involved in public applied anthropology.

For example, anthropologists study immigrants crossing the U.S.–Mexico border; street food vendors in Mumbai, India; climate change in the South Pacific islands; HIV/AIDS prevention programs in South Africa; financial firms on Wall Street; and Muslim judicial courts in Egypt. Anthropologists trace the spread of disease, promote economic development, conduct market research, and lead diversity training programs in schools, corporations, and community organizations. Anthropologists also study our human origins, excavating and analyzing the bones, artifacts, and DNA of our ancestors from millions of years ago to gain an understanding of where we've come from and what has made us who we are today.

ANTHROPOLOGY'S UNIQUE APPROACH

Anthropology today retains its core commitment to understanding the richness of human diversity. As we will explore throughout this book, the anthropologist's toolkit of research strategies and analytical concepts enables us to appreciate, understand, and engage the diversity of human cultures in an increasingly global age and, in the process, to understand our own lives in a more complete way.

The Nacirema. In his now-famous article "Body Ritual among the Nacirema" (1956), anthropologist Horace Miner helps readers understand the tension between familiar and strange that anthropologists face when studying other cultures. Miner's article examines the cultural beliefs and practices of a group in North America that has developed elaborate and unique practices focusing on care of the human body. He labels this group the "Nacirema."

Miner hypothesizes that underlying the extensive rituals he has documented lies a belief that the human body is essentially ugly, is constantly endangered by forces of disease and decay, and must be treated with great care. Thus, the Nacirema have established intricate daily rituals and ceremonies, rigorously taught to their children, to avoid these dangers. For example, Miner describes the typical household shrine—the primary venue for Nacirema body rituals:

> While each family has at least one shrine, the rituals associated with it are not family ceremonies but are private and secret. . . . The focal point of the shrine is a box or chest which is built into the wall. In this chest are kept the many charms and magical potions without which no native believes he could live. . . . Beneath the charm-box is a small font. Each day every member of the family, in succession, enters the shrine room, bows his head before the charm-box, mingles different sorts of holy water in the font, and proceeds with a brief rite of ablution. (Miner 1956, 503–4)

In addition, the Nacirema regularly visit medicine men and "holy-mouth men." These individuals are specialists who provide ritual advice and magical potions.

> The Nacirema have an almost pathological horror of and fascination with the mouth, the condition of which is believed to have a supernatural influence on all social relationships. Were it not for the rituals of the mouth, they believe that their teeth would fall out, their gums bleed, their jaws shrink, their friends desert them, and their lovers reject them. The daily body ritual performed by everyone includes a mouth-rite. It was reported to me that the ritual consists of inserting

A healing specialist conducts an elaborate ceremony, the facial treatment, a key body ritual among the Nacirema.

a small bundle of hog hairs into the mouth, along with certain magical powders, and then moving the bundle in a highly formalized series of gestures. (504)

Do these exotic rituals of a seemingly distant tribe sound completely strange to you, or are they vaguely familiar? Miner's descriptions of the Nacirema are intended to make the strange seem familiar and the familiar strange. "Nacirema" is actually "American" spelled backward. Miner's passages describe the typical American bathroom and personal hygiene habits: "Holy water" pours into the sink. The "charm-box" is a medicine cabinet. The Nacirema medicine men are doctors, and the "holy-mouth men" are dentists. The "mouth-rite" is toothbrushing.

Developing an anthropological perspective as we investigate the beliefs and practices of other cultures enables us to perceive our own cultural activities in a new light. Even the most familiar aspects of our lives may appear exotic, bizarre, or strange when viewed through the lens of anthropology. Through this cross-cultural training, anthropology unlocks our ability to imagine, see, and analyze the incredible diversity of human cultures. It also enables us to avoid the tendencies of **ethnocentrism**—that is, the impulse to use our own cultural norms to judge the cultural beliefs and practices of others.

To that end, anthropology has built upon the key concerns of early generations to develop a set of characteristics unique among the social sciences.

ethnocentrism

The belief that one's own culture or way of life is normal and natural; using one's own culture to evaluate and judge the practices and ideals of others.

Anthropology Is Global in Scope. Our work covers the whole world and is not constrained by geographic boundaries. Anthropology was once distinguished by the study of faraway, seemingly exotic villages in developing countries. But from the beginning, anthropologists have been studying not only in the islands of the South Pacific, in the rural villages of Africa, and among Indigenous peoples in Australia and North America, but also among factory workers in Britain and France, among immigrants in New York, and in other groups in the industrializing world. Over the last forty years, anthropology has turned significant attention to urban communities in industrialized nations. With the increase of studies based in North America and Europe, it is fair to say that anthropologists now embrace the full scope of humanity—across geography and through time.

Anthropologists Start with People and Their Local Communities. Although the whole world is our field, anthropologists are committed to understanding the local, everyday lives of the people we study. Our unique perspective focuses on the details and patterns of human life in the local community and then examines how particular cultures connect with the rest of humanity. Sociologists, economists, and political scientists primarily analyze broad trends, official organizations, and national policies, but anthropologists—particularly cultural anthropologists—adopt **ethnographic fieldwork** as their primary research strategy (see Chapter 3). They live with a community of people over an extended period to better understand their lives by "walking in their shoes."

The field's **cross-cultural and comparative approach** considers the life experiences of people in every part of the world, comparing and contrasting cultural beliefs and practices to understand human similarities and differences on a global scale. The global scope of anthropological research provides a comparative basis for contemporary humans to see the seemingly unlimited diversity of and possibilities for cultural expression, whether in family structures, religious beliefs, sexuality, gender roles, racial categories, political systems, or economic activities.

Anthropologists have constantly worked to bring often-ignored voices into the global conversation. As a result, the field has a history of focusing on the cultures and struggles of non-Western and nonelite people. In recent years, some anthropologists have conducted research on elites—"studying up," as some have called it—including financial institutions, aid and development agencies, medical laboratories, and doctors (Gusterson 1997; Ho 2009; Nader 1972; Tett 2010). But the vast majority of our work has addressed marginalized segments of society.

ethnographic fieldwork

A primary research strategy in cultural anthropology, typically involving living and interacting with a community of people over an extended period to better understand their lives.

cross-cultural and comparative approach

The approach by which anthropologists compare practices across cultures to explore human similarities, differences, and the potential for human cultural expression.

Once noted for the study of seemingly faraway and "exotic" people and places, anthropologists today increasingly study the complex interactions of diverse communities in global cities like New York.

Anthropologists Study People and the Structures of Power.

Human communities are full of people, the institutions they have created to manage life in organized groups, and the systems of meaning they have built to make sense of it all. Anthropology maintains a commitment to studying both the people and the larger structures of power around them. These include families, governments, economic systems, educational institutions, militaries, the media, and religions as well as ideas of race, ethnicity, gender, class, and sexuality.

To examine people's lives comprehensively, anthropologists consider the structures that empower and constrain those people both locally and globally. At the same time, anthropologists seek to understand the "agency" of local people— in other words, the central role of individuals and groups in determining their own lives, even in the face of overwhelming structures of power.

Anthropologists Believe That All Humans Are Connected.

Anthropologists believe that all humans share connections that are biological, cultural, economic, and ecological. Despite fanciful stories about the "discovery" of isolated, seemingly "lost" tribes of "stone age" people, anthropologists suggest that there are no truly isolated people in the world today and that there rarely, if ever, were any such people in the past. Clearly, some groups are less integrated than others into the global system currently under construction. But no group is completely isolated, and for some, their seeming isolation may be of recent historical origins. In fact, when we look more closely at the history of so-called primitive tribes in Africa and the Americas, we find that many were complex state societies before colonialism and the slave trade led to their collapse.

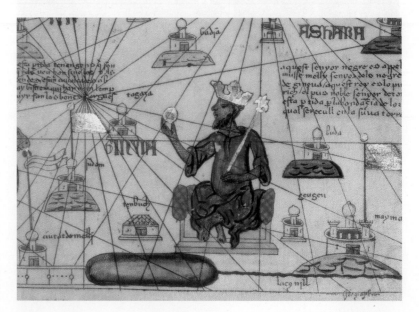

The King of Mali, West Africa, in 1375, is shown seated at the center of his vast kingdom—a key point along trade routes stretching across Africa and into the Middle East and beyond.

Human history is the story of movement and interaction, not of isolation and disconnection. Yes, today's period of rapid globalization is intensifying the interactions among people and the flows of goods, technology, money, and ideas within and across national boundaries, but interaction and connection are not new phenomena. They have been central to human history. Our increasing connection today reminds us that our actions have consequences for the whole world, not just for our own lives and those of our families and friends.

What Lenses Do Anthropologists Use to Gain a Comprehensive View of Human Cultures?

Explain how the four fields of the discipline of anthropology form its comprehensive view of human cultures.

One of the unique characteristics of anthropology in the United States is that it has developed four "lenses" for examining humanity. Constituting the **four-field approach**, these interrelated fields are biological anthropology, archaeology, linguistic anthropology, and cultural anthropology. Taken together, they represent a holistic approach to examining the complexity of human origins and human culture, past and present.

four-field approach

The use of four interrelated disciplines to study humanity: biological anthropology, archaeology, linguistic anthropology, and cultural anthropology.

Paleoanthropologists trace the history of human evolution by reconstructing the human fossil record. Here, Ketut Wiradyana unearths a fossilized human skeleton buried in a cave in Indonesia's Aceh province.

holism

The anthropological commitment to look at the whole picture of human life—culture, biology, history, and language—across space and time.

Holism refers to anthropology's commitment to look at the whole picture of human life—culture, biology, history, and language—across space and time. Anthropologists conduct research on the contemporary world and also look deep into human history.

Because we analyze both human culture and biology, anthropologists are in a unique position to offer insight into the roles of "nature" and "nurture." How do biology, culture, and the environment interact to shape who we are as humans, both individually and as groups? The four-field approach is key to implementing this holistic perspective within anthropology.

BIOLOGICAL ANTHROPOLOGY

biological anthropology

The study of humans from a biological perspective, particularly how they have evolved over time and adapted to their environments.

Biological anthropology, sometimes called *physical anthropology*, is the study of humans from a biological perspective—in particular, how they have evolved over time and adapted to their environments. Both the fossil record and genetic evidence suggest that the evolutionary line leading to modern humans split between 5 and 6 million years ago from the one leading to modern African apes. Modern humans thus share a common ancestor with other primates such as apes and monkeys. In fact, genetic studies reveal that humans share 97.7 percent of their DNA with gorillas and 98.7 percent with chimpanzees. Through a complex evolutionary process that we are learning more about every day, *Homo sapiens* (the group of modern humans to which you and I belong) evolved in Africa fairly recently in the grand scheme of things—probably less than 200,000 years ago— and gradually spread across the planet (Larsen 2021).

paleoanthropology

The study of the history of human evolution through the fossil record.

Biological anthropology has several areas of specialization. **Paleoanthropology** traces the history of human evolution by reconstructing the human fossil record. Thus, paleoanthropologists excavate the teeth, skulls, and other bones of our human ancestors and analyze them to track changes in human physical form over time. From these fossils they map changes in key categories such as overall body size, cranial capacity, hand structure, head shape, and pelvic position. Such changes reveal developments in walking, diet, intelligence, and capacity for cultural adaptation. Since the late 1970s, paleoanthropologists have also used molecular genetics to trace changes in human ancestors over time. The sequencing of DNA allows us to measure how closely humans are related to other primates and even to follow the movement of groups of people through the flow of genes. For instance, mitochondrial DNA (passed on from mother to child) indicates that modern *Homo sapiens* first appeared in Africa around 150,000 years ago and migrated out of Africa 100,000 years ago. This DNA evidence generally matches the findings of the archaeological record.

primatology

The study of living nonhuman primates as well as primate fossils to better understand human evolution and early human behavior.

Primatology is another specialization within biological anthropology. Primatologists study both living nonhuman primates and primate fossils to see what clues their biology, evolution, behavior, and social life might provide about our own, particularly about early human behavior. Careful observation of primates in their natural habitats and in captivity has offered significant insights into sexuality, parenting, sex differences, cooperation, empathy, intergroup conflict, aggression, conflict resolution, toolmaking, and problem-solving.

Biological anthropologists also study the diverse human physical forms that have evolved over time. Humans come in all shapes and sizes. Our differences range from body size and facial shape to skin color, height, blood chemistry, and susceptibility to certain diseases. Biological anthropologists attribute general patterns of human physical variation to adaptation to different physical environments as humans spread from Africa across the other continents. Variations in skin color, for instance, can be traced to the need to adapt to different levels of ultraviolet light as humans migrated away from the equator.

However, studies of human biology show that physical similarities far outweigh the differences among the world's people. In fact, there is more variation *within* what are assumed to be "groups" than there is *between* groups. This is clearly evident in terms of the thorny concept of race. A biologically distinct race would include people in a group who share a greater statistical frequency of genes and physical traits than people outside the group. Biological anthropologists find

Primatologist Jane Goodall studies chimpanzee behavior in an African nature preserve.

no evidence of distinct, fixed, biological races. Rather, there is only one human race. Attempts to identify distinct biological races are flawed and arbitrary, as no clear biological lines exist to define different races. Racial categories, which vary significantly from culture to culture, are loosely based on a few visible physical characteristics such as skin color, but they have no firm basis in genetics (Larsen 2021; Mukhopadhyay, Henze, and Moses 2007). We will return to this discussion of the biological and social dimensions of race in Chapter 5.

ARCHAEOLOGY

archaeology

The investigation of the human past by means of excavating and analyzing artifacts.

Archaeology involves the investigation of the human past by means of excavating and analyzing material remains (artifacts). Some archaeologists study the emergence of early states in places such as Egypt, India, China, and Mexico. They have unearthed grand sites such as the pyramids of Egypt and Mexico and the terra-cotta warriors guarding the tomb of China's Qin Dynasty emperor. Others focus on the histories of less spectacular sites that shed light on the everyday lives of people in local villages and households.

prehistoric archaeology

The reconstruction of human behavior in the distant past (before written records) through the examination of artifacts.

Archaeology is our only source of information about human societies before writing began (around 5,500 years ago). Because we are unable to travel back through time to observe human behavior, **prehistoric archaeology** seeks to reconstruct human behavior in the distant past (before written records) from artifacts that give significant clues about our ancestors' lives. Campsites, hunting grounds, buildings, burials, and garbage dumps are rich sources of material. There, archaeologists find tools, weapons, pottery, human and animal bones, jewelry, seeds, charcoal, ritual items, building foundations, and even coprolites (fossilized fecal matter). Through excavation and analysis of these material remains,

Prehistoric garbage dumps provide rich sources of material for understanding the cultural practices of human ancestors. Today, "garbologists" also learn about contemporary culture by examining what people throw away, including in large landfills like the one pictured here. What might an anthropologist 200 years from now learn about your community by studying its garbage?

archaeologists reconstruct family and work life. What animals did the people eat? What seeds did they plant? What tools and crafts did they make? Coprolites reveal a great deal about the local diet. Burial sites provide significant data about how people treated their elders and their dead, what rituals they may have practiced, and their ideas about the afterlife. Archaeological evidence can suggest trade patterns, consumption habits, gender roles, and power stratification.

Unlike prehistoric archaeology, which looks at the time before writing, **historic archaeology** explores the more recent past and often combines the examination of physical remains and artifacts with that of written or oral records. Historic archaeologists excavate houses, stores, factories, sunken slave ships, and even polar ice caps to better understand recent human history and the impact of humans on the environment. For example, recent excavations of former plantations of the enslaved in the southern United States, combined with historical records such as deeds, census forms, personal letters, and diaries, have provided rich insight into the lives of enslaved Africans in the seventeenth and eighteenth centuries. Students in the North Atlantic Biocultural Organisation's international field school conduct excavations in Iceland that reveal not only historical information about the settling of the North Atlantic but also data on major changes in the contemporary global climate. Core samples from borings drilled through glaciers reveal sediments deposited from the air over thousands of years as the glaciers formed; such samples allow archaeologists to track global warming and the impact of greenhouse gases on climate change.

historic archaeology
The exploration of the more recent past through an examination of physical remains and artifacts as well as written or oral records.

LINGUISTIC ANTHROPOLOGY

Linguistic anthropology involves the study of human language in the past and the present. Languages are complex, vibrant, and constantly changing systems of symbols through which people communicate with one another. Languages are very flexible and inventive. (Consider how English has adapted to the rise of the Internet to include such new words and concepts as *spam*, *instant messages*, *texting*, *Googling*, *Zoom*, *Instagram*, *TikTok*, *Snapchat*, and *FaceTime*.) Language clearly reflects people's ideas of and experiences with the world. But linguistic anthropologists suggest that language may also limit and constrain people's views of the world. In other words, can we think clearly about something if we don't have an adequately sophisticated language for it?

linguistic anthropology
The study of human language in the past and the present.

Language is perhaps the most distinctive feature of being human. It is key to our abilities to learn and share culture from generation to generation, to cooperate in groups, and to adapt to our environments. While some animals—including dolphins, whales, bees, and ravens—have a limited range of communication, human language is more complex, creative, and extensively used.

Linguistic anthropology includes three main areas of specialization. **Descriptive linguists** carefully describe and analyze languages and their component parts.

descriptive linguists
Those who describe and analyze languages and their component parts.

For example, some descriptive linguists spend years in rural areas helping local people construct a written language from their spoken language. **Historic linguists** study how language changes over time within a culture and as it moves across cultures. **Sociolinguists** study language in its social and cultural contexts. They examine how different speakers use language in different situations or with different people. They explore how language is affected by factors such as race, gender, age, class, or other relationships of power. Consider current changes in American English. For example, speakers are increasingly using a gender-neutral third-person singular pronoun, *they*, when referring to a person with an unknown, nonbinary, or fluid sex or gender identity. This is a distinct shift from past language norms that required using *he or she* rather than the plural *they*. Sociolinguists would explore these changes: How are these linguistic norms changing? Who uses *they*? Who resists using it? How do these changes reflect changing American norms of gender and sexuality? We will explore sociolinguistic issues like these further in Chapter 4.

CULTURAL ANTHROPOLOGY

Cultural anthropology is the study of people's everyday lives and their communities—their behaviors, beliefs, and institutions. Cultural anthropologists explore all aspects of human culture, such as war and violence, love and sexuality, child-rearing and death. They examine what people do and how they live, work, and play together. But they also search for patterns of meaning embedded within each culture, and they develop theories about how cultures work. Cultural anthropologists examine how local communities interact with global forces.

Ethnographic fieldwork is at the heart of cultural anthropology. Through **participant observation**—living and working with people on a daily basis, often for a year or more—the cultural anthropologist strives to see the world through the eyes of others. Intensive fieldwork has the power to educate the anthropologist by (1) making something that may at first seem very unfamiliar into something that ultimately is quite familiar and (2) taking what has been very familiar and making it seem very strange. Through fieldwork, anthropologists look beyond the taken-for-granted, everyday experience of life to discover the complex systems of power and meaning that all people construct. These include the many systems we will cover throughout this book: gender, sexuality, race, ethnicity, religion, kinship, class, and economic and political systems.

Cultural anthropologists analyze and compare ethnographic data across cultures in a process called **ethnology**. This process looks beyond specific local realities to see more general patterns of human behavior and to explore how local experiences intersect with global dynamics. Ultimately, through intensive ethnographic fieldwork and cross-cultural comparison, cultural anthropologists seek to help people better understand one another and the way the world works.

What Is Globalization, and Why Is It Important for Anthropology?

Describe globalization and its four key dynamics.

The term **globalization** refers to the worldwide intensification of interactions and increased movement of money, people, goods, and ideas within and across national borders. Growing integration of the global economy has driven the rapid globalization of the past fifty years. Corporations have relocated factories halfway around the world. People are crossing borders legally and illegally in search of work. Goods, services, ideas, and viruses—both biological and digital—are flowing along high-speed transportation and communication networks. People, organizations, and nations are being drawn into closer connection.

Globalization is not an entirely new phenomenon. Intensification of global interaction occurred in earlier eras as communication and transportation breakthroughs brought the world's people into closer contact. The present period of globalization, however, has ushered in a level of interaction previously unknown.

Globalization has not resulted in the broad improvements to local communities that its proponents originally imagined. As we will see in Chapter 10, the economic expansion and growth associated with globalization has also created significant global economic inequalities as billions of people are left out of these advances. At the same time, as we will see in Chapter 12, key characteristics of globalization, particularly innovations in communication and transportation, have enabled grassroots social and nongovernmental movements to build networks and coalitions across national boundaries to address problems created by economic globalization.

GLOBALIZATION AND ANTHROPOLOGY

Globalization and anthropology have always been intricately intertwined. As we have noted, the field of anthropology emerged in the mid-nineteenth century during an earlier era of globalization. At that time, technological innovations in transportation and communication enabled a period of colonial encounter, the slave trade, and the emerging capitalist economic system while facilitating deeper interactions of people across cultures. Early anthropologists sought to organize the vast quantity of information being accumulated about people across the globe. Unlike most contemporary anthropologists who conduct research in the field, however, they did so primarily from the comfort of their own homes and meeting halls.

Today, another era of even more dynamic globalization is transforming the lives of the people whom anthropologists study in every part of the world. And, as we will see throughout this book, globalization is also transforming how

globalization
The worldwide intensification of interactions and increased movement of money, people, goods, and ideas within and across national borders.

anthropologists conduct research and communicate their findings. To understand these sweeping changes, we must understand the key dynamics of globalization at play in the world today (Inda and Rosaldo 2002; Kearney 1995; Lewellen 2002; Trouillot 2003).

GLOBALIZATION: KEY DYNAMICS

Globalization today is characterized by several key dynamics: time-space compression, flexible accumulation, increasing migration, and uneven development, all of which are happening at an accelerating pace. These dynamics are reshaping how humans adapt to the natural world and how the natural world is adapting to us.

time-space compression

The rapid innovation of communication and transportation technologies associated with globalization that transforms the way people think about space (distances) and time.

Time-Space Compression. According to the theory of **time-space compression**, the rapid innovation of communication and transportation technologies has transformed the way we think about space (distances) and time. Jet travel, supertankers, superhighways, high-speed railways, telephones, computers, the Internet, digital cameras, and cell phones have condensed time and space, changing our sense of how long it takes to do something and how far away someplace or someone is. The world no longer seems as big as it used to.

Consider these examples of a changing sense of time. Today we can fly from New York to Paris in eight hours or from Los Angeles to Hong Kong in twelve. A letter that once took ten days to mail from Texas to Kenya can now be attached as a PDF and emailed instantaneously with a few clicks of a mouse. We instant message, text, Zoom, Snapchat, and FaceTime. These kinds of changes have

Globalization has accelerated the movement of people within and between countries. Here, Congolese refugees arrive on the coast of Lake Albert in Uganda in 2018.

transformed not only how long it takes us to do something but also how quickly we expect other people to do things. For example, how much time do you have to respond to an email or a text message before someone thinks you are rude or irresponsible?

Flexible Accumulation. A second characteristic of today's globalization, **flexible accumulation**, reflects the fact that advances in transportation and communication have enabled companies to move their production facilities and activities around the world in search of cheaper labor, lower taxes, and fewer environmental regulations—in other words, to be increasingly flexible about the way they accumulate profits (see Chapter 10). Companies in developed countries move their factories to export-processing zones in the developing world, a process called *offshoring*. An iPhone is made from parts built by 200 companies in over two dozen countries that are then shipped to China for assembly. Once the phones are assembled, they are sold around the world.

Other corporations shift aspects of their work to employees in disparate parts of the world, a process called *outsourcing*. Phone and computer companies hire English-speaking operators and technicians in Manila to answer customers' questions called in on 800 numbers. X-rays, CT scans, and MRIs taken in Colorado may be read and interpreted by doctors in Bangalore, India. Clearly, flexible accumulation allows corporations to maximize profits, while time-space compression enables the efficient management of global networks and distribution systems (Harvey 1990).

> **flexible accumulation**
> The flexible strategies that corporations use to accumulate profits in an era of globalization, enabled by innovative communication and transportation technologies.

Increasing Migration. A third characteristic of globalization is **increasing migration**, the accelerated movement of people both within countries and between countries. In fact, recent globalization has spurred the international migration of more than 258 million people, 51 million of them to the United States alone (see Chapter 10; United Nations Department of Economic and Social Affairs, Population Division 2020). An estimated 740 million more are internal migrants within their own countries, usually moving from rural to urban areas in search of work (International Organization for Migration 2022). The Chinese government counts 245 million internal migrants floating in China's cities, drawn by construction projects, service jobs, and export-oriented factories (Chang 2017; Liang, Li, and Ma 2014).

> **increasing migration**
> The accelerated movement of people within and between countries.

In countries from Pakistan to Kenya to Peru, rural workers migrate to urban areas seeking to improve their lives and the lives of their families back home. This movement of people within and across national borders is stretching human relationships and interactions across space and time. Immigrants send money home, call and email friends and family, and sometimes even travel back and forth. Migration is building connections between distant parts of the world, replacing face-to-face interactions with more remote encounters and potentially reducing the hold of the local environment over people's lives and imaginations.

uneven development
The unequal distribution of the benefits of globalization.

Uneven Development. Globalization is also characterized by **uneven development**. Although many people associate globalization with rapid economic development and progress, globalization has not brought equal benefits to the world's people. Some travel the globe for business or pleasure; others are limited to more local forms of transportation. Although 3.9 billion people now have Internet access, the distribution is uneven. In developing countries, 3.5 billion people remain offline, representing more than half of their population. And only 19.5 percent of the 1 billion people living in the least-developed countries have Internet access. Europe, North America, and Asia account for the vast majority of high-tech consumption, while areas of Africa are marginalized and excluded from the globalization process (International Telecommunication Union 2018). Such uneven development and uneven access to the benefits of globalization reflect the negative side of changes in the world today.

Although the global economy is creating extreme wealth, it is also creating extreme poverty. Fully half of the world's population continues to live in poverty. And nearly 700 million people live in extreme poverty, surviving on less than $1.90 each day (World Bank 2019). Even in the United States, the wealthiest country in the world, 38.3 million people, including 11.7 million children, experience food insecurity, a number that increased dramatically during the COVID-19 pandemic (United States Department of Agriculture 2020). In Chapter 10, we will explore the possibility that the rapid growth seen in globalization actually *depends on* uneven development—extracting the resources of some to fuel the success of others.

How Is Anthropology Changing Today?

Analyze how the author's fieldwork exemplifies how globalization has changed anthropology.

The field of anthropology has changed significantly in the past forty years as the world has been transformed by globalization. Just as the local cultures and communities we study are changing in response to these forces, our focus and strategies must also change.

CHANGING COMMUNITIES

Globalization is changing the communities we study. Today, vulnerable people and cultures are encountering powerful economic forces that are reshaping family, gender roles, ethnicity, sexuality, love, health practices, and work patterns. Debates over the effects of globalization on local cultures and communities are intense. Critics of globalization warn of the dangers of homogenization and the loss of traditional local cultures as products marketed by global companies flood into local communities. (Many of these brands originate in Western countries, including Coca-Cola, Microsoft, McDonald's, Levi's, Disney, Walmart, CNN, and Hollywood.) Yet globalization's proponents note the new exposure to diversity of people, ideas, and products that is now available to people worldwide, opening possibilities for personal choice that were previously unimaginable. As with the case of Filipino community pantry movement—and as we will see throughout this book—although global forces are increasingly affecting local communities, local communities are also actively working to reshape encounters with globalization to their own benefit: fighting detrimental changes, negotiating better terms of engagement, and embracing new opportunities.

CHANGING ENVIRONMENT

Perhaps the most distinctive characteristic of modern humans is our ability to adapt—to figure out how to survive and thrive in a world that is swiftly changing. Change has been a constant. So has human adaptation, both biological and cultural.

Our species has successfully adapted genetically to changes in the natural environment over millions of years. We walk upright on two legs. We have binocular vision and see in color. We have opposable thumbs for grasping. Our bodies also adapt temporarily to changes in the environment on a daily basis. We sweat to keep cool in the heat, tan to block out the sun's ultraviolet rays, shiver to generate warmth in the cold, and breathe rapidly to take in more oxygen at high altitudes.

As our ancestors evolved and developed greater brain capacity, they invented cultural adaptations—tools, the controlled use of fire, and weapons—to navigate the natural environment. Today, our use of culture to adapt to the world around us is incredibly sophisticated. In the United States, we like our air conditioners on a hot July afternoon and our radiators in the winter. Oxygen masks deploy for us in sky-high airplanes, and sunscreen protects us against sunburn and skin cancer. Mask wearing, physical distancing, and vaccine production and distribution have been adaptations to the spread of COVID-19. These are just a few familiar examples of adaptations our culture has made. Looking more broadly,

Actual stomach contents of a baby albatross on the remote Midway Atoll, 2,000 miles from the nearest continent. Thousands die as their parents feed them lethal quantities of floating plastic trash that they mistake for food as they forage in the polluted Pacific Ocean.

the worldwide diversity of human culture itself is a testimony to human flexibility and adaptability to particular environments.

Shaping the Natural World. To say that humans adapt to the natural world is only part of the story. Humans actively shape the natural world as well. As we will explore further in Chapter 11, humans have planted, grazed, paved, excavated, and built on at least 40 percent of Earth's surface. Our activities have caused profound changes in the atmosphere, soil, and oceans. Humans' impact on the planet has been so extensive that scholars in many disciplines have come to refer to the current historical period as the **Anthropocene**—a distinct era in which human activity is reshaping the planet in permanent ways. Whereas our ancestors struggled to adapt to the uncertainties of heat, cold, solar radiation, disease, natural disasters, famines, and droughts, today we confront changes and social forces that we ourselves have set in motion. These include climate change, global warming, water scarcity, overpopulation, extreme poverty, biological weapons, and nuclear missiles. They pose the greatest risks to human survival. As globalization accelerates, it escalates the human impact on the planet.

Today, human activity already threatens the world's ecological balance. We do not need to wait to see the effects. For example, Earth's seemingly vast oceans are experiencing significant distress. In the middle of the Pacific Ocean sits a floating island of plastic the size of Texas, caught in an intersection of ocean currents. The plastic originates mainly from consumers in Asia and North America. Pollution from garbage, sewage, and agricultural fertilizer runoff, combined with

Anthropocene

The current historical era in which human activity is reshaping the planet in permanent ways.

overfishing, rising water temperatures and increasing acidity caused by carbon dioxide, has caused a 50 percent decline in marine populations over the past fifty years (World Wildlife Fund 2015). These sobering realities are characteristic of today's global age and the impacts of increasing globalization.

Humans and Climate Change. Human activity is also producing accelerating **climate change**. Driven by the increase of greenhouse gases in the atmosphere, largely from the burning of fossil fuels, global warming is already reshaping the physical world and threatening to radically change much of modern human civilization (Intergovernmental Panel on Climate Change 2020). Changing weather patterns have already begun to alter agricultural patterns and crop yields. Global warming has spurred rapid melting of polar ice and glaciers, and the pace is increasing as sea levels begin to rise.

climate change

Changes to Earth's climate, including global warming produced primarily by increasing concentrations of greenhouse gases created by the burning of fossil fuels.

Anthropologists' attention to climate change has taken on added urgency as the people and places we study are increasingly affected. Half of the world's population lives within fifty miles of a coast, so the implications of sea-level rise are enormous—especially in low-lying delta regions. Bangladesh, home to more than 150 million people, will be largely underwater. Miami, parts of which already flood during heavy rainstorms, will have an ocean on both sides. Should all the glacier ice on Greenland melt, sea levels would rise an estimated twenty-three feet.

How will the planet cope with the growth of the human population from 8 billion in 2020 to more than 9.8 billion in 2050? Our ancestors have successfully adapted to the natural world around us for millions of years, but human activity and technological innovation now threaten to overwhelm the natural world beyond its ability to adapt to us.

CHANGING RESEARCH STRATEGIES

Anthropologists are also changing their research strategies to reflect the transformations affecting the communities we study (see Chapter 3). Today, it is impossible to study a local community without considering the global forces that affect it. Thus, anthropologists are engaging in more multisited ethnographies, conducting fieldwork in more than one place in order to reveal the linkages between communities created by migration, production, or communication. My own research is a case in point.

Multisited Ethnography: China and New York. When I began my fieldwork in New York City's Chinatown in 1997, I anticipated conducting a yearlong study of Chinese immigrant religious communities—Christian, Buddhist, and Daoist—and their role in the lives of new immigrants. I soon realized, however, that I did not understand why tens of thousands of immigrants

MAP 1.2
Fuzhou/New York

Rural Fuzhou villagers worship at a Chinese temple constructed with funds sent home by community members working in the United States.

from Fuzhou, China, were taking such great risks—some hiring human smugglers at enormous cost—to come and work in low-paying jobs in restaurants, garment shops, construction trades, and nail salons. To figure out why so many were leaving China, one summer I followed their immigrant journey back home.

I boarded a plane from New York to Hong Kong and on to Fuzhou, the capital of Fujian Province on China's southeast coast. From Fuzhou, I took a local bus to a small town at the end of the line. A ferry carried me across a river to a three-wheeled motor taxi that transported me across dirt roads to the main square of a rural fishing village at the foot of a small mountain. I began to hike up the slope and finally caught a ride on a motorcycle to my destination.

Back in New York, I had met the master of a temple, an immigrant from Fuzhou who was raising money from other immigrant workers to rebuild their temple in China. He had invited me to visit their hometown and participate in a temple festival. Now, finally arriving at the temple after a transcontinental journey, I was greeted by hundreds of pilgrims from neighboring towns and villages. "What are you doing here?" one asked. When I told them that I was an anthropologist from the United States, that I had met some of their fellow villagers in New York, and that I had come to learn about their village, they began to laugh. "Go back to New York!" they said. "Most of our village is there already, not here in this little place." Then we all laughed together, acknowledging the irony of my traveling to China when they wanted to go to New York—but also marveling at the remarkable connection built across the 10,000 miles between this little village and one of the most urban metropolises in the world.

Over the years I have made many trips back to the villages around Fuzhou. My research experiences have brought to life the ways in which globalization is transforming the world and the practice of anthropology. Today, 70 percent of the village population resides in the United States, but the villagers live out time-space compression as they continue to build strong ties between New York and China. They travel back and forth. They build temples, roads, and schools back home. They transfer money by wire. They call, text, Zoom, WeChat, and post videos online. They send children back to China to be raised by grandparents in the village. Parents in New York watch their children play in the village using webcams.

In Fuzhou, local factories built by global corporations produce toys for Disney and McDonald's and Mardi Gras beads for the city of New Orleans. The local jobs provide employment alternatives, but they have not replaced migration out of China as the best option for improving local lives.

These changes are happening incredibly rapidly, transforming people's lives and communities on opposite sides of the world. But globalization brings uneven benefits that break down along lines of ethnicity, gender, age, language, legal status, kinship, and class. These disparities give rise to issues that we will address in depth throughout this book. Such changes mean that I as an anthropologist have to adjust my own fieldwork to span the entire reality of the people I work with, a reality that now encompasses a village in China, the metropolis of New York City, and many people and places in between (Guest 2003, 2011). And as you will discover throughout this book, other anthropologists are likewise adapting their strategies to meet the challenges of globalization. Learning to think like an anthropologist will enable you to better navigate our increasingly interconnected world.

Toolkit

Thinking Like an Anthropologist
Living in a Global Age

As you begin your exploration of anthropology, the Filipino community pantry food activists discussed in this chapter may provide you with a powerful image to keep in mind and challenge you to think more anthropologically about the world and its people. How are we all connected in a global age? At the City University of New York where I teach, 40 percent of our 275,000 students come from families that earn less than $20,000 a year. Before the pandemic, one-fifth of our students were estimated to experience food insecurity. During the pandemic, job loss, transportation shutdowns, campus closures, and housing instability exacerbated the situation. Does your college or university keep statistics on student hunger? How does it address this situation? Several of my students began serving as food navigators during the pandemic, counseling classmates on how to access food benefits from the college, city, and state. They were working as part of a program called Swipe Out Hunger, which was started by students at the University of California, Los Angeles, in 2010 and now operates on 130 campuses across the United States. Originally designed to encourage students with extra meal swipes or dining dollars to donate them to peers, the program has now expanded to food counseling and lobbying for legislation to end student hunger. How does the work of these U.S. students relate to the work of Ana Patricia Non in our opening story? What are the commonalities? The differences?

How would you use the tools of anthropology to think more deeply about global food crisis and its local realities in Manila, New York, or the place you live? *Cultural Anthropology: A Toolkit for a Global Age* is designed to help you explore the richness of human diversity, uncover your conscious and subconscious ideas of how the world works (or should work), and develop strategies for living, working, and learning in an environment where diversity is a part of daily life.

Solving the challenges that face the human race in your lifetime will require greater engagement, interaction, and cooperation—not more isolation and ignorance. The future of the planet requires everyone to develop the skills of an anthropologist if our species is to thrive and, perhaps, even to survive. These skills include cross-cultural knowledge and sensitivity, perceptiveness of other people, understanding of systems of meaning and power, and consciousness of one's own culture, assumptions, beliefs, and power. By the end of this book, you will have many of the skills needed to think carefully about these questions:

- What is anthropology?

- Through what lenses do anthropologists gain a comprehensive view of human cultures?

- What is globalization, and why is it important for anthropology?

- How is anthropology changing today?

You also will discover that the study of anthropology helps you rethink many of your assumptions about the world and how it works. For the magic of anthropology lies in unmasking the underlying structures of life, in spurring the analytical imagination, and in providing the skills you need to be alert, aware, sensitive, and successful in a rapidly changing—and often confusing—multicultural and global world.

Key Terms

anthropology (p. 9)

ethnocentrism (p. 12)

ethnographic fieldwork (p. 13)

cross-cultural and comparative approach (p. 13)

four-field approach (p. 15)

holism (p. 16)

biological anthropology (p. 16)

paleoanthropology (p. 16)

primatology (p. 16)

archaeology (p. 18)

prehistoric archaeology (p. 18)

historic archaeology (p. 19)

linguistic anthropology (p. 19)

descriptive linguists (p. 19)

historic linguists (p. 20)

sociolinguists (p. 20)

cultural anthropology (p. 20)

participant observation (p. 20)

ethnology (p. 20)

globalization (p. 21)

time-space compression (p. 22)

flexible accumulation (p. 23)

increasing migration (p. 23)

uneven development (p. 24)

Anthropocene (p. 26)

climate change (p. 27)

Chapter 2
Culture

Learning Objectives

- Define culture and its key characteristics.

- Outline the historical development of the culture concept.

- Describe the ways that power is embedded in the culture concept.

- Explain how biology relates to culture and human behavior.

- Analyze how a culture of consumerism is created.

- Employ the concept of globalization to understanding contemporary culture change.

How did a simple piece of fabric—a face mask—become a cultural battlefield?

The international scientific and medical community considers wearing a face mask to be one of the simplest and most effective ways that people can avoid respiratory infections and reduce their risk of infecting others. But during the global COVID-19 pandemic, in countries like Brazil, the United Kingdom, Mexico, and the United States, masks became highly symbolic and highly politicized. In June 2021, Brazilian president Jair Bolsonaro, maskless and waving to the crowds, led a throng of 12,000 anti-mask motorcyclists on a ride through the streets of São Paulo. From atop a sound truck in the city's Ibirapuera Park, Bolsonaro spoke to a largely unmasked (but helmeted) audience to denounce the use of masks among vaccinated people, an assertion disputed by public health experts.

The culture of mask wearing proved to be a divisive point across the world. Brazilian president Jair Bolsonaro denounced the use of masks by vaccinated people. He organized a group of anti-mask motorcyclists to reinforce this sentiment.

Brazil has struggled to fight off the coronavirus. Low vaccination rates and limited vaccine availability have combined with Bolsonaro's efforts to minimize the dangers of COVID-19 to create the third highest infection and death rates in the world, behind only those of the United States and India. Still, Bolsonaro and local Brazilian politicians have fought over what restrictions might best protect the country's population. After Bolsonaro's motorcycle ride and speech in the city park, the city of São Paulo fined him the equivalent of $110. São Paulo requires mask wearing in public spaces, even by a president.

The coronavirus relies on human behavior to spread. After initial COVID-19 outbreaks in 2020, and before the introduction of vaccines, countries like Italy, France, Germany, Hong Kong, South Korea, Senegal, Liberia, Rwanda, and New Zealand successfully employed social distancing, hand washing, isolation contact tracing, and mask wearing to curb the virus's spread. Hong Kong residents, familiar with managing infectious disease outbreaks, quickly and uniformly donned masks and maintained social distance long before their government imposed mandates to do so. Over the first five months of the pandemic, the densely populated city of 7.5 million had a total of 4,300 infections and only sixty-three deaths. In contrast, New York City, population 8.8 million, with no previous mask-wearing experience, delayed its mask mandate for a month during the peak of its infections and deaths. During its first five months up against the virus, the city suffered 233,000 infections and 23,602 deaths. In these cases, different cultural attitudes toward mask wearing, among other factors, had a significant impact on infection rates and deaths.

Today in the United States, most Americans have adopted regular mask wearing to protect against the spread of COVID-19 and its variants. Yet despite ongoing community transmission, a vocal minority continues to reject this simple, effective tool: They refuse to wear masks in stores, bars, and churches; march in protests and attend political rallies without them; demand to send their unvaccinated children to school without them; and shout at one another to put them on or take them off. As anthropologists, we might consider how meanings associated with masks have shifted so quickly. Before COVID-19, masks in the United States were often associated with tough guys, bandits, bank robbers, construction workers, professional wrestlers, dentists, and surgeons. How did masks become items of contestation about values like masculinity, femininity, freedom, individualism, liberty, strength, weakness, collective responsibility, and care for family? How did a core value like freedom become associated with the expression of individual liberties rather than a commitment to public health and a collective effort to keep everyone free from the virus during the pandemic?

Anthropologists work to understand complex and diverse human behaviors and experiences. We conduct reasoned, careful research into people's cultures, norms, values, symbols, and ways of seeing the world. We carefully consider the cultural organizations people create to promote and sustain certain cultural norms and values. And we look at the strategies people use to challenge and renegotiate those norms. This chapter will give you a new set of tools—both research strategies and analytical perspectives—to make better sense of the mask battles in the United States and cultures around the world; to recognize how powerful cultural institutions like governments, political parties, public health officials, the media, religion, schools, and the family have been working to establish and contest the meanings of masks; and, if you choose, to engage with this cultural phenomenon to make your community, your country, and your world safer.

In this chapter, we will apply an anthropologist's perspective to culture and consider its crucial role in shaping how we behave and what we think. In particular, we will consider:

- **What is culture?**
- **How has the culture concept developed in anthropology?**
- **How are culture and power related?**
- **How much of who you are is shaped by biology, and how much by culture?**
- **How is culture created?**
- **How is globalization transforming culture?**

By the end of this chapter, you should have a clear sense of how anthropologists think about culture and use culture to analyze human life. By exploring this seemingly familiar concept, you can become conscious of the many unconscious patterns of belief and action that you accept as normal and natural. You can also begin to see how such patterns shape your everyday choices and even your basic conceptions of what is real and what isn't. By examining the rich diversity and complexity of human cultural expressions, you may also begin to grasp more fully the potential and possibilities for your own life.

What Is Culture?

Define culture and its key characteristics.

When people hear the word *culture*, they often think about the material goods or artistic forms produced by distinct groups of people—Chinese food, Middle Eastern music, Indian clothing, Greek architecture, African dances. Sometimes people assume that culture means elite art forms such as those displayed in museums, operas, or ballets. But for anthropologists, culture is much more: It encompasses people's entire way of life.

How is culture learned and taught? Here, kindergartners learn Mandarin Chinese at the New York Chinese School.

Culture is a system of knowledge, beliefs, patterns of behavior, artifacts, and institutions that are created, learned, shared, and contested by a group of people. Culture is our guide for understanding and interacting with the people and the world around us. It includes shared norms, values, symbols, mental maps of reality, and material objects, as well as structures of power—including the media, education, religion, and politics—in which our understanding of the world is shaped and negotiated. We will explore these concepts over the next few pages. A cultural group may be large or small, and it may have within it significant diversity of region, religion, race, gender, sexuality, class, generation, and ethnic identity. It may not be accepted by everyone living in a particular place or time. But ultimately, the culture that we learn has the potential to shape our ideas of what is normal and natural, what we can say and do, and even what we can think.

CULTURE IS LEARNED AND TAUGHT

Humans do not genetically inherit culture. We learn culture throughout our lives from the people and organizations that surround us. Anthropologists call the process of learning culture **enculturation**. Some aspects of culture we learn through formal instruction: English classes in school, religious education, visits to the doctor, history lessons, dance classes. Other processes of enculturation are informal—even unconscious—as we absorb culture from family, friends, and the media. All humans are equally capable of learning culture and of learning any culture they are exposed to. And while the process of social learning and passing information across generations is not unique to humans, humans have developed a unique capacity for culture.

How is culture shared and contested? National Football League players Eli Harold, Colin Kaepernick, and Eric Reid sparked controversy by kneeling during the shared singing of the national anthem to contest police violence against African Americans.

Humans establish cultural institutions as mechanisms for enculturating their members. Schools, medical and legal systems, media, and religious institutions promote the ideas and concepts that are considered appropriate behavior and thinking.

CULTURE IS SHARED YET CONTESTED

No individual has their own culture. Culture is a shared experience developed as a result of living as a member of a group. Through enculturation, humans learn how to communicate and establish patterns of behavior that allow us to live in community, often in close proximity and sometimes with limited resources. Cultures may be shared by groups large and small. For example, anthropologists may speak of Indian culture (1.3 billion people), of U.S. culture (320 million people) or of the culture of the Yanomami tribe (several thousand people) living in the Amazonian rainforest. There may be smaller cultures within larger cultures. For instance, your college classroom has a culture, one that you must learn in order to succeed academically. A classroom culture includes a shared understanding of what to wear, how to sit, when to arrive or leave, how to communicate with classmates and the instructor, and how to challenge authority, as well as formal and informal processes of enculturation. If your class meets virtually, online classroom culture may require you to understand camera and microphone use and expectations for participation in chats, polls, and breakout rooms.

Although culture is shared by members of groups, it is also constantly changing. Just as cultural institutions serve as structures for promoting enculturation, they also serve as arenas for debating and challenging core cultural beliefs and behaviors. Debates erupt over school curriculums, mask mandates, medical practices, media content, religious customs, and government policies as members of a culture engage in sometimes dramatic confrontations about their collective purpose and direction.

CULTURE IS SYMBOLIC AND MATERIAL

Through enculturation, the members of a culture develop a shared body of cultural knowledge and patterns of behavior. The elements of a culture powerfully frame what its participants say, what they do, and even what they think is possible and impossible, real or unreal. Though anthropologists no longer think of culture as a discrete, unique possession of a specific group of people, most argue that any given culture has a common core, at least among certain more dominant groups within the culture. Norms, values, symbols, and mental maps of reality are four elements that an anthropologist may consider in attempting to understand the complex workings of a culture.

norms

Ideas or rules about how people should behave in particular situations or toward certain other people.

Norms. In a culture, **norms** are ideas or rules about how people should behave in particular situations or toward certain other people—what is considered "normal" and appropriate behavior. Norms may include what to wear on certain occasions, what you can say in polite company, how younger people should treat older people, whom you can date, who can own guns, or, as the opening story in this chapter demonstrated, where and when to wear masks. Many norms are assumed, not written down. We learn them—consciously and unconsciously— and incorporate them into our patterns of daily living. Other norms are formalized in writing and made publicly available, such as a country's laws, systems of medical and business ethics, and the code of academic integrity at your college or university. Norms may vary for segments of the population, imposing different expectations on men and women, for instance, or children and adults. Cultural norms may be widely accepted, but they also may be debated, challenged, and changed, particularly when norms enforced by a dominant group disadvantage or oppress a minority within the population.

Consider the question of whom you can marry. Cultures have clear norms based on ideas of age, kinship, sexuality, race, religion, class, and legal status that specify which kinds of partners are normal and which are not. Let's consider some extreme cases.

In Nazi Germany, the Nuremberg Laws passed in 1935 banned marriage or sexual relations between German Jews and other persons with German or related blood. From 1949 to 1985, South Africa's apartheid government, dominated by White lawmakers, declared marriage and sex between White people and people of mixed race, Asian people, and Black people to be a crime under the Prohibition of Mixed Marriages Act and the Immorality Act. In the history of the United States, as many as forty states passed anti-miscegenation laws that barred interracial marriage and sex. Such laws targeted marriages between Whites and non-White partners—primarily Black people, but also Asians and Native Americans. Only in 1967 did the U.S. Supreme Court unanimously rule (in *Loving v. Virginia*) that these laws were unconstitutional, thereby striking down statutes that were then still on the books in sixteen states (all the states in which slavery was once legal plus Oklahoma).

Cultural norms may discourage *exogamy* (marriage outside one's "group") and encourage *endogamy* (marriage within one's "group"). Think about your own family. Who could you bring home to your parents? Could you cross boundaries of race, ethnicity, nationality, religion, class, or gender? Although U.S. culture has very few formal rules about whom one can marry—with some exclusions related to age and certain kinship relations—cultural norms still powerfully inform and enforce our behavior.

Most people, though not all, accept and follow a culture's norms. If they choose to challenge the norms, other members of the culture have means for enforcing its standards, whether through shunning; institutionalized punishment, such as fines or imprisonment; or, in more extreme cases, violence and threats of violence. For example, in 1958, Richard and Mildred Loving, an interracial couple, married in Washington, D.C., but were arrested when they returned to Virginia. During their trial, the judge gave them a choice of going to prison, divorcing, or moving out of the state. The Lovings ultimately brought suit in *Loving v. Virginia* to challenge the illegality of interracial marriage.

Values. Every culture promotes and cultivates a core set of **values**—fundamental beliefs about what is important, what makes a good life, and what is true, right, and beautiful. Values reflect shared ultimate standards that should guide people's behavior as well as goals that people feel are important for themselves, their families, and their community. What would you identify as the core values of U.S. culture? Individualism? Independence? Care for the most vulnerable? Freedom of speech, press, and religion? Equal access to social mobility?

As with all elements of culture, cultural values are not fixed. They can be debated and contested. And they may have varying degrees of influence. For example, if you pick up a newspaper in any country, you will find a deep debate about cultural values. Perhaps the debate focuses on modesty versus public displays of affection in India, economic growth versus environmental pollution in China, or land settlement versus peace in the Middle East. In the United States, while the value of privacy is held dear, so is the value of security. The proper balance of the two is constantly being contested and debated. Under what conditions should the U.S. government be able to breach your privacy—by eavesdropping on telephone calls and emails or unlocking your iPhone, for instance—in order

values
Fundamental beliefs about what is important, what makes a good life, and what is true, right, and beautiful.

to ensure your safety? To what extent should a government, hospital, restaurant, or college restrict individual freedoms to ensure public health?

Ultimately, values are not simply platitudes that express people's ideals about the good life. Values are powerful cultural tools for clarifying cultural goals and motivating people to act. When enshrined in law, values can become powerful political and economic tools. Values can be so potent that some people are willing to kill or die for them. During the COVID-19 pandemic, some people have been so committed to the value of individual freedom that they risked their health and life rather than taking a government-approved vaccine or wearing a mask.

Symbols. Cultures include complex systems of symbols and symbolic actions—in realms such as language, art, religion, politics, and economics—that convey meaning to those who share the culture. We are immersed in worlds of symbols that we create. And symbols are central to human culture. In essence, a **symbol** is something that stands for something else. For example, language enables humans to communicate abstract ideas through the symbols of written and spoken words as well as unspoken sounds and gestures (see Chapter 4). People wave, whistle, nod, smile, give two thumbs up, give thumbs down, give someone the middle finger. Pre-pandemic, people shook hands, but now people may also touch elbows, bump fists, or simply maintain social distance. These symbols are not universal, but within their particular cultural context they convey certain meanings.

Much symbolic communication is nonverbal, action-based, and unconscious. Religions include powerful systems of symbols that represent deeper meanings to their adherents. Consider mandalas, the Koran, the Torah, the Christian cross, holy water, statues of the Buddha—all carry greater meanings and value than the physical material they are constructed of. National flags, which are mere pieces of

symbol
Anything that represents something else.

Money is symbolic: Only 10 percent of the world's money exists in tangible form. Here, traders move money electronically at Euronext stock exchange in Amsterdam, the Netherlands.

colored cloth, are symbols that stir deep political emotions. Even money is simply a symbolic representation of value guaranteed by the sponsoring government. It has no value except in its symbolism. Estimates suggest that only about 10 percent of money today exists in physical form. The rest moves electronically through banks, stock markets, and credit accounts (Graeber 2011). Symbols change in meaning over time and from culture to culture. Not understanding another culture's collective understandings—that is, their sets of symbolic actions—can lead to embarrassing misunderstandings and cross-cultural miscues.

Mental Maps of Reality. Along with norms, values, and symbols, another key component of culture is **mental maps of reality**. These are "maps" that humans construct of what kinds of people and what kinds of things exist. Because the world presents our senses with overwhelming quantities of data, our brains create shortcuts—maps—to navigate our experiences and organize all the data that come our way. A road map condenses a large world into a manageable format (one that you can hold in your hands or view on your portable GPS system) and helps us navigate the territory. Likewise, our mental maps organize the world into categories that help us sort out our experiences and what they mean. We do not want all the details all the time. We could not handle them anyway. From our general mental maps, we can then dig deeper as required.

> **mental maps of reality**
> Cultural classifications of what kinds of people and things exist, and the assignment of meaning to those classifications.

Our mental maps are shaped through enculturation, but they are not fixed. Like other elements of culture, they can be challenged and redrawn. Today, globalization continues to put pressure on mental maps of reality as people on the planet are drawn into closer contact with the world's diversity. We will examine these transformations throughout this book, especially in the chapters on language, race, ethnicity, gender, sexuality, and kinship.

Mental maps have two important functions. First, *mental maps classify reality*. Starting in the eighteenth century, European naturalists such as Carolus Linnaeus (1707–1778) began creating systems of classification for the natural world. These systems included five kingdoms subdivided into phylum, class, order, family, genus, and species. Through observation (this was before genetics), these naturalists sought to devise a logical framework to organize the world into kinds of things and kinds of people. In a similar way, our cultures' mental maps seek to classify reality—everything from units of time to what is considered food to who is considered a relative. Often, however, a culture's mental maps are drawn from the distinct vantage point of those in power.

A culture creates a concept such as time. Then we arbitrarily divide this concept into millennia, centuries, decades, years, seasons, months, weeks, hours, morning, afternoon, evening, minutes, seconds. Categories of time are assumed to be scientific, universal, and "natural." But mostly they are cultural constructs. The current Gregorian calendar, which is used in much of the world, was introduced in 1582 by the Catholic Church, but its adoption occurred gradually; it was accepted in the United States in 1756, replacing the earlier Julian calendar, and in China in 1949. Still today, much of China relies on the traditional lunar calendar in which months and days align with the waxing and waning of the moon. According to this calendar, New Year's Day shifts each year. So do Chinese holidays and festivals. Even in the Gregorian calendar, the length of the year is modified to fit into a neat mental map of reality. A year (how long it takes Earth to orbit the sun) is approximately 365.2425 days long, so every four years the Gregorian calendar must add a day, creating a leap year of 366 days rather than 365.

As these examples demonstrate, categories that seem completely fixed and "natural" are in reality flexible and variable, showing the potential role of culture in defining our fundamental notions of reality.

Mental maps of reality become problematic when people treat cultural notions of difference as being scientifically or biologically "natural." Race is a key example. As we will see in Chapter 5, the notion of race is assumed in popular culture and conversation to have a biological basis. There is, however, no scientific basis for this assumption. The particular racial categories in any given culture do not correlate directly to any biological differences. Although most people in the United States would name White, Black, Latino, Asian, and perhaps Native American people as distinct races, no genetic line marks clear differences among these groups. The classifications are created by and are specific to our culture. Other cultures draw different mental maps of the reality of human physical variation. The Japanese use different racial categories than we do in the United States. Brazilians have more than 500 racial classifications.

Second, *mental maps assign meaning to what has been classified.* Not only do people in a culture develop mental maps of things and people, they also place

What does it mean to be a child laborer in your culture? (*Left*) A boy in Dhaka, Bangladesh, makes balloons for export. (*Right*) A girl in Nangarhar province, Afghanistan, works at a brick-making factory.

values and meanings on those maps. For example, we divide the life span into categories—that is, infants, children, adolescents, teenagers, young adults, adults, and seniors—but then we give different values to different ages. Some carry more respect, some more protection, and others more rights, privileges, and responsibilities. In the United States, these categories determine at what age you can marry, have sex, drink alcohol, drive, vote, go to war, stand trial, retire, and collect Social Security and Medicare benefits. Anthropologists warn that by assuming our mental maps of reality are natural, fixed, and universal, we risk misunderstanding and disregarding others' cultural values.

CULTURAL APPROPRIATION

In recent years, debates about cultural appropriation have flooded media reports and social media feeds. Stories have focused on Halloween costumes, prom dresses, and sports teams' mascots. But what does cultural appropriation mean from an anthropological perspective? How can an anthropological perspective inform our conversations and actions?

Throughout the history of our discipline, anthropology has studied many forms of cultural borrowing between individuals and groups. Early anthropologists examined the wide occurrence of *diffusion*—the movement of cultural forms, practices, values, and technologies from one setting to another. Diffusion has occurred widely between groups of relatively equal status in human history, a movement that has often prompted innovations and changes in the cultural practices of the receiving group. Anthropologists have also considered cultural exchanges framed by more unequal power dynamics. *Acculturation* has been used to describe the mutual influencing of two unequal groups that have come into continuous firsthand contact—for instance, under colonialism. Similarly, *assimilation* has been used to describe a powerful group's imposition of its cultural practices upon an economically, politically, or demographically weaker target group.

From an anthropological perspective, **cultural appropriation** refers to the unwanted taking of an important cultural practice or body of knowledge from one group by another, more dominant group. The cultural appropriation of Native American iconography and sacred symbols by U.S. sports teams provides a clear example. A number of large non–Native American corporations and institutions, including schools and colleges, have fraudulently claimed a connection to Indigenous people and their cultures, religious practices, symbols, and crafts for commercial profit. The National Football League's Washington Commanders, for instance, used a racial slur directed at Native Americans as its team name for eighty-seven years. The team placed that slur and other Native American images on helmets, uniforms, tickets, merchandise, and advertising, generating enormous profits for the team's owners and shareholders while denigrating

cultural appropriation
The unwanted taking of cultural practices or knowledge from one group by another, more dominant group.

and damaging the broader Native American community. The team dropped the offensive name in 2020 after years of widespread protests and condemnation by Native Americans and their allies.

As we will discuss later in this chapter, power is key to analyzing the dynamics of cultural appropriation. Appropriation occurs when a more powerful group takes aspects of a subordinate group's culture for personal or corporate gain, using those taken elements in ways considered offensive to members of the source community. In the process of cultural appropriation, the taking group improves its status and power while creating negative consequences for the group of origin: harmful stereotypes; stripping of heritage, artifacts, and resources; and a deep sense of grief, loss, and violation (Jackson 2021).

How Has the Culture Concept Developed in Anthropology?

Outline the historical development of the culture concept.

The concept of culture has been central to anthropology ever since the English anthropologist Edward Burnett Tylor (1832–1917) crafted his definition in the opening paragraph of his 1871 book *Primitive Culture*: "Culture or Civilization, taken in its wide ethnographic sense, is that complex whole which includes knowledge, belief, art, morals, law, custom and any other capabilities and habits acquired by man as a member of society."

Tylor understood culture to be a unified and complex system of ideas and behavior learned over time, passed down from generation to generation, and shared by members of a particular group. Over the past century and a half, culture has become more than a definition; it is now a key theoretical framework for anthropologists attempting to understand humans and their interactions.

EARLY EVOLUTIONARY FRAMEWORKS

Edward Burnett Tylor and James Frazer (1854–1941) of England and Lewis Henry Morgan (1818–1881) of the United States were among the leading early anthropologists who worked to professionalize a field long dominated by wealthy collectors of artifacts. They sought to organize the vast quantities of data about the diversity of cultures worldwide that were being accumulated through colonial and missionary enterprises during the nineteenth century. These anthropologists were influenced by Charles Darwin's theory of biological evolution, which maintains that the diversity of biological species resulted from gradual change over time in response to environmental pressures. Thus, they suggested that the vast diversity of cultures represented different stages in the evolution of human culture.

Early anthropologists suggested that all cultures would naturally evolve through the same sequence of stages, a concept known as **unilineal cultural evolution**. They set about plotting the world's cultures along a continuum from most simple to most complex using the terms *savage*, *barbarian*, and *civilized*. Western cultures were, perhaps too predictably, considered the most evolved or civilized. By arranging cultures along this continuum, early anthropologists believed that they could trace the path of human cultural evolution, understand where some cultures had come from, and predict where other cultures were headed.

Tylor and others developed the theory of unilineal cultural evolution at least in part to combat the prevalent racist belief that many non-Europeans were of a different species. Today, however, the theory has been criticized as racist itself for ranking different cultural expressions in a hierarchy, with European culture, considered the ideal, at the apex (Stocking 1968). Franz Boas, a key figure in American anthropology, and Bronisław Malinowski, a Polish anthropologist who spent most of his life teaching in England, represent two main schools of anthropology that moved beyond the evolutionary framework for viewing cultural differences.

AMERICAN HISTORICAL PARTICULARISM

Franz Boas (1858–1942) conducted fieldwork among the Kwakiutl Indigenous people of the Pacific Northwest of the United States and Canada before becoming a professor of anthropology at Columbia University in New York and a curator of the American Museum of Natural History. Boas rejected unilineal cultural evolution, its generalizations, and its comparative method. Instead, he advocated for an approach that today we call **historical particularism**. He claimed that cultures arise from different causes, not uniform processes. According to Boas, anthropologists could not rely on an evolutionary formula to explain differences among cultures and instead must study the particular history of each culture to see how it developed. Evolutionists such as Tylor, Frazer, and Morgan argued that similarities among cultures emerged through independent invention as different cultures independently arrived at similar solutions to similar problems. Boas, in contrast, while not ruling out some independent invention, turned to the idea of diffusion—the borrowing of cultural traits and patterns from other cultures—to explain apparent similarities.

Boas's belief in the powerful role of culture in shaping human life is evident in his early twentieth-century studies of immigrants. His research with the children of immigrants from Europe revealed the remarkable effects of culture and environment on their physical forms, challenging the role of biology as a tool for discrimination. As a Jewish immigrant himself, Boas was particularly sensitive to

British anthropologist Edward Burnett Tylor.

unilineal cultural evolution
The theory proposed by nineteenth-century anthropologists that all cultures naturally evolve through the same sequence of stages from simple to complex.

historical particularism
The idea, attributed to Franz Boas, that cultures develop in specific ways because of their unique histories.

the dangers of racial stereotyping, and his work throughout his career served to challenge White supremacy, the inferior ranking of non-European people, and other expressions of racism.

Boas's students Ruth Benedict (1887–1948) and Margaret Mead (1901–1978) continued his emphasis on the powerful role of culture in shaping human life and the need to explore the unique development of each culture. Benedict's popular studies *Patterns of Culture* (1934) and *The Chrysanthemum and the Sword* (1946) explored how cultural traits and entire cultures are uniquely patterned and integrated. Mead conducted research in Samoa, Bali, and Papua New Guinea and became perhaps the most famous anthropologist of the twentieth century, promoting her findings and the unique tools of anthropology to the general American public.

Mead turned her attention particularly to enculturation and its powerful effects on cultural patterns and personality types. In her book *Coming of Age in Samoa* (1928), she explored the seeming sexual freedom and experimentation of Samoan young people and compared it with the repressed sexuality of young people in the United States, suggesting the important role of enculturation in shaping behavior—even behavior that is imagined to have powerful biological origins. Mead's controversial research and findings throughout her career challenged biological assumptions about gender, demonstrating cross-cultural variations in expressions of what it meant to be male or female and contributing to heated debates about the roles of women and men in U.S. culture in the twentieth century.

BRITISH STRUCTURAL FUNCTIONALISM

Between the 1920s and 1960s, in a rejection of unilineal cultural evolution, many British social anthropologists viewed anthropology more as a science and fieldwork more as a science experiment that could focus on the specific details of a local **society**. These anthropologists viewed human societies as living organisms, and through fieldwork they sought to analyze each part of the "body." Each aspect of society—including kinship, religious, political, and economic structures—fit together and had its unique function within the larger structure. Like a living organism, a society worked to maintain an internal balance, or equilibrium, that kept the system working. Under this conceptual framework, called **structural functionalism**, British social anthropologists employed a synchronic approach in order to control their science experiments—analyzing contemporary societies at a fixed point in time without regard to historical context. By isolating as many variables as possible, especially by excluding history and outside influences such as neighboring groups or larger national or global dynamics, these anthropologists sought to focus narrowly on the culture at hand.

American anthropologist Ruth Benedict.

society

The focus of early British anthropological research whose structure and function could be isolated and studied scientifically.

structural functionalism

A conceptual framework positing that each element of society serves a particular function to keep the entire system in equilibrium.

Early practitioners of this approach included Alfred Radcliffe-Brown (1881–1955), who drew on his own work among the Indigenous people of the Andaman Islands of India (1922) and of Australia (1930), and E. E. Evans-Pritchard (1902–1973) and his classic ethnography of the Sudan, *The Nuer* (1940), which we will consider further in Chapters 3 and 10. Bronisław Malinowski (1884–1942) used an early form of functionalism in his ethnography of the Trobriand Islands, *Argonauts of the Western Pacific* (1922), discussed in more detail in Chapter 3. Later, British anthropologists, including Max Gluckman (1911–1975) in his work on rituals of rebellion and Victor Turner (1920–1983) in his work on religious symbols and rituals, critiqued earlier structural functionalists for ignoring the dynamics of conflict, tension, and change within the societies they studied. Their intervention marked a significant turn in the study of society and culture by British anthropologists.

CULTURE AND MEANING

One predominant view within anthropology in recent decades sees culture primarily as a set of ideas or knowledge shared by a group of people that provides a common body of information about how to behave, why to behave that way, and what that behavior means. The anthropologist Clifford Geertz (1926–2006), a key figure in this **interpretivist approach**, urged anthropologists to explore culture primarily as a symbolic system in which even simple, seemingly straight-forward actions can convey deep meanings.

interpretivist approach
A conceptual framework that sees culture primarily as a symbolic system of deep meaning.

In a classic example, Geertz (1973c) examines the difference between a wink and a twitch of the eye. Both involve the same movement of eye muscles, but a wink carries a meaning, which can change depending on the context in which it occurs—it may imply flirting, including a friend in a secret, or slyly signaling agreement. Deciphering a wink's meaning requires a complex, collective (shared) understanding of unspoken communication in a specific cultural context. Collective understandings of symbols and symbolic actions enable people to interact with one another in subtle yet complex ways without constantly stopping to explain themselves.

Geertz's essay "Deep Play: Notes on the Balinese Cockfight" (1973a) describes in intricate detail a cockfight—a common activity even today in local communities across Bali, a small island in the South Pacific. Geertz describes the elaborate breeding, raising, and training of the roosters; the scene of bedlam at the fight; the careful selection of the birds; the rituals of the knife man, who provides the razors for the birds' feet; the fight itself; the raucous betting before and during the fight; and the aftermath, with the cutting up of the losing cock and the dividing of its parts among participants in the fight.

thick description
A research strategy that combines detailed description of cultural activity with an analysis of the layers of deep cultural meaning in which those activities are embedded.

Geertz argues that such careful description of cultural activity is an essential part of understanding Balinese culture. But it is not enough. He claims that we must engage in **thick description**, looking beneath the surface activities to see

MAP 2.1
Bali

the layers of deep cultural meaning in which those activities are embedded. The cockfight is not simply a cockfight. It also represents generations of competition among the village families for prestige, power, and resources within the community. It symbolizes the negotiation of those families' prestige status and standing within the larger groups. For Geertz, all activities of the cockfight reflect these profound webs of meaning, and their analysis requires extensive description that uncovers those meanings. Indeed, according to Geertz, every cultural action is more than the action itself; it is also a symbol of deeper meaning.

Geertz's culture concept has provided a key theoretical framework for anthropological research. But, as we will see in the following section, it has also been criticized for not adequately considering the relations of power within cultures and the contested processes by which cultural meanings—norms, values, symbols, mental maps of reality—are established.

How Are Culture and Power Related?

Describe the ways that power is embedded in the culture concept.

As you have just read, anthropologists for many years focused primarily on culture as a system of ideas. But more recent scholarship has pushed anthropology to consider the deep interconnections between culture and power in more sophisticated ways (Foucault 1977; Gramsci 1971; Wolf 1982), and the chapters of this book take this challenge seriously.

power

The ability or potential to bring about change through action or influence.

Power is often described as the ability or potential to bring about change through action or influence, either one's own or that of a group or institution. This may include the ability to influence through force or the threat of force. Power is embedded in many kinds of social relations, from interpersonal relations, to institutions, to structural frameworks of whole societies. In effect, power is everywhere, and individuals participate in systems of power in complex ways. Throughout this book, we will work to unmask the dynamics of power that are central to all aspects of culture, including race and racism, ethnicity and nationalism, gender, human sexuality, economics, and family.

Anthropologist Eric Wolf (1923–1999) urged anthropologists to see power as an aspect of all human relationships. Consider the relationships in your own life: teacher/student, parent/child, employer/employee, landlord/tenant, lender/borrower, boyfriend/girlfriend. Wolf (1990, 1999) argued that all such human relationships have a power dynamic. Though cultures are often assumed to be composed of groups of similar people who uniformly share norms and values, in reality people in any given culture are usually diverse, and their relationships are complicated.

Preparations for a cockfight
outside a Hindu temple in Bali.
How do you analyze the deep
webs of meaning at play in any
cultural event?

Power in a culture reflects **stratification**—uneven distribution of resources and privileges among the culture's members—that often persists over generations. Some people are drawn into the center of the culture. Others are ignored, marginalized, or even annihilated. Power may be stratified along lines of gender, racial or ethnic group, class, age, family, religion, sexuality, or legal status. These structures of power organize relationships among people and create a framework through which access to cultural resources is distributed. As a result, some people are able to participate more fully in the culture than others. This balance of power is not fixed; it fluctuates. By examining how the resources, privileges, and opportunities of a culture are shared unevenly and unequally, we can begin to use culture as a conceptual guide to power and its workings.

stratification

The uneven distribution of resources and privileges among members of a group or culture.

POWER AND CULTURAL INSTITUTIONS

One key to understanding the relationship between culture and power is to recognize that a culture is more than just a set of ideas or patterns of behavior shared among a collection of individuals. A culture also includes the powerful institutions that these people create to promote and maintain their core values. Ethnographic research must consider a wide range of institutions that play central roles in the enculturation process. For example, schools teach a shared history, language, patterns of social interaction, notions of health, and scientific ideas of what exists in the world and how the world works. Religious institutions promote moral and ethical codes of behavior. The media convey images of what is considered normal and valued. Other prominent cultural institutions that reflect and shape norms and values include the family, medicine, government, courts, police, and the military.

These cultural institutions are also locations where people can debate and contest cultural norms and values. In 2003, an intense debate erupted in France about Muslim girls wearing headscarves to public schools. Although few girls actually wore headscarves, the controversy took on particular intensity in the aftermath of the events of September 11, 2001, the invasions of Afghanistan and Iraq, and terrorist incidents in Europe. For many non-Muslim people in France, the wearing of head coverings represented a grave danger to French society, particularly its commitment to equality for women, its history of ethnic assimilation, and its tradition of the separation of church and state. Passage of a law banning the headscarf from public schools was intended as a signal (to people both inside and outside France) of the country's commitment to these principles. But many Muslim girls believed that wearing the headscarf also expressed a commitment to French values—the country's commitment to religious freedom and liberty.

Despite legal challenges, strikes by students, and street demonstrations in opposition to the law, in 2004 the French government banned any clothing in public schools that indicates particular religious beliefs. Although the language of the law was broadly stated to include all religions, everyone understood that Muslim girls' headscarves were the target. France's public schools had become the venue for debating, contesting, and enforcing key French cultural norms and values (Bowen 2006). As we will see, cultural institutions such as schools are not only places where norms are enforced but also places where powerful ideas of what is normal and natural are shaped. Do you see parallels to current U.S. debates about mask mandates and mask wearing in public schools?

A young Muslim woman with two French flags pulled over her head covering marches in Paris against a French ban on religious symbols, including headscarves, in public schools.

HEGEMONY

The Italian political philosopher Antonio Gramsci (1891–1937) described two aspects of power. *Material power*, the first component, includes political, economic, or military power. It exerts itself through coercion or brute force. The second aspect of power involves the ability to create consent and agreement within a population, a condition that Gramsci (1971) called **hegemony**.

Gramsci recognized the tremendous power of culture—particularly the cultural institutions of media, schools, and religion—to shape what people think is normal, natural, and possible and thereby directly influence the scope of human action and interaction. Cultures, which develop slowly over time, include a shared belief system of what is right, what is wrong, and what is normal and appropriate. In this hegemony of ideas, some thoughts and actions become unthinkable, and group members develop a set of "beliefs" about what is normal and appropriate that come to be seen as natural "truths." The French sociologist Michel Foucault (1926–1984), in *Discipline and Punish* (1977), described this hegemonic aspect of power as the ability to make people discipline their own behavior so that they believe and act in certain "normal" ways, often against their own interests, even without a tangible threat of punishment for misbehavior.

Earlier in this chapter, we discussed anti-miscegenation laws in the history of the United States. These laws drew upon cultural beliefs in "natural" biological differences among races and the seemingly unnatural, deviant practice of intermarriage. Despite the elimination of these formal laws, a certain hegemony of thought remains: Many in U.S. culture still see interracial marriage as unthinkable and undoable. As evidence, consider U.S. intermarriage rates. According to the U.S. Census Bureau (2016), there were 5,818,000 interracial married couples in 2016, only 10.2 percent of all marriages in the United States.

Clearly, although U.S. culture has very few formal rules about whom one can marry, cultural norms combined with long-term geographic and institutional patterns of segregation still powerfully inform and enforce our behavior. As this example shows, views against interracial marriage do not require legal sanction to remain dominant, hegemonic norms.

hegemony
The ability of a dominant group to create consent and agreement within a population without the use or threat of force.

HUMAN AGENCY

Although hegemony can be very powerful, it does not completely dominate people's thinking. Individuals and groups have the power to contest cultural norms, values, mental maps of reality, symbols, institutions, and structures of power—a potential known as **agency**. Cultural beliefs and practices are not timeless; they change and can be changed. Cultures are not biologically determined; they are created over time by particular groups of people. By examining human agency, we see how culture serves as a realm in which battles over power take place—where

agency
The potential power of individuals and groups to contest cultural norms, values, mental maps of reality, symbols, institutions, and structures of power.

people debate, negotiate, contest, and enforce what is considered normal, what people can say, do, and even think.

Although a culture's dominant group may have greater access to power, resources, rights, or privileges, the systems of power such groups create are never absolute, and their dominance is never complete. Individuals and groups with less power or no power may contest the dominant power relationships and structures, whether through political, economic, religious, or military means. At times, these forms of resistance are visible, public, and well organized, including negotiations, protests, strikes, or rebellions. At other times, the resistance may be more subtle, discreet, and diffuse. For example, James Scott's book *Weapons of the Weak: Everyday Forms of Peasant Resistance* (1985) identifies strategies that people in very weak positions use to express their agency and to resist the dominant group.

How Much of Who You Are Is Shaped by Biology, and How Much by Culture?

Explain how biology relates to culture and human behavior.

Biology is important. We live in our bodies, after all. We feel, smell, taste, hear, and see the world around us through our bodies. We communicate with and through our bodies. And we have certain biological drives that are essential for survival. All humans must eat, drink, and sleep. But current research in physical and cultural anthropology shows that no matter how strong our biological needs or our hormones, odors, and appetites might be, culture and the environment in which we live exert powerful influences on what we think, on how we behave, on the shape and functions of our individual bodies, and even on how humans have evolved over time.

NATURE AND NURTURE

Popular discourse in the United States often assigns biology—and usually genes—the primary role in determining who we are. Anthropological research, however, consistently reveals the powerful roles that culture and environment together play in shaping our lives and bodies. Human genetic codes are 99.9 percent identical, so if behavior were entirely driven by our genes, we should expect to find very similar—even universal—behavioral responses to biological influences. Instead, we find remarkable physical and behavioral variety across cultures. Even the most basic human activities, such as eating, drinking, and sleeping, are carried out in remarkably distinct ways. All humans must do these things. But shared biological needs do not ensure shared cultural patterns.

Of course, food and liquid enter the body through the mouth and get digested in the stomach and intestines. But what goes in and how it goes in are other stories. Perhaps you find dog or snake or pony to be inedible, although these are delicacies in other cultures. Many people in China dislike cheese, a staple of North American and European diets. Even how, where, and how many times a day you eat and drink varies from culture to culture. You may use forks, knives, spoons, chopsticks, or hands. You may eat once a day, three times a day, or—like many Americans—six times a day (breakfast, coffee break, lunch, afternoon snack, dinner, midnight snack). You may prefer caviar or a Happy Meal.

Everyone sleeps each day, but some people sleep six hours a night, others eight. Some people take a midday nap. Many college students average six hours of sleep a night during the week and ten on the weekends. Whom you sleep with also varies by culture, with variations including spouses, parents and children, siblings, mothers and children, grandparents and grandchildren. All these patterns vary by culture, and even within a culture they may vary by age, gender, and class. Despite the cross-cultural evidence of human behavioral variation, many people believe that basic patterns of human behavior, intellectual capacity, and psychological tendencies are determined by biology, from warfare and sexuality to the shortage of women in math and science careers.

Most anthropologists have been highly critical of approaches that significantly overstate the importance of a genetic inheritance fixed in deep evolutionary time and that underestimate the role of culture and the environment in shaping human physical and behavioral diversity (McKinnon and Silverman 2005). Although contemporary genetic discoveries are opening up new realms of understanding about human biology, we are not close to linking certain genes or groups of genes with particular behaviors or characteristics. At best, we can imagine these connections based on contemporary patterns of behavior. But it often appears just as likely that contemporary notions of human nature are being projected back onto a mythological version of human prehistory that never existed.

We do have, however, much clearer indications of how cultural patterns and beliefs shape human behavior. In the debate over the origins of gender inequality in the upper echelons of math and science careers, we might look instead to gender stereotyping in the classroom, enculturation of girls, and conscious and unconscious gender bias in hiring and promotion practices. It may feel more comfortable to trace inequality to innate biological differences; a link might enable us to dismiss or excuse the inequality as "natural." But there is no biological evidence of this link. The current evidence is that these patterns of inequality and stratification are culturally constructed and completely changeable.

FROM HUMAN BEINGS TO HUMAN BECOMINGS

Contemporary anthropological research calls for a much more complex view of human evolution and life span development that incorporates multiple architects of the human physical form and behavior. An emerging synthesis looks at genes as part of a developmental history in which biology and culture are deeply entangled in a dynamic and ongoing biocultural process of change (Fuentes 2013). For instance, the emerging field of **epigenetics** explores how the environment into which one is born can directly affect the expression of genes during one's lifetime. In particular, epigenetics examines variations caused not by changes in the actual DNA sequence but by environmental factors that switch genes on and off and affect how cells read genes. These epigenetic marks may change in response to many of the processes anthropologists frequently study—nutrition, stress, disease, social inequality, and migration (Fuentes 2013; Thayer and Non 2015; Wade and Ferree 2015). Additionally, research shows that our bodies do not function in isolation as discrete biological units, despite what our popular culture narratives would lead us to believe. The human body contains approximately 100 trillion cells. About 90 percent are independent microorganisms that live within our bodies and form what has come to be known as the **human microbiome**. This microbiome plays a key role in many bodily functions, including human digestion, vitamin production, drug metabolism, and immunity (Palsson 2013; Warinner and Lewis 2015). Some scholars suggest that these new ways of thinking about the body and gene expression should lead us to think of ourselves not as human beings—shaped long ago by a completed evolutionary process— but as human *becomings* who are continually evolving and adapting, both on the species level and within the individual life span (see Ingold and Palsson 2013).

epigenetics

An area of study in the field of genetics exploring how environmental factors directly affect the expression of genes during one's lifetime.

human microbiome

The complete collection of microorganisms in the human body's ecosystem.

CONNECTING CULTURE AND BEHAVIOR

While direct links between specific genes and behavior have proven difficult to identify, we have much clearer indications of how cultural patterns and beliefs shape human behavior. Culture is learned from the people around us. It is not written into our DNA. Instead, we are born with the ability to learn any culture that we might be born into or move into. We have the ability to learn any language and master any set of beliefs, practices, norms, or values. This may seem obvious, but it is a crucial principle to understand as we examine the many cultural patterns in our own experience that we often assume to be normal, even natural. Such cultural practices are not universal to all humans. Rather, they are uniquely created in each culture. Recognition of this fact allows us to question common assumptions about the biological basis of most, if not all, human behavior, and instead to consider how learned patterns of belief and practice have been created and how they might be changed. Later in this book, in the chapters on race, ethnicity, gender, family, and human sexuality, we will explore the intersections of biology and culture in further detail.

As popular as it may be to think that genetics is the primary driver of our development as humans, even our long evolutionary process has been deeply influenced by culture. Ultimately, it is culture that has made us human and enabled us to evolve physically and in our patterns of relationship with others. For example, with the development of simple stone tools as early as 2.5 million years ago, culture allowed our ancestors to adapt to the world around them. Stone tools (in particular, hand axes and choppers) enabled our ancestors to butcher meat more quickly and efficiently, thereby providing higher quantities of protein for the developing brain and influencing the direction of our physical adaptation. In cases such as these, the power of culture to direct and modify biological instincts is indisputable. Over time, cultural adaptations—from control of fire, to the development of language, to the invention of condoms and birth control pills—have replaced genetic adaptations as the primary way humans adapt to and manipulate their physical and social environments.

How Is Culture Created?

Analyze how a culture of consumerism is created.

Culture does not emerge out of the blue. It is learned and taught through the process of enculturation. It is created over time, shaped by people and the institutions they establish in relationship to the environment around them. Culture is not fixed. It is invented, changed, contested, and negotiated. Nor is it bounded.

It moves and flows across regions and between people. You will help create many cultures over the course of your life, even if on a small scale. Humans create cultures every time we form a new group, whether a classroom, club, nonprofit, business, or family. How does a new group establish a set of norms, values, symbols, mental maps of reality, and relationships of power? Just as we have examined the relationship between culture and power, we can analyze the processes through which culture is created (Moussa, Newberry, and Urban 2021). Let's consider the consumer culture that has become so central to contemporary life.

CREATING CONSUMER CULTURE

In many parts of the world, consumerism has become more than an economic activity. It is a way of life, a way of looking at the world—a culture. The culture of consumerism includes norms, values, beliefs, practices, and institutions that have become commonplace and accepted as normal and that cultivate the desire to acquire consumer goods to enhance one's lifestyle (McCracken 1991, 2005).

Advertising, marketing, and financial services industries work to transform the cultural values of frugality, modesty, and self-denial into patterns of spending and consumption associated with acquiring the material goods of a middle-class lifestyle. Many key cultural rituals now focus on consumption. In the United States, holidays such as Valentine's Day, Mother's Day, and Father's Day all promote the purchase of gifts, as do birthdays, weddings, and anniversaries. Christmas, which in early U.S. history featured public drinking, lewd behavior, and aggressive begging, by the nineteenth century was being transformed into a family-centered ritual of gift giving from parents to children. Moreover, the invented character of Santa Claus was promoted as the mythical mediator of gift exchange and the symbol of Christmas consumer marketing (Nissenbaum 1996). The culture of consumerism has become so powerful that it successfully promotes spending and consumption even when people don't have money.

ADVERTISING

Used as a powerful tool of enculturation, advertising teaches how to be "successful" in consumer culture, how to be cool and normal. Social media influencers champion products assured to make us popular. Commercials promise that clothes, perfume, deodorant, haircuts, and expensive gifts will bring us love. Having our teeth straightened and whitened will help us network. A large, expensive car and proper insurance will protect our families and make us responsible and mature adults. Magazines, television shows, and films promote stars we are encouraged to emulate. If only we could dress like them and imitate their lifestyles, then we would be more desirable. The culture of consumerism tells us that having these things will bring us better friends, better sex, stronger families, higher-paying jobs, fancier houses, faster cars, sharper picture definition, and truer sound quality.

The advertising industry is key in shaping cultural norms and values around shopping while arousing our desires for goods and services. Consider that children in the United States watch up to 40,000 television commercials a year (Vitelli 2013). In addition, they are bombarded with advertising on the Internet, social media, video games, and YouTube videos. Many children's television programs are themselves thinly disguised advertisements for products featuring their characters, from lunch boxes to clothing to action figures.

Advertising appears before and during movies in the theater, at sporting events, in department stores and shopping malls, on billboards, and in store windows. Your favorite websites and social media are covered with advertisements. So are your clothes. Even your classroom is full of advertisements that you most likely do not notice: all the labels and tags on computers, pens, notebooks, backpacks, food packaging, and soda cans. Owning certain products and brands becomes symbolic of happiness, love, beauty, and success, or at least the potential for upward social mobility.

FINANCIAL SERVICES AND CREDIT CARDS

The financial services industry makes sure that once our desires are aroused, we have access to money to make our dreams a reality—at a small price. With the advent of computers and the deregulation of banking in the 1970s, credit cards burst on the scene, transforming the financial environment. Banks, chain stores, and financial services corporations carry out intensive marketing to promote their cards. In 2022, Americans carried $838 billion dollars of credit card debt (Latham 2022).

College students are a key target of the credit industry, which promotes credit cards on campus and through the mail regardless of students' ability to repay any debts they accrue. Credit cards grease the wheels of consumer culture. To pay them off, we need to intensify our participation: Work harder. Make more money. Then we can shop more. As credit card limits max out, banks and mortgage companies encourage homeowners to refinance their homes, taking out second mortgages to pay for day-to-day expenses and speculating that housing prices will remain high and continue to increase. Underlying these shifts is the fundamental drive of contemporary capitalism toward perpetual growth. People need to buy, make, invest, and profit more and more each year if the economy is to keep growing. And so contemporary capitalism invests heavily to arouse our desire and promote the expansion of the culture of consumerism.

How Is Globalization Transforming Culture?

Employ the concept of globalization to understanding contemporary culture change.

Cultures have never been made up of completely isolated or bounded groups of people located in a particular place. As we discussed in Chapter 1, cultures have always been influenced by flows of people, ideas, and goods, whether through migration, trade, or invasion. Today's flows of globalization are intensifying the exchange and diffusion of people, ideas, and goods, creating more interaction and engagement among cultures. Let's consider three key interrelated effects of globalization on local cultures: homogenization, the global flows of culture through migration, and increased cosmopolitanism.

THE GLOBAL AND LOCAL IN TENSION: HOMOGENIZING OR DIVERSIFYING

The expansion of global corporations, products, and markets has led some anthropologists and cultural activists to warn of the rise of a homogenized global culture dominated by McDonald's, Levi's, Coca-Cola, CNN, Hollywood, and U.S. cultural values. Will the spread of Western goods, images, and ideas diminish the diversity of the world's cultures as foreign influences inundate local practices, products, and ways of thinking? Certainly, global encounters of people, ideas, and things are influencing local cultures and communities. But instead of homogenization, the result of globalization is often hybridization, a mixing or incorporation and reworking of the influences of other cultures into a community's beliefs and practices. Global encounters may even transform global practices and commodities to reflect more local cultural character.

Consider McDonald's. Launched in the 1940s in San Bernardino, California, today McDonald's operates nearly 40,000 restaurants in 119 countries. Though McDonald's is a global brand, as the company has expanded it has adapted its menu in response to local tastes, culinary traditions, laws, and religious beliefs. In Egypt, where McDonald's has more than seventy locations, the menu includes McFalafel Sandwiches. In Morocco and other parts of the Middle East, the McArabia, a grilled chicken sandwich, is served on flatbread. McDonald's serves a teriyaki McBurger in Japan, McSpaghetti in the Philippines, and certified halal food in Malaysia. It has kosher stores in Israel, McCurrywurst hot sausages in Germany, and the McBurrito in Mexico.

To many people in developing countries, elements of global culture like McDonald's symbolically represent the opportunity for economic advancement and participation in the idealized middle-class, consumerist lifestyle associated with these products. In *Golden Arches East: McDonald's in East Asia* (1998), James Watson suggests that East Asians in Tokyo, Japan; Seoul, Korea; Hong Kong; Beijing, China; and Taipei, Taiwan, go to McDonald's not so much for the food but to participate in what they view as a middle-class activity. By eating out and eating Western fast food, they hope to align themselves with the Western middle-class norms and values to which they aspire (Yan 2004).

A McDonald's restaurant in downtown Manila, capital of the Philippines, advertises the McDo Rice Burger, a local product added to McDonald's standard global menu.

MIGRATION AND THE GLOBAL FLOWS OF CULTURE

The large-scale movement of people within and across national boundaries associated with contemporary globalization reveals that cultures are not necessarily bound to particular geographic locations. People migrate with their cultural beliefs and practices. They incorporate the cultural practices of their homelands into their new communities. They build links to their homelands through which culture continues to be exchanged.

Robert Smith's book *Mexican New York* (2006) reveals one example of the deep transnational connections—links across national borders—that have become increasingly common in today's globalizing world. Direct flights physically link immigrants living in the suburbs of New York City to their hometowns in Mexico in five hours. Telephone calls, emails, and videoconferences connect families and communities. The Mexican town of Tihuateca relies heavily on money sent back from villagers in New York City to build roads, water systems, and schools. Community leaders travel between countries to strengthen relationships, promote projects, and raise funds. In Boston, meanwhile, immigrants from India, Pakistan, Ireland, and Brazil maintain intense connections with their home communities, particularly through transnational religious practices. And a charismatic preacher from Brazil can lead thousands of Brazilians gathered in a Boston auditorium in worship by satellite hookup (Levitt 2007). These stories and many others reveal how global flows of people are transforming local cultures in both the sending and the receiving countries (Appadurai 1990; see also Chapter 10).

INCREASING COSMOPOLITANISM

A third significant effect of globalization on culture is that the increasing flows of people, ideas, and products have allowed worldwide access to cultural patterns that are new, innovative, and stimulating. Local cultures are exposed to a greater range of cultural ideas and products—such as agricultural strategies and medicines, to name just two. Globalization means that communities in the most remote parts of the world increasingly participate in experiences that bridge and link cultural practices, norms, and values across great distances, leading to what some scholars have called a new cosmopolitanism.

Cosmopolitanism is a very broad, sometimes global, outlook, rather than a limited, local one—an outlook that combines both universality and difference (Appiah 2006). The term is usually used to describe sophisticated urban professionals who travel and feel at home in different parts of the world. But anthropologist Lila Abu-Lughod's study *Dramas of Nationhood: The Politics of Television in Egypt* (2005) explores the emergence of cosmopolitanism even among Egypt's rural poor. Her book explores the role of television dramas—much like American soap operas, but more in tune with political and social issues—in creating ideas

In a globalizing age, local cultures are increasingly exposed to a vast array of people, ideas, and products. Here, a montage of images from a day on Egyptian television, with channels from Egypt and across the Middle East, includes comedy and music from Lebanon, old Egyptian films, American entertainment, and news and religious discussion programs.

MAP 2.2
Egypt

of a national culture, even among rural Egyptians, and crafting the identity of the new Egyptian citizen.

Abu-Lughod's ethnography of television pushes us to move beyond notions of single cultures sharing a set of ideas and meanings distinct from those of other cultures in an era of mass media, migration, and globalization. Television, she argues, "is an extraordinary technology for breaking the boundaries and intensifying and multiplying encounters among life-worlds, sensibilities and ideas" (2005, 45). By the 1990s, there were 6 million television sets in Egypt, and more than 90 percent of the population had access. In this reality, television provides material—produced somewhere else—that is consumed locally; it is inserted into, mixed up with, and interpreted by local knowledge and systems of meaning.

Even though poverty prevents the people in Abu-Lughod's study from fully participating in the consumer culture of commodities promoted by television programming and commercials, they are not untouched by these features of cosmopolitanism.

The influences of globalization ensure that even in rural Egyptian peasant culture, the knowledge of other worlds comes not only from television but also from foreign friends, tourists, visiting scholars and anthropologists, relatives migrating to find work in cities, imported movies and electronics, and even teachers trained by the Egyptian state and their approved textbooks. This is just one example of the powerful effects of the intersection of culture and globalization. No matter where you look in the twenty-first century, you are sure to find some elements of this intersection.

Toolkit

Thinking Like an Anthropologist
Analyzing Mask Wearing in American Culture

Every day, culture is all around us. It informs our thoughts and actions; guides us through complex interactions in our families, schools, jobs, and other personal relationships; and even shapes the way we perceive reality. Thinking like an anthropologist can help you to better understand yourself and those around you and to analyze your own culture and other cultures you encounter in this globalizing world.

In thinking about the controversies that have arisen about mask wearing in U.S. culture and around the world, as discussed in the chapter opener, consider the questions we have raised about culture:

- **What is culture?**

- **How has the culture concept developed in anthropology?**

- **How are culture and power related?**

- **How much of who you are is shaped by biology, and how much by culture?**

- **How is culture created?**

- **How is globalization transforming culture?**

Perhaps you or someone you know has been involved in a controversy about mask wearing during the pandemic. Or perhaps you have been particularly moved by reading about a similar incident, perhaps in a school. Drawing on your own experience, how can the key questions of this chapter help you think more deeply about masking in American culture? As anthropologists, we can analyze mask wearing during the pandemic as a system of meaning, with norms, values, symbols, and mental maps of reality. We can also analyze it as a system of power, including not only individual actions but also the cultural institutions—social, political, economic—that create, promote and sustain it and the social movements that challenge and contest it. We can consider the social life of the masks involved. We can examine the assumed links between mask wearing and biology. And we can place mask wearing within a global perspective. By thinking like an anthropologist, you are better prepared to understand and analyze this complex cultural phenomenon and, if you are so inclined, take concrete steps to shape the future.

Key Terms

culture (p. 36)

enculturation (p. 36)

norms (p. 38)

values (p. 39)

symbol (p. 40)

mental maps of reality (p. 41)

cultural appropriation (p. 43)

unilineal cultural evolution (p. 45)

historical particularism (p. 45)

society (p. 46)

structural functionalism (p. 46)

interpretivist approach (p. 47)

thick description (p. 47)

power (p. 48)

stratification (p. 49)

hegemony (p. 51)

agency (p. 51)

epigenetics (p. 54)

human microbiome (p. 54)

Chapter 3
Fieldwork and
Ethnography

Learning Objectives

- Define fieldwork and its fundamental principles.

- Trace the development of fieldwork in the discipline's history.

- Summarize the key fieldwork strategies, skills, and perspectives.

- Demonstrate knowledge of ethnographic writing principles and forms.

- Describe the ethical concerns associated with fieldwork and ethnographic writing.

- Analyze the impact of globalization on fieldwork strategies today.

Over many years, anthropologist Nancy Scheper-Hughes invested herself in trying to understand the lives of the women and children of one particular shantytown in Brazil. Her research resulted in numerous articles and an award-winning ethnography, *Death Without Weeping: The Violence of Everyday Life in Brazil* (1992). Scheper-Hughes's efforts reflect the deep commitment of anthropologists to *ethnographic fieldwork*—a research strategy for understanding the world through intense interaction with a local community of people over an extended period.

Anthropologist Nancy Scheper-Hughes
researched survival strategies of mothers and
children in a Brazilian shantytown.

MAP 3.1
Brazil

Burial of an infant in the Alto do Cruzeiro favela in northeast Brazil. How did anthropologist Nancy Scheper-Hughes make sense of the "death without weeping" that she found in this poor community?

Scheper-Hughes first arrived in Brazil's Alto do Cruzeiro (Crucifix Hill) in 1965 as a Peace Corps volunteer to assist in community development and health promotion. That year, a severe drought had created food and water shortages, and a military coup had spread political and economic chaos throughout the country. In the Alto, more than 350 babies died in 1965 out of a total population of a little more than 5,000. Scheper-Hughes later wrote, "There were reasons enough for the deaths in the miserable conditions of shanty-town life. What puzzled me was the seeming indifference of Alto women to the death of their infants and their willingness to attribute to their own tiny offspring an aversion to life that made their deaths seem wholly natural, indeed all but anticipated" (1989, 10).

This puzzle crystallized her research agenda as she returned to the Alto many times over the ensuing years to conduct ethnographic fieldwork. Scheper-Hughes found that it was possible to reduce diarrhea and dehydration-induced death among infants and toddlers in the shantytown with a simple solution of sugar, salt, and water. But it was more difficult to convince a mother to rescue a child she perceived as likely to die, a baby she already thought of as "an angel rather than a son or daughter." The high expectancy of death led mothers to differentiate between infants whom they saw as "thrivers and survivors" and those seen as born already "wanting to die." Scheper-Hughes found that in this environment, part of learning to be a mother was learning which babies to let go of and which ones it was safe to love.

Scheper-Hughes's experience in the Alto led her to rethink "mother love." What does the idea of mother love mean in the impoverished context of Alto do Cruzeiro?

Scheper-Hughes suggests that Alto women were doing what must be done given their context, where the real dangers were "poverty, deprivation, sexism, chronic hunger, and economic exploitation." Reflecting on this high-risk environment, she asks, "If mother love is, as many psychologists and some feminists believe, a seemingly natural and universal maternal script, what does it mean to women for whom scarcity, loss, sickness, and deprivation have made that love frantic and robbed them of their grief, seeming to turn hearts to stone?" (1989, 14).

Their experience, suggests Scheper-Hughes, compares more aptly to a battlefield or an overcrowded emergency room where actions are guided by the practice of triage—prioritizing the treatment of those who can be saved. "In their slowness to anthropomorphize and personalize their infants, everything is mobilized so as to prevent maternal overattachment and, therefore, grief at death. The bereaved mother is told not to cry, that her tears will dampen the wings of her little angel so that she cannot fly up to her heavenly home" (16). Scheper-Hughes suggests that in these difficult conditions, Alto women are left with no choice but to find the best way to carry on with their lives and nurture those children who have the best chance of survival.

What can you learn about fieldwork by reading about Scheper-Hughes's research? A middle-class woman from the United States, Scheper-Hughes traveled to one of the poorest places in the world, learned the language, lived in the community, built relationships of trust, accompanied local people through the births and deaths of their children, and searched for meaning amid the pain. As you might imagine, the fieldwork experience can become more than a strategy for understanding human culture. Fieldwork has the potential to radically transform the anthropologist. Can you imagine making the same commitment Scheper-Hughes did?

The term *fieldwork* implies going out to "the field" to do extensive research. Although in the history of anthropology this has often meant going a long way from home, as Scheper-Hughes did, contemporary anthropologists also study human culture and activities in their own countries and local contexts. By exploring the practice of fieldwork, you will gain a deeper understanding of how anthropologists go about their work. In particular, in this chapter we will consider:

- **What is unique about ethnographic fieldwork, and why do anthropologists conduct this kind of research?**
- **How did the practice of fieldwork develop?**
- **How do anthropologists get started conducting fieldwork?**
- **How do anthropologists write ethnography?**
- **What moral and ethical concerns guide anthropologists in their research and writing?**
- **How have fieldwork strategies changed in response to globalization?**

By the end of the chapter, you will see both how professional anthropologists employ fieldwork strategies and how fieldwork can provide a valuable toolkit for gathering information to make decisions in your own life. Fieldwork skills and strategies can help you navigate the many unfamiliar or cross-cultural experiences you will encounter at work or school, in your neighborhood, or in your family. And hopefully you will see how key fieldwork strategies can help you become a more engaged and responsible citizen of the world.

What Is Unique about Ethnographic Fieldwork, and Why Do Anthropologists Conduct This Kind of Research?

Define fieldwork and its fundamental principles.

ethnographic fieldwork

A primary research strategy in cultural anthropology that typically involves living and interacting with a community of people over an extended period to better understand their lives.

Ethnographic fieldwork is the unique set of practices that anthropologists—particularly cultural anthropologists—have developed to put people first as we analyze how human societies work. Chemists conduct experiments in laboratories. Economists analyze financial trends. Demographers crunch census data. Historians pore over records and library archives. Sociologists, economists, and political scientists analyze trends, quantifiable data, official organizations, and national policies. But anthropologists start with people and their local communities. Even though the whole world is our field, our unique perspective first focuses on the details and patterns of human life in the local setting.

FIELDWORK BEGINS WITH PEOPLE

Through fieldwork, we try to understand people's everyday lives, to see what they do, and to understand why. By living with others over an extended period, we seek to understand their experiences through their eyes. We participate in their activities, take careful notes, conduct interviews, take photographs, and record music. We make maps of communities, both of the physical environment and of family and social relationships. Although careful observation of the details of daily life is the first step, through intensive fieldwork anthropologists look beyond the taken-for-granted, everyday experience of life to discover the complex systems of power and meaning that people construct to shape their existence. These include the many systems discussed throughout this book: gender, sexuality, race, ethnicity, religion, kinship, and economic and political systems. Learning to ask good questions is key to successful fieldwork. This requires careful preparation and study before going to the field. It also requires careful listening once in the field to adjust one's questions to new information and unexpected circumstances. As we extend our analysis as anthropologists, we try to see how local lives compare to the lives of others and fit into larger human patterns and global contexts.

FIELDWORK SHAPES THE ANTHROPOLOGIST

Fieldwork experience is considered an essential part of an anthropologist's training. It is the activity through which we learn the basic tools of our trade, earn credibility as effective observers of culture, and establish our reputation as full members of the discipline. Engaging in fieldwork teaches us the basic research strategies of our discipline and hones those skills: careful listening and observation, asking meaningful questions, engagement with strangers, cross-cultural interaction, and deep analysis of human interactions and systems of power and inequality. We learn empathy for those around us, develop a more global consciousness, and uncover our own ethnocentrism. Indeed, fieldwork is a rite of passage, an initiation into our discipline, and a common bond among anthropologists who have been through the experience.

Fieldwork transforms us. In fact, it is quite common for anthropologists entering the field to experience *culture shock*—a sense of disorientation caused by the overwhelmingly new and unfamiliar people and experiences encountered every day. Over time, the disorientation may fade as the unfamiliar becomes familiar. But then, many anthropologists feel culture shock again when returning home, where their new perspective causes previously familiar people and customs to seem very strange. Through this cross-cultural training, anthropology provides the tools to unlock our cultural imaginations, to move beyond our ethnocentrism, to see the incredible diversity of the world's cultures, and to consider the full potential of human life.

FIELDWORK AS SOCIAL SCIENCE AND AS ART

Fieldwork is a strategy for gathering data about the human condition, particularly through the life experiences of local people in local situations. Fieldwork is an experimental setting for testing hypotheses and building theories about the diversity of human behavior and the interactions of people with systems of power—a scientific method for examining how the social world really works. As such, anthropologists have developed techniques such as participant observation, field notes, interviews, kinship and social network analysis, life histories, and mapping—all of which we will discuss in this chapter.

But fieldwork is also an art. Its success depends on the anthropologist's more intuitive abilities to negotiate complex interactions, usually in an unfamiliar cultural environment; to build relationships of trust; to make sense of patterns of behavior; and to be conscious of their own biases and particular vantage point. Ethnographic fieldwork depends on the ability of an outsider—the anthropologist—to develop close personal relationships over time in a local community and to understand the everyday experiences of often-unfamiliar people. It requires the anthropologist to risk being changed in the process—the risk of mutual transformation. Successful ethnographic fieldwork also depends on the anthropologist's ability to tell the subjects' stories to an audience that has no knowledge of them in ways that accurately reflect the subjects' lives and shed light on the general human condition.

FIELDWORK INFORMS DAILY LIFE

MAP 3.2
Tucson/New York

Anthropologist Brackette Williams suggests that fieldwork can even be a kind of "homework"—a strategy for gathering information that will help the anthropologist make informed decisions in order to act morally and to weigh in advance the likely consequences of their actions. Williams studied homelessness and begging in New York City and Tucson, Arizona, over a period of several years. She began with some very practical questions about whether to give to homeless people asking for money on the subway she took to work in New York City every day.

Her research started with careful observation of all the people involved, including people experiencing homelessness and others on the subway, particularly those deciding to give or not to give. She continued with informal and formal interviews, careful note taking, and background reading. In the process, she began to identify a clear set of stories and begging styles and to examine the complicated set of responses made by people on the subway who were being asked for money.

Williams suggests that this approach to her daily dilemma was not only an interesting use of her ethnographic fieldwork skills and training but also "socially required homework" for anyone who confronts complex problems in daily life, whether with family, friends, school, work, or politics. Can you imagine using this strategy to explore a problem, puzzle, or question in your life?

How Did the Practice of Fieldwork Develop?

Trace the development of fieldwork in the discipline's history.

EARLY ACCOUNTS OF ENCOUNTERS WITH OTHERS

Descriptive accounts of other cultures existed long before anthropologists came on the scene. For centuries, explorers, missionaries, traders, government bureaucrats, and travelers recorded descriptions of the people they encountered. For example, nearly 2,500 years ago, the Greek historian Herodotus wrote about his travels in Egypt, Persia, and the area now known as Ukraine. In the thirteenth century, the Venetian explorer Marco Polo chronicled his travels from Italy across the silk route to China. And the Chinese admiral Zheng He reported on his extended voyages to India, the Middle East, and East Africa in the fifteenth century, seventy years before Christopher Columbus arrived in the Americas. These are just a few of the many early accounts of encounters with other peoples across the globe.

NINETEENTH-CENTURY ANTHROPOLOGY AND THE COLONIAL ENCOUNTER

The roots of anthropology and fieldwork lie in the intense globalization of the late nineteenth century. At that time, the increased international movement of Europeans—particularly merchants, colonial administrators, and missionaries—generated a broad array of data that stimulated scientists and philosophers of the day to make sense of the emerging picture of humanity's incredible diversity (Stocking 1983). They asked questions such as: Who are these other people? Why are their foods, clothing, architecture, rituals, family structures, and political and economic systems so different from ours and from one another's? Are they related to us biologically? If so, how?

Fieldwork was not a common practice at the beginning of our discipline. In fact, many early anthropologists, such as Edward Burnett Tylor (1832–1917), are now considered "armchair anthropologists" because they did not conduct their own research; instead, they worked at home in their armchairs analyzing the reports of others. One early exception was Lewis Henry Morgan (1818–1881), who conducted fieldwork among Native Americans in the United States. As we discussed in Chapter 2, Tylor and Morgan were leading figures in attempts to organize the accumulating data, to catalogue human diversity, and to make sense of the many questions it raised. These men applied the theory of unilineal cultural evolution—the idea that all cultures would naturally evolve through the same sequence of stages from simple to complex and that the diversity of human cultural expression represented different stages in the evolution of human culture, stages which could be classified in comparison to one another.

Early anthropologists encountered a world of people already in motion. The 1375 Catalan Atlas shows the world as it was then known. It depicts the location of continents and islands as well as information on ancient and medieval tales, regional politics, astronomy, and astrology.

THE PROFESSIONALIZATION OF SOCIAL SCIENTIFIC DATA GATHERING AND ANALYSIS

Succeeding generations of anthropologists in Europe and North America rejected unilineal cultural evolution as being too Eurocentric, too ethnocentric, too hierarchical, and lacking adequate data to support its grand claims. Anthropologists in the early twentieth century developed more-sophisticated research methods—particularly ethnographic fieldwork—to professionalize social scientific data gathering.

Franz Boas: Fieldwork and the Four-Field Approach.

In the United States, Franz Boas (1858–1942) and his students focused on developing a four-field approach to anthropological research, which included gathering cultural, linguistic, archaeological, and biological data. Boas's early work among the Indigenous Kwakiutl people of the Pacific Northwest of the United States and Canada firmly grounded him in the fieldwork process, as he learned about Kwakiutl culture through extensive participation in their daily lives, religious rituals, and economic activities. After settling in New York City in the early twentieth century as a professor of anthropology at Columbia University and curator of the American Museum of Natural History, Boas (and his students) embarked on a massive project to document the Native American cultures being devastated by the westward expansion of European settlers across the continent.

Often called **salvage ethnography**, Boas's approach involved the rapid gathering of all available material, including historical artifacts, photographs, recordings of spoken languages, songs, and detailed information about cultural beliefs and practices—from religious rituals to family patterns, gender roles to political structures. With limited time and financial resources, these ethnographers often met with a small number of elderly informants and focused on conducting oral interviews rather than observing actual behavior. Despite the limitations of this emerging fieldwork, these early projects built upon Boas's commitment to historical particularism when investigating local cultures (see Chapter 2) and defined two continuing characteristics of American anthropology: the four-field approach and **cultural relativism** (Stocking 1989).

Bronisław Malinowski: Fieldwork and Participation.

Across the Pacific Ocean, Bronisław Malinowski (1884–1942) went even further than Boas in developing cultural anthropology's research methods. Malinowski, a Polish citizen who later became a leading figure in British anthropology, found himself stuck for a year on the Trobriand Islands as a result of World War I. His classic ethnography, *Argonauts of the Western Pacific* (1922), has become most famous for its examination of the Kula ring, an elaborate system of exchange. The ring involved thousands of individuals across many islands, some of whom traveled hundreds of miles by canoe, in an exchange of Kula valuables (in particular, shell necklaces and armbands).

Argonauts also set new standards for fieldwork. In the opening chapter, Malinowski proposes a set of guidelines for conducting fieldwork based on his own experience. He urges fellow anthropologists to stay for a long period in their field sites, learn the local language, get off the veranda (that is, leave the safety of

salvage ethnography

Fieldwork strategy developed by Franz Boas to collect cultural, material, linguistic, and biological information about Native American populations being devastated by the westward expansion of European settlers.

cultural relativism

Understanding a group's beliefs and practices within their own cultural context, without making judgments.

American anthropologist Franz Boas in Inuit clothing during fieldwork in the Pacific Northwest of North America, 1883.

British anthropologist Bronisław Malinowski at a bachelor's house in Kasanai, Trobriand Islands, ca. 1915–18.

their front porch to mingle with the local people), engage in participant observation, and explore the mundane "imponderabilia of actual life"—the seemingly commonplace, everyday items and activities of people and their communities. Using these strategies enabled Malinowski to analyze the complex dynamics of the Kula ring, both its system of economic exchange and its social networking.

Although some of these suggestions may seem obvious to us a century later, Malinowski's formulation of a comprehensive strategy for understanding local culture was groundbreaking and has withstood the test of time. Of particular importance has been his conceptualization of **participant observation** as the cornerstone of fieldwork. For anthropologists, it is not enough to observe from a distance. We must learn about people by participating in their daily activities, walking in their shoes, seeing through their eyes. Participant observation gives depth to our observations, provides intimate knowledge of people and their communities, and helps guard against mistaken assumptions based on observation from a distance (Kuper 1983).

participant observation

A key anthropological research strategy involving both participation in and observation of the daily life of the people being studied.

E. E. Evans-Pritchard and British Social Anthropology. Between the 1920s and 1960s, many British social anthropologists viewed anthropology as a science designed to discover the component elements and patterns of society (see Chapter 2). Fieldwork was their key methodology for conducting their scientific experiments. Adopting a *synchronic approach*, they sought to control their experiments by limiting consideration of the larger historical and social context in order to isolate as many variables as possible.

E. E. Evans-Pritchard (1902–1973), one of the leading figures during this period, wrote a classic ethnography in this style. In *The Nuer* (1940), based on his research with a group of rural Sudanese people over eleven months between 1930 and 1936, Evans-Pritchard systematically documents the group's social

MAP 3.3
The Nuer Region of East Africa

British anthropologist E. E. Evans-Pritchard seated among Nuer men and boys in southern Sudan, ca. 1930.

structures—political, economic, and kinship—and captures the intricate details of community life. But later anthropologists have criticized his failure to consider the historical context and larger social world. Indeed, the Nuer in Evans-Pritchard's study lived under British occupation in the Sudan, and many Nuer participated in resistance to British occupation despite an intensive British pacification campaign against the Sudanese during the time of Evans-Pritchard's research. Later anthropologists have questioned how he could have omitted such important details and ignored his status as a British subject when it had such potential for undermining his research.

Margaret Mead: Fieldwork and Public Anthropology. Margaret Mead (1901–1978), a student of Franz Boas, conducted pioneering field-work in the 1920s, famously examining teen sexuality in *Coming of Age in Samoa* (1928) and, later, the wide diversity of gender roles in three separate groups in Papua New Guinea (1935). Perhaps most significant, however,

MAP 3.4
Samoa

Mead mobilized her fieldwork findings to engage in crucial scholarly and public debates at home in the United States. At a time when many in the United States argued that gender roles were biologically determined, Mead's fieldwork testified to the fact that U.S. cultural norms were not found cross-culturally but were culturally specific. Mead's unique blend of fieldwork and dynamic writing provided her with the authority and opportunity to engage a broad public audience and made her a powerful figure in the roiling cultural debates of her generation.

American anthropologist Margaret Mead with a mother and child in the Admiralty Islands, South Pacific, 1953.

Zora Neale Hurston: Fieldwork in the American South. Zora

Neale Hurston (1891–1960), perhaps best known as a leading literary figure in the Harlem Renaissance of the early twentieth century, was, like Margaret Mead, a student of Franz Boas at Barnard College and Columbia University. While Mead conducted fieldwork in the South Pacific, as part of his salvage ethnography project Boas sent Hurston to the American South, particularly Florida, to conduct intensive fieldwork on Black folk culture. Hurston, who grew up

Zora Neale Hurston's literary style was grounded in her distinctly anthropological approach.

in Eatonville, Florida, just north of Orlando, traveled throughout central and northern Florida, across the southeastern United States, and later to Jamaica, the Bahamas, and Honduras. In reams of field notes, photographs, audio recordings, and film reels, Hurston documented folk tales, stories, sayings, work songs, religious rituals, character sketches, life histories, spirituals, blues music, and other ethnographic material, culminating in her book *Mules and Men* (1935) on southern Black folklore and folk religion. Though Hurston had been sent to conduct salvage ethnography on what Boas and others incorrectly considered a dying and even inferior cultural tradition, her work captured the vitality of local storytelling as central to the ongoing construction of a dynamic Black cultural tradition and community identity.

Hurston proved to be several generations ahead of her time in anthropology: She conducted research in her own community rather than in a distant place years before that became common. She broke with anthropological writing expectations, writing for a popular rather than a scholarly audience by merging inventive literary conventions with her rich ethnographic data. Her fieldwork and its characters—loggers, migrant farm workers, turpentine boilers, bootleggers, and juke joint operators—provided rich material for her creative work for years to come. Over the course of her career, she published four novels, other nonfiction books, more than fifty stories, essays, and collections of poetry, and she directed numerous plays and ethnographic films.

The People of Puerto Rico: A Turn to the Global. During the 1950s, a team of anthropologists headed by Julian Steward (1902–1972) and including Sidney Mintz (1922–2015) and Eric Wolf (1923–1999) engaged in a collaborative fieldwork project at multiple sites on the island of Puerto Rico. Steward's resulting ethnography, *The People of Puerto Rico* (1956), marked the beginning of a significant anthropological turn away from studies of seemingly isolated, small-scale, nonindustrial societies toward studies that examined the integration of local communities into a modern world system. In particular, the new focus explored the impacts of colonialism and the spread of capitalism on local people. Mintz, in *Sweetness and Power* (1985), later expanded his fieldwork interests in Puerto Rican sugar production to consider the intersections of local histories and local production of sugar with global flows of colonialism and capitalism. Wolf, in *Europe and the People Without History* (1982), continued a lifetime commitment to reasserting forgotten local histories—or the stories of people ignored by a European-dominated history—into the story of the modern world economic system. Historically, Wolf argued, local cultures have been interconnected on the world level, not isolated from one another. And their unique histories have themselves shaped global processes and interactions, not just been shaped by them.

Annette Weiner: Feminism and Reflexivity. In the 1980s, anthropologist Annette Weiner (1933–1997) retraced Malinowski's footsteps to conduct a new study of the Trobriand Islands sixty years later. Weiner quickly noticed aspects of Trobriand culture that had not surfaced in Malinowski's writings. In particular, she took careful note of the substantial role women played in the island economy. Whereas Malinowski had focused his attention on the elaborate male-dominated system of economic exchange among islands, Weiner found that women had equally important economic roles and equally valuable accumulations of wealth.

Anthropologist Barbara Myerhoff with two members of the Aliyah Senior Citizens' Center in Southern California, the focus of her book *Number Our Days*.

reflexivity

A critical self-examination of the role the anthropologist plays and an awareness that one's identity affects one's fieldwork and theoretical analyses.

In the course of her fieldwork, Weiner came to believe that Malinowski's conclusions were not necessarily wrong but were incomplete. By the time of Weiner's study (1988), anthropologists were carefully considering the need for **reflexivity** in conducting fieldwork—that is, a critical self-examination of the role of the anthropologist and an awareness that who one is affects what one finds out. Malinowski's age and gender influenced what he saw and what others were comfortable telling him. By the 1980s, feminist anthropologists such as Weiner and Kathleen Gough (1971), who revisited Evans-Pritchard's work with the Nuer, were pushing anthropologists to be more critically aware of how their own position in relationship to those they study affects their scope of vision.

Barbara Myerhoff: A Turn to Home. The first book written by Barbara Myerhoff (1935–1985), *Peyote Hunt* (1974), traces the pilgrimage of the Indigenous Huichol people across the Sierra Madre of Mexico as they retell, reclaim, and reinvigorate their religious myths, rituals, and symbols. In her second book, *Number Our Days* (1978), Myerhoff turns her attention closer to home. Her fieldwork focuses on the struggles of older Jewish immigrants in a Southern California community—particularly the Aliyah Senior Citizens' Center, through which her subjects create and remember ritual life and community as a means of controlling their daily activities and faculties as they age. Their words pour off the pages of Myerhoff's book as she allows them to tell their life stories. As a character in her own writing, Myerhoff traces her interactions and engagements with the members of the center and reflects poignantly on the process of self-reflection and transformation that she experiences as a younger Jewish woman studying a community of older Jews.

Coming nearly fifty years after Hurston's fieldwork, *Number Our Days* marks a broader turn in anthropology from the study of the "other" to the study of the self—what Victor Turner calls in his foreword to Myerhoff's book "being thrice-born." The first birth is in our own culture. The second birth immerses the anthropologist in the depths of another culture through fieldwork. Finally, the return home is like a third birth as the anthropologist rediscovers their own culture, now strange and unfamiliar in a global context.

ENGAGED ANTHROPOLOGY

Over the past thirty years, an increasing number of anthropologists, including Nancy Scheper-Hughes, whose work bookends this chapter, have identified their work as **engaged anthropology**. Engaged anthropologists intentionally seek to apply the research strategies and analytical perspectives of the discipline to address the concrete challenges facing local communities and the world at large. In this regard, engaged anthropology challenges the assumptions that anthropology, as a science, should focus on producing objective, unbiased, neutral accounts of human behavior and that anthropologists should work as disengaged observers while conducting research. Engaged anthropologists argue that in a world of conflict and inequality, social scientists must develop an active, politically committed, and morally engaged practice. Engaged anthropology, then, is characterized by a commitment not only to revealing and critiquing but also to confronting systems of power and inequality. Design, implementation, and analysis of research involve close collaboration with colleagues and co-researchers in the community. Advocacy and activism with local communities on matters of mutual concern are central tenets of engaged anthropology (Scheper-Hughes 1995; Speed 2006).

> **engaged anthropology**
> Application of the research strategies and analytical perspectives of anthropology to address concrete challenges facing local communities and the world at large.

As we have seen in the work of Boas and Mead, for example, this form of engagement is not new to anthropology. The field has had a strong strain of engagement since its inception. As early as 1870, John W. Powell, the first director of the U.S. Bureau of Ethnology, testified before Congress about the genocide of Native Americans following the United States' westward expansion and construction of the railroads. Hurston vividly illuminated the culture and folklore of the early twentieth-century African American diaspora (1935, 1938; McClaurin 2007; King 2019). Lakota anthropologist Beatrice Medicine (1924–2005) long advocated for the rights of women, children, Native Americans, and gay, lesbian, and transgender people. In recent decades, this focus on engagement, advocacy, and activism has become increasingly central to anthropologists' research strategies (Low and Merry 2010).

How Do Anthropologists Get Started Conducting Fieldwork?

Summarize the key fieldwork research strategies, skills, and perspectives.

Today, cultural anthropologists call on a set of techniques designed to assess the complexity of human interactions and social organizations. You probably use some variation of these techniques as you go about daily life and make decisions for yourself and others. For a moment, imagine yourself doing fieldwork with Nancy Scheper-Hughes in the Brazilian shantytown of Alto do Cruzeiro. How would you prepare yourself? What strategies would you use? How would you analyze your data? What equipment would you need to conduct your research?

PREPARATION

anthropologist's toolkit

The tools needed to conduct fieldwork, including information, perspectives, strategies, and even equipment.

Prior to beginning fieldwork, anthropologists go through an intense process of preparation, carefully assembling an **anthropologist's toolkit**: all the information, perspectives, strategies, and even equipment that may be needed. We start by reading everything we can find about our research site and the particular issues we will be examining. This *literature review* provides a crucial background for the experiences to come. Following Malinowski's recommendation, anthropologists also learn the language of their field site. The ability to speak the local language eliminates the need to work through interpreters and allows us to participate in the community's everyday activities and conversations, which richly reflect local culture.

Before going to the field, anthropologists search out possible contacts: other scholars who have worked in the community, community leaders, government officials, perhaps even a host family. A specific research question or problem is defined and a research design created. Grant applications are submitted to seek financial support for the research. Permission to conduct the study is sought ahead of time from the local community and, where necessary, from appropriate government agencies. Protocols are developed to protect those who will be the focus of the research. Anthropologists attend to many of these logistical matters following a preliminary visit to the intended field site before fully engaging in the fieldwork process.

Finally, we assemble all the equipment needed to conduct our research. Today this aspect of your anthropologist's toolkit—most likely a backpack—might include a notebook, pens, camera, voice recorder, maps, cell phone, batteries and chargers, dictionary, watch, and identification.

STRATEGIES

Once in the field, anthropologists apply a variety of research strategies for gathering quantitative and qualitative data. **Quantitative data** include statistical information about a community—data that can be measured and compared, including details of population demographics and economic activity. **Qualitative data** include information that cannot be counted but may be even more significant for understanding the dynamics of a community. Qualitative data consist of personal stories and interviews, life histories, and general observations about daily life drawn from participant observation. Qualitative data enable the ethnographer to connect the dots and answer the questions of why people behave in certain ways or organize their lives in particular patterns.

Central to a cultural anthropologist's research is participant observation. By participating in our subjects' daily activities, we experience their lives from the perspective of an insider. Through participant observation over time, we establish **rapport**—relationships of trust and familiarity with members of the community we study. The deepening of that rapport through intense engagement enables the anthropologist to move from being an outsider toward being an insider. Over time in a community, anthropologists seek out people who will be our advisors, teachers, and guides—sometimes called **key informants** or cultural consultants. Key informants may suggest issues to explore, introduce community members to interview, provide feedback on research insights, and warn against cultural miscues. (Again, quoting from Scheper-Hughes: "Ze Antonio advised me to ignore Nailza's odd behavior, which he understood as a kind of madness that, like the birth and death of children, came and went.")

Another key research method is the *interview*. Anthropologists are constantly conducting interviews while in the field. Some interviews are very informal, essentially gathering data through everyday conversation. Other interviews are highly structured, closely following a set of questions. Semi-structured interviews use those questions as a framework but leave room for the interviewee to guide the conversation. One particular form of interview, a **life history**, traces the biography of a person over time, examining changes in the person's life and illuminating the interlocking network of relationships in the community. Life histories provide insight into the frameworks of meaning that individuals build around their life experiences. **Surveys** can also be developed and administered to gather quantitative data on key issues and to reach a broader sample of participants but rarely do they supersede participant observation and face-to-face interviews as the anthropologist's primary strategy for data collection.

Anthropologists also map human relations. **Kinship analysis** enables us to explore the interlocking relationships of power built on family and marriage (see

quantitative data

Statistical information about a community that can be measured and compared.

qualitative data

Descriptive data drawn from nonstatistical sources, including personal stories, interviews, life histories, and participant observation.

rapport

Relationships of trust and familiarity that an anthropologist develops with members of the community under study.

key informant

A community member who advises the anthropologist on community issues, provides feedback, and warns against cultural miscues. Also called cultural consultant.

life history

A form of interview that traces the biography of a person over time, examining changes in the person's life and illuminating the interlocking network of relationships in the community.

survey

An information-gathering tool for quantitative data analysis.

kinship analysis

A fieldwork strategy of examining interlocking relationships of power built on marriage and family ties.

social network analysis

A method for examining relationships in a community, often conducted by identifying whom people turn to in times of need.

field notes

The anthropologist's written observations and reflections on places, practices, events, and interviews.

mapping

The analysis of the physical and/or geographic space where fieldwork is being conducted.

built environment

The intentionally designed features of human settlement, including buildings, transportation and public service infrastructure, and public spaces.

Chapter 9). In more urban areas where family networks are diffuse, a **social network analysis** may prove illuminating. One of the simplest ways to analyze a social network is to identify whom people turn to in times of need.

Central to our data-gathering strategy, anthropologists write detailed **field notes** of our observations and reflections. These field notes take various forms. Some are elaborate descriptions of people, places, events, sounds, and smells. Others are reflections on patterns and themes that emerge, questions to be asked, and issues to be pursued. Some field notes are personal reflections on the experience of doing fieldwork—how it feels physically and emotionally to be engaged in the process. Although the rigorous recording of field notes may sometimes seem tedious, the collection of data over time allows the anthropologist to revisit details of earlier experiences, to compare information and impressions over time, and to analyze changes, trends, patterns, and themes.

Sophisticated computer programs can assist in the organization and categorization of data about people, places, and institutions. But in the final analysis, the instincts and insights of the ethnographer are key to recognizing significant themes and patterns.

MAPPING

Often, one of the first steps an anthropologist takes upon entering a new community is to map the surroundings. **Mapping** takes many forms and produces many different products. While walking the streets of the field site, the ethnographer develops a spatial awareness of where people live, work, worship, play, and eat and of the space through which they move. After all, human culture exists in real physical space. And culture shapes how space is constructed and used. Likewise, physical surroundings influence human culture, shaping the boundaries of behavior and imagination. Careful observation and description, recorded in maps, field notes, audio and video recordings, and photographs, provide the material for deeper analysis of these community dynamics.

Urban ethnographers describe the power of the **built environment** to shape human life. Most humans live in a built environment, not one made up solely or primarily of nature. By focusing on the built environment—what we have built around us—scholars can analyze the intentional development of human settlements, neighborhoods, towns, and cities. Growth of the built environment is rarely random. Rather, it is guided by political and economic choices that determine funding for roads, public transportation, parks, schools, lighting, sewers, water systems, electrical grids, hospitals, police and fire stations, and other public services and infrastructure. Local governments establish and enforce tax and zoning regulations to control the construction of buildings and approved uses. Mapping the components of this built environment may shed light on key dynamics of power and influence in a community.

Anthropologists turn to quantitative data to map who is present in a community, including characteristics such as age, gender, family type, and employment status. This demographic data may be available through the local or national census, or, if the sample size is manageable, the anthropologist may choose to gather the data directly by surveying the community. To map historical change over time in an area and to discern its causes, anthropologists also turn to archives, newspaper databases, minutes and records of local organizations, historical photos, and personal descriptions, in addition to census data.

Mapping today may be aided by online tools such as satellite imagery, geographic information system devices and data, online archives, and electronic databases. All can be extremely helpful in establishing location, orientation, and, in the case of photo archives, changes over time. On their own, however, these tools do not provide the deep immersion sought by anthropologists conducting fieldwork. Instead, anthropologists place primary emphasis on careful, first-hand observation and documentation of physical space as a valuable strategy for understanding the day-to-day dynamics of cultural life.

Student-made maps of blocks along East Broadway, a street on Manhattan's Lower East Side that serves as both a gateway into the country and the economic hub for Chinese immigrants seeking a foothold in the United States today.

SKILLS AND PERSPECTIVES

Successful fieldwork requires a unique set of skills and perspectives that are hard to teach in the classroom. Ethnographers must begin with open-mindedness about the people and places they study. We must be wary of any prejudices we might have formed before our arrival, and we must be reluctant to judge once we are in the field. Boas's notion of cultural relativism is an essential place to begin: Can we see the world through the eyes of the people we are studying? Can we understand their systems of meaning and internal logic? The tradition of anthropology suggests that cultural relativism must be the starting point if we are to accurately hear and retell the stories of others.

A successful ethnographer must also be a skilled listener. We spend a lot of time in conversation, but much of that time involves listening, not talking. The ability to ask good questions and to listen carefully to the responses is essential. A skilled listener hears both what is said and what is not said. **Zeros** are the elements of a story or a picture that are not told or seen—key details omitted from the conversation or key people absent from the room. Zeros offer insights into issues and topics that may be too sensitive to discuss or display publicly.

A good ethnographer must be patient, flexible, and open to the unexpected. Sometimes sitting still in one place is the best research strategy because it offers opportunities to observe and experience unplanned events and unexpected people. The overscheduled fieldworker can easily miss the mundane imponderabilia that constitute the richness of everyday life. For instance, I have a favorite tea shop in one Chinese village where I like to sit and wait to see what happens.

At times, the most important, illuminating conversations and interviews are not planned ahead of time. Patience and a commitment to conducting research over an extended period allow the ethnographic experience to come to us on its own terms, not on the schedule we assign to it. This is one of the significant differences between anthropology and journalism. It is also a hard lesson to learn and a hard skill to develop.

A final perspective essential for a successful ethnographer is openness to the possibility of **mutual transformation** in the fieldwork process. This is

zeros
Elements of a story or a picture that are not told or seen and yet offer key insights into issues that might be too sensitive to discuss or display publicly.

mutual transformation
The potential for both the anthropologist and the members of the community being studied to be transformed by the interactions of fieldwork.

What is the global journey of Mardi Gras beads? (*Left*) Hands of a Chinese woman burned, cracked, and stained from making beads in sweatshop conditions. The beads are exported for sale in the United States at the annual Mardi Gras festival in New Orleans, Louisiana. (*Right*) Young American women exchange nudity for the beads in New Orleans' French Quarter during Mardi Gras.

risky business because it exposes the personal component of anthropological research. It is clear that by participating in fieldwork, anthropologists alter—in ways large and small—the character of the community being studied. But if you ask them about their fieldwork experience, they will acknowledge that in the process they themselves become transformed on a very personal level—their self-understanding, their empathy for others, their worldviews. The practice of participant observation over time entails building deep relationships with people from another culture and directly engages the ethnographer in the life of the community.

Nancy Scheper-Hughes could not have returned unchanged by her research experience. The people of Alto do Cruzeiro would not let her simply observe their lives; they made her work with them to organize a neighborhood organization to address community problems. Indeed, the potential for the fieldworker to affect the local community is very great. So is the potential for the people being studied to transform the fieldworker.

ANALYSIS

As the fieldwork experience proceeds, anthropologists regularly reflect on and analyze the trends, issues, themes, and patterns that emerge from their carefully collected data. One framework for analysis that we will examine in this book is power: Who has it? How do they get it and keep it? Who uses it, and why? Where is the money, and who controls it? The anthropologist Eric Wolf thought of culture as a mechanism for facilitating relationships of power—among families, genders, religions, classes, and political entities (1999). Good ethnographers constantly assess the relations of power in the communities they study.

Ethnographers also submit their local data and analysis to cross-cultural comparisons. We endeavor to begin from an **emic** perspective—that is, to understand the local community on its own terms. But the anthropological commitment to understanding human diversity and the complexity of human cultures also requires taking an **etic** perspective—viewing the local community from the anthropologist's perspective as an outsider. This provides a foundation for comparison with other relevant case studies. The overarching process of comparison and assessment, called ethnology, uses the wealth of anthropological studies to compare the activities, trends, and patterns of power across cultures. The process enables us to better see what is unique in a particular context and how it contributes to identifying larger patterns of cultural beliefs and practices. Perhaps the largest effort to facilitate worldwide comparative studies is the Human Relations Area Files at Yale University (http://hraf.yale.edu/), which has been building a database of ethnographic material since 1949 to encourage cross-cultural analysis.

emic
An approach to gathering data that investigates how local people think and how they understand the world.

etic
Description of local behavior and beliefs from the anthropologist's perspective in ways that can be compared across cultures.

How Do Anthropologists Write Ethnography?

Demonstrate knowledge of ethnographic writing principles and forms.

After gathering data through fieldwork, anthropologists must decide how to tell the stories of the people they study. Although ethnographic films are a vibrant part of our field, most anthropologists make their contributions through ethnographic writing—either articles or books. The art of ethnographic writing has been a particularly hot topic within anthropology for the past twenty-five years, and both style and content have changed dramatically since Malinowski and Evans-Pritchard published their books in the early twentieth century.

Ethnography has changed as anthropology has changed. More women and people of color are writing, bringing their unique perspectives into the anthropological discourse. More people from non-Western countries are writing, challenging the position of Western writers as unquestioned authorities on other cultures. And with better communication systems, people are reading what we write about them, even when we write it halfway around the world. This has had a profound effect on the conversations between author and subject and on the ethnographer's final product.

It is unavoidable that what we write will in some way provide only a limited view of the lives of those we study. The process of collecting, organizing, and analyzing our data presumes not only that we present facts but also that we choose which facts to present, which people to highlight, and which stories to tell. As authors, we have the power to interpret the people and their experiences to our audience. This is an awesome and sometimes overwhelming responsibility, which often leaves the ethnographer at a loss for how to proceed. In researching my book *God in Chinatown*, for instance, I conducted more than one hundred interviews, each lasting one hour or more. The process of selecting certain stories and specific quotations was arduous.

POLYVOCALITY

polyvocality

The practice of using many different voices in ethnographic writing and research question development, allowing the reader to hear more directly from the people in the study.

Changes in ethnographic fieldwork and writing over recent decades have sought to make the process more participatory and transparent. Today, most ethnographic projects involve people from the community in the research process and include their voices more directly in the written product.

Polyvocality—the use of many voices in ethnographic writing, including quotations—allows the reader to hear directly from the people in the study and, by bringing their stories to life, makes them more vibrant and available to the reader. Anthropologists also increase polyvocality in their research by inviting key informants to help design the research, including interview and survey questions. Others may be invited to read sections of the manuscript as it is being drafted. In contemporary ethnographic writing, the author's voice also comes out more clearly. Ethnographies have moved from the style of Evans-Pritchard (1940) toward that of Geertz (1973a)—from being a scientific report toward being thick description and an interpretation of what is observed.

REFLEXIVITY

In recent years, the practice of reflexivity—self-reflection on the experience of doing fieldwork—has become more prevalent in written ethnographies. Contemporary writers make an effort to reveal their own position in relation to their study so that readers can assess what biases, strengths, or handicaps the author may have. The ethnographer's age, gender, race/ethnicity, nationality, sexuality, and religious background may have a direct impact on the ease with which they establish rapport or gain access to the research community and on the successful analysis of their findings. A careful ethnographer must address these issues in the research design and implementation and may choose to reflect on them in the written report.

ETHNOGRAPHIC AUTHORITY

Ultimately, the ethnographer must wrestle with the question of ethnographic authority: What right do they have to present certain material, make certain claims, and draw certain conclusions? That authority is not automatically given, so writers make efforts, often early on in the ethnography, to establish their credentials and identify the grounds on which readers should trust them and the decisions they made during fieldwork and writing. These attempts to establish ethnographic authority include discussions of the length of time engaged in the study, language skills, special training and preparation, research design and implementation, and the quality of the relationships with subjects in the study. The quality and persuasiveness of the writing can also be significant in establishing the ethnographer's credibility. The inclusion of direct quotes can confirm the author's conclusions, provide more direct access to the fieldworker's data, and enable the reader to better assess the author's conclusions.

Anthropologists today write for a wide variety of audiences, including students, colleagues, and other specialists in the field. We also write for the people we study. In today's world of global communication, the people we are writing about often read our work, even across barriers of language and geography. People expect to see their lives accurately portrayed and their community's concerns appropriately expressed. Balancing the expectations and needs of these at times contradictory audiences makes the ethnographer's task quite complicated.

What Moral and Ethical Concerns Guide Anthropologists in Their Research and Writing?

Describe the ethical concerns associated with fieldwork and ethnographic writing.

Anthropologists often face moral and ethical dilemmas while conducting fieldwork. These dilemmas require us to make choices that may affect not only the quality of our research but also the people we study. Indeed, the moral and ethical implications of anthropological research and writing are of deep concern within the discipline and have been particularly hot topics at various times in its history. As a result, the American Anthropological Association (AAA) has developed an extensive set of ethical guidelines, which you can view at www.aaanet.org.

DO NO HARM

At the core of our ethics code is the mandate to do no harm. Even though as anthropologists we seek to contribute to general human knowledge and perhaps shed light on a specific cultural, economic, or political problem, we must not do so at the expense of the people we study. In fact, this issue spurred the creation of the AAA's code of ethics. The organization's website presents a great variety of advice about the anthropologist's responsibility to the people being studied.

Several key examples in the history of anthropology demonstrate the importance of the "do no harm" mandate. After World War II, anthropology as a discipline was criticized for intentionally and unintentionally aiding the European

The relationship of anthropology to colonialism and war has been complicated. During the Vietnam War, for instance, some anthropologists were criticized for collaborating with the U.S. military occupation and counterinsurgency efforts. (*Left*) An American soldier in rural Vietnam, 1967. (*Right*) Recently, the controversy continued as the U.S. military's Human Terrain Systems program (2007–14) recruited anthropologists to help troops understand local culture and make better decisions in the field.

colonial encounter, assisting colonial administrators and military agents by providing detailed descriptions and analysis of local populations, many of which were actively engaged in struggles against colonial rule. Anthropology was also taken to task for helping to create an image of colonial subjects as unable to govern themselves and in need of Western guidance and rule (Asad 1973). During the Vietnam War in the 1960s, some anthropologists were rebuked for collaborating with the U.S. military occupation and counterinsurgency efforts. In the 1970s, the AAA experienced internal political turmoil as it addressed accusations of covert research conducted in Southeast Asia by anthropologists (Petersen 2015; Price 2004; Wakin 1992; Wolf and Jorgensen 1970).

More recently, the ethical practices of two American researchers, anthropologist Napoleon Chagnon and geneticist/physician James Neel, who worked among Brazil's Indigenous Yanomami people (Chagnon 1968) in the 1960s and following, have come into question. In his book *Darkness in El Dorado* (2000), journalist Patrick Tierney claimed, among other things, that Chagnon and Neel compromised their subjects' health to see how unprotected Indigenous populations would respond to the introduction of infectious disease. Later investigations did not support Tierney's most serious charges, and the AAA's original findings against Chagnon and Neel were rescinded. The controversy, however, stimulated a significant debate within the field about the code of ethics expected of all anthropologists.

More recently, the U.S. military has actively recruited anthropologists to serve as cross-cultural experts in Iraq and Afghanistan, renewing impassioned debates within the discipline about the proper role of anthropologists in military and covert operations. Through the Human Terrain Systems program, between 2007 and 2014 the U.S. military recruited, trained, and deployed anthropologists to be embedded with combat units and to advise military commanders on building local community relationships. Though this program has ended, a similarly controversial project, the U.S. Department of Defense's Minerva Research Initiative, which funds social science research of benefit to U.S. military planning and operations, has raised concerns among anthropologists (Gusterson 2008). The role of anthropologists in military-sponsored "nation building" projects has been supported by some (McFate 2005) but criticized by many others, who have warned of the "weaponizing of anthropology"—turning anthropological research strategies and knowledge into a tool of war (Price 2011).

OBTAIN INFORMED CONSENT

One of the key principles for protecting research subjects involves obtaining **informed consent**. It is imperative that those whom we study agree to participate in the project. To do so, they must understand clearly what the project involves and the fact that they have the right to refuse to participate. After all, anthropological research is not undercover investigation using covert means and deception.

informed consent
A key strategy for protecting those being studied by ensuring that they are fully informed of the goals of the project and have clearly indicated their consent to participate.

The anthropologist's hallmark research strategy is participant observation, which requires establishing rapport—that is, building relationships of trust over time. To develop rapport, the subjects of our studies must be clearly informed about the goals and scope of our projects and must willingly consent to being a part of them.

U.S. federal regulations protect human subjects involved in any research, and proposals to conduct research on humans, including anthropological research, must be reviewed by the sponsoring organization. Such regulations were originally designed to cover medical research, but anthropologists—whether students or professionals—now participate in these institutional reviews before conducting research.

ENSURE ANONYMITY

anonymity

Protecting the identities of the people involved in a study by changing or omitting their names or other identifying characteristics.

Anthropologists take precautions to ensure the privacy and safety of the people they study by providing **anonymity** in research notes and in publications. We frequently change the names and disguise the identities of individuals or, at times, whole communities. For example, Nancy Scheper-Hughes disguises the identities of people and places in Brazil to protect the community and individuals she worked with (for example, "the market town that I call Bom Jesus da Mata"). Anonymity protects the people in our studies who may be quite vulnerable and whose lives we describe in intimate detail. This consideration becomes particularly important and sometimes controversial when research involves illegal activities—for instance, Claire Sterk's ethnography about prostitution (2000) or Philippe Bourgois's work with drug dealers in New York City (2003).

How Have Fieldwork Strategies Changed in Response to Globalization?

Analyze the impact of globalization on fieldwork strategies today.

The increased movement of people, information, money, and goods associated with globalization has transformed ethnographic fieldwork in terms of both its process and its content.

CHANGES IN PROCESS

Changes in communication and transportation have altered the ongoing relationship between the anthropologist and the community being studied. Global communication allows the fieldworker and the community to maintain contact long after the anthropologist has left the field, facilitating a flow of data, discussions, and interpretation that in the past would have been very difficult to continue. The expansion of global transportation networks further increases the opportunities for personal interactions between an anthropologist and someone from the researched community outside the original research setting.

RISE OF DIGITAL ETHNOGRAPHY

Before COVID-19, only a small percentage of anthropological research projects focused on digital worlds, including online gaming, virtual communities, and social networking sites. For example, in the aftermath of the killing of Michael Brown in Ferguson, Missouri, in 2014, anthropologists Yarimar Bonilla and Jonathan Rosa (2015) explored the use of social media as a powerful platform for political activism. What they described as "hashtag activism" on Twitter, YouTube, Instagram, and Vine created shared digital moments across a large and disparate population of activists and helped document and challenge police brutality and the misrepresentation of Black bodies in the mainstream media.

In an era of intensifying globalization, most ethnographic projects have included at least some digital component, as our interlocutors send texts, post on Facebook, and send money online. But COVID-19 upended anthropological research by limiting our primary research methods, including in-person participant observation and interviews. Research strategies requiring social proximity became not only impractical but also potentially dangerous for those we work with. The global pandemic has pushed us to further adapt our research strategies to include digital components like Zoom interviews; participant observation in online chat groups, Facebook pages, and Twitter feeds; and observation of online communities and virtual activism even from halfway around the world. The extent and durability of these shifts over time is still uncertain.

CHANGES IN CONTENT

Globalization has also deeply affected fieldwork content. No longer can an anthropologist study a local community in isolation from global processes. As even the most remote areas are affected by intensifying globalization—whether through media, tourism, investment, migration, or global warming—ethnographers are increasingly integrating the local with the global in their studies. In some cases, particularly in studies of migration, ethnographic fieldwork is now multisited, encompassing research in two or more locations to more fully represent the scope of the issue under study.

Nancy Scheper-Hughes's career reflects many recent changes in ethnographic fieldwork. Her earliest research, introduced at the beginning of this chapter, focused on local life in the Brazilian shantytown Alto do Cruzeiro. She has

A middleman and two young Filipino men with scars; each of the two men has sold a kidney as part of the global trade in human organs.

carefully monitored changes in the community in the ensuing years, including dramatic recent improvements in infant mortality rates stemming from Brazilian economic growth and direct government promotion of local health-care services (Scheper-Hughes 2013), and she is reporting these changes in a revised and updated version of her classic ethnography *Death Without Weeping*.

Scheper-Hughes's other recent work places Alto do Cruzeiro in the middle of an illicit global trade in harvested human organs (Scheper-Hughes 2002). While she continues to explore the richness of local life in Brazil, she has expanded her scope to examine how the experiences of the poor in one community are mirrored in the lives of poor people in many other countries and are linked by a gruesome global trade driven by demand from the world's economic elite. Scheper-Hughes first began hearing rumors while working in northeast Brazil: rumors of the abduction and murder of poor children, whose bodies—minus heart, lungs, liver, kidneys, and eyes—would later be found on roadsides, in sugarcane fields, or in hospital dumpsters. Later, as she began writing articles about these organ-stealing rumors, other anthropologists reported similar stories of organ theft in Central and South America, India, Korea, Eastern Europe, and many parts of Africa.

Reflecting on the meaning of these stories, Scheper-Hughes writes, "To the anthropologist . . . working closely with the urban poor, the rumors spoke to the ontological insecurity of people 'to whom almost anything could be done.' They reflected everyday threats to bodily security, urban violence, police terror, social anarchy, theft, loss, and fragmentation. Many of the poor imagined, with some reason as it turns out, that autopsies were performed to harvest usable tissues and body parts from those whose bodies had reverted to the state" (Scheper-Hughes 2002, 36).

As an engaged medical anthropologist, Scheper-Hughes has spent countless hours investigating the extensive illegal international trade in smuggled human organs. Contemporary globalization, especially the time-space compression of transportation and communication, enables trafficking networks to spread across national boundaries and around the world. These same cornerstones of globalization have allowed Scheper-Hughes and her organization, Organs Watch, based at the University of California, to develop an extensive global network of anthropologists, human rights activists, transplant surgeons, journalists, and government agencies that have collaborated to address issues of human organ trafficking in India, Pakistan, Israel, South Africa, Turkey, Moldova, Brazil, the Philippines, and the United States.

As a member of two World Health Organization panels on transplant trafficking and transplant safety, Scheper-Hughes has seen firsthand the global search for kidneys: the often-poor kidney sellers, the kidney hunters who track them down, and the kidney buyers willing to cross borders, break laws, and pay as much as $150,000 in advance to the organ brokers for a chance at a new kidney and a new life. In 2009, the U.S. Federal Bureau of Investigation arrested a Brooklyn rabbi who had been arranging kidney sales, highlighting the deep integration of illegal international organ trafficking into developed-country markets where, for example, more than 100,000 Americans linger on a kidney waiting list, struggling through dialysis to stay alive, and where the wait times for a donor in some parts of the country are as long as nine years.

The trajectory of Scheper-Hughes's career from fieldwork in a small favela in Brazil to fieldwork in international organ-trafficking networks reflects many of the transformations that have shaped anthropological fieldwork over the last forty years. No local community can be viewed as isolated. Anthropologists must consider each local fieldwork site in light of the myriad ways in which local dynamics link to the world beyond. Today, fieldwork includes attention to global flows, networks, and processes as anthropologists trace patterns across national and cultural boundaries while keeping one foot grounded in the lives of people in local communities.

Toolkit

Thinking Like an Anthropologist
Applying Aspects of Fieldwork to Your Own Life

You don't have to go to Brazil to use the skills of an anthropologist. Maybe you will be inspired by this book—or by a language you study, a professor whose class you take, or a new friend you meet—to explore a culture in another part of the world. Or maybe you will apply these skills nearer to home. In Chapter 1, you were asked to begin seeing yourself as a budding anthropologist, one who is already working hard to understand the complicated, globalizing world and how you fit into it. Fieldwork skills are the key to navigating what lies ahead of you.

As you think back to the fieldwork of Nancy Scheper-Hughes, remember the questions we asked at the beginning of the chapter:

- **What is unique about ethnographic fieldwork, and why do anthropologists conduct this kind of research?**

- **How did the practice of fieldwork develop?**

- **How do anthropologists get started conducting fieldwork?**

- **How do anthropologists write ethnography?**

- **What moral and ethical concerns guide anthropologists in their research and writing?**

- **How have fieldwork strategies changed in response to globalization?**

Consider how the concepts we have discussed can be applied not only by professional anthropologists but also by each one of us in our daily lives.

You already use many of the strategies, skills, and perspectives of ethnographic fieldwork to navigate your daily journey through life. Whether in your family, your workplace, or your school, you have to understand the people with whom you interact. You participate and observe, establish rapport, listen, interview, gather life histories, and map out family and social networks. If you keep a journal or diary, you have already started taking field notes about the people and cultural patterns around you. You are constantly assessing who has power, how they got it, and how they use it. While you may already use many of these tools, the goal of this chapter has been to show the rigor with which they can be applied if you take fieldwork seriously and to enable you to apply them in a more systematic and self-aware way in your daily life.

Key Terms

ethnographic fieldwork (p. 68)

salvage ethnography (p. 72)

cultural relativism (p. 72)

participant observation (p. 73)

reflexivity (p. 78)

engaged anthropology (p. 79)

anthropologist's toolkit (p. 80)

quantitative data (p. 81)

qualitative data (p. 81)

rapport (p. 81)

key informant (p. 81)

life history (p. 81)

survey (p. 81)

kinship analysis (p. 81)

social network analysis (p. 82)

field notes (p. 82)

mapping (p. 82)

built environment (p. 82)

zeros (p. 84)

mutual transformation (p. 84)

emic (p. 85)

etic (p. 85)

polyvocality (p. 86)

informed consent (p. 89)

anonymity (p. 90)

Chapter 4
Language

Learning Objectives

- Define language and its key elements.

- Describe how language shapes thought and culture.

- Analyze how systems of power relate to language.

- Assess the impact of globalization on languages.

To promote integration, assimilation and national unity, future immigrants will be required to learn English . . . prior to admission.

—President Donald Trump,
May 16, 2019

In 2010, the state of Arizona passed a law requiring police officers to arrest anyone whom they had a "reasonable suspicion" of being an undocumented immigrant. If such a person could not prove their legal status, they were to be detained immediately. This law touched on a very contentious issue. Arizona lawmakers argued that it responded to the federal government's failure to monitor borders and protect U.S. citizens from foreigners—who they worry will take their jobs and endanger their neighborhoods. The statement quoted above echoes this sentiment, revealing how many people

Could the language you use have marked you with a "reasonable suspicion" of being undocumented under a 2010 Arizona law?

closely link increasing language diversity with social upheaval. Civil rights activists, however, questioned how police would arrive at a "reasonable suspicion" that a person is undocumented. They feared that law enforcement officers would rely on the person's looks (skin color), clothing, or language. Would someone who spoke Spanish or who spoke English with a Spanish accent be more likely to be arrested and detained? Is language an effective screen for legal status or citizenship?

Debates about language have been raging in the United States for decades. More than thirty states have passed English-only laws limiting classroom instruction, driver's license exams, road signs, and even health warnings to one language. The U.S. House of Representatives has passed legislation several times declaring English to be the national language of the United States, although these bills have never been signed into law. The United States, historically, has been a country of many languages: Spanish, French, Dutch, German, Italian, Chinese, not to mention hundreds of Native American languages and hundreds of others spoken by contemporary immigrants. Spanish has been spoken in what is now the U.S. South and Southwest since the 1500s, when the Spanish conquistadors Francisco Vázquez de Coronado and Hernán Cortés explored and colonized the area on behalf of the Spanish Crown. How has language come to be such a hot-button issue in the United States today?

Nearly 7,000 languages are currently in use in the world. Through linguistic anthropology, one of the four fields of anthropology, we explore not only the details of a language's vocabulary and grammar but also the role of language in people's lives—both as individuals and as communities. Languages are not just abstract concepts with ideal forms perfectly displayed in a dictionary or a textbook. Languages are also dynamic and alive. Communication is a social act. Words are part of actions. We call a friend, text a classmate, tell a story, say a prayer, ask a favor. Human language uses an infinite number of forms to communicate a vast array of information. We communicate through poetry, prose, gestures, signs, touch, text messaging—even anthropology textbooks. Not only can we communicate content in great detail, but we also have the wondrous capacity to share the content of our imaginations, our anger, fear, joy, and the deepest longings of our souls.

Humans are born with the ability to learn language—not a particular language, but whatever languages they are exposed to as they grow up. Languages are learned through enculturation—through interactions with others. Exactly what we learn and the context in which we learn it vary widely. Languages change and grow, constantly adapting to the needs and circumstances of the people who speak them. Although the number of languages shrinks every year under the pressures of globalization, the remarkable diversity of human language reflects humans' dramatically different ways of perceiving, thinking about, and engaging with the world. Because languages are deeply embedded in culture, they also become arenas where norms and values are created, enforced, and contested; where group identity is negotiated; and where systems of power and status are taught and challenged.

In this chapter, we will consider how linguistic anthropologists study human language and communication. In particular, we will ask:

- **What is language and where does it come from?**
- **How does language shape our ways of thinking?**
- **How do systems of power intersect with language and communication?**
- **What are the effects of globalization on language?**

By the end of the chapter, you will have a better understanding of how language works, have the conceptual tools to analyze the role of language in your personal life and within your language community, and comprehend the forces that will shape language and communication in our increasingly global future.

What Is Language and Where Does It Come From?

Define language and its key elements.

All animals communicate in some fashion, often relying on a *call system* of sounds and gestures that are prompted by environmental stimuli. Ants share information through chemical trails and pheromones. Bees dance to communicate distance and direction to flower petals and nectar. Dogs growl or bark to express hostility or warning. And a border collie named Betsy, featured on the cover of *National Geographic* magazine, could recognize more than 340 distinct words and commands (Morrell 2008). Dolphins produce complicated vocal signals—clicks, whistles, squeaks, trills. Whales have been found to "sing"—to create a vocalization that appears to have a unique tune or accent for each clan or pod of whales.

Although these are all examples of communication—a sender providing information to a receiver—they are not symbolic language as humans use it. Human **language** is a system of communication that conveys information using symbols—such as words, sounds, and gestures—organized according to certain rules. These symbols have deep historical and cultural meaning, yet human language is remarkably flexible and creative, rapidly adapting to changes in human life and the environment.

language

A system of communication organized by rules that uses symbols such as words, sounds, and gestures to convey information.

All animals communicate in some fashion. A border collie named Betsy could recognize more than 340 distinct words and commands.

Do nonhuman primates have the capacity to create human language? Koko, a gorilla, with Francine Patterson, learned more than 400 signs in sign language.

THE ORIGINS OF HUMAN LANGUAGE

In searching for the evolutionary origins of human language, anthropologists, particularly primatologists, have investigated language use and communication among our nearest primate relatives—chimpanzees, orangutans, and other great apes—with some surprising results. In their natural habitats, primates produce an astonishing array of vocalizations to communicate information about food, sex, and potential predators. Nonhuman primates lack the physical apparatus to create human sounds and human speech. Specifically, their ability to manipulate their vocal cords, tongues, and lips is far more limited than that of humans. But do they have the mental capacity to create human language?

Landmark studies have explored this possibility by teaching primates American Sign Language rather than spoken English. Because chimps, gorillas, orangutans, and other primates use their hands extensively to express themselves, the theory was that sign language might more accurately reflect their cognitive capacity for language.

A chimpanzee named Washoe was the first to use sign language, mastering more than 130 different signs (Gardner, Gardner, and Van Cantfort 1989). Koko, a gorilla, learned more than 400 signs (Patterson 1978). Chantek, an orangutan, mastered several hundred signs and could understand some spoken English. Reports indicated that some primates had an ability to move beyond rote memorization of certain signs—they seemed to have a more humanlike capacity to lie, swear, tell jokes, invent new words by combining signs, and even try to teach language to others (Fouts 1997; Miles 1993).

Scholars disagree about the implications of research on nonhuman primate language capacity. Certainly, chimpanzees, gorillas, and orangutans can master rudimentary language signs and can even, at times, exhibit key aspects of human language skills. Their language use reflects *productivity*, meaning that they can use known words to invent new word combinations. Their language can also exhibit *displacement*—that is, the ability to use words to refer to objects not immediately present or events happening in the past or future. But, fundamentally, these primates do not use language in the human sense. In their natural habitats, they do not create and use basic language elements. They cannot achieve the extremely complex human language system that enables us to store and pass on to succeeding generations huge quantities of information not embedded in our genes (Miles 1993; Sebeok and Umiker-Sebeok 1980; Terrace et al. 1979).

How did human language capacity evolve? Recent genetic studies have examined the role of the FOXP2 gene variant in activating and inactivating key human speech capacities, an evolutionary development that appears to be essential to human speech. Such genetic analysis suggests the emergence of human language within the past 150,000 years.

Archaeological evidence, including fossilized brain casts from archaic *Homo sapiens* known as Neandertals (who lived from about 130,000 to about 30,000 years ago) and even earlier *Homo* species, reveals the presence of neurological and anatomical features necessary for speech. Our early human ancestors' capacity to cooperate in hunting and toolmaking also suggests that some language ability may have existed over 2 million years ago, before the evolution of *Homo sapiens*. Cultural evidence supporting extensive language use by modern humans appears around 50,000 years ago, including art, tools, and other technologies that required language to facilitate their transmission from generation to generation. The modern human capacity for group cooperation and the transmission of cultural knowledge would have conferred a significant advantage in adapting to less hospitable natural environments and increased the species' potential for survival.

Historical linguistics is the study of the development of language over time, including its changes and variations. By analyzing vocabulary and linguistic patterns, historical linguists trace connections between languages and identify their origins. For example, through comparative analysis of vocabulary, syntax, and grammar, we know that Spanish and French historically developed from their parent language, Latin. English, German, Dutch, and Scandinavian languages evolved from an earlier proto-Germanic language. Both Latin and proto-Germanic branched out from an even earlier language called Proto-Indo-European, which was spoken more than 6,000 years ago and also gave birth to the languages spoken today in Greece, India, Iran, and Eastern Europe (Mallory and Adams 2006; McWhorter 2001).

> **historical linguistics**
> The study of the development of language over time, including its changes and variations.

Over thousands of years of adaptation, growth, and change, human language developed more along the lines of a **language continuum** rather than into distinct languages. In a language continuum, people who live near one another speak in a way that is mutually intelligible. The farther apart places are, the more the language varies, but it tends to be at least partially mutually intelligible to those living nearby. Although language continuums have been disrupted to some extent over centuries by migration and the strengthening of nation-states, they still exist in many parts of the world. For instance, a strong language continuum exists between Italy and France. If you were to walk northward from village to village beginning at the southern tip of Italy and then northwest into France, you would find that people at either end of the journey would not be able to communicate with one another—their languages would be mutually unintelligible. But along the journey, the local residents of each village you pass through would be able to understand their neighbors in the nearby villages. Changes would be evident from location to location, but communication would be mutually intelligible.

> **language continuum**
> The idea that variation in languages appears gradually over distance so that groups of people who live near one another speak in a way that is mutually intelligible.

HOW LANGUAGES WORK

Language is a system of symbols. It is a system of otherwise meaningless sounds, marks (writing), and gestures that are made meaningful by a group of people—a **speech community**—through their collective history and cultural traditions. **Descriptive linguistics** is the study of the construction of those sounds, their meanings, and their combination into forms that communicate meaning. Descriptive linguists work to describe the elements and rules of a particular language.

A number of years ago, I accompanied a linguist as she conducted research in a village in the mountains of the Philippines where the residents had no writing system for their local language. Over the course of two years, she had learned to speak the language, and she was in the process of creating a system for representing it in writing using the International Phonetic Alphabet. She lived in the village, participated in local activities, and made close friends. She regularly recorded conversations in the community and recruited two key informants, a man and a woman, who had become her teachers and interlocutors as she worked to formally describe their language's elements and rules.

Where would you begin? Perhaps you would work your way from the most simple aspects of the language to the most complex. A language has a limited number of **phonemes**—the smallest units of sound that can make a difference in meaning. For instance, the English letters *b* and *p* sound very similar, but using one or the other will convey a significant difference in meaning. If you fail to carefully distinguish between these phonemes, you might mistakenly switch them and end up saying something you don't mean—calling something *pig* instead of *big*, for example. The study of what sounds exist and how they are used in a particular language is called **phonology**.

Morphemes are the smallest units of sound that carry meaning on their own. (Phonemes, in contrast, have no meaning of their own.) So, for instance, the morphemes *cow* and *horse* can convey meaning without needing additional sounds. The study of the patterns and rules of how sounds combine to make morphemes is called **morphology**. In human languages, we combine morphemes to form phrases and sentences, relying on specific patterns and rules called **syntax**. For example, following Standard American English syntax, we place a possessive pronoun before the noun, not afterward. We would say or write *my pig*, not *pig my*—although the latter pattern might be syntactically appropriate in another language. **Grammar** encompasses the combined set of observations about the rules governing the formation of phonemes, morphemes, and syntax that guide language use.

speech community

A group of people who come to share certain norms of language use through living and communicating together.

descriptive linguistics

The study of the sounds, symbols, and gestures of a language and their combination into forms that communicate meaning.

phonemes

The smallest units of sound that can make a difference in meaning.

phonology

The study of what sounds exist and how they are used in a particular language.

morphemes

The smallest units of sound that carry meaning on their own.

morphology

The study of patterns and rules of how sounds combine to make morphemes.

syntax

The specific patterns and rules for combining morphemes to construct phrases and sentences.

grammar

The combined set of observations about the rules governing the formation of phonemes, morphemes, and syntax that guide language use.

NONVERBAL COMMUNICATION: KINESICS AND PARALANGUAGE

To fully describe and understand another language, a linguist must master more than its spoken and written elements. Human language is accompanied by and embedded in a *gesture–call system* made up of nonverbal elements that convey significant amounts of information. These elements include body movements, noises, and tone of voice, as well as *proxemics*, cultural understandings about the use of space, and *haptics*, the culturally acceptable rules of touch. **Kinesics**, the study of the relationship between body movements and communication, explores all the facial expressions, gestures, and postures that convey messages with or without words. For example, nods, handshakes, bows, and arms folded tightly across the chest all communicate information, although their meanings are not universal; they vary from culture to culture. The thumbs-up and the "okay" hand signals used in North America are considered rude gestures in certain other cultures. North Americans point with their fingers, but Filipinos point with their lips. Have you ever had the experience of making a motion or gesture that someone else misunderstood? If so, what was the cultural context?

Signed languages, including American Sign Language, though they involve elaborate and meaningful movements, are not part of the gesture–call system described here. They are instead considered to be languages themselves, expressed visually rather than aurally. In contrast to the less formalized expressions of the gesture–call system, signed languages maintain a set of formalized rules akin to those usually associated with spoken and written languages.

Human language is also accompanied by **paralanguage**—an extensive set of noises (such as laughs, cries, sighs, yells) and tones of voice that convey significant information about the speaker. Paralanguage indicates whether the speaker

kinesics

The study of the relationship between body movements and communication.

paralanguage

An extensive set of noises (such as laughs, cries, sighs, and yells) and tones of voice that convey significant information about the speaker.

Humans have been communicating in writing for thousands of years. (*Left*) Ancient Egyptian stele with hieroglyphs, ca. twenty-seventh to twenty-fifth century BCE. (*Right*) Rune stone on Adelsö Island near Stockholm, Sweden, eleventh century CE.

Did you ever wonder why emoticons and emojis developed in emails and text messages?

is (for example) happy, sad, angry, tired, scared, disgusted, or enthusiastic. Try saying the sentence "The exam is on Thursday" using each of these tones of voice. The effect on communication is really quite stunning.

As much as 90 percent of emotional information is communicated through body movements and paralanguage. No wonder that email and text messaging have developed an extensive set of emoticons and emojis—symbols that indicate the emotional content intended by the sender. Email and text messaging are beneficial developments in that they allow rapid response over distances great and small in our globalizing world, and they are increasingly used in the business world and personal life. But because they are devoid of the kinesics and paralanguage that play such key roles in face-to-face human communication, they significantly increase the potential for misunderstandings. Do you trust email or text messaging to communicate your most intimate thoughts? Can you remember an instance when they failed to adequately convey your meaning?

How Does Language Shape Our Ways of Thinking?

Describe how language shapes thought and culture.

The power of language to shape human thought and culture has been a hot topic in linguistic anthropology for many generations. Linguistic anthropologists have considered questions such as: Is there an underlying, genetically structured grammar to all languages? Do languages evolve in response to local environments? Do vocabularies and classifications of reality embedded in a language affect how its speakers think and see the world? In this section, we will look at research on the relationships among language, thought, and culture.

LANGUAGE, THOUGHT, AND CULTURE

linguistic relativity

The notion that all languages will develop the distinctive categories necessary for those who speak them to deal with the realities around them.

A signature concept in linguistic anthropology—linguistic relativity—traces its roots to Franz Boas's ethnographic work among Indigenous populations of North America. Boas emphasized learning and preserving language as central to the anthropological endeavor and extended his concept of cultural relativism (see Chapter 3) to language. Specifically, Boas argued that each language had to be studied on its own terms and not in relation to the familiar classifications and categories of European languages. Boas's notion of **linguistic relativity** held that one cannot predict how languages will classify the world, only that they will develop distinctions and categories necessary for those who speak them to deal with the realities around them (Duranti 2009).

The idea that different languages shape different ways of thinking and acting was more fully developed by Boas's student Edward Sapir and later by Sapir's student Benjamin Lee Whorf. Their work, later deemed the **Sapir-Whorf hypothesis**, proposed that languages establish certain mental categories, classifications, or maps of reality—almost like a grammar for organizing one's worldview—that in turn shape people's ways of perceiving the world (Sapir and Swadesh 1946). Whorf's linguistic research with the Hopi, a Native American group in the southwestern United States, suggested that the Hopi language differs from English both in vocabulary and in basic grammatical categories that are key to conceptualizing how the world works. For instance, rather than using separate verb tenses expressing past, present, and future, the Hopi language combines past and present into one. Whorf suggested that this pattern reflects a different conceptualization of time and a unique worldview in which past and present reflect lived reality while the future is hypothetical or potential (Carroll 1956; Ahearn 2017).

Sapir-Whorf hypothesis
The idea that different languages create different ways of thinking.

The Challenge of Translation: Reading "Shakespeare in the Bush."

Laura Bohannan explores the challenges that different vocabulary and conceptualizations of the world pose for translation between languages and cultures. She relates her discoveries in her article "Shakespeare in the Bush: An American Anthropologist Set Out to Study the Tiv of West Africa and Was Taught the True Meaning of *Hamlet*" (1966). While Bohannan was conducting fieldwork in a small village in Nigeria, Tiv elders asked her to tell them a story from her own culture. She attempted to explain *Hamlet*, one of the classic stories of English literature, but time and again was unable to translate directly from English to Tiv. Words such as *chief* and *leader* hold distinctly different meanings and roles in the two cultures; the English concept of *chief* does not translate to the Tiv cultural worldview, and vice versa. The "dead" in Hamlet do not translate because the Tiv have no concept of ghosts. Instead, they imagined Shakespeare's characters as beset by witchcraft.

As Bohannan attempted to use Tiv words to tell Shakespeare's story, the original meanings of the English words became blurred, and the standard message of *Hamlet* was lost in translation. Bohannan's insights as related in "Shakespeare in the Bush" reveal both the power of our environment to shape our language and the power of our language to shape the way we see the world.

MAP 4.1
Nigeria

LANGUAGE ADAPTABILITY

Contemporary studies in linguistic anthropology suggest that although the vocabulary and grammar of the language we learn may influence how we see the world, language does not control or restrict our thinking. Languages are dynamic. They change and adapt as the natural and cultural worlds shift. Humans creatively invent new words and concepts to describe and discuss the changing world as they experience it. Evidence of this adaptability can be found lexicon

All the words for names, ideas, and events that make up a language's dictionary.

in a language's **lexicon**—all the words for names, ideas, and events that make up a language's dictionary—and in its *registers*—specialized vocabulary and linguistic repertoires, that develop within a particular group of people to describe their unique cultural practices (Ahearn 2021).

Thus, the Indigenous Aymara in Bolivia have 200 names for potatoes, reflecting the potato's role as a major source of food in their diet. The Nuer of Sudan, studied by E. E. Evans-Pritchard (1940), relied on cattle in their economy, political system, and kinship structures and so developed more than 400 words to distinguish different types of cattle. In today's globalizing world, a specialized vocabulary has emerged to describe and engage in digital communication. Words such as *mouse, modem, laptop, Wi-Fi, download,* and *attachment*—even *email, text,* and *tweet*—are very recent creations designed to facilitate communication among people working in the digital communication age.

Even descriptions of the color spectrum vary across and within cultures, seemingly according to need. Anthropologist Robin Lakoff (2004) examined how color terms in American English have expanded over the last fifty years, a trend being promoted by the fashion and cosmetics industries. An extensive color vocabulary is not uniform among Americans. It varies primarily by gender: Women are far more likely than men, for instance, to be able to distinguish between salmon and peach, teal and turquoise, or cranberry and dusky orange. A similar gender-based vocabulary exists in American sports language. Men are far more likely than women to use the common basketball terms such as *slam dunk, back door, box out, zone, dish, reverse layup, in the bonus, in the paint, isolation play, from downtown!,* and *and one!* This highly specialized set of terms and distinctions, whether used directly in reference to basketball or as metaphors, permits complex communication about complicated human activity but is applicable in extremely limited scenarios.

Clearly, language, including vocabulary, provides people with categories for recognizing and organizing the world. But language also reflects reality. Language is not rigidly structured or controlling. It is remarkably flexible and fluid, responding to changes in the surrounding culture and enabling us to describe and analyze our world with remarkable specificity.

How Do Systems of Power Intersect with Language and Communication?

Analyze how systems of power relate to language.

Language comes alive when people communicate with one another. But languages are deeply embedded in the patterns of particular cultures. What people actually say and how they say it are intricately connected to the cultural context, to the speakers' social position, and to the larger systems of power within which the language operates. A related linguistic field called **sociolinguistics** pioneered the study of how culture shapes language and language shapes culture, particularly the intersection of language with cultural categories and systems of power such as age, race, ethnicity, sexuality, gender, and class (Wardhaugh 2009). Linguistic anthropologists have built upon this tradition by expanding ethnographic research and focusing on ways that both cultural categories and speech acts are culturally constructed and changing.

sociolinguistics
The study of the ways culture shapes language and language shapes culture, particularly the intersection of language with cultural categories and systems of power such as age, race, ethnicity, sexuality, gender, and class.

LANGUAGE, DIALECT, AND LANGUAGE IDEOLOGIES

Politics and power can play key roles in how we evaluate a system of communication. For instance, how do we distinguish between a language and a **dialect**? Is it purely on a linguistic basis? The distinction is not always simple. Human languages vary widely in spoken and written form and in accent, pronunciation, vocabulary, and grammar. Yet, from the perspective of linguistic anthropology, all languages serve as effective communication tools for the people who speak them.

dialect
A nonstandard variation of a language.

The categorization and evaluation of certain ways of speaking as dialects and others as languages can frequently be traced to the exertion of power—the political power of the nation, the state, and the media—and the stratification among racial and ethnic groups. Naming something a dialect generally places it in a subordinate relationship to its associated language. Yiddish linguist Max Weinreich reputedly once said that a language is a dialect with an army and a navy. In other words, the elevated status associated with a language derives not from its superior linguistic form or communication capacity but from its ability to establish—perhaps impose through force, if necessary—a particular form as the norm by which to judge other ways of speaking. A particular language variation or way of speaking may be elevated in a culture as the **prestige language**—that is, the one associated with wealth, success, education, and power.

prestige language
A particular language variation or way of speaking that is associated with wealth, success, education, and power.

Today, we are taught to think that all people in France speak French and that those in Italy speak Italian. This is a definition of language based more on power—the establishment of national borders—than linguistics. In this case, the border between languages is established not by mutual intelligibility but by politics. It is just as likely, because of the language continuum, that people in the villages on either side of the France–Italy border can understand one another. Of course, the people on the French side may be considered to be speaking a "dialect" of French, whereas "standard French" (based on the French spoken in Paris) is promoted through the government, the schools, and the national media. In effect, "standard French" has an army and a navy. The local language spoken in the village on the France–Italy border does not. The language continuum between France and Italy has been disrupted in recent years by the French government's efforts to impose a standard dialect across the country. But new laws passed by the European Union have guaranteed that national governments must recognize minority languages within their borders and have given new standing to local languages.

French sociologist Pierre Bourdieu proposes that language skills serve as a type of cultural capital—a resource or asset available to language users that can be converted into financial capital, such as wages and benefits. Mastery over language brings a set of resources that enable the individual to be more successful. Bourdieu notes that linguistic standards are established and reinforced by a culture's educational institutions, government, media, and religious organizations. They may be taught in schools, used in national media broadcasts such as radio and television, or selected as a sign of competence in business hiring practices. Other language variations are then judged against the norm of the prestige language, and their speakers—often said to be speaking a dialect—are associated with inferior positions within the culture (Bourdieu 1982, 1984).

As the story at the beginning of this chapter illustrates, the United States is home to speakers of nearly 400 languages, including 150 distinct Native American languages whose origins predate European conquest (U.S. Census Bureau 2015). Some 40 million people speak Spanish at home (U.S. Census Bureau 2018). The 38 million immigrants in the United States bring unprecedented language diversity, though 90 percent of the children of immigrants learn to speak English proficiently (Pew Research Center 2013).

Although globally the English language varies widely in pronunciation, vocabulary, and grammar, in the United States—through national television, radio, and the educational system—the Midwestern accent and grammar have come to characterize the prestige language variation against which all other variations are judged. This variety of English is sometimes called Standard Spoken American English (SSAE) or simply Standard American English (SAE). As we explored in this chapter's opening story, judgments about language can have consequences well beyond the realm of communication.

code switching

Switching back and forth between one linguistic variant and another, or one language and another, depending on the cultural context.

In cultures with distinct language variations, dialects, styles, and accents, individuals may become skilled at **code switching**—that is, switching back and forth between one variation and another according to cultural context. Code switching takes many forms. Bilingual speakers, for instance, code switch as they shift from language to language to express certain thoughts or emotions (Woolard 1989; Koven 2007).

Educational systems tend to resist acknowledging speech variations as equally effective, instead choosing to promote a prestigious version as the inherent best one. (For instance, think about the linguistic standards your instructor used to grade your last English paper.) In educational environments, as a result, students, teachers, and administrators all learn to switch frequently from informal to formal styles of speaking and writing as required. Talking with friends in the hallway may assume a very different form than responding to a professor's query in class. Writing a text message or a tweet elicits a distinctly different writing style than polishing a research paper for a class assignment does.

In analyzing the relationship of language to systems of power, linguistic anthropologists use the concept of **language ideology**. As we will discuss later in chapters on race, gender, and sexuality, ideologies are sets of beliefs, ideas, and assumptions—often incorrect—about what is normal and natural in the world. These ideologies are then used to explain and justify patterns of inequality. Similarly, language ideologies are beliefs and conceptions about language—for instance, what is considered standard or nonstandard—that often serve as strategies for rationalizing and justifying patterns of stratification and inequality (Ahearn 2017). Language ideology is clearly present in the chapter opening story. Consider how language ideologies also come into play in the following examples of African American English, Inverted Spanglish, and gendered speech.

language ideology
Beliefs and conceptions about language that often serve to rationalize and justify patterns of stratification and inequality.

LANGUAGE AND RACE

African American English. Linguistic anthropologists and other scholars of language have extensively studied one particular form of English that is spoken by millions of African Americans in the United States. At times, this variation has been referred to as Black English, Black English Vernacular, African American Vernacular English, or African American English (AAE). The language habits of African Americans in the United States are not homogenous: They vary according to region, gender, social class, and age, and not all African Americans speak AAE. Even among those who do, there are significant differences.

AAE is perhaps the most stigmatized variation of SAE, mistakenly criticized as broken or flawed English and associated with urban African American youth. But from a linguistic perspective, AAE is a complete, consistent, and logical variation of the English language with a unique history and a distinct and coherent pronunciation, vocabulary, and grammar. Studies by Labov (1972a) and other scholars have carefully demonstrated that AAE is a sophisticated linguistic system with clear rules and patterns (Table 4.1).

Scholars disagree about the exact origins of AAE. Some trace its vocabulary and grammar to the West African linguistic roots of enslaved people who were forced to work in the American colonies. Others trace its heritage to nonstandard English used by poor English immigrants who interacted with enslaved African workers in the plantation system of the American South. The creole languages—blends between the Indigenous language and the colonial language—found in Jamaica, Trinidad, Barbados, and Guyana that developed during and after the slave trade may also have been potential sources of the unique forms that AAE has taken (Green 2002; Rickford and Rickford 2000).

TABLE 4.1

Contrasts between Standard American English and African American English

STANDARD ENGLISH	STANDARD ENGLISH CONTRACTION	AFRICAN AMERICAN ENGLISH VERNACULAR
You are ready	You're ready	You ready
He is ready	He's ready	He ready
We are ready	We're ready	We ready
They are ready	They're ready	They ready

Source: William Labov. 1972a. *Language in the Inner City: Studies in the Black English Vernacular.* Philadelphia: University of Pennsylvania Press.

Despite its stigmatization within certain parts of American society and the intense cultural pressure to assimilate to SAE, AAE has not only survived and developed but also become a symbol of identity and solidarity for many within the African American community. John Rickford and Russell Rickford (2000) document how this "Spoken Soul"—spoken by African Americans of all ages across the United States and closely associated with African American identity and culture—comes alive in the African American community. Indeed, it is vibrant in homes, schools, streets, and churches and on the airwaves. It represents a culture, history, and worldview that are distinct from White culture and ways of speaking.

The linguistic status of AAE entered prominently into the U.S. national debate in 1996. At that time, the Oakland Unified School District in California recommended recognizing it under the name Ebonics—from *ebony* ("black") + *phonics* ("sounds")—as a distinct language. The district also recommended supporting student speakers of AAE as if they were learning SAE as a second language in school. The goal was to use AAE as a bridge for students as they mastered SAE. In response, critics from across the country warned that the "teaching of Ebonics" in U.S. public schools would undermine the use of SAE, which they considered central to U.S. national identity, unity, and progress.

Under pressure, the Oakland school district revised its plan, but the controversy effectively obscured its efforts to address a local problem with national implications—the struggles of African American children to succeed in school. Today, resistance to recognizing AAE continues, creating negative stereotypes that undermine efforts to understand the unique linguistic character of AAE and the struggles that young AAE speakers may have in educational settings dominated by SAE. In fact, the debate about English language diversity and the place of SAE in U.S. culture continues through efforts at the local, state, and national levels (Ahearn 2012).

Here, the Oakland, California, Task Force on the Education of African American Students presents a resolution on Ebonics in public education, on January 12, 1997.

Looking Like a Language, Sounding Like a Race. In his book *Looking Like a Language, Sounding Like a Race* (2021), Jonathan Rosa examines how language ideologies shape the racialization of young Latinx people. In particular, he explores the importance of educational settings, with their emphasis on language standardization, as premier sites for asserting normative U.S. language ideologies and shaping Latinx identity. Between 2007 and 2010, Rosa conducted fieldwork in a new Chicago-area high school in which 90 percent of the 1,000 students were classified as Mexican or Puerto Rican and almost all the non-Latinx students were classified as African American. Public schools, Rosa notes, are required by city, state, and federal government mandate to preserve English as the primary language of instruction and administration. As a result, even though students and staff regularly spoke Spanish at school, Spanish was treated as a handicap to overcome rather than a resource to develop among English language learners and students in bilingual programs. School administrators established explicit goals to transform Spanish-speaking students from "at-risk youth" into "young Latino professionals," what Rosa describes as an intersectional mobility project in which speaking standardized English was seen as a central component to assimilation and success in the dominant U.S. English language culture. Rosa's research documents the strategies that students deploy to navigate this complex landscape of language and race, in which Spanish equates to race—sounds like a race—and Latinx people are deemed to look like a language, including a wide range of linguistic repertoires that challenge ideas of their language and educational deficiency.

In one innovation, Latinx students in Rosa's study deploy what he calls Inverted Spanglish to resist racialization and marginalization in their school and community. By speaking Spanish words using English pronunciation, students engaged in a strategic parody of the speech of White people. As students simultaneously revealed their "unaccented" English ability and their familiarity with Spanish, they disclosed their expansive, crossover linguistic skills and their deep understanding of their location in U.S. racial and linguistic dynamics.

On a visit to a restaurant near the school, students became annoyed by how White customers disrespected Latinx waiters and waitresses and loudly expressed their irritation at being forced to communicate in Spanish. Two students proceeded to stage an impromptu intervention. In a performance intended to be overheard by the White customers and by the employees with whom they empathized, the students engaged in the following Inverted Spanglish parody.

DIANA: Donday esta el banyo? (Spanish: "Donde esta el bano?"; "Where is the bathroom?") *Walter points in the direction of the bathroom.*

DIANA: Moochus Gracias. (Spanish: "Muchas gracias"; "Thank you.")

WALTER: Di nada. (Spanish: "De nada"; "It's nothing.")
(see table in Rosa 2021, 163)

Walter and Diana drew on the hyper-anglicized "White voice" to pronounce their Spanish words to intentionally make the White customers feel uncomfortable about their behavior. Their strategy turned the linguistic tables and highlighted the customers' language practices. Rosa argues that the students revealed their linguistic dexterity by deploying Inverted Spanglish. In their display of both "unaccented" English ability and intimate familiarity with Spanish, they claimed both Spanish and English as their own. And by expressing solidarity with the restaurant's Latinx staff, they helped create a shared U.S. Latinx ethnolinguistic identity while challenging the racializing forces that attempt to position them, and all Latinxs, on the margins of Americanness.

LANGUAGE AND GENDER

Ethnic and racial dynamics are not the only sources of tension in communication. If you've ever walked away from a conversation with someone of the opposite sex and thought to yourself, *That person has no idea what I'm talking about!*, you are not alone. Bookstores are full of titles that promise to help you figure it out: *Men Are from Mars, Women Are from Venus* (Gray 2004), *The 5 Love Languages: The Secret to Love That Lasts* (Chapman 2010), *You Just Don't Understand: Women and Men in Conversation* (Tannen 2001). Clearly, women and men are developing different patterns of language use. How and why?

There is no hard evidence that the brains of men and women are wired in a way that produces gender differences in language and other behavior. But linguistic anthropologists have examined the powerful role of culture in shaping language. In this instance, language and gender are intricately intertwined in personal and public conversations, among groups of men or groups of women, and in mixed-gender talk. In particular, linguists use two main theoretical frameworks for analyzing these patterns. These frameworks are sometimes known as the *difference model* and the *dominance model*.

Linguist Deborah Tannen's popular book *You Just Don't Understand: Women and Men in Conversation* (2001) is built on the difference model. Tannen suggests that conversations between men and women are basically a form of cross-cultural communication. Between the ages of five and fifteen, boys and girls grow up in different linguistic worlds. At the time when most children are developing and perfecting their communication skills, boys and girls are operating in largely segregated gender groups. Girls mostly hang out in small groups, indoors, in more intimate conversations. Boys tend to play in larger groups, often outdoors, and compete with one another for group status, often through verbal jokes, stories, and challenges. These patterns, according to Tannen, are reinforced in later years through socializing, sports, and work. No wonder that boys and girls have a difficult time communicating with each other when they finally begin to look for relationships. It is as if they have grown up in two different cultures, two different worlds.

But is miscommunication always rooted in misunderstanding? Or are there real, underlying conflicts between the genders that lead to the miscommunication (Cameron 2007)? Other linguistic anthropologists, working from the dominance model, examine how the cultures of communication learned by boys and girls intertwine with gender dynamics throughout the larger culture: at home, school, work, and play, and even through religion. According to these scholars, if gender stratification and hierarchy are prevalent in the larger culture (see Chapter 7), and if men are generally in positions of superiority, then language will reflect men's dominance and may play a key role in enabling it (Lakoff 2004; West 1998).

Research on mixed-gender communication over the past thirty years has consistently shown that many men adopt linguistic strategies that allow them to establish and maintain dominance in conversation and in social interaction. Men are more likely to use dominant speech acts such as commands, explanations, contradictions, criticisms, challenges, and accusations. Women are more likely to ask, request, agree, support, accommodate, accept, and apologize. Men are more likely to interrupt other speakers to insert their ideas or concerns, express doubts, or offer advice.

Despite stereotypes to the contrary, men also tend to dominate conversations through the amount of talking they do. Men claim more "air time" than women in meetings, seminars, boardrooms, and classrooms—especially in public forums where they see some possibility of maintaining or increasing their power and status. Working from the dominance model of mixed-gender communication, many linguistic anthropologists suggest that language and gender, as reflected in the communication patterns of men and women, are intricately connected to patterns of stratification in the culture at large (Holmes 1998).

Does "No" Really Mean "No"? Don Kulick's (2003) study of the use of the word *no* in sexual relations, published before the #MeToo movement rose to prominence, considers how words can take on different meanings depending on the gender of the speaker and the listener. What does "no" mean when a woman says it to a man who desires sex? In court cases involving rape or sexual harassment, men regularly state that they have misunderstood a woman's refusal of their sexual advances. They often blame the victim for not being clear enough with her "no." How can this miscommunication be possible? After all, "no" means "no." Or does it?

According to Kulick's findings, some men apparently think a woman's "no" actually means "yes" or "keep trying." Kulick suggests that men don't hear the actual word but instead hear what they think the word is supposed to mean. Specifically, his study suggests that men in a patriarchal (male-dominated) culture may not even hear a woman's "no" because it does not make sense within their cultural expectations of women as sexual objects. Within U.S. cultural formulations of gender roles and sexuality, women are imagined to say "no," to resist, when they actually mean "yes." Is it possible that, based on their gender, the men and women in your class might even react differently to hearing the results of this study?

The power of culture to shape the meaning of language can have implications for men as well. Men in U.S. culture are expected to say "yes" to women's sexual initiatives, never "no." With a "no," the man risks undermining his masculine identity, perhaps raising questions about his sexuality. A simple and straightforward linguistic expression—*No!*—struggles for clarity in the murky cultural context of gender relationships and power (MacKinnon 1993). As U.S. colleges and universities struggle to address widespread incidents of sexual harassment and abuse and seek to empower students to communicate more directly and successfully about their intentions and desires, attention to the intersections of language, gender, and power become increasingly important.

He, She, They. Language changes. Despite the efforts of dictionary boards and linguistic councils to codify a language at a particular moment, human modes of communication are never static. As we have discussed, sociolinguists are interested in how and why changes happen.

Today, changing norms of gender and sexuality are reshaping language use around the world, particularly in response to movements for gender equity

and inclusiveness. In Argentina, people have been shifting common references for Argentine men and women, *Argentinos* and *Argentinas*, to *Argentines*, a gender-neutral term that does not exist in traditional Spanish grammar. A parallel movement among U.S. politicians, scholars, and activists has introduced the term *Latinx* to replace *Latino*, the masculine form of the word often used to encompass all people, and the more awkward use of *Latino/a*.

Pronouns are lodged deep in our cognition and reinforced by constant use from childhood. Yet their use is changing, too. In many Swedish preschools, teachers substitute the gender-neutral term *hen* for gendered pronouns like *he* or *she* or simply call children "friends." In the United States, momentum has built, especially among younger people, to use a gender-neutral third-person singular pronoun, *they*, when referring to a person whose sex or social gender is unknown or fluid. This is a distinct shift from past language norms that required using *he or she* rather than the formally plural *they*. Here, the rejection of dominant gender designations has a distinctly political and cultural project, namely to contest rigid gender expectations and to create space for members of trans and gender-nonbinary communities to find an avenue of self-expression in a deeply binary culture. In some circles, identifying one's pronouns in letter and email signatures or Zoom screen names has become common practice to signal this open space. Transgressing familiar linguistic rules in this way reaches beyond strictly grammatical debates to contest assumed norms and values and to shift the culture's binary mental maps of gender and sexuality.

As the examples discussed above indicate, language and power intersect in many arenas. Socioeconomic class, educational environments, racial/ethnic group status, and gender are just some of these. Clearly, languages evolve as human groups use them, adapt them, contest them, or surrender them to more prevalent forms. The current age of globalization will provide even more opportunities for languages to meet and either mix or remain largely unchanged.

Did you ever wonder why men and women struggle to communicate with each other? Are their brains wired differently for language, or have they grown up in different social worlds learning different communication skills?

What Are the Effects of Globalization on Language?

Assess the impact of globalization on languages.

The movement of people throughout human history has played a role in the way that languages change and develop. As people move, elements of vocabulary and grammar are loaned to and imposed on populations that come into contact. Languages are full of loanwords that have been adopted from others. The encounter of linguistic communities is occurring with increasing rapidity in the contemporary era of globalization. Still, approximately 7,000 languages resound around the world today (Figure 4.1). A few have hundreds of millions of speakers. Most have a few thousand. However, globalization is consolidating language use among a small group of languages while threatening the extinction of thousands of others (Table 4.2).

DIMINISHING LANGUAGE DIVERSITY

The current pattern of increasing global interconnection threatens to diminish language diversity worldwide. In an earlier era of globalization, colonialism spread English, Spanish, Portuguese, French, Dutch, German, and Russian beyond Europe to people around the globe. Because these former colonial languages provide points of access to the current global economic and political system, many of them continue to expand today. In addition, increasing migration to urban centers often leads speakers of less widely used languages to assimilate to and adopt the more widely used language. The more prominent languages—including the former colonial languages and other regional or national languages—dominate global media, including television, radio, print, and digital media. Through this dominance, they are crowding out the less widely used languages and their speakers.

As a result of these dynamics, today the eight most prominent languages are spoken by more than 40 percent of the world's population. The top ninety-four languages account for 80 percent of humanity. The 4,000 least widely used languages, in total, account for only 0.12 percent of the world's language users (Simons 2019). English has a unique position in the world at the moment, with as many as 2 billion speakers. Many of these are nonnative speakers who learn English as a second language because of its central role in universities, medicine, computing, entertainment, and intergovernmental relationships. English is currently a prestige language that provides effective access to international economic activity and political engagement.

FIGURE 4.1

World Languages by Country, 2019

The languages of the world are spread across countries in ways that may surprise you. Take a moment to identify the twenty countries with the most language diversity and the country with the least language diversity.

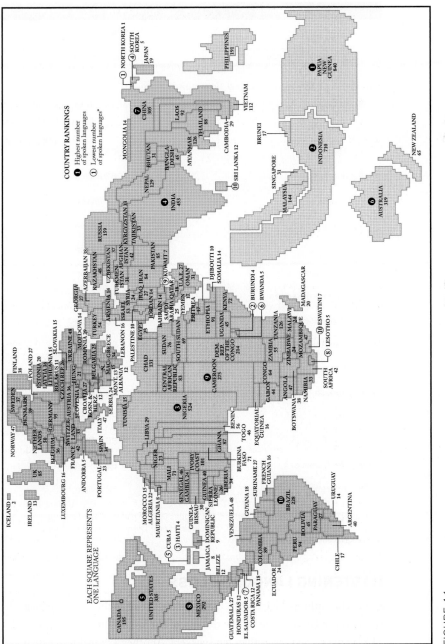

Source: Simons, Gary F. and Charles D. Fennig (eds.). 2019. *Ethnologue: Languages of the World*, 22nd ed. Dallas, TX: SIL International. Online version: www.ethnologue.com.

TABLE 4.2
Top Twenty World Languages, 2021

	LANGUAGE	NUMBER OF NATIVE SPEAKERS
1.	English	1,348 million
2.	Mandarin Chinese	1,120 million
3.	Hindi	600 million
4.	Spanish	543 million
5.	Standard Arabic	274 million
6.	Bengali	268 million
7.	French	267 million
8.	Russian	258 million
9.	Portuguese	258 million
10.	Urdu	230 million
11.	Indonesian	199 million
12.	Standard German	135 million
13.	Japanese	126 million
14.	Marathi	99 million
15.	Telugu	96 million
16.	Turkish	88 million
17.	Tamil	85 million
18.	Yue Chinese	85 million
19.	Wu Chinese	82 million
20.	Korean	82 million

Source: Simons, Gary F., David M. Eberhard, and Charles D. Fennig (eds.). 2021. *Ethnologue: Languages of the World*, 24th ed. Dallas, TX: SIL International. Online version: https://www.ethnologue.com/guides/ethnologue200.

HASTENING LANGUAGE LOSS

Linguistic anthropologists warn that as many as half of the 7,000 languages in the world today could be lost by the end of the twenty-first century. In 2019, 114 languages had fewer than ten speakers. Another 329 had fewer than one hundred speakers. Together, these 443 languages represent almost 7 percent of the world's languages (Simons 2019). They have very little chance of survival and face almost certain language death. This is the outcome of **language loss**. On average, one language is lost every ten days (Harrison 2007). The most rapid disappearances are in northern Australia, central South America, the Pacific Northwest of North America, and eastern Siberia; this group also includes the Native American languages spoken in Oklahoma and the southwestern United States.

Languages develop over time to enable human groups to adapt to a particular environment and to share information that is essential to their local culture. When a language is lost, when it is crowded out by more widely used languages, we lose all of the bodies of information and local knowledge that had been developed—perhaps over thousands of years—by that community. Within a language is embedded rich knowledge about plants, animals, and medicines. Within a language is embedded a particular group's unique way of knowing the world and thinking and talking about the human experience.

LANGUAGE REVITALIZATION

Most languages have never been written down. Does this surprise you? If you are a speaker of one of the more prominent languages, such as English, perhaps it does. As many of the less widely used languages face extinction, some groups are undertaking efforts to preserve them in written form.

Documenting a local language may involve years of work in a detailed and painstaking process that draws on all the basic skills of fieldwork and descriptive linguistics. One of the most extensive efforts to create written records of small languages is the work of a group called the Summer Institute of Linguistics (SIL), which together with its partner, the Wycliffe Bible Translators, trains missionaries in linguistic and anthropological methods and sends them to the field, often to remote areas, to live with a community and create a written language in order to translate the Christian Bible into the local language.

Some linguistic anthropologists consider SIL's work to be controversial. They are concerned that the Christian nature of the project means that certain aspects of local culture—including Indigenous religious beliefs, ritual language, songs, and art connected to local religion—are at risk of being ignored and extinguished. Other scholars acknowledge the significant data that would be lost if SIL translators were not doing the detailed work of documenting hundreds of local languages that are threatened with extinction in small communities worldwide. Despite this controversy, SIL has succeeded in producing a widely used compendium of all the world's languages, called *Ethnologue*. Although it started with only forty entries in 1951 as a language guide for Christian missionaries, in 2022 *Ethnologue*'s twenty-fifth edition catalogued 7,151 languages (Simons 2022).

language loss
The extinction of languages that have very few speakers.

Preserving Endangered Languages. Information technology is beginning to transform how linguistic anthropologists document and preserve endangered languages, creating new opportunities for revitalization. Consider the Native American Lakota language. Its approximately 25,000 speakers live primarily in tribal areas scattered across North and South Dakota, as well as in cities, towns, and rural areas throughout the United States. Their tribally owned lands are in some of the poorest U.S. counties. Few children learn Lakota today, threatening the language with eventual extinction. So the Lakota have placed a high priority on preserving their language and culture and increasing Lakota language use among young people. Linguists have been working to document the Lakota language by collecting and preserving language samples, cultural knowledge, and artifacts. Some have even done intensive immersion in the Lakota language. But limited resources, combined with the geographic dispersion of Lakota speakers, have inhibited these efforts.

In 2009, a small local company, LiveAndTell, built an online digital platform for Lakota language preservation and instruction. Using participatory social media technology similar to that of YouTube and Flickr, LiveAndTell created opportunities for Lakota speakers to collaborate, create, and share digital artifacts. Families wrote family stories and posted photos, audio recordings, videos, and online annotations. School research projects were uploaded to community sites. In these ways, the dispersed Lakota language community has created an online archive of the living language. For instance, one contributor posted a

Globalization threatens the loss of many smaller local languages and, with them, their local knowledge and ways of understanding the world. (*Left*) A Seri herbalist carries home lavender from the desert. The Seri are an Indigenous people in Mexico. (*Right*) Ramona Dick is an elder in the Washoe tribe, which is based in Nevada and California. As a child, she refused to be sent to a school where students were required to speak only English.

picture of a car and then tagged each part—steering wheel, mirror, tire, and so on—with the Lakota name and an audio file of its pronunciation. Entries like these provide detailed linguistic information that is not available in standard dictionaries and may never come to light in formal oral interviews with professional linguists (Arobba et al. 2010).

Humans are born with the ability to learn language. But exactly what we learn and the context in which we learn it vary widely. Languages change and grow, they are taught, debated, and contested. Humans are constantly adapting language to meet the needs of local communities and global interactions. And while today local languages are under increasing stress, the continuing diversity of human languages provides a vivid portrait of the dramatically different ways humans perceive, consider, and engage the world. As we have seen throughout this chapter, linguistic anthropologists are deeply engaged in the analysis and understanding of the role language plays in human life and in understanding the transitions and changes that are facing the human linguistic landscape in an era of increasing globalization.

Toolkit

Thinking Like an Anthropologist
Language, Immigration, and U.S. Culture

As you encounter the complexities of language in daily life—communicating with a loved one, collaborating with classmates from other places, studying abroad, working with people in multinational corporations, debating immigration policy, or understanding gender in classroom dynamics—thinking like an anthropologist can help you better understand your own experiences and those of others. First, take a moment to review the questions we asked at the beginning of this chapter:

- **What is language and where does it come from?**

- **How does language shape our ways of thinking?**

- **How do systems of power intersect with language and communication?**

- **What are the effects of globalization on language?**

In our opening story, we considered how language has entered the immigration debates in Arizona. Now that you have been studying anthropology—and in this chapter, linguistic anthropology—how would you analyze the underlying issues at play in this debate? Why has language become such a hot-button issue in U.S. politics? How is English intertwined with notions of American identity, class, and belonging? The long-held model of incorporating new immigrants into U.S. culture—the melting pot that blends everyone's diversity into one big stew—now competes with a salad bowl metaphor in which immigrants don't blend in completely but contribute their unique diversity to a multicultural salad. This new model has encountered resistance, particularly from people who fear a fragmentation of U.S. culture.

Language use has become symbolic of these larger debates. Studies consistently show that the children of immigrants grow up speaking English as their first language, not the language of their parents' country of origin (Portes, Fernandez-Kelly, and Haller 2009). Yet the debate over language instruction in education continues. Along with Arizona's restrictive immigration laws, the Arizona Department of Education has seen a 180-degree turn in its policies for bilingual education programs. Facing a teacher shortage in the 1990s, Arizona recruited thousands of bilingual teachers to lead bilingual classes for the tens of thousands of students who may have grown up speaking Spanish at home. Many of the new teachers were recruited from Latin America, and their first language was Spanish. Then, in 2000, Arizona voters passed a referendum mandating that instruction of nonnative English speakers be in English only. In 2010, the state adopted further policy changes, including new fluency standards for teachers focused on pronunciation and writing. Teachers who were unable to meet the new standards were removed from the classrooms of nonnative English speakers (Jordan 2010).

The Arizona education debates reveal how language functions as more than a system of symbols that enable people to communicate. Language is also a key cultural arena in which norms are established, values are promoted, and relationships of power are negotiated.

Key Terms

language (p. 99)

historical linguistics (p. 101)

language continuum (p. 101)

speech community (p. 102)

descriptive linguistics (p. 102)

phonemes (p. 102)

phonology (p. 102)

morphemes (p. 102)

morphology (p. 102)

syntax (p. 102)

grammar (p. 102)

kinesics (p. 103)

paralanguage (p. 103)

linguistic relativity (p. 104)

Sapir-Whorf hypothesis (p. 105)

lexicon (p. 106)

sociolinguistics (p. 107)

dialect (p. 107)

prestige language (p. 107)

code switching (p. 108)

language ideology (p. 109)

language loss (p. 119)

Part 2

What lies beneath the surface of any beautiful scene? The project of anthropology includes unmasking the structures of power—the deep complexities of how humans organize themselves in groups. In Part 2, we will explore the structures of race, ethnicity, gender, sexuality, kinship, and class in order to help you develop the analytical tools to see more deeply, navigate more carefully, and engage more fully with the world around you. Here, young Black people in London participate in a Black Lives Matter march.

Unmasking the Structures of Power

Chapter 5
Race and Racism

Learning Objectives

- Define race and the flawed biological assumptions often associated with it.

- Compare the construction of race across cultures.

- Explain the unique cultural construction of race in the United States.

- Analyze racism in terms of both individual actions and institutional systems of power.

On the evening of May 25, 2020, Derek Chauvin and three other Minneapolis, Minnesota, police officers violently arrested unarmed forty-six-year-old African American George Floyd outside a neighborhood deli, Cup Foods. For nine minutes and twenty-nine seconds, Chauvin, who is White, held his knee directly on Floyd's neck, while Floyd, who was handcuffed and lying face-down on the street, called out, "I can't breathe." Two other officers knelt on his back for part of the time. The fourth officer prevented onlookers from intervening. George Floyd died as a result.

George Floyd's murder by a Minneapolis police officer reverberated across the world. In Gaza City, Palestine, a street mural expresses transnational solidarity.

Seventeen-year-old Darnella Frazier, standing nearby, courageously filmed a graphic ten-minute video of the murder. Other bystanders pleaded with the officers to get off. The statement issued by the Minneapolis Police Department immediately after the killing noted only: "man dies after medical incident during police interaction." It also claimed that Floyd had physically resisted the officers. Frazier's video clearly contradicted the misleading police report and became key courtroom evidence a year later in the trial of Derek Chauvin. Chauvin—a nineteen-year veteran of the Minneapolis Police Department who had been the subject of eighteen previous complaints and had been formally disciplined twice—was convicted of murder and manslaughter and sentenced to twenty-two and half years in prison. He was the first White police officer in Minnesota to be charged in the death of a Black civilian. The City of Minneapolis settled a wrongful death lawsuit with the Floyd family for $27 million. The U.S. Department of Justice indicted all four officers for violating George Floyd's civil rights.

George Floyd's murder sparked a racial justice uprising demanding an end to repeated and systemic police violence against people of color. Millions of people marched in hundreds of towns and cities across the United States, despite the rapid spread of the COVID-19 pandemic that spring, becoming the largest series of civil rights demonstrations in the country's history. Protests spread around the world. Black Lives Matter activists called for rethinking what makes a community truly healthy and safe. They demanded defunding local police departments and reinvesting those funds in efforts to end the daily violence of poverty, mass incarceration, poor housing, underfunded schools, and discriminatory health-care practices affecting communities of color. By adopting George Floyd's cry, "I can't breathe," they simultaneously condemned patterns of racist police violence and the ways that the coronavirus moves along lines of race and class to unequally attack the lungs of people of color across the country and around the world.

The torrent of deadly encounters between police and African Americans across the country—including, notably, the tragic events in Minneapolis—and the growth of the Black Lives Matter movement have continued to push race and racism directly into the U.S. national spotlight. Race and racism are incredibly difficult topics of conversation in U.S. culture, whether we are in a classroom, a courtroom, a religious setting, the halls of Congress, the streets of Minneapolis, or our own local communities. How do we create opportunities to explore ideas of race and the way those ideas shape our lives and culture? In a country that likes to think of itself as color-blind, how do we as anthropologists make sense of the continuing inequalities in income, wealth, education, access to health care, police enforcement, and incarceration rates that break so clearly along color lines (Shanklin 1998)?

Anthropologists view race as a framework of categories created to divide the human population. Western Europeans originally developed this framework as part of their global expansion beginning in the 1400s (Sanjek 1994). As they encountered, mapped, and colonized people in Africa, Asia, the Pacific, and the Americas, Europeans placed them into an "international hierarchy of races, colors, religions and cultures" (Trouillot 1994, 146). The exact labels and expressions have varied over time and place as colonial powers engaged with local cultures and confronted local resistance. But the underlying project—to stratify people into groups based on assumed natural differences in intelligence, attractiveness, capacity for civilization, and fundamental worth in relation to people of European descent—has been remarkably consistent (Mullings 2005a).

As we will explore in this chapter, anthropologists today find no scientific basis for classifications of race. Genetically there is only one race—the human race, with all its apparent diversity. Yet despite consistent efforts over the last century by anthropologists and others to counter the inaccurate belief that races are biologically real, race has remained a powerful framework through which many people see human diversity and through which those in power organize the distribution of privileges and resources. Race—which is scientifically not real—has become culturally real in the pervasive racism found across many parts of the globe, including the United States.

Over the past 500 years, race as a way of organizing the world has been put to destructive use, wreaking an enormous toll on both its victims and its proponents. Race and racism have justified the conquest, enslavement, forced transportation, and economic and political domination of some humans by others. Today, race and racism have become so integral to patterns of human relations in many parts of the world that inherited racial categories may seem to be natural, and the inequality built on racism may seem to represent "real" differences among "real" races.

In this chapter, we will critique arguments for the existence of discrete biological human groups called "races." We will consider the roots of race and racism in the European colonial past and the different ways they are expressed in various places today. We will examine the construction of race in the United States over the past 400 years and the ways race and racism continue to shape U.S. culture. And we will explore how race and racism intersect with class and other systems of power. In particular, we will consider the following questions:

- **Do biologically separate races exist?**

- **How is race constructed around the world?**

- **How is race constructed in the United States?**

- **What is racism?**

race

A flawed system of classification, with no biological basis, that uses certain physical characteristics to divide the human population into supposedly discrete groups.

We will examine **race** as a flawed system of classification, created and re-created over time, that uses certain physical characteristics (such as skin color, hair texture, eye shape, and eye color) to divide the human population into a few supposedly discrete biological groups and attributes to those groups unique combinations of physical ability, mental capacity, personality traits, cultural patterns, and capacity for civilization. Drawing on anthropological research, however, we will see that racial categories have no biological basis. We might even say that races, as a biological concept, do not exist. The danger in this statement about biological race is that it may lead us to the mistaken conclusion that race does not exist. On the contrary, race as a cultural construction has very real consequences.

Race is a deeply influential system of thinking that affects people and institutions. Over time, imagined categories of race have shaped our cultural institutions—schools, places of worship, media, political parties, economic practices—and have organized the allocation of wealth, power, and privilege at all levels of society. Race has served to create and justify patterns of power and inequality within cultures worldwide, and many people have learned to see those patterns as normal and reasonable. So, in this chapter, we will also examine **racism:** individuals' thoughts and actions, as well as institutional patterns and policies, that create or reproduce unequal access to power, privilege, resources, and opportunities based on imagined differences among groups (Omi and Winant 1994).

racism

Individuals' thoughts and actions and institutional patterns and policies that create or reproduce unequal access to power, privilege, resources, and opportunities based on imagined differences among groups.

By the end of the chapter, you will have the anthropological tools to understand not only the flaws in arguments for biologically discrete races but also the history and current expressions of race and racism globally and in the United States. This first chapter of the section "Unmasking the Structures of Power"

addresses race and racism. The following chapters address ethnicity and nationalism, gender, sexuality, and kinship. Each of these systems of power—its ideas and institutions—shapes individual life chances and creates societal patterns of inequality by differentially allocating access to rights, privileges, assets, and opportunities. While examining each system of power in its own right, we will also consider the elaborate intersections among them as they work together to create inequality. For instance, how did race, gender, and class intersect to shape the disastrous encounter between George Floyd and Derek Chauvin on a Minneapolis street corner? In recent years, this attention to **intersectionality** has become increasingly prominent in anthropological research and analysis. Over the course of this chapter and the chapters that follow, our discussion will prepare you to apply these anthropological tools and perspectives, if you so choose, to engage in efforts against racism and other systems of inequality on your college campus, in your community, and throughout the world.

intersectionality

An analytic framework for assessing how factors such as race, gender, and class interact to shape individual life chances and societal patterns of stratification.

Do Biologically Separate Races Exist?

Define race and the flawed biological assumptions often associated with it.

Many of us were enculturated to believe that "race" refers to distinct physical characteristics that mark individuals as clearly belonging in one group and not in another. However, anthropologists see race very differently. Contemporary

What can you know about a person's genetic makeup based on their outward appearance? Variations of skin color or other visible characteristics often associated with race are shaped by less than 0.1 percent of our genetic code. Contrary to certain stereotypes, they do not predict anything else about a person's genetic makeup, physical or mental capabilities, culture, or personality.

studies of human genetics reveal no biologically distinct human groups. We can state this with certainty despite centuries of scientific and pseudoscientific effort to prove the existence of distinct biological races, and despite the widespread popular belief that different races exist. In fact, humans are almost identical: We share more than 99.9 percent of our DNA with one another. The small differences that do exist are not distributed in any way that would correspond with popular notions of separate races. Racial categories are not fixed in nature but, as we will explore later in this chapter, have changed constantly over time as people have created and perpetuated them through individual and collective action (Ossorio and Duster 2005).

First, however, let's explore some of the science behind race.

FUZZY BOUNDARIES IN A WELL-INTEGRATED GENE POOL

Some biological anthropologists have compared modern humans to a little village that has grown very quickly. Throughout the short 200,000-year history of modern humans, we have basically been functioning as one enormous, interconnected gene pool, swapping genetic material back and forth (by interbreeding) quite freely within the village. Over the years, our family trees have intersected again and again.

If you trace your own family back for thirty generations—parents to grandparents to great-grandparents, and so on—you will find that in less than a thousand years, you have accumulated 1 billion relatives. It is not hard to imagine the myriad and unpredictable exchanges of genetic material among that large a group. Now extend your family tree back 100,000 years—the time it has taken for a few small groups of humans to migrate out of Africa and populate the entire planet. It is easy to imagine the billions of times this growing population has exchanged genetic material. Such deep integration of the human gene pool means that no clear and absolute genetic lines can be drawn to separate people into biologically discrete "racial" populations.

As a result of this gene flow, human variation changes gradually over geographic space in a continuum (what biological anthropologists refer to as a *cline*), not by abrupt shifts or according to clearly marked groups. Even skin color, perhaps most frequently imagined to demarcate separate races, in fact varies so gradually over geographic space that there are no clear boundaries between one population and another, nor color groupings that distinguish one population from another. If you flew from western Africa to Russia, you would notice distinct variations in physical human form between the population where you boarded the plane and the population where you disembarked. But if you walked from western Africa to Russia, there would never be a point along the way where you could stop and say that the people on one side of the road are of one race and the people on the other side are of a different race.

Perhaps more surprising, a person from western Africa who starts walking toward Russia may have more in common genetically with someone at the end of their trek than they do with a neighbor at home. This seems hard to imagine because we have been enculturated to believe that a very small number of traits—including skin color, hair texture, and eye color and shape—can serve to categorize people into distinct groups and predict larger genetic patterns. This is a flawed assumption. The human gene pool continues to be highly integrated. Minor genetic variations such as skin color cannot be used to predict anything else in an individual's genetic makeup. People in a particular region of the world whose ancestors have inhabited that area for an extended period of time may have some increased likelihood of genetic similarity because of the greater probability that those who are geographically closer will swap genetic material. But group boundaries are fuzzy and porous. People move and genes flow. Ultimately, group genetic probabilities cannot predict the genetic makeup of any individual in the group.

THE WILD GOOSE CHASE: LINKING PHENOTYPE TO GENOTYPE

In considering human physical diversity, biological anthropologists distinguish between genotype and phenotype. **Genotype** refers to the inherited genetic factors that provide a framework for an organism's physical form; these factors constitute the total genetic endowment that the organism, in turn, can pass down to its descendants. In contrast, **phenotype** refers to how genes are expressed in an organism's physical form (both visible and invisible) as a result of its genotype's interaction with environmental factors, such as nutrition, disease, and stress.

The widespread belief that certain phenotypes, such as skin color, are linked to physical and mental capabilities, personality types, or cultural patterns is incorrect but deeply ingrained and difficult to reimagine.

As individuals, we may make snap judgments based on phenotypical traits that we erroneously assume indicate a person's "race"; with a quick glance we may think we know something significant about that individual. On the basis of phenotype alone, we may consider someone to be smarter, faster, stronger, safe or dangerous, better at business, better at math, a better dancer or singer, more prone to alcoholism, more artistic, more susceptible to certain diseases, a better lover. You might call this the "White Men Can't Jump" or "Asians Are Better at Math" way of thinking about race and genes. But what can we really tell about someone from these superficial characteristics?

A relatively small number of genes control the traits frequently used today to distinguish one "race" from another—skin color, eye shape, or hair texture, for

genotype

The inherited genetic factors that provide the framework for an organism's physical form.

phenotype

The way genes are expressed in an organism's physical form as a result of genotype interaction with environmental factors.

instance. As a result, in the short history of modern humans, these genes have been able to change rapidly in response to the environment. For example, as humans moved out of Africa and across the globe into a wide variety of physical environments, traits such as skin color, which are shaped by a relatively small cluster of genes, were more susceptible to environmental pressures and adapted more quickly. In contrast, traits such as intelligence, athletic or artistic ability, and social skills appear to be shaped by complex combinations of thousands or tens of thousands of genes, so they have been much less susceptible to environmental pressures. Adaptations in skin color were not accompanied by adaptations in, say, intelligence, musical ability, or physical ability. It is important to note that genetic research consistently shows that the genes that influence skin color, eye shape, or hair texture are not linked to any other genes and cannot predict anything about the rest of a person's underlying genotype (Mukhopadhyay, Henze, and Moses 2007).

Jonathan Marks, a leading biological anthropologist, compares the problem of sorting people into races with the problem children might have of sorting blocks into categories. Imagine that you start with a pile of blocks and ask a group of children to sort them into "large" and "small." They might agree on some—the largest and the smallest. But others in between might be harder to classify. "The fact that the blocks can be sorted into the categories given, however, does not imply that there are two kinds of blocks in the universe, large and small—and that the child has uncovered a transcendent pattern in the sizing of the blocks. It simply means that if categories are given, they can be imposed upon the blocks" (Marks 1995, 159).

The same is true for humans and the concept of race. If you give people a limited range of categories for skin color groups, they will be able to place many people into these categories. Some individuals who lie in the boundaries may be more difficult to categorize. But would this exercise uncover some deep, intrinsic, genetic pattern about humans? No, because traits like skin color are not linked to any other particular set of genes and cannot predict anything else about a person's underlying genotype.

How Is Race Constructed around the World?

Compare the construction of race across cultures.

Racial categories are human constructs; they are not found in nature. Yet they have become so deeply internalized that they feel natural and provide one of the most powerful frameworks through which we experience the world (Mukhopadhyay, Henze, and Moses 2007). Anthropologists examine race and racism on a global scale and thus from different angles, identifying their regional similarities and variations and, in the process, revealing how these concepts have evolved and might be changed through individual and collective action.

RACE AND THE LEGACY OF COLONIALISM

Contemporary global expressions of race and racism are deeply rooted in the systems of classification that western Europeans created as they expanded their colonial empires into Africa, Asia, the Pacific, and the Americas beginning in the 1400s. **Colonialism** became the centerpiece of European global economic activity, combining economic, military, and political control of people and places to fuel Europe's economic expansion and to enhance the continent's position in the emerging global economy (see Chapter 10). The classification of people based on phenotype, particularly skin color, became the key framework for creating a hierarchy of races—with Europeans at the top—that falsely linked people's looks with assumptions about their intelligence, physical abilities, capacity for culture, and basic worth. Eventually this framework served to justify colonial conquests, the transatlantic slave trade, and the eradication of much of the Indigenous population of the Americas (Gregory and Sanjek 1994).

colonialism
The practice by which a nation-state extends political, economic, and military power beyond its own borders over an extended period of time to secure access to raw materials, cheap labor, and markets in other countries or regions.

Taking a global perspective, anthropologists often refer to "racisms" in the plural, reflecting the variety of ways race has been constructed among people in different places. Locally and nationally, racisms and systems of racial classification are complex frameworks that derive from encounters among colonialism and local cultural patterns, global migration, and specific movements of resistance. Even though racializing systems around the world may all have their roots in European colonialism, they manifest themselves differently in different places and at different times.

Racial frameworks and systems of racism have changed significantly over the last century. After World War II, colonial-era racist political and legal structures shifted as national liberation movements rose up against occupations by foreign powers. In addition, anti-racist liberation movements in this postcolonial period challenged long-term patterns of race and racial discrimination. Notably, the anti-apartheid movement in South Africa resisted dominant White rule, eventually reversing decades of legal structural discrimination and violence. The civil rights movement challenged more than 300 years of race-based inequality in the United States. Today, globalization has brought about new experiences of race and racism (as we will see in the case studies that follow).

Indeed, in today's global world, flexible accumulation produces new relationships between corporations and workers, the migration of workers within countries and across borders yields new racial formations, and time-space compression enhances communication tools that can be employed to resist traditional hierarchies while perpetuating old racial frameworks on a global scale. Racisms today, though rooted in similar historical realities, are shifting as they intersect with other systems of power, whether those are ethnicity, gender, sexuality, kinship, or class (Mullings 2005a). The exact expression of these constructs varies from culture to culture and place to place depending on why races were originally invented and how they have been used to establish and maintain hierarchies of power.

Class, Gender, and Hundreds of Races in Brazil.

Brazil provides another site to explore the cultural construction of race and its intersection with social stratification. The United States and Brazil are today the two largest multiracial countries in the Western Hemisphere, although they have traveled two very different paths in framing racial identities and hierarchies. By the time Brazil outlawed slavery in 1888, the country had the largest African population in the New World. This situation reflected the grim fact that during and after Brazil's time as a colony of Portugal (1500–1815), 40 percent of all Africans in the transatlantic slave trade were taken to Brazil to work on Portuguese plantations and mines. Brazil was the last country in the Americas to outlaw slavery—a full generation after the U.S. Emancipation Proclamation in 1863.

Today, Brazilians describe the human physical diversity called "race" in great detail. Although Brazil's system of racial classification is color-coded, its color terminology is uniquely expansive, encompassing hundreds of categories (Freyre 1933; Harris 1964, 1970). Terms include *alva* (pure white), *alva-escuro* (off-white), *alva-rosada* (pinkish white), *branca* (white), *clara* (light), *branca morena* (darkish white), *branca suja* (dirty white), *café* (coffee colored), *café com leite* (coffee with milk), *canela* (cinnamon), *preta* (black), and *pretinha* (lighter black; Fluehr-Lobban 2006). Brazilian race categories thus represent a nuanced continuum of appearance rather than a few rigid groups, as those used in the United States do.

Brazil's population of Europeans, Africans, and Indigenous people has a long history of interracial mixing. The Portuguese colonial government promoted assimilation and did not bar **miscegenation**—that is, interracial marriage. As a result, many single Portuguese men who settled in Brazil chose to intermarry. Nor has Brazil applied the rule of hypodescent—the "one drop of blood" rule— that in the United States meant that having even one Black ancestor out of many could mark an individual as Black (see "The Rule of Hypodescent" later in this chapter). As a result, a Brazilian family may include children who are categorized as various shades of white, brown, and black.

Race in Brazil is not solely a function of skin color. In fact, race intersects closely with class—including land ownership, wealth, and education—in determining social status. Because of the power of class, a Brazilian's racial position can be modified by their level of affluence. Affluence can shift a Brazilian's racial identity in spite of skin color and other supposedly "racial" markers (Walker 2002).

miscegenation

A demeaning historical term for interracial marriage.

Some scholars refer to Brazil as a "racial democracy" and extol the nation as an exceptional example of racial harmony (Freyre 1933; Harris 1964; Kottak 2006). Brazil's government abolished the use of racial categories in the 1930s and constitutionally banned racism in 1951. The complex and fluid color classifications—and the absence of political and legal mechanisms to establish and enforce a clear color line between Black and White—are seen as a sign of tolerance. In addition, the incorporation of key African cultural practices as symbols of the Brazilian nation (including carnival, samba, Candomblé religious practices, capoeira, and specific cuisine) is often cited as supporting evidence for the racial democracy thesis (Downey 2005).

MAP 5.1
Brazil

Other scholars have noted that despite the appearance of racial democracy, inequality exists in almost every area of Brazilian life and is directly linked to color. Darker-skinned Brazilians face higher levels of exclusion and injustice, and a systemic correlation exists between color and economics. Most of the poor are Afro-Brazilians. Most of the rich are White. Racial democracy may instead be simply a myth that serves as a cornerstone of Brazil's national denial of the existence of racism (Harrison 2002b; Roth-Gordon 2016; Smith 2016).

In *Laughter Out of Place* (2003), anthropologist Donna Goldstein writes about poor working women from the bleak favela (shantytown) ironically named Felicidade Eterna ("eternal happiness"). These women support their families as domestic workers for middle-class Brazilian families who live in the affluent sections of Rio de Janeiro. Gloria, poor and dark skinned, raising fourteen children, including nine of her own, works as a domestic servant, shopping, cooking, and cleaning. She earns $5 a day—just enough to feed herself and her family. The pay is off the books, so she has no legal labor protections, no insurance, and no pension. Goldstein links the contemporary culture of domestic work, particularly the employer–domestic servant relationship, to the historic institution of slavery in Brazil. Middle-class families enjoy a kind of learned helplessness similar to that of the slave owner—allowing their workers to do the dirty, manual chores. The employer–domestic servant relationship, like the owner–slave relationship, is characterized by domination, strict rules, and social separation.

How do Brazil's marginalized and oppressed people make sense of their lives—lives overburdened with poverty, violence, and work at the bottom of a global hierarchy of race, class, and gender, yet lives that also display dignity and resilience? Goldstein explores the role of laughter and humor as means to cope with persistent brutality. She particularly notes a humor that recognizes life's absurdities and ironies and provides perspective to a sense of injustice. She recalls, for instance, the awkwardness of "laughter out of place," as domestic workers and employers laugh at different times and for different reasons when they watch the local soap operas that dramatize middle-class Brazilian life. The distinctive life experiences of worker and employer create vastly different viewing experiences, casting the televised dramas of the Brazilian middle class in sharp contrast to the traumas of the domestic workers living in the favela—a contrast so absurd as to evoke laughter out of place.

How Is Race Constructed in the United States?

Explain the unique cultural construction of race in the United States.

Race is perhaps the most significant way of marking difference in U.S. culture. References to race can be found on census forms, school applications, and birth certificates, as well as in the media and casual conversation. Race is also a key framework that shapes the allocation of power, privilege, rewards, and status in the United States, and it infuses all of our political, economic, religious, recreational, educational, and cultural institutions (Smedley 1993). Yet it is one of the least discussed topics in U.S. culture and one of the most difficult to explore, even in anthropology. How do we begin to engage this difficult dialogue?

RACE AND THE U.S. CENSUS

The U.S. census, taken every ten years since 1790, provides a fascinating window into the changing conception of "race." The 1850 census had three categories: White, Black, and Mulatto. Mulatto referred to people of mixed race. The 1870 census expanded to five categories to incorporate new immigrants from China and to count the Native American population: White, Black, Mulatto, Chinese, and Indian (Native American). Respondents did not identify their own race; instead, census workers assigned them to a racial category based on their appearance.

By 1940, the census form had eight categories, eliminating the option for mixed race and adding more categories from Asia, including Hindu, a religion: White, Negro, Indian, Chinese, Japanese, Filipino, Hindu, and Korean. The 2020 census form included fourteen separate "race" boxes. Respondents could check one, many, or all of them.

This brief look at changes in the census form provides clear indications that race has been and still is an evolving human construction. The changing race categories do not reflect a change in human genotype or phenotype but changes in how the government organizes the diversity of people within its borders. The census construction of race reflects the U.S. government's power to establish certain categories and to apply those categories to make decisions about government resources.

The name of every person whose place of abode on the first day of June, 1870, was in this family.	DESCRIPTION.		
	Age at last birth-day. If under 1 year, give months in fractions, thus, 3/12.	Sex.—Males (M.), Females (F.).	Color.—White (W.), Black (B.), Mulatto (M.), Chinese (C.), Indian (L.)
3	4	5	6

What can changes in the U.S. census form tell us about the shifting concepts of race? Here, compare parts of the U.S. census Questionnaire, 1870, and the U.S. census Questionnaire, 2020.

Racial categories under debate provide a glimpse of the nation's changing future. For instance, increased immigration from Latin America, Asia, the Pacific Islands, and the Middle East has complicated both the census form and discussions about race in the United States. Note the rapid expansion of options in the census for people from Asia.

The position of Hispanics is also in flux. Beginning with the 2000 census, for instance, the "Hispanic" category was removed from the race question. In effect, "Spanish/Hispanic/Latino" became a unique ethnic group with its own separate question. Unlike other ethnic groups—for example, Irish, Welsh, Italians, or Greeks—the census form now suggests that Hispanics are the only U.S. ethnic group that could be of any race. It remains to be determined whether U.S. culture will move beyond the underlying Black/White dichotomy or whether the current flux is simply a reorganizing of new immigrants into that dichotomy (Rodriguez 2000).

HISTORY OF U.S. RACIAL CATEGORIES: CONSTRUCTING WHITENESS

The U.S. racial system developed at the intersection of slavery and the European conquest of Indigenous peoples of the North American continent. From its origins, American colonial life was built on the importation of indentured workers from Europe and enslaved people from Africa, along with the expropriation of land from Native Americans. Intensive agricultural work, particularly in the U.S. South, required a reliable and plentiful labor supply. Native Americans suffered quick and brutal extermination in other parts of the Americas through

NEGROES,
TO BE SOLD

A Parcel of young able bodied Negro Men, one of whom is a Cooper by Trade, two Negroes Wenches, and likewise two Girls, one of 12 Years old, and the other 16, the latter a good Seemſtreſs, and can be well recommended.

(*Left*) An advertisement for a slave auction, June 23, 1768. (*Right*) A slave family picking cotton in the fields near Savannah, Georgia, ca. 1860s.

White supremacy

The belief that White people are biologically different from and superior to people of other races.

Whiteness

A culturally constructed concept originating in 1691 Virginia designed to establish clear boundaries of who is White and who is not, a process central to the formation of U.S. racial stratification.

forced labor, violence, and disease, but they largely resisted forced labor in the North American colonies. European indentured laborers were in short supply. So imported enslaved Africans became the preferred workforce. Over 300 years, millions were forcibly transported to the Americas through the transatlantic slave trade.

The unique system of slavery that emerged relied not only on the legal right of landholders to enslave other people but also on the widespread acceptance of **White supremacy**—the belief that non-Whites were biologically different, intellectually inferior, and not fully human in a spiritual sense. Reflecting these ideas, the U.S. census from 1790 to 1860 counted each enslaved person as only three-fifths of a person. Only in 1868, upon ratification of the Fourteenth Amendment to the U.S. Constitution, did this practice come to an end. Subsequently, the 1870 census was the first to count all people as whole people.

The term *White* was itself a construction, first appearing in a public document in reference to a separate race in 1691 in Virginia. Colonial laws created and rigidly regulated **Whiteness**, establishing sharp boundaries of who was White and who was not. Intermarriage was outlawed—a practice that the U.S. Supreme Court did not overturn until 1967. Mixing was punished by the loss of White status.

Anthropologist Pem Buck's *Worked to the Bone* (2001) documents the ways in which White privilege was invented in early 1700s Virginia to prevent rebellion among poor, landless Whites who were beginning to join with enslaved African workers against the European economic elite. Elites introduced a set of privileges reserved for White people—the right to own a gun, livestock, and land; the right to obtain freedom at the end of indenture; the right to discipline Black people; and eventually the right to vote. These legal privileges were designed to ensure the cooperation of poor working Whites and White indentured servants, who together constituted a majority of the early colonial populations, and to drive a wedge between the European and African laborers who had much in common.

Efforts to eliminate slavery spread rapidly but unevenly after the American Revolution (1775–83), culminating in the Civil War (1861–65) and President Abraham Lincoln's 1863 Emancipation Proclamation. Yet long-established patterns of unequal treatment and entrenched ideas of White racial superiority persisted, providing the foundation for continuing inequality, discrimination, and White dominance. **Jim Crow** segregation laws throughout the South legally enforced the boundaries between White and Black Americans in housing, education, voting rights, property ownership, and access to public services such as transportation, bathrooms, and water fountains. Vigilante White-supremacist groups such as the Ku Klux Klan, founded in 1866, emerged to enforce through violence and terror what they considered to be the natural racial order. Especially in the South, lynchings became a widespread means to intimidate Blacks, enforce segregation, and ensure behavior that Whites considered normal and appropriate. Between 1870 and the 1940s, untold thousands of African American men and women were tortured and brutally murdered (Brundage 1993).

Jim Crow

Laws implemented after the U.S. Civil War to enforce segregation legally, particularly in the South, after the end of slavery.

A segregated summer social event—an annual barbecue—on an Alabama plantation, ca. 1935.

THE RULE OF HYPODESCENT

Imposition of the rule of hypodescent has been key to drawing and maintaining racial boundaries since the days of slavery, when one single drop of "black blood"—that is, one African ancestor—constituted Blackness. *Hypo* literally means "lower." Through **hypodescent** the race of children of mixed marriages is assigned to the lower or subordinate category of the two parents—or, in many cases, the subordinate category of any one of many ancestors.

Hypodescent rules were enshrined in the laws of many U.S. states and backed by the U.S. Supreme Court. Consider the 1982 court case of Susie Phipps. Born looking "White," Phipps grew up assuming she was White. But when she requested a copy of her birth certificate in 1977, she found herself listed as "colored." A 1970 Louisiana law mandated that a person be designated Black if their ancestry was even one-thirty-second Black—referring to any one of their thirty-two most recent ancestors. Phipps lost a court challenge to this categorization because the state produced evidence that she was three-thirty-seconds Black—more than enough to satisfy the 1970 legal standard. Both the Louisiana Supreme Court and the U.S. Supreme Court refused to review the lower court's ruling and allowed the decision to stand (Fluehr-Lobban 2019; Jaynes 1982). Phipps's case reveals the process through which U.S. categories of race have been

hypodescent

Sometimes called the "one drop of blood rule"; the assignment of children of racially "mixed" unions to the subordinate group.

A 1903 cartoon from the magazine *Judge* illustrates anti-immigrant sentiment at the turn of the twentieth century. A tide of newcomers—Riff Raff Immigration—representing the criminal element of other countries washes up on American shores, to the displeasure of Uncle Sam, presenting a "danger" to American ideas and institutions.

created and the tortured legal logic employed to assign individuals to particular racial categories. Also on full display are (1) the state's central role in establishing and maintaining boundaries between the races it has constructed and (2) the powerful influence of the legacies of slavery and past discrimination on the present (Omi and Winant 1994).

Although hypodescent is no longer enforced in law, it is still widely practiced in U.S. culture. A prominent contemporary example would be U.S. president Barack Obama. His mother was a White woman from Kansas (she was also an anthropologist). His father was a Black man from Kenya in East Africa. They met as students in Hawaii, where Obama was born. Though 50 percent of his genes came from his father and 50 percent from his mother, the concept of hypodescent still shapes the way some people regard Obama's race. Likewise, Vice President Kamala Harris has most frequently been identified in the media as Black, even though her father immigrated to the United States from Jamaica and her mother immigrated from India. How do you see the rule of hypodescent at work in the construction of Harris's racial identity?

RACE AND IMMIGRATION

For four centuries, the boundaries of Whiteness in the United States have been carefully guarded, and a group's admission to that category has been rare and difficult. When the nation encountered diverse immigration from Asia and eastern and southern Europe beginning in the nineteenth century, debate raged about where the newcomers fit: Were the Chinese White? Were the Irish, Germans, Greeks, Italians, eastern Europeans, Jews, and Catholics really White, or were they biologically distinct from earlier immigrants from England, France, and the Nordic countries? Where would people from Mexico, Central America, and South America be placed in the U.S. racial framework?

The struggle to guard the boundaries of Whiteness in order to protect the power and privileges reserved for White people has been particularly intense at certain times in history, generating passionate debate and sparking a sentiment of **nativism**—that is, the desire to favor native inhabitants over new immigrants. Nativists in the nineteenth century fought particularly hard to preserve the so-called racial purity of the nation's Anglo-Saxon origins. Riots, violence, discrimination, and anti-immigrant sentiment were commonplace.

nativism

The favoring of certain long-term inhabitants, namely White people, over new immigrants.

Chinese and Irish Immigrants: What Race? Chinese immigrants first arrived in large numbers in the 1850s to work in California's gold mines, on its farms, and in railroad construction. Because they constituted the first group of Asians to come to this country, other residents struggled to place them in the U.S. racial hierarchy. European immigrant laborers saw the Chinese as

competitors for jobs and branded them the "Yellow Peril"—a "race" that could not be trusted. Federal and state governments treated the Chinese immigrants ambivalently at best and often with great hostility.

Today, most people consider Italians, the Irish, Greeks, and eastern Europeans to be White, but none of these groups was received as White when they first came to the United States. They initially faced discrimination, prejudice, and exclusion because they were not Anglo-Saxon Protestants. When the Irish immigrants arrived in the 1840s and 1850s, they were poor, rural, Catholic, landless, and fleeing intense poverty and disease as a result of the Irish potato famine. Thus, they were seen as an inferior race (Ignatiev 1995).

Confronted with increasing immigration and diversity, the U.S. legal and political systems struggled to create and apply consistent definitions of who was White and who was not. Consider the 1923 U.S. Supreme Court case in which Bhagat Singh Thind, an upper-class Sikh immigrant from India, applied for U.S. citizenship. Despite the 1790 U.S. law limiting the right to naturalization (that is, the right to become a citizen) to Whites, Thind argued that as a part of the original "Aryan" or Caucasian race, he was White. Even though the justices agreed with his claim of Aryan or Caucasian ancestry, the Court found that Thind was not White as used in "common speech, to be interpreted in accordance with the understanding of the common man" (Lopez 2006, 66). Popular anti-immigrant and nativist sentiment had overcome even the racial pseudoscience prevalent at the time.

How exactly did the Irish, Italians, and eastern European Jews become "White"? Their increasing numbers, their intermarriage with members of other White groups, and their upward class mobility created conditions for inclusion in the White category. Karen Brodkin's book *How the Jews Became White Folks* (1998) offers additional insights into the Whitening process of immigrants after World War II. At that time, the U.S. economy was emerging virtually unscathed from the war's destruction, unlike its competitors in Europe and Japan. And rapid growth in the U.S. economy was supporting an unparalleled expansion of the nation's middle class. Brodkin suggests that an extensive government program to reintegrate soldiers after the war paved the road to upward mobility for many U.S. citizens.

Indeed, the GI Bill of Rights provided a wide array of programs to 16 million returning soldiers, who were primarily White and male. The benefits afforded to veterans included preferential hiring, financial support during the job search, small-business loans, subsidized home mortgages, and educational benefits such as college tuition and living expenses. Newly trained and educated veterans quickly filled the growing U.S. economy's need for professionals, technicians, and managers—jobs that offered opportunities for upward mobility and, thus, racial mobility. These educational opportunities, the dramatic rise in home ownership, and the expansion of new corporate jobs dramatically enlarged the U.S. middle class. The simultaneous elevation of living standards and financial assets of both native Whites and new European immigrants softened earlier boundaries of Whiteness and allowed the status of many immigrants to shift from racially non-White to ethnically White.

Middle Easterners. Racial categories continue to be created and contested in the United States today. Where, for example, do people from the Middle East fit? Are Saudis, Iranians, Afghanis, Kurds, Syrians, Turks, and Egyptians "White," African American, or Asian? The shifting characterization of people from the Middle East—especially after the terrorist attacks of September 11, 2001, and the ensuing "war on terror"—reveals newly contested terrain in the race debate and demonstrates how conceptions of race in the United States are constantly changing.

In a study of fourth graders in Brooklyn, New York, after the September 11 attacks, Maria Kromidas (2004) explores how nine-year-old children engage issues of race, religion, and region to create racial categories, assign certain people (both children and adults) to them, and enforce those boundaries through language, humor, and social interaction.

Using the common U.S. census categories, the school that Kromidas studied could be described as 28 percent Black, 1 percent White, 46 percent Hispanic, and 25 percent Asian. But these four categories do not reveal the diversity of the school and its neighborhood—a diversity that makes the students' formulations of race all the more complicated. Although the students and the surrounding community are predominantly African American and second- and third-generation Latino, a significant part of the population is composed of new immigrants from Nigeria, Bangladesh, Guyana, Jamaica, and the Dominican Republic.

In light of the events of September 11, students in the elementary school seem preoccupied with the potential danger from a perceived enemy—one they see racially as "brown, foreign, strange, and Muslim" (Kromidas 2004, 29). Though the children do not consider their Muslim classmates to be "evil" or "terrorists," they do take note of these classmates' identities as never before. Kromidas ("MK" in the dialogues below) notes in particular the equation of enemies with Indians, Pakistanis, or Afghans, and eventually all Arabic ("Ara-back") people. Here we see a racial construction, a lumping together of unrelated people based on a general phenotype—in this case, skin color.

Consider the following small-group student discussions:

EXAMPLE 1

SHERI: We were talking about who started it first, and if they kill a lot of White people.... I mean a lot of people we got to go to war right then.

MK:	Who are they?
SHERI:	The Indians.
MK:	The Indians?
SHERI:	I don't know—that's what I call them.
JONATHAN:	The Pakistans!
MK:	The Pakistans?
SODIQ:	The Afghanistans!
MK:	The Afghanistans?
JOSEPH:	The terrorists.

Later that afternoon:

EXAMPLE 2

SHERI:	I feel sorry for the Afghanistan people.
SUSANNA:	Why do you feel sorry after what they did?
SHERI:	Because they gonna die!
	(*Most of the class breaks up with laughter.*)
LATISHA:	(*standing up*) I feel happy!
	(*laughter*)
LATISHA:	No, no, no . . . because they want to kill our people, they're going to die, too. They want to have a party when we die, so we should celebrate! [*referring to news clips of street celebrations in the Middle East after September 11*]
ANUPA:	If they die, it will be better for us.
MK:	Who are they?
ANUPA:	The Araback people.
MARISELA:	The Afghanistans have always hated the Americans. I know because I always watch the news. (Kromidas 2004, 18–19)

These conversations yield some interesting observations. First, the students have taken on images presented in the media and from the conversations of adults around them; second, the students manipulate those images to create patterns of exclusion in their own context. Through their conversations, language groups, social interactions, and friendship networks, the students seek to clarify boundaries and to include and exclude newcomers according to what they see as racial characteristics. In the racial maps of the United States, South Asian Americans and Arab Americans do not have a clear place. Kromidas suggests that in the classroom, as in U.S. culture at large, the fourth graders of New York City are creating a new racial category and placing people in it. The category is generally defined as not White, not Black, but brown: foreign, strange, Muslim, and possibly enemy.

Before September 11, "Middle Eastern" was not considered a separate race in the United States. Officially, the government's Office of Management and Budget classifies people of Middle Eastern descent as White, along with people of European and North African descent. But the **racialization** (that is, giving a racial character) of Middle Easterners in U.S. culture after September 11, as reflected in Kromidas's study of fourth graders in Brooklyn, suggests a movement away from Whiteness.

Advertising and the Construction of Asian American Racial Identity.

In *Advertising Diversity: Ad Agencies and the Creation of Asian American Consumers* (2015), anthropologist Shalini Shankar explores the subtle role that advertising and media representation play in constructing and reproducing the racial category of Asian or Asian American, which refers to the 15 million people of Asian descent now living in the United States.

In 1965, new U.S. immigration laws dramatically diversified the pool of people coming to the United States, which included significant numbers of people arriving from Asia. Asian Americans' rising economic prosperity soon drew attention from marketers, and by the 1970s, small, niche advertising firms had emerged to target these consumers. A new generation of ad executives, many of Asian descent, began to market themselves as experts uniquely positioned to aid clients in this emerging sector of multicultural advertising. They argued that their intuitive, embodied understanding of being Asian would allow them to successfully deploy Asian language, culture, symbols, and group-specific imagery to successfully attract Asian American consumers, build brand allegiances, and make money for their clients.

Over the ensuing decades, ad execs have drawn on U.S. census data to bolster the case for targeting Asian American consumers. Increasing numbers of prosperous and upwardly mobile Asian Americans, they argued, would become model consumers. Shankar's study shows how advertising agencies and executives have contributed to the naturalization of this new racial category—making "Asian American" seem like a natural grouping rather than one constructed in the U.S. context. Although 4.6 billion people live in fifty-one Asian countries, advertisers consistently homogenize differences among Asians, including differences of nationality, region, language, and religion. They also blur differences of class, gender, and sexuality within Asian countries in order to create a broader target market. According to Shankar, "In order to make money, ad executives have to define, manipulate and underscore the significance of race. To do so, they must project the most attractive and appealing versions of race, those that let them play up favorable cultural and linguistic attributes compatible with brand identities, but downplay those that would threaten the status quo of an allegedly post-racial America" (2015, 41).

Shankar hopes that this multicultural advertising might play an anti-racist role by undermining stereotypes of Asian Americans as "forever foreign" and normalizing them as valuable consumers. But through advertising, race and racial differences have become valuable, marketable commodities that turn a profit for both advertisers and advertising agencies. In the process, Shankar warns, this celebration of diversity may divert attention away from prejudices and inequalities that underpin racial stratification in the United States.

WHITENESS TODAY

Popular conversations about race and racism tend to focus on the experiences of people of color. Whiteness is typically ignored, perhaps taken for granted. But analyzing race in the United States requires a careful look at Whiteness. Anthropologists refer to "White" as an unmarked category—one with tremendous power, but one that typically defies analysis and is rarely discussed. Recent scholarship, however, has been moving Whiteness into mainstream debates about race in the United States (Hargrove 2009; Harrison 1998, 2002a; Hartigan 1999; Marable 2002; Mullings 2005a; Roediger 1992).

White Privilege. Although the events of the U.S. civil rights movement occurred well before most of today's college students were born, the media images of African Americans being blocked from attending White schools, riding in the front of the bus, sitting at department store lunch counters, or drinking from "Whites-only" water fountains remain etched in our collective cultural memory. Although the overt signs declaring access for "Whites only" have been outlawed and removed, many patterns of interpersonal and institutional behavior have resisted change.

In her article "White Privilege: Unpacking the Invisible Knapsack" (1989), anthropologist Peggy McIntosh writes of "an invisible package of unearned assets" that White people have inherited as the legacy of generations of racial discrimination. Through these assets, Whites have become the beneficiaries of cultural norms, values, mental maps of reality, and institutions. Unearned advantages and unearned power are conferred systematically and differentially on one group over others, whether those benefits lie in health, education, housing, employment, banking and mortgages, or the criminal justice system.

McIntosh articulates an extensive list of these privileges, ranging from the mundane to the profound. They include (1) going shopping without being followed or harassed by store security; (2) seeing people of your "race" widely represented in the news, social media, and educational curricula; (3) swearing, dressing in secondhand clothes, or not answering letters or emails without having people attribute these choices to bad morals, poverty, or the illiteracy of your "race"; (4) feeling confident that you have not been singled out by race when a police officer pulls you over or an airport security guard decides to conduct a full-body scan; and (5) criticizing the government and its policies without being considered an outsider.

As we have discussed in this chapter, since the early European settlement of North America, the boundaries of Whiteness have been carefully constructed and guarded. Today, the privileges associated with Whiteness still pass down from generation to generation. They are simply harder to see. Acknowledging this fact enables us to analyze the functioning and effects of race and racism as a complete system.

As McIntosh writes, "For me white privilege has turned out to be an elusive and fugitive subject. The pressure to avoid it is great, for in facing it I must give up the myth of meritocracy. If these things are true, this is not such a free country, one's life is not what one makes it; many doors open for certain people through no virtues of their own" (1989, 12). Moving forward, McIntosh urges students to distinguish between (1) the positive advantages that we wish everyone could have and that we can all work to spread and (2) the negative types of advantages that, unless challenged and corrected, will always reinforce current racial hierarchies.

Not all people of European descent benefit equally from the system of White privilege. Whiteness is also stratified along deep, intersecting lines of class and region, gender and sexuality. In a study of a town she calls Shellcracker Haven, southwest of Gainesville, Florida, anthropologist Jane Gibson (1996) explores the process through which a community of poor White people has been systematically cut off from their local means of making a living. By imposing restrictions—all of which benefit large-scale businesses—on fishing, gaming, trapping, and agricultural activities, the Florida state government and its agencies have gradually prevented Shellcracker Haven's residents from making a living on the land or nearby water.

MAP 5.2
Florida

Gibson argues that these policies of disenfranchisement have been rationalized by stereotypes promoted by state authorities. Such stereotypes portray the local people as "White trash," "swamp trash," and "crackers"; as dirty, skinny, shoeless, toothless, illiterate, and unintelligent. The stereotypes deflect attention from the skewed distribution of wealth and power and the uneven investments in roads, education, and health care that result from state policies. Poor Whites are a subordinated group, distinct from successful middle- and upper-class Whites in the state. In the current age of globalization, economic restructuring and global competition are further undermining the White privilege of many poor and working-class Whites as manufacturing jobs leave the United States.

Anthropologists of race in the United States have studied the often "unmarked" category of Whiteness. The privileges of Whiteness in the United States are not experienced uniformly but rather are stratified along deep lines of class, region, gender, and sexuality.

What Is Racism?

Analyze racism in terms of both individual actions and institutional systems of power.

Having considered how concepts of race are constructed in the United States and globally, we now turn to consider how ideas of race are used to construct and maintain systems of power that we call racism. Racism draws on the culturally constructed categories of race to rank people as superior or inferior and to allocate access to power, privilege, resources, and opportunities differentially.

TYPES OF RACISM

Racism has both individual and institutional components, held together by an ideology—a potent set of ideas.

individual racism

Personal prejudiced beliefs and discriminatory actions based on race.

Individual Racism. On an interpersonal level, **individual racism** is expressed through prejudiced beliefs and discriminatory actions. Being prejudiced involves making negative assumptions about a person's abilities or intentions based on the person's perceived race. Discrimination involves taking negative actions toward a person on the basis of their perceived race. Individual racism may be expressed through disrespect, suspicion, scapegoating, and/or violence ranging from police brutality to hate crimes (Jones 2000). Individual, personally mediated acts of racism may be intentional or unintentional. They may be acts of commission (things that are done) or acts of omission (things that are left undone).

Individual racism can also be expressed through microaggressions. **Microaggressions** refer to common, everyday verbal or behavioral indignities and slights that communicate hostile, derogatory, and negative messages about someone's race, gender, sexual orientation, or religion. Racial microaggressions in the U.S. context include subtle slights, snubs, or insults directed toward people of color, often by White people who are unaware that they have transgressed against someone: moving a handbag, checking a wallet, locking a car door, changing seats, commenting, "You speak English well," or asking, "Where do you come from?" These actions and comments may communicate that someone is considered different, a stranger, prone to criminality, or not to be trusted. Underlying these acts of "othering"—making someone feel as if they do not belong—is a hidden cultural curriculum through which people have been taught certain biases associated with race, gender, sexual orientation, or religion, which are then acted out intentionally or unintentionally. Research has shown that the cumulative and recurring experience of microaggressions over a lifetime can create intense psychological and physical stress and harm (Sue 2010, 2015).

microaggressions
Common, everyday verbal or behavioral indignities and slights that communicate hostile, derogatory, and negative messages about someone's race, gender, sexual orientation, or religion.

Institutional Racism. Racism is more than individual prejudiced beliefs or discriminatory acts. It also includes **institutional racism,** sometimes called *structural racism*—patterns by which racial inequality is structured through key cultural institutions, policies, and systems. These include education, health, housing, employment, the legal system (legislatures, courts, and prison systems), law enforcement, and the media. Institutional racism originates in historical events and legal sanctions. But even when it is outlawed, it can persist through contemporary patterns of institutional behavior that perpetuate the historical injustices (Cazenave 2011; Feagin and Feagin 2011; Jones 2000; Neubeck and Cazenave 2001).

institutional racism
Patterns by which racial inequality is structured through key cultural institutions, policies, and systems.

In the United States, stratification along racial lines is a legacy of discrete historical events that include slavery, Jim Crow legal segregation, expropriation of Indigenous lands, and immigration restrictions. Through these legal forms of institutional racism, political, economic, and educational systems were organized to privilege Whiteness. Today, despite the elimination of legal racial discrimination and segregation, persistent individual and institutional racism mean that patterns of inequality still break along color lines. Such racism is evident in employment rates, income and wealth differentials, rates of home ownership, residential patterns, criminal sentencing patterns, incarceration rates, the application of the death penalty, infant mortality, access to health care, life expectancy, investments in public education, college enrollments, and voting rights (Alexander 2012).

For example, the U.S. educational system has been a site of intense contestation over race and racism. In 1896—three decades after the end of slavery—the Supreme

Court ruled in *Plessy v. Ferguson* that state-sponsored segregation, including in public schools, was constitutional as long as the separate facilities for separate races were equal. Across the South, individual White school administrators often refused, on overtly racist grounds, to allow children of color—Black, Hispanic, Asian—entrance to school buildings. But these individual actions alone did not constitute the total system of racism at work. They were systematically supported and enforced by government institutions: local boards of education, legislators, local police with guns and dogs, and court systems—including the U.S. Supreme Court.

Only in 1954, in the case of *Brown v. Board of Education*, did the Supreme Court reverse itself, declaring unanimously that state laws establishing separate public schools for Black and White students were unconstitutional and that separate educational facilities were inherently unequal. At the time, seventeen states, primarily across the South, required racial segregation. Sixteen prohibited it. Even after the Supreme Court ruling banned segregated schools, the federal government was forced to intervene in states like Mississippi and Arkansas, where it deployed National Guard troops to escort students to classes in order to end racist practices and protect student safety.

Contemporary racial disparities in school funding reveal how historical patterns of institutional racism can continue long after discrimination has been declared illegal (Miller and Epstein 2011). In 2003, the New York State Court of Appeals, the state's highest court, uncovered a long-standing disparity in state funding for public schools in New York City and its suburban areas. New York City public schools, with high proportions of students of color, received an

A racially segregated classroom in Monroe Elementary School, Topeka, Kansas, March 1953. Students Linda Brown (*front right*) and her sister Terry Lynn (*far left, second row back*), along with their parents, initiated the landmark civil rights lawsuit *Brown v. Board of Education*.

average of $10,469 per student, whereas schools in more affluent, predominantly White suburbs received $13,760 per student. The courts ordered New York State to provide $9.2 billion for capital improvement of New York City school buildings and to increase its annual education budget by up to $5.6 billion to cover the costs of redressing this inequality. Only in 2021 did the state agree to settle this matter and fully comply with the court's requirements.

Racial Ideology. Racism relies on a third component—a set of popular ideas about race, or a **racial ideology**—that allows the discriminatory behaviors of individuals and institutions to seem reasonable, rational, and normal. Ideas about the superiority of one race over another—shaped and reinforced in school systems, religious institutions, government, and the media—caused people in the United States to believe that slavery was natural, that the European settlers had a God-given right to "civilize" and "tame" the American West, and that segregation in schools was a reasonable approach to providing public education. As these ideas became ingrained in day-to-day relationships and institutional patterns of behavior, they ultimately provided the ideological glue that held racial stratification in place.

racial ideology

A set of popular ideas about race that allows the discriminatory behaviors of individuals and institutions to seem reasonable, rational, and normal.

Today, social scientists note that contemporary racial ideologies are much more subtle, often drawing on core U.S. values of individualism, social mobility, meritocracy, and color blindness to make their case. In his book *Racism without Racists* (2010), sociologist Eduardo Bonilla-Silva critiques the contemporary calls in U.S. culture for color blindness—that is, the elimination of race as a consideration in a wide range of institutional processes, from college admissions to the reporting of arrests by police. The ideology of color blindness suggests that the best way to end discrimination in the post–civil rights era is to treat individuals as equally as possible without regard to race. Bonilla-Silva warns that while the desire to transcend race by adopting a stance of color blindness appears reasonable and fair, the approach ignores the uneven playing field created by centuries of legal racism in areas such as wealth, property ownership, education, health, and employment. A color-blind ideology, Bonilla-Silva suggests, may actually perpetuate racial inequality by obscuring the historical effects of racism, the continuing legacy of racial discrimination, and the entrenched patterns of institutional behavior that undergird racism today.

In a country like the United States, which prides itself on being a meritocracy (a system that views people as a product of their own efforts and in which equal opportunity is available to all), the continuing existence of racism and skin-color privilege in the twenty-first century is difficult for many people to acknowledge. When the dominant culture celebrates the ideals of individualism and equal access to social mobility, it is ironic that for many people, success depends not only on hard work, intelligence, and creativity but also on the often unrecognized and unearned assets—cultural, political, and economic—that have accrued over hundreds of years of discrimination and unequal opportunity based on race.

Intersections of Race and Other Systems of Power. It is important to note the powerful intersection of race and other systems of power. Intersectionality provides a framework for analyzing the many factors—especially class and gender—that determine how race is lived and how all three systems of power and stratification build on and shape one another (Feagin and Sikes 1994).

In the 1990s, anthropologist Leith Mullings led a study, the Harlem Birth Right Project, that considered the impacts of race, class, and gender on women's health and infant mortality. The study focused on central Harlem, at that time a vibrant, primarily African American community in northern Manhattan, New York City (Mullings 2005b; Mullings and Wali 2001). Of particular concern, infant mortality rates in Harlem were twice the rate of New York City's overall. Previous studies (e.g., Schoendorf, Hogue, and Kleinman 1992) had demonstrated that African American women of all class levels have more problematic birth outcomes than do White women of similar class status. Even college-educated African American women experience infant mortality at twice the rate of college-educated White women. This observation suggested that factors other than education and social status were at work.

Mullings's research team examined how the underlying conditions of housing, employment, child care, and environmental factors, as well as the quality of public spaces, parks, and even grocery and retail stores, might affect the health outcomes being reported in Harlem, where both working-class and middle-class women lived. Since the early 1990s, Harlem has been hard hit by dramatic changes in New York City's economy. Manufacturing jobs with middle-class wages have been lost to flexible accumulation (see Chapters 1 and 10) as New York City–based companies relocate production overseas. Meanwhile, job growth in the metropolitan area has occurred in the high-wage financial sector and in the low-wage service sector. Throughout the 1990s, government social services were cut back while public housing and transportation were allowed to deteriorate.

The effects on working-class and middle-class women in Mullings's study were notable, with many, especially pregnant women, suffering increased physical and mental stress. Inadequate, overpriced, and poorly maintained private and public housing forced many working-class mothers and their children to be constantly on the move, searching for affordable housing and sharing living spaces with friends and relatives to make ends meet. The need to fight regularly for needed repairs drained time and energy from hardworking women holding multiple low-wage jobs while juggling work and child care. A shortage of steady, well-paying jobs meant that women had very little income security or benefits, so they often pieced together a living from multiple sources. Middle-class women, many of whom were employed in the public sector, were also increasingly subject to layoffs as local governments downsized. The study also found that heavy pollution in the Harlem area, including airborne pollutants from a sewage treatment plant and six bus depots, contributed to elevating the child asthma rate to four times the national average (Mullings 2005b; Mullings and Wali 2001).

The Harlem Birth Right Project illustrates a powerful application of the intersectional approach. It reveals how inequality of resources (class), institutional racism, and gender discrimination combine to affect opportunities for employment, housing, and health care in the Harlem community. It also shows how these factors are linked to elevated health problems and infant mortality.

Mullings points out the many forms of collaboration that women in Harlem use to resist these structures of inequality and survive in their chosen community. Calling this the *Sojourner syndrome*, she links the agency of contemporary African American women to the life story of Sojourner Truth. Truth was born into slavery in the late 1790s and was emancipated in 1827 after experiencing physical abuse and rape and watching many of her children be sold away from her. Subsequently, she became an itinerant preacher for the abolition of slavery, building coalitions with White abolitionists and later participating in the early women's rights movement. The stories of the women in Harlem today, like Sojourner Truth's, reflect the determination and creativity required to overcome interlocking constraints of racism, sexism, and class inequality.

Mother and child, Harlem, New York. How do class, race, and gender intersect to affect people's life chances?

In response to increasing gun violence in 2016, people organized a march in Magnificent Mile, a neighborhood in Chicago, to commemorate lives lost.

West Side, Chicago

MAP 5.3
West Side, Chicago

INJURY AND RESILIENCE

In *Renegade Dreams: Living through Injury in Gangland Chicago* (2014), anthropologist Laurence Ralph looks beneath the media narrative of violence, decay, and disease that so often characterizes stories of urban Chicago to illuminate a community's resilience amid injury and unjust circumstances. Ralph spent three years conducting ethnographic fieldwork in an area on Chicago's West Side that he calls "Eastwood." This low-income, working-class, predominantly African American neighborhood of just over 40,000 residents occupies just under four square miles, yet it disproportionately figures in the reports of journalists, scholars, and government officials interested in urban issues. Ralph originally moved to Eastwood to study gang violence. He volunteered at an anti-violence program and visited churches, hospitals, rehabilitation programs, and social welfare agencies. He spoke with people living with HIV, those wounded by gang bullets, and others struggling with drug addiction.

In *Renegade Dreams*, Ralph carefully details the historical, political, and economic context in which Eastwood residents today are entangled—how the legacy of institutional racism in housing, employment, education, and law enforcement continues to shape much of Eastwood today.

Recounting an interview with Aaron Smalls of Chicago's Department of Planning, Ralph describes Smalls's conclusion that Eastwood was "doomed for failure." Neighborhood housing was crumbling. Half its residents lived below the poverty line. Half were unemployed, a rate three times higher than the average in Chicago and five times higher than the national average. Many had not finished high school. Fifty-seven percent were in some way caught up in the criminal justice system, either in jail, on parole, or under house arrest. The facts were all true. But the conclusion did not match Ralph's ethnographic findings.

One of Ralph's key informants, Justin Cone, navigated Eastwood in a wheelchair. He had been shot in the spine during a gang-related incident. Cone worked at an anti-violence program, but he aspired to join the Crippled Footprint Collective, a group of young Black men who now use wheelchairs who talk to at-risk high school youth about the perils of gang life and the lifelong injuries that can be sustained from near-fatal gun violence. In Eastwood, far more shooting victims survive than are killed. They live with their injuries forever. Like members of the Collective, Cone refused to succumb to despair and aspired to do more to end gang violence.

Ralph also discovered the diverse, surprising alliances that arose in the community. When real estate developers proposed demolishing dilapidated neighborhood homes to build new housing, an alliance of grandmothers, church leaders, and gang members with their crews joined to resist the developers, the displacement of long-term residents, and neighborhood change. The gang members' participation in constructive community work pushed Ralph to recognize that the stereotypical portrayal of dangerous, threatening gangs is an overly simplistic narrative that is too often imposed from outside the community. In the community, a gang member may also be the grandson of an older neighborhood resident facing eviction. These complex identities are too often obscured by external assessments.

After three years in the community, Ralph chose to focus his study on the nature of injury, particularly the injuries and disabilities caused by violence. Many of the injuries experienced in Eastwood are physical: disease, violence, broken limbs, paralysis, and the physical harm caused by addiction. These are the injuries so often discussed, pathologized, and obsessed over by government officials, scholars, and the media. But Ralph also explores other injuries: the anxieties of parents and kids navigating the violent vulnerabilities of life, stray bullets, peer pressure, and predatory police. These encumbrances follow them through their lives, weigh them down, and affect their future prospects.

By exploring the landscape of injury in the Eastwood neighborhood, Ralph identifies the community's most unexamined resource. Out of injury, Ralph found, came dreams, aspirations, and imaginations of a different future. During his time in Eastwood, he found people who dreamed dreams of resilience: safe passage to school; a stable job; affordable, livable housing; a healthy environment; or the opportunity to become an anti-violence activist. In Eastwood, he found people who recognized the reality that systemic change is difficult and that dreams don't always come true. Despite the statistical odds against them and the cumulative impact of generations of institutional racism, Eastwood residents determinedly imagined alternative futures for themselves and their community. They dreamed as acts of defiance. They dreamed renegade dreams.

Ralph's ethnographic study of Chicago's African American community reveals the power of local communities of color to mobilize and engage in political activism. It also demonstrates how such groups can contest stereotypes of urban Black communities and practices of racial discrimination and exclusion, whether those involve housing, policing, or the environmental and community impacts of public infrastructure projects.

In this chapter, we have begun our work as budding anthropologists to unmask the structures of power, starting with race and racism. We have seen how flawed ideas of "race" serve as rationales for very real systems of power built around racial stratification both in the United States and around the world. As globalization, particularly global migration, brings cultural systems of meaning and stratification into closer contact, your ability to analyze and engage dynamics of race and racism will prove to be increasingly important. In the following chapters, we will consider other systems of power—including ethnicity, gender, sexuality, kinship, and class—and their points of mutual intersection with race.

Toolkit

Thinking Like an Anthropologist:
Shifting Our Perspectives on Race and Racism

As you encounter race and racism in your life—on campus, in the classroom, at the workplace, in the news, or in your family—thinking like an anthropologist can help you to better understand these experiences. As you untangle this knotty problem, remember to think about the big questions we addressed in this chapter:

- **Do biologically separate races exist?**

- **How is race constructed around the world?**

- **How is race constructed in the United States?**

- **What is racism?**

After reading this chapter, you should be better equipped to engage the challenges of race and racism. As you think back on the story of George Floyd and the events in Minneapolis, Minnesota, how would you apply the ideas of this chapter to assist your analysis and inform your responses?

How can an anthropological approach to the study of race and racism help us analyze and confront these contentious issues? How can we learn a language about race and racism that will allow us to talk and work together across lines of race, gender, sexuality, class, and political perspective to confront the continuing American legacy of racism? As we have seen throughout this chapter, the anthropological study of race not only examines the social construction of race and the establishment of systems of racism but also takes seriously movements against racism that emerge from communities of color and their allies. How can you begin to engage these crucial issues of our time and to apply these anthropological concepts to your life today?

Key Terms

Chapter 6
Ethnicity and Nationalism

Learning Objectives

- Define ethnicity and ethnic identity from an anthropological perspective.

- Describe how ethnicity is created and activated rather than biologically determined.

- Explain how ethnicity and the nation are related.

One million Rohingya refugees have fled their homes in Myanmar (also known as Burma) in recent years. Driven out by a systematic military campaign of murder, torture, rape, and imprisonment, Rohingya have escaped by boat to India, Malaysia, and Indonesia and by foot across the Naf River to makeshift refugee camps in neighboring Bangladesh. Thousands more are internally displaced in western Myanmar, their villages burned and homes destroyed.

The mostly Muslim Rohingya have faced decades of discrimination and repression under successive governments, including earlier waves of violence in 2012 and 2016. With the most recent atrocities, Myanmar's military appears determined to drive out the Rohingya ethnic minority group in an act of genocide and erase them from the nation's history.

What can religious refugees tell us about ethnicity and nationalism? Rohingya refugees walk along a muddy rice field after crossing the border into Bangladesh to escape the violence in their native Rakhine State in Myanmar.

This level of interethnic conflict and state-sponsored violence has not always been the norm in Myanmar. After the country achieved independence from Britain in 1948, the government officially listed the Rohingya among the nation's 135 ethnic groups, issued citizenship identification cards, and granted them the right to vote. But the 1982 Citizenship Law effectively stripped Rohingya of citizenship and reversed their official recognition as an ethnic minority group. Later, the government stopped issuing birth certificates to Rohingya babies and excluded Rohingya from the country's census. Today, the Rohingya are one of the largest stateless populations in the world.

Ethnic Rohingya leaders assert deep roots in Myanmar's Rakhine State, stretching back over 1,000 years. But the Rohingya's adversaries brand them as interlopers in the majority Buddhist kingdom—illegal Muslim immigrants brought from neighboring Bengal to farm and mine under British colonial rule (1824–1948). Misled by anti-Rohingya propaganda, many in the majority Buddhist Bamar ethnic group fear the Rohingya are part of a militant Muslim crusade to wipe out the Buddhist religion.

How can anthropological ideas about ethnicity, nationalism, colonialism, and the nation-state help us think more deeply about the plight of the Rohingya people and ethnic and religious minorities in other places?

While ethnicity is often popularly imagined to have deep historical and perhaps biological roots, anthropological research instead reveals the ways in which ethnicity is constructed over time through complex political, economic,

MAP 6.1
Rakhine State, Myanmar

Many Rohingya refugees have settled into makeshift camps in Bangladesh. Here, Rohingya boys from the Kutupalong Rohingya Refugee Camp attend school.

and cultural processes, thickly entangled in the aftereffects of colonialism. As we will see throughout this chapter (and also in Chapter 12), over the past 400 years, as countries competed for raw materials, cheap labor, and markets, they forcibly redrew the political map of the world without regard for local realities of ethnicity, language, history, village, or family life.

Of the nearly 200 nation-states in the world today, fewer than one-third existed in their current form fifty years ago. Dozens of states, including Myanmar, were created after World War II as nationalist movements won independence from European and Japanese colonial powers in Asia, the Middle East, and Africa. Dozens more were created in central Asia and eastern Europe following the collapse of the former Soviet Union and the breakdown of previously socialist states in the 1990s (Robbins and Dowty 2019).

Today, Myanmar is a conglomeration of territories and people largely consolidated by the British in the nineteenth century. Myanmar's Rakhine State, home to the majority of Rohingya, had previously been a wide-open, largely autonomous, rural frontier area that straddled the Burmese and Bengali worlds. But when the British added Myanmar to their sprawling British Indian empire, they imposed rigid new borders and governing structures. Across the globe, including in the case of Rwanda, which we will consider later in the chapter, colonial rulers strengthened their political control by enforcing a rigid system of ethnic classification, discouraging interaction between groups, and pitting one group against another. Ethnic identities and political borders that had once been quite fluid became formal and hard. At independence, Myanmar inherited a territory and a population cobbled together under British rule, not one that had organically emerged from local realities of group, religious, or linguistic identity.

The story of the Rohingya opens avenues for exploring the complex intersection of ethnicity, nationalism, colonialism, the nation-state, and citizenship from an anthropological perspective. In particular, we will ask three key questions:

- **What does "ethnicity" mean to anthropologists?**
- **How and why is ethnicity created, mobilized, and contested?**
- **What is the relationship of ethnicity to the nation?**

After reading this chapter, you will have the tools to understand and analyze the role of ethnicity and nationalism in your own life and in communities and countries worldwide.

What Does "Ethnicity" Mean to Anthropologists?

Define ethnicity and ethnic identity from an anthropological perspective.

We hear the word *ethnicity* all the time. The press reports on "long-held ethnic conflicts" that shatter the peace in Rwanda, Iraq, India, and the former Yugoslavia. We check boxes on college applications and U.S. census forms to identify our ethnicity or race. We shop in the "ethnic foods" aisle of our super-sized grocery store to find refried beans, soy sauce, pita, and wasabi. Our use of *ethnicity* is not particularly consistent or terribly clear. In recent years in the United States, *ethnicity* has been increasingly substituted for *race* when describing group differences, perhaps to deflect attention from difficult discussions about racism. *Ethnic* is often paired with *minority*, a term signifying a smaller group that differs from the dominant, majority culture in language, food, dress, immigrant history, national origin, or religion. But this usage ignores the ethnic identity of the majority. The same lack of clarity is true for our use of the terms *nation*, *nationalism*, and *nation-state*, all of which often blur together and at times seem indistinguishable from *ethnicity*.

ETHNICITY AS IDENTITY

Over a lifetime, humans develop complex identities that connect to many people in many ways. We build a sense of relationship, belonging, and shared identity through connections to family, religion, hometown, language, shared history, citizenship, sports, age, gender, sexuality, education, and profession. These powerful identities influence what we eat, who we date, where we work, how we live, and even how we die. **Ethnicity** is one of the most powerful identities that humans develop: It is a sense of connection to a group of people whom we believe share a common history, culture, and (sometimes) ancestry and who are distinct from others outside the group (Ericksen 2010; Jenkins 1996). Ethnicity can be seen as a more expansive version of kinship—the culturally specific creation of relatives—that includes a much larger group and extends further in space and time. As we will see in this chapter, the construction of ethnicity, like the construction of kinship, is quite complicated, moving well beyond easy equation with biological ancestry. In this chapter, we will explore the ways ethnicity may be perceived, felt, and imagined by a group as well as the ways it may be imposed on a group by others.

With the intensification of globalization and the increasing flows of people, goods, and ideas across borders, one might anticipate that the power of ethnicity to frame people's actions and to influence world events would diminish. Instead,

ethnicity

A sense of historical, cultural, and sometimes ancestral connection to a group of people who are imagined to be distinct from those outside the group.

ethnicity seems to be flourishing—rising in prominence in both local and global affairs. Why is it so powerful? When threatened or challenged, people often turn to local alliances for support, safety, and protection. Ethnicity is one of the strongest sources of solidarity available.

As the effects of globalization intersect with systems of power at the local level, many people turn to ethnic networks and expressions of ethnic identity to protect their way of life in the face of intense pressures of homogenization. Ethnicity can also serve political purposes on the national and local levels. As we will see later in this chapter, political elites and other social actors may impose or enforce ethnic distinctions or use calls for ethnic solidarity to mobilize support against perceived enemies inside and outside the nation-state. Rather than diminishing in the face of globalization, ethnicity emerges even more powerfully in specific situations of conflict, tension, and opportunity.

CREATING ETHNIC IDENTITY

Anthropologists see ethnicity as a cultural construction, not as a natural formation based on biology or inherent human nature. Fredrik Barth (1969) describes ethnicity as the "social organization of cultural difference." In other words, people construct a sense of ethnicity as they organize themselves in relation to others whom they perceive as either culturally similar or culturally different. Ethnic identity starts with what people believe about themselves and how others see them. It begins to form early and continues to take shape throughout our lives. People learn, practice, and teach ethnicity. Anthropologists who study it seek to understand how it is created and reinforced, how boundaries are constructed, how group identity is shaped, and how differences with others are mobilized and perpetuated (Jenkins 2008). Who do you consider to be in your ethnic group? Who belongs to a different group?

In what ways do stories, paintings, and even Thanksgiving turkey floats help create an American ethnic identity? (*Left*) A 1914 depiction of the first Thanksgiving at Plymouth, Massachusetts, often assumed to have occurred 300 years earlier. (*Right*) Native American scholar and activist Vine Deloria Jr., whose book *Custer Died for Your Sins: An Indian Manifesto* challenges popular versions of the American origin myth.

origin myth

A story told about the founding
and history of a particular group
to reinforce a sense of common
identity.

Ethnic identity is taught and reinforced in a number of ways. One key method is through the creation and telling of **origin myths.** By myth, we do not mean a fable or a legend but rather a story with meaning. In the United States, the "American" origin myth includes stories of historical events—such as the landing of the *Mayflower*, the first Thanksgiving, the Boston Tea Party, the American Revolution, the Civil War, the settling of the West—that are retold to emphasize a shared destiny as well as shared values of freedom, exploration, individualism, and multiculturalism. The American origin myth of the first Thanksgiving is ritually enacted each year with a national holiday. Schoolchildren produce dramas and artwork based on textbook stories. Families gather to feast, usually eating certain traditional foods. Nationally televised parades and sporting events add to the ritual's celebratory character. However, origin myths—like all elements of culture—are continuously promoted, revised, and negotiated. For example, recent years have seen more open discussion of the brutal conquest of Native Americans by European colonial settlers (Deloria 1969; Dunbar-Ortiz 2015) and, in books such as Howard Zinn's *A People's History of the United States* (2005), more challenges to classic representations of the American origin myth.

ethnic boundary marker

A practice or belief used to
signify who is in a group and who
is not; usually not clearly fixed
or defined and may change over
time.

People create and promote certain **ethnic boundary markers** in an attempt to signify who is in an ethnic group and who is not. These may include a collective name; shared cultural practices such as food, clothing, and architecture; belief in a common history and ancestors; association with a particular territory; a shared language or religion; and an imagination of shared physical characteristics. But ethnic boundaries are usually not clearly fixed or defined. No group is completely homogenous: Not everyone imagined to be inside the group is the same, and not everyone imagined to be outside the group is noticeably different. Group boundaries can be quite porous, as people move between groups through marriage, migration, and adoption. Identity, including ethnic identity, can be fluid and flexible, reflecting shifting alliances and strength over time and according to need. Groups may vanish in situations of war or violence. New ethnic groups may come into existence when part of an existing group splits off or two groups form a new one (Ericksen 2010).

situational negotiation of
identity

An individual's self-identification
with a particular group that can
shift according to social location.

Because ethnicity is not biologically fixed, self-identification with a particular ethnic group can change according to one's social location. This occurs through a process called **situational negotiation of identity.** For example, the Rohingya in our chapter-opening story might have chosen to be Rohingya, Burmese, Muslim, or simply residents of Rakhine State. At different points during their lives, they may choose to identify with any of these, depending on the situation. Have you ever had the experience of identifying with a different aspect of your identity as you moved between groups or locations?

Constructing Indian Identity in the United States. The immigration experience profoundly affects ethnicity and ethnic identification. New immigrants reshape their home-country ethnic identification to build alliances and solidarity in their new host country. In her book *From the Ganges to the Hudson* (1995), anthropologist Johanna Lessinger explores how a new Indian ethnic identity is created and publicly demonstrated through consumption, public festivals, and Indian immigrant media in New York City. Indian immigrants arrive in New York from all corners of their homeland, speaking different languages, following diverse cultural practices and religions, and reflecting class and caste stratifications. In India, a country of more than 1.2 billion people, these individuals would identify with different ethnicities shaped by geography, language, food, and cultural practices. But in New York, they all begin the process of becoming Indian American.

New York City's Little India, a bustling shopping district in Jackson Heights, Queens, has become the symbolic center of Indian immigrant life and a key to the construction of Indian ethnic identity in the United States. Vibrant with the sights, sounds, and smells of India, the streets are lined with Indian grocery and spice shops, Indian restaurants, clothing and jewelry stores, travel agencies, music and video distributors, and electronics stores. Indian immigrants come from all parts of New York City and the metropolitan region to walk the streets of Little India and shop, eat, and take in the many symbols of "home."

Here, Indian immigrants have created a wide-ranging infrastructure—including ethnic associations, religious temples, cultural societies, newspapers, television programming, and major public festivals—that supports and promotes the construction of a unified Indian ethnic identity in their new homeland. One

India

New York, NY

MAP 6.2
New York/India

of the largest festivals is the India Day Parade held in late August to mark India's nationhood and independence from British colonialism. Like the dozens of ethnic parade celebrations in New York each year, Indian immigrant community organizations, business owners, and hometown associations sponsor marching bands, singers, dancers, banners, and a vast array of colorful floats. Holding a public festival like the India Day Parade is a powerful way to stake a claim to a place in the multiethnic mosaic that is New York—to send a clear signal to all New Yorkers, including the political establishment, that Indians are here, are organized, and want to be taken seriously.

Ethnic boundaries are often fluid, messy, and contested. For example, exactly who is Indian American? For more than fifteen years, until 2010, the South Asian Lesbian and Gay Alliance (SALGA) requested permission to march in the India Day Parade only to be denied by parade organizers. Members of SALGA held demonstrations each year along the parade route, holding signs that read, "We are also Indians!" Despite the parade organizers' desire to build a broad-based Indian American identity and coalition, they were willing to declare SALGA not Indian enough to participate in the event. In this situation, sexuality became a more powerful boundary marker than country of origin or ethnic identity. The public rift over the India Day Parade symbolized the contestation of ethnic boundary markers—a struggle that deeply divides many Indian immigrants and their children—and the debate involved in defining who is Indian in the United States.

How and Why Is Ethnicity Created, Mobilized, and Contested?

Describe how ethnicity is created and activated rather than biologically determined.

Ethnicity is not necessarily a pressing matter in the daily lives of many of the world's people, but it can be activated when power relationships undergo negotiation in a community or a nation. In times like these, people call on shared ideas of ethnicity to rally others to participate in their causes, whether those causes involve ensuring self-protection, building alliances, constructing economic networks, or establishing a country. Ethnicity can also be activated by charismatic entrepreneurs of ethnicity who seek support from co-ethnics in their fight for political, economic, or military power against real or perceived enemies. The sections that follow illustrate how ethnicity can be harnessed for either harmful or beneficial outcomes.

ETHNICITY AS A SOURCE OF CONFLICT

Anthropologists explore the complex ways culture can be invented, transformed into ethnicity, and mobilized in situations of ethnic conflict (Eller 1999). The anthropological study of ethnic conflict requires an open-mindedness to new ideas of how ethnicity is formed and how it works—ideas that may be at odds with our everyday usage of the terms *ethnicity* and *ethnic groups*. Rogers Brubaker, in his book *Ethnicity without Groups* (2004), warns against "groupism" when studying ethnicity. Anthropologists may anticipate that we will work with clearly defined, homogenous groups that have fixed boundaries and will act in a unified fashion. But this is not what we find when we explore ethnicity on the local level. Ethnicity is much more complicated, involving people with many perspectives, disagreements, and at times competing loyalties. The strong bonds of ethnicity that we associate with ethnic groups may wax and wane.

Why do the power and intensity of ethnicity sometimes crystallize into ethnic conflict? To answer this question, Brubaker encourages paying attention to ethnic group-making projects, such as those we will see in the cases of Rwanda and the former Yugoslavia. Such projects occur when **identity entrepreneurs**—political, military, and religious leaders—promote a worldview through the lens of ethnicity. They use war, propaganda, and state power to mobilize people against those whom they perceive as dangerous. Ethnicity may not actually be the problem. Rather, the struggle for wealth and power uses the convenient narrative of ethnic difference to galvanize a population to collective action. Once the wedge of ethnic difference has been driven into a population and used to achieve power, it can be self-perpetuating and extremely difficult to undo. In these instances, ethnic conflict may intensify into violent acts, including **genocide**—the deliberate and systematic destruction of an ethnic or religious group (Eller 1999; Ericksen 2010; Scheper-Hughes and Bourgois 2004).

identity entrepreneurs
Political, military, or religious leaders who promote a worldview through the lens of ethnicity and use war, propaganda, and state power to mobilize people against those whom they perceive as a danger.

genocide
The deliberate and systematic destruction of an ethnic or religious group.

Mobilizing Ethnic Differences in Rwanda.
In 1994, the East African country of Rwanda was shattered by a horrific genocide involving two main groups, the Hutu and the Tutsi. Over a few months, as many as 1 million Tutsi and an unknown number of moderate Hutu died in a slaughter perpetrated by extremist Hutu death squads. In a country of only 7 million people before the genocide, where Hutu made up 85 percent of the population and Tutsi 15 percent, how did this tragic genocide occur? How did Tutsi and Hutu, who have lived together in the region for generations and centuries, come to perceive such clear differences between them and choose to act on those differences in such violent ways?

Before the imposition of German and Belgian colonial rule in the early twentieth century, Hutu and Tutsi were distinguished mainly by occupation and social status. Hutu were primarily farmers; Tutsi were cattle owners. The two groups shared a common language and religious affiliations. Intermarriage was quite

MAP 6.3
Rwanda

common. Children of mixed marriages inherited their father's identity. Although Tutsi were later stereotyped as taller and thinner than Hutu, it is not possible to distinguish between members of the two groups by looks alone.

It was common practice among colonial governments worldwide to choose one native group to serve as the educated, privileged intermediaries between the local population and the colonial administration. In Rwanda, the Belgian colonial government (1919–62) elevated Tutsi to the most influential positions in society—to the exclusion of Hutu leaders. In an attempt to rationalize its prejudicial behavior, in the 1920s the Belgian colonial government hired scientists to measure Hutu and Tutsi anatomy—including skull size—so as to physically differentiate between the two groups. These flawed studies, based on the Western pseudoscience of eugenics, declared that Tutsi were taller, bigger brained, and lighter skinned—closer in physical form to Europeans and thus "naturally" suited to the role assigned to them by the Belgian colonial government.

To maintain and enforce this segregation, in 1933 the Belgian colonial government issued national identity cards that included the category "ethnicity." Even after independence in 1962, Rwandan officials continued to use the identity cards, forcing all citizens to be labeled as Hutu, Tutsi, Twa (a small minority population), or naturalized (born outside Rwanda). The cards were discontinued only in 1996 after the genocide.

Many Hutu resented the Belgians' decision to elevate the Tutsi to power in the colonial government. Periodic protests in the early years of colonial occupation were followed by a major uprising against Tutsi elites in 1956. In 1959, the Hutu seized power and forced many Tutsi into exile in neighboring countries. At independence in 1962, the Hutu consolidated power and implemented repressive policies toward the Tutsi. A full-blown civil war erupted in 1990. Subsequently, a 1993 United Nations–backed cease-fire collapsed when a plane carrying the Rwandan president, a Hutu, was shot down in April 1994.

What followed was an extensive genocide campaign by Hutu extremists who blamed the Tutsi for the death of their president. Rwandan radio broadcast instructions to kill all Tutsi, including spouses and family members, as well as any Hutu moderates who were unwilling to cooperate. Hutu civilian death squads implemented the "Hutu Power" genocide program, a deliberate and seemingly long-planned extermination of Tutsi. Tutsi and moderate Hutu were killed largely by hand with machetes and clubs after local officials gathered them up into schools and churches. Hutu death squads used the Rwandan identity cards to identify Tutsi victims for extermination.

What role did ethnicity play in the Rwandan genocide? Western press and government reports referred to the extermination as "tribal violence," the result of "ancient ethnic hatreds" and a failed nation-state. However, we can see how colonial European policies constructed and enforced notions of difference

between Hutu and Tutsi—including notions of physical and mental difference—that were not deep-rooted historical patterns but that nonetheless later served to rationalize genocide (Mamdani 2002). Indeed, the twentieth-century history of Rwanda reveals how local ethnic relationships can be broken down and reconstituted in enduring ways by a foreign superpower that weaponizes ethnicity to divide and rule—and how those new patterns of ethnicity can be mobilized to fuel a struggle for economic, political, and military power (Eller 1999).

Rwandan identity cards listing each citizen's ethnic identity were discontinued only in 1996 after the genocide of as many as 1 million Tutsi.

Remaking Identity: Hutu Refugees in Tanzania.

In neighboring Burundi, where Tutsi outnumber Hutu, a series of massacres in the 1970s drove many Hutu refugees to Tanzania. Anthropologist Liisa Malkki's ethnography *Purity and Exile: Violence, Memory and National Cosmology among Hutu Refugees in Tanzania* (1995) focuses on the lives of Hutu refugees in a remote resettlement camp and their experiences of atrocity, displacement, and exile. Through a year of fieldwork, Malkki collected dozens of life histories, which she calls mythico-histories—stories through which refugees worked to remake sense of their past, present, and future.

Through these mythico-histories, Hutu refugees reimagined their conceptions of community, history, and ethnic identity, often in stark contrast to both

MAP 6.4

Tanzania

Tutsi accounts of the conflict and Western accounts of the colonial history in Rwanda and Burundi. Hutu instead described how their essential nature had emerged through the experience of atrocity and exile. Their stories told not of victims and outcasts but of a distinct Hutu people with a long history as Burundians, while the Tutsi were foreign usurpers. In their narratives, the trials of dispossession and dislocation prepared their "nation in exile" for a restoration to Burundi. To reinforce this sense of Hutu identity, refugees held to certain purity practices while in exile—discouraging intermarriage, preserving their language, and acquiring official recognition as refugees rather than blending into the surrounding Tanzanian community.

By recounting Hutu refugees' mythico-histories, Malkki sheds light on the dilemmas of displaced people in a world that assumes the nation-state is the natural frame for viewing ethnicity and ethnic identity. In the process, she captures the creative strategies that displaced people deploy to sustain themselves and imagine a better future. When considering the intersections of ethnicity, ethnic conflict, and the nation-state, Malkki urges us to move beyond easy explanations of contemporary conflicts as inevitable or natural outcomes of ancient tribal hatreds. Instead, Malkki's work pushes us to see the complex histories and processes of identity making that are often obscured by labels like "refugee" and "ethnic conflict" (Haugerud 1998; Malkki 1995; Roseberry 1997).

Orchestrating Ethnic Conflict in the Former Yugoslavia.
The disintegration of the former Yugoslavia in the late 1980s and early 1990s catalyzed a devastating civil war that harnessed ethnicity as a powerful weapon of conflict and hatred. The war began in 1992 among Catholic Croats, Orthodox Christian Serbs, and Bosnian Muslims as national political leaders scrambled for control over land and power. The region is one of the most ethnically diverse in the world, and the area's national boundaries have shifted constantly over the past 150 years. But in direct contrast to journalistic accounts of the 1992–95 war, which traced the conflict's origins to ancient ethnic hatreds that condemned the country's people to an endless cycle of violence, Norwegian anthropologist Tone Bringa has offered a different perspective. In her ethnography *Being Muslim the Bosnian Way* (1995), she declares, "The war was not created by those villagers. . . . The war has been orchestrated from places where the people I lived and worked among were not represented and where their voices were not heard" (5).

Bringa began her fieldwork in 1987 in a diverse Muslim-Catholic village in central Bosnia. She carefully describes the integrated social structures of daily village life—including the roles of women, religion, and the family—and pays particular attention to how Muslims practiced their faith. Bringa did not find a village populated with people who had always hated one another. They spoke the same language, went to school together, traded in the same local market,

MAP 6.5
Bosnia

and shared village life as friends and neighbors. Bringa pointedly notes that despite the usual tensions any small community would face, these people of different faiths had lived together peacefully for 500 years.

Significant change occurred in the community during the short time of Bringa's fieldwork. When she began her research, local Muslims based their identity on differences in religious practices from those of their Catholic neighbors. The emphasis was on practices such as scheduling of worship, prayer, and holiday celebrations, not on religious beliefs and convictions. However, these perceptions of self and others changed as war broke out and state leaders imposed new ethnic and cultural policies. Gradually, local Muslims were forced to identify less with their local community and more with the religious beliefs of other Bosnian Muslims, and they had to turn to the outside Muslim world as a source of solidarity and support.

When Bringa returned to the village in the spring of 1993—revealed in riveting scenes from her documentary film *Bosnia: We Are All Neighbors* (1993)—to her horror, she found that almost every Muslim home had been destroyed by Croat forces with assistance from local Croat men of the village. All 400 Muslims in the village (two-thirds of its population) had fled, been killed, or been placed in concentration camps. **Ethnic cleansing**—efforts of one ethnic or religious group to remove or destroy another group in a particular geographic area—had shattered the dynamic and peaceful fabric of village life that had prevailed only a few years earlier. As Bringa writes in the preface to her book, "My anthropological training had not prepared me to deal with the very rapid and total disintegration of the community. . . . [T]his war has made sense neither to the anthropologist nor to the people who taught her about their way of life" (Bringa 1995, xviii). Her second documentary, *Returning Home: Revival of a Bosnian Village* (Bringa and Loizos 2002), examines the return of some of the Muslim refugees and the attempt to reconstruct the village life that was destroyed by civil war. In Bringa's account of Bosnian village life, we can see the vulnerability of local ethnic identities to manipulation by outside political and military forces (Coles 2007; Eller 1999).

Bosnian Muslim women comfort one another near coffins of family members, victims of "ethnic cleansing," exhumed from a nearby mass grave.

ethnic cleansing

Efforts by representatives of one ethnic or religious group to remove or destroy another group in a particular geographic area.

ETHNICITY AS A SOURCE OF OPPORTUNITY

Ethnicity is not only mobilized to rally support in times of conflict, as we have seen in the examples of Rwanda, Tanzania, and Bosnia. Ethnicity can also be mobilized to create opportunities, including economic opportunities both locally

Each year, half a million tourists visit the Dai Minority Park in China's southwestern Yunnan Province. This is one of many ethno-parks owned and operated by members of China's Han majority (96 percent of the population), who market the nation's fifty-five ethnic minorities to a primarily middle-class Han clientele (Chio 2014). Here, tourists can live in Dai-style houses, eat ethnic meals, and participate in reenactments of ritual celebrations such as the water festival, pictured here, originally an annual three-day festival but now performed every day for the entertainment of visitors. How might ethno–theme parks benefit the Chinese government's goal of national unity? How do you think they affect the local communities?

and globally. People eat at ethnic restaurants, listen to ethnic music, and decorate their homes and offices with ethnic furnishings. Some ethnic groups are branding themselves and becoming ethno-corporations in order to capitalize on their ethnicity. Ethno–theme parks, cultural villages, and ecotourism all promote the ethnic experience to attract investors and customers (Chio 2014; Nelson 1999). (In contrast, for an example of a majority group's marketing of minority theme parks, see the group of images above.)

Puerto Rican Farmworkers, Ethnicity, and United States Agriculture. In *Colonial Migrants at the Heart of Empire: Puerto Rican Workers on U.S. Farms* (2020), anthropologist Ismael García-Colón draws upon decades of fieldwork to document the history of Puerto Rican laborers on mainland U.S. farms. Of particular interest are the strategies these workers use to construct ethnic identities and ethnic communities amid rural U.S. communities where their presence has often been unwelcome. Puerto Rico has been a U.S. colonial territory since 1898, when the United States claimed the Caribbean island and its people in the Spanish-American War. Though Puerto Ricans were granted U.S. citizenship in 1917, the United States has refused to recognize Puerto Rico as a state. As a result, Puerto Rican farmworkers have an ambiguous status on the mainland. Despite their citizenship and the essential farm work they provide, Puerto Ricans have often been seen as outsiders to mainstream American society.

García-Colón's research focuses on one of a number of significant waves of Puerto Rican migration to cities and more rural communities. Beginning in 1948, hundreds of thousands of rural, often poor, Puerto Rican farmers responded to an aggressive program to recruit them as laborers on mainland U.S. farms. Over the following decades, the Farm Labor Program—a collaboration of the Puerto Rican and United States governments—filled U.S. farm labor shortages by contracting and transporting Puerto Rican farmers, often as seasonal workers, to grow and harvest everything from apples, mushrooms, and potatoes to cranberries and tobacco on orchards and farms up and down the Eastern Seaboard. As a government initiative, the Farm Labor Program established relatively generous labor contracts for Puerto Rican workers that assured their preferential hiring ahead of undocumented immigrants and noncitizen guest workers. Ironically, however, employers often avoided hiring Puerto Rican workers because of their citizenship status, fearing that they would be harder to control than more vulnerable undocumented workers or guest workers.

The arrival of Puerto Rican migrant farmworkers in predominantly White, rural communities contributed significantly to the Latinization of the U.S. farm labor force. It also drew considerable resistance from many local residents. Puerto Rican farmworkers sought economic opportunities for themselves and their families, aspiring to the American dream of social mobility and a middle-class lifestyle. Despite their U.S. citizenship status and their essential role in the farm economy, however, their position as Spanish-speaking, mixed-race, culturally Latino colonial subjects commonly marked them as outsiders. Puerto Rican migrants living in rural communities, where they were often the first non-White residents, commonly faced hostility and marginalization, surveillance and violence. Faced with unsafe and unfair working conditions, withholding of wages, or threats and intimidation, many workers simply abandoned their contracts, relocated to U.S. cities, or migrated back to Puerto Rico.

Colonial Migrants at the Heart of Empire focuses significant attention on the labor conditions experienced by Puerto Rican migrant farmworkers. As

García-Colón documents, many lived in grim labor camps on the farms, where they worked, ate, lived, shopped, and sought entertainment. Isolated on farm property, these labor camps kept a largely unwanted population invisible to the broader public. The all-encompassing nature of the camps circumscribed the workers' social and economic activity, making them more vulnerable to employer tactics such as overcharging for food and other goods while shortchanging wages.

García-Colón recounts the ways that, despite employer exploitation and marginalization within the broader rural community, Puerto Rican migrant workers used these farm labor camps as centers of resistance and organizing efforts to improve local working conditions. Mobilization among extended family and friendship networks was key. So were strategies to create and mobilize a sense of shared ethnic identity amid the largely White, rural communities where farmworkers experienced prejudice and racism almost on a daily basis. Farmworkers also drew upon their ethnic bonds to create ethnic-based businesses, particularly in the service and food industries, that kept financial resources within the community. This ethnic infrastructure allowed the Puerto Rican community to support one another and provided alternatives to the exploitative farm labor camp conditions.

The desire for Puerto Rican foods created one such opportunity for ethnic mobilization. The food provided by farm owners in the labor camps was often unfamiliar, tasteless, and boring. An extensive network of small Puerto Rican food entrepreneurs and businesses quickly emerged around the camps, and these enterprises, in turn, supported a related network of small businesses to supply the food sellers. This ethnic infrastructure not only provided an alternative to the owners' tightly controlled labor camp food system but also established employment opportunities outside of farm labor. Furthermore, by creating an alternative, ethnic-oriented economy, Puerto Rican farm laborers were able to build upon ties of ethnic solidarity to keep more money within their community rather than pouring it back into the farm labor camp system.

Although the flow of Puerto Rican farm labor into the United States has declined in recent years, thousands continue to pursue these opportunities and experience the difficulties of being an outsider in their own country. Their journeys, including their creative efforts to mobilize ethnic identities and infrastructures, provide key insights into the complex experiences of Latinos in the rural United States today.

ASSIMILATION VERSUS MULTICULTURALISM: ETHNIC INTERACTION IN THE UNITED STATES

The United States has an extremely complicated history when it comes to people of different geographic origins, religions, skin colors, and ethnic backgrounds. The relationship of "ethnic" and "American" (as applied to the United States) remains controversial today. From the outset, immigration from various regions in Europe, the enslavement and forced migration of Africans, and the conquest of Native American peoples made the United States one of the most ethnically diverse countries in the world. But these diverse groups and additional waves of immigrants over the past 200 years have experienced vastly different paths to incorporation into U.S. culture. In fact, these paths have often followed color lines that divide people of lighter and darker complexions and that came to be rigidly enforced as race.

Scholars for many years used the **melting pot** metaphor to describe the standard path into U.S. culture. In the melting pot, cultural minorities adopt the patterns and norms of the dominant culture and eventually cease to exist as separate groups—a process scholars call **assimilation**. Eventually, all cooked in the same pot, diverse groups become assimilated into one big stew. According to this metaphor, tens of millions of European immigrants from dozens of countries with myriad languages, cultures, and religious practices have been transformed into ethnic Whites through marriage, work, education, and the use of English.

But in reality, the melting pot has never been completely successful in the United States, even for people of European descent. The creation of Whiteness, as we saw in Chapter 5, was often contentious and difficult, marked by intense rivalries and violence. Nathan Glazer and Daniel Patrick Moynihan's landmark study *Beyond the Melting Pot* (1970) found a failure to reach complete assimilation among European immigrants and their descendants as late as the third generation. And many scholars suggest that the melting pot metaphor never meaningfully represented the experiences of Native Americans and people of African descent.

The incredibly diverse flows of immigration to the United States since 1965 have made earlier, familiar categories increasingly inadequate to capture the rapidly shifting ethnic character of the nation's population today. For many Africans, Native Americans, Latinos, and Asian immigrants, the United States has resisted their assimilation into the dominant culture, regardless of their educational level or socioeconomic status. Yet, as discussed in Chapters 5 and 10 (on race and the global economy, respectively), immigrants and their children are creating new ethnic identities and new ways of becoming American. Today, a multiculturalist narrative competes with the melting pot metaphor to represent the role of ethnicity in U.S. culture. **Multiculturalism** refers to the process through which new immigrants and their children enculturate into the dominant national culture and yet retain an ethnic culture. In multiculturalism, both identities may be held at the same time.

Tensions over which model should become dominant in the U.S. ethnicity story—assimilation or multiculturalism—are constantly rising to the surface. For example, White nationalist movements promote anti-immigrant laws and violence. Attempts to establish English as the official language of towns, states, and

melting pot
A metaphor used to describe the process of immigrant assimilation into U.S. dominant culture.

assimilation
The process through which cultural minorities accept the patterns and norms of the dominant culture and cease to exist as separate groups.

multiculturalism
A pattern of ethnic relations in which new immigrants and their children enculturate into the dominant national culture yet retain an ethnic culture.

even the U.S. federal government can be seen as an effort to mandate language assimilation into the melting pot and a reassertion of the dominant culture's centrality against the growing trend toward multiculturalism (Rumbaut and Portes 2001).

What Is the Relationship of Ethnicity to the Nation?

Explain how ethnicity and the nation are related.

Almost all people today imagine themselves as part of a nation-state. But this has not always been the case. **States**—regional structures of political, economic, and military rule—have existed for thousands of years, beginning in the regions now known as Iraq, China, and India. But the nation-state is a relatively new development. The term signifies more than a geographic territory with borders enforced by a central government. **Nation-state** assumes a distinct political entity whose population shares a sense of culture, ancestry, and destiny as a people. **Citizenship** refers to legal membership in a nation-state. Though the term **nation** once was used to describe a group of people who shared a place of origin, today the word *nation* is often used interchangeably with *nation-state*. **Nationality** is an identification with a group of people thought to share a place of origin. **Nationalism** emerges when a sense of ethnic community combines with a desire to create and maintain a nation-state in a location where that sense of common destiny can be lived out (Gellner 1983; Hearn 2006; Wolf 2001).

IMAGINED COMMUNITIES AND INVENTED TRADITIONS

Across the world over the past 200 years, people have shifted their primary associations and identifications from family, village, town, and city to an almost universal identification with a nation or the desire to create a nation. Yet despite our contemporary assumptions that identifying with an ethnic group or a nation is a tradition with a deep history, anthropological research reveals that most ethnic groups and nations are recent historical creations, that our connection to people within these groups is recently imagined, and that our shared traditions are recently invented.

Political scientist Benedict Anderson (1983) conceived of the nation as an **imagined community**. He called it "imagined" because almost all of the people within it have never met and most likely will never meet. They may be separated by sharp divisions of class, politics, or religion and yet imagine themselves to have

state

An autonomous regional structure of political, economic, and military rule with a central government authorized to make laws and use force to maintain order and defend its territory.

nation-state

A political entity, located within a geographic territory with enforced borders, where the population shares a sense of culture, ancestry, and destiny as a people.

citizenship

Legal membership in a nation-state.

nation

A term once used to describe a group of people who shared a place of origin; now used interchangeably with nation-state.

nationality

An identification with a group of people thought to share a place of origin.

nationalism

The desire of an ethnic community to create and/or maintain a nation-state.

imagined community

The invented sense of connection and shared traditions that underlies identification with a particular ethnic group or nation whose members likely will never all meet.

a common heritage and collective responsibility to one another and their nation. This sense of membership in an imagined national community can be strong enough to lead people into battle to protect their shared interests.

Historians Eric Hobsbawm and Terence Ranger (1983) suggest that nations are not ancient configurations but instead are recent constructions with invented traditions. Nations may evoke a sense of deep history and inspire a broad sense of unity, but they are, in fact, relatively new. For example, we imagine the French nation-state to have a deep and unitary history, but prior to the 1800s, the French were a scattered collection of urban and rural people who spoke different languages, celebrated different holidays and festivals, practiced different religions, and held primary loyalty not to the French state but to their city, town, village, or extended family. It was two national infrastructure projects, launched in the early 1800s, that ultimately played key roles in inventing a French nation.

First, a new education system was introduced on a national scale. Its textbooks promoted a shared sense of French history, and perhaps most important, all schools used the Parisian dialect of French as the medium of instruction. This created a standard national language—a lingua franca—that facilitated communication among the population. Second, the construction of an extensive network of roads and railways integrated rural areas into a national market economy. This new transportation infrastructure promoted the rapid flow of goods between agricultural and industrial sectors and allowed the regular movement of workers between countryside and city, thereby providing a national labor pool for France's growing economy. These national infrastructure projects proved crucial to transforming the diverse people living within the territorial boundaries of modern-day France into a French people with a common sense of identity, history, language, and tradition (Weber 1976).

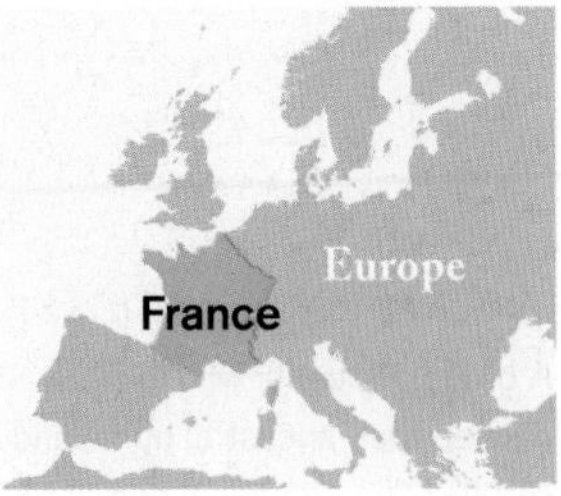

MAP 6.6
France

Globalization and Transnational Citizenship in Eritrea.

Today, globalization is reshaping the ways in which nation-states operate and are experienced within and beyond their borders. For example, Victoria Bernal's ethnography *Nation as Network* (2014) explores the recent history of Eritrea, a small multiethnic nation in the Horn of Africa, and how Eritrean out-migration in recent decades has combined with new media technologies to transform notions of the nation-state and citizenship.

War and violence have been constant for Eritreans in recent decades, from the country's struggle for independence to ensuing border wars with neighboring states. The country's citizens have faced increasing militarization and repression by the Eritrean state.

Given these circumstances, tens of thousands of Eritreans have chosen to move abroad in search of economic opportunities and political stability. Scattered

MAP 6.7
Eritrea

French classroom, 1829. What role can education play in creating a sense of common nationality?

over many countries and continents, they have formed what immigration scholars call a **diaspora**—an extensive network of Eritreans living outside their ancestral homeland yet maintaining emotional and material ties to home—through which they continue to participate passionately in Eritrean politics and economic life. They send money to family members back home. They make investments. And through a dynamic network of websites, blogs, and social media, they connect with one another, debate Eritrean politics, mobilize actions and campaigns, and communicate their political views to the Eritrean state and a wider audience of nongovernmental organizations and human rights groups. Eritrean political and economic elites actively cultivate the diaspora's involvement and rely on their financial contributions to support Eritrea's welfare and warfare.

Bernal documents how the activities of the Eritrean diaspora create new opportunities to experiment with political expression, including dissent and other activities that would not be safe in Eritrea itself. New communication technologies enable Eritreans in diaspora to participate in a kind of "infopolitics" in which the management of information becomes a central aspect of power relations between the state and its citizens. Their online presence creates an alternative public sphere in which they can challenge Eritrea's authoritarian government, question the narratives of the country's mainstream media, and more generally undermine practices of secrecy and censorship. In the process, this transnational network of Eritreans participates robustly in the building of Eritrea as a nation—both in the struggle over Eritrean economic and political priorities and in the making and remaking of the conceptual boundaries of the Eritrean state, Eritrean citizenship, and Eritrean identity (Bernal 2014; Ivana 2015).

ANTI-COLONIALISM AND NATIONALISM

At times, efforts to imagine a national identity among a diverse group of people gain strength through the need—perceived or real—to join together against the threat of a common enemy. The outsiders—"others" who do not belong to the group—may be stereotyped along lines of religion, race, language, ethnicity, or political beliefs. War is the most dramatic strategy for evoking nationalism and mobilizing a population for the project of nation building.

Through their colonial conquests over more than 400 years, the emerging nation-states of Europe and, later, Japan in Asia, redrew the political borders of much of the world to suit their own economic and political interests. In the search for raw materials, cheap labor, and markets for their expanding economies, they mapped out territorial boundaries without regard to local ethnic, political, economic, or religious realities (see Chapter 10 on the global economy). In the process, colonial activity disrupted long-established and complex local and regional social, economic, and political relationships. Colonialism had a particularly negative impact on Indigenous people around the world who faced forced labor, relocation, forced assimilation, violence, and genocide (Maybury-Lewis 2002).

The destruction of European and Japanese economies during World War II (1939–45) weakened the colonial powers' ability to control their colonies. As a result, national independence movements that had been gaining strength in colonies throughout Asia, Africa, the Middle East, Latin America, and the Caribbean before World War II—and that had developed military capabilities and guerrilla fighting tactics during the war—were strongly positioned to turn their efforts toward liberating their countries from their colonial occupiers. The anti-colonialist efforts led to a rise of nationalism in former colonies as disparate populations banded together to reassert local control (Cesaire 1955; Fanon 1961).

The following case study from Iraq explores the challenges experienced by emerging nations in the postcolonial period and will expand your understanding of the intersection of nation, nationalism, nation building, and the modern nation-state. Can you identify in this example the key concepts introduced in this chapter?

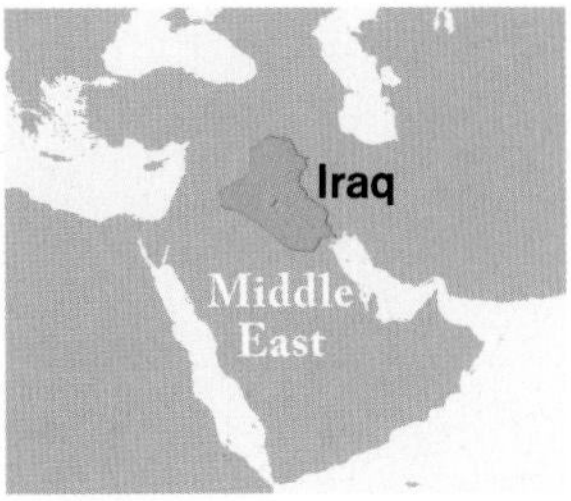

Are There Any Iraqis in Iraq? After the U.S. invasion and occupation of Iraq in 2003 and the overthrow of Iraqi president Saddam Hussein, news reports featured stories of ethnic violence among Sunni, Shia, and Kurds—violence that the media portrayed as the true obstacle to democracy and peace. The front pages of newspapers and the leads on evening news told stories of seemingly endless and senseless suicide bombings, roadside explosives, armed militias, kidnappings, assassinations, and warfare. Elections were held, but the elected officials, torn by

MAP 6.8
Iraq

intense ethnic, religious, and political differences, were unable to form a functioning government. Typical of the way the Western press reports on supposed ethnic conflicts around the world—whether in Rwanda, Sudan, Sri Lanka, India, or the former Yugoslavia—deep and long-standing ethnic and religious cleavages in Iraq were blamed for an environment in which civil war and government collapse were almost inevitable.

Why, after so many years of U.S. economic and military support, have the Iraqi people struggled to form a strong government and military and stop the violence? Aren't there any Iraqis in Iraq—people who would put the country first, ahead of other ethnic or religious differences?

Iraq does not have an ancient history as a nation. Although cities such as Baghdad have an ancient history in the region of Mesopotamia, sometimes called the "cradle of civilization," the country of Iraq did not exist before World War I. Even then, Iraq was not formed through local initiative. A secret treaty between France and Great Britain (the Sykes-Picot Agreement), signed during World War I, carved up their opponent, the Ottoman Empire, to form many of the countries we find in the Middle East today. With Russia's consent, the two European powers drew national borders—including those of present-day Iraq—to meet their needs for economic access, trade routes, and political control. The powers mapped out these borders with little regard for the history, politics, religions, and ethnic makeup of the local populations.

With a mandate from the new League of Nations in 1920, the British established a monarchical government in the new state of Iraq and recruited and empowered leaders from the minority Sunni population to run it. Members of the Shia and Kurd populations, excluded from leadership roles in the government, actively fought for independence from British colonial occupation. Britain subsequently granted full independence to Iraq in 1932 (with the exception of another brief military occupation during World War II), but the Sunni minority retained control of the government until the fall of Saddam Hussein in 2003.

After the U.S. military occupied Iraq in 2003, the people of Iraq inherited a collapsed state structure and confronted the prospects of nation building in a country under foreign occupation that had experienced decades of state-sponsored violence. Yet media representations of Iraq consistently trace its problems to the roots of ethnic conflict. Social scientists from many fields question these simple storylines that portray deep ethnic and religious hatreds as the cause of Iraq's current difficulties (Ericksen 2010). Ethnicity, they warn, should never be seen that simply or monolithically. A more careful examination may find that (1) ethnic and religious lines are not drawn so clearly, and (2) other identities based on factors such as region, family, and class—even international relations—may also play key roles in the unfolding of events.

With a weak state unable to provide security to its population, people turn to other strategies for mobilizing support, safety, and the means for achieving a livelihood (Eller 1999).

As globalization creates flows of people, ideas, goods, and images across borders and builds linkages among local communities worldwide, we might anticipate that ethnicity and nationalism—which are associated with local and national identities—would have less capacity to shape people's lives and influence how people make decisions. Instead, in many parts of the world, we see an intensification of ethnic and national identities and related conflicts. Understanding the processes through which ethnicity and nationalism are imagined and mobilized and their traditions are invented, often over relatively short periods of time, can provide a set of tools for analyzing the role of ethnicity in our world today.

Toolkit

Thinking Like an Anthropologist:
Who Is an American?

In the opening story of the Rohingya and in the ethnographic examples throughout the chapter, we have seen how ethnic identity and nationalism continue to be imagined, built, nurtured, taught, learned, promoted, negotiated, and contested. And we have explored an anthropological perspective on three questions that connect the concepts of ethnicity and nationalism:

- **What does "ethnicity" mean to anthropologists?**
- **How and why is ethnicity created, mobilized, and contested?**
- **What is the relationship of ethnicity to the nation?**

Few of us are aware of the roles ethnicity and nationalism play in our lives or how our culture works to promote them. For instance, a former Facebook employee, Frances Haugen, revealed in 2021 that Facebook had been used by Myanmar's military and civil society groups to promote misinformation and to amplify violence against the Rohingya. As you learn to think like an anthropologist, can you begin to see the process of ethnic identity construction at work in your own life and in the major debates of the culture that surrounds you? Consider these recent debates about who is and who is not an American:

- Despite an official birth certificate and other clear evidence that former U.S. president Barack Obama was born in the state of Hawaii on August 4, 1961, more than 20 percent of Americans surveyed in a September 2015 poll by CNN/ORG claimed that he is not a U.S. citizen, and 29 percent expressed their belief that Obama is a Muslim, despite his repeated professions of Christian faith (CNN/ORC International 2015). How is that possible?

- Some leading politicians want to change the Fourteenth Amendment of the U.S. Constitution. The amendment was passed after the Civil War to protect African Americans by ensuring that anyone born in the United States is granted full rights of citizenship. Children born in the United States to undocumented Hispanic parents are the target of these recent suggested changes to the Constitution. Some people fear that immigrant parents intentionally give birth on U.S. soil so they can become citizens when their child attains the age of twenty-one. Do you think the U.S. Constitution should be amended to address this issue? Or is this debate simply a substitute for a larger struggle over who belongs to U.S. culture and who does not? How should a child's nationality and citizenship be defined?

• In recent years, leading political candidates have evoked notions of ethnicity, nationalism, and citizenship to rally voters, suggesting that Muslims should be banned from immigration to the United States; that 10–15 million undocumented immigrants living in the United States, including children who accompanied them and who have grown up in the United States, should be deported; that Muslim mosques should be placed under surveillance; and that the United States should only accept Syrian refugees if they are Christian. What role do ethno-political identity entrepreneurs play in attempts to define immigrants and Muslims, in particular, as ethnic outsiders in the United States?

After reading this chapter, you should be better prepared with the anthropological tools you need to understand the ways in which ethnicity and nationalism work in your life and in your imagined communities—whether they are built around your family, religion, hometown, ethnic group, or nation-state.

Key Terms

ethnicity (p. 164)

origin myth (p. 166)

ethnic boundary marker (p. 166)

situational negotiation of identity (p. 166)

identity entrepreneurs (p. 169)

genocide (p. 169)

ethnic cleansing (p. 173)

melting pot (p. 177)

assimilation (p. 177)

multiculturalism (p. 177)

state (p. 178)

nation-state (p. 178)

citizenship (p. 178)

nation (p. 178)

nationality (p. 178)

nationalism (p. 178)

imagined community (p. 178)

diaspora (p. 180)

Chapter 7
Gender

Learning Objectives

- Define sex and gender from an anthropological perspective.

- Explain the diversity of biological sex beyond the male–female binary.

- Describe how gender works as a system of power that includes stratification and ideologies.

- Assess how globalization is reshaping gender roles and stratification in local contexts.

Sarah Rose Huckman, a student at the University of New Hampshire, is a prominent public speaker, a vlogger on YouTube, and an activist for transgender rights. Sarah grew up in the small town of Ossipee, New Hampshire, population 4,372, after being adopted from Cambodia. Assigned male at birth, she understood herself to be female from a young age. In the seventh grade, she came out publicly as transgender. At Kingswood High School, Sarah was a four-sport athlete, competing on the girl's division Nordic ski, winter indoor track, spring track, and cross-country teams. When she first began to compete in high school, the New Hampshire Interscholastic Athletic Association (NHIAA), which sets athletic policy for the state's high schools, only permitted transgender students who had undergone gender reassignment surgery to compete on teams consistent with their gender identity

---

Sarah Rose Huckman, student-athlete and transgender rights activist, testifying in support of HB 1319 which would prohibit discrimination based on gender identity.

rather than their sex assigned at birth. Doctors have not recommended such surgery for transgender youth. Sarah's parents worked with GLBTQ Legal Advocates and Defenders and the NHIAA to allow individual school districts to make that determination locally. Still, the policy's language potentially allowed other schools to challenge Sarah's eligibility.

For three years, Sarah served on the New Hampshire Legislative Youth Advisory Council and advocated for the passage of New Hampshire House Bill 1319 to explicitly extend New Hampshire's nondiscrimination protections to transgender and gender nonconforming people. In testimony before the New Hampshire House Judiciary Committee, Sarah said, "we all want a future where we are judged on the merits of hard work and being good citizens, and no one is treated differently because of their gender identity. . . . This bill is a critical starting point for acceptance and inclusion in our communities, and will allow me, and so many others, to truly live free in our beloved state!"

In 2018, New Hampshire passed HB 1319. A year later, the state explicitly extended protections for transgender and gender nonconforming students to all public high schools. In 2021, the documentary *Changing the Game* followed the journey of Sarah and two other transgender teen athletes, Mack Beggs and Andraya Yearwood, as they struggled against policies, laws, and angry adults to pursue their dreams of being student athletes.

While some U.S. states, like New Hampshire, explicitly prohibit discrimination against transgender athletes, and other states are silent, legislators in a growing number of states have introduced bills to ban transgender youth from participating in school sports consistent with their gender identity, requiring them instead to compete based on the sex listed on their birth certificates. Such bans have been enacted in Idaho, South Dakota, Arkansas, Mississippi, Alabama, Tennessee, West Virginia, and Texas, among others.

In contrast, at the U.S. federal level, the Supreme Court ruled in a 6–3 decision on June 15, 2020, that employment discrimination based on gender identity and sexual orientation is illegal under Title VII of the 1964 Civil Rights Act, which outlaws discrimination in the workplace on the basis of race, color, religion, sex, and national origin. Following the Court's reasoning, in June 2021, the U.S. Department of Education stated that the Title IX policies that prohibit discrimination on the basis of sex in educational institutions that receive federal funds also protect students on the basis of sexual orientation and gender identity.

As anthropologists, how do we analyze these cultural battles about the boundaries of gender identity, whether they are waged over youth sports, bathroom use, workplace discrimination, marriage, or transgender teens' access to gender affirming health care? How do we engage the real-life impacts of these policy debates on the lives of millions of gender nonconforming young people and adults both in the United States and globally?

Questions of gender—that is, the characteristics and identities associated with masculinity and femininity in a particular culture and the ways those characteristics intersect with dynamics of power—are central to the practice of anthropology. Since the pioneering work of Margaret Mead challenged U.S. cultural assumptions about human sexuality and gender roles (see Chapter 3), anthropologists, especially feminist anthropologists, have been at the forefront of attempts to use the tools and analysis of anthropology to analyze the role of gender in crucial contemporary debates, social movements, and political struggles. Over the last fifty years, **gender studies**—the study of how gender identities and expressions are shaped by and affect one's life chances—has become one of the most significant subfields of anthropology. Indeed, anthropologists consider the ways in which gender is constructed to be a central element in every aspect of human culture, including sexuality, health, family, religion, economics, politics, sports, and individual identity formation.

As we have seen throughout this book, people create diverse cultures with fluid categories to define complex aspects of the human experience. The same holds true for gender. While binary gender identities and expressions have provided a central framework in the history of gender studies, more recent scholarship has expanded to consider nonbinary, gender nonconforming, gender-fluid, genderqueer, and transgender expressions. Even biological sex is far more fluid and complex than many people realize. As we will see later in this chapter, particularly in our discussion of the experiences of intersex individuals, nature creates diversity, not rigid categories. As globalization transforms gender roles and gender relations on both the local level and a global scale, anthropologists play an essential role in mapping the changing gender terrain of the modern world. In this chapter, we will explore these issues in more detail:

- **What is gender?**
- **Are there more than two sexes?**
- **How do anthropologists explore the relationship between gender and power?**
- **How is globalization transforming gender roles and stratification?**

By the end of this chapter, you will be better prepared to understand the roles that sex and gender play in the culture around you, including in the classroom, in the family, in the workplace, in places of worship, and at the ballot box. You will also be able to apply anthropological insights into gender issues as they emerge in your own life—insights that will serve you well as a romantic partner, spouse, parent, student, teacher, worker, manager, and community leader in our increasingly global world.

gender studies

The study of how gender identities and expressions are shaped by and affect one's life chances.

What Is Gender?

Define sex and gender from an anthropological perspective.

"That's just the way guys are," some women sigh when a man says or does some stereotypical "man" thing. "Women!" a man may exclaim, hands in the air, as if all the other guys in the room know exactly what he means. But what *do* they mean? Is there some essential male or female nature that differentially shapes our personalities, emotions, patterns of personal relationships, career choices, leadership styles, and economic and political engagements?

DISTINGUISHING BETWEEN SEX AND GENDER

Much of what we stereotypically consider to be "natural" male or female behavior—driven by biology—might turn out, upon more careful inspection, to be imposed by cultural expectations of how men and women should behave. To help explore the relationship between the biological and cultural aspects of being men and women, anthropologists distinguish between sex and gender. **Sex,** from an anthropological viewpoint, refers to the culturally agreed upon physical differences between male and female human beings, especially the biological differences related to human reproduction. **Gender** is composed of the expectations of thought and behavior that each culture assigns to people of different sexes.

Historically, biological science has tended to create distinct binary mental maps of reality for male and female anatomy. Three primary factors have generally been considered in determining biological sex: (1) genitalia, (2) gonads (testes and ovaries, which produce different hormones), and (3) chromosome patterns (women have two X chromosomes; men have one X and one Y). Within this binary framework, human males and females are said to display **sexual dimorphism**—that is, they differ physically in primary sexual characteristics as well as in secondary sexual characteristics such as breast size, hair distribution, and pitch of voice. Men and women also differ in average weight, height, and strength. An average man is heavier, taller, and stronger than an average woman. Women on average have more long-term physical endurance and live longer.

But sexual dimorphism among humans is far from absolute. In fact, human male and female bodies are much more similar than they are different (Fedigan 1982; Ogden et al. 2004). Many biological characteristics associated with human sexual dimorphism fall along a continuum—a range—in which men and women overlap significantly. Not all men are taller than all women, though many are. Not all women live longer than all men, though most do.

sex

The culturally agreed upon physical differences between male and female, especially biological differences related to human reproduction.

gender

The expectations of thought and behavior that each culture assigns to people of different sexes.

sexual dimorphism

The phenotypic differences between males and females of the same species.

As we will see later in this chapter, primary characteristics of biological sex do not always fit into the two assumed categories of male and female. Millions of people are born with some combination of male and female genitalia, gonads, and chromosomes. This suggests the need to reconceptualize one of our most rigid mental maps of reality—the one separating male and female—in order to more accurately reflect the full range of human physical variation, including many who identify as intersex and those born with ambiguous genitalia.

As is the case with sex, in the United States, gender is learned and taught in a mostly binary framework that assumes humans fit naturally into neat categories of male and female, masculine and feminine. As we will see throughout this chapter, cross-cultural anthropological research reveals that a diversity of **gender identities**—each person's internal experience and understanding of their own gender—and **gender expressions**—how a person expresses or presents themselves in relationship to gender, whether in their behavior, appearance, name, or pronouns—undermines a strictly binary approach. Diverse expressions of gender and the wide range of gender nonconforming, gender-fluid, **transgender,** and genderqueer identities stretch far beyond the boundaries of the traditional binary male–female gender system. As we seek to understand and engage gender as a system of power, the term **cisgender** has emerged to draw attention to the unexamined gender norms, roles, identities, and privileges of people whose gender identity and expression correspond with their birth sex, much as attention to Whiteness enables a more complete analysis of race and racism (Valentine 2007; West and Zimmerman 1987, 2009; Darwin 2017).

What is the role of biology in shaping gender identities and behaviors? Research consistently reveals that biology and culture closely intertwine—and even that culture can shape biology. Culture, for instance, constantly shapes and reshapes our bodies throughout our lives, whether through nutrition, exercise, stress, exposure to disease, or social stimulation. Our bodies are designed to respond to our environments and life experiences. Our DNA, for instance, can be turned on and off by environmental factors. Our brains are constantly reshaped by the stimuli they receive. Even our hormone production is closely tied to the experiences we have with others. Testosterone levels rise and fall in response to what is going on around us. Studies have shown that if fathers are actively involved with their children, their bodies respond in ways that help them be good dads (Kuzawa et al. 2009; Muller et al. 2009; Wade and Ferree 2015).

Cross-cultural anthropological research challenges common assumptions that biology determines behavior. Knowing a person's biological sex does not enable

As the visibility of transgender and nonbinary individuals has increased in the United States, social media companies like Facebook now include an expanded list of possible gender expressions to reflect the expanding cultural definition of gender.

gender identity

Each person's internal experience and understanding of their own gender.

gender expression

How a person expresses or presents themselves in relationship to gender, whether in their behavior, appearance, name, or pronouns.

transgender

People whose gender identity and expression do not correspond with the biological sex category they were assigned at birth.

cisgender

People whose gender identity and expression correspond with the biological sex category they were assigned at birth.

Gender roles, even those stereotypically associated with male strength and aggression, are in flux across the globe. Here, U.S. Marines Sergeant Savanna E. Malendoski patrols in Helmand Province, southern Afghanistan.

us to predict what roles that person will play in a given culture. In some cultures, people with two X chromosomes do most of the cooking, farming, public speaking, and ritual activity; in others, people with one X and one Y chromosome fill those roles. Alternatively, the tasks may be done by both but stratified by power and prestige. In many Western cultures, for instance, both XX and XY cook. But women tend to cook in the home, while men predominate as restaurant chefs. Clearly, this is not a biologically driven division of labor. What could be the cultural reasons?

Even roles stereotypically associated with male strength and aggression do not fit an assumed binary gender division. Women do heavy labor—like women in many parts of the world who rise early to carry water drums miles from the well to their homes. Even the predominance of men in violence and warfare is shifting as militaries in many parts of the world increasingly rely on women soldiers. Because biology cannot predict the roles that men and women play in a given culture, anthropologists consider how gender is constructed culture by culture, and they explore the implications of those constructions for individuals in each context.

THE CULTURAL CONSTRUCTION OF GENDER

cultural construction of gender

The ways humans learn to perform and recognize behaviors as masculine or feminine within their cultural context.

Humans are born with biological sex, but we learn gender. From the moment we're born, we begin to learn culture, including how to walk, talk, eat, dress, think, practice religion, raise children, respond to violence, and express our emotions in gendered ways (Mauss 1979). We learn what kinds of behavior are perceived as masculine or feminine. Thus, anthropologists refer to the **cultural construction of gender.**

Family, friends, the media, doctors, educational institutions, religious communities, sports, and law all enculturate us with a sense of gender that becomes normative and seems natural. For example, parents "do gender" with their children. They assign them boy or girl names; dress them in gendered clothing, colors, and jewelry; and give them the "right" haircuts. Parents even speak to their children in gendered tones of voice. As we see gender being performed all around us, we learn to perform it in our turn. In these ways gender is taught, learned, performed, and policed.

Over a lifetime, gender becomes a powerful, and mostly invisible, framework that shapes how we see ourselves and others (Bern 1981, 1983). Our relationships with others become an elaborate gendered dance of playing, dating, mating, parenting, and loving that reinforces our learned ideas of **masculinity** and **femininity** and establishes differing roles and expectations. Gender is a potent cultural system through which we organize our collective lives—not necessarily on the basis of merit or skill but on the constructed categories of what it means to be a man or a woman (Bonvillain 2007; Brettell and Sargent 2009; Lorber 1994; Rubin 1975).

masculinity
The ideas and practices associated with manhood.

femininity
The ideas and practices associated with womanhood.

Teaching Gender in the United States: Boys, Girls, and Youth Sports.
Sports is a key cultural arena in which individuals learn gender roles. A study of children playing coed T-ball provides insights into how gender in the United States is subtly and not-so-subtly taught, learned, and enforced through youth sports (Landers and Fine 1996). In T-ball, the precursor to baseball and softball, kids hit a ball off a stationary, upright plastic stick (a tee) rather than a ball thrown from a pitcher.

Landers and Fine found that T-ball coaches established a hierarchy of opportunity, training, and encouragement that favored boys over girls. Boys consistently received more playing time than girls, played positions (such as shortstop or first base) that provided more opportunities to touch the ball and develop their skills, and had more opportunities to practice hitting the ball at the plate. Boys frequently received coaching advice, while girls' mistakes went uncorrected. Parents and other players supported this hierarchy of training and opportunity and, along with the coaches, offered less or more encouragement along gender lines. For example, boys received more words of praise for their successes. These hierarchies were apparent not only between boys and girls but within gendered groups as well. Among the boys, praise and opportunity were unequally distributed: Those who were already stronger, faster, better coordinated, or more advanced in their skills were favored over those who were not as advanced. Moving beyond the T-ball experience, the researchers noted that ideal forms of masculinity and manliness are taught, learned, and enforced on the baseball field as well, promoting aggressiveness, assertiveness,

competitiveness, physical strength and skill, and a drive to succeed and win (Landers and Fine 1996).

Did you ever participate in youth sports, either in the United States or in another country? If so, what was your experience like? Did your parents sign you up for certain sports—basketball, soccer, lacrosse, football, wrestling, ice hockey, dance, gymnastics, figure skating, cheerleading? If so, what role might their ideas of gender have played in their choice? How might the gender enculturation process in sports and physical play affect gender nonconforming, genderqueer, or trans kids? In considering Landers and Fine's study, can you see the ramifications of such gender training on individuals' attitudes and behaviors as they become adults with responsible roles in family, work, and politics?

While recognizing the physical differences between men and women—modest as they are when considering the diversity of the whole human population—how do we factor in the role of culture when considering gender differences in sports and athletic performance? Gender enculturation in sports and physical play begins early and happens in varied settings. I remember taking my toddler son to the playground and watching as other parents encouraged their little boys to run, climb, and jump while urging their little girls to play nicely in the sandbox. Starting in everyday settings like this, perhaps we can begin to imagine the cumulative effects of parental expectations, peer pressure, and media images on girls' motivation to engage in intense physical activity and competition or boys' willingness to express emotions, play with dolls, or take care of younger siblings. As a result, sports may reflect less about real physical differences in speed, endurance, and strength and more about how a given culture constructs and maintains gender and sex norms. Today, as training and opportunities increase, women are closing the performance gap with men in many sports. The gap between male and female marathon winners, for instance, has rapidly closed to less than ten minutes, and women are improving their times faster than men. But inequality of opportunity along gender lines persists through sports culture, including unequal access to coaching, nutrition, training facilities, and financing. As a result, definitive comparisons between women and men athletes cannot be made at this time (Wade and Ferree 2015).

Constructing Masculinity in a U.S. High School. Since the 1970s, gender studies have focused primarily on women. Recent studies, however, have begun to explore the gender construction of male identity as well as the broader construction of masculinity. The ethnography described here touches on several key aspects of this complex process.

C.J. Pascoe's ethnography *Dude, You're a Fag* (2007) explores the construction of gender—and particularly masculinity—in a suburban, working-class, racially diverse high school in north-central California. Calling someone a fag, what Pascoe calls "fag discourse," occurred almost exclusively among White male students in a daily banter of teasing, bullying, and harassment. Basing her conclusions on interviews with students, Pascoe found that calling someone a fag was not about whether someone was or was not gay; instead, it was directed at guys who danced like girls, cared about their clothing, seemed too emotional, or did something incompetent. In other words, White male students directed the epithet at other males who were not considered sufficiently masculine. Gay guys were tolerated as long as they were not effeminate, as long as they could throw a football around. Among the teenagers in Pascoe's study, fag discourse became a powerful tool for enforcing the boundaries of masculinity—a disciplinary mechanism for making sure "boys are boys" through the implied threat of abuse or violence.

Moreover, Pascoe points out that masculinity is not always associated with men. Girls can act masculine as well. She describes a group of "masculine" girls who play on the girls' basketball team and "perform masculinity" in how they dress, display their sexuality, and dominate public spaces around the school. Jessie, a lesbian, is also homecoming queen and president of the student council. Her popularity appears to be related to her performance of masculinity. In these contexts, masculinity and dominance are linked to women's bodies, not to men's. Pascoe thus points out the ways in which both guys and girls can perform masculinity and how girls can adopt masculinity to gain status (Bridges 2007; Calderwood 2008; Wilkins 2008).

THE PERFORMANCE OF GENDER

Recently, anthropologists have moved from focusing on gender roles toward examining **gender performance.** Gender roles can mistakenly be seen as reflecting stable, fixed identities that fall in one of two opposite extremes—male or female. But

gender performance
The way gender identity is expressed through action.

anthropologists increasingly see gender as a continuum of behavior that ranges between masculine and feminine. Rather than being something fixed in the psyche, gender is an identity that is expressed through action (Butler 1990).

My students, when identifying stereotypical masculine and feminine characteristics, often create something similar to the following list:

- *Masculine*: aggressive, physical, tough, competitive, sports oriented, testosterone driven, strong, unemotional

- *Feminine*: gentle, kind, loving, nurturing, smart, persuasive, talkative, enticing, emotional

But we know that both women and men can display any of these characteristics, and any individual may display various characteristics at different times depending on the setting. A man may perform his masculinity—his gender—differently when watching football with his buddies than when out on a date. Indeed, people regularly make choices—conscious and unconscious—about how they will express their gender identity, for whom, and in what context. This is why we say that gender is performed (Butler 1990; Weston 2001; Valentine 2007).

Machismo in Mexico. The construction of masculinity does not necessarily yield a rigid result, as the following study reveals. In *The Meanings of Macho* (2007), Matthew Gutmann examines what it means to be a man, *ser hombre*, for the men and women of a small neighborhood in Mexico City. Common understandings of *machismo* as the concept has spread around the world feature stereotypes of self-centered, sexist, tough guys. When "macho" is applied to men in Latin America, especially working-class Mexican men, these stereotypes can also include insinuations of violence, drug use, infidelity, and gambling. However, Gutmann's research in a working-class community reveals a complex male world of fathers, husbands, friends, and lovers that does not fit the common stereotypes.

For the men Gutmann studied, machismo and masculinity constitute a shifting landscape. What it means to be a man (or a woman) in the community can depend on the particular man or woman or the particular circumstance. One of Gutmann's key informants, the elderly Don Timo, rails against effeminate men but has himself crossed stereotypical gender boundaries by actively helping to raise his children. Two other informants, Tono and Gabriel, who are tough young men, argue about a

What does it mean to be macho? Here, a father holds his baby in Oaxaca, Mexico.

father's proper role in buying children's Christmas presents. These examples illustrate the fluidity of male identity in the population that Gutmann studied.

Ultimately, Guttmann discovered such complex male identities that he found it impossible to use any simple formula to describe a typical Mexican man, a Mexican urban working-class man, or a macho Mexican. Instead, the men in the community he studied worked out their roles together with women, debating and deciding about household chores, child rearing, sex, the use of money, work outside the home, and the use of alcohol (Limon 1997; Parker 1999). How do these processes take place in your own family?

Viewing gender as a performance enables us to broaden our thinking beyond easy dichotomies and universal characteristics of "man" and "woman." And by approaching gender this way, we can more easily see that stratification based on gender is not fixed and natural; rather, it emerges as a result of decisions to arrange access to power, privilege, and resources in particular ways.

MAP 7.1
Mexico City

Are There More Than Two Sexes?

Explain the diversity of biological sex beyond the
male–female binary.

As our earlier discussion of sexual dimorphism indicated, primary characteristics of biological sex do not always fit neatly into the two assumed categories of male and female. In fact, scholars recognize more than two biological sexes, as discussed below. Moreover, even when we can identify a person's biological sex, we cannot predict what gender roles that person will play in a given culture. Subsequently, sex does not always correlate with society's assumptions around gender.

A THEORY OF FIVE SEXES

Biologist Anne Fausto-Sterling (1993, 2000) has proposed a theory that sheds light on the issue of fluidity versus rigidity in conceptualizing categories of biological sex and their relationship to gender identity. In her article "The Five Sexes: Why Male and Female Are Not Enough," Fausto-Sterling describes the middle ground between these two absolute categories. This middle ground encompasses a diversity of physical expressions along the continuum between male and female that are described as **intersex.**

A review of medical data from 1955 to 2000 suggests that "approximately 1.7% of all live births do not conform to [the] ideal of absolute sex chromosome, gonadal, genital and hormonal dimorphism" (Blackless et al. 2000, 151). Using these statistics, we may estimate that millions of people are born with some

intersex

The state of being born with a combination of male and female genitalia, gonads, and/or chromosomes.

combination of male and female genitalia, gonads, and chromosomes. Some have a balance of female and male sexual characteristics—for instance, one testis and one ovary. Others have female genitalia but testes rather than ovaries. Still others have male genitalia with ovaries rather than testes.

Most Western societies ignore the existence of middle sexes. More commonly, they legally require a determination of male or female to be made at birth. Furthermore, since the 1960s, Western medicine has taken the extreme steps of attempting to "manage" intersexuality through surgery and hormonal treatments. According to the 2000 American Academy of Pediatrics policy statement on intersex surgery, "the birth of a child with ambiguous genitalia constitutes a social emergency" (American Academy of Pediatrics 2000, 138). Medical procedures—most performed before a child comes of age and can decide for themselves—aim to align intersex infants' sex characteristics with the cultural norm for either males or females, although about 90 percent of the surgeries make ambiguous male anatomy into female. Decisions are often based on the size of the penis: The smaller the phallus, the more likely it is that the surgery will reassign the person as female. These interventions represent what French social scientist Michel Foucault ([1976] 1990) has referred to as *biopower*—the power of the state to regulate the body—in this case through control of biological sex characteristics in order to meet a cultural need for clear distinctions between the sexes.

These medical interventions have faced increasing criticism both within the medical profession and among advocacy and support groups such as the Intersex Society of North America (www.isna.org), InterConnect (https://interconnect .support/), and interACT: Advocates for Intersex Youth (https://interactadvocates .org). Such groups have worked to educate the public and the medical community about the experiences of intersex people, particularly about their right to control decisions about their sexual and gender identities. In 2006, *Pediatrics*, the journal of the American Academy of Pediatrics, published new guidelines that urge practicing greater patient-centered care, avoiding "elective" surgery until the person is old enough to make their own decision, and eliminating misleading and outdated language (such as *hermaphrodite*) that distracts from treating the whole person.

The presence of middle sexes suggests that we must reconceptualize one of our most rigid mental maps of reality—the one separating male and female. In the process, perhaps we will recognize that just as gender is culturally constructed, our ideas of human biology have been culturally constructed as well. Acknowledgment of a diversity of physical expressions along the continuum between male and female may, in turn, allow for a less dualistic and more holistic approach to understanding the complex relationship between biology and gender (Davis 2015).

ALTERNATE SEXES, ALTERNATE GENDERS

Cross-cultural studies show that while many cultures fix sexuality and gender in only two distinct categories, many others allow room for diversity. Certainly, the gender binary is being contested in U.S. culture as trans experiences are increasingly integrated into mainstream media and popular culture, for instance, via the television shows *Orange is the New Black*, *Transparent*, and *Pose*. In India, even though the country's dominant system for mapping sex and gender strongly emphasizes two opposite but complementary roles (male and female), Indian culture also recognizes many alternative constructions. Hindu religion acknowledges these variations in myth, art, and ritual. Hindu myths feature androgynous and intersex figures, and Hindu art depicts a blending of sexes and genders, including males with wombs, breasts, or pregnant bellies. In terms of Hindu ritual, the following discussion explores the role of one alternative group, known as *hijras*, in expressing gender diversity in India.

The Role of *Hijras* in Hindu Ritual. *Hijras* are religious followers of the Hindu Mother Goddess Bahuchara Mata, who is often depicted and described as transgender. Most *hijras* are born as men, though some may be intersex. In *Neither Man nor Woman: The Hijras of India* (1998) and subsequent writing, Serena Nanda has analyzed these individuals and their role in demonstrating gender diversity.

Hindu religious myth, art, and ritual acknowledge alternative gender constructions like this depiction of Ardhanari, an androgynous deity composed of Shiva and his consort Parvati.

Through ritual initiation and, for some, extensive ritual surgery to remove their penis and testicles (an operation now outlawed in India), *hijras* become an alternative sex and gender. Culturally, they are viewed as neither man nor woman, although they tend to adopt many characteristics of the woman's role. Because of their transgression of cultural and religious boundaries, they are at once feared and revered. Many live in *hijra* religious communities on the margins of Hindu society. *Hijras* often face extreme discrimination in employment, housing, health, and education. Many support themselves through begging, ritual performances, and sex work. Violence against them is not uncommon, particularly against *hijra* sex workers.

At the same time, *hijras* are revered as auspicious and powerful ritual figures. They perform at weddings and at birth celebrations—particularly at the birth of a son. They not only bless the child and family but also entertain the celebrants and guests with burlesque and sexually suggestive songs, dance, and comedy. Their life in the middle ground between strong cultural norms of male and female contributes to their ritual power (Nanda 1998; Saria 2021). These insights underscore the potential for more complex understandings of sex and gender that move beyond assumptions of two discrete categories of male and female, masculine and feminine.

Two-Spirits in Native North American Cultures. According to accounts written over the past 100 years, many Native North American cultures have had traditions of gender diversity. Such traditions have supported a gender alternative now commonly referred to as Two-Spirits (Roscoe 1991; Williams 1992). Some of these transgender men and women adopted roles and behaviors of the opposite gender. In certain cases, people considered them to have both feminine and masculine spirits. Often they were considered to have supernatural powers and thus held special privileges in the community.

Since 1990, the term *Two-Spirits*, a direct borrowing from the Ojibwe language, has risen in popular and scholarly usage after being proposed by participants of the third annual Native American/First Nations Gay and Lesbian Conference in Winnipeg, Canada. No common term exists across Native cultures for alternative gender patterns, nor are the historical or contemporary practices indicated by these terms by any means uniform. Instead, many different terms have served to represent local expressions of alternative gender and sexuality among Native Americans—for example, *winkte* (Lakota), *kwido* (Tewa), and *nadleeh* (Navajo; Jacobs 1997).

Current studies of sex and gender diversity in contemporary Native American communities attempt to de-romanticize the accounts offered by earlier anthropologists, historians, and other social scientists of a tolerant Native American life for those who were not heterosexual. These idealized views do not match the experiences of many gay, lesbian, transgender, or Two-Spirit Native Americans today who have experienced homophobia or transphobia rather than acceptance both within and beyond their Native American communities (Jacobs 1997).

How Do Anthropologists Explore the Relationship between Power and Gender?

Describe how gender works as a system of power that includes stratification and ideologies.

Although gender is often regarded as affecting individuals on a personal basis—for instance, how you negotiate relationships with people you date, study with, or work for—anthropology illuminates how gender structures relationships of power that have far-reaching effects. Understanding these processes becomes increasingly important as individuals and cultures experience heightened interaction in today's global age (Mascia-Lees 2009).

BOUNDARIES OF GENDER AND SEXUALITY AT THE CANADIAN BORDER

In his book *Real Queer? Sexual Orientation and Gender Identity Refugees in the Canadian Refugee Apparatus* (2015), York University anthropologist David Murray explores the Canadian government's high-stakes process for assessing asylum claims based on sexual orientation, gender identity and expression, and sex characteristics (SOGIESC). Claimants face a daunting double challenge. They must first prove their identity. Then they must prove that they faced persecution in their countries of origin. The Canadian government has welcomed lesbian, gay, bisexual, and transgender refugees for more than twenty years, and it has more recently expanded its framework to include gender identity and gender expression. Still, many applicants are turned down. Through intensive ethnographic fieldwork with asylum seekers, court officers, and a number of well-established LGBTQ and immigrant social service agencies and support groups in Toronto, Murray examines the complex process through which SOGIESC refugee claimants navigate the Canadian refugee apparatus, establish a credible story line, and convince the Canadian Immigration and Refugee Board (IRB) that they are, as Murray frames it, "real" queer.

Murray's book focuses on arrivals from Latin America, the Caribbean, Africa, and Eastern Europe who petition for refugee status after crossing the border into Canada. Their expressions of gender and sexuality vary widely across cultures, defying easy international definition and creating inconsistencies in an adjudication system heavily informed by normative Western notions of gender and sexuality. In this context, refugee claimants deploy a wide array of creative strategies to learn about and prepare for their immigration hearings. Many join refugee support groups to gather information, make friends, and find safe spaces in an unfamiliar country. They seek out the advice of social workers, lawyers, and fellow refugees. Most volunteer with an LGBTQ, HIV/AIDS-focused, or other community organization while they await their hearing in the hope of receiving a reference letter from the group that can be used to help establish their credibility. But Toronto's nonprofits have a complicated, if carefully cultivated, role in this arena. They do serve as advocates and frequently write letters of support for many volunteers, which can serve as key pieces of evidence in their cases. But Murray criticizes the groups for engaging in a kind of surveillance for the state, effectively becoming informal screeners for the Canadian IRB of a claimant's legitimacy.

In most cases, the asylum seeker's case depends heavily on their personal narrative. Credible documents proving repressive conditions in their home countries may be partial or completely unavailable, so how they present themselves in formal hearings often determines the outcome. Lawyers, LGBTQ support workers, and nonprofit staff may help SOGIESC applicants understand the process and structure of the hearings. They may also help them tell their stories in ways that will appear to the court to be credible and authentic. Convincing stories are best told in the right order and with the necessary components. Over time, successful claimants learn to present themselves in ways that conform to preconceptions of an authentic SOGIESC refugee in the eyes of refugee workers, other refugees, and decision makers. Murray notes the particular importance of aligning these stories with the dominant Canadian national narrative. If Canadians, and most importantly, the personnel of the Canadian IRB, view refugees' home countries as backward, homophobic, and repressive, while Canada stands out as an international safe haven where all are welcome, then refugee claimants must credibly align their stories within that narrative. This can be particularly challenging for claimants who have fond memories of home, despite having to flee, and those who have experienced homophobia and racism in Canada after arrival.

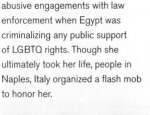

Activist Sarah Hegazi sought asylum in Canada after abusive engagements with law enforcement when Egypt was criminalizing any public support of LGBTQ rights. Though she ultimately took her life, people in Naples, Italy organized a flash mob to honor her.

Murray reflects on the particular difficulties that SOGIESC refugees have telling compelling and authentic narratives. Their stories frequently involve intimate, emotional narratives about desires, identities, practices, experiences, and journeys that are extremely private, frequently violent, and often previously unspoken or even unspeakable. How does a refugee claimant learn to present these intimate details successfully and credibly in the formalized, legalistic environment of the Canadian IRB? At times, some SOGIESC individuals, especially those with more fluid gender identities, may choose to present an identity and a narrative that is not authentic in order to avoid speaking about some details of their lives or in order to align their stories with IRB expectations and formal guidance on who is "real" queer and who is not. By exploring the experiences of refugee claimants crossing this highly regulated nation-state border, Murray, whose book has since contributed to a rethinking of Canadian refugee guidelines, sheds light on the unique challenges of translating gender identities and experiences, concepts of biological sex, and expressions of sexuality across cultures and countries.

REVISITING EARLY RESEARCH ON MALE DOMINANCE

A quick look at some statistics reveals the current contours of women's struggles worldwide: Sixty percent of the world's poorest people are women and girls. More than half of all children unable to attend school are girls. The chance of dying because of pregnancy in sub-Saharan Africa is 1 in 196, but in the developed world it is only 1 in 6,250. Young women ages fifteen to twenty-five are being infected with HIV/AIDS three times faster than men in the same age group. Women are disproportionately affected by environmental degradation. Only 25 percent of the world's parliamentarians are women (United Nations Women 2020). It is not hard to conclude from these facts that gender plays a key role in power relationships on many levels and in many arenas.

As gender studies emerged in anthropology in the 1970s, one of the first targets of research was the apparent universality of male dominance across cultures. In searching for an explanation for what appeared to be women's universally low status, anthropologist Sherri Ortner (1974) proposed the existence of a pervasive, symbolic association of women with nature and men with culture (which was more highly valued). Ortner argued that the biological functions of reproduction, breast-feeding, and child rearing associated women with nature and placed them at a consistent disadvantage in negotiating relationships of power.

At the same time, Michelle Rosaldo (1974) saw the gender roles of men and women across cultures as being split between public and private spheres. Women, constrained by their role in reproduction, were confined to the private, or domestic, sphere—including the home, family, and childbearing. Men tended to dominate the public sphere—politics, economic exchange, and religious ritual. Because wealth and social status accrued to activities in the public sphere, men gained and maintained more power, privilege, and prestige than women did. Some scholars speculated that these patterns were rooted in the human evolutionary past—a proposition we will challenge later in this chapter. Others suggested that they might derive from men's superior physical strength (see also Chodorow 1974).

As scholars looked more carefully at women's lives in particular cultures, however, the picture became even more complicated. Previous assumptions

In contrast to Malinowski's earlier study (1922), why did feminist anthropologist Annette Weiner's research (1976) find Trobriand Island women engaged in significant economic activity, including the elaborate exchange of banana leaf bundles and banana fiber skirts (*left*), as well as participation in the yam harvest festival (*right*)?

MAP 7.2
Trobriand Islands

about universal male dominance, including the gendered division of labor and uniformly separate spheres of activity and power, were revealed to be historically inaccurate, overly simplistic in their reading of contemporary cultures, and prone to overlooking the specific contexts of stratification and inequality (Leacock 1981). This was true not only for women's lives but for men's as well, where wealth, power, and prestige were stratified both within and between gender groups (Quinn 1977; Rosaldo 1980).

Feminist scholars also began to revisit earlier anthropological research. Perhaps not surprisingly, these scholars discovered the significant role of women in cultures that earlier anthropologists had reported to be uniformly dominated by men. In one important reconsideration of a classic anthropological text, Annette Weiner (1976) revisited Bronisław Malinowski's research on the Trobriand Islands (see Chapter 3), an archipelago of coral atolls just east of Papua New Guinea in the South Pacific. When Weiner reexamined the economic practices of the Trobriand Islands in the 1970s with an eye to the role of gender in shaping economic activity, she found that Malinowski's research was incomplete. In *Women of Value, Men of Renown: New Perspectives in Trobriand Exchange* (1976), Weiner describes the much more complex and significant roles of Trobriand Island women in economic exchange, kinship, and ritual life. These exchanges were closely interconnected with the yam exchanges that Malinowski had described, but his failure to see the significance of the women's activity engendered an inaccurate view of them as inconsequential to Trobriand economic life.

The emerging anthropological scholarship of gender in the 1970s provided new tools for Weiner to overcome gender blindness and, instead, see the fullness of Trobriand culture. She wrote:

Any study that does not include the role of women—as seen by women—as part of the way the society is structured remains only a partial study of that society. Whether women are publicly valued or privately secluded, whether they control politics, a range of economic commodities, or merely magic spells, they function within that society, not as objects, but as individuals with some measure of control. (Weiner 1976, 228)

Weiner's example and admonition resonate throughout anthropology today.

GENDER STEREOTYPES, GENDER IDEOLOGY, AND GENDER STRATIFICATION

Gender studies' emphasis on the cultural construction of gender challenges anthropologists to explore the dynamics of specific cultures to understand what processes serve to construct gender in each society. Today, anthropologists are asking questions like: What are the processes that create **gender stratification**—an unequal distribution of power in which gender shapes who has access to a group's resources, opportunities, rights, and privileges? What are the gender stereotypes and gender ideologies that support a gendered system of power (Brodkin 2007)?

Gender stereotypes are widely held and powerful, preconceived notions about the attributes of, differences between, and proper roles for women and men in a culture. Men, for instance, may be stereotyped as more aggressive, whereas women might be seen as more nurturing. These stereotypes create important assumptions about what men and women might expect from one another. **Gender ideology** is a set of cultural ideas—usually stereotypical—about men's and women's essential character, capabilities, and value that consciously or unconsciously promote and justify gender stratification. Gender stereotypes and ideologies vary from culture to culture, though their effects may appear similar when viewed through a global lens.

We now consider two ways in which gender ideologies have influenced thinking in U.S. culture.

The Egg and the Sperm. Emily Martin (1991) has explored the ways in which cultural ideas about gender—that is, gender ideologies—have influenced how biologists have understood, described, and taught about human reproduction. In particular, Martin discusses what she calls the fairy tale of the egg and the sperm. By examining the most widely used college biology textbooks at the time of her research, Martin found that the distinct roles of eggs and sperm were described in stereotypical ways, even if those descriptions did not match up with more recent scientific findings.

gender stratification

An unequal distribution of power in which gender shapes who has access to a group's resources, opportunities, rights, and privileges.

gender stereotypes

Widely held preconceived notions about the attributes of, differences between, and proper roles for men and women in a culture.

gender ideology

A set of cultural ideas, usually stereotypical, about the essential character of different genders that functions to promote and justify gender stratification.

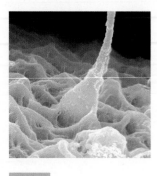

Are the stories you have been told about the meeting of the sperm (blue) and the egg (pink) drawn from biological research or cultural gender stereotypes?

The textbooks that Martin studied described the aggressive sperm as being propelled by strongly beating tails, searching for the egg in competition with fellow ejaculates, and attacking and penetrating the protective barriers of the egg to fertilize the passive, waiting, receiving egg.

Yet Martin cites biology research that reveals a very different dynamic. The tail of the sperm actually beats quite weakly and does not propel the sperm forward. Instead, the tail serves only to move the head from side to side enough to keep the sperm from getting stuck on all surfaces except the egg. When the egg and the sperm do connect, the sperm is not the assertive aggressor. Rather, adhesive molecules on both create a chemical bond that keeps them attached. Then, the sperm and egg work in tandem. The sperm secretes a dissolving fluid that allows it to move toward the egg's nucleus. At the same time, the egg draws the sperm in and actually moves its own nucleus to meet the sperm and better enable fertilization. Thus, rather than displaying active and passive roles, the egg and the sperm appear to be mutually active partners in an egalitarian relationship.

According to Martin, writing in the early 1990s, images of the egg and sperm found in popular and scientific writing have commonly been based on cultural stereotypes of male and female. Moreover, the scientific language of biology has promoted these gender stereotypes. Men are considered more active, vigorous, adventurous, and important than women, who are seen as passive, receptive, nurturing, less valuable, and less significant. Martin warns that by reading stereotypical feminine and masculine behavior into our accounts of eggs and sperm, we enshrine these gender roles in nature—we make them seem natural. In turn, when this narrative becomes a common description of nature, it reinforces culturally constructed gender patterns, roles, and hierarchies. Such a process of misinformation might cause someone to believe, mistakenly: "Of course those characteristics of men and women are natural and normal—they show up at the very beginning with the behavior of the sperm and the egg!"

Man the Hunter, Woman the Gatherer. Another familiar story that lies at the heart of U.S. gender ideologies is the tale of Man the Hunter, Woman the Gatherer. This fiction is frequently invoked to explain contemporary differences in gender roles by referencing the effects of human evolution. In our deep past, the story goes, human males—being larger and stronger than females—hunted to sustain themselves, their sexual partners, and their offspring (Lee and Devore 1968; Lee 2003). Hunting required aggression, inventiveness, dominant behavior, male bonding, mobility, time away from the home, and less time with offspring—all patterns that we imagine have become hardwired into the human brain or imprinted on human DNA. The ancient pleasure of killing animals supposedly shaped the human male psyche's predilection for aggression and violence and continues to drive men today. Women, in contrast, were gatherers (Dahlberg

Ancient petroglyphs (rock carvings) discovered in the mountains north of the Saudi Arabian city of Ḥā'il appear to depict a hunting party. Were they men, as hunter-gatherer stereotypes would suggest?

1981). They collected fruits, seeds, and nuts and were more sedentary, home oriented, child centered, nurturing, cooperative, talkative, and passive.

This story, closely associated today with the field of evolutionary psychology, underlies much contemporary thinking about the origins and "naturalness" of gender relations. Contemporary gender roles, divisions of labor, and stratifications of power, resources, rights, and privileges are assumed to have emerged directly from physical or mental differences that developed during human evolution. So, for instance, because early human males were hunters 2 million years ago, today modern human men prefer to go off to work, compete in the marketplace, and leave child rearing and housecleaning to the women. Quite simple, really—or is it?

Despite the popularity of this scenario in explaining contemporary male and female behavior, anthropological evidence does not support it. Yes, food foraging—hunting, scavenging, and gathering—was our ancestors' primary survival strategy for millions of years before the introduction of agriculture 10,000 years ago. Hundreds of thousands of people still live in societies where food foraging is a significant means of making a living. But no contemporary foraging societies or nonhuman primate groups display the division of labor described in the Man the Hunter, Woman the Gatherer story. In known foraging societies, women are not sedentary or passive members of the group (Stange 1997).

Though men appear to have done 70 percent of the hunting, it is not even clear that hunting was the foundational activity of early human groups. In fact, human patterns of group interaction more likely developed through the gathering and sharing of plant and seed resources. Archaeological evidence reveals that early hominid teeth were adapted to an omnivorous diet—most likely of plants, seeds, and meat, depending on what food was available in a particular season or area. Hunting would have contributed to this foundation when available, rather than the reverse. Meat may have been a part of the diet, but there is no conclusive evidence that our earliest human ancestors hunted prey themselves. Just as likely, they scavenged meat left behind by other predators (Fedigan 1986).

Anthropologists have found no evidence to prove the existence of historical patterns of male dominance, including the protection of dependent women and children. Instead, contemporary food-foraging cultures and the archaeological record on gender roles reveal a highly flexible division of labor that enabled human groups to adapt quickly to changing conditions. In fact, a flexibility of roles rather than a clear division of labor may more properly characterize male–female relationships over human evolutionary history. Based on the evidence currently available, Man the Hunter, Woman the Gatherer—much like Martin's description of the fairy tale of the egg and the sperm—appears to be the result of a modern-day cultural myth about gender projected back onto human evolutionary history. This "history," in turn, serves to imbue contemporary gender patterns with an appearance of inevitability and "naturalness" (Fedigan 1986).

Despite the archaeological, physical, and cultural evidence that anthropologists have accumulated to debunk the Man the Hunter, Woman the Gatherer myth, it is still a daunting task to shake free of the popular idea in U.S. culture that men and women have some essential—and essentially different—nature that was shaped in our deep past. The stereotypical "boys will be boys" and "that's just a girl thing" approach to gender differences has become a powerful gender ideology, deeply ingrained in the day-to-day conversations, expectations, relationships, work patterns, pay packages, promotions, and political activities of contemporary life.

Perhaps it is simpler to believe that our genetic blueprint predetermines who we are as men and women. Perhaps this belief in the inevitability of gendered cultural patterns makes us feel better about the gender inequality structured into our cultural practices and institutions. Why try to change what is "inevitable and natural"? But if these cultural ways of thinking about gender mask gender's essential changeability, then the burden lies more heavily on the individual, the community, and the body politic to challenge patterns of power, privilege, and prestige drawn along gender lines.

CHALLENGING GENDER IDEOLOGIES AND STRATIFICATION

Women challenge and resist gender stereotypes, ideologies, inequalities, and violence directly and indirectly through creative local strategies, often building movements from the bottom up. Although lacking the global media attention or global solidarity afforded to international social movements, these local initiatives begin with women's culture-specific experiences (Abu-Lughod 2000).

Mothers of "The Disappeared" in El Salvador.

Between 1977 and 1992, the Central American country of El Salvador was torn by a brutal civil war. Threatened by calls for economic equality and political openness, the government unleashed military and military-related death squads in a campaign of violence and terror that targeted students, peasants, union leaders, and anyone else critical of its policies. All who expressed opposition to government policies were labeled subversive and subject to reprisal.

MAP 7.3

El Salvador

Over the course of the civil war, the military assassinated, imprisoned, tortured, raped, and "disappeared" tens of thousands of Salvadorans. One in every 100 was murdered or disappeared. The late 1970s were marked by particularly brutal campaigns. Every morning, residents of the capital city awoke to the sight of dead bodies—visibly tortured—left lying in the streets or dumped on the outskirts of town by the death squads. Many were disappeared—that is, detained and never seen again.

The grassroots women's organization CO-MADRES (The Committee of Mothers and Relatives of Political Prisoners, Disappeared, and Assassinated of El Salvador) emerged against this backdrop. The committee was one of a number of "motherist" groups across Central America in which the mothers of victims mobilized for human rights and against violence. Originally founded in 1977 by nine mothers, CO-MADRES quickly grew to include teachers, workers, students, lawyers, housewives, and shopkeepers—still mostly mothers, but with a few fathers as well. CO-MADRES became one of the first groups in El Salvador to challenge the brutal actions of the government and the military.

Initially, the women of CO-MADRES focused on demanding information from government, military, and paramilitary groups about family members who had been incarcerated, assassinated, or disappeared. The women occupied government buildings, demonstrated in public parks and plazas, and held hunger strikes to exert pressure on the state. Searching for their missing relatives, they demanded access to prisons and prisoner lists, uncovered clandestine cemeteries, and formed alliances with international human rights groups to publicize the Salvadoran government's atrocities.

As they became better organized, the women of CO-MADRES began to participate in movements for greater democratization, particularly demanding the inclusion of women at all levels of El Salvador's political decision-making bodies. Eventually, along with other feminist movements emerging globally, CO-MADRES began to address concerns about the prevalence of gender-based violence and rape and the absence of sex education and sexual autonomy for women in El Salvador.

CO-MADRES continued to work throughout the Salvadoran civil war despite attacks on the organization and its leaders by the government and its allies. CO-MADRES offices were bombed on multiple occasions. A majority of active CO-MADRES members and all of its leaders were detained, tortured, and raped: Forty-eight were detained, five assassinated, and three disappeared. In El Salvador, rape became a common experience for the women activists of CO-MADRES and for urban and rural Salvadoran women, whether they participated in a social movement or not.

CO-MADRES activist Alicia Panameno de Garcia, in an interview with anthropologist Lynn Stephen ("LS" in the dialogue below), shared how rape had become a widely used weapon of state-sponsored torture and how psychologically difficult it was to talk about it openly, even with other women victims:

DE GARCIA: Rape was one of those things we didn't really think about. We weren't really prepared for it happening to us. We didn't think that the military would systematically be using these practices. So the first few women were detained and they were raped and because we are taught that women are supposed to be pure, they didn't talk about that. They didn't say, "They did this to me."

LS: They didn't talk about it?

DE GARCIA: Yes. But little by little we discovered it. The women started talking about it. They had to because it had consequences for their health. They needed medical assistance and when we would give people medical aid we started discovering that every one of the women had been raped. (Stephen 1995, 818)

Over time, the CO-MADRES members found that detained men were also being raped as part of their torture. The men were even more reluctant to talk about it than the women.

Eventually, CO-MADRES created a space for women to discuss their experiences publicly, to bring the sexual brutality of the military out into the open, and to talk about their fears—particularly that their husbands would abandon them. Working with other human rights organizations, the group began a process of holding the state accountable for these violations and calling into question discriminatory legal codes that provided no rights to rape victims.

The story of CO-MADRES is just one example of the determined, creative, and often risk-filled efforts that women undertake across the globe to address gendered expressions of inequality, stratification, and violence. In an evolving response to their experiences in the midst of El Salvador's civil war, the women

of CO-MADRES created a social movement that integrated traditional cultural expressions of femininity—ideas of motherhood, child rearing, and sacrifice for one's children—with direct confrontation of military death squads and government authorities as they demanded equality for women and sought to protect their families and their communities (Martin 1999; Molyneux 1999; Stephen 1995).

How Is Globalization Transforming Gender Roles and Stratification?

Assess how globalization is reshaping gender roles and stratification in local contexts.

Beginning in the 1980s, anthropologists turned their attention to the impacts of globalization on women and gender dynamics in local economies. Flexible accumulation—relocation of the production process through both offshoring factories and outsourcing jobs—has spurred increasing migration of women from rural areas to work in urban, coastal, export-oriented factories established by foreign corporations searching for cheap labor, low taxes, and few environmental regulations. As both local and national economies have continued to undergo rapid transitions, these women have had to negotiate between traditional gender expectations and the pressure to engage in wage labor to support themselves and their families (Mills 2003).

IMPACTS ON WOMEN IN THE LABOR FORCE

Working women in various parts of the globe have experienced similar challenges at the volatile intersection of globalization and local realities (Fernández-Kelly et al. 1983).

MAP 7.4
Barbados

Carla Freeman's *High Tech and High Heels in the Global Economy* (2000) explores the gendered production processes in export factories on the Caribbean island of Barbados. Many women there work in the informatics industry: They do computer data entry of airline tickets and insurance claims, and they key in manuscripts for everything from romance novels to academic journals. Instead of toiling in garment or electronics sweatshops, these women enjoy working in cool, air-conditioned, modern offices. Freeman asks whether the comfortable conditions in the data-processing factories represent an improved position in the global economy for Barbadian women or whether this new factory formation is simply another expression of women's exploitation through flexible accumulation.

Key distinctions separate the Barbadian informatics workers from those in other studies. They enjoy improved work conditions. As wives, mothers, and heads of households, rather than young, single, temporary sweatshop workers, they have won concessions from the company that include transportation, higher levels of job security, and more flexible work hours to care for their families. Freeman labels these women "pink-collar" workers because they fall between the blue-collar work done on the sweatshop factory floor and the white-collar work carried out in the higher-wage environment of the front office.

Despite the improved working conditions and social status for Barbadian women working in informatics, the company owners strive to extract maximum efficiency from them. Supervisors walk the floor and observe through glass windows to ensure continual surveillance. Managers calculate the keystrokes of each computer terminal. Wages are no higher than those of the typical sweatshop worker; in some cases, they are lower. The skills of data entry are not transferable to higher-wage clerical work. Women often need to take on additional work sewing, selling in the market, or working in beauty salons to support their families.

Freeman explores the ways in which the Barbadian women express their agency in the face of the informatics factory controls. These women use their status working with computers in air-conditioned offices to negotiate a different class status in the local community. They use clothing to fashion their local identities as well. Indeed, the women workers are preoccupied with fashion: They wear colorful, tailored skirt suits with jewelry, high heels, and the latest hairstyles. With their clothes, these women perform a professional and modern gender identity that enhances their local reputations and distinguishes them from other low-wage workers in garment and textile factories.

Freeman's research adds to scholarly findings that women factory workers are not simply victims of the exploitative practices of flexible accumulation. Instead, by engaging these capitalist practices directly, women assert their own desires and goals in ways that transform the interaction between the local and the global (England 2002; Richman 2001).

GENDERED PATTERNS OF GLOBAL MIGRATION

Globalization spurs the migration of women seeking to support themselves and their families. Women are moving as never before within and between countries in a largely invisible flow. Each year, tens of millions of women leave their homes and travel to urban areas to seek jobs in cities and export-processing factories in their own countries. Millions more leave developing countries in search of work abroad to support their families back home. As an alternative to finding jobs in export-processing factories, many women immigrants work as nannies, cleaning ladies, maids, or home health aides in North America, Europe, Asia, and the Middle East. In so doing, they fill the shortage of what is known as "care work" in wealthier countries (Hondagneu-Sotelo 2001).

Pei-Chia Lan's (2006) study of Filipino and Indonesian care workers laboring for newly rich families in Taiwan reveals the ways women—both employers

Globalization is reshaping the lives of working women as corporations search the world for cheap labor, low taxes, and fewer environmental restrictions. But are women reshaping globalization? Here, women labor in an international call center in Barbados.

MAP 7.5
Taiwan, the Philippines, and Indonesia

and workers, madams and maids—create new flows of global migration that destabilize traditional gendered and patriarchal roles in surprising ways.

As Taiwan's economy has expanded, first-generation Taiwanese career women, many from newly middle-class, dual-income families, have opted to meet their traditional filial and patriarchal family obligations as mother, wife, and daughter-in-law by hiring transnational migrant women domestic workers to do what was expected of their mothers in previous generations. Consuming transnational domestic labor—specifically the care work of Filipino and Indonesian women—allows them to move into the male workforce while still satisfying traditional expectations of womanhood.

In contrast, Filipino and Indonesian women convert their transnational migration and domestic labor into remittances that provide the major source of support for their families at home. In the process, they assert new status roles as primary breadwinners, though their absence—often for years at a time—severely limits their ability to fulfill the more traditional roles of mother, wife, and daughter. Lan calls these immigrant domestic workers "global Cinderellas"—women who dream of escaping poverty and finding freedom through care work abroad yet whose emancipation is built upon oppression and exploitation within their employer's home.

Anthropologists, whether studying gender, sexuality, kinship, race, ethnicity, religion, or any other cultural construct, seek to understand the rich diversity of human bodies and human lives, both past and present, to unlock the pre-suppositions that reside in mental maps of reality. As we analyze gender, we strive to unmask the structures of power that create unequal opportunities and unequal access to rights and resources along gender lines. These inequalities are far from natural, essential aspects of human life and human community. Rather, they are cultural constructs established in specific historical moments and cultural contexts. Through a careful analysis and exposure of gender as a culturally constructed system of power—not a fixed and natural pattern of human relationship—anthropologists hope to participate in opening possibilities for all humans to live to their full potential.

Toolkit

Thinking Like an Anthropologist:
Broadening Your View of the
Cultural Construction of Gender

In this chapter, we considered the story of Sarah Rose Huckman and her experience in youth sports. How do we think anthropologically about the move in many states to ban transgender athletes from competing in sports according to their gender identity?

Nearly 8 million high school students play on a school or community sports team, comprising 57 percent of all high school students. Since the enactment of Title IX laws in the 1970s that required equal opportunity for women in federally funded organizations and activities, girls' participation in high school sports has increased from fewer than 300,000 to 3.5 million. If you've ever participated in youth sports, you know that young people have a wide range of athletic abilities. Some fear that transgender athletes will have an unfair physical advantage over cisgender athletes, particularly cisgender women athletes. But on a national level, we can see that transgender teen athletes are not dominating youth sports. In fact, most laws targeting transgender athletes are being passed in states where no complaints have been filed.

Discrimination and stereotyping mean that most gender nonconforming young people never participate in sports. Discrimination and violence make it difficult for transgender and gender nonconforming youth to even stay in school. As many as a third drop out. Transgender youth are at elevated risk for suicide. The camaraderie and teamwork of sports often provides stability and fun for those who participate. If we acknowledge that the spate of state-level legislation targeting transgender and gender nonconforming youth athletes is not aimed at defending cisgender athletes from unfair advantage, we might instead consider these controversies as elements of a decades-long contestation in American culture over gender roles, gender identity, gender expression, and "proper" expressions of masculinity and femininity. Sports are a key cultural arena in which individuals learn gender roles and in which gender is taught, learned, and enforced. Perhaps these bills are more about power over particular bodies and the desire to control and define the terms of debate in this arena of rapid cultural change.

As you reflect on these issues, consider how the big questions that have organized this chapter may help you analyze the situation more deeply:

- **What is gender?**

- **Are there more than two sexes?**

- **How do anthropologists explore the relationship between gender and power?**

- **How is globalization transforming gender roles and stratification?**

Anthropologists consider gender a central element in every aspect of human culture, including education, the workplace, sexuality, health, family, religion, politics, and identity formation. In this chapter, we have explored how anthropologists examine the role of gender in contemporary debates and global political struggles.

Having read this chapter, are you able to take a fresh look at gender in your own life? Perhaps you can see how culturally constructed notions of gender have been replicated in patterns of inequality in cultural institutions ranging from education to the workplace. Use these tools in your anthropological toolkit and see how your view of the world, particularly the gendered world, might be transformed.

Key Terms

gender studies (p. 189)

sex (p. 190)

gender (p. 190)

sexual dimorphism (p. 190)

gender identity (p. 191)

gender expression (p. 191)

transgender (p. 191)

cisgender (p. 191)

cultural construction of gender (p. 192)

masculinity (p. 193)

femininity (p. 193)

gender performance (p. 195)

intersex (p. 197)

gender stratification (p. 205)

gender stereotypes (p. 205)

gender ideology (p. 205)

Chapter 8
Sexuality

At Columbia University's graduation ceremony in May 2015, Emma Sulkowicz lugged a fifty-pound, dark-blue, extra-long twin mattress across the platform to receive her diploma. Carrying the mattress—the kind Columbia uses in its dorms—was the final act of a nine-month-long senior project for her visual arts degree called "Carry That Weight," designed to protest the university's refusal to expel the male student she accused of raping her in her dorm room. She carried the mattress with her wherever she went on campus all year. By her own rules, she was not allowed to ask for help carrying it, though she was allowed to accept help when offered. The *New York Times* art critic

Emma Sulkowicz, a Columbia University student, carried a mattress across campus for nine months to protest the university's lack of action after she reported being raped during her sophomore year.

Roberta Smith (2014) described the performance as "a woman with a mattress, refusing to keep her violation private, carrying with her a stark reminder of where it took place."

Following Sulkowicz's lead, in October 2014 Columbia students carried twenty-eight mattresses onto campus, one for each of the plaintiffs who had filed a federal Title IX complaint alleging that the university discouraged students from reporting sexual assault, that sanctions were too lenient, and that perpetrators were not removed from campus, leaving survivors to encounter their attackers in dormitories and classrooms. The students were fined $471 to clean up the mattresses left outside the university president's home. Later that month, a group called Carry That Weight organized a national day of action during which students carried mattresses on 130 campuses, joining an increasingly effective anti-rape movement that is working to shatter the silence about widespread sexual assaults on campus.

Surveys reveal that as many as one in five women college students will experience some form of assault (Fisher, Daigle, and Cullen 2010; Hirsch and Khan 2020; Sanday 1990). College administrations are scrambling to address the crisis under the mandate of Title IX of the Education Amendments of 1972, which aims to ensure gender equality in federally funded institutions. In September 2014, the University of California instituted an affirmative consent policy for sexual encounters between students on all of its campuses. Such policies, originally pioneered by Antioch College in Ohio in the early 1990s, require more explicit communication between sexual partners, including a clear "yes" at every step of the encounter. This shift in the standard of consent from "no means no" to "only yes means yes" has now been adopted at institutions of higher education across the United States, reflecting a growing effort to bring the resources of educational institutions to bear on the troubled intersection of sexuality and power in American culture.

What are your own experiences of the intersection of sexuality and power? Have you heard stories like Emma Sulkowicz's on your own college campus? In 2017, the hashtag #MeToo went viral on social media as women stepped forward to share their stories of sexual assault and harassment. Within the first twenty-four hours, it had been tweeted 500,000 times and used by 4.7 million people in 12 million posts on Facebook. Community activist Tarana Burke began using the phrase *Me Too* in 2006 to empower women, especially young and vulnerable women, to speak out and change cultural practices, policies, and laws around sexual assault. Its message is: "You are not alone. Don't be ashamed." The 2017 #MeToo movement challenged inappropriate sexual behavior and policies in Hollywood, the music industry, science, academia, politics, sports, medicine, financial services, religion, and the military. The hashtag trended in over 85 countries, and the movement took on life around the world.

Sexuality is a profound aspect of human life, one that stirs intense emotions, deep anxieties, and rigorous debate. The U.S. population holds widely varying views of where sexuality originates, what constitutes appropriate sexual expression, and what sexuality's fundamental purpose is. It is fair to say that our cultural norms and mental maps of reality are in great flux, and have been for several generations, in response to theological shifts, medical advances, and powerful social movements promoting the equality of women and gay, lesbian, bisexual, transgender, and queer individuals.

Sexuality involves more than personal choices about who our sexual partners are and what we do with them. It is also a cultural arena within which our desires are expressed, socialized, and even thwarted. And it is an arena in which people debate ideas of what is moral, appropriate, and "natural" and use those ideas to create unequal access to society's power, privileges, and resources. Indeed, conflicts about sexuality often intersect with multiple systems of power, including those based on gender, religion, race, class, and kinship.

Anthropologists have a long but uneven history of studying human sexuality. Bronisław Malinowski (1927, 1929) and Margaret Mead (1928, 1935), like other early anthropologists writing in the 1920s and 1930s, considered human sexuality to be key to understanding the cultures they studied, so they wrote extensively about their research findings on human sexuality across cultures. Mead's work with young people in the islands of the western Pacific challenged prevailing norms of gender and sexual expression in the United States, which were assumed to reflect universal traits immutably fixed in nature.. Rather, anthropological research began to reveal the vast scope and diversity of human sexuality across time and space and the broad arc of potential human sexual expression.

After World War II, however, anthropological interest turned away from explicit attention to sexuality and focused instead on related issues of marriage, kinship, and the family. Since the 1980s, sexuality has reemerged as a key concern in anthropology (Herdt 1981, 1987; Rubin 1984), paralleling a rise of interest in the wider academic community spurred by the successes of the U.S. women's movement in the 1960s and 1970s, the emergence of gay and lesbian studies in the 1980s (Weston 1993), and the development of queer theory in the 1990s (Boellstorff 2007; Boellstorff and Howe 2015; Weiss 2011). Recently, anthropological scholarship has more intently considered the diverse expressions of sexuality in cultures worldwide, including in Western cultures, and how those expressions are being shaped by the intersection of local practices and globalization.

In this chapter, we examine the extensive body of work that anthropologists have compiled primarily in this latter period. In particular, we consider the following questions:

- **What is sexuality and where does it come from?**
- **What is the scope of human sexuality when seen in a global perspective?**

- **How has sexuality been constructed in the United States?**
- **How is sexuality an arena for working out relations of power?**
- **How does globalization influence local expressions of sexuality?**

By the end of this chapter you should have a broader understanding of the vast diversity of human sexuality across cultures. You should be able to discuss the roles of nature and culture in shaping human sexuality. Furthermore, you should be able to recognize how norms of sexuality are created and used to control people's bodies and desires and to organize the way cultures work. And you should be able to incorporate anthropological insights as you seek to better understand the role of sexuality in your own life and in your relations with others.

Sexuality is all around us in U.S. culture. Here, a Calvin Klein billboard uses sexuality to sell underwear. Where have you encountered sexuality today?

What Is Sexuality and Where Does It Come From?

Define sexuality from an anthropological perspective.

Text three friends and ask them to define *sexuality*. You will most likely get three very different responses. Perhaps this is not surprising in a culture where sexuality is omnipresent but rarely discussed carefully. In 1998, U.S. president Bill Clinton famously said of his liaison with White House intern Monica Lewinsky, "I did not have sexual relations with that woman." He chose those words presumably because he and Lewinsky had not had intercourse. But did they have sex? Such careful word choice by a sitting president giving testimony under oath reveals the challenges of defining behavior that is not only a physiological process but also a cultural construction whose meaning can vary widely.

Consider the following data. A 1999 survey of college students at a large midwestern university asked: "Would you say you 'had sex' with someone if the most intimate behavior you engaged in was . . . ?" The survey results showed that even college students do not agree about what *having sex* means. Kissing (2 percent) and petting (3 percent) clearly did not constitute having sex for almost all respondents. Oral "sex" (40 percent) constituted sex for many but not most. For 20 percent of respondents, perhaps influenced by dominant heterosexual norms, anal penetration did not constitute having sex. Fully 99.5 percent of respondents indicated that vaginal intercourse did constitute having sex (Sanders and Reinisch 2006). As this study shows, even within one population group—in this case, college students at one university—there can be disagreement over the meaning of the most physical aspects of sexual relations.

For the purposes of this chapter, we will define **sexuality** from two key perspectives. First, sexuality is the complex range of desires, beliefs, and behaviors that are related to erotic physical contact, intimacy, and pleasure. Second, sexuality is the cultural arena within which people debate ideas of what kinds of physical desires and behaviors are morally right, appropriate, and "natural" and use those ideas to create unequal access to status, power, privileges, and resources.

sexuality

The complex range of desires, beliefs, and behaviors that are related to erotic physical contact, and the cultural arena within which people debate what kinds of physical desires and behaviors are right, appropriate, and natural.

THE INTERSECTION OF SEXUALITY AND BIOLOGY

Clearly, biology plays a key role in shaping sexuality, for sexuality includes distinct physiological processes. But how much of human sexuality is shaped by our nature? As we will see, exactly how our genetic inheritance shapes our desires, attractions, identities, practices, and beliefs is quite complicated and subject to heated debate.

People sometimes think that sexuality is the most "natural" thing in the world. After all, every species must reproduce or face extinction, right? Therefore, many assume that the sexual instincts and behaviors of other animals provide an indication of the natural state of human sexuality unencumbered by the overlays of culture.

Yet research reveals that human sexuality is actually a distinct outlier in the animal kingdom. In his article "The Animal with the Weirdest Sex Life" (1997), scientist and author Jared Diamond suggested that human sexuality is completely abnormal by the standards of the world's estimated 8.7 million animal species and 5,400 mammal species. Diamond identified many ways in which humans differ from most other mammals:

- Most other mammals live individually, not in pairs, and meet only to have sex. They do not raise children together, and usually the males do not recognize their offspring or provide paternal care. In contrast, most humans engage in long-term sexual partnerships and often co-parent the couple's joint offspring.

- Most mammals engage in public sex, whereas humans, as a rule, have sex in private.

- Most mammals have sex only when the females of the species ovulate, at which time they advertise their fertility through visual signals, smells, sounds, and other changes in their behavior. Human women, however, may be receptive to sex not only during ovulation but also at other times during their menstrual cycle.

- Humans are one of the few species to have sex face to face.

• Possibly most intriguing, humans, dolphins, and bonobos (a species of ape) are the only mammals that have sex for fun rather than exclusively for reproduction. In fact, in contemporary U.S. culture, humans seem to do it mostly for fun.

By the standards of most mammals (including great apes, to whom we are most closely related), we humans are the sexual outliers. Despite the common belief that clues to the essentials of human sex drives and behaviors may be found in "nature," Diamond makes clear that humans have developed a sex life that lies far outside the natural framework of that of our mammal relatives. If other animals' sex lives do not provide clues to the roots of our sexuality, what can human biology tell us about the genetic and hormonal roots of sexual desire and sexual behavior?

One school of thought, which draws heavily on evolutionary psychology, focuses on the ways in which human evolution has created biological drives that are embedded in the genes that shape the human brain and control the body's hormones. These drives work automatically—instinctively—to ensure the reproduction of the species. Human sexuality is thought to rely heavily on the expression of these biological drives (Buss [1994] 2016).

Physical anthropologist Helen Fisher draws on many of these ideas to explore the complex biological roots of human sexuality in her book *Why We Love: The Nature and Chemistry of Romantic Love* (2004), particularly the relationship of body chemistry to human sensations of love. Fisher suggests that through evolution, humans have developed a set of neurochemicals that drive an "evolutionary trajectory of loving" (93). These neurochemicals guide us through three distinct phases of falling in love: finding the right sexual partner, building a relationship, and forming an emotional attachment that will last long enough to raise a child. First, testosterone—found in all people—triggers the sense of excitement, desire, arousal, and craving for sexual gratification that we call "lust."

Then, our bodies release the stimulant dopamine, and possibly norepinephrine and serotonin, to promote the feelings of romance that develop as relationships deepen. Eventually, the hormones oxytocin and vasopressin generate the feelings of calm and security that are associated with a long-term partnership; Fisher calls these feelings "attachment." These phases, she suggests, are built into our biological systems to ensure the reproduction of the human species, and they play key roles in shaping human sexuality.

Despite remarkable developments in genetic science, including the ability to map the human genome (the whole human genetic structure), there are limits to its ability to predict individual human behavior, including sexual behavior. Yes, the frequency of certain behaviors in the human population may suggest an underlying biological component. But it is extremely difficult to directly trace links between specific genes and specific behaviors. So, for instance, geneticists have not been able to identify a "straight" gene, a "gay" gene, or any cluster of genes that determines sexual orientation (Fausto-Sterling 2012).

Furthermore, we know that genes do not work in isolation from their surroundings. As discussed in Chapter 2, humans are a biocultural species, shaped by the interaction of genes, environment, and culture. Our bodies and minds, which are not fully formed at birth, bear the imprint of this interaction. Beginning in the womb, our genes interact with the nutrients, sounds, emotions, and diseases that surround and infuse us. The exact effects of the interaction of biology, culture, and environment are extremely difficult to measure, and this is particularly true in relation to complex human sexual desires and behaviors.

Even within the parameters of Fisher's study, we cannot predict a particular man's level of sexual desire for a particular partner by measuring his level of testosterone. Attraction, desire, and even lack of interest are not only biologically driven but also triggered by a vast array of cultural factors—including responses to the potential partner's age, religion, class, race, education, and employment prospects—or previous positive or negative experiences that may shape the body's physiological response to certain stimuli. So, although biology clearly plays a role in human sexuality, exactly how it manifests itself in each individual and how it interacts with the environment and culture is not as clear as many popular descriptions of sexuality suggest.

SEXUALITY AND CULTURE

A second school of thought, one we will consider in more detail throughout the rest of this chapter, focuses on the ways in which the people, events, and physical and cultural environments around us shape—or construct—our sexual desires and behaviors. These feelings and actions may have roots in human evolution, but they are shaped by our experiences and surroundings. For instance, humans are enculturated from birth to channel sexual feelings and desires into a limited

How do people, events, and the cultural environment around us shape our sexual desires and behaviors? (*Clockwise from top left*) Advertisements featuring sex and love; plaintiff Jim Obergefell speaks on June 26, 2015, after the U.S. Supreme Court rules that same-sex couples have a constitutional right to marry; a sex education class at Highland School District in Yakima, Washington.

number of acceptable expressions. Culture shapes what people think is natural, normal, and even possible. Parents, family, friends, doctors, religious communities, sex education classes, the media, and many other individual and institutional actors all play a role in shaping how we imagine and express our sexuality and what those expressions mean to others. Thus culture both guides and limits, encourages and thwarts our sexual desires and imaginations.

Anthropologists also trace the ways in which, through culture, human groups arrange the diversity of human sexuality into a limited number of categories that are imagined to be discrete (such as gay and straight), thereby masking the actual diversity and fluidity of human expressions of sexuality. Where an individual is assigned within these categories has direct consequences for their life chances. The meanings that certain sexual desires and behaviors acquire in a particular culture may affect people's access to social networks, social benefits, jobs, health care, and other resources and can make people vulnerable to discrimination, marginalization, and violence (Harding 1998; Ore 2010).

It is important to note that the perspectives of evolutionary biology and cultural constructionism discussed in this section need not be mutually exclusive. Rather, they reflect different research emphases into the roots and contemporary expressions of human sexuality.

What Is the Scope of Human Sexuality When Seen in a Global Perspective?

Describe the diversity of human sexuality over time and across cultures.

A look at human sexuality over time and across cultures reveals significant diversity in (1) how, where, when, and with whom humans have sex and (2) what certain sexual behaviors mean. This diversity challenges Western culture-bound notions and suggests ways of reinterpreting assumed cultural categories of sexuality. The discussions that follow offer examples of alternative constructions of sexuality in Suriname, Nicaragua, and Japan.

SAME-GENDER "*MATI* WORK" IN SURINAME

In *Politics of Passion* (2006), cultural anthropologist Gloria Wekker explores the lives of Black, working-class Creole women in the port city of Paramaribo, Suriname, a former Dutch colony on the northern coast of South America. Writing about the sexual choices Surinamese women make, Wekker (like Roger Lancaster and Anne Allison, whose work we will encounter later in this chapter) challenges the dominant thinking about sexual identity in Western scholarship and social movements by describing a much more flexible and inclusive approach specific to the local Paramaribo context.

Wekker's study focuses on *mati*—women who form intimate spiritual, emotional, and sexual relationships with other women. Wekker estimates that three out of four working-class Black women in Paramaribo engage in "*mati* work" at some point in their lives, establishing relationships of mutual support, obligation, and responsibility with other women—sometimes living in the same household, sometimes separately, and often sharing the responsibilities of child rearing. In contrast to Western notions of fixed, "either/or" sexual identities, *mati* may engage in sexual relationships with both women and men—sometimes simultaneously, sometimes consecutively. Their relationships with men may center on having children or receiving economic support, but frequently *mati* choose a "visiting" relationship rather than marriage in order to maintain their independence.

Born in Suriname and trained as an anthropologist in the United States and the Netherlands, Wekker also writes about the transfer of *mati* work to the Netherlands. In recent decades, young Surinamese women have emigrated from the former colony to its former colonizer in search of economic opportunities. There, *mati* work frequently takes the form of relationships between young

MAP 8.1
Suriname

Women join a parade in the port city of Paramaribo, Suriname, on the northern coast of South America.

immigrants and older Black women of Surinamese parentage who have established Dutch citizenship. Wekker describes these relationships as often fraught with complicated power dynamics involving differential age, class, and citizenship status. Yet she notes that this *mati* work does not parallel European ideas of lesbianism.

Wekker argues that Western scholarship mistakenly links all sexual acts between individuals of the same gender to a notion of "homosexual identity"—a permanent, stable, fixed sexual core or essence, whether inborn or learned, that is counterposed to an equally fixed and opposite heterosexual identity. In the Western framework, a person is either/or. The *mati* of Paramaribo, Wekker argues, approach their sexual choices very differently, regarding sexuality as a flexible behavior rather than a fixed identity. Their behavior is dynamic, malleable, and inclusive—both/and—rather than exclusive.

Wekker urges students of sexuality to not impose Western views about sexuality—what she considers "Western folk knowledge"—on the rest of the world but to understand local realities of sexuality with the goal of rethinking same-gender behavior in cross-cultural perspective. She recommends focusing attention on the variation of people's behaviors rather than imagining one uniform expression of same-gender sexual behavior. Furthermore, thinking cross-culturally, she argues that research and analysis of same-gender sexuality must recognize that identical physical sexual acts between same-gendered people may be understood in multiple ways and have vastly different social significance in different cultures and historical periods (Brown 2007; Stone 2007; Wekker 2006, 1999).

MACHISMO AND SEXUALITY IN NICARAGUA

Cultural anthropologist Roger Lancaster explores similar themes in *Life Is Hard: Machismo, Danger, and the Intimacy of Power in Nicaragua* (1994), in which he considers expressions of sexuality in a working-class neighborhood in Managua, Nicaragua, during the 1980s. In particular, he examines the concept of machismo—which can be defined as a strong, sometimes exaggerated performance of masculinity. This concept, which Lancaster sees as central to the Nicaraguan national imagination, shapes relationships not only between men and women but also between men and other men. Machismo creates a strong contrast between aggression and passivity. "Real" men—masculine men—are aggressive. But a real man's macho status is always at risk. Machismo must be constantly performed to retain one's social status.

MAP 8.2
Nicaragua

Lancaster was particularly intrigued by how machismo affects sexual relations between men. Generally, in U.S. culture, any man who engages in a same-gender sexual behavior is considered gay. But in the Nicaraguan community that Lancaster studied, only the men who receive anal intercourse are pejoratively called *cochon*—"queer, gay." The *machista*, the penetrator, is still considered a manly man—an *hombre-hombres*—under the rules of machismo. For it is the *machista*'s role to achieve sexual conquest whenever possible with whoever is available, acting out machismo and enhancing his status by dominating a weaker person. Among Nicaraguan men, the intersection of sexuality and power creates a culturally constructed system of arbitrary and unequal value for male bodies in which machismo privileges the aggressive, assertive *machista* penetrator over the passive, receptive, penetrated *cochon*.

Lancaster points out that in Nicaragua, the same acts that in the United States would be seen to reveal one's "essential" sexual orientation are interpreted differently. In fact, active, aggressive men enhance their masculinity and macho status even if they engage in same-gender sexual activity (Lewin 1995; Perez-Aleman 1994; Rouse 1994).

SEXUALITY AND PLEASURE IN CORPORATE JAPAN

In Tokyo's fashionable Roppongi district, elegant hostess bars attract groups of white-collar "salary men" for evenings of high-priced entertainment organized and paid for by their employers at elite Japanese corporations (who may spend up to 5 percent of company budgets on entertainment). These are not sex clubs, but they are still part of the commercialized sex industry—only selling the idea of sex, not physical sex. In her ethnography *Nightwork: Sexuality, Pleasure, and Corporate Masculinity in a Tokyo Hostess Club* (1994), anthropologist Anne Allison draws on four months of fieldwork in one club to explore the relationship between sexuality, masculinity, and Japan's capitalist corporate culture. At the clubs, hostesses

MAP 8.3
Tokyo

serve as the focal point of the party. They pour drinks, light cigarettes, flatter, and banter to enhance the clients' pleasure. Discussion of the hostess is also a central feature of the party, as men engage in sexual banter and innuendo about her personal and physical attributes, especially her breasts.

Despite the highly charged sexual atmosphere at the club, Allison suggests that corporate trips to hostess clubs are not primarily about sex. Rather, gathering in these spaces—outside the office and outside the home and family life—is about stimulating and channeling the men's sexual desire in the service of strengthening corporate culture and office relationships. All the talk about breasts is not about heterosexuality but about building homosocial relationships with other men. Sexual innuendo transforms women hostesses into sexual objects—a status seemingly all men agree on—and turns men's laughter and banter into a unifying process of male identity construction and bonding. Ideally, difference and discord in the workday can be dissolved into sexual conversation after hours. Allison suggests that in the highly ritualized expression of male dominance and male privilege performed in the hostess bars, the service purchased is not the eroticization of the woman but the eroticization of the men. The hostess does not deliver a sex act but through her banter, service, and submissive role instead projects an image of the potent and pleasing man who is powerful and desirable. Ultimately, this nightwork—whether performed by the hostess or by the men desperately attempting to have fun in an atmosphere of forced camaraderie and pretend sexuality long after the regular workday is over—fosters a particular form of masculinity, corporate masculinity, that serves the interests of contemporary Japanese businesses by channeling men's sexuality and desire into work (Curtis 1996; Davidson 1997; Ogasawara 1995).

How Has Sexuality Been Constructed in the United States?

Examine the construction of sexuality in the United States.

The studies discussed throughout this chapter reflect what anthropologist Kath Weston has called the vast ethnocartography of human sexuality (Weston 1993). As we turn our attention to the United States, research reveals the uniquely Western cultural history of a dual-category system of describing sexual orientation. In recent years, scholarship of race and racism in the United States has turned its attention to the historical and contemporary construction of the category of Whiteness, a process central to the formation of U.S. racial stratification. In a similar way, the anthropology of sexuality in the United States has turned its attention to the historical and contemporary construction of heterosexuality (D'Emilio and Freedman 1998).

THE INVENTION OF HETEROSEXUALITY

Historian Jonathan Katz (2007) argues that heterosexuality as it is practiced and understood in contemporary U.S. culture is a fairly recent invention. The *Oxford English Dictionary Supplement* lists the first U.S. usage of the term in 1892. Because words provide clues to cultural concepts, Katz suggests that the lack of earlier citations in popular or scientific sources in the United States indicates that the idea of heterosexuality had not achieved widespread cultural currency in the nineteenth century.

Does this mean that women and men in the United States were not engaging in opposite-gender sexual activity before the invention of this word? Katz suggests instead that heterosexuality as we think of it is not the same as reproductive intercourse between a man and a woman. Instead, what we call "heterosexuality" today is a particular arrangement between the sexes that—although not excluding reproductive intercourse—involves ideas about the practice and purpose of sex that have not always been socially authorized. For instance, early references to heterosexuality often described it as a perversion of the natural order because of its association with sex for pleasure rather than for procreation. The nineteenth-century Victorian ideal of sexuality, heavily influenced by Christian teachings, considered sex to be for procreation alone. Sex for pleasure represented a danger to the purposes of God. Masturbation—clearly nonprocreative—was considered a life-threatening, depleting form of self-abuse.

Only in 1892 did the translation of German psychiatrist Richard von Krafft-Ebing's influential work *Psychopathia Sexualis* first introduce to the U.S. scene the modern sense of heterosexuality as erotic feelings for the opposite sex and "homosexuality" as erotic feelings for the same sex. This marked a significant shift in the scientific community, supported by a growing number of medical doctors, toward the new idea of sexuality for pleasure rather than exclusively for procreation.

Sexology. A scientific study of sexuality, called *sexology*, began to emerge in Europe and the United States in the late nineteenth century. This field of study played a central role in the establishment of heterosexuality as the dominant erotic ideal and in the gradual process of dividing the population into distinct heterosexual and homosexual groups. Twentieth-century studies led by Alfred Kinsey, William Masters and Virginia Johnson, and Shere Hite used interviews, questionnaires, observation, and participation to explore the sexual lives of thousands of primarily White U.S. residents. Their studies produced surprising results.

Sex researchers William Masters and Virginia Johnson, pictured here interviewing a couple in 1969, challenged common assumptions about U.S. sexual practices.

Kinsey and later sexologists found that human sexuality did not fit into simplistic categories. Same-gendered attraction, fantasies, and experiences were much more common than previously thought. Furthermore, sexual behaviors could shift over the course of a lifetime, spanning both same-gender and opposite-gender sexual activity. Rather than finding a sharp dichotomy between heterosexuality and homosexuality, research revealed diversity, flexibility, and fluidity along a continuum of sexual behavior (Hubbard 1990; Kinsey, Pomeroy, and Martin 1948).

Despite their arguments for the recognition of diversity and fluidity in human sexual behavior, sexology studies reinforced the emerging popular and scientific consensus that because it was the sex most people were having, heterosexuality was the functional norm for human sexuality (Hubbard 1990; Katz 2007).

Over the course of a century, heterosexuality gradually came to be seen as the norm—the presumed "natural" state—against which to judge all other expressions of sexuality. Today, cultural notions of sexuality are in flux, yet a particular version of heterosexuality continues to be constructed and contested.

WHITE WEDDINGS

White Weddings: Romancing Heterosexuality in Popular Culture (2008), by sociologist Chrys Ingraham, is not a book about wedding ceremonies. It is about wedding culture and what Ingraham calls the "wedding industry"—the vast network of commercial activities and social institutions that market 2.2 million weddings a year in the United States. The wedding industry and wedding culture, Ingraham argues, provide insights into how U.S. culture gives meaning to marriage and, in the process, constructs contemporary understandings of heterosexuality.

Constructing Heterosexuality. It's hard to turn on the television, go online, or check out at the local grocery store without encountering some reminder of U.S. society's fascination with weddings. Bridal magazines, popular tabloids, television shows, and commercials in every medium saturate the culture with images of spectacles of excess that will, they promise, lead to everyone's fairy-tale ending of happily ever after. Wedding consultants push wedding announcements, bridal showers, wedding halls, floral arrangements, diamond rings, rehearsal dinners, receptions, gifts and favors, caterers, photographers, bands, limousines, and glamorous honeymoons to romantic destinations. Wedding registries orchestrate the delivery of just the right gifts of kitchenware, china, household furnishings, and every appliance imaginable. The average bridal gown (mostly made in third-world garment shops by women who will never have a white wedding), including alterations, headpiece, and veil, will cost $1,259. In 2022, the average U.S. couple will spend more than $30,433 on their big day. Altogether, the annual $70 billion wedding industry wields enormous social and economic power (Wedding Stats 2022).

Ingraham reminds her readers that brides are not born. They are made. Every girl in U.S. culture, almost from birth, is bombarded with cultural symbols and messages about what it will take to have her very own white wedding. Barbie dolls and other toy-industry favorites model the perfect bride, complete with accessories (including Ken?) for the perfect white wedding. Disney movies, feature films, and television shows celebrate weddings as key life moments (and central plot devices) and essential cultural symbols. Every broadcast season features a spate of elaborate made-for-television weddings, especially on shows struggling in the ratings.

What is your idea of a perfect wedding? Here, a woman adjusts a bridal gown at a wedding fair in Bucharest, Romania, where the wedding industry has grown despite an economic crisis.

From childhood, girls are tutored in preparation for the "you may kiss the bride" moment, learning to apply makeup, wear high heels, send valentines, go on dates, and select a prom dress. Boys learn to buy flowers and corsages, wear tuxedos, pay for dates, lead during the first dance, buy an engagement ring, and initiate sex. But no matter where you think human sexuality originates, it is clear that these behaviors do not occur in nature. They are constructed in culture. Through the wedding industry and wedding culture, Ingraham suggests, we learn what it means to be heterosexual.

Inequality and Unequal Access. What do weddings tell us about the construction of heterosexuality in U.S. culture? Building on recent feminist scholarship, Ingraham suggests that white weddings, and the marriages that result, offer insights into the gendered power dynamics embedded in the normative patterns of heterosexuality that have developed since the late nineteenth century. These power dynamics disadvantage women while being largely obscured by the idealism and romance that U.S. culture wraps around these institutions. Historically, the institution of heterosexual marriage included legal stipulations that effectively made women the economic and sexual property of their husbands. This assumption continues to be ritualized in contemporary U.S. weddings by the father "giving away" the bride to her soon-to-be husband, exchanging the woman between two men. Today, patterns of inequality are not legally sanctioned but still significant both in the workplace and in the gendered division of labor in the home.

Ingraham selected the book title *White Weddings* to highlight the issues of class and race that also are embedded in the workings of the wedding industry and the fairy tale of the wedding ritual. White weddings are not available to all. The women sewing wedding dresses, the young men mining diamonds, and the staff serving dinner on the Caribbean honeymoon island cannot afford a white wedding. Nor does the industry depict a diverse population in its advertising, insinuating that white weddings are primarily for White folks. Actually, most Americans cannot afford the average U.S. wedding; they incur significant debt for the ceremony and the honeymoon to launch their marriage (Ingraham 2008; Milkie 2000; Siebel 2000).

LESBIAN AND GAY COMMITMENT CEREMONIES

The U.S. Supreme Court legalized same-gender marriage in 2015. In *Recognizing Ourselves* (1998), anthropologist Ellen Lewin opened a window into both the personal and the political dynamics of gay and lesbian commitment ceremonies before they were legalized.

For some couples in Lewin's study, commitment ceremonies, holy unions, and weddings were a form of resistance against the cultural norms and legal standards that denied gay men and lesbians the recognition of their lives and loves. The public performances of these ceremonies allowed them a chance to speak of their anger and sorrow, to refuse to be marginalized and mistreated, and to challenge the dominant patterns of heterosexuality and gender stratification in mainstream U.S. culture. Many also saw their ceremonies as part of the efforts to legalize same-gender marriage and to advocate for the legal, health, and economic benefits associated with heterosexual marriages.

For others, their commitment ceremonies expressed more personal and intimate feelings—a decision to recognize themselves, to celebrate their love, and to call their communities to participate in supporting their relationships. Through public ceremonies long reserved for heterosexual couples, gay men and lesbians declared they were already part of local communities, schools, religious congregations, families, and workplaces—that they belonged.

Today, U.S. marriage patterns, and relationship patterns more generally, are shifting rapidly. Placed in historical perspective and in light of our anthropological perspectives on the fluidity and malleability of human sexuality, perhaps we can view these shifts not as some new and surprising contestation of age-old "natural" patterns but as the most recent rethinking of human sexuality in U.S. culture. If so, we might then be better prepared to analyze the underlying intersections of sexuality and power in our own personal and political lives.

How Is Sexuality an Arena for Working Out Relations of Power?

Analyze how sexuality and power intersect.

As we have noted, sexuality is more than an expression of individual desires and identities. French philosopher and social scientist Michel Foucault (1978) described sexuality as "an especially dense transfer point for relations of power." By this he meant that in every culture, sexuality—like race, ethnicity, class, and gender—is also an arena in which appropriate behavior is defined, relations of power are worked out, and inequality and stratification are created, enforced, and contested.

Indeed, cultural institutions ranging from governments to religious bodies attempt to regulate many aspects of sexuality, including marriage and divorce; monogamy and polygamy; the age of consent; the definition of incest; reproductive rights; the rights of gay men, lesbians, and bisexual and transgender persons; pornography; and prostitution. A consideration of "who is allowed to do what with whom and when" exposes the intersections of sexuality and power in a culture. Attention to intersectionality—the ways in which systems of power interconnect to affect individual lives and group experiences—offers a fundamental shift in how social scientists study inequality and stratification, including how we think about sexuality. In this section, we consider several case studies that reflect on these intersections.

INTERSECTIONS OF RACE AND SEXUALITY FOR BLACK GAY WOMEN

Mignon Moore's study *Invisible Families* (2011) explores the impact of the intersection of race and sexuality on the identities, relationships, and families of Black gay women in the United States. Moore notes that, historically, race has framed Black women's political, economic, and religious identities (see also Dill 1983; Higgenbotham 1992). And whereas many middle-class White lesbian couples experience sexuality as the primary framework that shapes their identity, many in the Black lesbian community (including African American, Afro-Caribbean, and African immigrant women) find that race—perhaps as much as, if not more than, sexuality—is the primary framework that shapes their identity.

In an interview with Moore, Zoe Ferron (a pseudonym), an African American woman born in 1960 in Brooklyn, New York, reflects on how the identities of race, gender, and sexuality describe her:

> If I had to number them one, two, three? Probably Black and lesbian—real close, to be honest with you. I don't know which would come up as one. Probably Black. Woman last. . . . Because that is just what it is. People see your Blackness, and the world has affected me by my Blackness since the very inception of my life. . . . My sexuality is something that developed later on, or I became aware of later on, [because] I think *it's always been what it's been*, but I think that it was just something that developed in my psyche. But being Black is something that I've always had to deal with: racism since day one and recognizing how to navigate through this world as a Black person, and even as a Black woman. (Moore 2012, 33)

The intersection of race and sexuality becomes particularly meaningful as Black gay women participate in Black or gay communities that define themselves around just one or the other of these identities.

Moore notes that before the 1980s, gay sexuality in communities of color was rarely articulated in public settings. And only infrequently was it recognized as a component of the community's larger experiences of discrimination and struggle. Instead, openly gay sexuality was perceived to flout notions of "respectability"—virtue, modesty, discipline, responsibility—that had developed within the Black

A couple share a laugh while playing cards with their daughter and son at home in Chicago, Illinois.

middle class and that its leadership promoted as important tools to combat racist stereotypes in the workplace, political arena, and family life (Shaw 1996; Wolcott 2001). Moore points to a strong reluctance during that period on the part of gay Black people to challenge community expectations about respectability by creating families together.

How do the women in Moore's study navigate the Black middle-class politics of respectability in order to both live their sexuality openly and maintain strong community connections? Moore suggests that by risking the disruption of this particular version of respectability, Black women who live openly as lesbians—forming families, getting married, becoming mothers, and raising children—offer an alternative manifestation of respectability at the intersection of sexuality and race.

Can you see how the intersection of race and sexuality may differentially affect one's life choices and opportunities? In your own life, how is your sexuality shaped by its intersection with other systems of power—perhaps age, gender, race, class, or religion?

SEXUAL CITIZENS

As discussed at the beginning of the chapter, sexual assault is pervasive on college campuses across the country. Anthropologist Jennifer Hirsch and her colleague Shamus Khan conducted ethnographic research with 150 undergraduate students at Columbia University between 2015 and 2017—including students who self-identified as gay, lesbian, straight, bisexual, trans, queer and asexual—to better understand their sexual lives on campus and to investigate what leads to the widespread incidence of sexual assault. In listening to students' stories and conducting fieldwork on and off campus, Hirsch and Khan learned that 36 percent of women and 15 percent of men had experienced some form of nonconsensual sexual contact by their senior year. Twenty percent of women and 6 percent of men reported having been raped. Previous studies have found that 90 percent of rapes are committed by someone the victim knows, usually a boyfriend, former boyfriend, coworker, classmate, friend, or acquaintance (Fisher, Cullen, and Turner 2000).

Hirsch and Khan's book *Sexual Citizens: A Landmark Study of Sex, Power, and Assault on Campus* (2020) seeks to uncover the deep cultural roots beneath sexual violence and assault. How are students' experiences shaped and created by their interpersonal relationships, precollege histories, organizations they are a part of, and the surrounding culture? Eliminating assault, Hirsch and Khan argue, will require shifting attention from individual bad actors to the systems that make sexual assault a predictable consequence of how our society is organized—systems that normalize assault and create conditions of vulnerability.

Hirsch and Khan's study reveals that assault happens at a complex intersection of students' sexual projects, their sense of self as sexual citizens, and their physical location within particular sexual geographies. Each person, they suggest, has a *sexual project*, some more developed than others, that answers the question: Why do you want sex? Students' responses cited pleasure, intimacy, connecting with others, acquiring sexual experiences, exploring sexual identity, having children, or achieving social status. Sexual projects are embedded within other projects, like going to college or preparing for work and family life. Despite the significance of sex in students' stories, few had been given any guidance from their family or community about how to think and talk about what they wanted from sexual experiences and what kind of sexual projects fit their values. This vacuum created uncertainty and vulnerability at key moments in their sexual encounters.

Hirsch and Khan's study also examines the impact of particular *sexual geographies*—including the campus design, buildings, college-life areas, residential dorms, access to buildings, access to alcohol, fraternities, Greek-life policies, even furniture. How do the physical spaces through which students move shape their sexual experiences and create conditions of vulnerability that lead to sexual assault? Space influences actions and interactions. What is the effect, for instance, when a dorm room has only one chair and a second person must sit on the bed? Hirsch and Khan urge more careful attention to systemic design features in discussions of sexual assault prevention.

Hirsch and Khan's study also reveals a limited sense of sexual agency or control—what the authors call *sexual citizenship*—among the students. How can a culture, a college, and a country create sexual citizens—that is, individuals with a clear sense of both their right to freely exercise their own sexual projects and their obligation to treat their partner's sexual projects with dignity and respect? Hirsch and Khan's work reveals that sexual encounters occur at the complex intersection of many systems of power—not only gender and sexuality but also age, race, wealth, knowledge of campus, and previous sexual experience. A clear sense of sexual citizenship and self-determination, or lack thereof, significantly affects students' ability to navigate those complicated power dynamics.

Hirsch and Khan recommend that institutions at all levels—the family, school, religion, the university, and the state—devote renewed attention to promoting sexual citizenship, including a commitment to a rethought, comprehensive sex education program for young people. As described by students in Hirsch and Khan's study, today's sex education programs commonly present sex as scary and dangerous, focus on sexually transmitted infections and unwanted pregnancies, and encourage abstinence—in sum, they suggest that young people are not ready to become sexual citizens. Few students reported receiving formal instruction about birth control, how to say no to sex, the right to make one's own reproductive decisions, or how to resist peer pressure. Conventional sex education was particularly irrelevant to the sexual experiences and identities of LGBTQ students.

Hirsch and Khan note the importance of shifting these conversations. The average age of one's first sexual encounter in the United States is seventeen, and this number has been stable for about four decades. Overall, young people are actually having less sex. But the average age of marriage, if young people get married at all, has risen significantly: from twenty-three in 1960 to thirty for men and twenty-eight for women today. As a result, a full decade may pass between when young people first have sex and when they get married. Old norms and educational patterns have not prepared young people for sexual citizenship in this new reality. In this context, Hirsch and Khan argue that preparation to be fully empowered sexual citizens is an essential element of both achieving individual sexual self-determination and eliminating sexual assaults on campus.

SEX, DISABILITY, AND SOCIAL JUSTICE IN DENMARK AND SWEDEN

Anthropologists Don Kulick and Jens Rydstrom explore the intersections of state power and sexuality in their book *Loneliness and Its Opposite: Sex, Disability, and the Ethics of Engagement* (2015), focusing on the constraints on and potential for sexuality among severely disabled people in Denmark and Sweden. In recent decades, the disability rights movement has successfully advocated for access to physical spaces, jobs, social services, and other public arenas where people with disabilities have commonly faced discrimination and marginalization. But the more private realm of the erotic lives of people with disabilities has often been ignored or viewed with discomfort or anxiety. Should a person with severe

MAP 8.4
Denmark and Sweden

"I want a family—a marriage, children, the whole thing. 'Family' is happy is strong." Nick Hogan of Australia, one of an estimated 7 million people around the world with Down syndrome. What can we do to support people with disabilities as they form attachments with other people, including attachments that involve sexual pleasure and love?

disabilities hope to have a meaningful sex life? And how can that be possible for someone who needs assistance to perform most basic life activities, such as eating, bathing, and going to the bathroom?

Denmark and Sweden are two liberal welfare states with similar cultural histories, considered to be sexually progressive and at the forefront of the global movement for disability rights. Both countries commit significant portions of their budgets to social services (30 percent) and provide disability pensions, housing in group homes, or personal assistance to those who desire to live independently. But these two neighboring countries take distinctly different approaches to the erotic lives of people with disabilities. In Denmark, their sexuality is acknowledged, discussed, and facilitated. In Sweden, as in the overwhelming majority of countries around the world, the erotic lives of people with disabilities are denied, repressed, and discouraged. Their desires for sexual pleasure are ignored. These adults with disabilities are commonly treated as children whose erotic desires and sexual behaviors are seen as inappropriate or even dangerous to their own well-being.

Kulick and Rydstrom's study focuses specifically on severely disabled people, including those with intellectual and physical disabilities, limited mobility in their limbs, and limited verbal language abilities who live in group homes. In Sweden, staff are trained to discourage the erotic lives of their residents, to never "wake the sleeping bear" (that is, to avoid all mention of sexuality), and to shut down erotic feelings when they do arise. In stark contrast, the group homes in Denmark promote welcoming attitudes and affirmative policies regarding sex. Denmark supports a network of advocates, sexual advisors, social workers, medical professionals, educators, and counselors who work toward recognizing and facilitating the sexual desires and practices of people with disabilities. The government sponsors an eighteen-month training course to become a sexual advisor. An elaborate set of national recommendations, *Guidelines about Sexuality—Regardless of Handicap*, discusses how these advisors can help people with disabilities engage in such activities as having sex with a partner, masturbation, or purchasing sexual services from a sex worker.

Ultimately, Kulick and Rydstrom are most interested in the impact of state policies on the lives of women and men with disabilities and their potential to develop, explore, and thrive as sexual human beings. Kulick and Rydstrom frame this as an ethical question—a matter of social justice. What can we do to support people with disabilities as they form attachments with other people, including attachments that involve sexual pleasure and love? And how can we foster the circumstances that allow each individual to realize a life of human dignity? This, Kulick and Rydstrom argue, is the true measure of a just society.

How Does Globalization Influence Local Expressions of Sexuality?

Assess how globalization is affecting individual expressions and local understandings of sexuality.

Local understandings of sexuality are undergoing dramatic shifts as they intersect with national, regional, and international economic policies, immigration practices, and political movements influenced by processes of globalization (see Curtis 2009). For example, time-space compression (see Chapter 1) is facilitating the movement of people—particularly men—within countries and across national borders in search of sexual pleasure. In addition, disruptions of local economies are pushing women to find wage labor to support themselves and their families. And international campaigns for gay and lesbian rights, often initiated in Western countries, are shaping a global conversation about sexuality and the human rights of sexual minorities worldwide. At the same time, groups opposing gay and lesbian sexuality are promoting their own agendas on a global platform.

The following study offers insights into the intersection of the local and global when it comes to sexuality. This is an arena that most of us view as deeply personal but that today crosses national borders in the company of economic flows, immigrant journeys, international tourism, and global rights campaigns.

GLOBALIZATION, SEXUALITY, AND THE MIGRATION OF MEXICAN GAY MEN

Migration across the U.S.–Mexico border has dominated the news in recent years. But the intense focus on border walls, migrant caravans, and drug smuggling obscures the actual lives, journeys, and motivations of the immigrants themselves. How do we move beyond stereotypes and political rhetoric to understand the impact of globalization on the lives of people on both sides of the U.S.–Mexico border?

In *Pathways of Desire: The Sexual Migration of Mexican Gay Men* (2018), Héctor Carrillo illuminates the lives of gay Mexican men and the journeys that take them to the United States, an aspect of migration that has largely fallen outside social science research and popular debate. Through interviews with 150 gay men and participant observation in places where they socialize, Carrillo and his team trace the men's migration journeys from life in the towns and villages of Mexico to their arrival and incorporation in the gay community of Hillcrest in San Diego, California. How does sexuality shape their migration? How does migration shape their sexuality?

Discussions of gender and sexuality in the scholarly literature about Mexican migration to the United States have mainly focused on heterosexual migrants. Heterosexual men move for work opportunities. Their journeys represent rites of passage that mark their masculinity, ambition, and worthiness as marriage partners. Heterosexual women seek reunification with relatives—parents, husbands, children—who preceded them on the cross-border journey. Or, as seen in more recent studies, women migrate to gain autonomy and to challenge the entrenched patterns of gender inequality that characterize their relationships with their husbands, boyfriends, and fathers.

For the men in Carrillo's study, whom he refers to as sexual migrants, sexual motivations for migration intertwine with desires for economic advancement and family reunification. Despite Mexico's growing gay communities, gay men consistently point to their desire to live a fully gay life and experience a kind of sexual freedom that would be hard to achieve at home.

Gay migrants often rely on the same social and family networks and resources that heterosexual migrants use to facilitate their journeys. Immigration scholars often note a culture of migration (see Chapter 13) that develops in certain communities as more residents relocate within countries or across borders. Money and messages sent back home, along with return visits by successful immigrants,

MAP 8.5
Hillcrest, San Diego, California and Mexico

spur the imagination of other residents. New financial resources and new social capital—networks of friends, family, and fellow villagers already in the United States; knowledge about migration routes; and strategies for incorporation into U.S. communities—motivate more people, especially young people, to move.

But gay Mexican men also draw on alternative resources, what Carrillo calls a "gay culture of migration," that include LGBTQ+ social networks in Mexico and the United States. Through them, sexual migrants activate gay and lesbian acquaintances, friends, boyfriends, and sex partners to access a kind of "gay social capital" to facilitate travel, meet human smugglers, find housing and jobs, and obtain information about the U.S. legal and health care systems.

Carrillo notes the central role of Hillcrest, a neighborhood in San Diego, as a safe landing place for new immigrants and a key site for mobilizing such social capital. Gay friends and acquaintances play a crucial role as cultural ambassadors, helping new arrivals learn about Latino gay support groups, gay dance clubs and bathhouses, the Metropolitan Community Church (a nondenominational LGBTQ+ church with congregations throughout the United States and abroad), gay Catholic groups, and health services (including HIV/AIDS treatment and support groups).

In Hillcrest, new arrivals also begin the process of becoming sexual citizens, understanding and enacting their sexual rights and duties in a new country and community. The neighborhood's many rainbow flags, gay bars, and other cultural institutions provide a setting in which gay men can openly hold hands without fear of harassment, violence, or arrest. This public expression of same-sex intimacy marks a new political framework of freedom, belonging, and acceptance that many have not previously experienced. At the same time, traveling outside San Diego, new arrivals quickly find that not all of the United States is like Hillcrest. Homophobia and anti-gay violence are not uncommon. Full participation in their community is further limited by their undocumented status, encounters with racial prejudice, and their ever-present vulnerability to arrest and deportation.

Immigrants transform the cultures where they settle. The same is true of the Mexican men in Carrillo's study, who identify sexual passion as the unique characteristic they bring to intimate relationships with White American gay men. They trace this trait to Mexican culture, particularly their upbringing in close-knit families where the group's needs come before the individual's needs and where unity, connection, and respect are central to daily life and survival. In contrast, they find White American gay men to be calculating, detached, and even shallow in their interpersonal relationships. This they link to the erosion of American family values in a highly materialistic and individualistic culture. Mexican gay migrants wear their reputation as passionate, intimate lovers as a badge of honor as they interact sexually and romantically with "the locals" in San

Diego. And as vulnerable immigrants with limited power to shape their own lives, they also wield it as a tool for critiquing the mainstream American culture they are working so hard to join.

Globalization has propelled Western norms of sexuality around the world. But Carrillo's study reveals how cross-border migration flows—also stimulated by globalization—are reshaping sexuality in the San Diego gay community, as Mexican gay migrants bring unique perspectives on sexuality from their home communities to the United States and into the global gay landscape. The actual lives of migrants, in this case sexual migrants, reveal deeper complexities of globalization, the immigrant journey, and the contributions of gay Mexican men to creating both local and global gay cultures.

In this chapter, we have considered the vast scope and diversity of human sexuality across cultures, time, and space. The sexual dimensions of human diversity in turn challenge us to expand our imaginations about the potential for human sexuality available to us. But as we have seen throughout this chapter, human sexuality is more than the personal choices we make about our sexual partners and how we express our erotic desires. The anthropological lens and a global perspective have enabled us to see that sexuality encompasses complex relationships not only between individuals but also between individuals and the larger culture. We have examined how elements of human sexuality are culturally constructed—formed in relationship to particular people, cultural norms, and expectations. Rather than representing sharply drawn, fixed, and oppositional identities that align with two discrete categories, sexuality is diverse, flexible, and fluid.

We have also seen that the construction of human sexuality—how it is perceived and valued—is a highly contested process. Debates rage and decisions are made about human sexuality that affect people's life chances and access to power, privileges, rights, and resources. Certain rights or benefits may be granted or restricted based on assumptions about sexual preferences or sexual behavior. Given this reality, sexuality has become a key cultural location within anthropology for analyzing, understanding, and contesting systems of stratification and inequality, including those that arise from sexuality's intersections with other systems of power, such as race, gender, ethnicity, nationality, religion, kinship, and class.

Toolkit

Thinking Like an Anthropologist:
Sexuality in Your Life

Sexuality is all around us. Turn on the television, search the Internet, check out at the grocery store, or drive down an interstate highway, and you will find sexuality all around you in reality shows, websites, magazines, and billboard advertisements. At times, the presence of sexuality in U.S. culture is so pervasive as to be overwhelming. In such an environment, how do you begin to make sense of what sexuality means for you on a personal level and for U.S. culture on a political level?

Remember to consider the big questions that have organized this chapter:

- **What is sexuality and where does it come from?**
- **What is the scope of human sexuality when seen in a global perspective?**
- **How has sexuality been constructed in the United States?**
- **How is sexuality an arena for working out relations of power?**
- **How does globalization influence local expressions of sexuality?**

Think again about the story that opens this chapter. In what ways do sexuality and power intersect on your college campus? If, as anthropologist Eric Wolf argues (see Chapter 2), every relationship is embedded in complex dynamics of power, how do you navigate intersections of sexuality with gender, age, class, race, or religion? Has your college or university created opportunities to discuss matters of sexuality?

Certainly, attention to sexual violence on college campuses has increased. Terms such as *date rape* and *domestic violence* have become part of the national conversation, and many colleges and universities have implemented policies on sexual harassment and sexual conduct. Still, many women experience sexual harassment, violence, and rape while in college (Fisher, Daigle, and Cullen 2010; Sanday 1990). While these policies attempt to address extreme expressions of the intersection of power with sexuality, conversations about sexuality can be far more wide-ranging.

Until recently, most sexual offense policies have been based on the assumption that *no* means *no*. Most legal definitions of rape have assumed that if a person does not consent or is incapable of consent for any reason, then any sexual activity with them is considered rape. Now, newer affirmative consent policies that define consent as an ongoing process require intimate partners to obtain verbal consent at each new level of physical intimacy.

An affirmative consent policy requires a dramatic shift in thinking about intimate sexual encounters. It also commands a new attention to shifting the power dynamics that underlie current patterns of gender and sexuality in the culture at large. Imagine if all forms of coercion—physical and psychological coercion; the pressures of norms, obligations, and expectations; and the fear of ridicule or abandonment—were removed from the equation, enabling people to engage in sexual intimacy only when they really wanted to. What if *yes* really meant *yes* (Friedman and Valenti 2008)?

Although anthropology may not be able to help you decide whom to date or when to do what and where, it does offer a set of tools—perspectives and insights—that may help you think more clearly about what it all means, identify the cultural frameworks within which you negotiate your desires and decisions, and imagine what your full range of options may be when you consider your sexuality within a global perspective. Questions of sexuality run deep in U.S. cultural conversations. Having thought through key issues of sexuality from an anthropological perspective, are you better prepared to engage in the debates and advance the conversation?

Key Term

sexuality (p. 223)

Chapter 9
Kinship, Family, and Marriage

Learning Objectives

- Define the key anthropological concepts related to kinship.

- Describe ethnographic examples of the global diversity of kinship formations.

- Assess how ideas of kinship are shaped by the nation-state.

- Analyze how globalization is reshaping global expressions of kinship.

"I'm Alan. I'm 27. I'm a sperm seeker." Zhang Alan (an alias), who lives in the Chinese capital, Beijing, is unsure about marriage but would like to have a child. As an unmarried woman, however, she is barred by the Chinese government from accessing the nation's sperm banks. Instead, she made a video about her search for a sperm donor and posted it on the Internet. A number of men responded positively but Alan eventually chose a friend to be her donor (Zhang 2019).

For more than forty years, China's government has sought to define the family by carefully controlling who can have children and how many they can have. Large extended families have long been central to Chinese culture, serving as an economic engine as well as providing intergenerational support for children and the elderly. But in 1980, faced with a population boom that threatened economic

---

China's government prohibits unmarried women from accessing sperm banks. Pictured here is the Jiaen fertility hospital in Beijing.

growth, the Chinese government sought to orchestrate a cultural shift by implementing a "one child per family" policy. All families, whether urban or rural, rich or poor, would be strictly limited to one child. Government-sponsored neighborhood committees enforced these mandates with peer pressure, government agencies imposed economic fines, and state-run companies and schools withheld job opportunities, health care, and education from those who transgressed. Some local officials resorted to more draconian enforcement measures, including sterilization campaigns and forced abortions.

In 2016, faced with imminent population decline, the Chinese government fully reversed its one child per family policy. Estimates suggest that by 2100, China's population of 1.4 billion will be reduced by almost half. In May 2021, new government regulations allowed all married couples to have three children per family. But over the course of the one child policy, smaller families became the norm in much of China. More educated women are now delaying marriage and having fewer children. Increasing wealth has reduced reliance on children as a source of retirement support. State policies have led to a culture shift that new policies are not likely to alter.

Despite the state's urgent moves to incentivize more births, it still preserves certain restrictions on the family form by privileging married heterosexual couples. It provides access to reproductive technology, improved maternity leave, and workplace protections for expectant mothers—but only to couples within state-approved family structures. Unmarried couples, single parents, and same-sex partners are excluded from these benefits. Single women, like Beijing's Zhang Alan, are barred from accessing reproductive technologies such as sperm banks, in vitro fertilization, and freezing eggs, and thus they are left to organize their families outside the approved policies of the state.

Zhang Alan's story and her experience of trying to form a family in China raise key questions about our most important human relations, relations that we sometimes call "family" and that anthropologists have explored under the category of kinship. What is a family? Who is "related" to whom? Who decides? Is kinship biological or chosen? What are the relationships between systems of power, like national governments, and the family?

Humans live in groups. As a species, we rarely live alone or in isolation. Kinship is perhaps the most effective strategy humans have developed to form stable, reliable, distinct, and deeply connected groups that can last over time and through generations.

kinship

The system of meaning and power that cultures create to determine who is related to whom and to define their mutual expectations, rights, and responsibilities.

Kinship is the system of meaning and power created to determine who is related to whom and to define their mutual expectations, rights, and responsibilities. Of course, humans also form groups through work, religion, education, and politics. But families and kinship networks provide a unique system of support and nurture, ensure reproduction of the next generation, protect group assets, and influence social, economic, and political systems.

Many people in Western cultures assume that kinship groups have a biological basis and arise around the **nuclear family** of mother, father, and children. But when we examine these assumptions in a cross-cultural context, they show themselves to be a Euro-American ideal that not even those cultures have realized. Kinship groups come in a variety of shapes and sizes: We trace our connections through biological ancestors. We create kinship relations through marriage and remarriage. We adopt. We foster. We choose families of people who care about us. Sometimes we even imagine everyone in our nation to be part of one big kinship community.

nuclear family
The kinship unit of mother, father, and children.

In the twenty-first century, we are vividly aware of new forms of family life as kinship relations shift, closing off familiar patterns and opening up new ones. The image of a mother, father, and two kids gathered around the dining room table every evening for a home-cooked meal and conversation may be familiar as a cultural icon, but for many people, the experience of family is more complicated. Families are made, taken apart, reconstructed, and blended. Gay and lesbian couples and their families are achieving increased acceptance and official recognition. New reproductive technologies—including artificial insemination, in vitro fertilization, and surrogacy—continue to stretch our ideas of kinship and families by showing how human culture, through science and technology, is shaping biological relationships.

Although the term *kinship* may be unfamiliar to you, the subject material is not. Through kinship studies, anthropologists examine the deepest and most complicated aspects of our everyday lives—our relationships with the people who are often closest to us, including our mothers, fathers, brothers, sisters, grandparents, cousins, husbands, wives, partners, and children. These are the people we live with, eat with, count on for support, and promise to take care of when they are in need. We pour our emotions, creative energy, hopes, and dreams into these relationships. Many of the most emotionally vibrant moments of our lives—from joy and love to anger and pain—occur at the intersection of individual and family life: birthdays, holiday celebrations, shared meals, weddings, illnesses, and funerals. Through kinship, we see our lives as part of a continuum. We look back to see the history of the people we come from, and we look ahead to imagine the relatives and families yet to be.

At the same time, kinship is deeply intertwined with forces beyond the everyday activities of family and home. In our families, we also learn basic patterns of human behavior—how to treat one another, how to act in groups, how to navigate differences of age, gender, ethnicity, and sexuality. This enculturation shapes our lives outside the household, including the ways we think about gender roles, the division of labor, religious practices, warfare, politics, migration, and nationalism. Because cultural norms, values, and social structures are always evolving, kinship and family also become places of contestation, experimentation, and change that reflect and shape debates within the larger culture.

The study of kinship is one of anthropology's unique innovations for thinking about how culture works. In this chapter, we will explore the following questions about kinship:

- **How are we related to one another?**
- **Are biology and marriage the only bases for kinship?**
- **How are ideas of kinship linked to the nation-state?**
- **How is kinship changing in the modern world?**

We will examine the many strategies people use to form kinship groups, and we will consider the implications of kinship's changing expressions in the twenty-first century. By the end of this chapter, you should be ready to interpret your own family tree—not just by creating a list of relatives but also by considering how those ties are formed and what role your kin play in shaping who you are as an individual and as a member of society. You will also be prepared to understand and analyze how debates about kinship shape important aspects of our individual and collective lives locally, nationally, and globally.

How Are We Related to One Another?

Define the key anthropological concepts related to kinship.

Who are you related to? As we saw in Chapter 5, all humans are closely related genetically, sharing more than 99.9 percent of our DNA. Despite this close biological "kinship" among all humans, closer to home we tend to organize our personal relationships more specifically through systems of common biological descent, marriage, love, and choice. As you will discover throughout this chapter, cultures organize kinship relationships in a variety of ways. Some will be familiar to you, and others will not. All are equally valid.

DESCENT

descent group

A kinship group in which primary relationships are traced through certain consanguineal ("blood") relatives.

One way that humans construct kinship groups is by tracking genealogical descent. In **descent groups**, primary relationships are with certain consanguineal relatives (what U.S. culture refers to as "blood" relatives). These would include your mother, father, sister, brother, grandparents, children, and grandchildren as well as your uncles and aunts who are your parents' siblings—but not your uncles

and aunts who are married to your parents' siblings. Descent groups are often imagined as long chains of connections from parent to child that reach back through many generations to a common ancestor or group of ancestors and forward to imagined future generations.

Early anthropological studies through the mid-twentieth century assumed the descent group to be central to the social structure of most nonindustrial cultures outside Europe and North America (Evans-Pritchard 1951; Fortes 1949; Malinowski 1929, 1930; Radcliffe-Brown 1950). Anthropologists of that period expected to find extended descent groups that stretched back over many generations and worked together. Such groups were considered key to understanding each culture's economic, political, and religious dynamics because of the way kinship was understood to be a foundation for other large social networks extending beyond the immediate family into all aspects of cultural life. We will consider one classic example, the Nuer, later in this section.

In contrast, most European and North American cultures do not use descent to organize social groups. Although we may keep track of our ancestors over a few generations, we do so bilaterally—through both the mother's and the father's relatives—and we have generally not constructed large social networks based on kinship connections. In the United States, the Rockefeller, Kennedy, and Bush families might loosely qualify as descent groups. They stretch back over a few generations, tracing roots to a much more recent common ancestor (either John D. Rockefeller, Joseph Kennedy, or Prescott Bush), and although they are now subdivided into smaller segments, they still maintain strong enough connections that they sometimes function together on common economic, social, political, or ritual activities and projects. But such descent groups are extremely rare in North America.

Anthropologists distinguish two types of descent groups: lineages and clans. **Lineages** can clearly demonstrate genealogical connections through many generations, tracing the family tree to a founding (apical) ancestor. **Clans** likewise

What does a descent group look like? (*Left*) The Pham family gathers with Xuyen Pham (*Far right*), from whom they are descended. (*Right*) A Bush family portrait at the White House, 2005, including, seated from right, then governor of Florida Jeb Bush, former U.S. president George H. W. Bush, and, fourth from right, then president George W. Bush.

lineage

A type of descent group that traces genealogical connection through generations by linking persons to a founding ancestor.

clan

A type of descent group based on a claim to a founding ancestor but lacking genealogical documentation.

claim connection to a founding ancestor, but they do not provide the same genealogical documentation. Descent groups may be *matrilineal*, constructing the group through female ancestors, or *patrilineal*, tracing kinship through male ancestors. Both matrilineal and patrilineal patterns reflect *unilineal* descent because they build kinship groups through either one line or the other. In contrast, *ambilineal* descent groups—including Samoans, Maori, Hawaiians, and others in Southeast Asia and the Pacific—trace kinship through both the mother and the father. This alternative pattern is sometimes called *cognatic* or *bilateral*.

Most people in the world practice patrilineal descent to formally track kin group membership. At the same time, many people, for practical reasons, still build kinship networks bilaterally through both parents, even when tracing descent unilineally. Are you aware of how your own family traces descent?

The Nuer of Southern Sudan.
The Nuer people of southern Sudan in northeast Africa constitute a classic representation of the descent group. British anthropologist E. E. Evans-Pritchard studied this group in the 1930s (Evans-Pritchard 1951). At the time of his research and until the later part of the twentieth century, the Nuer were primarily a pastoral, cattle-herding people that moved between settlements throughout the year to adapt to rainy and dry seasons. The Nuer were a **patrilineal descent group**: Both boy and girl children were born into the group, but membership could only pass to the next generation through the sons who inherited membership through their fathers. Nuer clans were *exogamous*—meaning that marriages within the group were not permitted. Large clans were divided into lineages, although lineages were extensive enough to spread over several villages.

Cattle were the center of Nuer economic life. They were owned by men, but they were milked by women as well as by boys who had not yet reached the age of initiation into the descent group. A successful marriage proposal often required the groom to provide cattle in exchange for the bride.

The patrilineal kinship structures of clans and lineages provided the primary structure for Nuer political and economic activity. In the villages, the lineages collectively owned land, fisheries, and pastures. Ceremonial leadership of Nuer group life was organized under sacred ritual leaders, but these individuals did not control the social networks built around kinship and cattle, so they were not the driving force in Nuer culture (Stone 2009).

Searching for Kinship Patterns.
As early anthropologists gathered kinship data from cultures worldwide, they developed a limited number of general categories that facilitated comparison. Across vast geographic distances and language differences, only four primary systems were identified to classify relatives in the parental generation: *lineal, bifurcate merging, generational,* and *bifurcate collateral*. When beginning with the ego's generation (the ego being the central character

patrilineal descent group

A kinship group in which membership passes to the next generation from father to son.

MAP 9.1
The Nuer Region of East Africa

The Nuer of Sudan are a classic representation of a descent group. (*Top left*) A Nuer man, his sons, and cattle outside the family homestead, 1930s (photo by E. E. Evans-Pritchard). (*Top right*) A Nuer family homestead, 2007. (*Bottom left*) Nuer men leaping (beside Evans-Pritchard's tent) in a dance that often took the form of mock battles between village groups. Dances accompanied marriages and provided courtship opportunities for Nuer youth. (*Bottom right*) Nuer women dancing at the bride's family homestead at a contemporary Nuer wedding.

and starting point in tracing kinship relationships—for example, you in your own family tree), anthropologists found only six different ways of organizing relatives, in which the variation centered on the classification of siblings and cousins. Each of these six were named after a key group in which the pattern occurred: Inuit, Hawaiian, Sudanese, Omaha, Crow, and Iroquois (Figure 9.1).

FIGURE 9.1

Kinship Naming Systems

Early anthropologists identified only six general patterns worldwide for classifying relatives when beginning with the ego's generation: Inuit Hawaiian, Sudanese, Omaha, Crow, and Iroquois.

INUIT

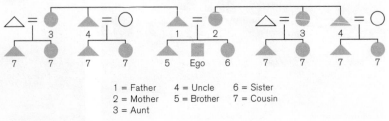

1 = Father   4 = Uncle   6 = Sister
2 = Mother   5 = Brother   7 = Cousin
3 = Aunt

The Inuit kinship naming system is the most common in Europe and North America. Only members of the nuclear family are given distinct terms. Aunts and uncles are distinguished from parents but not by side of the family. All cousins are lumped together.

HAWAIIAN

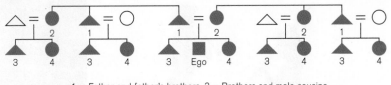

1 = Father and father's brothers 3 = Brothers and male cousins
2 = Mother and mother's sisters 4 = Sisters and female cousins

The Hawaiian system is the least complicated. The nuclear family is deemphasized, and relatives are distinguished only by generation and gender.

SUDANESE

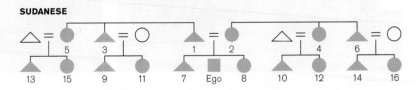

The Sudanese kinship system is the most complex. Each category of relative is given a distinct term based on genealogical distance from ego. There can be eight different cousin terms, all of which are distinguished from ego's brother and sister.

Source: Dennis O'Neil, "Kin Naming Systems: Part 1, The Nature of Kinship," http://anthro.palomar.edu/kinship/kinship_5.htm.

Generalized systems of kinship classification can be very useful for identifying and comparing broad patterns of social structure. But anthropologists have found that actual, local kinship patterns do not always match the generalized models. The ways in which human groups trace connections between generations—in other words, how they construct genealogies—can be messy and far from exact. Genealogies are full of gaps, interruptions, disruptions, uncertainties, and imagined or assumed connections. Some groups have extensive genealogies, but even these carefully constructed records may be partly mythical and based on limited

OMAHA

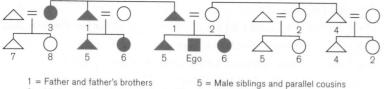

1 = Father and father's brothers
2 = Mother and females on mother's side
3 = Females on father's side
4 = Males on mother's side

5 = Male siblings and parallel cousins
6 = Female siblings and parallel cousins
7 = Male cross cousins
8 = Female cross cousins

The Omaha, Crow, and Iroquois naming systems trace kinship through unilineal descent—either patrilineally or matrilineally—so distinguishing between cousins takes on importance. The Omaha system is typical of kinship patterns traced through patrilineal descent.

CROW

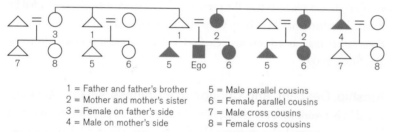

1 = Father and father's brothers
2 = Mother and mother's sisters
3 = Females on father's side
4 = Male on mother's side

5 = Male siblings and parallel cousins
6 = Female siblings and parallel cousins
7 = Male cross cousins
8 = Female cross cousins

The Crow system is typical of kinship patterns traced through matrilineal descent.

IROQUOIS

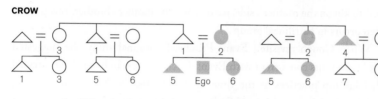

1 = Father and father's brother
2 = Mother and mother's sister
3 = Female on father's side
4 = Male on mother's side

5 = Male parallel cousins
6 = Female parallel cousins
7 = Male cross cousins
8 = Female cross cousins

The Iroquois kinship system can be traced either matrilineally or patrilineally. Note the same term is used for father and father's brother and for mother and mother's sister, reflecting shared membership in lineages.

recollections or partial history. In contrast, other groups have extremely shallow genealogical memories that span only two or three generations. Segments of these descent groups may no longer live together or act together. Other relatives may have been forgotten or excluded from the main line through conflict. Political, economic, and/or military upheaval, colonial interventions, and the establishment of modern nation-states may have disrupted collective memory and records. Or kinship patterns may have changed over time as groups adapted to external pressures. As a result, these groups' knowledge of individual ancestors and even whole generations may have been lost.

Once again, the Nuer are an excellent example. Despite representing one of the six key cross-cultural variations in kinship studies (Sudanese), their day-to-day kinship practices did not exactly match the clear patrilineal descent model that might be imagined on a Nuer family tree. Evans-Pritchard determined that the Nuer inherited formal group membership through patrilineal descent, but he and Kathleen Gough (1971), who revisited the study a generation later, found that most Nuer individuals continued to trace kinship relations through both parents. These bilateral kinship relationships created by marriage were often just as important as those created through descent. Specifically, while women married into the Nuer descent group and produced children for that group, they also provided their children with close connections to kin on the mother's side, particularly the mother's brother. This pattern often occurs in patrilineal groups.

When Gough revisited Evans-Pritchard's original study, she suggested that local events concurrent with Evans-Prichard's research may have affected Nuer kinship practices at the time. In the 1930s, the Nuer were resisting British colonial occupation of Sudan. In addition, they were involved in a conquest of the neighboring Dinka ethnic group. Additional intense conflicts existed among Nuer groups. Gough suggests that these tensions, conflicts, and disruptions may have intensified Nuer attention to kinship and marriage patterns as they attempted to reinforce group identity and assimilate outsiders. Gough also suggests that the particular expressions of kinship recorded by Evans-Pritchard may have been adaptations to political and economic conditions rather than an entrenched, changeless kinship norm (Gough 1971; see also Stone 2009).

MAP 9.2
Fuzhou

Kinship, Descent, and Change in a Chinese Village. As Gough found in her work with the Nuer, political factors can shape efforts to construct kinship—a pattern I also uncovered in my own research in a Chinese village. When I conducted fieldwork in the late 1990s, I thought I had found a classic, Nuer-style patrilineal descent group. Ninety percent of the men in the village had the surname *Chen* and traced their origins back to the founding Chen—the apical ancestor—whom they believed had settled in the area more than 700 years earlier. The village children, boys and girls, were all named Chen. But the Chen daughters were all to be married out to men in neighboring villages. The Chen men were to marry women from the same neighboring villages, who would then move in with them at home. The Chen family temple was the largest ancestral hall in the village and served as the center for venerating Chen ancestors. Until the 1960s, village lands, including agricultural plots and fisheries, were held in common by the Chen lineage, which acted like a small corporation. Male elders

allocated access to the collectively owned village property to the other males in the descent group during an annual lineage meeting.

Although the village appeared to be a textbook case of patrilineal descent, kinship is always a bit more complicated and interesting than anthropologists first imagine. In the late 1960s, family and temple ancestral records were destroyed as part of a chaotic and brutal national political movement known as the Cultural Revolution—a modernization campaign promoted by the Chinese government to throw out the old and bring in the new. Only in the 1990s did political and economic conditions improve enough for local villagers to consider reconstructing their lost records. An older village member who had become a university professor in the provincial capital accepted the task of writing and publishing a local village history book called a *zupu* ("gazetteer"). His research included an effort to reconstruct the village genealogy and the Chen line of descent. Funding came from villagers working abroad, particularly in the United States.

When the research was complete, however, the devastating impact of the Cultural Revolution became apparent. Without written records, the reconstructed descent-based genealogy relied primarily on oral histories stored in the memories of village elders. Many vividly recalled their parents' and grandparents' generations. Some had heard stories of a few prominent Chen villagers whose earlier travel, business success, or scholarship had made them famous in the villagers' collective memory. Of course, the apical ancestor, his sons, and a few of their immediate descendants had been remembered. Unfortunately, most of the generations prior to 1900 had been left blank. The genealogical details, if they had ever existed, had been destroyed during the Cultural Revolution.

Migration has also challenged the Chen descent group's ability to maintain kinship connections, especially in the context of the current global age. In fact, fully 70 percent of the villagers—most between the ages of eighteen and fifty—have left China since the early 1980s to seek their fortunes in the United States, Japan, South America, Canada, Europe, and the Middle East. Some return to visit their hometown. Most marry and have children in their new host country. According to the rules of the patrilineal descent group, all children born to villagers working abroad still belong in the descent group, and males can pass on that membership to the next generation. But faced with such a massive out-migration and global diaspora of the lineage, how would the Chen descent group keep track of its most far-flung members?

New York is the primary international destination for people from the village. There, with the support of village leaders in China, immigrants have created a village hometown association to rebuild and strengthen hometown kinship ties. The association enables villagers to reconnect, provide mutual support, share information, and use their kinship networks to improve their immigrant experience. Association leaders also keep track of fellow villagers, their marriages, and their offspring. They report these developments back to the Chen family elders in China for proper recording. Through this process, long-held village strategies for kinship formation and group building are adapting to the challenges of international migration, spurred by globalization. Modern communication and transportation technologies are enabling Chinese villagers to innovatively extend their notions of patrilineal descent, both spatially beyond China's national boundary and temporally forward into the future.

Certainly, the forces of globalization, including migration and time-space compression, are placing stress on kinship systems worldwide. Members of kinship groups commonly relocate temporarily or permanently to nearby factories or to jobs abroad, seeking improved economic and educational opportunities or fleeing natural disasters and political upheavals. Although the generalized kinship categories developed by an earlier generation of anthropologists have provided insights into broad patterns of kinship, anthropologists who study kinship today confront more fluid, flexible, and creative kinship patterns.

MARRIAGE AND AFFINAL TIES

affinal relationship

A kinship relationship established through marriage and/or alliance, not through biology or common descent.

A second way humans form kinship groups, distinct from descent or consanguineal groups, is through marriage—what anthropologists refer to as **affinal relationships**. Unlike the construction of kinship groups through descent, which links direct genealogical ancestors and descendants, marriage builds kinship ties between two people who are (usually) not immediate biological kin. Marriage also creates a relationship between the spouses' respective kinship groups, called "in-laws" in U.S. culture. The new kinship group created through marriage is linked through affinity and alliance, not through shared biology and common descent.

Something like marriage exists in every culture, but the exact contours and characteristics of these relationships vary widely—so widely, in fact, that it is difficult to say that any one characteristic is universal. **Marriages** create socially recognized relationships that may involve physical and emotional intimacy, sexual pleasure, reproduction and raising of children, mutual support and companionship, and shared legal rights to property and inheritance. The bond of marriage may also serve to create connection, communication, and alliance between groups.

Marriages take many forms, including arranged marriages and companionate marriages. **Arranged marriages**, orchestrated by the families of the involved parties, continue to be prominent in many cultures in Asia, the Pacific, the Middle East, and Africa. Arranged marriages are even common among some religious groups in the United States and, in a sense, among some segments of the upper class, who send their children to elite private schools to meet future partners and encourage in-group marriage. These traditional marriages ensure the reproduction and continuation of the kinship group and build alliances with other kin groups. Thus, the couple's parents may view the economic and political consequences of the marriage as too important to be left to the whims of two young people. In this context, marriage becomes a social obligation and a symbol of commitment to the larger kinship group rather than a mechanism for personal satisfaction and fulfillment. Alliance marriages of this sort require extensive negotiation to balance the needs of the group and the intimate personal feelings of the individuals being married. Bonds of affection may develop in an arranged marriage, but this is not the primary goal.

What about Love? Today, marriage patterns are changing rapidly. Younger generations are increasingly thinking of love, intimacy, and personal pleasure—not social obligation—as the foundation on which to build families and kinship relations. Love—and what anthropologists call **companionate marriages**, which are built on love—is the ideal to be achieved (Chan 2006; Gregg 2003; Inhorn 1996; Rebhun 1999; Wardlow 2006; Yan 2003).

Cross-cultural ethnographic research reveals diverse local expressions of companionate marriage but shows that young people around the world are increasingly framing marriage in terms of love, in contrast to the marriage patterns of their parents (Hirsch 2007). Consider for a moment how your own views on marriage compare to those of your parents and grandparents.

On a global scale, changing notions of marriage are combining with expanding economic opportunities for women to spur a rapid rise in divorce

marriage
A socially recognized relationship that may involve physical and emotional intimacy as well as legal rights to property and inheritance.

arranged marriage
Marriage orchestrated by the families of the involved parties.

companionate marriage
Marriage built on love, intimacy, and personal choice rather than social obligation.

MAP 9.3
Brazil

and marriage dissolution. Melanie Medeiros's (2014) ethnographic study of the small town of Brogodo in the rural interior of Northeast Brazil reveals the local impact of these transformations. Populated by Afro-Brazilian descendants of enslaved people and plantation workers, Brogodo's economy shrank drastically in the early twentieth century because of the decline of the mining industry, leaving residents to rely primarily on small-scale farming and remittances from relatives in urban areas. When the adjacent region was declared a national park in 1985, however, the growing ecotourism industry generated better-paying local jobs—particularly for women, who were recruited to work as receptionists, waitresses and housekeepers. Economic opportunities for men were more limited, as tour guide positions went primarily to bilingual outsiders. Medeiros's survey of local households in Brogodo found that 40 percent of couples were separated or divorced—and 95 percent of those dissolutions occurred at the request of women. Interviews confirmed that women's increased economic independence, combined with shifting expectations about gender roles and marriage, was driving up the rate of marital dissolution in Brogodo.

polygyny

Marriage between one man and two or more women.

polyandry

Marriage between one woman and two or more men.

monogamy

A relationship between only two partners.

Monogamy, Polygyny, and Polyandry. Cultural rules, often inscribed in law, may determine who is a legitimate or preferred marriage partner. They may even determine how many people one can marry. Historically, some cultures, such as the Nuer of Sudan or the Brahmans of Nepal, practiced **polygyny**—several marriages involving one man and two or more women. In a few cultures, including the Nayar of India and the Nyimba of Tibet and Nepal, **polyandry** has been common—marriages between one woman and two or more men (Goldstein 1987). Most marriages in the world demonstrate **monogamy**—marriage (usually) between one man and one woman, though, as

The Nyimba of Nepal practice polyandry. Here, a woman (*Center*) stands with her two husbands (on either side of her) and her father (*Far left*). Why do different marriage systems emerge in different cultures?

of 2022, thirty-one countries also legally recognize same-sex marriages, as we will discuss later in the chapter.

Even where monogamous marriages are the norm, it is common for people to marry more than one person in their lifetime. How does this happen? Marriages may be interrupted by divorce or death. In these cases, individuals who marry again reflect a process called *serial monogamy* in which monogamous marriages follow one after the other.

Incest Taboos. Just as some form of marriage exists in essentially all cultures, all cultures have some form of **incest taboo**, or rules that forbid sexual relations with certain close relatives. Such taboos relate to nuclear family members: parents and children, siblings, and grandparents and grandchildren. Incest taboos also affect marriage patterns. A few historical examples of brother–sister marriage exist: among the Inca of Peru, among certain traditional Hawaiian groups, and among ancient Egyptian royalty (perhaps to preserve family control over wealth and power). But these cases are rare. Incest taboos universally prohibit marriage between siblings and between parents and children. But can a person marry a cousin?

incest taboo

Cultural rules that forbid sexual relations with certain close relatives.

Beyond the nuclear family, incest taboos vary from culture to culture. In some contemporary cultures, including parts of China, India, the Middle East, and Africa, *cross-cousins* (children of a mother's brother or father's sister) are preferred marriage partners, but *parallel cousins* (children of a father's brother or a mother's sister) are excluded. Even in the United States, incest rules regarding marriage between cousins vary from state to state. Nineteen states allow *first-cousin* marriages (between the children of two siblings). More distant cousins are not excluded from marriage under U.S. law. No other country in the Western world prohibits first-cousin marriage. Moreover, although it is illegal in the United States to marry a *half-sibling* (a brother or sister with whom one shares a parent), this is not illegal in many other cultures. Can you think of anyone in your family or a friend's family who is married to a cousin?

Even though the incest taboo is universal, its origins are unclear. Some scholars have suggested that the taboo arises from an instinctive horror of sex with immediate family members that developed during our evolutionary history (Hobhouse 1915; Lowie 1920). But studies of primates do not reveal a consistent incest taboo that humans might have inherited (Rodseth et al. 1991). Furthermore, if this instinctive horror existed, then it seems likely that humans would not need to create taboos to restrict incest.

Other theories have addressed the issue from different perspectives. For example, anthropologist Bronisław Malinowski (1929) and psychologist Sigmund Freud (1952) both suggested that incest taboos might have developed to protect the family unit from sexual competitiveness and jealousy, which would disrupt cooperation. However, neither scholar could substantiate this claim with historical or contemporary ethnographic data. Another theory suggests that incest taboos arose out of concern that inbreeding would promote biological degeneration and genetically abnormal offspring (Morgan 1877). However, incest taboos predate the development of population science and the understanding of human genetics.

Even using contemporary genetic information, the science does not support the assumptions behind the incest taboo. For instance, incest does not create defective genes. If a harmful trait runs in the family, systematic inbreeding will increase the possibility of the defective gene being passed along and amplified in the gene pool, but there are few actual historical human examples of this kind of inbreeding over generations. Genetic studies of consanguineous unions (between "blood" relatives) show some increased risk of congenital defects, but only within the studies' margins of error. These risks are actually less than the risk of congenital defects in children whose mothers are over the age of forty, yet this older population is not prohibited from marrying or giving birth (Bennett et al. 2002). Therefore, despite the universal existence of incest taboos, they vary widely in extent, and no consensus exists as to their origins or exact purpose.

Other Marriage Patterns. Beyond explicit incest taboos, all cultures have norms about who is a legitimate or preferred marriage partner. In some groups, including most descent groups, marriage tends to reflect **exogamy**, meaning marriage to someone outside the group. Other groups practice **endogamy**, requiring marriage inside the group. Although kin group exogamy is more prevalent, endogamy exists in numerous cultures. It is practiced, for example, within the Indian caste system and within whole ethnic groups, as evidenced by both historical and contemporary U.S. marriage patterns.

exogamy

Marriage to someone outside the kinship group.

endogamy

Marriage to someone within the kinship group.

In the United States, we practice *kindred exogamy*: We avoid, either by force of law or by power of tradition, marriage with certain relatives. At the same time, we also follow clear patterns of class, race, and religious endogamy. Indeed, most marriages occur between people of the same economic class, the same religious tradition, and within the same race (U.S. Census Bureau 2021). As noted in Chapter 2, interracial marriages were outlawed for most of U.S. history, and only in 1967 did the U.S. Supreme Court rule anti-miscegenation laws unconstitutional. Although interracial marriage is legal today, intense patterns of racial endogamy continue.

Most monogamous marriages occur between one man and one woman, but there are important exceptions, including female marriage among the Nuer of Sudan and the Nandi of Kenya. Today, same-sex marriage is increasingly gaining acceptance globally, and it is legally recognized in the Netherlands, Belgium, Canada, Spain, South Africa, Norway, Sweden, Argentina, Iceland, Portugal, Denmark, France, Brazil, Uruguay, New Zealand, the United Kingdom, Luxembourg, Ireland, Greenland, Colombia, Finland, Germany, Malta, Australia,

Austria, Taiwan, Ecuador, Costa Rica, Switzerland, and Chile. In the United States, as of June 2015, same-sex marriages are legal in all fifty states.

Whether arranged or not; whether monogamous, polygynous, or polyandrous; and whether between people of the same or opposite gender, marriages may be accompanied by an exchange of gifts—most commonly, bridewealth and dowry—used to formalize and legalize the relationship. Though most contemporary Western cultures view marriage as an individual matter entered into by a couple who are romantically in love, in many non-Western cultures, marriages focus on the establishment of strategic alliances, relationships, and obligations between groups—namely, the bride's kin and the groom's kin. Bridewealth and dowry gifts formalize and legalize marriages and establish the relationship between these groups.

Bridewealth—common in many parts of the Middle East and Africa, where it often involves the exchange of cattle, cash, or other goods—is a gift from the groom and his kin to the bride's kin. Often thought of as a means to compensate her family for the loss of the bride, bridewealth agreements also establish reciprocal rights and obligations of the husband and wife, give legitimacy to their children, and assign the children to the husband's family. Even with the exchange of bridewealth, though, marriages may not always remain stable. Incompatibility, infertility, and infidelity can threaten the marriage agreement and trigger a return of the bridewealth. In this way, bridewealth can stabilize the marriage by establishing a vested interest for both extended families in the marriage's success (Stone 2009).

Through a **dowry**, the bride's family gives gifts to the groom's family on the occasion of marriage. Common in India, a dowry may be part of a woman's family inheritance that the woman and her new husband can use to establish their household. In many cases, dowries are seen as compensation to a husband and his family for taking on the responsibility of a wife, perhaps because of women's relatively low status in India or because upper-class and upper-caste women are not supposed to work. Today, gifts often include personal and household items. Compulsory dowries are no longer legal in India (since 1961), but dowries are still quite common as part of the public process of transferring rights and legitimizing alliances. In some unfortunate instances where the dowry is considered insufficient, the bride may become the victim of domestic violence. In extreme cases, this may lead to the murder or suicide of the bride, sometimes through bride burning or self-immolation. Such practices have come under severe criticism and are targeted by both Indian and international human rights groups that are committed to protecting the rights and lives of Indian women (Stone 2009).

While interracial relationships are legal in the United States today, intense patterns of racial endogamy (marriage within the same group) continue. Here, Mildred and Richard Loving embrace at a press conference the day after the U.S. Supreme Court ruled in their favor, June 13, 1967, in *Loving v. Virginia*, overturning Virginia's laws banning interracial marriage.

bridewealth

The gift of goods or money from the groom's family to the bride's family as part of the marriage process.

dowry

The gift of goods or money from the bride's family to the groom's family as part of the marriage process.

Are Biology and Marriage the Only Bases for Kinship?

Describe ethnographic examples of the global diversity of kinship formations.

Cross-cultural ethnographic research reveals diverse strategies for constructing kinship ties that do not involve direct biological connection or marriage alliances. As you will see, the range of strategies underscores the fluid, socially constructed aspect of kinship in many cultures.

HOUSES, HEARTHS, AND KINSHIP: THE LANGKAWI OF MALAYSIA

MAP 9.4
Langkawi

Among Malay villagers on the island of Langkawi, studied by Janet Carsten in the 1990s, kinship is not only given at birth but also acquired throughout life (Carsten 1997). The Langkawi house and its hearth—where people gather to cook and eat—serve as places to construct kinship. In particular, Langkawi kinship is acquired through co-residence and co-feeding. In the local thinking, "blood" is formed by eating food cooked at home. Other bodily substances, specifically breast milk and semen, are regarded as forms of blood. Thus, a husband and wife gradually become more similar by living and eating together. Sisters and brothers have the closest kinship relationship in childhood because they grow up in the same household eating the same food, but as they marry and move out of the shared home, their "blood" becomes less similar.

The Malay ideal is to marry someone close in terms of genealogy, geography, social status, or disposition. But perhaps because of the Langkawis' history of mobility, as well as the arrival of settlers in their outlying region of the Malay state, local notions of kinship have allowed new people to become close kin by living and eating together. For example, many children in the community have grown up spending significant time in homes with adults other than their birth parents. This fostering has been common for nieces, nephews, grandchildren, and others who are welcomed into the foster family and treated on an equal basis with those born into the family.

In addition, Langkawi understandings of fostering have often included expressions of hospitality in the community, whether one is a short-term or long-term visitor, a visiting student, or a distant relative. Villagers assume that all those who live together and eat together, regardless of their backgrounds, gradually come to resemble one another physically. The ideal guest—successfully fostered—stays for a long time, becomes part of the community, marries a local person, and raises children. In this way, the individual fully enters the kin group. This flexible

process has built kinship relations that do not require the connection of biology or marriage. Instead, "[h]ouses and their hearths are the sites of the production of kinship" (Carsten 1997, 128; Carsten 2004; Peletz 1999; Stone 2009).

Among the Langkawi in Malaysia, kinship is created by sharing meals prepared in the family hearth and living together in the same house.

CREATING KIN TO SURVIVE POVERTY: BLACK NETWORKS NEAR CHICAGO, ILLINOIS

Kinship can even be a means to survive poverty, as Carol Stack's *All Our Kin: Strategies for Survival in a Black Community* (1974) demonstrates. This ethnography is a classic in anthropological kinship studies. Through deep involvement in an impoverished urban African American community called the Flats in a town outside Chicago, Stack uncovered residents' complex survival strategies based on extended kinship networks.

MAP 9.5
Chicago

Although the federal government's 1965 Moynihan Report, titled "The Negro Family: The Case for National Action," had branded the Black family as disorganized, dysfunctional, and lost in a culture of poverty of its own making, Stack found otherwise. She uncovered a dynamic set of kinship networks based on mutual reciprocity through which residents managed to survive conditions of intense structural poverty and long-term unemployment.

These kinship networks included biological kin and *fictive kin*—those who became kin. They stretched among households and across generations, extending to include all those willing to participate in a system of mutual support. Members provided child care. They loaned money to others in need. They took in children who needed a foster home for a while. They borrowed clothes. They exchanged all kinds of things when asked. They cared for one another's sick or aging family members. Despite survival odds stacked against them in a community with few jobs, dilapidated housing, and chronic poverty, residents of the Flats succeeded in building lifelines for survival through their extended kinship networks (McAdoo 2000; Taylor 2000).

How Are Ideas of Kinship Linked to the Nation-State?

Assess how ideas of kinship are shaped by the nation-state.

References to the nation often invoke powerful metaphors of homeland, motherland, fatherland, and ancestral home, effectively entwining notions of kinship and family with the power of the nation-state. These concepts evoke ideas of family that can then be used to consolidate political force and build a sense of common nationality and ethnicity. Indeed, Benedict Anderson, in *Imagined Communities* (1983), marvels at the ability of nation-states to inspire a common national or ethnic identity among people who have never met, most likely never will meet, and have little in common socially, politically, or economically. Yet many people feel so connected to their country that they are even willing to die for it. How does this idea of the "nation" gain such emotional power? Janet Carsten (2004) suggests that nationalism draws heavily on ideas of kinship and family to create a sense of connection among very different people.

Like membership in many families, citizenship in the nation generally derives from birth and biology. Citizenship may be conveyed through direct descent from a current citizen. Another key pathway to membership in some nations, available to immigrants and other outsiders, is through marriage. Over time, members of the nation come to see themselves as part of an extended family that shares a common ancestry and a deep biological connection. As the boundaries blur among kinship, nationalism, and even religion, these powerful metaphors shape our actions and experiences (Carsten 2004).

REPRODUCING JEWS: ISSUES OF ARTIFICIAL INSEMINATION IN ISRAEL

In Israel, we can see how women serve as key players in defining and maintaining kinship connections and reproducing Judaism and the Israeli nation-state. Susan Kahn's ethnography *Reproducing Jews: A Cultural Account of Assisted Conception in*

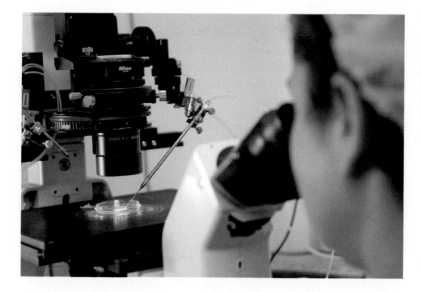

What is the relationship between kinship and the nation-state? A lab technician looks through a microscope while fertilizing egg cells at a fertility clinic in Tel Aviv, Israel.

Israel (2000) provides a dramatic example of the powerful intersections among reproduction, kinship, religion, and the state. For historical and religious reasons, Jewish women in Israel have felt great pressure to reproduce the family and the nation. Israel's national health policies have heavily favored increased reproduction. The national health insurance, for instance, has subsidized all assisted reproductive technologies, and it does not promote family planning services to prevent pregnancy. Today, the country has more fertility clinics per person than any other nation in the world, and it was the first to legalize surrogate motherhood.

MAP 9.6
Israel

Kahn's study examines a small but growing group of single Jewish mothers who are giving birth through artificial insemination. Because Jewishness passes down matrilineally from mother to child, what happens when a child is conceived through assisted reproductive technologies? These matters are of vital importance to the reproduction of Judaism and the state of Israel and, thus, have been debated intensely by Jewish rabbis and Israeli state policy makers alike. Some scenarios are straightforward. For instance, in the eyes of the Israeli state, any children conceived through artificial insemination and born to unmarried Jewish women are legitimate citizens. The line of descent and religious inheritance through the mother is clear. As evidence, the state provides these unmarried mothers with a wide range of support, including housing, child care, and tax breaks.

But other scenarios spur complex disagreements about religion and nationality. What is the effect on citizenship and religious identity when non-Jewish men donate sperm to Jewish women? Who is considered to be the father—the sperm donor or the mother's husband? When Jewish women carry to term eggs from non-Jewish women, who is considered to be the mother—the donor of the egg or the woman who carries the egg to term? The situation is equally complicated if a non-Jewish surrogate mother carries the embryo of a Jewish woman that was fertilized by a Jewish man through in vitro fertilization.

Much is at stake in these arguments for the Jewish religion and for the state of Israel. Decisions about kinship in these cases of assisted reproductive technologies intersect with heated debates about how Judaism is reproduced and how Israel is populated. In fact, these decisions have implications not only for the Jewish religion but also for notions of ethnic and national belonging and for the pathways to legal citizenship in the state of Israel (Feldman 2001; Finkler 2002; Nahman 2002; Stone 2009).

How Is Kinship Changing in the Modern World?

Analyze how globalization is reshaping global expressions of kinship.

Kinship patterns are rapidly changing around the world in response to cultural shifts, changing gender roles, new imaginations of marriage, technological advances, and processes of globalization.

THE NUCLEAR FAMILY: THE IDEAL VERSUS THE REALITY

The nuclear family concept developed in Western industrialized cultures as families adapted to an economic system that required increased mobility to follow job opportunities wherever they might lead. Though people are born into a **family of orientation** (in which they grow up and develop life skills), when they reach adulthood, they are expected to detach from their nuclear family of orientation, choose a mate, and construct a new nuclear **family of procreation** (in which they reproduce and raise their own children). These "detachable" nuclear family units are extremely well adapted to a culture that prioritizes economic success, independence, and mobility over geographic stability and intergenerational continuity. Anthropologists like David Schneider have shown how this view of the nuclear family has become entrenched as the standard against which to judge other family forms (Schneider 1980).

Historical studies suggest that the nuclear family's status as the cornerstone of U.S. culture may be more myth than reality (Coontz 1988, 1992). Although the nuclear family came into prominence during a unique period of economic expansion after World War II, it had not played a major role in the kinship

family of orientation
The family group in which one is born, grows up, and develops life skills.

family of procreation
The family group created when one reproduces and within which one rears children.

history of the United States before that time. The idealized nuclear family of the twentieth century did not exist for the early colonists; it emerged as nineteenth-century industrialization spurred increased mobility by smaller family units and undermined extended family groups. Even at its height in the mid-twentieth century, participation in the nuclear family model was far from universal. It was limited to a minority of Americans, particularly those in the White middle class (Carsten 2004; Coontz 1988, 1992; Stone 2009).

Current kinship patterns in the United States are changing rapidly, just as they are in many other parts of the world. A wide variety of newly constructed family forms and kinship networks are emerging (Figure 9.2). Families are creatively renegotiating kinship after divorce, constructing new relationships to include stepparents, stepchildren, stepsiblings, multiple sets of grandparents, and extended households of former spouses. Unmarried couples are living together. Same-sex couples are having or adopting children. Families are supplementing biological connections and affinal marriage connections with alternative family forms based on friendship, respect, and mutual support. New reproductive technologies are yielding families of choice through in vitro fertilization, artificial insemination, and surrogacy. These patterns reflect new residential and interpersonal relationships that contrast sharply with the imagined privacy and separation associated with the nuclear family ideal.

CHOSEN FAMILIES

Kath Weston's (1991) ethnographic study of the construction of gay and lesbian families in San Francisco in the 1980s, *Families We Choose*, revealed how chosen families can take on the characteristics of stability, continuity, endurance, and permanence to become "real" when biological families are inadequate or fail. Not surprisingly, chosen families come in many shapes and sizes. Gay and straight friends, biological children, children adopted formally and informally, and former lovers all can become kin. Close friends can become family. Support networks and caregivers can take the place of biological kin and become kin themselves. In chosen families, love, compassion, and the hard work of care over time make kinship very real (Bolin 1992; Lewin 1992).

THE IMPACT OF ASSISTED REPRODUCTIVE TECHNOLOGIES

Discussions of technologies that assist in human reproduction—such as sperm and egg donation, in vitro fertilization, surrogacy, and cloning—have filled the popular media, religious publications, courtrooms, and legislative halls of government. The emergence of these technologies raises questions about the rights of parents who use them and of children born as a result. Culture, in the form of

medical technology, is now shaping biology. The long-term implications of this shift for our ideas and experience of kinship and family are unclear, but they deserve consideration (Franklin 1997).

Reproductive technologies are not new. Most, if not all, cultures have had techniques for promoting or preventing conception or enabling or terminating pregnancy, including fertility enhancements, contraceptives, abortion, and cesarean surgeries. Over the last thirty years, technological innovations have opened new avenues for scientific intervention in the reproductive process and the formation of kinship. DNA testing can now determine the identity of a child's father with remarkable certainty, erasing doubts about paternity. Medical tests can now identify the sex of unborn children, a practice that has become problematic in parts of India and China where a strong cultural preference for male children has led to the early termination of many female fetuses (Davis-Floyd and Dumit 1997). Across the globe, when reproductive technologies become increasingly specialized, the implications for cultural constructs such as family and kinship become progressively more complex.

Increasingly, people are creating kinship through choice. Here, a gay couple in Chengdu, China, share their home with their adopted son, daughter-in-law, and grandson.

FAMILIES OF SAME-SEX PARTNERS

Same sex partners and their families have become increasingly woven into the fabric of U.S. cultural norms and values. Television shows and movies routinely include gay characters and their families. Celebrities like Elton John, Jillian Michaels, Niecy Nash, Ricky Martin, Wanda Sykes, Karamo Brown, Alec Mapa, and Neil Patrick Harris raise children with their same-sex partners. The United Methodist Church ordained its first openly gay bishop, Karen Oliveto, in 2016. And when a high school in Louisiana canceled its senior prom in 2010 rather than allow a graduating student to bring her girlfriend as her date, a group of parents organized an alternative prom so the girls could attend.

Still, cultural debates about sexuality and same-sex marriage in the United States are intense and by no means settled among certain segments of the population. Within the debate we can see the contestation of cultural norms and values. Opponents raise concerns that these alternative kinship patterns will cause the breakdown of the traditional family and that the acceptance of same-sex relationships will lead to social disorder.

Drawing on generations of cross-cultural research on kinship, marriage, and the family, in 2004 the American Anthropological Association issued the following statement:

> The results of more than a century of anthropological research on households, kinship relationships, and families, across cultures and through time, provide no support whatsoever for the view that either civilization or viable social orders depend upon marriage as an exclusively heterosexual institution. Rather, anthropological research supports the conclusion that a vast array of family types, including families built upon same-sex partnerships, can contribute to stable and humane societies. (American Anthropological Association 2004)

From a cross-cultural perspective, we see that there is no single definition of marriage, but many. As anthropologist Linda Stone notes, "From a global, cross-cultural perspective, those who seek same-sex marriage are not trying to redefine marriage, but merely to define it for themselves, in their own interests, as people around the world have always done" (Stone 2009, 271).

TRANSNATIONAL MIGRATION, KIN CARE, AND AGING IN GHANA

Today's unprecedented migration flows of people searching for work have spread generations of families across national boundaries and, in turn, affected kinship structures around the globe. Anthropologist Cati Coe's early research, detailed in her book *The Scattered Family* (2013), focuses on the transnational kinship practices of immigrants from Ghana, West Africa, who live and work in the United States. In Ghanaian culture, family strategies of kin care, including care for children and the elderly, have been highly valued. But transnational migration and parenting strategies have forced a reworking of many older patterns. For example, in addition to sending money to support their families back home, many Ghanaians working in the United States also send their young children back to Ghana. To these parents, allowing their children to grow up in the care of grandparents in an extended family environment seems preferable to raising them in a situation characterized by the uncertainties of immigrant sojourns. Physically separated from their children, mothers and fathers working abroad hope that material and financial support will be adequate evidence of their parental love within these transnational families.

In a Ghanaian culture known for its respect of elders, government policy on aging has placed almost exclusive responsibility for the care of the country's senior citizens on family and kin—a policy that has remained constant despite

Women exercise at a weekly group meeting for the elderly in the rural town of Bankoe, Ghana.

significant shifts in national and global economic and social realities. In recent years, rural to urban migration within Ghana has made urban centers younger and turned many rural areas into de facto retirement communities. Women are increasingly working outside the household. Longer life spans have meant a reshaping of intergenerational relations as families reorganize to provide synchronized care for children, grandparents, and even great-grandparents, whose lives now intertwine.

Coe's most recent work, *Changes in Care: Aging, Migration, and Social Class in West Africa* (2019), extends her earlier research to focus directly on the impact of transnational family configurations on the elderly and the experience of aging in Ghana. What happens, Coe asks, when the kinship system of care for frail and elderly relatives is disrupted by transnational migration, particularly when previous economic instabilities and internal migration have already altered these kinship repertoires?

Coe's research brings to light the many creative ways that Ghanaian families and local communities are adapting long-standing familial practices to a contemporary globalized setting. In urban areas, Coe's study finds that wealthy elites and some in the middle class supported by international remittances are fueling the rise of residential nursing homes and commercial care services—an outsourcing of kin care that would have been unimaginable in Ghanaian culture only a few years ago. In more rural areas, families and communities, also sometimes supported by remittances, are creating adult day care centers. These facilities, many operated by local churches, give elders a space to congregate for social interaction, singing, music, and exercise, and they serve as points of contact for those needing additional services like health care. As Coe notes, the transnational parenting strategies of Ghanaians working abroad are not so much undermining long-established family kin care practices as they are contributing to innovations in more traditional practices that have been changing for some time in response to the effects of globalization.

Toolkit

Thinking Like an Anthropologist
Kinship in Personal and Global Perspective

We experience kinship all the time, although we may not use that term to describe it. Kinship is close to home, for it comes alive in the people we live with, eat with, play with. It is vital as we experience the most dramatic periods of our personal lives. You will continue to make kinship and family relationships—perhaps through marriage, having children, and choosing close friends who ultimately become family. Thinking like an anthropologist can help you better understand these experiences. And in today's globally interconnected world, understanding the vast diversity of kinship patterns may help you navigate relationships with classmates, friends, family, and colleagues. As you do so, keep in mind the questions that have guided our discussion in this chapter:

- **How are we related to one another?**
- **Are biology and marriage the only bases for kinship?**
- **How are ideas of kinship linked to the nation-state?**
- **How is kinship changing in the modern world?**

In thinking about the complex kinship issues described at the beginning of this chapter, how can we apply this chapter's ideas to better understand the situation of families in China and, more generally, any future changes in the constructs of kin and family? Who is related to whom? Who decides? What role does the state play in defining kinship? Is kinship primarily biological, or can family be chosen? Who constitutes your own family? As you traced your family tree, did you see that kinship is not only about creating a list of relatives but also about understanding the many ways those ties are formed and the role that kin play in shaping you as an individual and as a member of society? These tools of anthropological analysis will become increasingly important to you as you engage changing concepts of kinship in cultures across the globe during the twenty-first century.

Key Terms

kinship (p. 250)

nuclear family (p. 251)

descent group (p. 252)

lineage (p. 253)

clan (p. 253)

patrilineal descent group (p. 254)

affinal relationship (p. 260)

marriage (p. 261)

arranged marriage (p. 261)

companionate marriage (p. 261)

polygyny (p. 262)

polyandry (p. 262)

monogamy (p. 262)

incest taboo (p. 263)

exogamy (p. 264)

endogamy (p. 264)

bridewealth (p. 265)

dowry (p. 265)

family of orientation (p. 270)

family of procreation (p. 270)

Part 3

The world is changing rapidly in the twenty-first century. People are on the move, spurred by changes in the global economy, political systems, communication and transportation infrastructures, and more. At Tongi Station on the outskirts of Dhaka, Bangladesh, hundreds of people sit on the roof of an overcrowded train to travel homeward for Eid al-Fitr, a Muslim festival marking the end of the fasting month of Ramadan.

Change in the Modern World

বাংলাদে

Chapter 10
The Global Economy

Learning Objectives

- Define what an economy is from an anthropological perspective.

- Describe how trade and colonialism have shaped the global economy.

- Understand core theories anthropologists use to explain the modern world economy.

- Explain the key organizing principles of the global economy.

- Analyze the global economic connections between workers and consumers.

- Apply the theories of key thinkers on class and inequality to real-life situations.

- Use anthropological concepts to explain the relationship between migration and the economy.

Where does your chocolate come from?
A young man on an eastern Côte d'Ivoire
farm breaks cocoa pods to extract the beans
used to make chocolate.

Do you know where your last chocolate bar came from?

Côte d'Ivoire, West Africa, exports 40 percent of the world's cocoa, which is used to make chocolate. Much of the country is covered in tropical forest, amid which are plantations that farmers carved out with hand tools. Seven million Ivoirians make a living farming cocoa and coffee. Although the global price for cocoa—set on the commodities market in New York City—is relatively high, Côte d'Ivoire's farmers see little return for their work. The bulk of the profits go to transnational agricultural corporations, such as U.S.-based Cargill, Archer Daniels Midland (ADM), and the Swiss firm Barry Callebaut. These corporations buy cocoa beans and process them into chocolate products to be eaten worldwide. Few local farmers in Côte d'Ivoire can afford a chocolate bar.

In recent years, Côte d'Ivoire has been riven by poverty, civil war, and conflict over cocoa and coffee revenues. In a fiercely contested election in 2010, Alassane Ouattara defeated incumbent Laurent Gbagbo for the presidency. Gbagbo's regime had relied on high taxes on cocoa and coffee farmers to subsidize its excesses and to fund Gbagbo's paramilitary hit squads. The election of Ouattara, a former deputy director of the International Monetary Fund (IMF), gave Ivoirians hope for a more secure and prosperous future. But Gbagbo refused to acknowledge his loss in the election and remained ensconced in the presidential palace. By clinging to power and stirring ethnic violence, Gbagbo pushed the country toward civil war.

To undercut Gbagbo's financial base, Ouattara called on international corporations to embargo Côte d'Ivoire's coffee and cocoa exports, claiming that Gbagbo used profits from the sales to fund his armed resistance. Giant U.S. agribusiness corporations eventually pledged to cooperate, but they refused to allow independent inspection of their exports. Many nongovernmental organizations (NGOs) charged that Côte d'Ivoire was circumventing the embargo by shipping its coffee and cocoa overland to neighboring Mali and Burkina Faso, which were reselling the goods to the same corporations.

As fighting between Gbagbo's and Ouattara's supporters escalated in 2011, the French military, returning to its colonial role, stormed the airport outside Abidjan, the country's economic capital and primary port. The French had established a colony in Côte d'Ivoire in 1840 to enter the ivory trade and to build coffee and cocoa plantations. Even after Côte d'Ivoire's independence in 1960, however, the French maintained a strong economic and military presence there. In the hope of limiting violence in the civil war, France joined with the United Nations to create a demilitarized zone stretching across the country. French and U.N. soldiers then isolated the presidential palace, still occupied by the defeated Gbagbo, until forces loyal to new president Ouattara ousted Gbagbo from the residence and arrested him. Despite continuing hostility between supporters of Gbagbo and Ouattara, in 2012 the country's economy began to

What role have chocolate revenues played in the recent conflict in Côte d'Ivoire? Here, soldiers loyal to newly installed president Alassane Ouattara patrol after the arrest of former president Gbagbo.

recover (Monnier 2013; North 2011). In recent years, cocoa production has stabilized, France and China have launched large infrastructure projects, and the International Cocoa Organization has moved its headquarters from London to Abidjan. Despite ongoing tension and violence, in 2018 President Ouattara declared amnesty for those involved in the 2010–11 postelection violence, stalling many investigations. In 2019, the International Criminal Court acquitted Gbagbo of crimes against humanity and war crimes.

The conflict in Côte d'Ivoire reveals many of the complex dynamics of today's global economy: (1) the interconnectedness of farmers in rural West Africa with chocolate eaters and coffee drinkers worldwide; (2) the tension-filled relationship between nation-states and transnational corporations; (3) the strategic military interventions, often by former colonial powers, that serve to police local political affairs and global economic flows; (4) the power of global financial markets to determine the prices of coffee and cocoa and thus the quality of life for small farmers; and (5) the link between consumers and producers through global commodity chains that have blurred notions of distinct national territories.

To fully understand the modern world economy, we must examine the concept of an economy as well as the historical developments that underlie today's global economy. In this chapter, we will explore the following questions:

- **What is an economy, and what is its purpose?**
- **What are the roots of today's global economy?**
- **How did the modern world economic system emerge?**
- **What are the dominant organizing principles of the global economy today?**

Côte d'Ivoire

Africa

MAP 10.1
Côte d'Ivoire

- How does today's global economy link workers with consumers worldwide?

- How do anthropologists analyze class and inequality?

- How is today's global economy reshaping migration?

By the end of this chapter, you should be able to analyze the major economic patterns of the contemporary global economy and assess its underlying principles. Armed with this information, you will be better prepared to make choices about your own lifestyle as a consumer and to engage in debates about how to create a sustainable economic system as the growing human population places increasing pressure on the Earth's resources.

What Is an Economy, and What Is Its Purpose?

Define what an economy is from an anthropological perspective.

economy

A cultural adaptation to the environment that enables a group of humans to use the available land, resources, and labor to satisfy their needs and to thrive.

At the most basic level, an **economy** is a cultural adaptation to the environment—a set of ideas, activities, and technologies that enables a group of humans to use the available land, resources, and labor to satisfy their basic needs and, if organized well, to thrive. Of course, today the concept of an economy seems much more complicated. But what is an economy at its core?

Anthropologist Yehudi Cohen (1974) describes an economy as a set of adaptive strategies that humans have used to provide food, water, and shelter to a group of people through the production, distribution, and consumption of foodstuffs and other goods.

Cohen suggests five primary adaptive strategies that developed at different times and places: food foraging, pastoralism, horticulture, agriculture, and industrialism. By reviewing these strategies, we can begin to understand that the current consumption-based global economy—with its emphasis on industrial production (even in agriculture), consumption, and technology—is only one of many possible variations.

FROM FORAGING TO INDUSTRIAL AGRICULTURE: A BRIEF SURVEY OF FOOD PRODUCTION

food foragers

Humans who subsist by hunting, fishing, and gathering plants to eat.

Food Foraging. Before the domestication of plants and animals around 10,000 years ago, all humans were **food foragers**. They made their living by hunting, fishing, and gathering nuts, fruit, and root crops; in fact, humans evolved into

our current physical form as food foragers. Mobility was key: Small, egalitarian groups followed the movement of large animals and/or the seasonal growth of fruits, vegetables, and nuts to secure their survival. Throughout human history, food foragers have ranged over a remarkable variety of habitats, from the most hospitable to the most extreme.

Today, few people make their primary living from food foraging. Most food foragers now incorporate farming and the domestication of animals. The remaining food foragers often live in the most marginal of the Earth's environments—cold places, forests, islands—where other economic activity and other strategies for food production are not sustainable. Food foragers in recent times have included the Inuit of Canada and Alaska, Aboriginal Australians, and inhabitants of African and South American rain forests (e.g., Lee 1984; Turnbull [1971] 2020).

Pastoralism, Horticulture, and Agriculture.
Cohen identifies three adaptive strategies for food production in nonindustrial societies: pastoralism, horticulture, and agriculture.

Pastoralism involves the domestication and herding of animals for food production. **Horticulture** is the cultivation of plants for subsistence through nonintensive use of land and labor. Horticulturalists use simple tools such as sticks and hoes to cultivate small garden plots. Land is generally rotated in and out of use to exploit more fertile ground. Horticulturalists frequently employ *slash-and-burn agriculture*—also called swidden farming—to clear land for cultivation, kill insects that may inhibit crop growth, and produce nutrient-rich ash that serves as fertilizer.

Agriculture requires an intensive investment in farming and well-orchestrated land-use strategies. Irrigation, fertilizer, draft animals, and machinery, such as

pastoralism
A strategy for food production involving the domestication and herding of animals.

horticulture
The cultivation of plants for subsistence through nonintensive use of land and labor.

agriculture
An intensive farming strategy for food production involving permanently cultivated land to create a surplus.

A Chinese-owned farm in Angola, southern Africa, produces corn for export to China, a reflection of industrial agriculture in today's global economy.

plows and tractors, provide the technology and labor for successful agriculture. Through agriculture, humans produce enough food on permanently cultivated land to satisfy the immediate needs of the community and to create a surplus that can be sold or traded.

Whereas hunter-gatherer societies tended to be largely egalitarian, the rise of intensive agriculture in nonindustrial cultures led to social stratification. Social distinctions included large landholders, wealthy merchants, owners of small businesses, and peasants and landless tenants working on large farms and estates as wage laborers.

Industrial Agriculture. Recent decades have seen remarkable progress in feeding the growing world population. Although portions of the world continue to face famines and food shortages, these are not a result of inadequate food production but, rather, of unequal distribution of the food that is produced.

industrial agriculture

Intensive farming practices involving mechanization and mass production of foodstuffs.

Despite increased food production, **industrial agriculture** and agribusinesses have yielded complicated results. For example, chemical fertilizers and pesticides pose dangers to workers and to local water resources. Antibiotics that keep poultry and livestock healthy in industrial production facilities seep into the human food chain. Genetic engineering to combat crop disease also reduces crop diversity, making crops more susceptible to harsh weather and pests in the long term. Food irradiation, used to increase food shelf life, poses potential safety and health hazards. Overall, industrial agriculture requires extremely high energy input to support machinery, irrigation, pesticides, fertilizer, and transportation costs—in many cases, more calories of energy than the food actually provides when it is consumed.

Can the planet support our projected population growth and consumption of natural resources? Can our contemporary economy meet current human needs, given the limitations of the natural environment? We will consider these questions throughout this chapter and in Chapter 11, "Environment and Sustainability."

DISTRIBUTION AND EXCHANGE

All cultures have developed patterns for the distribution and exchange of goods and information produced by their members. In fact, the exchange of goods and ideas appears to be central to the workings of culture, establishing patterns of interaction and obligation among people. Anthropologists recognize three main patterns of exchange: market exchange, reciprocity, and redistribution.

Market Exchange. Today, patterns of distribution and exchange are heavily influenced by economic markets that facilitate the buying and selling of land, natural resources, goods, services, labor, and ideas. Contemporary markets range in size and scope from village markets in India to the New York Stock Exchange on Wall Street. Though some people may *barter*—that is, directly exchange goods and services, one for the other—most contemporary economic transactions are based on an exchange medium, or some form of money. In recent human history, the medium of exchange has varied. Items such as salt, precious stones, shells, livestock, precious metals such as gold or silver, coins—and, most recently, paper money, digital transfers of money, and cryptocurrencies—have served to make payments for goods and services (Davies 2005; Wolf 1982).

Reciprocity. Transactions characterized by **reciprocity** involve an exchange of resources, goods, and services among people of relatively equal status. Such exchanges, including gift giving, create and reinforce social ties between givers and receivers, fulfill social obligations, and often raise the prestige of the gift giver. Anthropologists identify three types of reciprocity defined by the social distance between exchange partners: generalized reciprocity, balanced reciprocity, and negative reciprocity (Sahlins [1974] 2004; Service 1966).

Generalized reciprocity encompasses exchanges in which the value of what is exchanged is not carefully calculated and the timing or amount of repayment is not predetermined. Generalized reciprocity is common among close kin or close friends, serving as an expression of personal connection while reinforcing family and social networks. You may often experience generalized reciprocity without recognizing it: offering to take someone to the airport without expecting exact or timely reciprocity; borrowing a pen or sheets of paper; offering some of your food to a friend. Likewise, parents provide for their children—food, shelter, education, clothes, protection— without calculating the value or expecting repayment on predetermined terms.

Balanced reciprocity occurs between people who are more distantly related. This type of exchange includes norms about giving, accepting, and reciprocating. The giver expects the gift to be accepted and then to receive something in return. The recipient has an obligation to accept the gift (or is otherwise considered rude

reciprocity
The exchange of resources, goods, and services among people of relatively equal status to create and reinforce social ties.

or ungrateful) and reciprocate promptly with a gift of equal value. The goal of exchanges based on balanced reciprocity is to build and maintain social relationships, often beyond the immediate kin group.

Negative reciprocity refers to a pattern of exchange in which the parties seek to receive more than they give, reaping a material advantage through the exchange. Whereas general and balanced reciprocity are based on relationships of trust and familiarity, negative reciprocity occurs among people who are strangers, antagonists, and enemies with opposing interests. Through hard bargaining, cleverness, deception, or cheating, the parties hope to minimize their cost and maximize their return.

redistribution

A form of exchange in which accumulated wealth is collected from the members of the group and reallocated in a different pattern.

Redistribution. Finally, **redistribution** is a form of exchange in which goods are collected from the members of the group and reallocated in a different pattern. Redistribution requires the collected goods to flow through a central location—a chief, a storehouse, or a central government—where they can be sorted, counted, and redistributed. In small-scale societies, redistribution brings prestige to the community leader as food and goods collected from the leader's supporters are reallocated to support the general populace or to establish alliances with outside groups. You have experienced redistribution directly if those in your family who earn wages share their earnings with those who do not in order to provide all members with food and shelter.

Redistribution may increase or decrease the inequality of wealth and resources within a group. In fact, many cultures have *leveling mechanisms*—practices and organizations that level out resources within the group. In the United States, for example, as in many other nation-states, redistribution is enacted through local, state, and federal tax codes. The government collects money and then reallocates and redistributes the nation's wealth to provide services (for example, the military) and infrastructure (for example, roads and bridges). Leveling mechanisms enact a cultural commitment to the collective good that aspires to safety, health, education, food, and shelter for all group members irrespective of class.

What Are the Roots of Today's Global Economy?

Describe how trade and colonialism have shaped the global economy.

Recent centuries have intensified the integration of all humanity into an interconnected global economy. Economic anthropology—the study of human economic activity and relations—views the world through the lens of movement

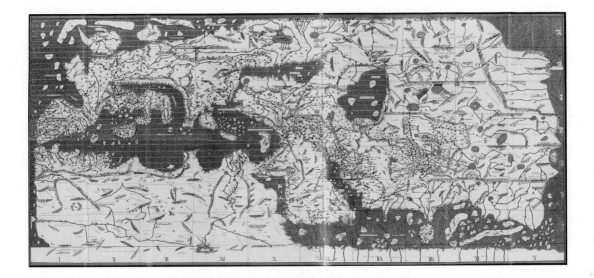

rather than through the perspective of fixed and discrete groups. But not all of these connections have been smooth and easy. Many have been—and still are—contentious and unequal.

EARLY LONG-DISTANCE TRADE ROUTES

More than 2,000 years ago, long-distance trade routes connected Asia, the Middle East, Africa, and Europe in a dynamic international network of economic exchange (Abu-Lughod 1989; Braudel [1979] 1992; Frank 1998; Schneider 1977; Wolf 1982). Movement was slow, but long-distance trade conveyed luxury items, such as silk, spices, tea, and gunpowder, across vast territory encompassing Asia, the Middle East, Europe, and Africa. China led the world in the production and export of silk, porcelain ceramics (china), tea, fruit, drugs, cotton, tobacco, arms and powder, copper and iron products, zinc, and cupronickel (Abu-Lughod 1989; Frank 1998). Before long, Europe's elite were seeking greater access to China's desirable commodities.

By the time Columbus sailed in 1492, Europe's elite needed more than a shorter trade route to Asia to enter the world economy. Although China wanted or needed very little from the West, Europeans increasingly sought its export commodities. As a result, European trade in Asia created surpluses for China, whose exports constantly surpassed its imports. China demanded payment of all deficits in silver and gold, setting off an intense global competition for these scarce resources.

Thus, acquisition of silver and gold was high on the Europeans' agenda in the Caribbean and the Americas. They systematically plundered the Mayan and Aztec kingdoms as well as other Indigenous peoples as they conquered the South

Long-distance trade routes have connected Asia, the Middle East, Europe, and Africa for more than 2,000 years. The Tabula Rogeriana, a map of trade routes through northern Africa, Europe, the Indian Ocean, and much of Asia, was written in Arabic and attributed to the Arab geographer Muhammad al-Idrisi, 1154.

American continent. They enslaved local populations in order to extract precious minerals. Between 1500 and 1600, the supply of silver in circulation in Europe increased eightfold (Robbins 2013). The gold and silver plundered from the Americas enabled Europeans to buy a seat on the economic train based in Asia (Frank 1998; Spence 2013).

COLONIALISM

Europe's economic engagements between 1500 and 1800 relied primarily on extensive maritime trade within the existing global economic system. Private corporations, such as the British East India Company and the Dutch West India Company—and their private armies—led the expansion of trade and later seized large swaths of territory around the world to further advance their economic activity. The early European conquest of the Caribbean and the Americas launched an era of colonial domination in the nineteenth and early twentieth centuries that eventually touched every part of the globe.

colonialism

The practice by which states extend political, economic, and military power beyond their own borders over an extended period of time to secure access to raw materials, cheap labor, and markets in other countries or regions.

Under **colonialism**, European powers redrew the map of the world and fundamentally reorganized the political and economic balance of power on a global scale. Europeans' advanced military weaponry and strategies, developed through years of continental warfare and naval battles, gave them an advantage that enabled them to dominate others in the colonial era. Beginning in the 1500s, European colonialism played a pivotal role in establishing the framework for today's global economic system.

THE TRIANGLE TRADE

triangle trade

The extensive exchange of enslaved people, sugar, cotton, and furs between Europe, Africa, and the Americas that transformed economic, political, and social life on both sides of the Atlantic.

The **triangle trade** that emerged in the 1500s among Europe, Africa, and the Americas was an extensive exchange of goods, people, wealth, food, diseases, and ideas that transformed economic, political, and social life on both sides of the Atlantic (Figure 10.1). While it brought western Europeans the resources they needed to grow their national economies and to expand their role in international trade, it simultaneously decimated elaborate, well-established political, economic, and social systems in Africa and the Americas.

Europeans established a plantation economy in the Caribbean and South America to produce sugar for export to Europe. Columbus had carried sugar to the Caribbean, which, along with Brazil, offered an ideal climate for sugarcane cultivation. Colonial plantation production transformed sugar from a luxury item to a key component of the European diet. Sugar also sweetened three other key commodities in the triangle trade—all stimulants (drugs): coffee, tea, and cocoa (Mintz 1985).

The expansion of Spanish and Portuguese sugarcane plantations could not be sustained by local populations in the Caribbean and South America, which had been decimated by European diseases and the grueling conditions of forced labor.

FIGURE 10.1
The Triangle Trade

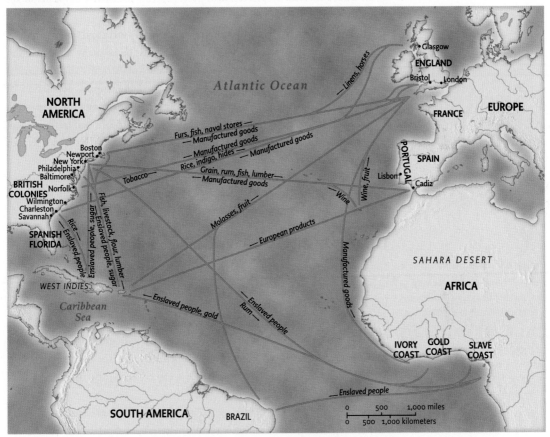

So, plantation owners turned to the transatlantic slave trade to supply their labor needs. Between the sixteenth and eighteenth centuries, millions of Africans were sold into slavery and transported across the Atlantic to work on these sugarcane plantations. Later, rising demand for cotton for England's textile industry would require more laborers for cotton plantations in the southern region of what is now the United States. This pressure further stimulated demand for enslaved Africans. Many—perhaps millions—of people died in the traumatic passage across the Atlantic, and millions more died in inhuman conditions of incarceration and slavery after arriving in the Americas. The uncompensated labor of enslaved Africans, extracted under brutal conditions, subsidized the economic growth and development of Europe and the American colonies for more than 350 years.

In North America, the fur trade, particularly in beaver pelts, pulled the continent into the global economy. European trappers established trading relationships with Native Americans, swapping beaver pelts for European finished products such as guns, metal tools, and textiles. The fur trade was not as lucrative as the trade with Asia in spices, silk, or porcelains, but an active European market for fur coats and hats created steady demand.

The decimation of the Indigenous populations in North and South America and the Caribbean (estimated by some scholars to be as many as 15 million people), combined with the relocation of millions of Africans and the arrival of millions of European immigrants, transformed the human population of the New World over a period of a few centuries. Furthermore, the large-scale migration of Europeans and the forced migration of Africans had lasting repercussions in their home communities as well. The conquest of Native American lands, genocide of Indigenous people, and enslavement of Africans relied on intertwined ideologies of White supremacy, patriarchy, and religious destiny to establish, expand, and justify a hierarchy of exploitation central to the European colonial enterprise (Robbins 2013; Trouillot 1994; Wolf 1982).

THE INDUSTRIAL REVOLUTION

Industrial Revolution

The eighteenth- and nineteenth-century shift from agriculture and artisanal skill craft to machine-based manufacturing.

The **Industrial Revolution** in the eighteenth and nineteenth centuries drove the next phase of European colonial activity. As European economies, led by Great Britain, shifted toward machine-based manufacturing, the new industries relied heavily on the raw materials, cheap labor, and open markets of the colonies. At the same time, Europe's expanding cities, combined with growing colonies, provided markets for goods produced in Europe's factories. The huge profits from the transatlantic triangle trade provided the capital necessary to fund Europe's industrial transformation.

Industrial expansion of the capitalist economy created intense competition among European countries for raw materials, cheap labor, and markets. Throughout the nineteenth and early twentieth centuries, Great Britain, France, the Netherlands, Belgium, Russia, Japan, and other countries all raced to divide nonindustrial regions of the world into colonies that would secure their economic growth. In the process, European countries redrew the political map of the world—especially in Asia, Africa, and the Middle East—and restructured the global economy to serve their expanding industrial activities.

ANTI-COLONIAL STRUGGLES

Local populations resisted colonialism with mixed success. Independence movements used strategies of rebellion, resistance, and negotiation to achieve their goals. Their approaches ranged from nonviolent actions, such as those led by Mohandas Gandhi in the Indian struggle against British colonialism, to violent uprisings, such as those in the Algerian quest for independence. Frequently, external factors such as wars, economic crises, and international pressures aided independence movements by creating conditions for their success.

Independence movements throughout the Americas brought changes to the colonial system. The United States declared independence from Great Britain in 1776, eventually winning it through the Revolutionary War. The people of Haiti, a highly profitable Caribbean French colony known for its sugarcane, coffee, cocoa, indigo, and cotton plantations, declared independence in 1804 and became the first independent former colony to be ruled by people of African descent. In Latin America, Brazil declared independence from Portugal in 1822. By 1825, most of Spain's colonies in South America had achieved independence.

Ultimately, World War II created conditions for the success of national independence movements and the collapse of the colonial system. For example, Japanese occupation destroyed much of the European colonial infrastructure in Asia and inspired organized national resistance movements. These forces led efforts toward national independence when the war ended. On a global scale, the war-ravaged economies and political institutions of the European colonial powers could no longer sustain their colonial enterprises, especially in the face of organized resistance movements. Between 1945 and 1991, more than one hundred former colonies gained their independence.

But as we have seen in the opening story about Côte d'Ivoire, and as we will see throughout the remainder of this chapter, despite the formal end of the colonial era, patterns of relationship established under colonialism—from migration and economics to military involvement—continue to influence both former colonies and colonizers.

How Did the Modern World Economic System Emerge?

Understand core theories anthropologists use to explain the modern world economy.

With the end of the colonial era, many people believed that the former colonies—wealthy in natural resources and freed from colonial control—would see rapid economic growth. But such growth, as well as diminished poverty and the possibility for income equality, has proved elusive. Why have patterns of inequality established under colonialism persisted into the current era?

CONFLICTING THEORIES

Modernization theories, which became popular following World War II, predicted that with the end of colonialism, less-developed countries would follow the same trajectory as the industrialized countries and achieve improved standards of living. Certainly, the rise of industrial capitalism in Europe beginning in the late eighteenth century had spurred spectacular advances in production and a sense of optimism about the possibilities for dramatic material progress—in other words, **development** (Larrain 1989). As decolonization approached, politicians and economists in industrialized nations began to strategize about how to develop the economies of the colonies of Britain, France, Portugal, and other European powers (Leys 1996). The modernization model was assumed to be the key. Progress, modernization, and industrialization would be the natural path of economic development throughout the global capitalist economy, though this process would need nurturing through foreign aid and international investment.

After World War II, policy theorists and planners believed that scientific and technological expertise could help replicate the European and North American style of development across the globe. Through an array of new international aid agencies and financial institutions, such as the World Bank, the IMF, and the United Nations, wealthy nations worked with emerging national governments in former colonies to develop programs they hoped would stimulate growth, alleviate poverty, and raise living standards. Development projects often emphasized state investment in infrastructure as an engine of economic growth, focusing on the construction of ports, roads, dams, and irrigation systems (Cowen and Shenton 1996; Edelman and Haugerud 2005).

But by the 1960s, **dependency theory** had emerged as a critique of modernization theory. Scholars from Latin America, in particular, argued that a new kind of colonialism—**neocolonialism**—had emerged (Cardoso and Faletto 1969; Frank 1969). Dependency theorists argued that despite the end of colonialism, the underlying economic relations of the modern world system had not changed. These scholars introduced the term **underdevelopment** to suggest that poor countries were not poor because of some fundamental structural flaw (such as inadequate natural resources) but because their participation in the global economy left them underdeveloped. The global economy was still structured to extract resources from less-developed countries and transfer them to developed, industrialized countries. Thus, dependency theorists argued, underdeveloped countries should break their dependency on the global economic system and build up and protect their own self-sufficient national economic activities.

underdevelopment

The term used to suggest that poor countries are poor as a result of their relationship to an unbalanced global economic system.

CORE AND PERIPHERY

Immanuel Wallerstein (1974) introduced to these debates a *modern world systems* analysis. According to Wallerstein, the nations within the world economic system occupy core, semiperiphery, and periphery positions (Figure 10.2). The **core countries**—primarily industrialized former colonial states—dominate the world system by extracting cheap labor and raw materials from periphery countries and sending them to the industrialized core. Finished products, with value added in the manufacturing process, are then returned to markets in the periphery. Core countries control the most lucrative economic processes, including the financial services sectors.

core countries

Industrialized former colonial states that dominate the world economic system.

FIGURE 10.2
The Core/Periphery Division of the World

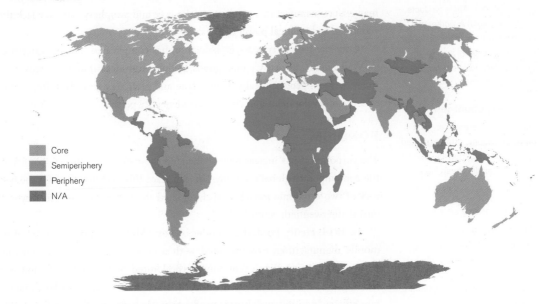

Source: Core/Periphery Division of the World. The Geography of Transport Systems. https://transportgeography.org/?page_id=1381.

Where does your iPhone come from? The journey of an iPhone illustrates Wallerstein's concepts of core, semiperiphery, and periphery. (*Left*) Factory workers at the Foxconn plant in Shenzhen, South China, where many iPhones, iPads, and other Apple products are made. (*Right*) A worker at a rare earth mine in Inner Mongolia; rare earth elements are vital to the manufacture of electronics, including iPhones.

periphery countries

The least developed and least powerful nations; often exploited by the core countries as sources of raw materials, cheap labor, and markets.

semiperiphery countries

Nations ranking in between core and periphery countries, with some attributes of the core countries but with less of a central role in the global economy.

Periphery countries—among the least developed and least powerful nations—serve primarily as sources of raw materials, agricultural products, cheap labor, and markets for the economic activities of the core. Established economic, political, and military patterns ensure the steady transfer of wealth, natural resources, and human resources from the periphery to core, contributing to underdevelopment. **Semiperiphery countries** occupy a middle position. They may have developed some industry, may draw resources from the periphery, and may export manufactured products to the core and periphery, but they lack the economic and political power of the core.

Over the past forty years, globalization has complicated the neat categories of Wallerstein's theory. Capital, goods, people, and ideas flow less predictably today between geographically defined core and periphery areas. But the realities of uneven development and entrenched inequality persist.

FORDISM

The corporation has increasingly challenged the nation-state for supremacy in the contemporary global economy. We can trace this dynamic through the history of two economic models that dominated the U.S. economy (and beyond) during the twentieth century.

In 1914, Henry Ford, the founder of Ford Motor Company, a U.S. automobile manufacturer, experimented with a new strategy for profit making within the industrializing economy of the United States. Ford is famous for refining the factory assembly line and the division of labor in order to facilitate efficiency in industrial mass production. Perhaps equally significant, at a time when many U.S. manufacturers were exploiting immigrant workers with low wages and long work hours to maximize profits, Ford took a different approach.

Ford made several key innovations. Most important, he introduced a $5, eight-hour workday—a living wage that he hoped would create a worker who was loyal to the company, dependable on the job, and cooperative with management in the grueling, repetitive work environment of the assembly line. Ford also believed that every Ford worker should be able to buy a Ford car. Higher wages and shorter hours, he felt, would create a new pool of consumers with enough income and leisure time to purchase and enjoy a car. Ford sought to form a new social compact between labor and capital that would benefit his corporation. These were the central aspects of **Fordism**.

Fordism took hold firmly after World War II with growing cooperation among corporations, labor, and government. The latter stepped in to regulate corporate responsibility for worker health and safety and, eventually, environmental impact. An income tax structure with high marginal rates for the very wealthy moderated the growth in income inequality. Wages and benefits, along with corporate profits, rose steadily through a long postwar boom that drove a rapid expansion of the middle class through the early 1970s.

Fordism
The dominant model of industrial production for much of the twentieth century, based on a social compact between labor, corporations, and government.

FLEXIBLE ACCUMULATION

Industrial economic activity in the late 1960s and 1970s began to shift away from the Fordist model toward what geographer David Harvey (1990) has called "strategies of flexible accumulation" to address shrinking corporate profits brought about by increased global competition and a global recession.

Flexible accumulation refers to the increasingly flexible strategies that corporations use to accumulate profits in an era of globalization. In particular, these strategies include *offshoring* (relocating factories anywhere in the world that provides optimal production, infrastructure, labor, marketing, and political conditions) and *outsourcing* (hiring low-wage laborers in periphery countries to perform jobs previously done in core countries). Using these strategies, corporations were able to bypass high production costs, organized labor, and environmental laws in the core industrial cities and core countries.

flexible accumulation
The increasingly flexible strategies that corporations use to accumulate profits in an era of globalization, enabled by innovative communication and transportation technologies.

Under flexible accumulation, corporations—even highly profitable ones—eliminated jobs in old core industrial centers such as New York City, Chicago, and Detroit. Instead, they began offshoring their factories, reopening them in places such as Mexico, the Caribbean, South Korea, and Taiwan. In the 1980s, they began to relocate factories to China to take advantage of even lower wages, lower taxes, and weaker environmental restrictions. Today, Walmart has more than 7,000 factories in China that produce goods for its stores worldwide.

Who answered your last call for tech support? Here, a call center agent in the Philippines talks to a client in the United States, an example of how jobs are being outsourced from core countries to low-wage destinations under flexible accumulation.

Recent strikes by Chinese workers demanding higher wages and better working conditions have led some corporations to relocate again, opening new factories in Thailand, Cambodia, Vietnam, and Bangladesh. Over the past forty years, strategies of flexible accumulation have transformed the local factory assembly line into a global assembly line. And as workplace patterns shift in response to the COVID-19 pandemic, corporations will outsource an increasingly wide array of jobs.

What Are the Dominant Organizing Principles of the Global Economy Today?

Explain the key organizing principles of the global economy.

Flows of capital, goods, and services associated with flexible accumulation have built on old colonial patterns and have made use of advances in transportation and communication technologies (time-space compression). But other forces—including powerful international financial institutions and international and regional trade agreements—are also helping to move all people and nations toward one free market with minimal barriers. Drawing on the economic philosophy of *neoliberalism*, these institutions and agreements have created a strong international financial and policy framework, one that promotes an even deeper integration of nations and local communities into the contemporary global economy.

CAPITALISM, ECONOMIC LIBERALISM, AND THE FREE MARKET

The work of the Scottish economist and philosopher Adam Smith (1723–1790) and the British economist John Maynard Keynes (1883–1946) provided key intellectual counterpoints that have shaped economic debates about the functioning of capitalism in the twentieth century. In *The Wealth of Nations* (1776), Adam Smith promoted economic liberalism through his ideas of laissez-faire ("leave it alone") capitalism. In Smith's view, free markets and free trade, being liberated from government intervention, would provide the best conditions for economic growth: They would unleash competition to maximize profits. In contrast, Keynes later argued that capitalism would work best when the government had a role in moderating capitalism's excesses and ensuring the basic welfare of all citizens (Keynes [1936] 2007).

After World War II, leading Western governments applied Keynesian economic philosophy to rebuilding their war-torn economies and establishing development projects to stimulate growth in former colonies. Keynesian economics began to lose popularity in the 1970s in the wake of a global recession. But today it maintains a role in government policies that stimulate economic activity through public investment in infrastructure projects and the employment of civil servants and those that seek to regulate the excesses of corporate and financial activities and to moderate the most extreme effects of capitalism on the population through the provision of a social safety net and investment in health, education, and housing.

NEOLIBERALISM

Economic liberalism, building on Smith's philosophy, has reemerged since the 1970s as a guiding philosophy for the global economy. This **neoliberalism**, associated with conservative fiscal and political policies in the United States, views the free market—not the state—as the main mechanism for ensuring economic growth. Neoliberal policies focus on promoting free trade on a global scale, eliminating trade barriers, and reducing taxes, tariffs, and most government intervention in the economy. Neoliberalism promotes the privatization of public assets (such as publicly owned utilities and transportation systems) and an overall reduction, if not privatization, of government spending on health, education, and welfare.

neoliberalism
An economic and political worldview that sees the free market as the main mechanism for ensuring economic growth, with a severely restricted role for government.

Since the 1980s, powerful international financial institutions have promoted neoliberal policies. These institutions are the International Monetary Fund (IMF), the World Bank, and the World Trade Organization, which was founded in 1995 to replace the Global Agreement on Trade and Tariffs. The Allied nations established the IMF and the World Bank after World War II to regulate financial

What are the most effective strategies for building a healthy economy? Here, protestors in Greece demonstrate against government austerity measures.

and commercial relations among the industrial powers and to provide loans for modernizing national economies ravaged by the war. In the latter role, these institutions often subsidized national development efforts, including infrastructure projects such as ports, roads, dams, and irrigation systems.

Critiques of Neoliberal Policies. Debates continue over the effectiveness of neoliberal policies. In particular, there is skepticism in many countries about the notion that facilitating competition and profit making through free trade, free markets, and privatization promotes improved economic opportunities for most of the world's people. Leaders of underdeveloped countries, scholars, and activists have argued that these policies are the centerpiece of an ever-evolving global economic system that promotes uneven development and ensures that wealthy countries remain wealthy and poor countries remain poor (Krugman 2015; Sachs 2005; Stiglitz 2010). Much of Latin America has repaid its debts to the IMF and has rejected neoliberal economic strategies. The World Social Forum, an annual international meeting of social movements and NGOs, explores alternatives to neoliberal economic policies and the negative aspects of globalization.

THE (IN)STABILITY OF GLOBAL FINANCIAL MARKETS IN THE TWENTY-FIRST CENTURY

In late 2008, the United States experienced its worst financial collapse in more than seventy years. At the center of the crisis was a massive credit bubble created by millions of high-risk mortgages and other complex new financial instruments. In the years leading up to 2008, bankers seeking new investment vehicles for their clients bundled millions of individual mortgages into new financial instruments—derivative contracts—that could themselves be traded, bought, sold, exchanged, and insured. People buying the derivatives were making a bet on the future value of the new asset (Tett 2009).

The U.S. financial collapse of 2008 and its subsequent impact on other countries indicated a significant shift in the global economy. Anthropologists of finance suggest that the circulation of capital has become the driving force behind the global expansion of capitalism in the twenty-first century. As a result, while the total gross domestic product of the global economy was estimated to be $84.7 trillion in 2020 (World Bank 2020), the face value of derivatives circulating through the global financial markets is now estimated to be at least $610 trillion (Bank for International Settlements 2021). Financial firms and global capital markets increasingly shape economic and political realities in every part of the world (Ho 2009; LiPuma and Lee 2004; Zaloom 2006).

CRYPTO AND THE RISE OF VIRTUAL CURRENCIES

Cryptocurrencies—decentralized digital or virtual currencies secured through encryption—emerged in the late 2000s as a disruptive alternative to traditional money at a time of tremendous upheaval and innovation in global financial systems. Anthropologists have long recognized that all mediums of exchange—whether beads, pieces of paper, coins, lumps of precious metals, mortgage-backed securities, or digital and virtual cryptocurrencies—rely heavily on trust. Users must trust that a currency will retain its value, that others will trade for it, and in today's complex financial systems, that banks, financial advisors, investment houses, and governments will operate with integrity. The 2008 fiscal crisis, discussed in the previous section, undermined trust in the traditional banking system. Simultaneously, the technological innovations of the iPhone (launched in 2007) and other smartphones brought together voice, text, web browsing, camera, optical scanning, GPS, and immense data capabilities in ways that transformed communication systems and reshaped the financial services industry.

In this context, Bitcoin launched in 2009 to create a decentralized money system separate from government-issued currencies. The unregulated space in which Bitcoin and other cryptocurrencies exist transfers users' trust from banks to blockchain technology. Blockchains provide a secure and decentralized public accounting ledger of virtual cryptocurrency transactions by using a string of numbers and letters to maintain an electronic, permanent transaction history for each crypto asset. Banks, governments, or other trusted third parties are no longer needed.

Today cryptocurrencies like Bitcoin and Ethereum have gained a foothold in the global financial system. In 2021, El Salvador became the first country to allow consumers to use the cryptocurrency in all transactions (alongside its other official currency, the U.S. dollar). A number of U.S. businesses, such as Home Depot and Microsoft, have begun to accept cryptocurrencies. Cryptocurrencies are even more popular as an investment vehicle. India, for instance, has as many as 20 million investors in cryptocurrencies, many of whom are young professionals. Trust in cryptocurrencies is not absolute, however. Concerns include wild valuation fluctuations, security breaches, the impact of regulation, overconsumption of energy to mine Bitcoin and its impact on the environment, plus the potential of cryptocurrencies to enable criminal activities like terrorism, organized crime, and the purchase of illegal goods such as weapons and drugs. Other digital technologies have already transformed how we experience our social world. In what ways do you see cryptocurrencies transforming the culture of money and the financial world (Ceraldi 2018; Maurer 2015)?

MAP 10.2
Kenya

Mobile Money in Kenya. While cryptocurrencies like Bitcoin and Ethereum have captured the public imagination, anthropologists have been researching virtual currencies and mobile technologies that are transforming local economies and money use. In her ethnography *Reimagining Money: Kenya in the Digital Finance Revolution* (2021), anthropologist Sibel Kusimba explores how the everyday use of the M-Pesa mobile phone–based payment system became central to Kenyan life, replacing cash and transforming local economies over the past twenty years, while still cultivating Kenyan values of "wealth-in-people." In the late 1990s, mobile phones spread rapidly throughout East Africa in what Kusimba considers to be one of the most rapid technology diffusions in human history. In rural areas, phones owned by local shopkeepers and rented or loaned in the community filled gaps in technology ownership. Prepaid airtime could be purchased on encoded scratchcards available in every marketplace. In a unique local innovation—soon picked up by mobile phone company Safaricom—users began sending prepaid airtime codes via text message. For a fee, local agents, often local shopkeepers in rural markets or urban malls, would then exchange airtime codes for cash.

Building on this airtime exchange system, in 2007 Safaricom introduced the mobile transfer service M-Pesa. M-Pesa allows users to send Kenyan currency, rather than airtime, via text message. With only a national ID card and a SIM card—no smartphone or Internet connection required—a resident can set up an individual account with Safaricom. Local mobile money/airtime agents, usually shopkeepers, take cash, convert it into e-money, and add it to one's Safaricom account balance, where it can be kept in the account or texted to another phone. On the other end, the e-money can be redeemed for cash through another local agent. Unlike Bitcoin and other cryptocurrencies, the value transferred through M-Pesa never became a separate currency. It is simply a digitized representation of the Kenyan currency, the shilling. In another contrast with decentralized cryptocurrencies, the M-Pesa system is operated by Safaricom, a mobile phone provider partly owned by the Kenyan government.

Thinking anthropologically, Kusimba argues that rather than disrupting local communities and cultural patterns, the M-Pesa system has reinforced long-held and important Kenyan systems for creating kinship relations, financial ties, reciprocity, and value. Kenya's economy long relied on pastoralism, particularly the raising and exchange of cattle, sheep and goats that served as pastoralists' main monetary system (Schneider 1979). The birth of new cows meant more money in the system that could be redistributed through an exchange of livestock, often at marriages or other rites of passage. The circulation of livestock knit society together and led to the accumulation of deep and broad financial ties. Wealth, however, lay not in the money or value of the livestock. Wealth lay in the cultivation of an extensive network of personal relationships that could be called upon at a later time. Wealth lay in the accumulation of these financial ties, or what local Kenyan communities called "wealth-in-people." Kusimba's ethnography shows how the exchange system enabled by M-Pesa, like the pastoralist system of exchange and value that preceded it, is used to maintain extensive social networks and financial ties. The circulation of mobile money and airtime allows for the accumulation of "wealth-in-people" in a time when family networks are often organized over great distances.

How Does Today's Global Economy Link Workers with Consumers Worldwide?

Analyze the global economic connections between workers and consumers.

Through much of recent human history, markets have been places where farmers and craftsmen, traders and consumers exchanged products, ideas, information, and news, linking local communities to one another and to faraway communities for the benefit of all (Polanyi [1944] 2001). Today, local markets around the world are more deeply integrated with each other as social and material **commodities** often flow across national borders (Hannerz 1996). Although **commodity chains**—the hands an item, (commodity) passes through between producer and consumer— used to be primarily local, globalization has extended their span across territories and cultures, intensifying the connection between the local and global in ways previously unimaginable (Haugerud, Stone, and Little 2000). Tsukiji Fish Market, until recently the largest fish market in the world, is a prime example.

commodity

A good that can be bought, sold, or exchanged in a market.

commodity chains

The hands an item passes through between producer and consumer.

MAP 10.3
Tokyo

TSUKIJI: FISH MARKET AT THE CENTER OF THE WORLD

Tsukiji Fish Market, which until 2018 stood in the heart of downtown Tokyo, Japan, was the center of a massive global trade in seafood and a cultural icon of Japanese cuisine. Each day, 60,000 traders gathered to auction bluefin tuna from Maine, eel from southern China, octopus from West Africa, salmon from Canada, and shellfish from California. Tsukiji's seafood made its way into restaurants, supermarkets, and homes across Japan, feeding Tokyo's 22 million people and many more throughout the country. But Tokyo and the Tsukiji Market were also the center of an intricate global trade in seafood.

The Japanese people's desire for sushi and sashimi has established Japan as the world's main market for fresh tuna. And Japanese cultural influence has spurred the consumption of sushi in other countries. At the same time, rising demand in Japan has led to overfishing and the decimation of the local tuna fishery. Forty years of time-space compression have facilitated an extension of the tuna commodity chain to previously unconnected places and people. Advances in transportation and communication—refrigerated trucks and cargo jets traveling international routes, along with cell phones, faxes, and the Internet—have promoted an integrated network of fishermen, buyers, and shippers. The search for the perfect tuna has now expanded to the North Atlantic, the Mediterranean, and Australia.

Anthropologist Theodore Bestor's study (2004) of the transnational tuna trade, particularly in Atlantic bluefin tuna, takes him to coastal Maine and the Mediterranean coast of Spain to reveal a complex view of global markets. The stories of these global commodity chains—what Appadurai (1986) calls tracing the "social life of things"—illustrate how the modern world economic system

Where does your tuna fish come from? Here, a tuna fish auction at Tsukiji Fish Market, Tokyo, Japan, 2007.

works. Tsukiji Market and the movement of tuna to it enhance our understanding of Wallerstein's ideas of an integrated, but increasingly complicated, world system. Goods, money, ideas, and even people (or, in this case, tuna) flow from periphery to core. But assumptions of a fixed core and periphery, as well as expectations of a predictable flow of raw materials, are called into question. In the story of tuna and sushi, natural resources flow to consumers at the center of the global market and at the end of the global commodity chain. But in this story, Japan is the core. The Atlantic seaboards of North America and Europe are the periphery (Bestor 2001, 2004; Jacobs 2005; Stevens 2005).

How Do Anthropologists Analyze Class and Inequality?

Apply the theories of key thinkers on class and inequality to real-life situations.

Inequality exists in every contemporary culture, and each society develops its own patterns of **stratification** that differentiate people into groups or classes. Such categories serve as the basis for unequal access to wealth, power, resources, privileges, and status. As discussed in other chapters, these systems of power and stratification may include race, ethnicity, gender, sexuality, kinship, age, legal status, or ability/disability. In addition, systems of social class create and sustain patterns of inequality that structure the relationships between rich and poor, between the privileged and the less well-off. By **class** we refer to a system of power based on wealth, income, and status that creates an unequal distribution of the society's resources—usually moving wealth steadily upward into the hands of an elite. Systems of class stratify individuals' life chances and affect their possibilities for upward social mobility.

stratification

The uneven distribution of resources and privileges among members of a group or culture.

class

A system of power based on wealth, income, and status that creates an unequal distribution of a society's resources.

THEORIES OF CLASS

We turn now to consider three key theorists of class and inequality. European social philosophers Karl Marx and Max Weber, writing in the nineteenth and early twentieth centuries in the context of the Industrial Revolution, are separated by a century from French sociologist Pierre Bourdieu, whose late twentieth-century writings are based in the context of a much more complicated and advanced capitalist economic system.

Karl Marx: Bourgeoisie and Proletariat. Karl Marx (1801–1882) distinguished between two distinct classes of people. The **bourgeoisie**, or

bourgeoisie

Marxian term for the capitalist class that owns the means of production.

capitalist class, owned the **means of production**—the factories, machines, tools, raw materials, land, and financial **capital** needed to make things. The **proletariat**, or working class, lacked land to grow their own food, tools to make their own products, and capital to build workshops or factories. Unable to make their own living, they sold their work—their labor—to capitalists in return for wages.

Marx identified labor as the key source of value and profit in the marketplace. Owners sought constantly to increase their income by forcing workers to toil faster, longer, and for lower wages, thereby reducing the costs of production and increasing the difference between production costs and sale prices. The surplus value created by the workers could then become profit for the owner. In this relationship, capitalists increased their wealth by extracting the surplus labor value from workers. Recognition of these two fundamentally different positions within the economy—two different classes—was essential to Marx's understanding of power relations in a culture.

Today, anthropologists apply Marx's ideas to analyze class and power in contemporary society while acknowledging that capitalism has grown much more complex since Marx's time. Intense competition has grown among capitalists, notably between those in the manufacturing and financial sectors. Small-business owners and farmers now own the means of production, technically making them part of Marx's bourgeoisie, but they do not possess the same access to capital as others in that class. The working class—the proletariat—is divided along lines of race, gender, and ethnicity. Moreover, increasing global circulation of capital is drawing local cultures and communities into class-based relationships that did not exist even a generation ago.

Can you apply Marx's understanding of class to a fast-food restaurant? The median full-time salary for a fast-food worker is $23,860 with no benefits. The store manager, earns a $56,590 median salary annually plus benefits, serves the owner by ensuring that the most surplus labor value possible can be extracted from the workers (U.S. Bureau of Labor Statistics 2020).

Many contemporary social scientists recognize a middle class of professionals and managers (white-collar workers) that has emerged between capitalists and the working class (blue-collar workers). But others who take a stricter Marxian view of class argue that professionals and managers are still members of the pro-letariat (Buck 2009; Durrenberger and Erem 2010). They may have more power in the workplace and substantially higher incomes, but they still sell their labor to the bourgeoisie. These managers, government officials, military, police, and even college professors receive special privileges from the bourgeoisie. But for the capitalist class, it is worth the price of extending these privileges to gain the middle class's cooperation in organizing, educating, and controlling the working class, thereby maximizing the capitalists' extraction of profits.

Together with Friedrich Engels, Marx wrote the *Communist Manifesto* (1848), a political pamphlet urging workers to recognize their exploited class position and to unite in opposition to the proletariat–bourgeoisie relationship emerging in the capitalist system. Marx noted, however, that developing a class consciousness among workers—a political awareness of their common position in the economy that would allow them to unite to change the system—would be extremely difficult. Why? The *ideological superstructure* of society—arts, culture, religion, politics, or, contemporarily, Hollywood, social media, virtual reality, and even the notion of the American Dream—distracts people from recognizing the *economic base* that is the true root of their struggles. And the proletariat's contin-uous struggle simply to make ends meet, as well as the creative means used by the bourgeoisie to keep the proletariat divided, works against a unified challenge to the stratification of society.

Max Weber: Prestige and Life Chances.
Max Weber (1864–1920) added consideration of power and prestige to Marx's concern for economic strat-ification of wealth and income. By **prestige**, Weber referred to the reputation, influence, and deference bestowed on certain people because of their member-ship in certain groups (Weber [1920] 1946). Thus, certain occupations may hold higher or lower prestige in a culture—for instance, physicians and farm workers. Prestige, like wealth and income, can affect life chances. Prestige rankings affect how individuals are treated in social situations, their access to influential social networks, and their access to people of wealth and power.

Weber saw classes as groups of people whose life chances are determined by similar sets of factors. By **life chances**, Weber referred to the opportunities that individuals have to improve their quality of life and realize their life goals. Life chances are determined by access not only to financial resources but also to social resources such as education, health care, food, clothing, and shelter. Class position—relative wealth, power, and prestige—determines access to these resources. According to Weber, members of a class share common life chances,

prestige

The reputation, influence, and deference bestowed on certain people because of their membership in certain groups.

life chances

An individual's opportunities to improve their quality of life and realize life goals.

experiences, and access to resources as well as similar exposure and vulnerability to other systems of stratification. For Weber, however, class stratification doesn't just happen. Instead, he suggests that stratification is created and enforced by the state: The state holds the monopoly on the legitimate use of force, and class-based societies and elite control of the means of production would not be possible without the exercise of state power through police, tax collectors, and even the military.

Pierre Bourdieu: Education and Social Reproduction. Pierre Bourdieu (1930–2002) studied the French educational system to understand relationships among class, culture, and power ([1970] 1990). Throughout much of the world, education is considered the key to upward social mobility within stratified societies. **Social mobility** refers to one's change of class position—upward or downward—in stratified societies. Theoretically, the *meritocracy* of education—whereby students are deemed successful on the basis of their individual talent and motivation—should provide all students an equal opportunity to advance. Instead, Bourdieu's research uncovered a phenomenon of **social reproduction** in the schools: Rather than providing opportunities for social class mobility, the educational system helped reproduce existing social relations by passing class position from generation to generation in a family.

What factors in schools work against the meritocratic idea and instead serve to limit a person's life chances? First, a family's economic circumstances make a difference. But Bourdieu identified two additional key factors: *habitus* and *cultural capital*.

Bourdieu described **habitus** as the dispositions, self-perceptions, sensibilities, and tastes developed in response to external influences over a lifetime that shape one's conceptions of the world and where one fits into it. Habitus is taught and learned from an early age and is culturally reinforced through family, education, religion, socioeconomic status, and the media. It is not fixed or predetermined, but it is so deeply enculturated and embedded that it becomes an almost instinctive sense of one's potential. Habitus emerges among a class of people as a set of common perceptions that shape expectations and aspirations and guide individuals in assessing their life chances and potential for social mobility. Many major life decisions—for instance, the choice of college education or career—are made on the basis of habitus.

Cultural capital is another key to the social reproduction of class. Bourdieu defined **cultural capital** as the knowledge, habits, and tastes learned from parents and family that individuals can use to gain access to scarce and valuable resources of society. For example, family wealth can create cultural capital for children. With enough money, parents can give their children opportunities to travel abroad, learn multiple languages, take music lessons, join sports clubs, go to concerts and museums, have enriching summer experiences, and build social

social mobility

The movement of one's class position upward or downward in stratified societies.

social reproduction

The phenomenon whereby social and class relations of prestige or lack of prestige are passed from one generation to the next.

habitus

Bourdieu's term to describe the self-perceptions, sensibilities, and tastes developed in response to external influences over a lifetime that shape one's conceptions of the world and where one fits in it.

cultural capital

The knowledge, habits, and tastes learned from parents and family that individuals can use to gain access to scarce and valuable resources in society.

networks with others who have similar opportunities. The less wealthy may pass along existing cultural capital through inexpensive activities like reading, while others may divert additional financial resources toward activities that build cultural capital for their children. These opportunities create the social skills, networks, and senses of power and confidence that are essential for shaping class position and identity in stratified societies. Family wealth enables children to perpetuate cultural capital, including by fostering the high motivation and sense of possibility that are crucial for academic success. Schools reward cultural capital. In the process, they reproduce social class advantage.

CLASS AND INEQUALITY IN THE UNITED STATES

Anthropologists have studied the construction of class and its effects across the spectrum of U.S. culture—in rural, urban, and suburban settings and in relationship to race and gender. Ethnographic studies like those presented here explore class and income inequality in local contexts and their impact on the life chances of real people in local communities.

Poor Whites in Rural Kentucky. In *Worked to the Bone: Race, Class, Power, and Privilege in Kentucky* (2001), anthropologist Pem Davidson Buck provides a dynamic introduction to intersectionality. She analyzes the intersections of class, race, and gender through the history of the poor White population in two rural Kentucky counties. Here, the privileges often associated with Whiteness in the United States have been severely limited by class. Buck traces the development of

MAP 10.4
Kentucky

Miners in Hazard, Kentucky, sit in a "break car" that will carry them down a coal mine shaft for their daily work shift. How does their sweat "trickle up"?

an economic system built on tobacco cultivation, coal mining, and manufacturing that has created a class hierarchy in which "sweat is made to trickle up" (13). In other words (reflecting Marx's theory), the surplus value of workers' labor drains upward into the hands of successive layers of elites.

According to Buck, numerous historical events and processes contributed to this development. The construction of race in Kentucky through slavery, share-cropping, and Jim Crow legislation served to persuade European laborers that they should value their Whiteness and align their primary identities with the White elite rather than build solidarity with laborers of other races. The dispos-session of Native Americans from their land consolidated elite control over the territory's natural resources. Later, poor and working-class Whites were enticed by the elites with promises of White privilege to view all newcomer groups (such as Jews, Catholics, Irish, and later immigrants) with suspicion as outsiders, ethnic "others," and "White trash" rather than as potential allies in the struggle for fair value, wages, and compensation for their work.

Buck writes about life in central Kentucky from a personal perspective. She and her husband bought land in the rolling farm country, choosing to not pursue careers and instead to try to live off the land. They grew food in their garden, raised goats and dairy calves, and took various jobs shoveling corn or stripping tobacco on a large farm to make ends meet. Buck's husband eventually took a job with a plumbing and heating supply company, and later they started a small plumbing and heating business of their own. All told, they spent twelve years living under the poverty line and producing most of their own food.

Buck—who drew on her own middle-class cultural capital to escape poverty—chronicles the ways the construction of class relies on a complex man-ufacturing of what it means to be White. Whiteness has been a continuously evolving smokescreen, she claims, adjusted and readjusted to the changing needs of the elites. But as the local economy of the rural United States becomes further integrated into the global economy, and as the sweat of local workers trickles fur-ther and further up, even the privileges of Whiteness are not enough to protect those who live at or below the poverty line and whose fingers are already "worked to the bone." Research suggests it is also not inevitable. By examining both sta-tistical and ethnographic material, anthropologists seek to reopen a conversation about the roots of inequality—the obstacles to greater opportunity, social mobil-ity, and improved life chances in a culture that is reluctant to discuss class.

A LOOK AT THE NUMBERS

Economic statistics provide a sobering picture of inequality in the United States today. They also reveal the increasing concentration of income and wealth at the top rungs of the class ladder. In reviewing statistics related to class, we examine both income and wealth.

TABLE 10.1
Household Income Disparities in the United States

A) U.S. HOUSEHOLD INCOME BY PERCENTAGE, 2020	
Percentage of U.S. Households	**Household Income Range**
Top 5%	Above $273,739
Top 20%	Above $141,110
Second 20%	$85,077–$141,110
Middle 20%	$52,180–$85,076
Fourth 20%	$27,027–$52,179
Bottom 20%	Less than $27,026

B) DISTRIBUTION OF U.S. HOUSEHOLD INCOME, 1967 VERSUS 2020				
	Top 5% of Population	**Top 20% of Population**	**Bottom 40% of Population**	**Bottom 20% of Population**
1967	17.2%	43.6%	10.8%	4%
2020	23%	52.2%	8.1%	3%

Source: U.S. Census Bureau. 2020. "Historical Income Tables: Income Inequality, Tables H-1 and H-2 All Races." https://www.census.gov/data/tables/time-series/demo/income-poverty/historical-income-inequality.html.

Income. In society, **income** is what people earn from work, plus dividends and interest on investments along with earnings from rents and royalties. (A *dividend* is a payment by a corporation to its shareholders of a portion of corporate profits. *Interest* is a fee paid for the use of borrowed money—for example, interest that a bank pays to the holder of a bank savings account. *Rent* refers to payment to an owner as compensation for the use of land, a building, an apartment, property, or equipment. *Royalties* are income based on a percentage of the revenue from the sale of a patent, book, or theatrical work paid to the inventor or author.) Table 10.1a shows a breakdown of household income in the United States for 2020. Income patterns reveal how power is distributed in a society. As Table 10.1b illustrates, income distribution among the U.S. households shows a heavy concentration at the top. Do you know where your family fits in the national income range?

income
What people earn from work plus dividends and interest on investments along with earnings from rents and royalties.

Wealth. Another key indicator of the distribution of power in a society is **wealth**, or the total value of what someone owns—including stocks, bonds, and real estate—minus any debt, such as mortgage or credit card debt. Wealth may be accumulated, or it may be inherited, growing over generations. If wealth were evenly distributed, every U.S. household would have had $692,100 in 2016 (Board of Governors of the Federal Reserve System 2016).

Wealth is even more unevenly distributed than income. The widening gap in wealth has multiple causes. First, shifts in the U.S. tax code have lowered the top tax rate from 91 percent in the years from 1950 to 1963 to 37 percent

wealth
The total value of what someone owns, minus any debt.

beginning in 2018, allowing the wealthy to retain far more of their income (Tax Policy Center 2019). Second, wages for most U.S. families have stagnated since the early 1970s. Meanwhile credit card, education, and mortgage debt have skyrocketed.

Wealth is also stratified by race. Reflecting the devastating long-term effects of slavery and Jim Crow segregation on the African American community, as well as the difficult immigration experiences of most of the U.S. Hispanic population, White households have accumulated fifteen times the net worth of Black and Hispanic households.

THE ROOTS OF POVERTY

The U.S. Census Bureau reported that 37.2 million people—11.4 percent of the U.S. population—were living in poverty in 2020 (U.S. Census Bureau 2021), including 16.1 percent of U.S. children under the age of 18. Why do people live in poverty in the United States—one of the wealthiest countries in the world?

Anthropologists and other social scientists have articulated numerous theories to explain poverty's origins and persistence. Two key theories have emerged: One focuses on poverty as pathology, and the other focuses on poverty as a structural economic problem.

Theories of poverty as pathology trace ongoing poverty to the personal failings of the individual, family, or community. Such theories—which most anthropologists reject—see these failings as stemming from a "culture of poverty"—a combination of dysfunctional behaviors, attitudes, and values that make and keep poor people poor (Lewis 1959, 1966; Wilson 1987).

Many anthropologists have critiqued the "culture of poverty" theory (Leacock 1971) and have proposed instead that poverty is a structural economic problem. If people are faced with no jobs, inadequate education and health care, and a systematic failure to invest in the infrastructure of impoverished neighborhoods and communities, then poverty cannot be changed by changing individuals' attitudes and values. What are often considered to be characteristics of a culture of poverty are actually characteristics of poverty itself; they have nothing to do with the attitudes, values, and life choices of those forced to live in poverty.

Anthropologists Judith Goode and Jeff Maskovsky (2001) trace the roots of contemporary poverty in the United States to the impact of global economic processes on the nation's economy. The growth of globalization and the expansion of global capitalism, they argue, have launched an economic restructuring in which corporations ship high-paying, blue-collar manufacturing jobs overseas in search of cheaper labor, lower taxes, and fewer environmental restrictions. The U.S. workforce has become more polarized between highly educated, well-paid professionals and managers, on the one hand, and undereducated workers who struggle with low pay, no benefits, and little job security, on the other. U.S. government policies and programs designed to regulate the economy, protect the most vulnerable, and provide opportunities for social mobility have been reduced, including public education, housing, and investment in infrastructure.

Intersections of Class and Race in a San Francisco High School

Anthropologist Savannah Shange explores the structural roots of poverty through an intersectional lens of race, gender, and class in her book *Progressive Dystopia: Abolition, Antiblackness, + Schooling in San Francisco* (2019). What, she asks, is to be done when the world simply doesn't work, when one lives in a dystopia of lessened life chances, limited health care, poor education, mass incarceration, wide-spread poverty and diminished life spans?

MAP 10.5
San Francisco

Shange conducted fieldwork at Robeson Justice Academy, a community-initiated high school serving one of the last working-class neighborhoods in San Francisco. The school's progressive curriculum is designed to offer low-income young people of color a liberating education designed around social justice themes and initiatives. San Francisco, imagined by many to be a leading liberal, progressive city, has suffered an exodus of Black residents in recent decades in the face of gentrification, redlining, urban renewal projects that have destroyed primarily Black neighborhoods, pollution, and other forms of racialized displacement. Shange reminds us that San Francisco, like other U.S. cities, is built upon a past that includes the genocide of the local Indigenous population and the long afterlife of slavery. By 2020, San Francisco's Black population had plunged to just 5.2 percent, compared to 12.4 percent in the United States nationally. Robeson's student body, now majority Latinx, reflects this shift.

Despite Robeson's lofty goals and sincere pursuit of multiracial uplift, Shange documents the school's struggle to serve its Black students. Black staff, students, and family are marginalized, those seen as disruptive are counseled to transfer out, and the border between the school and neighborhood is criminalized. Robeson's Black students face the highest suspension rates in the district and disproportionately high rates of disciplinary procedures and expulsions. Shange views these patterns within the national context of a school-to-prison pipeline in which zero-tolerance disciplinary policies disproportionately affect students of color, particularly Black students, leading to a cycle of arrests, detentions, and incarceration within the prison system.

In 2016, when a grand jury in Ferguson, Missouri, failed to bring charges against the officer who killed unarmed Black teenager Michael Brown, students at Robeson organized a protest. With the support of school administrators and teachers, students gathered on the basketball court with hands in the air, some holding signs that said "Hands up, Don't Shoot" and "Murder is Illegal—Arrest the Officer." The school website posted a photo of the action emblazoned with the title "#OurLivesMatter." Shange critiques this slogan's shift away from the original #BlackLivesMatter hashtag's focus on Black lives and Black bodies. But she also suggests that the demonstration reveals Robeson's fundamental failure in addressing racism and poverty. The demonstration, she argues, channeled student concerns into what can be done: basic demands like don't shoot unarmed civilians, protect Black and Brown youth from police violence, arrest those who kill other people. Shange identifies these as typical progressive strategies for addressing inequality: reform the system, win control over the mechanisms of the state, redistribute its resources in incremental progressive programs. But what if what *can* be done is not what *needs* to be done?

Educators and staff at Robeson are winning within the system. They provide a culturally competent, engaged, democratically oriented education designed to enact the best-case scenario for surviving and living in the world as it exists. Shange warns, however, that winning within the system is inadequate when the system itself, built over many generations, creates the dystopia—deep structural patterns of inequality, a world that doesn't work—in the first place. In such a dystopian scenario, she asks, is there any choice but to willfully defy systemic racism, disrupt patterns of exploitation and anti-Blackness, abolish state-sponsored practices of dispossession, and create something new? Building on anthropologist Leith Mullings's work on intersectionality (see Chapter 5), Shange's study confirms that class in the United States and elsewhere cannot be studied in isolation but, instead, must be considered together with other interlocking systems of power such as race. Only by analyzing the intersection of multiple systems of power can we see more clearly how class is lived and life chances are defined.

Discussions about the root causes of poverty continue today in both popular conversations and policy circles. Intense debate continues, for instance, over the appropriate role of government in addressing problems of persistent poverty. Arguments often draw on the distinction between seeing the roots of these problems in a culture of poverty or in a long-term structural system of exclusion built into government policies and economic practices. Can poverty be addressed through improved housing, provision of health care, education, and the creation of living-wage jobs (the structural causes)? Or must perceived patterns of dependency on government programs and services be addressed to confront an underlying culture that holds people back? You will encounter these questions in conversations with classmates and coworkers, and you will influence these debates at different points in your life—perhaps as you undertake community service as a college student or later as you participate in the U.S. political process.

CLASS AND INEQUALITY GLOBALLY

Uneven development is a central characteristic of globalization, particularly of the global capitalist system. The global economy has not brought equal benefits to the world's people; it has produced unprecedented wealth and widespread poverty. It appears that the rapid growth of globalization actually depends on uneven development—extracting the resources of some to fuel the success of others. Systems of class and caste are central to creating and maintaining these patterns of extraction, stratification, and uneven effects on individuals' life chances and possibilities for upward social mobility.

STREET VENDORS IN THE GLOBAL ECONOMY

Today's global economic transformations have led to historic levels of poverty in the world's poorest cities as rural dwellers move to urban areas in search of work. Anthropologist Daniel Goldstein (2016) explores the contours of class and inequality in his study of street vendors in the enormous Cancha outdoor market in Cochabamba, Bolivia. Goldstein focuses specifically on vulnerable street vendors and their small-scale commercial activities, or what scholars call the informal economy: the underground, and sometimes illegal, system of buying and selling that parallels the official economy.

The bright, colorful, and dynamic Cancha marketplace is the largest of its kind in Bolivia. Thousands of long-term merchants, known as *fijos*, sell their wares from narrow stalls in the market's central pavilion. At the same time, thousands of street vendors, locally known as *ambulantes*, rove the surrounding, traffic-clogged streets and packed sidewalks, alleyways, and passageways, hawking food, drink, watches, radios, DVDs, men's briefs, hardware, soap, cosmetics, bananas, rice—any small, portable item that might attract the attention of a local shopper or visiting tourist. While stall vendors and street vendors alike contribute to the dynamism and success of the market, their experiences stand in stark contrast. Tensions between the groups run high. Their furious competition for sales ensures that. But the *fijos* and *ambulantes* operate on unequal playing fields. For stall vendors, their fixed, permanent, and legal locations at the center of the market provide a more secure position in the local economy. Their stability and legal status create conditions for economic success and the potential, if all goes well, for upward economic mobility.

The street vendors of the Cancha, in contrast, work under much more tenuous and vulnerable conditions. They are harassed by police, insulted by motorists and pedestrians, preyed upon by shoplifters and muggers. State laws explicitly prohibit them from selling on the street. Goldstein argues that the marked growth of informal urban economic activity worldwide is produced not by the informal workers themselves but by the state's creation and regulation of economic and political conditions. What may appear to the outsider as chaotic, disorderly, or

The informal economy—small-scale, underground, and sometimes illegal—has become the primary economic activity in many poor countries. Here, street vendors and stall vendors compete for customers at the sprawling Cancha outdoor market in downtown Cochabamba, Bolivia.

MAP 10.6
Cochabamba

FIGURE 10.3
The World by Gross National Income per Capita, 2020

High income:	Upper-middle income:	Lower-middle income:	Low income:
$12,056	$3,896–$12,055	$996–$3,895	$995 or less

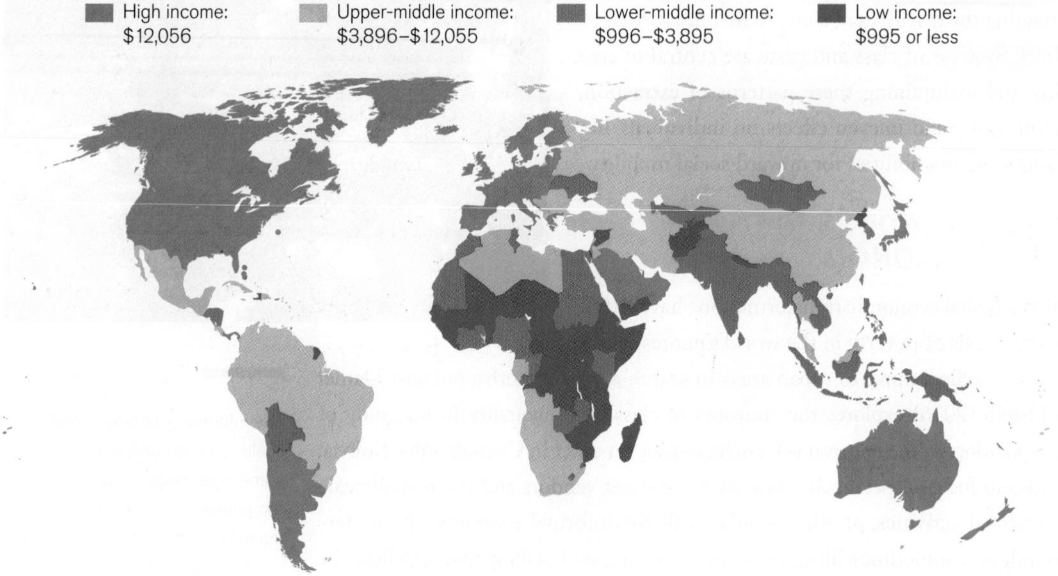

Source: The World Bank. 2020. World by Income and Region. datatopics.worldbank.org

even criminal and dangerous is not random at all. Rather, the state and its representatives create and benefit directly from the conditions of informality and illegality that turn urban small-scale entrepreneurs into criminals. Inconsistently enforced laws and regulations applied to poor city dwellers—an increasingly common pattern in the contemporary global economy—only increase workers' experience of uncertainty, insecurity, and vulnerability.

Despite the chaos and disorder built into the informal activity in the Cancha, Goldstein's ethnography reveals the determined efforts of street vendors—poor urban small business people—to scrabble together a living against the odds in the only way available to them—as precarious owners of the streets and sidewalks of the informal city.

Global statistics reveal the extremes of uneven development. In 2021, the world had 2,755 billionaires, up from 937 billionaires in 2010 (Dolan 2021). At the same time, almost 3.4 billion people—half of the world's population—struggle to meet basic needs. Of these, 736 million people live in extreme poverty, surviving on less than $1.90 each day. Nearly 2 billion people, or 26.2 percent of the world's population, live on less than $3.20 per day, which is considered the poverty rate in lower-middle-income countries (World Bank 2018). If household wealth were divided equally on a global basis, each household would have $26,754 (using 2000 data). Instead, 10 percent of the world's population owns 71 percent of all wealth on the entire planet. The wealthiest 20 percent of the world's population receives 75 percent of the total global income (Davies et al. 2009).

Growing global inequality affects the life chances of the world's population on many fronts, including hunger and malnutrition, health, education, vulnerability to climate change, and access to technology. Hunger is indeed a global problem. Although there is enough food in the world to feed everyone, it is unevenly distributed. Every day 821 million people go hungry—one out of every nine—and 150 million children under age five are malnourished (World Health Organization 2018).

Health and mortality are also areas of serious concern. In late 2021, the number of COVID-19 vaccine doses administered per one hundred people was eighteen times higher in high-income countries than in low-income countries (Anderson and Wakamo 2021). Preventable infectious diseases such as malaria, measles, and HIV/AIDS kill millions each year in poor countries. And in low-income countries, people are more likely to die in infancy and are eleven times more likely to die at birth than are people in wealthy countries. Moreover, people live longer in high-income countries, averaging a nearly eighty-one-year life span compared to a nearly sixty-three-year life span in low-income countries (World Health Organization 2019).

Despite the centrality of class-based stratification in the dynamics of globalization and its powerful effects on individuals' life chances and possibilities for social mobility, class remains arguably the most overlooked of the systems of power we have considered in this textbook. Careful attention to the theoretical approaches to class adopted by anthropologists, including ethnographic research and data analysis, will position you to engage issues of income and wealth inequality more fully as you participate in a rapidly globalizing world.

How Is Today's Global Economy Reshaping Migration?

Use anthropological concepts to explain the relationship between migration and the economy.

The past forty years have seen one of the highest rates of global migration in modern history, not only between countries but within them as well. The powerful effects of globalization have stimulated migration from rural areas to urban areas and from less-developed countries to more-developed countries. At the same time, time-space compression has transformed the migration experience: Rapid transportation and instantaneous communication enable some migrants to travel more cheaply and quickly than ever and to stay connected with folks back home. Flexible accumulation also stimulates migration by disrupting local economic, political, and social relationships while linking local communities to global economic processes (Massey et al. 2005; Portes and Rumbaut 2014; Sassen 1988, 2016). In 2019, the United Nations estimated that there were 271 million international migrants, plus hundreds of millions more internal migrants moving within their own national borders (United Nations Department of Economic and Social Affairs, Population Division 2019). The Chinese government estimates that more than 230 million people migrate internally in China alone (Liang 2012).

PUSHES AND PULLS

pushes and pulls

The forces that spur migration from the country of origin and draw immigrants to a particular new destination country.

The decision to migrate and the chosen destination are often shaped by **pushes and pulls**. People are pushed to migrate from their home community by poverty, famine, natural disasters, climate change, war, ethnic conflict, genocide, disease, or political or religious oppression. Those who are forced to migrate are often termed *refugees*. Uneven development in the global economy stimulates much of today's global migration. Frustrated by their inability to achieve life aspirations and meet the needs of their families at home, many people seek opportunities elsewhere (Portes and Rumbaut 2006).

Destinations are not chosen randomly, nor are all destinations equal. When considering migration, people are pulled to certain places by job opportunities, higher wages, educational opportunities for themselves and their children, access to health care, or investment opportunities. Family and friends who have already migrated provide encouragement and connections. At the same time, media such as television, music, and film, along with powerful advertising, promote the desire to live a Western, middle-class, consumer-oriented lifestyle.

BRIDGES AND BARRIERS

bridges and barriers

The factors that enable or inhibit migration.

Immigrants also encounter **bridges and barriers** that influence who moves and where they go. Bridges may include family networks, transportation links, government immigration policies, recruitment agencies, and even human smugglers. Barriers range from language difference and geographical distance to tightly regulated borders and expenditures for passports, visas, and transportation.

But why do people migrate? My own research, published in *God in Chinatown: Religion and Survival in New York's Evolving Immigrant Community* (2003), focuses on migrants from towns and villages near Fuzhou in southeastern China. In recent years, these individuals have come in large numbers: first to New York City to work in Chinese restaurants, garment shops, nail salons, and construction trades, and now spreading across the United States as they open takeout restaurants and all-you-can-eat buffets. In many towns and villages, as much as 50 to 70 percent of the population has migrated out, and hundreds of thousands of these migrants have come to and through New York.

Of the more than 1.4 billion people in China, why have people from the Fuzhou City area decided to migrate out? And why do so many go to New York City? The conditions are the same for Fuzhounese as they are for many rural people in China—small incomes, difficult farm labor, limited opportunities for upward mobility or education. And the attraction of New York City—in this case, the tremendous need for low-wage workers—exists in many big cities, not only in the United States but also in countries much closer to China.

In the back of a Chinese restaurant in New York City, I interviewed Chen Dawei, age nineteen, who had come from Fuzhou one year earlier and whose story sheds light on the Fuzhounese immigrant experience:

MAP 10.7
Fuzhou City

> I didn't really want to go to America. But everyone else my age had already gone. I didn't want to seem stupid. My parents really wanted to send me. They have a little shop on the main street. We aren't poor. But we don't make much money either. Making $1,500 a month as a delivery man for a Chinese restaurant in the United States sounds really good when your family is lucky to make that much in a whole year back home. I really didn't want to go. But people kept calling to say how well they were doing. Both of my uncles were already in the U.S. Lots of people were sending money back home. And people who got green cards would come back and build a nice home for their family. So my dad arranged with a snakehead (smuggler) to send me to New York. It cost $65,000. We borrowed some from my uncles. And some from friends who had already gone to New York. The rest we borrowed at really high interest. It will probably take me four or five years to pay it all off.

Can you identify the pushes, pulls, bridges, and barriers in Chen Dawei's migration story?

Chinese Restaurants and the Global Economy.

The journey of Fuzhounese immigrants does not end in New York City and may, in fact, continue to your college dorm or apartment front door. Have you ever wondered why chicken with broccoli is so inexpensive in your local Chinese restaurant? The answer lies along a street called East Broadway in Chinatown on the Lower East Side of Manhattan. There an entire migration industry draws Chinese

immigrants from the rural villages of the Fuzhou area to New York City and sets them on the move again to a Chinese restaurant near you.

Located along East Broadway are a cluster of services that facilitate the movement of Chinese immigrants. Offices for immigration lawyers, English language classes, driving schools, and producers of legitimate and illegitimate documents stand alongside doctors' offices, pharmacies, clothing stores, and gambling parlors. East Broadway's human smugglers help undocumented immigrants make their way across national borders. Phone card sales booths help workers keep in touch with family back in China. MoneyGram and Western Union wire-transfer offices help people send money back to family members in their home villages. Key to this migration industry are two dozen employment agencies that match newly arrived workers with Chinese restaurants across the country and another dozen long-distance buses that deliver Fuzhounese to those restaurants (Guest 2009).

This global flow of Fuzhounese is fraught with frictions. Chinese smugglers charge more than $80,000 to bring a person to the United States, leaving immigrants with huge debts that may take years to repay. Restaurant owners rely on vulnerable, underpaid workers to make their profit margins on inexpensive dishes such as chicken with broccoli. Workers often live and work in the restaurants, putting in twelve- to fourteen-hour days, six or seven days a week. Chinatown buses provide the link that moves workers between out-of-town jobs and the support system of the migration industry along East Broadway. As many as 50,000 individuals are circulating through this Chinese restaurant industry at any given time.

The movement of rural men and women from Chinese villages to the far reaches of the United States illustrates the deep interconnectivity of people in the modern world economic system. The demand for inexpensive Chinese food in Omaha, Nebraska, can pull young Chinese farmers across an ocean to help fill the demand of a global labor market and pursue their dreams of wealth and

FIGURE 10.4
Contemporary Global Migration Patterns

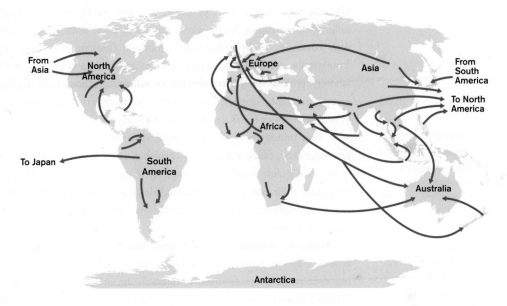

happiness for themselves and their families. That is the story behind your next dish of chicken with broccoli (Guest 2011).

GLOBAL MIGRATION PATTERNS

Globalization has intensified the volume and types of movement occurring within and across political boundaries (Trouillot 2003). But not every country is equally affected by today's global flow of migrants. Some are primarily sending countries; others are primarily receiving countries. Moreover, not all migration occurs across borders. Thus, a truly global perspective on migration must include both international and internal migration.

International migrants, or migrants who cross borders, exist around the globe, but they largely relocate to more-developed countries. Figure 10.4 shows the primary migration flows for receiving and sending countries. Internal migration refers to the movement of people within their own national borders. For example, urban-oriented development programs and the establishment of large-scale export processing zones in developing countries have provided the pulls for significant internal migration from rural to urban areas to fill new labor needs. Women workers, sought after by factory owners in export processing zones, constitute a high proportion of internal migrants.

TYPES OF IMMIGRANTS

Globally, migration includes people from a wide variety of class backgrounds, ranging from refugees fleeing war or natural disaster, to unskilled workers with little education, to well-educated doctors and elite corporate businesspeople. Immigration scholars often focus on immigrants' economic roles, whether as laborers, professionals, entrepreneurs, or refugees. Although not applicable to every immigrant journey, these categories delineate certain patterns that offer a general framework for analysis and comparison.

Labor immigrants, like the Fuzhounese, move in search of low-skill and low-wage jobs, filling economic niches that native-born workers will not fill. Labor immigrants constitute the majority of migrants in the world today. They may enter their new countries through legal or illegal channels, but they are drawn by employment opportunities that, though limited, provide jobs at wages higher than those available in their home economies.

Professional immigrants are highly trained individuals who move to fill economic niches in middle-class professions marked by shortages in the receiving country. Many professional immigrants are university students trained in Western-style professions who lack opportunities to implement their training at home. This migration is often referred to as a *brain drain*, for many of the most highly skilled professionals trained in developing (periphery) countries are enticed by wages and other opportunities to relocate to developed (core) countries.

Entrepreneurial immigrants move to new locations to conduct trade and establish businesses as merchants, restaurateurs, and small shopkeepers in countries worldwide.

labor immigrants

Persons who move in search of low-skill and low-wage jobs, often filling an economic niche that native-born workers will not fill.

professional immigrants

Highly trained individuals who move to fill economic niches in middle-class professions often marked by shortages in the receiving country.

entrepreneurial immigrants

Persons who move to a new location to conduct trade and establish a business.

Why are an increasing number of U.S. health-care professionals immigrants from India, the Philippines, and the Caribbean? Here, Dr. Saeid Ahmadpour performs a checkup on a baby at a clinic in Cheyenne Wells, Colorado.

A fourth type of immigrant, **refugees** are people who have been forced to migrate beyond their national borders because of political or religious persecution, armed conflict or other forms of violence, or natural or human-made disasters. The United Nations estimated a total of 26.6 million refugees worldwide in 2021 (United Nations High Commissioner for Refugees 2022).

Although refugee status technically applies to those who seek asylum in another nation, the experiences of *internally displaced persons* can be just as devastating. These experiences mirror those of international refugees, except they take place in the migrants' own countries.

In another phenomenon of globalization, time-space compression—notably, advances in communication and transportation—has transformed the migration experience by tying migrants more closely to their families and communities back home. Today, many migrants travel back and forth, send money through Western Union, and talk, text, and share videos and movies regularly with family and friends through KakaoTalk, LINE, Skype, WeChat, WhatsApp, Zoom, and other smartphone apps. These transnational immigrants actively participate in social, economic, religious, and political spheres across national borders. Contemporary globalization has intensified the webs of interaction, lowered the cost of travel and communication, and sped up the exchange of people, information, and money, thereby enabling some migrants to enjoy a lifestyle that spans national borders.

refugees
Persons who have been forced to move beyond their national borders because of political or religious persecution, armed conflict, or disasters.

Malian Migrants: Reshaping Globalization from the Ground Up.

Though international movements of people between continents and across oceans often capture public and scholarly attention, today significant movement occurs between neighboring countries. In *Migrants and Strangers in an African City* (2012), anthropologist Bruce Whitehouse focuses on migrants from Mali, a large West African nation of 17 million people. Though landlocked, Mali's position at the center of regional trade networks crisscrossing West and North Africa has a long history. Today, Malians, along with hundreds of thousands of other West Africans, have increasingly been on the move. Some have settled in developed Western countries, such as France, Spain, and the United States, or in Asian cities, such as Dubai, Bangkok, Hong Kong, and Guangzhou. Most, however, have relocated within the African continent—notably to Senegal, Côte d'Ivoire, Burkina Faso, Gabon, the Republic of the Congo, and South Africa.

Whitehouse begins his ethnography with the story of a small town in southern Mali that he calls Togotala. The town lies on an arid plain between desert to the north and forest to the south. With agricultural production being inadequate to meet the immediate needs of the Togotala population, and with no development assistance from the Malian government, the community has a history of producing merchants who enter regional trade networks in order to send remittances home to support their families and the community at large.

MAP 10.8
Mali and Republic of the Congo

Twice daily, battered buses arrive in Togotala carrying goods and passengers and providing the town's primary link to the outside world. A ride south to Mali's capital, Bamako, connects Togotala's merchants to an extensive transport network through which they can reach more-distant destinations. Whitehouse traces some of Togotala's residents southward to a large Malian community in Brazzaville, capital of the Republic of the Congo. A port city of 2.5 million residents on the northern bank of the Congo River, Brazzaville serves as the country's administrative, manufacturing, and financial center. It is also a transfer point for agricultural products, wood, rubber, and other raw materials coming from upriver onto the Congo–Ocean railroad that links Brazzaville to the seaport of Pointe-Noire. French colonialists originally brought West Africans to Brazzaville in the 1800s to serve as soldiers, porters, laborers, and messengers. But West Africans succeeded in creating parallel economic networks of merchants, traders, laborers, blacksmiths, leatherworkers, and traditional storytellers—economic networks that survived the end of colonialism in 1960. Today, a large community of Malians, mostly Muslim, work in Brazzaville as importers, shopkeepers, street vendors, entrepreneurs, and merchants in the diamond and jewelry trades.

Despite their long history in Brazzaville, Malians are treated as outsiders and strangers, segregated by language, social organization, and religion. A strong connection to home enables them to maintain a sense of place and belonging despite local marginalization and in the face of increasing mobility and spatial separation from their families and home communities.

Migrants, including the merchants of Togotala and other entrepreneurs across Africa, reveal creative individual responses to the intensification of interaction that is occurring worldwide. Actions by migrants such as the Malians in Brazzaville reveal the determined entrepreneurial strategies that local people use to bring the benefits of the global economy to their communities and to reshape globalization from the ground up.

Today, we have an economic system of astounding complexity. Our economic activity surpasses anything we might have imagined even fifty years ago. The global economy integrates all of the world's people to one extent or another into a global system of exchange. But does it work well for everyone? What are the criteria we might use to assess its effectiveness?

Entrepreneurial immigrants from Mali have built a vibrant community in Brazzaville, Republic of the Congo.

The global economy has achieved remarkable success over the past sixty years. For example, gross domestic product of the global economy rose from around $1 trillion in 1960 to $84.7 trillion in 2020 (World Bank 2020). School enrollment increased nearly 20 percent between 1970 and 2021 (World Bank 2022). Infant mortality rates dropped by more than 60 percent between 1990 and 2020 (World Bank 2022). And life expectancy nearly doubled over the last century, reaching 72.7 years in 2019 before the COVID-19 pandemic (World Bank 2022).

But the outlook is not all rosy. In 2019, 5.2 million children died from preventable or treatable causes, nearly half from malnutrition (World Health Organization 2020). In 2020, the world had nearly 768 million people going hungry each day and living in extreme poverty (United Nations 2021). The pandemic was expected to push another 100 million into extreme poverty (World Bank 2020). Clearly, global inequality continues to increase. Is the current trajectory of the global economy sustainable? And how can anthropologists help address these questions? We will consider these questions further in Chapter 11, "Environment and Sustainability."

Toolkit

Thinking Like an Anthropologist
Situating Yourself within the
Global Economy

Globalization of the world economy has transformed the way we live. As you analyze the global economy and your connection to it, consider again the questions we raised at the beginning of the chapter:

- **What is an economy, and what is its purpose?**
- **How did the modern world economic system emerge?**
- **What are the dominant organizing principles of the global economy today?**
- **How does today's global economy link workers with consumers worldwide?**
- **How do anthropologists analyze class and inequality?**
- **How is today's global economy reshaping migration?**

Our opening story of chocolate in Côte d'Ivoire highlighted both the complexities of the global economy and the connections it facilitates among people, states, and corporations worldwide. Chocolate—like coffee, tea, sugar, a laptop, or a smartphone—reveals both (1) the incredible potential of our globalized economy to create connections and (2) the unwelcome consequences of globalization that lead to imbalances and inequalities.

We have asked whether the global economy works well. Is it sustainable? How can we ensure the adequate distribution of resources necessary for human life—food, clean water, shelter, and health care? These are questions you will have to answer in your lifetime. And you will answer them by the life choices you make. For, as globalization continues to intensify, we are all connected in a web of constraints and opportunities. Your engagement with the global economy may not be constrained by poverty, illiteracy, or violence, but it could be constrained by cultural expectations—for instance, group and peer pressure about what you need to do to fit in, dress well, eat right, and travel from place to place. Do you really have the choice in U.S. culture to not consume? How you address these constraints and opportunities will make a difference.

The good news is that there are many points at which to intervene in the current patterns of the global economy, whether you work to save the forests, recycle, support fair trade, reevaluate your consumption patterns, organize to support the rights of workers around the world, or become an engineer focusing on clean manufacturing or a scientist developing renewable energy sources. Thinking like an anthropologist will help you to analyze your choices in a more informed and responsible way.

Key Terms

economy (p. 284)

food foragers (p. 284)

pastoralism (p. 285)

horticulture (p. 285)

agriculture (p. 285)

industrial agriculture (p. 286)

reciprocity (p. 287)

redistribution (p. 288)

colonialism (p. 290)

triangle trade (p. 290)

Industrial Revolution (p. 292)

modernization theories (p. 294)

development (p. 294)

dependency theory (p. 294)

neocolonialism (p. 294)

underdevelopment (p. 295)

core countries (p. 295)

periphery countries (p. 296)

semiperiphery countries (p. 296)

Fordism (p. 297)

flexible accumulation (p. 297)

neoliberalism (p. 299)

commodity (p. 303)

commodity chains (p. 303)

stratification (p. 305)

class (p. 305)

bourgeoisie (p. 305)

means of production (p. 306)

capital (p. 306)

proletariat (p. 306)

prestige (p. 307)

life chances (p. 307)

social mobility (p. 308)

social reproduction (p. 308)

habitus (p. 308)

cultural capital (p. 308)

income (p. 311)

wealth (p. 311)

pushes and pulls (p. 318)

bridges and barriers (p. 318)

labor immigrants (p. 322)

professional immigrants (p. 322)

entrepreneurial immigrants (p. 322)

refugees (p. 323)

Chapter 11
Environment and Sustainability

"We are not prepared to die. . . . We are not going to become the first victims of the climate crisis. Instead we are going to do everything to keep our heads above the water."

—*Mohamed Nasheed, former president,*
The Republic of Maldives

Learning Objectives

- Define the Anthropocene and its key characteristics.

- Describe the multispecies perspective in environmental anthropology.

- Assess how the environment is shaped by other systems of power.

- Explain how globalization is shaping the environment.

- Analyze ways today's global economy may be unsustainable.

For small island nations, climate change is not something in the future. Here, Maldivian president Mohamed Nasheed holds a cabinet meeting underwater to draw international attention to the impending crisis of sea levels rising. How vulnerable is your community to the effects of climate change?

In the Indian Ocean, 600 miles southwest of India, the 2,000 coral islands and atolls of the Maldives spread like gemstones over miles of open water. These are low-lying islands—the world's lowest country. The lives of its 430,000 citizens revolve around the sea. Exclusive tourist resorts ring the main islands, though fishing provides the islanders' primary livelihood.

For the Maldives and other small island nations, climate change is not something in the future. Ground level elevation in the Maldives averages about five feet above sea level. The highest point is eight feet. Already, rising seas are eroding coastlines, contaminating drinking water, and undermining food security. Rising water temperatures have caused the loss of 95 percent of the Maldives' coral reefs. Climate scientists project global sea levels may rise by at least six feet by the year 2100, in which case the Maldives will have disappeared completely into the sea.

Since serving as president of the Maldives, Mohamed Nasheed has taken a leading role in efforts to reverse the threat of global warming. At home he pledged to make the Maldives the first carbon-neutral country. To dramatize what will become of his nation without urgent climate action, he and his cabinet donned scuba gear to conduct a meeting twelve feet under water. Internationally he helped assemble a coalition of thirty-nine vulnerable small island states and built global alliances to push the world community to take urgent collective climate action. His message to world leaders was simple: Environmental realities connect all humans in today's global age. Though the Maldives contribute little to the environmental pollution that is driving climate change, its residents are among the first to suffer. But small islands do not exist in isolation from one another or from the rest of the world. Twenty-five percent of the world's population lives in low-lying coastal areas, including small island nations. Downtown Miami floods regularly at high tide. Lower Manhattan, New York City, is the same elevation as the Maldives. We are all in this together.

Swedish climate activist Greta Thunberg has questioned the ability of world leaders to address the environmental crisis facing the planet. "Since our leaders are behaving like children, we will have to take the responsibility they should have taken long ago," she said. "We have to understand what the older generation has dealt to us, what mess they have created that we have to clean up and live with. We have to make our voices heard" (Carrington 2018).

Thunberg began her climate protests alone outside the Swedish parliament in the summer of 2018. She then skipped school every Friday to continue the demonstrations. Her actions have inspired student strikes in over 100 countries to demand action on climate change. In response to criticism that kids should be in school, not protesting on the streets, one popular protest sign read, "We'll do our homework when you do yours."

Anthropologists have a long but uneven history of considering the physical environment and nonhuman actors in their research. Still, our field's historical

In August of 2018, fifteen-year-old Greta Thunberg, a Swedish high school student, led a school strike outside of the Swedish parliament building to protest the government's inaction on climate change. Her activism has inspired many climate-related protests from students around the world urging their lawmakers to take immediate action to combat climate change. Her sign reads, "School Strike for the Climate."

focus on rural areas and subsistence strategies provides a unique body of research on human relationships to the natural world that predates the current environmental moment. Bronisław Malinowski studied Trobriand gardens. E. E. Evans-Pritchard studied Nuer cows. Owen Lattimore wrote about Chinese water management and irrigation farming. Zora Neale Hurston interviewed migrant agricultural workers transforming Florida's Everglades swampland. Julian Steward considered how environmental factors shaped cultural adaptations by the Indigenous people of the Great Basin area of the American West, creating what Steward called a cultural ecology (Kopnina and Shoreman-Ouimet 2017; Townsend 2018).

Today, **environmental anthropology**—the study of how humans interact with the natural world around them—has taken on new urgency as the people and places anthropologists study are being radically affected by climate change. The planet is not just warming. It has warmed. Human production of carbon dioxide, largely from burning fossil fuels, has created a greenhouse effect in Earth's atmosphere, raising the planet's temperature, acidifying its oceans, and causing mass extinctions of species. Carbon emissions have created permanent, irreversible damage to Earth's ecosystems, defrosting the tundra, melting the Greenland and the West Antarctic ice sheets, and destroying coral reefs—changes that cannot be undone through technology. Today, environmental anthropologists are deeply engaged in work to understand the impact and scope of contemporary changes on local communities, think in new ways about the relationship between humans and nature, and see how local communities are working to shape their futures in a time of uncertainty (Guarasci, Moore, and Vaughn 2018).

environmental anthropology

The study of relations between humans and the environment.

In this chapter, we consider contemporary anthropological approaches to studying the environment. In particular, we consider the following questions:

- **What is the Anthropocene?**
- **How does a multispecies perspective change our worldview and our future?**
- **How do other systems of power shape the environment?**
- **How is the environment shaped by globalization?**
- **What if today's global economic system is not sustainable?**

Humans are facing a unique challenge to our survival. This chapter explores the roots of our current dilemma, including our deeply held ideas about nature and the processes by which humans have attempted to control and govern it. By the end, you will better appreciate how anthropologists' strategies of long-term field-work offer possibilities for understanding the complex interaction between local communities and global environmental forces. You will see how local communities are responding to these challenges, and you will have the tools to engage these issues in your own life.

What Is the Anthropocene?

Define the Anthropocene and its key characteristics.

Earth's atmosphere has been remarkably stable since the end of the last ice age 12,000 years ago, which marked the beginning of what geologists call the Holocene period. But the stable Holocene climate has shifted in recent years in response to human activity. The human impact on the planet is so extensive that scholars in many disciplines have come to refer to the current geological period as the **Anthropocene**—a distinct era in which human activity is reshaping the planet in permanent ways. Whereas our ancestors struggled to adapt to the uncertainties of the world around them, today we confront environmental changes and social forces that we ourselves have set in motion. These challenges—including climate change, drought, extreme poverty, widespread species extinction, and toxic pollution of air and water—pose a tremendous risk to human survival. As globalization intensifies, it escalates the human impact on the environment and threatens the world's ecological balance (Latour 2014).

Over the past hundred years, particularly since World War II, large swaths of the planet's observable landscapes and physical spaces have been remade. The spread of global capitalism and the expansion of consumer-based economies has

Anthropocene

The current geological era in which human activity is reshaping the planet in permanent ways.

led to a voracious consumption of Earth's resources—including fossil fuels, water, forests, minerals, and wildlife—well beyond what the planet can sustain. The benefits of global economic development have been uneven. Now, as environmental challenges mount, the impact is also uneven. Many who have not participated in or benefited from the reshaping of the planet are at the greatest risk. Inequality of wealth and environmental vulnerability are rapidly expanding along lines of race, gender, class, and ethnicity (Smith 2010; West 2016).

Finding solutions to the current crisis requires an accurate assessment of its root causes. The ethnographies that follow offer insights into humans' impact on the planet in the Anthropocene and reveal the complicated ways humans and nature are coproducing new ecosystems in response to global processes.

CONSUMING OCEAN ISLAND: RESHAPING THE PLANET

In *Consuming Ocean Island* (2014), anthropologist Katerina Teaiwa reveals key dynamics of the Anthropocene in a very personal story of globalization's effects on the physical contours of the planet and the lives of people in local communities. Her story revolves around the extraction of the mineral phosphate from the tiny South Pacific island of Banaba and the forced relocation of people who stood in the way. Phosphate is found in a limited number of places worldwide. Along with nitrogen and potassium, it is a key nutrient needed for crop growth, and when mined, crushed, and refined, phosphate rock becomes a powerful fertilizer. It is found in abundance and in highly concentrated form on 2.5-square-mile Banaba.

Between 1900 and 1980, foreign corporations, under the auspices of British colonial rule, sought to integrate Ocean Island (another name for Banaba) into the global colonial system and marketplace. Workers from other Pacific islands were first brought in to build docks, railroads, and processing stations. Then, over decades, they removed 90 percent of the island's surface, extracting 22 million tons of phosphate in a strip-mining operation that devastated the local population and ecology.

MAP 11.1
Banaba, Kiribati

Over the last century, phosphate-based fertilizers have transformed barren landscapes across the planet into abundant farmland, driving massive expansions of agriculture and literally feeding the growth of the human population—which has risen from 1.6 billion people in 1900 to 8 billion today. New Zealand and Australia were primary destinations for Ocean Island's phosphate. Crop dusters sprayed the powerful fertilizer on farms and grazing lands, allowing for abundant crops, thick turf, and well-fed sheep.

After World War II, the British forcibly relocated the Banaban people to Rabi Island in Fiji, where most continue to live today. The Banaban presence on

Ocean Island had interfered with the mining companies' extraction work and the British Empire's desire to expand global food supplies. Their removal cleared the way for the complete consumption of Ocean Island, a consumption that benefited corporate investors, industrial agriculturalists, and millions of people whose produce grew from Ocean Island's exported soil.

In exile, amid their dispossession and grief, these environmental refugees worked to rebuild their cultural practices and identity. The last phosphate shipment left Ocean Island in 1981. Today, 300 Banabans, supported by remittances from the Rabi Island community, have returned to care for the island and assert their continuing claim on the territory.

Teaiwa's account of colonial rule, corporate extraction, Indigenous dispossession, ecological destruction, and cultural resilience assembles an environmental history that links remote islanders with colonial governments, global corporations, and international markets. As a descendant of Native Banabans raised in Fiji and the daughter of a Banaban leader, Teaiwa's deeply personal story reveals the complex interplay between people and places across time and space. What does it mean to a people when their land and soil are literally removed and shipped to fertilize the land and pastures of other places? What are the spiritual effects? *Consuming Ocean Island* exposes the consequences of globalization for the physical contours of the planet and its people in the Anthropocene (Hattori 2016; Jones 2016; Melillo 2017; Parvulescu 2017).

THE PANAMA CANAL, HUMAN TECHNOLOGY, AND THE ENVIRONMENT

Technological innovations have been key to the transformation of the planet during the Anthropocene. The conquest of human engineering over nature has enabled the construction of Earth-changing transportation and information infrastructures such as canals, ports, dredged rivers, railroads, roads, pipelines, bridges, airports, undersea cables, orbiting communication satellites, and wireless Internet servers. These infrastructures have in turn made globalization possible today.

The Panama Canal, sometimes called the "big ditch," stands as one of the Anthropocene's boldest technological feats. Tens of thousands of workers between 1904 and 1914 dug through mountains, cut rain forest, and dammed rivers to slice the fifty-one-mile canal across the narrowest part of the Americas to link the Atlantic and Pacific Oceans. The canal's aquatic staircase of locks lifts more than 14,000 vessels a year eighty-five feet above sea level to cross the mountains of central Panama, speeding the movement of goods between oceans and around the world.

In *Beyond the Big Ditch: Politics, Ecology, and Infrastructure at the Panama Canal* (2014), anthropologist Ashley Carse considers the unexpected complications that arise when humans seek to use technology to dominate nature. The

Atlantic Ocean

Panama Canal

Panama

Pacific Ocean

MAP 11.2
Panama Canal, Panama

canal's technical elements and engineering achievements of locks, dams, and gates are famous. But Carse explores the canal's impact on local communities and landscapes by tracing the flow of water along the canal and across the populated watershed upstream. The construction and maintenance of the canal have reshaped the lives of rural Panamanian peasants who live near it. The canal's demand for water has reshaped the environment on which they rely.

The canal requires an enormous quantity of freshwater to move ships through its locks. Over 52 million gallons are needed for each ship, the equivalent of 500,000 Panamanians' daily water use. To provide a steady supply of that much water, construction crews dammed the Chagres River basin, creating a system of lakes, waterways, and reservoirs that now form the Panama Canal watershed and feed the canal's system of locks. At the headwaters of the Chagres River basin lie Panama's dense tropical rain forest. Its thick canopy of trees and undisturbed soils capture and retain the massive rains that then work their way gradually into the newly constructed water system. Before construction, the Chagres River had been an elaborate trading and transit route, intersecting with banana farms and railroad traffic. Flooding for the canal project disrupted the river-based economy, submerged entire riverside towns, and forced residents to relocate to the shoreline of the newly formed Gatun Lake at the top of the lock system.

The vast infrastructure projects associated with the Panama Canal had political, economic, and environmental implications far beyond the river basin. Just as canal engineers cut the Panama isthmus in half, they also cut the nation in half, leaving the government struggling to politically unify the country on both sides of the canal. The canal also split the country economically. Urban trading centers grew at key points along the canal, but the country's rural citizens, many of whom had been displaced by the creation of reservoirs, remained isolated from development in the canal zone.

Carse documents the conflicts that emerged as poor rural people, the Panama Canal administration, and Panama's government battled over the same natural resources. Small farmers cut down rain forests to clear new agricultural land, but less rain forest meant less water collected, stored, and fed into the reservoirs. Uncertain water supplies for the locks threatened canal traffic and led the Panama Canal administration to pressure the national government to alter its development programs. The government, in turn, enacted new conservation policies and agricultural restrictions to protect the rain forest.

The Panama Canal project reveals limits to the technological programs associated with the Anthropocene and globalization. The engineering feat of the canal and the natural features of the rain forest are intertwined. If there were no rain forest, there would be no canal. From entanglements of infrastructures and environments, new ecosystems may emerge. Carse also notes the long-term power of the environment to alter and overcome human technology. For without continuous maintenance and intervention on behalf of our engineering feats, the ever active, adapting environment will retake what has been built—roads, rails, dams, locks, canals, and all—in a constantly evolving ecosystem (Caroll 2016; Reynolds 2015; Victoria 2018).

How Does a Multispecies Perspective Change Our Worldview and Our Future?

Describe the multispecies perspective in environmental anthropology.

Western philosophy has long assumed a fundamental divide between humans and nature: Each operates in its separate realm, but humans may extract unlimited value from nature without consequence. This perception has been central to the emergence of the Anthropocene (Cronon 1995). In recent years, environmental anthropology has moved to repair this philosophical divide by exploring the ways that people, animals, plants, land, and water—together—create an interdependent ecosystem. To visualize that ecosystem, anthropologist Bruno Latour (2014) suggests that we think not about the whole planet but rather a narrow band that stretches only several miles above and below Earth's surface. This tiny ring in which we live is a crowded and deeply entangled space where creatures, water, soil, air, and natural processes interact to co-create our collective environment.

multispecies ethnography

Ethnographic research that considers the interactions of all species living on the planet in order to provide a more-than-human perspective on the world.

Today, environmental anthropologists increasingly engage in **multispecies ethnography** to explore these relationships and recenter the anthropological gaze on the intricate connections between all creatures on Earth, human and nonhuman. Anthropologist Donna Haraway (2016) calls for a rethinking of our basic notions of kinship to include all living beings great and small. Humans are embedded in vast ecosystems teeming with life—on which we rely for our survival. By illuminating our intimate relationships with our planetary co-inhabitants more clearly, multispecies ethnography hopes to help humans reimagine the future, which is currently threatened by an anthropocentric worldview (Blaser and Cadena 2018; Kirksey and Helmreich 2010; Ogden, Hall, and Tanita 2013).

The ethnographies that follow seek to break down the human–nature divide that has been so prominent in Western philosophical thought. These multispecies ethnographies instead foreground nature, placing humans firmly in the natural environment. By exploring the deep interconnections among humans and other living beings, they seek to open new possibilities for humans and all lifeforms that share our planet.

FLORIDA'S EVERGLADES

Laura Ogden's *Swamplife: People, Gators, and Mangroves Entangled in the Everglades* (2011) explores the complex cultural, political, and ecological history of Florida's Everglades. One of North America's most treasured landscapes, these south Florida wetlands, she argues, assemble and connect a multispecies community of people, animals, plants, land, and water in an active and evolving landscape. Ogden's research attempts to reinsert humans into our understanding of nature. Through oral histories, Ogden traces the lives of people she calls *gladesmen*—poor rural Whites who embodied a largely forgotten way of life in the Florida backcountry between the late nineteenth and mid-twentieth centuries. Ogden describes a gladesmen culture of hard work, close-knit families, and respect for one another's territories. Gladesmen lived close to nature and became part of the Everglades ecosystem and swamp life, and their primary source of income—alligator hunting—was enabled by their deep knowledge of the Everglades landscape. Ogden paints a vivid picture of hunting parties canoeing through the swamps, tracking alligators, probing underwater caves, hooking the animals with special poles, killing them, and stripping them of their valuable skins. In 1929 alone, an estimated 190,000 alligator hides were sold in Florida.

In the twentieth century, real estate developers, naturalists, and conservation scientists transformed the Everglades from a hunter's landscape into a politicized natural landscape. Efforts to protect endangered alligators undercut the gladesmen's subsistence strategies. Alligator management programs run by the Florida Fish and Wildlife Conservation Commission criminalized their traditional hunting practices and rebranded them poachers and outlaws. Gladesmen used their local knowledge to resist and defy state restrictions but ultimately faced displacement of their communities and ways of life.

In exploring swamp life, Ogden found a complex ecosystem in which—despite human efforts to tame, manage, and control the Everglades—nature is

MAP 11.3
Everglades, Florida

The Florida Everglades is an important ecosystem ecologically and culturally. The tangled roots of the mangrove forests (*left*) symbolize the complicated relationships between nature, gladesmen (*right*), and tradition.

alive and growing. She suggests the mangrove as a metaphor for the swamp life that characterizes the Everglades and coastal Florida. From the surface, the numerous plants seem distinct. But underwater, their roots form a nearly impenetrable mess, a mangle of numerous plants. And like mangrove roots, animals, plants, alligators, developers, snakes, mangroves, gladesmen, Native people, outlaws, and swampland are all entangled and enmeshed in the evolving ecosystem of the Everglades (Contessa 2013; Davis 2012; Lipset 2013; Lorimer 2013).

HOW FORESTS THINK

MAP 11.4
Upper Amazon Rain
Forest, Ecuador

By seeing the world through the eyes of a jaguar, how might we understand other species more deeply? In his multispecies ethnography *How Forests Think* (2013), Eduardo Kohn asks how nonhuman beings see, know, and think about the world. Kohn's fieldwork considers the ecological relationships between the Indigenous Quechua-speaking Runa people and the surrounding forest, wild creatures, and ancestor spirits of Ecuador's upper Amazon rain forest. One of his key Runa informants warns Kohn that while camping out in the forests during fieldwork, he should sleep face up. Why? Jaguars are known to prowl the forest at night and have been known to attack humans. But by sleeping face up, jaguars will see his eyes and know that he, too, is a living being capable of seeing and is not merely prey.

Kohn's work explores how multiple life-forms interact, connect, and communicate through nonlinguistic modes and shared ecological relations. Placing ourselves within the ecological context of forests and nonhuman animals, as Ecuador's Runa have, offers a possibility to see ourselves differently, more fully, and more completely entangled with active multispecies ecosystems around us (Reno 2015; Flores, Medinaceli, and Thiel 2016; Di Giminiani 2016).

MICROBES IN AN ALIEN OCEAN

Invisible methane-eating microbes thrive in deep-sea volcanic vents. This newly discovered life-form exists where there should be none—on the ocean floor, subject to the extreme temperatures and pressures of the ocean's depths. Yet there is speculation that this is where life on Earth began, among single-celled organisms called the Archaea—the ancient ones. The sea is teeming with microbial life-forms. While the ocean has often been imagined as a vast, primordial wilderness, its microbes are a massive force shaping the chemistry of the sea, the atmosphere, and life on the planet.

In *Alien Ocean: Anthropological Voyages in Microbial Seas* (2009), Stefan Helmreich sets out to understand the emerging scientific focus on the ocean's microbial ecology and the scientists who study these incredible creatures that inhabit the vast space of open oceans. Oceans are alien, in Helmreich's view, because deep-sea research is so dangerous and inaccessible. To observe the ocean's microbial life, scientists rely on remote viewing techniques, such as deploying robots to the ocean floor. Helmreich accompanied a three-person submersible research vehicle journeying 7,000 feet into the Pacific Ocean to see how this works.

Microbes challenge many of our assumptions about what is native and what is alien to our bodies. Microbes do not keep to themselves. They don't respect physical barriers or boundaries between organisms or species. In fact, 90 percent of the human body is composed of microbes—other organisms. That is, human bodies are not discrete, individual entities; human and nonhuman existence is tightly intertwined. Studies of ocean microbes stretch the boundaries of native and alien even further. Research shows that microbes in the alien ocean are genetically influenced not only by their parents' DNA but also by their neighbors'. Yes, genes transfer between generations, but they also transfer laterally between microbes. Research on ocean microbes thus reinforces findings in the field of epigenetics (see Chapter 2) about the power of the environment to shape the expression of genetic information in an organism.

Helmreich's multispecies ethnography, like Ogden's and Kohn's, works to center nonhuman life in the stories we tell about the world and its future. By imagining for a moment life without humans or life in which humans are deeply enmeshed with other nonhuman life, can we also imagine a new collective, entangled future that can move us beyond our current environmental destruction?

Invisible, essential microbes, found in deep-sea volcanic vents like the one pictured here, may hold the key to how life began on Earth.

How Do Other Systems of Power Shape the Environment?

Assess how the environment is shaped by other systems of power.

While much attention has been given to climate change driven by global warming, in the Anthropocene, anthropologists' thinking embraces an expansive notion of the environment that includes infrastructure, waste, pesticides, pollution, gentrification, and development—particularly the uneven impact of these factors along lines of race, class, sexuality, gender, and ethnicity. For instance, rising sea levels related to global warming are making cities such as Venice, Italy; Dhaka, Bangladesh; and New Orleans, Louisiana, especially vulnerable to floods. But the impact on certain people in those places will be determined by more than just the power of natural forces. The following ethnographies consider how environmental issues intersect with other systems of power and stratification to create unequal vulnerabilities to environmental events.

HURRICANE KATRINA: A NATURAL DISASTER?

On August 29, 2005, Hurricane Katrina slammed into the Louisiana coast. People in the United States watched their televisions in horror as the storm surge breached the New Orleans levee system and water flooded into the city's urban center, engulfing homes, businesses, and churches. After the storm, news broadcasts showed residents wading through fetid water to find food, Coast Guard helicopters rescuing stranded residents from rooftops, and tens of thousands of desperate people—including children, older adults, and disabled persons—begging to be rescued from the Superdome and the Convention Center, which had been designated as shelters of last resort but lacked food, water, and working bathrooms. The U.S. government, apparently crippled in its disaster response, took days to deliver emergency aid. More than a hundred countries offered assistance as the world watched, stunned by scenes in the wealthiest country in the world.

When Katrina struck the coast, the hurricane's center actually missed New Orleans. Yet the heavy rain and storm surge overwhelmed the city's aged pumping system, and 80 percent of the city flooded when the levees broke. The city's poorest residents—overwhelmingly African American—were the most severely affected and largely had to fend for themselves. More than half the population was displaced.

Anthropologist and geographer Neil Smith makes the point that there is no such thing as a natural disaster. Hurricanes, tsunamis, earthquakes, droughts, and volcanic eruptions are all natural events. Whether they become disasters, however, depends on social factors: location, vulnerability of the population, government preparedness, effectiveness of the response, and sustained reconstruction efforts. Technological projects to reshape the environment, like the levees in New Orleans, often lead to disasters for humans and other biological species. But the difference between who lives and who dies in a natural event is largely determined by social inequality (Smith 2010).

PESTICIDES, SEXUALITY, AND THE ENVIRONMENT

What happens when human-induced environmental change begins to have long-term consequences on people's bodies? Vanessa Agard-Jones (2013) investigates the impact of chemical pesticides and fertilizers on the environment and on the bodies of residents of the island of Martinique in the Caribbean. In both tropical and temperate regions, farmers have relied on aerial crop-dusting with chemical sprays to efficiently deliver fertilizers and pesticides. From 1972 to 1993, Martinican banana plantation workers also manually applied the carcinogenic pesticide Kepone to kill banana boxer weevils. More recently, owners have used crop-dusting to deliver chemical fungicides to the same plantations. The European Union, to which Martinique belongs by virtue of its status as a

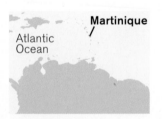

MAP 11.5
Martinique

During the 2013 Carnival festival in Martinique, the main parade figure, Vaval, was created to draw attention to debates over the effects of agricultural pesticides on the bodies of Martinicans. The figure in the center holds a lollipop that says "klordecone," and the champagne bottle reads "the end of the world," emphasizing the dire effects of these pesticides on the population of Martinique.

territory of France, banned crop-dusting in 2009, but the practice continued on the island. Today, these industrially produced chemical particles have contaminated Martinique's soil, water, and people.

Kepone is an internationally recognized carcinogen linked to male infertility and prostate cancer. According to the World Cancer Research Fund International, Martinique has the highest rate of prostate cancer in the world. Kepone is also known as a hormone-altering pesticide, specifically an endocrine disruptor that affects the production and functioning of estrogens in the human body. A direct link between environmental contamination and human endocrine disruption has not been firmly established, but many in Martinique fear that these chemicals will produce changes in human and nonhuman bodies. Concerns include a rise in male and female infertility, reproductive cancers, and birth defects in children.

Agard-Jones, whose fieldwork centers on gender-nonconforming people in Martinique, also notes how these concerns have mixed with anxieties about gender and sexuality. While some Caribbean countries criminalize same-sex relations and disallow gay relationships and marriage, under French law Martinique grants certain sexual rights to its citizens, including civil unions. But acceptance of alternative gender expressions and sexual behavior does not always follow the law. Despite legal protections, queer Martinicans often experience discrimination, harassment, and even violence. Within these complex gender and sexual politics, some Martinicans worry (without scientific substantiation) that the widespread environmental contamination on the island, especially by estrogen-like chemical compounds from crop-dusting, is now leading to the effeminizing of Martinican men and an increase in intersex births.

The intersection of the Kepone chemical contamination scandal with Martinique's complex gender and sexual politics came into full display during the island's 2013 Carnival celebration. Carnival is a festival of parades and revelry, colorful floats, raucous music and dance performances, and large papier-mâché effigies of local gods. The festivities also include overt displays of sexuality and gender transgression, as cross-dressing, cisgender men parody gay men and transgender people. Carnival is also a venue for public conversation and commentary about the big debates of the day. So in 2013, with the controversy over environmental toxins raging in public discourse and in the context of the French Parliament's decision to legalize same-sex civil unions, the creators of Vaval, the spirit of Martinique's Carnival, rendered this important parade figure as two twelve-foot-tall gay men walking arm in arm down the aisle to marriage. One held a champagne bottle emblazoned with the words "the end of the world." The other held a champagne glass with the word "Klordecone" (Kepone).

Citing anthropologist Michel-Rolph Trouillot, Agard-Jones writes that to understand how the world works, sometimes one must first examine the small places and the marginalized people, consider how they matter, and look out from the vantage point of these small places—and bodies—to see the world. At a time when so many in Western cultures are increasingly concerned about chemical pollutants, Agard-Jones's study of gender, sexuality, and the environment in Martinique pushes us to recognize how deeply our bodies are entangled in movements of chemicals that link our cells to plantations, colonial pasts, distant nation-states, and larger world systems.

How Is the Environment Shaped by Globalization?

Explain how globalization is shaping the environment.

Globalization, as we have discussed throughout this book, involves the intensification of interactions among people around the world as money, people, production, goods, and ideas increasingly flow within and across national borders. Despite fanciful stories of isolated people in distant lands, all humans today are connected. Contemporary anthropological studies of the environment further dramatize this point. Local environmental realities can be understood only within a global framework. Climate change and global warming affect us all. The following ethnographies explore how local environmental realities are entangled in global processes of markets, conservation, resource extraction, tourism, agriculture, and social movements.

CONSERVATION AND GLOBALIZATION

Since the 1970s, conservation scientists and international conservation organizations have mobilized to preserve endangered species and habitats in certain environmental hotspots across the globe. Paige West's ethnography *Conservation Is Our Government Now* (2006) explores one such project. On the South Pacific island of Papua New Guinea, the Research and Conservation Foundation (RCF) has worked with Indigenous Gimi groups to create the Crater Mountain Wildlife Management Area (CMWMA), a beautiful, rugged stretch of forests, ridges, valleys, and gardens around Bopoyan Mountain. This attempt at collaborative, community-based conservation engages scientists and local villagers in management of the area and protection of certain rare species, such as the bird of paradise, the cassowary, and the harpy eagle.

MAP 11.6
Papua New Guinea

In return for these efforts, conservation agencies have offered local residents, including the Gimi people, development projects designed to bring local products like traditional Gimi net bags to global markets. The Gimi hoped the arrangement would provide them with greater access to schoolteachers, medical supplies, health clinics, transportation to other islands, and ideas and goods beyond their local community.

West draws on her long-term fieldwork among the Gimi to question many of the basic assumptions of the CMWMA conservation effort, beginning with its ideas about nature itself. Efforts by international conservation organizations rely heavily on a classic Western philosophical approach that divides nature from culture, nature from humans. The nature to be conserved and protected is imagined as untouched, exotic, and spectacular. And to manage and conserve biodiversity for the global biological good, nature must be protected from the activities of local people.

West warns that this philosophical line between nature and culture (humans) obscures local realities. Perhaps for thousands of years, the Gimi and other local people have been living as part of this local ecosystem, not outside it. They understand the life cycle of the forest and its plants and animals. They have successfully managed and conserved the forest for their needs for generations without the help of outside intervention. For the past several hundred years, in fact, they have managed their ecosystem *despite* outside intervention from explorers, naturalists, and traders who have sought to explore it, study it, protect it, and sell it.

To understand this better, West recounts the story of English naturalist and adventurer A. R. Wallace. Wallace spent five months on the coast of Papua New Guinea in 1858 collecting skins and feathers from birds of paradise. He paid local villagers to hunt birds of paradise for him, though they delivered very few. Walking along the harbor, however, Wallace found foreign ships laden with birds of paradise. To his surprise, an extensive trade already existed between the island's interior and the coast. Regional traders moved birds of paradise and other "exotic" products from the "untouched" New Guinea interior of Wallace's imagination to be sold in an existing international market. As early as the seventeenth and eighteenth centuries, Portuguese, Dutch, French, and English navigators and explorers were procuring birds of paradise from Papua New Guinea for museums and private collections and to satisfy an expanding market for hat plumes. Rather than an isolated people living in a seemingly out-of-the-way place, the Gimi have managed their affairs and their ecosystem over a long period of globalization and global capitalist expansion.

Through the creation of the CMWMA, international conservationists sought to enlist local people in the management of protected areas and to transfer to them the burdens and responsibilities of biodiversity preservation. In contrast, the Gimi hoped partnership with outside conservation groups would provide basic support that their national government could not. Indeed, groups like the RCF have filled some of the gaps—maintaining health centers, bringing in teachers, and even managing local disputes. But with priority given to maintaining the region's biodiversity, RCF staff and other well-intentioned conservation scientists could not prioritize the Gimi notion of development. Rather, to promote conservation and preserve natural habitats, the Gimi's vision for development could not be allowed. As outside agencies asserted their power to distribute funds, establish geographic boundaries, and even rename places, conservation, for the Gimi, had become their government (Beilin 2011; Chan and Satterfield 2007; Hamilton-Smith 2007; Hitchner 2008; Walsh 2007).

ECOTOURISM IN ECUADOR'S AMAZON JUNGLE

In her book *Ecotourism and Cultural Production* (2013), anthropologist Veronica Davidov recounts her first visit to Ecuador's lowland jungle (the same region featured in *How Forests Think*, earlier in this chapter). For eight weeks she lived in a small village with Indigenous Kichwa (Quechua/Runa) people, learning their language and participating in cultural activities like making pottery, singing, and dancing. Afterward, Davidov traveled through Ecuador with her classmate Ariana, also a U.S. PhD student. Back in New York, Davidov received a phone call. After parting ways in Ecuador, Ariana had returned to the Indigenous village to visit her new friends, only to find that the village was empty. The villagers did not live there. Ariana tracked some villagers to a nearby town where they had apartments, but her former hosts became so uncomfortable that she did not stay long. Everything was different, she told Davidov. Village life for eight weeks had all been staged, and she had looked behind the curtain.

ecotourism
Tours of remote natural environments designed to support local communities and their conservation efforts.

Around the world, tens of thousands of wealthy Europeans, Americans, and Japanese engage in **ecotourism**—individual or group trips arranged by travel agents to experience the savanna in Africa, the Amazon rain forest in South America, or the Great Barrier Reef in Australia in an ecologically sustainable way. Ecotourism is promoted as a way for visitors like Davidov and Ariana to see the natural wonders of the world while supporting ecological conservation and cultural survival. Ecotourists hope their visits will provide alternative sources of income for local communities and so protect the environment from damage from extractive industries like oil drilling, mining, and logging.

Davidov's interviews with ecotourists reveal that they arrive in Ecuador with powerful fantasies of pristine rain forests populated by primitive Indians living in harmony with nature, isolated in a precapitalist world. Extractive industries threaten these rain forest Indians and their ecosystem, which, like endangered species, need to be rescued by international conservation organizations and the ecotourists themselves. Their jungle tours, toucan bird-watching, and participation in shamanic healing rituals are fun, but they also save the planet.

In contrast to these tourist fantasies, Davidov's research reveals marginalized yet competent Indigenous communities creatively navigating new cultural forms of globalization. Revenue from ecotourism opens the door to modernity and participation in the global economy. But it rewards an elaborate performance of the past that matches tourist fantasies. And it requires concealment of both the performance and the Indigenous people's new relationship to the global capitalist economy.

The Kichwa use ecotourism to create a new space within their historical and global realities. International oil companies first arrived in Ecuador in 1921, linking the Ecuadorian Amazon jungle to global processes of resource extraction. To supply oil to developed countries, companies have over the years clear-cut rain forests, driven roads through the thick jungle, and threatened both the fragile ecology and Indigenous ways of life. Today's encounter with globalization involves a complex and newly emerging transnational network of players.

Ecotourism has risen in popularity recently. But how do ecotourism fantasies match local conservation realities? (*Left*) A tourist learns a local practice with a member of the Huaorani people in the Ecuadorian Amazon. (*Right*) A company advertises ecotravel in Australia.

Western tourists, tour agencies, local entrepreneurs, conservation groups, local and global Indigenous activists, the Ecuadorian government's economic development expectations, and other resource extraction industries all play roles in creating new physical and cultural spaces. While roads cut by the oil industry scar the jungle, they also make ecotourism possible and facilitate collective action by Indigenous social movements. It is not unusual to find ecotourism sites situated near resource extraction sites and Indigenous villages and jungle lodges in close proximity to extractive infrastructure like oil wells, open pit mines, logging operations, and oil pipelines. In this complex configuration of local and global players, Davidov suggests that ecotourism may not function primarily as an alternative to resource extraction. Rather, ecotourism becomes a space where economic development, ecological conservation, and cultural survival come together to negotiate and cooperate about the future (Passariello 2015).

THE RIGHT TO NOT BE FUMIGATED IN THE FIELDS

Often overlooked in the global food supply chain of industrial agriculture and livestock production are the more than 1 billion rural, peasant farm workers, pastoralists, artisanal fishers, Indigenous people, and migrant farm workers who provide food to 70 percent of the world's population. Peasants and others who work in rural areas are also some of the world's most vulnerable people, exposed to the demands of large agricultural landholders, changing global food production patterns, and climate change.

International groups working on these issues define a *peasant* as a woman or man who relies on their own labor, family labor, or other small-scale labor collectives to produce food and agricultural products. Despite their role in food production, many peasants suffer from hunger and malnutrition. Today, 1 billion people, one-seventh of the world's population, suffer from food insecurity—not knowing where they will get an adequate supply of food for the day. Of those facing food insecurity, 75 percent are rural dwellers and 50 percent are peasant families. Twenty-five percent of the world's undernourished people live in cities, but many of them are migrants and children of migrants from rural peasant communities.

Peasants are key protectors of the environment because of their direct stewardship of the land. Unlike industrial agriculture and livestock production, which produces 25 percent of global greenhouse gas emissions, family farms use far less fossil fuels and water. Their smaller-scale production increases agrobiodiversity and increases carbon sequestration—the natural process of capturing excess atmospheric carbon in plants and soils. But intensifying droughts, floods, fires, and crop diseases undermine rural production and push farm workers to cities in search of wage labor. Climate change is a key factor in creating insecurity for small-scale farmers.

What can anthropology offer to meet these challenges of global food production, human rights, and environmental justice? For seventeen years, anthropologist Marc Edelman has worked with an international movement of peasant organizations to address the vulnerability and discrimination experienced by marginalized rural people. Their demands include basic human rights and rights specific to their situation: the right to farmland and to control of their seeds; the right to protection from land grabbing, discrimination, and criminalization of farm activists; and the right to not be fumigated with cancer-causing pesticides during crop-dusting.

On December 17, 2018, through the efforts of 180 nongovernmental organizations in eighty-one countries and working closely with scholars, international human rights lawyers, and U.N. experts, the United Nations finalized the Declaration on the Rights of Peasants and Other People Working in Rural Areas. This success, built through years of painstaking organizing across nation-states and economic sectors, expands existing U.N. human rights standards, including the original Universal Declaration of Human Rights passed seventy years earlier. Over the years, other U.N. agreements have been enacted to address the failure of current international law to safeguard the rights of women, children, migrants, disabled persons, and Indigenous peoples. The new Declaration on the Rights of Peasants raises the visibility of the conditions of rural populations, and it provides an internationally accepted legal framework that peasant organizations and rural social movements can invoke as they work on local levels to protect their rights to food, security, and health as well as safe, productive, sustainable agricultural environments and ecosystems (Edelman 2014, 2019).

STANDING ROCK, PIPELINES, AND GLOBAL OIL

In the early spring of 2016, protests erupted on the Standing Rock Sioux Reservation. Tribal members and their allies from across the country gathered to block the 1,172-mile, underground Dakota Access Pipeline (DAPL) and to demand that the U.S. government honor the 1868 Treaty of Fort Laramie, which protected Sioux land and water rights. Built by Energy Transfer Partners, the pipeline would carry 500,000 barrels of heavy crude oil a day from the Bakken oil fields in western North Dakota to southern Illinois, crossing under the Missouri and Mississippi Rivers and the tribe's drinking water supply in Lake Oahe. Oil would then pass to other pipelines on its way to refineries along the Gulf of Mexico and to global export.

Thousands of nonviolent protestors built encampments over the following year and engaged in acts of civil disobedience to defend Indigenous rights and stop the threat of pipeline spills to clean water and Native American burial grounds. In response, state police, National Guard, and private security forces employed by the energy company countered with riot gear, military equipment, bulldozers, attack dogs, surveillance drones, and water cannons in subzero temperatures to

MAP 11.7
Standing Rock Sioux Reservation, North Dakota

remove unarmed "water protectors." About 750 arrests were made and over 300 people were injured in the clashes, drawing national and international attention (Estes and Dhillon 2019).

Pipelines like DAPL have been essential infrastructure in an elaborate, century-long process of extracting and delivering exceptional quantities of fossil fuels to an expanding global economy. Global demand continues to soar even as reserves in the world's giant oil fields rapidly decline. So the current boom has turned to unconventional energy production from tar sands, deep-sea drilling, fracked natural gas, and shale oil. As a result, today the United States has surpassed Saudi Arabia and Russia as the world's largest fossil fuel producer. The conflict at Standing Rock and on many other Native territories in North America reflects the fact that 20 percent of U.S. fossil fuel reserves are on Native lands. And Native lands, unceded or treaty protected, stand in the path of many proposed pipelines in key energy corridors (Mitchell 2011).

In her article "Fighting Invasive Infrastructures: Indigenous Relations against Pipelines" (2018), anthropologist Anne Spice, a Tlingit member of Kwanlin Dun First Nation, notes that infrastructures like today's fossil fuel pipelines have historically been used as tools of **settler colonialism**—efforts to colonize and settle Indigenous people and land. Railroads facilitated westward colonial expansion into Native territories, transporting settlers in and extracting resources out. Dams flooded river estuaries and tribal villages. Today's highways are paved over extensive roadways and trade routes of Native American people (Dunbar-Ortiz 2015). Contemporary expansion of oil and gas infrastructure, Spice warns, is linked to the continued displacement and pacification of Native American people and expropriation of their lands.

settler colonialism

Displacement and pacification of Indigenous people and expropriation of their lands and resources.

In the twenty-first century, the U.S. and Canadian governments assert the imperative for continued settler colonialism of Native lands by labeling oil and gas pipelines critical infrastructure essential to their country's national (economic) security. Recently passed laws in various localities criminalize protest and resistance of pipelines as a form of terrorism. But Spice reminds us that Indigenous people have critical infrastructures, too—carefully balanced ecosystems of humans and nonhumans that are essential to Indigenous life and culture. Spice asks: What happens when the critical energy infrastructures of the nation-state clash with the critical infrastructures of Indigenous life? Specifically, what happens when the clean river water, spawning salmon, and wild bear that are central to the environmental infrastructure of Indigenous life are disrupted by the profit-oriented infrastructure of the state and corporate energy companies? Which should receive priority?

Anthropologist Jaskiran Dhillon (2018) links contemporary anti-pipeline resistance like the movement at Standing Rock with historical struggles for Indigenous rights and environmental protection. Indigenous scholars note that Native people in the Americas have already experienced 500 years of environmental devastation: mass killing of fur-bearing animals for the fur trade, slaughter of buffalo, state-sponsored warfare, expropriation of land, extraction of natural resources, taking of water rights for irrigation, and damming of rivers (Estes 2019). Today, Indigenous people across the world are leading social movements for environmental justice. Disruption of infrastructure projects, like the Standing Rock encampments, are a key strategy. In the time and space opened by resistance, Indigenous people hope to create possibilities to undo settler colonialism and restore the environmental relationships that will make survival on the planet possible.

What If Today's Global Economic System Is Not Sustainable?

Analyze ways today's global economy may be unsustainable.

Since at least the time of the earliest human settlements and the development of farming and pastoralism, humans' economic activities have affected their local environments. Human impact increased with an expanding population and was accelerated by the Industrial Revolution. Over the past 70 years, we have transformed our relationship with nature, and now our impact is being felt on a planetary scale. Scholars in many fields are asking if we have come to a crisis point where our model of economic growth is leading to ecological collapse.

THE HUMAN ECOLOGICAL FOOTPRINT

Humans have a huge ecological footprint (Table 11.1). The United Nations estimates that the world population, which was 2.5 billion in 1950, will increase from 8 billion in 2022 to 11.2 billion by 2100. Each day, we add 220,000 people. And each day, human consumption dramatically increases that footprint. Studies suggest that as early as 1980, humans began to use more resources than the planet could regenerate. Today, our consumption of the world's resources has stretched above 75 percent over sustainable levels. In other words, at our current rate of consumption, it would take 1.75 Earths to sustain our rate of resource use and absorb our pollution using prevailing technologies. This is what scientists call "ecological overshoot." The sobering reality is that for every human on the planet to have the ecological footprint of an American middle-class lifestyle, we would require five Earths (Global Footprint Network 2022).

The result is a scramble for natural resources—especially freshwater, oil, and coltan (a scarce metal ore used in cell phones and other electronic devices)—that

TABLE 11.1

Energy Consumption in Selected Countries, 2022

COUNTRY	TOTAL (10^{15} BTU)	PER CAPITA (10^6 BTU)
China	138.6	97.5
United States	97.6	300.4
Russia	32.8	225.6
India	30.4	22.7
Japan	19.4	152.1
Canada	15.0	410.0
Germany	14.0	170.1
Brazil	12.5	60.4
France	10.2	157.9
United Kingdom	8.1	122.7

Source: Worldometer. 2022. "Energy used today in the world." www.worldometers.info/energy/.

pits wealthy nations against poor nations. The ice sheets in the Himalayas that provide drinking water for billions of people in Pakistan, India, Myanmar, Cambodia, Laos, and Vietnam are shrinking from global warming. Underground aquifers that provide freshwater to billions more in China and the Middle East are being depleted faster than nature can replenish them. Environmental trends do not bode well for the global economy, raising the question: Are current trajectories sustainable?

SUSTAINABILITY

When anthropologists discuss *sustainability*, they refer to a society capable of reproducing itself indefinitely without undermining the conditions for its own existence. This includes social, economic, and environmental sustainability, all of which are linked. Certainly, many of the smaller-scale societies anthropologists studied in the early twentieth century met this criteria (Eriksen 2022).

Today, perhaps the biggest test for humanity will be whether the drive for constant, progressive development that has long been held as a central promise of the modern global economy will be sustainable. In 2005, the United Nations introduced a set of sustainable development goals supported by the assumption that achieving these goals would allow humanity to continue on the path of economic growth and expansion while simultaneously ensuring ecological viability. But anthropologists have regularly pointed out the flawed logic of that argument: A global capitalist economy built on expectations of growth and technological progress is actually creating the environmental damage that people are having to recover from.

In the twenty-first century, we will need to redefine the key threats to the future of humanity (Korten 2001, 2015). These are climate change, hunger, water shortages, costly oil, poverty, increasing inequality, rising food prices, the collapse of nation-states, and a lack of will to address these challenges urgently (Brown 2011a, 2011b; Worldwatch Institute 2015). Under the current conditions, anthropologists warn, it is not hard to imagine that an unsustainable economic system—and its attendant climate change, overexploitation of resources, mass extinctions, and environmental destruction—will bring about its own demise.

THE SUSTAINABILITY MYTH

In her book *The Sustainability Myth: Environmental Gentrification and the Politics of Justice* (2020), anthropologist Melissa Checker explores the underside of urban renewal and the "greening" of cities like New York. Under the mayoralty of Michael Bloomberg (2002–2013), New York City set out to reinvent itself as a leader in green urban revitalization and to become the world's most sustainable city. The city's PlaNYC 2030 initiative established goals to reduce carbon emissions, better manage stormwater overflows and energy use, reduce air pollution, plant 1 million trees, and create new waterfront parks, green spaces, 250 miles of bike lanes, and farmers markets. Its CoolRoofs program re-covered over 10 million square feet of city roofs with reflective paint that cooled inside temperatures and reduced the need for air conditioners. New regulations brought energy-efficient upgrades to new buildings. Buses, taxis, garbage trucks, police cars, and other city-owned vehicles were changed to hybrid or natural gas vehicles. Rezoning of formerly industrial waterfront sites and railroads in a number of the city's boroughs spurred new construction of residential and office towers.

Checker's primary research during that time, however, was with community-based environmental justice organizations on the North Shore of Staten Island, a community densely packed with toxic industrial sites in close proximity to low-income communities of color. Directly across the harbor, Manhattan's waterfront sparkled with new parks, bicycle lanes, farmers markets, and state-of-the-art, energy-efficient high-rise buildings. The city government, in contrast, continued to construct facilities for heavy industry and municipal waste on the North Shore. Checker's own neighborhood of Harlem housed five out of Manhattan's seven bus depots, two waste treatment plants, and scores of former factory sites commonly called brownfields that contained toxic chemicals.

Checker's book explores the intentional urban planning behind the dense cluster of industrial sites on Staten Island and in Harlem, which stand in marked contrast to the high-end, luxury developments and green spaces in the "sustainable city." In the process, she finds that building a sustainable city has gentrified many

Can Earth sustain the current global economy? Here, students join the International Youth Climate Strike in Washington, D.C., to demand action on climate change.

formerly working-class neighborhoods, forcing long-term low-income residents of color to relocate amid rising prices and taxes. Sustainability, she writes, became a shorthand for developing the kind of city attractive to the upper classes. Staten Island and Harlem were not forgotten: They simply became relocation sites for New York's industrial infrastructure and its pollutants, far away from areas of the city that were meant to be seen as luxurious, green, and attractive.

Checker's environmental research in New York City has deep roots in her earlier scholarship, notably her book *Polluted Promises: Environmental Racism and the Search for Justice in a Southern Town* (2005). Checker conducted fieldwork in a poor, predominantly Black community in Augusta, Georgia, that was also struggling with the effects of decades of toxic waste contamination by local factories. The toxins took a terrible toll on the environment and destroyed people's health.

Checker's account documents three decades of painstaking work by a community to improve living conditions and stop industrial pollution. Ultimately, Checker found, stakes for the community were much higher than ridding their neighborhood of chemical contaminants. Organizers also challenged persistent and systemic forms of racial discrimination that blamed bad health, education, and economic conditions on individuals rather than structural issues.

In Augusta, like in New York City, Checker found the promise of sustainable economic growth to be a myth built upon the ability of corporations and governments to externalize substantial costs of development onto marginalized communities, particularly communities of color.

WORLD ON THE EDGE

Time is short for our planet and the other species with which we live. Our current economic system risks pushing us closer to the edge. If we are on the edge, we are not yet over the cliff. But significant changes are needed to reestablish the balance between humans and our planet. We must slow population growth. We must leave fossil fuels in the ground. We must stabilize the global climate by rapidly shifting from petroleum-based, carbon dioxide–producing energy sources to renewable fuels, such as wind and solar power. Perhaps most fundamental, we need to reassess the culture of consumption that considers the acquisition of capital and things as a measure of self-worth and compensates for a lack of capital by buying on credit.

As a student, you can engage these issues on an individual and an institutional level. You can conserve energy and water, plant trees, use public transportation or a bike rather than a car, reduce how much you consume, and consider the hidden costs in all products that you buy. You can educate yourself about the threats to your friends, family, and future generations. Beyond changes in your lifestyle, you can engage these issues through the institutions around you. Challenge your college to conserve energy, recycle, invest in solar and wind power on campus, invest its endowment in renewable energy companies rather than carbon-generating oil companies, and offer courses on the relationship between economics and the environment. Work to elect leaders who support sustainability efforts. Invent technology to expand renewable energy capture and storage or remove carbon from the atmosphere. Find creative ways to engage religious institutions, local governments, stores, and corporations to adjust their institutional practices and cultures. Change, whether personal or institutional, is not easy. But it may not be a choice.

Toolkit

Thinking Like an Anthropologist: Making a Difference in Earth's Future

We know what is going on with the environment. We know the root causes of climate change, the acidification of oceans, and mass extinctions of species. The fossil fuel industry knew as early as the 1970s that pumping carbon dioxide into the atmosphere was changing the chemical composition of Earth's air and water and raising global temperatures. The U.N. Intergovernmental Panel on Climate Change, made up of the world's leading climate scientists, warns that to maintain a climate suitable for humans, we must reduce carbon emissions drastically by 2030 and reach zero emissions by 2050. We know what is happening and what needs to be done.

And still the world's political and economic leaders fail to act with urgency.

Perhaps it is the slow violence of environmental change (Nixon 2013). Glaciers thaw slowly. Greenhouse gas accumulates, oceans acidify, forests are depleted, and species become extinct slowly over years, decades, and centuries. The gradual violence of climate change has been relatively invisible to many in the world, with long dyings across time and space that sometimes only trickle into our awareness.

But even as climate events—hurricanes, wildfires, drought—become more destructive and frequent, we fail to act. Indian author Amitav Ghosh (2013) calls this the "great derangement." Perhaps the scale and intensity of contemporary climate events do not fit our mental maps of stable environmental reality, our notions of development and sustainability, our assumptions of what is normal. Perhaps our brains cannot handle the disconnect between our expectations of the world and the reality the future may have in store. And so we are deranged, unable to make sense of the changes happening before our eyes or to take the steps necessary to put the world back into order.

Or perhaps we have become too accustomed to the conveniences of the consumption-based, fossil fuel–driven economy to be able to imagine that a new world is possible and actually quite necessary.

What is the place of anthropology in the pressing environmental conversations and challenges of the twenty-first century? Now that you have read this chapter, how would you apply its ideas and analysis to gain a more complete understanding of the Maldives or the student protests in our opening story and the current global environmental challenges we face? Reconsider for a moment the key questions posed at the beginning of the chapter:

- **What is the Anthropocene?**
- **How does a multispecies perspective change our worldview and our future?**
- **How do other systems of power shape the environment?**
- **How is the environment shaped by globalization?**
- **What if today's global economic system is not sustainable?**

Anthropology's commitment to strategies of long-term, community-based fieldwork allows the study of the environment to move beyond structured surveys and global data analysis to a deeper, more complex understanding of local realities in global perspective. As we have seen throughout this chapter, local communities are developing creative strategies to resist and adapt to climate change. Not all humans are equally responsible for creating the climate changes facing the planet. And often the people least responsible bear the most significant impact. But they may also offer the most thoughtful solutions for amelioration.

Today, our planet no longer functions the way it did. Most scholars and activists agree that stabilizing the environment will require both concerted conservation efforts to stop polluting our air, seas, and land and technological innovations to reverse damage already done. Broad-based action will be required, drawing on expertise in every professional sector. Regardless of the career you choose, you will have an opportunity to engage debates about the environment and to make a difference in the future of your local community and of the planet.

Key Terms

environmental anthropology (p. 331)

Anthropocene (p. 332)

multispecies ethnography (p. 336)

ecotourism (p. 344)

settler colonialism (p. 348)

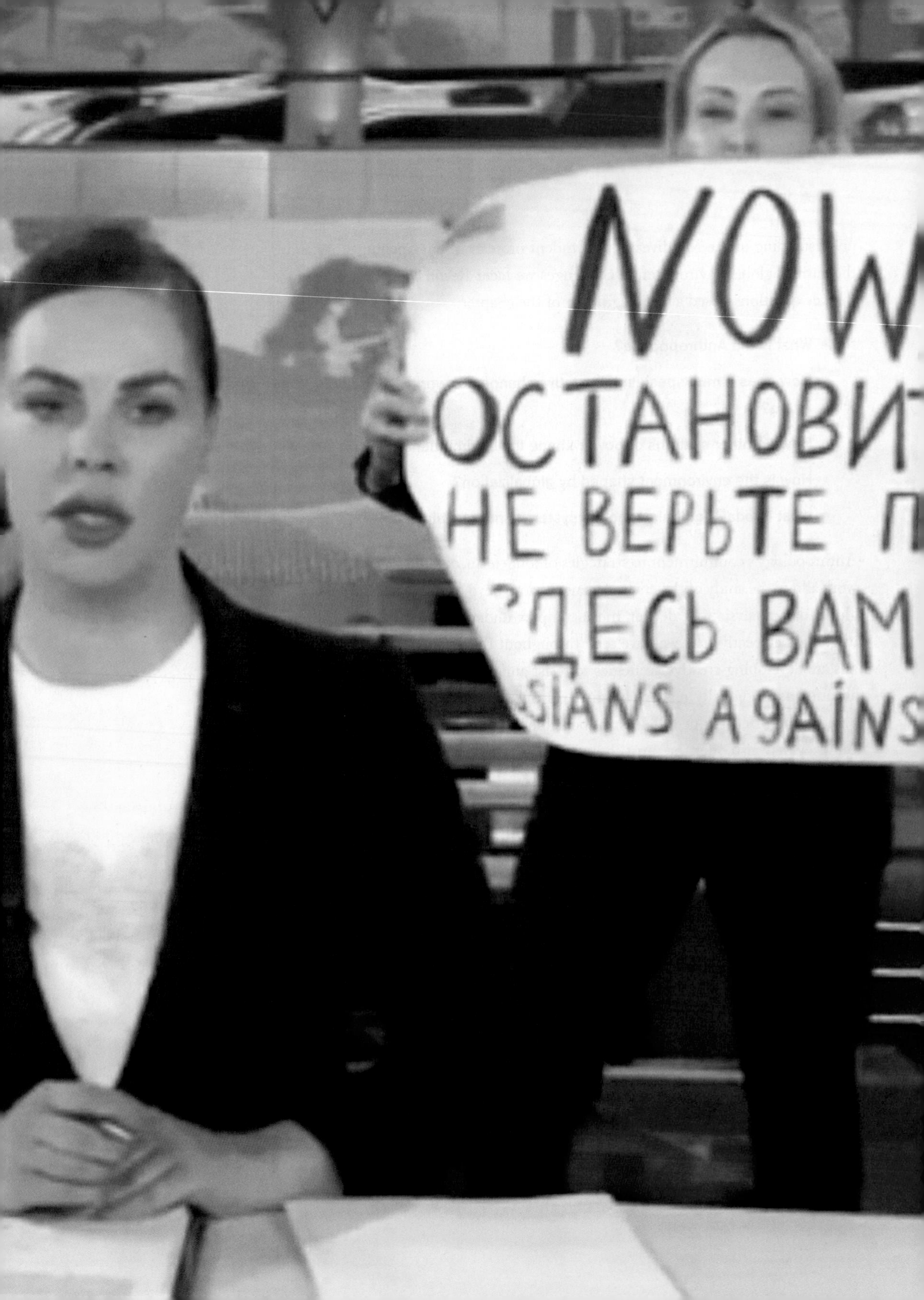
NOW
ОСТАНОВИТ
НЕ ВЕРЬТЕ П
ЗДЕСЬ ВАМ
SIANS A9AINS

Chapter 12
Politics and Power

Learning Objectives

- Describe anthropology's understanding of the origins of politics.

- Define the state from an anthropological perspective.

- Explain key ways globalization is affecting the state.

- Assess the origins of violence and war and their relationships to politics and the state.

- Demonstrate knowledge of ways people mobilize power outside the state's control.

War! What is it good for?

On February 24, 2022, the Russian government, led by President Vladimir Putin, sent nearly 200,000 soldiers to invade Ukraine, unleashing destruction and death in a horrific war with global implications. Ukraine's armed forces resisted fiercely in the face of overwhelming Russian bombardment. They pushed back initial Russian advances on the country's major cities, surprising many in Russia, Europe, and the United States who expected the vaunted Russian military to easily assert its dominance. Still, in those first months, more than 7 million people fled the onslaught for refuge in

---

As an act of protest against Russia's invasion of Ukraine, editor and journalist Marina Ovsyannikova held up a sign that reads: "NO WAR. Stop the War. Don't believe propaganda. They are lying to you here."

European countries to Ukraine's west, and as many as one-third of the country's 43 million people were displaced internally. Russian leaders' apparent plan for a quick strike to overthrow the Ukrainian government instead turned into a protracted, brutal, deadly war of attrition focused on eastern Ukraine's mineral- and energy-rich Donbas region.

Nineteen days after Russia invaded Ukraine, Marina Ovsyannikova, a long-time editor and journalist for Russia's state-controlled TV network Channel One, ran uninvited onto the set of a live broadcast. Standing behind the news anchor, she brandished a handwritten sign: "NO WAR. Stop the War. Don't believe propaganda. They are lying to you here." She shouted anti-war slogans for a few moments before the station switched programming. Pro-government Channel One is the main source of news for millions of Russians and has been central to promoting the state's current narrative about its "special military operation" in Ukraine. Ovsyannikova, whose father is Ukrainian and mother is Russian, was arrested for her actions, accused of being a British spy, interrogated, and fined for posting an anti-war online video message. Opposition to war within Russia—apparently widespread, though repressed—broke through the fog of war, at least momentarily.

In this global age, war has global implications. When the United States and members of the European Union placed economic sanctions on Russia with the goal of damaging its economy, the move sent shock waves through the global economy, too—disrupting supply chains of oil and gas, grain, car parts, and even lithium exports essential for the world's green energy transition. Global food and fuel prices skyrocketed. Global hunger increased. Western military contractors, funded by billions of dollars from U.S. and European governments, rushed weapons to Ukraine to arm men ages 18–60 whom the Ukrainian government had banned from leaving the country.

As anthropologists, how do we understand the politics of this (or any) war, its origins, and its impact? Why would Russia risk a large-scale war on its borders? For control over natural resources, access to warm-water ports, defense against encroachment from Western military alliances, or a political reunification of ethnic groups sharing cultural, linguistic, religious, and family ties? How did Ukraine, which has been independent of the former Soviet Union for only thirty years, mobilize education, media, legislation, history, and language to consolidate a distinct Ukrainian ethnic identity—an identity now activated in fierce opposition to the Russian invasion?

War is an extreme assertion of political power through violence. But who is it good for? Who wants it? Who decides when war starts? Who decides when war ends?

In 1940, in the midst of World War II, leading anthropologist Margaret Mead explored the roots of war in her essay "Warfare Is Only an Invention—Not a Biological Necessity." Addressing the common assumption that violence and war are essential aspects of human nature, Mead presented compelling ethnographic examples of people who did not go to war to settle disputes. Warfare is not a universal biological imperative, she argued, but rather a choice. Of the various reasons people cite for going to war—land, loot, prestige, honor, women—all can be satisfied without violence. Mead finds war a cultural invention. And a bad one at that. Surely, she ponders, humans must be able to invent a better, less violent way of negotiating power and resolving their differences.

Power is often described as the ability or potential to bring about change through action or influence—either one's own or that of a group or institution. War and violence may receive the most attention, but power—whether openly displayed or carefully avoided—is embedded in all human relationships, from the most mundane aspects of friendships and family relationships to the myriad ways humans organize institutions and the structural frameworks of whole societies (Wolf 1982).

The Greek philosopher Aristotle spoke of humans as political animals. By this he meant that we live with other people in communities through which we strive to organize ourselves to achieve the good life—not as hedonists seeking the maximization of individual pleasure but as a collective partnership (*koinonia*) seeking the good life, virtue, and beauty through community. Politics, then, in its most basic form, is simply the mobilization of people's beliefs into collective action. The presence of politics and power relations in the ebb and flow of daily life is a central focus of anthropological study. Although uprisings, demonstrations, and war may draw attention to the most public, dramatic, and violent aspects of politics, anthropologists also consider the multiple local forms of politics—the careful political interactions and activities that occupy much of daily life and are essential in making a community a decent place to live (Gledhill 2000; Kurtz 2001; Lewellen 2003).

Throughout this book, we explore power and its intersections with culture. We work to unmask the structures of power built on ideologies of race, gender, ethnicity, and sexuality and the institutions of kinship and religion. We also examine the power dynamics of class stratifications and the world economy. In this chapter, we explore power as it is expressed through political systems and processes: the ways humans have organized themselves in small groups, the role of the state in national and international politics—including war—and the ability of people (nonstate actors) to engage in politics and exercise power through individual actions and social movements outside the direct control of the state.

Demonstrators in New York's Time Square rally against Russia's invasion of Ukraine.

We consider the historical and contemporary approaches that anthropologists have taken toward these crucial issues and the ways in which globalization is shifting the dynamics of power and politics on local and global levels. In particular, we will examine the following questions:

- **How have anthropologists viewed the origins of human political history?**
- **What is the state?**
- **How is globalization affecting the state?**
- **What are the relationships among politics, the state, violence, and war?**
- **How do people mobilize power outside the state's control?**

While reading this chapter, you will analyze many expressions of politics and the ways in which aspects of power are expressed locally and globally today. You will consider how political anthropology can help you think more deeply about your own political expressions, including how you negotiate human relationships on the interpersonal, group, community, national, and global levels. You will examine the changing role of the state in local, national, and global affairs. You will also see how humans mobilize collectively through social movements to challenge the power of the state and the effects of globalization by advocating for social change and human rights. Finally, you will consider an anthropological debate about the roots of violence in human culture. The skills you acquire in this chapter will be valuable additions to your toolkit for living as a political actor and an engaged citizen in today's global world.

How Have Anthropologists Viewed the Origins of Human Political History?

Describe anthropology's understanding of the origins of politics.

Over the course of history, humans have organized themselves politically by using flexible strategies to help their groups survive and to make their communities better places to live. Our earliest human ancestors appear to have evolved in small, mobile, egalitarian groups of hunter-gatherers. Core human characteristics and cultural patterns emerged in these types of groups.

Beginning in the late 1800s, anthropologists studying politics and power focused primarily on small-scale, stateless societies in an attempt to understand human political history through the political activities of contemporary hunter-gatherers, pastoralists, and horticulturalists. But in the 1960s, as nation-states emerged to dominate political activity on a global scale, the anthropological gaze shifted significantly to encompass more complex, state-oriented societies and the processes by which local settings are politically incorporated into a larger context.

The specialized field of *political anthropology* took clear shape after World War II as anthropologists such as Meyer Fortes and E. E. Evans-Pritchard (1940), as well as other British social anthropologists (e.g., Gluckman 1954; Turner 1957), examined local political systems in Africa. Others looked closely

Qaanaaq, Greenland, dog teams and Inuit hunters traveling to a hunt. Once, food foraging was the primary way of life for humans and our ancestors, but today, food foragers are limited to the most remote areas of the planet.

at political systems in the Middle East and Asia (Barth 1959; Leach 1954) and among Indigenous peoples of the Americas (Redfield 1941; Wallace 1957).

As anthropologists undertook these studies of politics in many cultures, they attempted to create a common language, a typology that would enable them to communicate across cultural areas and compare and contrast their findings (Gledhill 2000; Lewellen 2003). The political anthropologist Elman Service (1962) classified the vast and varied world of political systems into four basic types: bands, tribes, chiefdoms, and states. Although considered too simplistic by anthropologists today, this framework shaped a previous generation of anthropological thinking about political systems. Service proposed that political systems develop through a natural, evolutionary progression from simple to complex and from less integrated to more integrated, with patterns of leadership evolving from weaker to stronger. Subsequently, when states emerged as the dominant political actors on the world stage, anthropologists hoped the examination of bands, tribes, and chiefdoms might provide insights into the origins and fundamental nature of the state.

BANDS

band

A small kinship-based group of foragers who hunt and gather for a living over a particular territory.

Anthropologists have used the term **band** to describe small, kinship-based groups of food foragers who move over a particular territory while hunting and gathering. Through archaeological evidence and the study of a few remaining band societies, anthropologists have identified key characteristics of band organization and leadership. A band might range in size from twenty to several hundred people, depending on the time of year and the group's hunting and ritual cycles. Bands break up and re-form regularly in response to conflicts among members and the development of new alliances.

Small, close-knit bands have served as the primary way of life not only for most modern humans over our 200,000-year history but also for our immediate ancestors. As a result, evolutionary biologists suggest that life in the band shaped the development of our earliest human characteristics and cultural patterns.

Politically, bands are highly decentralized, with decisions made primarily by consensus. Leaders emerge for a task at hand (organizing the hunt, moving the campsite, negotiating a conflict), with their leadership position resting on their skill, knowledge, generosity toward others, and level of respect within the band. With limited resources to compete for, bands have minimal stratification of wealth and power. But perhaps more important, bands require active cooperation among diverse groups of relatives and nonrelatives to successfully adapt to an unpredictable and shifting landscape. In turn, these early patterns may have embedded in humans a tendency toward egalitarian social and political organization rather than hierarchy.

In his book *Hierarchy in the Forest: The Evolution of Egalitarian Behavior* (1999), evolutionary biologist Christopher Boehm explores what life in bands can tell us about whether humans are fundamentally hierarchical or egalitarian. Drawing on ethnographic studies of contemporary and historical hunter-gatherer bands as well as archaeological findings, Boehm argues that the sharing of scarce resources, including food, was the most economically efficient—indeed, essential—economic strategy for hunter-gatherer bands. And this strategy could be sustained only through egalitarianism. Cooperative gathering of foods, coordinated game hunting, and reciprocal sharing went hand in hand with resisting hierarchy and domination as successful adaptations for humans living in hunter-gatherer bands. As a result, over the course of human evolutionary history, hunter-gatherer bands and tribal communities generated an egalitarian ethos that promoted generosity, altruism, and sharing while resisting upstarts, aggression, and egoism.

Despite serving as the predominant economic, social, and political structure over the course of human evolution, by the mid-twentieth century, only a few bands of food foragers remained. These groups were living in the most remote areas of the planet: the rain forests of South America, the arctic tundra of North America, and the deserts of Africa and Australia.

TRIBES

The term *tribe* is frequently used in contemporary media when describing civil wars or other conflicts among groups within a state. In discussions of tribal conflicts, tribal warfare, tribal factions, rifts, and alliances, *tribe* usually refers to a loosely organized group of people acting together outside the authority of the state under unelected leaders or big men/strong men and drawing on a sense of unity based on a notion of shared ethnicity. In many cases, current discussions use the term *ethnic group* instead of *tribe* (Ferguson 2011).

Most of these popular references to tribes imply that primitive, uncivilized, and violent peoples are engaging in conflict based on "ancient" tribal factions and hatreds. These faulty characterizations reflect the ethnocentric perspectives of observers who often operate from inside a state framework. They perpetuate the deeply problematic evolutionary assumption that less-complex political organizations are naturally less effective, stable, rational, and civilized than more-complex ones.

As originally formulated in political anthropology (Service 1962), the term *tribe* referred to a culturally distinct population, often combining several bands, that imagined itself as one people descended from a common ancestor and organized around villages, kin groups, clans, and lineages. Tribes in this sense appear to have emerged between 10,000 and 12,000 years ago as humans began to shift from food foraging to pastoralism and horticulture. Like bands, tribes are largely egalitarian, with a decentralized power structure and consensus decision-making. Leaders do emerge, sometimes called "village heads" or "big men" (Sahlins 1971), who garner the support of followers in several villages. But their power is limited. It is built and maintained through the leaders' personal achievements—such as conflict resolution, group organizing, success in war, and generosity of feasts and gifts—rather than awarded through political institutions.

In recent centuries, settler colonial states have sought to eliminate or assimilate Indigenous peoples and tribes in order to extract labor and natural resources from them and their lands. Today, no groups operate totally outside the framework of the state, and most have been incorporated to some extent into the nation-states that have come to dominate the global political landscape. Even a weak state or a failed state directly influences all those living within its borders. It is worth noting, however, that *tribe* today is also used in the self-naming and identity-building strategies of Indigenous groups, particularly Native Americans, as they continue to resist the ongoing dominance and extractive practices of the settler colonial state (Dennison 2017; Simpson 2014). In this context, today we might define a **tribe** more accurately as an Indigenous group of people with its own set of loyalties and leaders living to some extent outside the direct control of a centralized authoritative state.

CHIEFDOMS

Within Service's evolutionary typology of political systems, the **chiefdom**—an autonomous political unit composed of a number of villages or communities under the permanent control of a paramount chief (Carneiro 1981)—represented a transitional form between the simpler political structures of tribes and the more complex political structures of states. As in bands and tribes, the social relations of the chiefdom were built around extended kinship networks or lineages. The chiefdom might encompass thousands of people spread over many villages.

Unique to chiefdoms, leadership was centralized under a single ruling authority figure—a chief who headed a ranked hierarchy of people, asserted political control over a particular territory, and held authority to make and enforce decisions. In parts of Polynesia, for instance, chiefs functioned as full-time political specialists who resolved conflicts and organized collective economic activity. The permanent position of chief endured from generation to generation, often passing through direct descent and inheritance from father to son or through other kinship relationships. Religious rituals and beliefs often served to confirm the chief's authority.

Through feasts and festivals such as the potlatch, the chief gathered a portion of the collective bounty of the chiefdom's harvest or hunt and redistributed the communal wealth to the populace, thereby symbolically and practically

tribe

In the context of evolutionary typology of political systems, a culturally distinct, multiband population that imagined itself as one people descended from a common ancestor; today, more often used to describe an Indigenous group with its own set of loyalties and leaders living to some extent outside the control of a centralized authoritative state.

chiefdom

An autonomous political unit composed of a number of villages or communities under the permanent control of a paramount chief.

reinforcing the chief's central role among the people. Though group members' access to power and resources depended on their hierarchical relationship to the chief, the process of redistribution was key to moderating inequality and limiting conflict within the chiefdom.

THE PROBLEM WITH TYPOLOGIES

Though the typology of bands, tribes, chiefdoms, and states provided a basis for cross-cultural comparison, Service's evolutionary framework—assuming a steady progression from simple to complex and from primitive to civilized—frequently fails to capture the complexity and diversity of political practices and institutions reflected in ethnographic studies and the archaeological record. For instance, evidence now clearly suggests that across human history, groups of bands, tribes, and chiefdoms were never as isolated or homogeneous as mid-twentieth-century anthropologists proposed. In contrast, today we argue that movement, encounter, exchange, and change have been the hallmarks of human groups, both small and large, throughout human history.

Nor could twentieth-century political systems always be considered trustworthy representations of the human past, recent or distant. Certainly, by the time anthropologists began to enter the field in the late nineteenth century to document and classify people and their political systems, European colonial expansion—including violent encounters—had transformed peoples and their political structures across the globe. Colonialism, the slave trade, the conquest of Indigenous peoples of the Americas, military activity, missionary efforts, and global trade deeply influenced every political arrangement, from the most populous urban setting to the most rural village. It is safe to say that anthropologists have not observed a band, tribe, or chiefdom that has not been influenced by colonialism, the power of the state, and the forces of globalization. And today, no political arrangement of band, tribe, or chiefdom can operate outside the pervasive influence of the state.

What Is the State?

Define the state from an anthropological perspective.

As states took on an increasingly central role in shaping the local communities that anthropologists traditionally studied, political anthropologists turned their ethnographic attention to the state itself. Today, we typically define the **state** as an autonomous regional structure of political, economic, and military rule with a central government authorized to make laws and use force to maintain order and defend its territory.

state

An autonomous regional structure of political, economic, and military rule with a central government authorized to make laws and use force to maintain order and defend its territory.

Anthropologists link the origins of the state to the rise of agriculture. With fixed settlements, elite specialists emerged to manage increasingly complex economic activity (Wittfogel 1957), and warriors emerged to defend agricultural surpluses from marauders (Carneiro 1978). Some loosely configured states existed as early as 5,000 years ago in Mesopotamia and Egypt and somewhat later in China, Japan, the Indus Valley (which became parts of modern-day India, Pakistan, and Afghanistan), and portions of the Americas. Throughout most of human history, however, people organized themselves primarily through less-centralized, flexible bands, tribes, and chiefdoms.

The global landscape of contemporary states that now dominates local, regional, and international affairs reflects the impact of Western expansion over the past 500 years, particularly European imperial and colonial expansion (see Chapter 11). European colonialists deployed economic, political, and military force to redraw the political borders of much of the world to meet their economic needs. In this process, they carved states and territories out of geographic areas inhabited by Indigenous groups who were organized along lines of local kinship, political, and economic relations.

Most states in the world today did not exist before World War II—certainly not in their current configurations. In fact, few states are older than the United States, which officially formed in 1783. Most gained independence from colonial rule only in the decades immediately following World War II. By 2022, there were 195 independent states in the world recognized by the United Nations.

THE MODERN WESTERN-STYLE STATE

The type of state that has emerged since the sixteenth century, built largely on a Western model and expanded through colonization and globalization, developed with certain unique characteristics (Giddens 1985). Unlike earlier forms of the state, such as China's, which had relatively porous borders and loose administration, each modern state features a central administration designed to penetrate the everyday social life of its citizenry. A standing army asserts control over a

carefully defined territory. Administrative, communication, and military infra-structures define and enforce the state's borders. The state, rather than a big man or chief, serves as the source of laws and law enforcement. And the state demands the primary allegiance of residents within its borders, undermining other local networks based on kinship, religion, or ethnicity (Asad 1992). Today, global-ization, particularly the increasing flow of people, money, ideas, and things, is challenging states' capacity to control their borders and raising difficult debates about citizenship and belonging.

Externally, modern states compete economically and militarily with other states for resources and territory. Internally, each state seeks to establish a monop-oly on the legitimate use of force within a territorial domain (Weber 1919). For example, it enlists citizens' cooperation and pacifies resistance through expanded administrative power in police forces, the judicial system, tax collection, and reg-ulatory regimes (Giddens 1985). It also accomplishes these objectives via surveil-lance techniques and institutions such as prisons, hospitals, and asylums, through which individuals classified as deviant from the cultural norm are removed from mainstream society and disciplined (Foucault 1977).

One unique contribution of political anthropologists has been to study the processes of the state rather than its institutions and structures. Despite the illu-sion that the state is fixed, cohesive, and coherent, states are in fact constantly shaped and reshaped by elections, political campaigns, court rulings, creditors, legislation, and executive orders as well as daily interactions with individuals, communities, nonstate institutions, social movements, and other states. From this perspective, we can see that states are actually quite fluid, contested, and even fragile (Sharma and Gupta 2006).

How does the state become the ultimate authority within a particular ter-ritory? Anthropologists suggest that the state becomes real in the imaginations and experiences of people as they encounter it in a particular space. This spati-alization of the state (Ferguson and Gupta 2002)—the perception that the state fills a particular space, encompasses all aspects of culture, and stands above all other elements of society—is produced through mundane bureaucratic state practices. Citizens encounter the state in everyday acts of governance: policing, mail delivery, tax collection, mapping, surveys, issuance of passports, jury duty, voting, notarization, distribution of food to the poor, distribution of pension checks to the elderly. Through these routine and repetitive acts, the state comes to feel all-encompassing and overarching—a dynamic that James Ferguson and Akhil Gupta (2002) call "vertical encompassment." Representations of the state on the television and radio, as well as in newspapers and movies, all contribute to the construction of the state as concrete and real: They reinforce the conception of the state as the primary institution through which people experience social relations—family, community, civil society, economic exchange.

ASPECTS OF STATE POWER

The rituals and routines of the state also include overt practices of coercion. In fact, political philosopher Max Weber argued in 1919 that the fundamental characteristic of a state is its ability to establish a monopoly on the legitimate use of force in a particular territorial domain (Parsons 1964). States exert coercive power not only through military and police forces but also through the guarding and regulating of borders, the determining of criteria for citizenship, and the enforcing of discipline through rules, regulations, taxation, and the judicial system.

hegemony

The ability of a dominant group to create consent and agreement within a population without the use or threat of force.

State power is also established through **hegemony**, which is the ability of a dominant group to create consent and agreement within a population without the use or threat of force (Gramsci 1971). How is this done? As discussed in Chapter 2, cultural institutions of government, media, schools, and religions shape what group members think is normal, natural, and possible, thereby influencing and limiting the scope of human action and interaction. Group members develop a way of seeing the world—a set of beliefs about what is normal and appropriate—that subconsciously limits their life choices and chances. As discussed in Chapter 6, states reinforce this hegemony by promoting intense feelings of nationalism (a sense of shared history, culture, language, destiny, and purpose, often through invented traditions of holidays, parades, national songs, public ceremonies, and historical reenactments) to promote the perception of the state as a unified entity.

The hegemonic aspect of power can make group members discipline their own behavior, believing and acting in certain "normal" ways (often against their own interests), even without threat of punishment for misbehavior (Foucault 1977). Within the hegemony of ideas, some thoughts and actions actually become unthinkable and undoable. Others seem reasonable, necessary, and desirable; these include collective actions for the greater good of the "nation," even going so far as killing and being killed, as we have discussed in relation to the war in

Ukraine. Some modern states, however, are unable to gain the cooperation of their populace through consent and must resort to coercion. Where do you see this dynamic at work in the world today? How does the state become real for you? How are encounters with the state differentially shaped by one's race, gender, sexuality, citizenship, or immigration status?

How Is Globalization Affecting the State?

Explain key ways globalization is affecting the state.

Today, globalization presents serious challenges to the state, particularly in terms of flexible accumulation, time-space compression, and expanding migration. The boundaries of the state—its influence and control over internal and external affairs—appear to be shrinking in the face of pressures related to globalization and the neoliberalizing global economy.

INTERNATIONAL NONSTATE ACTORS CHALLENGE STATE SOVEREIGNTY

In a global economy with increasing flows of people, money, goods, and ideas, state borders are becoming more porous. As a result, states are increasingly struggling to control who and what enters and leaves their territories. State sovereignty—the right of the state to maintain self-determination within its borders—is being challenged by powerful international nonstate actors.

As discussed in Chapter 10, international financial institutions such as the World Bank, the International Monetary Fund, and the World Trade Organization, backed by the world's most developed economies, are pressuring states to adopt neoliberal economic policies. These policies include free markets; free trade; the free movement of goods, capital, and ideas; and access to local markets for transnational corporations. Furthermore, to receive development loans from international financial institutions, countries must privatize state-owned infrastructure such as ports, water systems, utilities, and transportation and to reduce state funding for social services, health care, and education. Neoliberal economists suggest that these changes, while lessening states' ability to control what flows across their borders, will enhance their ability to compete in the global economy.

Economic restructuring promoted by international financial institutions and implemented by the state has yielded a flourishing of civil society. This is evident

"Kayaktivists" who oppose Royal Dutch Shell's plans to drill for oil in the Arctic Ocean attempt to block Shell's Polar Pioneer drilling rig in Seattle's harbor. With a narrow summer window for arctic drilling, every day of delay reduces potential environmental damage.

in the phenomenon of people joining together to form local organizations and movements to protest the social upheaval and uneven development that have accompanied the institution of neoliberal economic policies. These nongovernmental organizations (NGOs), sometimes called **civil society organizations**, have become key players in challenging state policies and creating space through which activists can work together to access resources and opportunities for their local communities.

civil society organization

A local nongovernmental organization that challenges state policies and uneven development and advocates for resources and opportunities for its local community.

CIVIL SOCIETY ORGANIZATIONS GAIN A GLOBAL REACH

One key strategy of civil society organizations—which many states have viewed warily—has been to join forces with transnational movements and networks to recast local problems and conflicts as part of a global project for rights and resources. By connecting with groups outside their national borders, local civil society organizations can work with other activists, networks, and campaigns, such as Amnesty International, Human Rights Watch, Africa Watch, World Vision, and even international agencies like the United Nations. These linkages enable civil society organizations to advocate for local environmental concerns, demilitarization, women's rights, LGBTQ+ rights, human rights, and Indigenous rights—issues that also transcend the borders of the state.

Communication and transportation advances associated with time-space compression—from cell phones to Facebook, Twitter, and YouTube—facilitate the formation of these transnational networks. This process not only promotes the flow of observers, advisors, and participants into meetings and conferences but also stimulates global information flows of on-the-ground developments and organizing strategies. Working together, international coalitions mobilize global sentiment and bring pressure to bear on nation-states to address problems occurring within their borders. In this way, civil society coalitions challenge the ultimate claims of state sovereignty over intrastate affairs.

What Are the Relationships among Politics, the State, Violence, and War?

Assess the origins of violence and war and their relationships to politics and the state.

Perhaps no use of power is more troubling and challenging than violence, the "bodily harm that individuals, groups and nations inflict on one another in the course of their conflicts" (Ury 2002, 7). Conflict happens on the playground, in the classroom, on the job, and on the battlefield. As we look globally today, violent conflict seems not to be sporadic, but permanent—with continuous war in one place or another involving extraordinarily sophisticated tools and weaponry (Waterston 2009).

ARE HUMANS NATURALLY VIOLENT OR PEACEFUL?

For many centuries, the basic question of whether humans are naturally violent or peaceful has figured in discussions and debates about politics, war, and peace. Is there something in our evolutionary past that predisposes modern humans to behave in a particular way when confronted with conflict?

The main arguments can be simplified into three generalizations. First, some believe that organized human violence is a natural expression of the inherent human condition. In this view, human aggression and violence may be attributed to physiological factors such as testosterone, DNA, and neural wiring. A second conception of violence considers humans to be inherently peaceful. In this view, violence arises through cultural practices and patterns that overwhelm basic human nature. A third scenario places the roots of human violence in between nature and culture. For instance, humans may be naturally prone to violence but culturally capable of avoiding it. Or humans may be naturally peaceful and only culturally provoked into forsaking their nature. Or these two alternatives are evenly matched.

Challenging the Myth of Killer Apes and Aggressive Humans.

Some who see contemporary violence as a legacy of our evolutionary past point to common myths about aggressive primates and killer apes as evidence. If aggression, competition, and violence are part of our primate relatives' evolutionary development, they argue, then these impulses must be deeply ingrained in human nature as well. According to this view, aggression, competition, and violence linked to genes and hormones must be generated internally and instinctively released in social relations. Conflict, then, naturally drives individuals farther apart into competing groups.

Physical anthropologist Frans de Waal (2002, 2014), reviewing studies of living primate macaques, chimpanzees, and bonobos, points out patterns of behavior that directly challenge this myth. De Waal notes, for instance, that for social animals such as primates, a pattern of conflict and distancing would lead to everyone living alone, yielding ineffective relationships for individuals who rely on social cooperation for survival. In the primate social groups de Waal has reviewed, a far more complicated dynamic emerges in times of conflict. Rather than increased distance, reconciliation occurs on a regular basis. In fact, in twenty-five separate primate groups, researchers have observed increased attraction between opponents after fights, revealing powerful inclinations toward reconciliation among individuals who have a great deal to lose if their relationship deteriorates (e.g., Lappan 2014). Among bonobos, a primate group closely related to humans on a genetic level, sex is used to resolve conflicts. Bonobo conflicts and tensions occur in all combinations of female and male. So do reconciliations. Bonobos have a high rate of reconciliation and a low rate of violence.

Are humans naturally violent or peaceful? Despite myths of killer apes and aggressive humans, in primate studies, increased attraction is regularly observed between opponents after a conflict. Here, two female bonobos reconcile after a fight.

De Waal suggests that primates exercise various options for resolving conflicts, including avoidance, tolerance, and aggression. They deploy these options at various times depending on the situation, the partner, and the stakes. According to de Waal (2002), primate studies indicate that "aggression [is] not . . . the product of an inner drive but . . . one of the options that exists when there is a conflict of interest" (24). Ultimately, researchers may find that aggressive primate behavior has a genetic component, but this component does not operate in isolation, nor is it necessarily dominant. Equally natural among primates, including humans, are mechanisms for cooperation, conflict resolution, rechanneling of aggression, and reconciliation (de Waal 2002).

THE STATE AND THE INVENTION OF WAR

Political anthropologists actively explore the complicated cultural processes through which war is invented, learned, and enacted (Besteman 2002; Besteman and Cassanelli 1996; Farmer 2003; Ferguson 2002; Gusterson 1996, 2004; Lutz 2001; Waterston 2009). Over the past one hundred years, war has become far more than waging hand-to-hand combat or pulling a trigger at close range—actions that we might associate with aggression driven by hormones. Instead, modern warfare is considerably more premeditated and calculated, relying on computers, satellites, missiles, GPS tracking, and airborne drone strikes.

Today, anthropologists study a highly militarized world in which war seems normalized and permanent. Warfare has become one of the most visible of all human political institutions that reveals the state's pursuit of power. Warfare occurs not only between states but also within them, as those in power may mobilize the state military apparatus against fellow citizens. As we will see in Carolyn Nordstrom's work later in this chapter, we can no longer consider warfare to be a local military phenomenon. Indeed, modern warfare is embedded in a global system of war making. This fact pushes anthropologists to study the intersection of multiple factors that work to construct warfare as a reasonable means for resolving conflicts. These factors may be as disparate as economic stratification, ethnic identity formation, migration, weapons manufacturing and trade, and the imbalance between weak states and strong states as well as resource shortages involving oil, water, and land (Nugent and Vincent 2004).

Militarization. A growing body of anthropological literature has focused on **militarization**—the contested social process through which a civil society organizes for the production of military violence (Lutz 2004; see also Bickford 2011; Geyer 1989). Catherine Lutz, an anthropologist of militarization, in *Homefront: A Military City and the American Twentieth Century* (2001), describes how the processes of militarization include not only the production of material objects such as bullets, bombs, tanks, planes, and missiles but also the glorification of

militarization
The contested social process through which a civil society organizes for the production of military violence.

war and those who make war as states seek to shape their national histories and political culture.

Lutz warns that militarization left unchecked threatens to shape other cultural institutions to its own ends. For example, it influences research in physics, information technology, and psychology; it affects national budget priorities; it affects discussions and debates about gender and sexuality, race and citizenship, privacy and security; and it limits discussions in the news, online, or in the classroom.

Sierra
Leone

MAP 12.1
Sierra Leone

Making and Unmaking Child Soldiers in Sierra Leone. Between 1991 and 2002, a brutal civil war upended the lives of Sierra Leone's 7.5 million citizens: 50,000 people died in the fighting, 2 million refugees fled to neighboring Liberia and Guinea, 10,000 children became combatants. All of Sierra Leone's factions recruited child soldiers—boys and girls from all regions of the country. The children carried guns, commanded battles, and served as porters, messengers, cooks, spies, and "wives." Some were abducted and forced to join a faction. Others joined willingly, seeking an escape from poverty and their local encounters with violence.

In *Childhood Deployed: Remaking Child Soldiers in Sierra Leone* (2014), anthropologist Susan Shepler explores the experiences of these young people through her fieldwork in five reintegration centers for child soldiers run by international NGOs in the aftermath of war. Over the course of eighteen months, Shepler visited the centers, listened to young people's stories, and attended their classes and skill-training sessions.

The United Nations and other aid agencies, drawing on international understandings of the rights of children, have defined child soldiers as anyone under eighteen years old associated with an armed group, regardless of whether or not they were involved in combat. By definition, child soldiers were seen as children and innocent victims of war first, not combatants. Globalized Western concepts of "normal" childhood—innocence, carefree play, development and education—led U.N. programs to attempt to reunite families after the war and reintegrate child soldiers into their home communities and a lost childhood.

Shepler's research reveals the gap between international aid agencies' ideas and moral expectations of childhood and Sierra Leoneans' cultural beliefs and practices. While child labor is often illegal in Western countries, Sierra Leoneans expect children to work alongside adults, frequently as apprentices outside the family. Children are often breadwinners for the family and are seen as active participants in their own and their family's economic strategy. Also outside Western norms, they may be taken in by other families in a form of local fosterage and initiated into secret societies at young ages in order to receive hunting and ritual knowledge from elders.

These local cultural practices and beliefs, argues Shepler, shed light on the ways in which the recruitment and deployment of child combatants in Sierra Leone's civil war were consistent with local understandings of childhood and child–adult relationships. Shepler critiques international NGOs' failures to consider local notions of childhood in developing their programs for demobilization and reintegration. Are the former combatants simply innocent children, forced into war, and returning home to childhood? Or are they formerly powerful soldiers whose status in their community has now shifted, especially with respect to their power relationships to and dependence on their elders?

ANTHROPOLOGY ON THE FRONT LINES OF WAR AND GLOBALIZATION

In today's conflictual world, anthropologists have many opportunities to study current cases of warfare and violence in the context of pressures from globalization. Anthropologist Carolyn Nordstrom's work exemplifies contemporary anthropological contributions to this kind of study. Nordstrom focuses on the real, messy, local experiences of violence, resistance, survival, and creativity in actual communities where war occurs, not in the comfortable offices and remote institutions of military officials and political leaders. At the same time, she spotlights the complex web of local and foreign interactions and actors that drive war and make warfare a global phenomenon.

Mozambique. Between 1989 and 1996, Nordstrom made multiple visits to war-torn areas of Mozambique. The southeast African country's fifteen-year civil war after independence from Portugal claimed a million lives, mostly civilian. To reach rural and forested regions, she traveled with bush pilots making airlifts into war zones. In contrast to detached journalistic war reports, Nordstrom experienced firsthand the low-intensity conflict called "terror warfare" that targeted the country's civilian population through military attacks, hunger, and displacement.

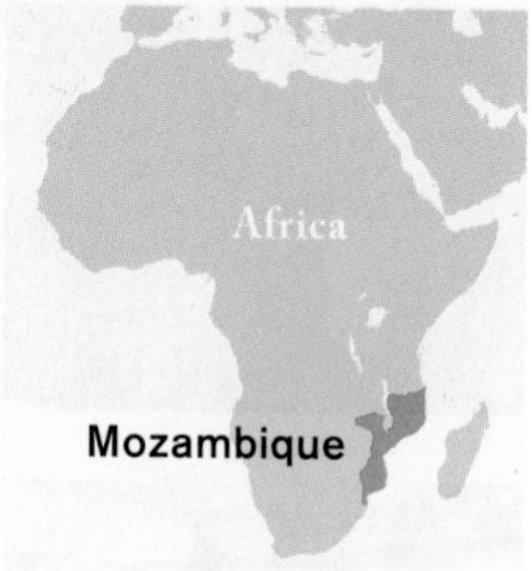

Rebel guerrillas and Mozambican government soldiers targeted the basic structures of Mozambican community life—hospitals, schools, and government offices as well as teachers, health-care professionals, religious authorities, and community leaders—in their acts of warfare. By destroying and disrupting these institutions, practices, and key practitioners of local culture, the forces of violence sought to undermine the local population's political will.

In her ethnography of civil war in Mozambique, *A Different Kind of War Story* (1997), Nordstrom recounts the determined creativity that local populations used to combat this terror and violence. In one village heavily targeted and frequently overrun by troops of both armies, most community leaders and service providers had fled as refugees to avoid potential assassination. Most resources and infrastructure had been destroyed. During the first severe attack on the village, however, one

Mozambique

MAP 12.2
Mozambique

remaining health-care practitioner gathered up as many medical supplies as she could carry and hid in the nearby bush until the soldiers left. Though the soldiers knew her name and searched for her, the villagers kept her secret, kept her safe. On the front lines of battle, soldiers passed through the village regularly in subsequent months. Yet the health worker remained, hiding her medical supplies, living a nomadic life on the outskirts of the area, and being protected by the villagers, who continued to carry their ailing members to her for treatment.

These actions by the health worker and the villagers typify the creativity that Nordstrom finds to be the most potent weapon against war—the determination to survive and resist, to continually refashion and reconstruct one's self, community, and world. Nordstrom concludes her ethnography by suggesting that if, as early political philosophers such as Thomas Hobbes proposed, violence is the "natural state" of human affairs when political institutions collapse, then war-torn regions such as Mozambique should be rife with scenes of aggression, acts of self-preservation, and individual attempts at survival in a

What is the life of a dangerous thing like a rifle, a bullet, or a bomb? (*Clockwise, from top left*) The Colt Defense factory in Hartford, Connecticut, makes the M16 and M4 rifles, the rifles of choice of the U.S. military; a gun poised and ready, in a refugee camp in Lebanon; the Eleventh International Defence Industry Fair, in Istanbul, Turkey, in 2013, which attracted 781 companies from 82 countries.

With globalization, an extensive network of individuals and industries circles the globe from one war to the next. (*Clockwise, from top*) Office of the U.N. High Commissioner for Refugees workers distribute blankets to Syrian refugees along the Jordan–Syria border, 2012; members of the media mark their flak jackets as gunfire rings out near the Tripoli Hotel in Lebanon, 2011; an Australian mercenary trains rebel recruits in Myanmar.

What Are the Relationships among Politics, the State, Violence, and War?   **377** dog-eat-dog world. Instead, Nordstrom consistently found people who resisted and defeated the political violence of war by attending to the day-to-day matters of their community—sharing food, healing wounds, repairing lives, teaching children, performing rituals, exchanging friendship, rebuilding places, and creatively reconstructing the everyday patterns that constitute a meaningful life (Englund 1999; Honwana 1999; Richards 1999).

The Global Business of War. In a later book, *Shadows of War* (2004), Nordstrom makes the case that standard notions of local wars fought by local actors over local issues are largely fiction. Through a comparative study of war and violence in Mozambique, Sri Lanka, South Africa, and Angola, she instead traces the extensive global networks of individuals and industries that feed and fuel local violence and war. Mercenary soldiers, foreign strategists, arms suppliers, businesspeople, underground marketeers, smugglers, humanitarian relief workers, researchers, propagandists, and journalists all circle the globe, moving from one war to the next. The United States, Russia, China, France, and Germany lead the world in global arms sales (SIPRI 2018).

Multitrillion dollar international financial networks support warfare. Illegal drugs, precious gems, weapons, food supplies, military training manuals, and medicines are moved by international networks of legitimate and illegitimate businesses and agencies that profit from war.

Thanks to globalization, the business of war now operates on a worldwide scale. It influences both the architects of war, who primarily engage the battle from a distance, and the people who suffer the consequences on a war's front lines. Discussing the local people affected by the business of war, Nordstrom notes that theirs are not the typical war stories recounted in the media. When war is portrayed only through the prism of weapons, soldiers, territory, and strategic interests won or lost, a more significant reality is ignored: the heroic efforts of people on the front lines who resist and maintain life in the face of violence and death (Finnstrom 2005).

How Do People Mobilize Power Outside the State's Control?

Demonstrate knowledge of ways people mobilize power outside the state's control.

Systems of power, including the state, are never absolute. Their dominance is never complete. Even when a culture's dominant groups and institutions are very powerful in terms of their ability to exercise force or to establish control through hegemony, they do not fully dominate people's lives and thinking. Individuals and groups with less power or no power may still contest established power relationships and structures through political, economic, religious, or military means and can challenge and change cultural norms, values, symbols, and institutions. This power is a potential that anthropologists call **agency** (see Holland and Lave 2001).

In displays of human agency, culture becomes the realm in which battles over power are waged, where people contest, negotiate, and enforce what is considered normal and what people can say, do, and even think. Because of human agency, cultures do not remain rigid and static. They change.

Efforts to change cultural patterns through expressions of agency take various forms, including individual strategies of everyday resistance, such as the "weapons of the weak" (Scott 1985) discussed in Chapter 2; collective efforts such as social movements; and alternative institutions to the state such as those based on religion.

agency
The potential power of individuals and groups to contest cultural norms, values, mental maps of reality, symbols, institutions, and structures of power.

SOCIAL MOVEMENTS

Social movements are collective group actions that seek to build institutional networks to transform cultural patterns and government policies. They often arise in response to uneven development, inequality, and injustice. Although social movements engage in contentious politics, usually outside the mainstream political process, to address specific social issues, they usually do not seek to overthrow the social order. The study of social movements is interdisciplinary, engaging not only anthropologists but also sociologists, political scientists, and historians (Edelman 2001).

Recently, the anthropological analysis of social movements has focused on local communities' responses to the forces of globalization. Factors such as the

social movement
Collective group actions that seek to build institutional networks to transform cultural patterns and government policies.

Activists in Kathmandu, Nepal, demand constitutional protections for Dalits who have been systematically marginalized by the region's caste system.

worldwide movement of capital and production through flexible accumulation, increasing migration within and across national borders, and rapidly increasing yet uneven rates of development have spurred the emergence of social movements as local communities have organized to protect their land, environment, human rights, and cultural identities in a changing economic and political context. Simultaneously, time-space compression has facilitated increased communication and cooperation among individuals, social movements, and NGOs, creating opportunities for a "globalization from below" (Falk 1993, 39).

Freedom Songs and Social Movements in South Africa. In the ethnography *You Can't Go to War without Song* (2022), Nigerian-born anthropologist Omotayo Jolaosho explores the role of singing, dance, and collective performance in South African social movements. Freedom songs and accompanying dances had played a central role in Black South Africans' decades-long struggle against apartheid, a system of institutionalized racial oppression established in 1948 that had allowed the country to become dominated by a small White minority. Apartheid was formally abolished in 1991, and the first multiracial elections were held in 1994. Jolaosho's study, based on sixteen months of ethnographic research living with and learning from South African women in 2009–2010, focused on the Anti-Privatisation Forum (APF), a grassroots social movement founded in 2000 to address the country's unfinished transition, namely the government's turn to neoliberal economic policies and its abandonment of the country's poorest people after the 1994 democratic transition.

Over a ten-year period, the APF mobilized a coalition of political activists, students, unions, community residents, and community organizations in a grassroots struggle in Johannesburg and its surrounding townships to shape government policies. The group opposed widespread evictions of poor people and the privatization of public infrastructure, water, and sanitation services, which led to dramatic service cuts to already impoverished citizens. It employed collective research projects, community meetings, solidarity activities, and mass direct actions, including the performance of freedom songs, as central strategies in the movement.

The distinctive genre of freedom songs, usually performed with movement as part of rallies and demonstrations, included lyrics and music that expressed the aspirations and fighting spirit of the country's freedom fighters. Jolaosho argues that freedom songs and their collective performance in protests, marches, and demonstrations empower social movements on multiple levels. Their musical structure, their lyrical themes, and their affirmation of collective identity provide a disruptive critique of broader society while also creating an invigorating, shared sensory experience among marginalized participants. Freedom songs literally erupt into public space, shattering the perception that impoverished South Africans—who are too often hidden from the consciousness of more affluent people—are invisible and inaudible.

Amid broader social silence and exclusion, marginalized demonstrators must go to dramatic lengths to make their anger and injury plain. Their "repertoires of contention," as Jolaosho names them, may include dances, songs, marches, rallies, occupations of municipal buildings and state officials' homes, and road barricades—sometimes with burning tires. These embodied transgressions of the public calm are designed to demand attention and swift action to correct injustices.

Jolaosho notes that by bringing their bodies fully into the struggle—integrating movement, objects, sounds, and emotions—protestors connect their activism directly with poor South Africans' bodily needs for water, housing, sanitation, electricity, and safety. At the same time, Jolaosho documents the profound effects of freedom songs, dances, and marches on the protestors themselves. The collective performances are invigorating and fortifying. They become an avenue for feeling and expressing deep emotions, especially when words fall short. The shared, embodied action helps marginalized demonstrators overcome their fear of police, of rubber bullets, of being shot, and of violence from counterdemonstrators. And they provide avenues for healing and catharsis. Jolaosho's rich ethnography and vibrant writing document the critical role of freedom songs and collective performances in mass mobilizations and social movements in South Africa and provide insights into similar repertoires of contention around the world (Jolaosho 2015, 2022).

Black Lives Matter. Anthropologists seek to understand how social movements arise, mobilize, and sustain themselves. Even though conditions of inequality and injustice are widespread in many parts of the world, movements for social justice develop only in certain situations. Anthropologists have investigated the material, human, cognitive, technical, and organizational resources necessary for social movements to succeed (McAdam, McCarthy, and Zald 1996). Recent attention has turned to the **framing process** of movements—specifically, how shared meanings and definitions arise to motivate and justify collective action.

framing process
The creation of shared meanings and definitions that motivate and justify collective action by social movements.

Actions by the Movement for Black Lives over the past decade illustrate the role of the framing process. How did activists and protestors using the slogan "Black Lives Matter" capture the attention of a nation (and beyond) and build a consensus for social action? What factors led to their success? The hashtag #BlackLivesMatter was first used in 2013 after the acquittal of George Zimmerman in the 2012 murder of Black teenager Trayvon Martin. The Movement for Black Lives captured national attention in 2014 after the murder of another Black teenager, Michael Brown, by a White police officer in Ferguson, Missouri. In Ferguson, thousands gathered in the streets to protest Michael Brown's death and long-standing patterns of discriminatory policing against people of color in their community. The murder of George Floyd by police in Minneapolis, Minnesota, in 2020 drew millions of people in hundreds of communities across the country and around the world to protest under the "Black Lives Matter" banner.

In support of Black lives, people collectively gathered online and in the streets to protest racism and police brutality toward Black people.

Anthropologist Jeffrey Juris (2012) suggests there are two keys to the success of contemporary social movements, both related to framing. First is the framing of the movement as simultaneously virtual and physical. And second is a framing of the movement's cause through compelling slogans. Social media draws a diverse group of people with shared concerns—in the case of the Movement for Black Lives, over racial justice—into shared physical spaces. Social media, email lists, websites, and collaborative networking tools facilitate new patterns of protest that build on and resonate with more traditional forms of action. As Yarimar Bonilla and Jonathan Rosa (2015) document in their pathbreaking article about the Black Lives Matter protests in Ferguson, "#Ferguson: Digital Protest, Hashtag Ethnography, and the Racial Politics of Social Media in the United States," social media was key to keeping the physical outdoor protests and occupations alive, vibrant, and relevant. In the process, the physical occupations became not only a protest tactic but also the "physical and communal embodiments of the virtual crowds of individuals aggregated through the viral flows of social media" (Juris 2012, 269).

Another key to the success of the Movement for Black Lives rests on its framing under the banner of Black Lives Matter. The slogan is a statement of outrage and a demand for equality. The statement's sentiment should be obvious, yet the country's history and current events reveal that it has not been realized. Over the past decade, activists using the Black Lives Matter framing have successfully organized a broad, decentralized political and social movement to directly challenge state policies and to indirectly shape public political discourse in a number of areas, including police brutality and the use of excessive force against people of color, budget reallocation from policing to community services focused on mental health and housing, and injustice built into the criminal justice system, particularly sentencing disparities that feed mass incarceration.

The Movement for Black Lives has been so successful in framing these debates and shifting public discourse that countermovements have attempted to undermine its framing by emulating it. Phrases like "All Lives Matter" or "Blue Lives Matter" are sometimes used as counterslogans to insinuate that Black Lives Matter is itself discriminatory in what should be a color-blind society. In response, Black Lives Matter activists continue to advance their framing by drawing attention to the many ways in which U.S. institutions and individuals have devalued Black lives over their 400-year history in the United States, up to and including today. In these ways, the Movement for Black Lives continues to use its framing to express outrage, demand justice, educate the public, and function as a laboratory for the production of alternative forms of democracy and community (Yancy and Butler 2015). Where have you heard this framing used in discussions about race, racism, and racial injustice?

ALTERNATIVE LEGAL STRUCTURES

In addition to overt social movements and subtle, covert forms of resistance, it is possible to challenge structures of power in an arena where the state usually holds clear authority: in matters of the law. But how do people organize alternative legal structures outside direct control of the modern state? What gives authority and legitimacy to alternative structures if they are not enforceable by the state's coercive power? Legal anthropologist Hussein Ali Agrama spent two years conducting ethnographic research on local courts and councils in Cairo, Egypt, to explore these questions (Agrama 2010, 2012).

Islamic Fatwa Councils in Cairo, Egypt. Agrama compared the operations of two key local sources of legal authority: (1) the personal status courts operated by the Egyptian state and (2) the Al-Azhar Fatwa Council, independently established in 1935 and one of the oldest and most established centers of Islamic authority. In the busy and crowded personal status courts, Egyptians of all walks of life appear before a judge, an official of the state, who makes legally binding rulings that draw on the Egyptian constitution and legal codes that are based on the principles of Islamic Sharia (law). In the equally busy and crowded Fatwa Council, held in a spacious room at the main entrance to the Al-Azhar

MAP 12.3
Cairo

mosque, seekers approach Islamic legal scholars and interpreters of Islamic law, or
muftis, for religious answers about matters of daily life. The muftis respond freely
with legally nonbinding answers to anyone who asks. Their decisions are called
fatwas—responses to questions about how to live ethically and rightly.

In comparing these two court systems, Agrama encounters a startling
dynamic. Both deal with an overlapping set of issues heavily focused on matters
of marriage, sex, divorce, reconciliation, and inheritance. Both draw their decisions from Islamic Sharia, although the personal status courts engage Islamic
law through the Egyptian constitution and legal code, whereas the muftis refer
directly to Sharia and other Islamic traditions in their fatwas. What interests
Agrama is that despite these basic similarities, the petitioners' responses to the
authorities' rulings are markedly different. The legally binding judgments of the
personal status court are generally looked on with great suspicion. People go
to great lengths to avoid the consequences of the court's decisions despite the
state's ability to coerce obedience to its judgments. In distinct contrast, the Fatwa
Council exercises great authority, even though seeking decisions from the council is not obligatory, a fatwa is not legally binding, and once issued, a fatwa does
not have to be obeyed. In fact, petitioners can seek more than one fatwa on
the same issue if they wish. But Agrama's research finds that petitioners take
fatwas very seriously, following the decisions even if they entail great difficulty
or unhappiness—despite no identifiable institutional enforcement mechanism.

What accounts for the differentiation between personal status courts and
the Fatwa Council? And how does a given fatwa acquire its authority without
the threat of coercive force? To understand the authority of the fatwa, Agrama
explores the complex interactions and expectations between seekers of fatwas

and the muftis that issue them. Contrary to popular impressions, fatwas are not merely designed to dispense points of correct doctrine in obedience to prescriptions found in Islamic Sharia. Rather, muftis seek to apply Islamic tradition and law to resolve particular problems, identify an effective solution, and point fatwa seekers toward a path forward. The process includes significant perplexities and uncertainties: The fatwa seeker arrives perplexed by their situation, and at least initially, the mufti is uncertain about how to respond. In this context, the mufti typically begins by asking for further information in an attempt to fully understand the context and facts as presented. The fatwa seeker approaches the mufti with the hope that they will have the skills to point the way out of the trouble, to offer a way forward—to discern and speak the right words.

In the end, both seeker and mufti share a collective responsibility for the success of the fatwa: The mufti must be sure to speak the right words, and the seeker must apply them correctly. Although the consequences of an incorrect fatwa may be most damaging for the seeker during their lifetime, the mufti is believed to bear responsibility for the outcome in the hereafter. Ultimately, the fatwa is meant to put the questioner on the right path forward, to offer direction and facilitate a journey on which the seeker can advance within the range of doctrine toward a Muslim ideal. Agrama suggests that it is careful and personal navigation of these complexities that engenders trust and conveys legitimacy on the muftis and their fatwas.

Despite the overarching presence of the state (Ferguson and Gupta 2002) and, in this case, the explicit presence of a state-run court, individuals and communities consistently seek alternative frameworks of authority through which to organize their lives. Agrama's study of the bustling Al-Azhar Fatwa Council in Cairo provides one compelling example and sheds light on local practices of the fatwa—practices that are increasingly popular within Egyptian society and the Muslim world more generally yet are frequently misunderstood in the West.

In this chapter's opening story of the Russian invasion of Ukraine, as well as in the ethnographic examples presented throughout this chapter, we have seen diverse strategies that humans use to exercise power through the medium of politics. Although war in Ukraine and political upheaval in the Middle East and various parts of the world readily draw the focus of the world media, Agrama's work in Cairo reminds us that human political activity occurs at many different levels during the course of daily life. Whether through the politics of the state, acts of war, social movements, or small-scale acts of resistance that James Scott (1985; see Chapter 2) labeled weapons of the weak, we have considered how anthropologists examine power and politics and the cutting edges of political activism that will continue to draw their interest in the future.

Toolkit

Thinking Like an Anthropologist
Applying Politics to Daily Life and Beyond

In each chapter of this book, we have investigated how human cultures construct, engage, and negotiate systems of power. We have considered the role of influential ideologies and structures of race, gender, ethnicity, class, kinship, and religion. In this chapter, we have explored how power is expressed and organized through political systems and processes. All human relationships and communities, large and small, involve politics. People are constantly negotiating the interpersonal and institutional balances of power.

Politics is not separate from daily life. We don't have to run for political office or start an online petition to be involved in politics. At its most basic level, politics encompasses all of the ways we organize ourselves to achieve what we most desire for our community: our family, friends, classmates, fellow citizens, the environment, and fellow inhabitants of planet Earth. As you learn to think like an anthropologist about politics and power, remember the opening questions that we have used to frame our inquiries:

- **How have anthropologists viewed the origins of human political history?**

- **What is the state?**

- **How is globalization affecting the state?**

- **What are the relationships among politics, the state, violence, and war?**

- **How do people mobilize power outside the state's control?**

If, as it appears, humans do not have an overwhelming and uncontrollable biological drive toward aggression and violence, then unlimited avenues open up to explore strategies for addressing problems that confront us today. These strategies include cooperatively engaging the challenging issues of our schools, communities, nations, and world and developing political responses that account for the unique cultural dynamics of local communities and specific groups.

As we have discussed, in this era of globalization, local political action can have global implications. Certainly, the challenge of climate change, discussed in Chapter 11, creates opportunities for political action on a local scale that can affect our planetary co-inhabitants on a global scale. Likewise, there are no climate-endangering activities anywhere in the world that do not directly affect all of the humans and other species on the planet. But what political strategies can be mobilized to bring a broad range of actors— activists, investors, civil society groups, and governments—into a collaborative movement with common strategies to address this existential challenge?

As a new generation of young people around the globe develop social networking and social media strategies for expressing their concerns and attempting to influence systems of power and politics, the networked nature of these movements also means that you, as a college student, have every possibility of becoming an anthropologist who engages the world.

Key Terms

band (p. 362)

tribe (p. 364)

chiefdom (p. 364)

state (p. 365)

hegemony (p. 368)

civil society organization (p. 370)

militarization (p. 373)

agency (p. 379)

social movement (p. 379)

framing process (p. 381)

ECONOMIC
INVESTMENT FOR
THE PEOPLE

NOT CORPORATIONS AND THE GREEDY!

REPAIRERS
OF THE BREACH   Poor People's Campaign   KAIROS CENTER

FULL BUILD BA
BETTER PLAN

3.2 MILLION JO

MANCHIN PLAN = 1.4 MILLION

REPAIRERS
OF THE BREACH   Poor People's Campaign   KAIROS CENTER

West Virginia
Poor
People's
Ca

UILD BA
TTER PLAN

OAK FLAT, SAC
ND OF THE APACH
MINING OPERATIONS

People's Campaign   KAIROS CENTER

Chapter 13
Religion

Learning Objectives

- Define religion from an anthropological perspective.

- Compare different theoretical approaches to the anthropological study of religion.

- Analyze the role of religion in meaning making and mobilizing power.

- Explain how globalization is changing religion.

"We gather on these streets in the spirit of the prophet Amos who declared: Hate evil, love good, and establish justice in the public square."

—Interfaith leaders, Poor People's Campaign March on Washington, D.C.

On the morning of Saturday, June 18, 2022, religious leaders from twenty faith groups joined to deliver a litany in front of the U.S. Capitol to begin a day-long rally against poverty organized by the Poor People's Campaign: A National Call for Moral Revival (PPC). People of faith joined tens of thousands of union workers, community organizers, students, scholars, gun safety advocates, and activists for voting rights, immigration reform, abortion rights, climate action, and LGBTQ rights.

Reverend Dr. William Barber, co-chair of The Poor People's Campaign, speaks at a rally in front of the United States Capitol.

They marched, sang, spoke, and prayed. They heard testimonials from poor and low-wage Americans. They called on Congress and the president to address long-term poverty in the United States. PPC co-chair and charismatic leader Reverend William Barber II, dressed in black clergy robes adorned with a large cross and a Native American pendant, exhorted the crowd like a revival preacher, "This level of poverty and greed in this the richest nation in the history of the world constitutes a moral crisis and a fundamental failure of the policies of greed." In soaring tones, he warned of the apocalyptic state of the nation and its government: "The regressive policies which produce 140 million poor and low-wealth people are not benign. They are forms of 'policy murder'." Poverty is not inevitable, Barber declared. There is enough for everyone. Instead, poverty is a public policy that must be challenged and changed.

Barber, pastor of Greenleaf Christian Church in Goldsboro, North Carolina, came to national prominence in 2013 as the leader of a civil disobedience campaign called Moral Mondays. Then president of North Carolina's state chapter of the NAACP, Barber convened protestors every Monday in the state capital, Raleigh, to fight against increasingly conservative policies restricting voting rights and decreasing support for health and education. Every Monday, demonstrators from across North Carolina gathered to engage in conversation and civil disobedience. Attendance ranged from 2,500 to 10,000 each week that the state legislature was in session. Many would enter the state legislature building to speak with lawmakers, and some were peacefully arrested. Over the course of the 2013 protests, for instance, 900 were arrested—including Barber, who, despite struggling with a lifelong spinal ailment, was arrested on so many occasions that he was eventually banned from the building. As Barber explained at one Moral Monday gathering, "(W)e have no other choice but to assemble in the people's house where these bills are being presented, argued, and voted upon in the hopes that God will move in the hearts of our legislators as he moved in the heart of Pharoah to let His people go."

Today's Poor People's Campaign draws inspiration from the 1968 Poor People's Campaign designed by Martin Luther King Jr. and the Southern Christian Leadership Conference. They planned to bring poor people to Washington, D.C., that June to make hunger and poverty visible to those in power and to demand an economic bill of rights for the nation's poor. Civil rights leaders, many of whom were motivated by their religious faith, had come to believe that the civil rights movement's gains in expanding voting rights and ending legal segregation had not improved material conditions for many Black Americans. They worried that the multiracial effort to alleviate poverty, including President Lyndon B. Johnson's War on Poverty, launched in 1964, had lost momentum as the U.S. government turned its attention to fighting a war in Vietnam. King himself had turned his rhetorical and organizing skills to fighting poverty and militarism, most notably in his speech against the Vietnam War in New York's Riverside Church on April 4, 1967. Exactly one year later, King was assassinated in Memphis, Tennessee, where he had traveled to support striking sanitation workers leading up to the Poor People's Campaign.

For some, the efforts of Barber and the Poor People's Campaign to engage with public policy and political activism—like King's efforts a generation ago—may seem like work unfit for spiritual leaders. But for these leaders and their congregations, the integration of theology, social analysis, and action in addressing the pressing issues facing humanity only continues a long tradition of engagement with matters important to the church's followers and to the world.

Religion plays a central role in human life and culture. Through the study of religion, anthropologists engage some of the deepest, most difficult, and most enduring human questions—about meaning, difference, power, love, sexuality, mortality, morality, human origins, and kinship. Religion has been a central interest of anthropologists since the beginning of our field (Frazer 1890; Tylor 1871). Research about religious beliefs and practices worldwide has explored an amazing diversity of beliefs, symbols, rituals, myths, institutions, religious experts, groups, deities, and supernatural forces. As you read about diverse religions in this chapter, some beliefs and practices may seem quite familiar. Others may be surprising or unexpected. Many might stretch your basic assumptions of what religion is and does.

In this chapter, we consider the anthropological approach to understanding the many groups, beliefs, and practices that are called "religion." In particular, we examine the following questions:

- **What is religion?**
- **What tools do anthropologists use to understand how religion works?**
- **In what ways is religion both a system of meaning and a system of power?**
- **How is globalization changing religion?**

By the end of the chapter, you will be able to investigate and analyze religion using the tools of an anthropologist. You will be better able to understand religion in your own life, in the growing religious pluralism of the United States, and in diverse religious expressions around the world. These skills will be increasingly valuable tools for living and working in the twenty-first century.

What Is Religion?

Define religion from an anthropological perspective.

When anthropologists talk about religion, what are we really talking about? Since the beginning of the discipline, anthropologists have attempted to create a universal definition that might apply to all religions' local manifestations. But the vast global diversity of these expressions makes defining religion a difficult task. Is there something present in all cultures that we can call "religion"?

SEEKING A WORKING DEFINITION

The unique anthropological approach to religion begins with the everyday religious practices of people in their local communities. Through fieldwork, anthropologists focus on the real religious worlds in which humans experience religion physically and express it through their actions. We may study a religion's history, theology, scriptures, and major figures, but we do so to understand their meaning and significance in the life of a community of people. Religion is not theoretical in people's daily activities. People make sense of the world, reach decisions, and organize their lives on the basis of their religious beliefs. Starting from these beginning principles, anthropologists also explore the myriad ways religion intersects with other systems of power, whether economics, politics, race, gender, or sexuality. And we explore how local religious expressions may be connected to larger religious movements or institutions.

Anthropologists have compiled a vast and diverse set of data on religious beliefs and practices worldwide. In general, we find that all local expressions of religion combine some, but not necessarily all, of the following elements:

- Belief in powers or deities whose abilities transcend those of the natural world and cannot be measured by scientific tools

- Myths and stories that reflect on the meaning and purpose of life, its origins, and humans' place in the universe

- Ritual activities that reinforce, recall, instill, and explore collective beliefs

- Powerful symbols, often used in religious rituals, that represent key aspects of the religion for its followers

- Specialists who help the average believer bridge everyday life experiences and the religion's ideals and supernatural aspects

- Organizations and institutions that preserve, explore, teach, and implement the religion's key beliefs

- A community of believers

What is religion? At the 600-year-old Prasanna Ganapathi Temple in Bangalore, India, a Hindu priest performs ritual blessings of new cars, auto rickshaws, and motorbikes to bestow divine protections on car and owner.

As a working definition, we might then say that a **religion** is a set of beliefs and rituals based on a vision of how the world ought to be and how life ought to be lived, often, though not always, focused on a supernatural power and lived out in community. (For an overview of the distribution of adherents to major world religions today, see Figure 13.1. Considering the range of religions shown there, perhaps you can begin to imagine the challenge inherent in creating a working definition to cover such a broad spectrum.)

As social scientists, anthropologists have largely been uninterested in questions of any religion's ultimate truth or falsity. Instead, we understand that religious worlds are real, meaningful, and powerful to those who live in them. Our task is to carefully illuminate those worlds for others by capturing their vivid inner life, sense of moral order, interactions with other systems of meaning and power, and dynamic public expressions—whether those expressions occur in a remote Chinese village temple or the most famous Catholic cathedral in Rome (Bowie 2006).

religion

A set of beliefs and rituals based on a vision of how the world ought to be and how life ought to be lived, often, though not always, focused on a supernatural power and lived out in community.

LOCAL EXPRESSIONS AND UNIVERSAL DEFINITIONS

Attention to local religious expressions complicates anthropologists' efforts to create a universal definition of religion. In a religious studies course, you would likely use a textbook that allocates one chapter for each of the largest world religions, including Christianity, Islam, Hinduism, Buddhism, Chinese religion, Sikhism, Judaism, and others. Each chapter might include an overview of the religion's history, theology, scriptures, major figures, and formal institutions. Under such an approach, drawing broad comparisons among the major religions can prove helpful in outlining the world's most established religious

FIGURE 13.1
Religion in Global Perspective

This chart shows the estimated relative distribution of adherents to the major world religions. It is worth noting, however, that few countries collect data on religious beliefs and practices; as discussed in the chapter, local religious expressions may not neatly fit these categories.

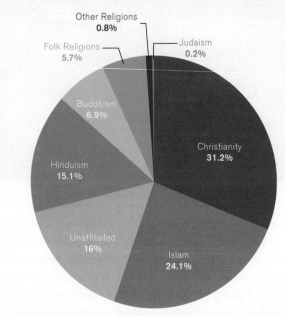

Other Religions
0.8%

Folk Religions
5.7%

Judaism
0.2%

Buddhism
6.9%

Christianity
31.2%

Hinduism
15.1%

Unaffiliated
16%

Islam
24.1%

Source: Pew Forum on Religion & Public Life. April 5, 2017. "The Changing Global Religious Landscape." Pew Research Center. www.pewforum.org/2017/04/05/the-changing-global-religious-landscape.

traditions and in understanding each religion's ideal expression. At the same time, it may obscure the creative and flexible ways people actually practice their religion—in many cases, ways that diverge from the ideal.

Indeed, local expressions and creative adaptations are often at the heart of anthropological research because they reveal how people make a religious tradition come alive in their own context. Consider Islam. Muslims and non-Muslims alike generally regard Islam as highly uniform wherever it is practiced—as a religion that would consistently manifest its core characteristics and definition regardless of location. For example, all Muslims are expected to follow the Five Pillars of Islam: making a declaration of faith, saying prayers five times a day, performing acts of charity, fasting during the holy month of Ramadan, and undertaking a pilgrimage to Mecca. In addition, all Muslims revere the authority of the Koran and the Prophet Muhammad. But on the local level, Muslims frequently expand these formal borders and develop modes of popular expression that may include distinctive devotional practices, life-cycle rituals, marriage customs, ritual clothing, and forms of veiling.

Awareness of the ways in which Muslim life and religious practice vary regionally and locally, such as between Sunni and Shia Muslims in the Middle East, can offer important insights to an anthropologist conducting research or to anyone seeking to build relationships across religious boundaries. The example that follows illustrates the possibility for local variation within a religious tradition that is often assumed to be universal in its expressions.

A Muslim Saint Shrine. Across India, certain popular expressions of Islam push the boundaries of what many people would consider traditional Islam. One example is Husain Tekri, a Muslim saint shrine, or *dargah*, named in memory of the martyred grandson of the Prophet Muhammad. (A **martyr** is a person who sacrifices their life for the sake of their religion.) Pilgrims from across northern India come to this shrine to remember Husain Tekri, to venerate the Muslim saints, and to participate in healing rituals. (A **saint** is an individual considered exceptionally close to God who is exalted after death.) Husain Tekri is part of the religious healing circuit of northern India along which both Hindu and Muslim pilgrims travel as they seek the saint or deity with the specific power to cure their ills.

Pilgrims to Husain Tekri may stay for a day or settle in nearby lodges and remain for days, months, or a year. They come in search of healing from suffering,

martyr
A person who sacrifices their life for the sake of their religion.

saint
An individual considered exceptionally close to God who is exalted after death.

Hindu and Muslim pilgrims at the Husain Tekri shrine in northern India breathe in incense to access the healing powers of the shrine.

illness, and financial ruin and for relief from the presence of evil spirits. The main daily ritual activity is the burning and distribution of *loban*—rocklike chunks of incense sold at the shrine and thrown onto red-hot coals eight times a day. As the white smoke of *loban* billows from the braziers, pilgrims—both men and women—are engulfed in the cloud, breathe in the smoke, symbolically consume the *loban*, and absorb its potency. Through pilgrimage and the ritual consumption of *loban*, pilgrims access the healing powers of the shrine. There, they believe, the power and mercy of the martyred Husain and his family enable them to escape their sick bodies, their mental anguish, and the malevolent spirits possessing them.

Surprisingly, pilgrims to the shrine of Husain Tekri are of many religious backgrounds—not only Muslim but also Hindu, Sikh, and Jain. Seeking healing across religious lines common in many parts of India, as pilgrims of various faiths try multiple religious systems to find the most successful means of healing, especially for illnesses beyond the powers of mainstream medicine (Bellamy 2011; Flueckiger 2006).

The example of Husain Tekri suggests that what often seem to be clearly defined, universally uniform, and consistent world religions are actually flexible and innovative at the local level. From an anthropological perspective, such local expressions of religion are no less complete, meaningful, or true than those taught in the most elite Muslim madrassa, Buddhist monastery, or Christian school of theology.

What Tools Do Anthropologists Use to Understand How Religion Works?

Compare different theoretical approaches to the anthropological study of religion.

Anthropologists have developed a set of key insights about how religion works that serve as a toolkit for understanding religion as we experience it in our fieldwork. These concepts may prove useful to you in thinking about religion in your own life and in your community, nation, and the world.

Anthropological theories of religion have been deeply influenced by the ideas of nineteenth- and twentieth-century social scientists Émile Durkheim, Karl Marx, and Max Weber. All three examined the connection between religion and the political and economic upheavals of their time: an Industrial Revolution that spurred massive shifts in land tenure patterns throughout western Europe; large-scale rural-to-urban migration; and high levels of unemployment, poverty, and disease. Through their writing, Durkheim, Marx, and Weber reshaped the study of religion, moving from the theological and cosmological orientation that dominated pre-twentieth-century European and North American thinking to focus on the role of religion in society. These thinkers have inspired generations of anthropologists, who have in turn expanded and refined these early theories.

ÉMILE DURKHEIM: THE SACRED AND THE PROFANE

Émile Durkheim (1858–1917) was a French sociologist who explored ideas of the **sacred** (holy) and the **profane** (unholy) as well as the practical effects of religious **ritual**. His work in these areas has provided key analytical tools for social scientists seeking to understand common elements across different religious movements and the practical application of religious ideas in the social life of religious adherents.

Developing the notion of a fundamental dichotomy between sacred and profane, Durkheim defined religion as "a unified system of beliefs and practices relative to sacred things, that is to say, things set apart and forbidden—beliefs and practices which unite into one single moral community called a Church, all those who adhere to them" ([1912] 1965, 62). Durkheim saw religion as ultimately social—something practiced with others—not private or individual. Through the collective action of religious ritual, group members reaffirm, clarify, and define for one another what is sacred and what is profane. Durkheim's famous study *Elementary Forms of Religious Life* (1912) examined the religious beliefs and practices of Indigenous Australians, whom he and others believed to have the most primitive culture of the time and thus to practice religion in a manner closest to its "original" forms. The Indigenous "elementary" religious beliefs and practices, he believed, could reveal the most basic elements of religion and shed light on religion's evolution into its present forms.

As western European societies experienced radical transformations in the late nineteenth and early twentieth centuries, Durkheim (1897) turned to the rising suicide rate at the time, particularly the problem of *anomie*—an alienation that individuals experience when faced with physical dislocation and the disruption of their social networks and group values. He wondered how society would overcome this crisis and reestablish its essential cohesion. Durkheim argued that religion, particularly religious ritual, plays a crucial role in combating anomie and addressing societal alienation and dislocation by creating social solidarity, cohesion, and stability. He saw religion as the glue that holds together society's many different pieces. Through ritual, Durkheim believed, society can regenerate its sense of social solidarity and connection. Ritual defines and reinforces collective ideas of the sacred and profane; thus, it reaffirms the community's sense of cosmic order, regenerates its social solidarity, and ensures the group's continued survival and growth.

sacred

Anything that is considered holy.

profane

Anything that is considered unholy.

ritual

An act or series of acts regularly repeated over years or generations that embodies the beliefs of a group of people and creates a sense of continuity and belonging.

French sociologist Émile Durkheim.

Girls kneeling during the *chisungu*, a coming-of-age initiation ceremony among the Bemba people of Zambia. Have you experienced a coming-of-age ritual or other rite of passage?

rite of passage

A category of ritual that enacts a change of status from one life stage to another, either for an individual or for a group.

MAP 13.1
Zambia

RELIGION AND RITUAL

Durkheim's work has influenced many anthropologists of religion. The focus on how individuals and communities manifest religion in their everyday lives—particularly, how they enact it through ritual—has become a cornerstone of the anthropological approach to the study of religion. Anthropologists are aware that religion is not so much talked about as it is *performed* in public displays, rites, and rituals—not so much thought about as *danced* and *sung*. Rituals make the beliefs and passions of a group of people come alive. When performed repeatedly over years and generations, as Durkheim suggested, they create a sense of continuity and belonging that defines a group and regenerates its sense of solidarity, history, purpose, and meaning.

Rites of Passage. French ethnographer and folklorist Arnold van Gennep (1873–1957) first theorized a category of ritual called a **rite of passage** that enacts a change of status from one life stage to another, either for an individual or for a group (van Gennep 1908). Religious rites of passage are life-transition rituals marking moments of intense change, such as birth, coming of age, marriage, and death.

Audrey Richards (1899–1984), a pioneering British woman in early male-dominated British anthropology, observed and recorded one such rite of passage in 1931 among the Bemba people of Zambia, central Africa. Their elaborate ritual, called the *chisungu*—a coming-of-age ceremony for a young teenage woman after her first menstruation and in preparation for marriage—was danced in eighteen separate ceremonies over one month in a ritual hut and the surrounding bush. Over fifty special *chisungu* songs and forty different pottery emblems were involved. The *chisungu*, exclusively a women's ritual, provided magical protection to the girl and her family from the physical dangers of puberty and the magical dangers associated with the first act of intercourse in legal marriage. Within the rituals, older women also passed down the songs, sacred stories, sacred teachings, and secret lore of Bemba womanhood, marking a clear change of status within the tribe from girl to woman (Richards 1956).

Victor Turner (1920–1983) built on Richards's pioneering work to explore why rituals and rites of passage are so powerful across religions and cultures. Drawing on his own research in Africa and on extensive comparisons of cross-cultural data, Turner theorized that the power of ritual comes from the drama contained within it, in which the normal structure of social life is symbolically dissolved and reconstituted. He identified three primary stages in all rites of passage. First, the individual experiences *separation*—physically, psychologically, or symbolically—from the normal, day-to-day activities of the group. This may involve going to a special ritual place, wearing special clothing, or performing actions such as shaving one's head. The second stage, **liminality**, involves a period of outsiderhood during which the ritual participant is set apart from normal society, existing on the margins of everyday life. From this position, the individual can gain a new perspective on the past, the present, or the future and thereby experience a new relationship to the community. The final ritual stage, *reaggregation* or *reincorporation*, returns the individual to everyday life and reintegrates them into the ritual community, transformed by the experience of liminality and endowed with a deeper sense of meaning, purpose, and connection to the larger group (Turner 1969).

Turner believed that all humans experience these rites of passage and that the experiences shape their perceptions of themselves and their community. Through them, he asserted, humans develop **communitas**: a sense of camaraderie, a common vision of what constitutes the good life, and perhaps most important, a commitment to take social action toward achieving this vision. Turner felt that the universal practice and experience of ritual reveals at the root of human existence an underlying desire for community and connection. Based on his cross-cultural investigation of the practice of rituals and rites of passage, Turner suggested that at the center of all human relationships lies a deep longing for shared meaning and connection, not a desire for self-preservation or material gain.

liminality

One stage in a rite of passage during which a ritual participant experiences a period of outsiderhood, set apart from normal society, that is key to achieving a new perspective on the past, present, and future community.

communitas

A sense of camaraderie, a common vision of what constitutes the good life, and a commitment to take social action toward achieving this vision that is shaped by the common experience of rites of passage.

Pilgrimage.
Turner applied his thinking about rites of passage to the study of religious pilgrimage, which he considered to be a unique form of religious ritual. Pilgrimage rituals—like those to Muslim saint shrines in northern India, as discussed earlier—exist in religions around the world. In a **pilgrimage**, adherents travel to sacred places as a sign of devotion and in search of transformation and enlightenment. For example, all Muslims are obliged to perform, if life circumstances allow, the hajj pilgrimage to Mecca. Jews, Christians, and Muslims all have pilgrimage sites in Jerusalem. Many Hindus travel to the holy city of Varanasi (Benares) to bathe in the Ganges River. Daoists climb Mount Tai in eastern China. The pilgrimage journey, Turner suggested, involves the same process of separation, liminality, and reincorporation associated with other rites of passage. Similarly, pilgrimage creates a shared sense of communitas among those who undertake the journey, even if years or entire generations separate the trips (Coleman 2021).

For Turner (1969), life in society is a process of becoming, not being; it is a process of change. He maintained that rituals, pilgrimages, celebrations, and even theatrical performances facilitate this process and have the potential to initiate and foster change—not only in the individual but also in the larger culture.

pilgrimage

A religious journey to a sacred place as a sign of devotion and in search of transformation and enlightenment.

Pilgrims circumambulate the Kaaba in Al Masjid al-Haram, the most sacred mosque in Islam, during the hajj, in Mecca, Saudi Arabia.

KARL MARX: RELIGION AS "THE OPIUM OF THE PEOPLE"

Karl Marx (1818–1883) was a German political philosopher. He is primarily known for his *Communist Manifesto* (with Friedrich Engels, 1848) and *Capital* (1867), a radical critique of the capitalist economics emerging in western Europe in the nineteenth century (see Chapter 10). However, Marx was also highly critical of the role of religion in society, famously calling religion "the opium of the people" (Marx and Engels 1957). What did he mean?

In a time of economic upheaval and intensifying social stratification, Marx warned that religion was like a narcotic: It dulled people's pain so they did not realize how serious the situation was. Religion, Marx argued, played a key role in keeping the proletariat—the working poor—from engaging in the revolutionary social change that he believed was needed to improve their situation.

Marx's statement that religion is "the opium of the people" fits within his larger social analysis. He believed that throughout human history, economic realities have formed the foundation of social life and have generated society's primary dynamics, including class stratification and class struggle. He called these economic realities "the base." In his view, all other institutions of culture (including family, government, arts, and, notably, religion) arise from and are shaped by economic realities and deep tensions of economic inequality and class struggle.

The role of these institutions, according to Marx, is to mask the material conditions and exploitation at the economic base and to contain—or provide a controlled release for—the tensions generated by class difference and class conflict. Religion, which Marx also called "the sigh of the oppressed," could provide to the downtrodden a sense of consolation that the sufferings of this life would end and be rewarded in heaven, thereby offering divine justification for the economic status quo.

Marx's overall focus on economics and power has pushed anthropologists to consider the relationship between religion and power. Contemporary studies move beyond Marx's idea that religion is merely an illusion that blinds people to economic realities; instead, such studies examine how religion can play a complex role in systems of power—both by exercising power through economic resources and the mobilization of religious personnel and by resisting systems of oppression through alternative ideas, symbols, and resources.

German political philosopher Karl Marx.

Religion and Cultural Materialism. Anthropologist Marvin Harris (1927–2001) built on Marx's analysis of the base, or infrastructure, and the way in which a society's material conditions shape its other components. Harris's theory of **cultural materialism** argued that material conditions, including technology and the environment, determine patterns of social organization. In this view, human culture is a response to the practical problems of earthly existence. In *Cows, Pigs, Wars, and Witches* (1974), Harris turned this perspective toward perplexing human behaviors, including why Hindus venerate the cow, why Jews and Muslims abstain from eating pork, and why some people believe in witches. Harris proposed that these practices might have developed in response to very practical problems as people sought to adapt to their natural environment.

cultural materialism

A theory that argues material conditions, including technology and the environment, determine patterns of social organization, such as religious principles.

Have you ever wondered why cows are considered sacred in India? Harris approached this question not through personal immersion in the worldviews of Indian Hindus but rather by exploring larger environmental forces—the cultural ecology—that might promote this cultural practice. If you visit India, you will find zebu cows—a large-humped cattle species found in Africa and Asia—wandering freely about city streets and rural areas. These cows eat food from market stalls, graze on sidewalk shrubs, and defecate indiscriminately. In a country with deep pockets of poverty and malnutrition, why are these cows left to roam and not slaughtered for nutritious, protein-rich beef?

Eating beef is prohibited in Hinduism, as is eating all meat. The cow, in Harris's view, became a symbol of *ahimsa*—the practice of nonviolence and respect for the unity of all life that is key to Hinduism, Buddhism, and Jainism.

MAP 13.2
India

How this tradition began is unclear, but today the holy mother cow is a symbol of health and abundance, and its image appears throughout Indian culture in media such as posters, movies, and carvings. The symbol also has a literal presence on streets and in fields.

Harris suggests that religious prohibitions protecting the cow have overwhelming practical applications in a culture that relies on agricultural production. Cows, after all, produce calves that grow up to be oxen, which Harris calls the tractor, thresher, and family car of the Indian agricultural system. Without an ox, a family has no way of planting, harvesting, preparing, or transporting its crops. Without an ox, a family loses the capacity to farm and eventually loses its land. Cows also produce vast quantities of dung, almost all of which can be recycled into fertilizer and cooking fuel. Religious dedication to *ahimsa* protects this resource even under the most difficult economic conditions. No matter how hungry the family may be in one season, keeping the cow alive ensures long-term survival.

For Harris, religiously based practices that appear to function in opposition to sound nutritional practices or economic development strategies may in fact be very rational cultural adaptations to the surrounding ecology. In India, the cow is extraordinarily useful. Its protection, especially during difficult economic times, may be essential to the long-term stability and survival of the Indian people and culture.

Think about any other religion, perhaps one you have an affiliation with. Can you apply the perspectives of Harris's cultural materialism to any of its practices and beliefs? Can you begin to imagine how certain material conditions of everyday life may have shaped patterns of religious belief and practice?

A sacred cow lies unperturbed and undisturbed in a busy intersection of Varanasi, India. Why is the cow sacred in India?

MAX WEBER: THE PROTESTANT ETHIC AND SECULARIZATION

Max Weber (1864–1920), a German sociologist, philosopher, and economist, considered religious ideas to be key to understanding the unique development of societies worldwide and the rise of industrial capitalism, particularly in western Europe.

Unlike Marx, who argued that economic realities ultimately shape society, Weber believed that ideas, including religious ideas, could be equally powerful. His book *Sociology of Religion* (1920) was the first sociological attempt to compare the world's religions. In it, Weber suggested that Asian religious beliefs and ethical systems had held Asian economies back from capitalist economic growth along the western European path. China, India, and other cultures had developed aspects of modern capitalism even earlier than western Europe did, but without a certain kind of ideological support, a more advanced capitalism had not evolved in Asia. Weber suggested that economic innovations alone could not explain the two regions' different paths.

In *The Protestant Ethic and the Spirit of Capitalism* (1905), Weber suggested that the ascetic values of self-denial and self-discipline that developed in western European Protestantism provided the ethic that was necessary for capitalism to flourish. Certain Protestant sects, including Calvinists, expressed their religious beliefs and values in a daily lifestyle of thrift, discipline, and hard work. In these ideas, Weber found evidence of the ethical and psychological framework necessary for the success of industrial capitalism.

Also key to the development of Western capitalism, according to Weber, was an evolution of religious ideas and practices toward increasing systematization: Tradition, sentiment, and charismatic leadership would be replaced by rational bureaucracies with intelligible and predictable rules. Weber imagined a gradual rationalization in religion that would evolve from (1) traditional religion based on magic and led by shamans to (2) charismatic religion based on the persuasive power of prophets such as Buddha, Jesus, and Moses and, finally, to (3) rational religion based on legal codes of conduct, bureaucratic structures, and formally trained religious leaders. He anticipated that this evolutionary process would be almost inevitable. But he warned that as society became more rationalized, it also risked becoming more **secular**—less religious—and thus losing the very spirit that had driven its success and development.

Scholars have debated Weber's secularization thesis for many years (Asad 1993; Berger 1999; Casanova 1994; Stark and Bainbridge 1985). Certainly, in western Europe today, religious identification among native-born residents continues to sink to record lows. In contrast, the United States stands as a striking exception to this pattern in industrialized countries, as religious beliefs and

German sociologist and philosopher Max Weber.

secular
Without religious or spiritual basis.

practices remain strong in both the native-born and immigrant populations. Between 1944 and 2011, polls consistently showed that nearly 90 percent of the U.S. population believed in God, and although there has been a slight dip among younger adults, 81 percent of Americans still believe in God (Gallup 2022). Even the assumed separation of church and state in the United States is far from absolute. Battles continue over the teaching of evolution in the science curriculums of public schools, fans at public high school football games in Texas rise to recite the Christian Lord's Prayer, and crowds at New York's Yankee Stadium stand during the seventh-inning stretch for a moment of silence to remember those serving in the U.S. military and then sing "God Bless America." In these instances, religious sentiments infuse public and political life, and public rituals of civil society take on sacred status (Bellah 1980).

Moreover, widespread revivals of religious ideas, organizations, and movements around the world in the face of increasing modernization—and at times in resistance to the homogenizing influences of globalization and Western culture—provide additional evidence that modernization does not always lead to secularization.

SHAMANISM

shamans

Local religious practitioners with abilities to connect individuals with supernatural powers or beings to provide special knowledge and power for healing, guidance, and wisdom.

Throughout much of human history, communities' religious needs have been served by **shamans**—local religious practitioners with special abilities to connect individuals with supernatural powers or beings. More formal religious organizations with trained specialists and elaborate moral rules and ritual practices are fairly recent, spanning 2,000 to 3,000 years at most with the rise of Hinduism, Buddhism, Judaism, Christianity, and Islam. The term *shaman* derives from the name given to healing specialists among the seminomadic people of Siberia, but it has since been applied to healers, spiritualists, witches, and witch doctors in cultures worldwide.

Shamans live as part of the local community and participate in daily activities and work, but they are called on at times to perform special rituals and ceremonies. They often gain their powers through special training or experience that involves passing through a journey or test of spirit, such as illness, isolation, physical pain, or an emotional ordeal. Through rituals involving prayers, meditation, songs, dance, pain, or drugs, shamans enter a trance, often at will. While entranced, they implore deities and powers to take action or to provide special knowledge and power that may assist individuals or the community at large—whether in the form of healing, medicinal advice, personal guidance, protection from illness or other attack, fortune telling, or control over the weather.

Although the role of the shaman is generally associated with small agricultural or seminomadic societies, shamans today often relocate to contemporary urban settings along with their immigrant communities. A variation of the shaman role also occurs in more formal religious organizations, as trained religious specialists seek to intervene with deities on behalf of adherents or assist adherents in practices of prayer and meditation through which they seek healing or guidance.

RELIGION AND MAGIC

Anthropology has a long history of studying cultures in which magic is practiced and witches are real (Frazer 1890). **Magic** involves the use of spells, incantations, words, and actions in an attempt to compel supernatural forces to act in certain ways, whether for good or for evil. Magic is part of cultural practices in every part of the world. And religion, almost everywhere, contains some components of magic.

magic
The use of spells, incantations, words, and actions in an attempt to compel supernatural forces to act in certain ways, whether for good or for evil.

E. E. Evans-Pritchard: Rethinking the Logic of Magic.
E. E. Evans-Pritchard (1902–1973), a British anthropologist who conducted extensive fieldwork in Africa's southern Sudan region, challenged Weber's rationalization thesis that assumed modernization and the rise of science would bring increasing rationality to cultures and their religious practices, thereby leading to a decrease in practices of magic. Instead, Evans-Pritchard's research among the tribal Azande people from 1926 to 1930 found that their use of magic was not an irrational expression but a component of a highly organized, rational, and

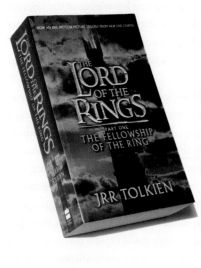

The success of J. R. R. Tolkien's *Lord of the Rings* and J. K. Rowling's *Harry Potter* series has revealed a vast appetite in Western culture for magic, witches, and wizards, at least in their fantastical literary and cinematic forms.

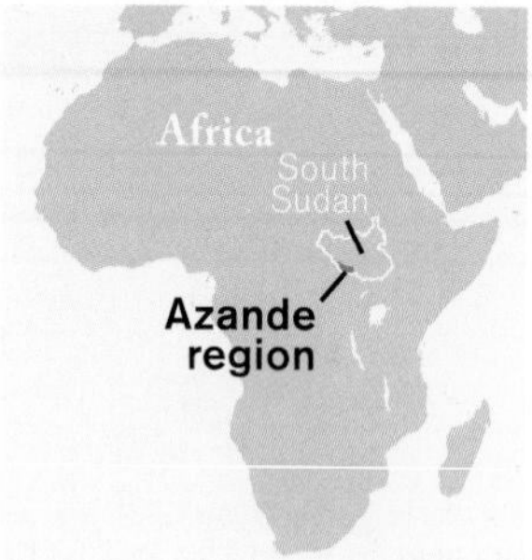

logical system of thought that complemented science in understanding how the world works.

In *Witchcraft, Oracles, and Magic among the Azande* (1937), Evans-Pritchard describes in careful detail the elaborate religious system of the Azande in which magic, witchcraft, and poison oracles are central elements of daily life and conversation. The Azande trace all misfortunes to witchcraft. Their witchcraft does not involve rituals, spells, or medicines. Instead, it is a psychic power that may be used consciously or unconsciously by a witch—a woman or a man—to cause misfortunes or death. Witchcraft is inherited from a parent, and a witch's body contains a witchcraft substance (which the Azande described to Evans-Pritchard as an oval, blackish swelling or bag near the liver) that cannot be detected during life but can be found during an autopsy.

Magic among the Azande, in contrast to witchcraft, is performed consciously through rites, spells, the preparation of herbal medicines, and other magical techniques. Magic has its own power and can be used to combat witchcraft. If people perceive that witchcraft is being deployed against them, they may consult a witch doctor—almost always a man—who will use magic and medicines to try to thwart the work of the witch.

Witchcraft, Oracles, and Magic among the Azande is considered one of the outstanding works of anthropology in the twentieth century. It is both an exquisitely detailed ethnography and a basis for rethinking the role of magic in society: Evans-Pritchard challenges the ethnocentric views of Western scholars who dismiss magical practices as irrational and illogical when compared to modern, rational, Western scientific strategies for accumulating knowledge of the external world. He contends instead that Azande ideas that may seem exotic, strange, and irrational to Europeans in actuality formed consistent, comprehensive, and rational systems of thought within the context of the Azande's daily lives and social structures.

Among the Azande, magic explained things that did not make sense otherwise, particularly the experience of misfortune; it provided an alternative theory of causation that supplemented the theory of natural causation. Magic helped explain what could not be explained by the scientific study of nature. Evans-Pritchard presented the case of a wooden granary structure that collapsed and injured several people seated underneath it. Science could explain how insects had damaged the wood, which led to the collapse. But science could not explain why the people who were injured were sitting in that particular location at that particular time. For the Azande, witchcraft and magic could explain this misfortune.

Evans-Pritchard argued that the Azande saw no contradiction between witchcraft and empirical knowledge. For them, witchcraft and magic provided a rational and intellectually consistent explanation for what science could not explain. Belief in witchcraft only appears inconsistent and irrational,

MAP 13.3
Azande region,
South Sudan

Evans-Pritchard chided his Western colleagues, when it is examined like a museum object on a shelf, outside the context of daily life.

Paul Stoller: _In Sorcery's Shadow_. In the ethnography _In Sorcery's Shadow_ (1987), anthropologist Paul Stoller and his co-author, Cheryl Olkes, extend Evans-Pritchard's commitment to respecting and understanding others' systems of knowledge—even if they at first appear irrational, unreasonable, and incomprehensible. Stoller takes Evans-Pritchard's work on magic and sorcery (another term for witchcraft) to a deeper, more personal level through direct engagement in the beliefs and practices of those he studied.

In the late 1970s, Stoller arrived in the Songhay region of the Republic of Niger, West Africa, to learn about the role of religion in community life there. Through intensive fieldwork covering five visits over eight years, his deep involvement in a world of magic, spirits, sorcery, and spirit possession prevalent in the Songhay and surrounding regions eventually led to his initiation as a sorcerer's apprentice. He memorized magical incantations. He ate special foods needed for his initiation. He ingested medicinal powders and wore magical objects to protect himself from antagonistic sorcerers. And he indirectly participated in an attack of sorcery that temporarily paralyzed the intended victim.

Stoller's fieldwork led him to reflect on the transformative and deeply personal experience of conducting research into people's religious worlds:

> For me, respect means accepting fully beliefs and phenomena which our system of knowledge often holds preposterous. I took my teachers seriously. They _knew_ that I used divination in my personal life.

MAP 13.4
Songhay region, Niger

A sorcerer preparing a written tablet for a customer in the Songhay region of Niger.

They *knew* that I had eaten powders to protect myself. They *knew* I wore objects to demonstrate my respect for the spirits. They *knew* I had an altar in my house over which I recited incantations. They liked the way I carried my knowledge and power and taught me more and more. (Stoller 1987, 228)

The anthropological commitment to long-term, in-depth participant observation brings many of us into close contact with the beliefs, practices, and emotions of those whom we study, an intimacy that often reveals the vibrant power of religion in their lives and leaves one marked by the encounter.

George Gmelch: Baseball Magic. If reading about the work of Evans-Pritchard and Stoller leaves you relieved that you live in a Western world in which magic mostly appears in children's books and movies, research by anthropologist and former Minor League Baseball player George Gmelch may surprise you. It turns out that beliefs and practices of magic are more common in U.S. culture than you might think.

Gmelch's study of baseball in the United States (2017) explores the rituals, taboos, and sacred objects of magic that permeate the game. He finds that they reflect the kinds of beliefs and activities that are prevalent in all sports.

Baseball players use charms such as special clothes or jewelry, and they believe that good magic is contagious. If a ritual or charm works one time, perhaps the magical conditions for success will be re-created if it's used again. Thus, players repeat certain actions to help them succeed: Pitchers touch the bill of their cap, wear good-luck charms, or never touch the foul line between home plate and first base when moving between the pitcher's mound and the dugout. Batters wear the same shirt or underwear, or use the same movements over and over again in the batter's box, to capture the magic of previous success.

In What Ways Is Religion Both a System of Meaning and a System of Power?

Analyze the role of religion in meaning making and mobilizing power.

Many people in Western cultures think of religion as a primarily personal matter. In the United States, for instance, doctrines promote an ideal of the separation of church (that is, religion) and state (politics). But as we saw in Chapter 2, any

analysis of a cultural system that focuses solely on its underlying meanings risks ignoring how power is negotiated within the system and how the system engages other structures of power within the culture. This observation applies to our study of religion as well.

RELIGION AND MEANING

Building on the themes of Weber's *Protestant Ethic and the Spirit of Capitalism*, anthropologist Clifford Geertz (1926–2006), in his essay "Religion as a Cultural System" (1973b), suggests that religion is essentially a system of ideas surrounding a set of powerful **symbols**. Hindus, for example, consider the cow sacred because by protecting it they symbolically enact the protection of all life. Other widely recognized religious symbols include the cross for Christians, the Torah scroll for Jews, and the holy city of Mecca for Muslims. In Geertz's view, each symbol has deep meaning and evokes powerful emotions and motivations in the religion's followers. Why?

These symbols acquire significance far beyond the actual material they are made of. Objects of wood, metal, rock, or paper come to represent influential explanations about what it means to be human and where humans fit in the general order of the universe. Symbols, with their deep pool of meaning, create a sense of order and resist chaos by building and reinforcing a larger worldview—a framework of ideas about what is real, what exists, and what that means.

Magic rituals, taboos, and sacred objects are used constantly in American sports. (*Left*) Former New York Mets reliever Turk Wendell's magical practices included always leaping over the baseline when walking to the mound, brushing his teeth between innings, chewing black licorice while pitching, and wearing a necklace decorated with the teeth of wild animals he had hunted and killed. (*Right*) Professional golfer Paula Creamer believes that wearing pink during the final round of tournaments will bring her good luck.

symbol

Anything that represents something else.

We can see symbols at work in various religious contexts. For Christians, the bread and wine served in the communion ritual are more than actual bread and wine. They symbolically recall the death and resurrection of Jesus, the power of God to overcome death, and the promise to Jesus's followers of everlasting life beyond the suffering of this world. Communion also recalls the fellowship of all Christian believers who share in the benefits of God's sacrifice and cultivates a sense of connection with people around the world. For Jews, the Torah scroll is more than a composite of paper and ink. It represents the holy word of God as revealed through the prophets, the story of a covenant between God and the people of Israel, an agreement that in return for faithfulness God will provide liberation from captivity, the establishment of a nation of people, and abundant life. For Hindus, the cow is venerated because it represents the Hindu practice of *ahimsa*—nonviolence toward all living things. In a practical sense, this means that no leather may enter the temple and all shoes must remain outside the temple door. Even these acts are symbolic of Hindus' belief that all life is sacred and that attention to this fact will transform the practicing individual and lead to their reincarnation as a more sentient being.

RELIGION AND POWER

Anthropologist Talal Asad, in his book *Genealogies of Religion* (1993), criticizes Geertz's explanation of religion. Asad bases his inquiry on questions such as these: How did religious symbols get their power? Who or what gave them their authority? What gives religion the power and authority to have meaning in people's lives? After all, Asad asserts, symbols do not have meaning in and of themselves. He suggests that religion and religious symbols are actually produced through complex historical and social developments in which power and meaning are created, contested, and maintained. What historical processes have given the cross, the Torah, the hajj, and the cow their symbolic power? Without understanding these particular **authorizing processes**, Asad claims, we cannot understand what really makes religion work.

authorizing process
The complex historical and social developments through which symbols are given power and meaning.

Asad argues that most definitions of religion are not universal. Instead, he claims, they are the creations of Western scholars based on western European ideas of what religion is and how it works—in particular, the way Christianity has developed in relationship to the state. Such scholars look for Western ideas of religion in the spiritual and ritual practices of other cultures. Asad warns that these attempts to create a universal definition impede our understanding of religion in other parts of the world. For instance, he suggests that Weber's assumptions about the arc of religious societies toward secularization are rooted in the way Western Christianity has developed—not in a universal pattern that we can assume exists in religions worldwide.

In the case of Islam, religious beliefs and political power are intricately intertwined in many countries, and national governments may seek to impose a version of Islamic religious law, the Sharia, through mechanisms of the state. Asad suggests that in these cases, Western understandings of religion that assume increasing secularization and separation of church and state may lead scholars and casual observers to dismiss other expressions of religion as irrational and backward. Instead, these other religious expressions are simply different—that is, outside the normative definition of religion established in Western scholarship. Asad states that scholars of religion must beware the power of universal definitions to obscure local realities. They must carefully examine how religion is expressed locally, how those expressions developed over time, and what has given those expressions the power and authority to be so meaningful to believers (Asad 1993).

Thinking like an anthropologist of religion, try to examine religious symbols from the perspectives of both Geertz and Asad. As you consider religious symbols in the culture around you—perhaps in your own religious tradition—can you begin to appreciate symbols' power to evoke intense emotions and motivations that put believers in touch with what feels "really real"? Can you begin to consider how particular symbols have been constructed, given meaning, and

A Jewish worshipper holds up a Torah scroll to receive a blessing at the Western Wall, Judaism's holiest prayer site, in Jerusalem's Old City. How does an object made of paper and ink become a powerful symbol with deep religious meaning?

authorized through particular historical and cultural processes?

BLURRING THE BOUNDARIES BETWEEN MEANING AND POWER

The work of both Geertz and Asad has influenced contemporary anthropological research on religion. We now consider local examples of religious activities and organizations in which meaning and power are intertwined and the boundaries between religion and other social systems of power are not rigid. As we consider these studies, can you begin to see how analyses of both meaning and power are essential to achieving a comprehensive picture of the role of religion in culture?

Religion and Revolution in Mexico. Charlene Floyd's (1996) research on the role of the Catholic Church in a revolutionary movement in the Chiapas region of southern Mexico provides another example of how meaning and power are expressed in religion. In Chiapas, one of the poorest states in Mexico, most children do not finish primary school, and many homes have no running water. The people are poor, but the land is rich: It holds large reserves of oil and natural gas, provides most of Mexico's hydroelectric power, and supports half of the country's coffee crop. The tension between an impoverished people, on the one hand, and rich natural resources extracted by Mexico's state and corporations, on the other, has not always found a smooth resolution.

In the early hours of January 1, 1994, some of the poor people of Chiapas, calling themselves "Zapatistas" (after the Mexican revolutionary Emiliano Zapata), covered their faces with bandanas and ski masks, marched into four Chiapas cities, and declared in a dramatic manifesto, "Today we say enough is enough!" Stunned by the uprising, the Mexican government and the economic leaders of Chiapas quickly accused the Catholic Church of inciting the rebellion. In particular, they blamed one of the bishops of Chiapas, Samuel Ruiz García, and his *catequistas*, or lay teachers. But how could a Catholic bishop and a group of lay teachers be accused of inciting a rebellion? Did they actually do so? In considering these questions, we must explore the Church's role in Mexican society.

Today, 90 percent of Mexicans identify as Catholic, a faith that has been a key component of Mexican national identity ever since Spanish colonizers forcibly imported it 500 years ago. In certain periods of Mexican history, religion and politics have been closely aligned. For example, a Catholic priest, Father Miguel Hidalgo y Costilla, is credited with providing the initial spark for the Mexican independence movement in 1810. Calling on the name of Mexico's Indigenous saint, the Virgin of Guadalupe, Father Hidalgo challenged his parishioners by asking, "Will you free yourselves?" Despite periods of alignment, Mexican

MAP 13.5
Chiapas region, Mexico

Catholic bishop Samuel Ruiz García of San Cristóbal in Chiapas, southern Mexico, and the Church's network of *catequistas* were accused by the Mexican government of inciting rebellion.

history has also seen ongoing tensions between the powerful institution of the Catholic Church (which has long been one of Mexico's largest landholders) and the Mexican state. The Church has been involved in Mexican political movements before, but did it have a role in the 1994 uprising in Chiapas? A quick look at recent Church history may shed light on this question.

In 1959, Pope John XXIII called for a Vatican Council to modernize the Catholic Church. By the end of this conference (1962–65), commonly called Vatican II, the Catholic Church had begun a dramatic revolution in theology and practice. In an attempt to redefine the Church as "the people of God" rather than an institution, Vatican II moved to make local congregations more accessible to laypeople. It permitted congregations to worship in their own local language rather than in Latin, and it encouraged priests and lay members to open the Church as a servant to the poor rather than an ally of the politically powerful.

Bishop Ruiz, head of the Diocese of San Cristóbal de las Casas in Chiapas, attended Vatican II and a subsequent meeting in 1968 of Latin American Catholic leaders. He returned to Mexico determined to implement the Church's new theology of liberation: He would put the Church to work to better the life conditions of the 1 million primarily Indigenous people in his diocese. The diocesan program for training lay teachers (*catequistas*) transformed its curriculum from a primary focus on Church doctrine, scriptures, law, liturgy, and music to include concerns of community life and social needs. By the time of the Zapatista uprising, the *catequistas* had grown from 700 to 8,000. Most were now elected by their local Indigenous communities, and they were deeply involved not only in traditional Catholic religious education but also in the empowerment of Indigenous people in their struggles against poverty. *Catequistas* developed prominent roles as community and political leaders, accompanying their constituents in efforts to eradicate poverty and landlessness in Chiapas and to open the state's political processes to greater participation from people at the grassroots.

Were Bishop Ruiz and the *catequistas* responsible for the 1994 Zapatista uprising? No accusations of their direct role in the uprising's leadership have been proven. But did the theology of liberation—which expressed the Catholic Church's desire for the empowerment of Indigenous people and the elimination of poverty—provide moral support and practical training to communities engaged in this struggle? If so, then the Catholic Church of Chiapas provides an instructive example for anthropologists of how we must consider the ways religious ideas and symbols engage with other systems of power to understand religion in all its fullness (Floyd 1996).

MAP 13.6
Afghanistan

Caravan of Martyrs: Religion, Politics, and Suicide Bombing.

In his book *Caravan of Martyrs: Sacrifice and Suicide Bombing in Afghanistan* (2017), anthropologist David B. Edwards, who has been studying Afghanistan for over forty years, explores complicated historical, cultural, and religious frameworks for thinking about suicide bombing. How is it that "men (and sometimes even women and children) would come to consider it a good thing to strap bombs onto their bodies, walk into crowded places, and trigger the bombs, knowing that they will lose their own lives and that they will take with them a large number of strangers" (Edwards 2017, 15)?

Edwards's fascination with Afghanistan began in the 1960s when his grandmother sent him a postcard of a camel caravan during her travels through the country. But since his first visit in 1978, Afghanistan has experienced unimaginable violence spurred by foreign occupations (Soviet Union, 1981–91; United States, 2001–21) and internal battles between Al-Qaeda, Osama bin Laden, and the Taliban in which Afghanistan and its people became proxies in broader global affairs.

The United States invaded Afghanistan after the September 11, 2001, suicide bombing airplane attacks on the World Trade Center in New York and the Pentagon in Washington, D.C. In response to U.S. occupation, bin Laden named suicide bombing an explicit strategy of "martyrdom operations against the enemy" (Edwards 2017, 14). As a result, bombing episodes in Afghanistan increased dramatically—rising from only two in 2003 to an average of one hundred a year toward the end of U.S. occupation in 2021.

Edwards asks the reader to consider suicide bombing in the context of the Afghan and Muslim notions of sacrifice and martyrdom. Sacrifice, closely tied to key cultural values of loyalty to family and the maintenance of honor, has always been a part of local customs and traditions in the region. But in the context of U.S. invasion, loyalty gradually shifted from kinship ties to Islamic political parties. As a result, just as Afghan tribesmen traditionally were obligated to defend their families and their land, they became obligated to defend Islam and the Afghan homeland. When that was not possible, revenge was often the next step—including revenge through self-sacrifice and martyrdom.

Suicide, suggests Edwards, is a form of ritual sacrifice. Such rituals require that one give something up to attain one's goal, whether religious or political. In Afghanistan, the ritual of suicide bombing came to include the sacrifice of oneself and others. This sacrifice must be witnessed by one's community so that the ritual is not individualized but understood as part of a collective action. Following Durkheim's work on ritual and religion, discussed earlier in this chapter, this collective action releases new energy into the group, transforming the profane

Afghan security officials inspect the site of a suicide car bomb in the capital city, Kabul, 2018.

into the sacred through the act of sacrifice and martyrdom. In Afghanistan, the ritual is more than just symbolic action: It has become a means of carrying out political struggle.

Edwards documents the many ways in which the U.S. invasion and occupation brought a degrading loss of honor to Afghan people. Drone strikes, night raids, household searches, armored convoys traversing Afghan terrain, the mixing of men and women, an ignorance of Afghan honor codes—all were degrading in their different forms. Drone warfare—launched at a distance by unseen and unassailable antagonists against defenseless individuals, families, and groups—was experienced as the most insidious humiliation to those honor bound to protect family and land. What could be an appropriate response in such asymmetrical warfare? It is in this context, Edwards argues, that suicide bombings came to be seen as the only way to recover one's honor in the community. Martyrdom, specifically the political act of striking an unjust oppressor, became the only way to fulfill the expectations of Islam.

Over the last twenty years of the U.S. occupation of Afghanistan, warfare radicalized the practice of martyrdom and martyrdom radicalized the practice of warfare. Radical sacrifice, of one's own life and that of others, changed the battlefield and the terms of battle. Ritualized death, while lamented, came to be actively sought out, even desirable. Suicide bombings became entrenched in everyday life. The perpetrators formed a caravan of people on a journey connected by a common purpose, but not a caravan of trade or commerce—a caravan of martyrs (Allison 2019; Malkasian 2017).

Think back to the discussions of religious expression in China and Mexico as well as your own experiences with religious communities. In what ways do those different religious contexts exemplify the blurring of boundaries between meaning and power?

How Is Globalization Changing Religion?

Explain how globalization is changing religion.

The forces of globalization—especially migration and time-space compression—are stretching and shaping religions and religious practices. Increasing immigration sometimes means that whole communities—their beliefs, religious architecture, religious leaders, and even their gods—relocate across national boundaries. Travel is broadening the encounters of people of different faiths. At the same time, information about religion is more widely available, and communication technologies enable religious institutions to transform their strategies for cultivating and educating participants. Cities, especially those serving as immigrant gateways, are generally the focal point of these encounters. It is here that new immigrants revitalize older religious institutions and construct new ones, often establishing deep ties to home and sophisticated networks of transnational exchange in the process.

RELOCATING RITUALS AND DEITIES FROM THE HOME COUNTRY

Globalization is transforming the ritual practices of religious communities large and small as congregations adapt to their members' mobility and the lively flow of ideas, information, and money across borders. These dynamics have rapidly spread the religious practices of a small, local Daoist village temple in rural China to New York and beyond through a network of Chinese restaurants across the United States. Today, thanks to globalization, the village temple's adherents and their local god have become international border–crossing immigrants.

Immigrant Chinese Gods. A few years ago, I walked into a little temple just off Canal Street in Manhattan's Chinatown as part of a project to map the Chinese religious communities in New York City (Guest 2003). Women and men, young and old, crowded into the noisy and smoky old storefront space, lighting incense, chatting with old friends, and saying prayers at the altar. Most were from the same small village in southeastern China, outside the provincial capital of Fuzhou. They had opened this temple to continue their religious practices in the United States and to serve as a gathering place for fellow immigrant villagers who lived and worked in and around New York City. Here, immigrants can reconnect with friends and relatives from their hometown, participate in rituals of devotion to their deities, and build networks of fellow devotees they may not have known before arriving in New York.

For a highly transient population, the temple serves as a center for exchanging information about jobs, housing, lawyers, doctors, employment agencies, and more. It operates a revolving loan fund to help members pay off smuggling debts or start up takeout restaurants. Through the temple, members contribute to building their home temple and support other charitable projects in their community back in China. Despite the undocumented status of many of these immigrants, the temple allows them to participate in civic activities and express themselves as contributing members of the community.

I later visited the home village temple in China to learn about village life and local religious traditions. One evening as I prepared to leave, the master of the temple expressed disappointment that I had not been able to meet the temple's spirit medium, a young woman who had a special relationship with the village's local god. He explained that on the first and fifteenth day of each lunar month, the local god possesses her and speaks through her to interpret the villagers' dreams and answer their questions: What name should I give my child? What herbal remedy will cure my ill? Will this woman be a good match for my son? When should I try to be smuggled out of China to the United States? I shared the master's disappointment at this missed opportunity and readily accepted his invitation to return on a future visit.

A year later I did return. The spirit medium, however, was gone. She and her husband, the temple master informed me, had moved to the United States and were now working in a restaurant in a place called "Indiana." I was disappointed again, but I expressed my concern that their departure may have disrupted a key element of temple life. The master then told me this story:

> Actually she still does it—only now it's from Indiana. Our believers
> work in restaurants all over the United States and some are still here
> in China. When they want to ask the advice of the god, they just pick
> up their cell phones and call. The spirit medium keeps careful records
> of their questions and dreams. Then on the first and fifteenth of the
> lunar month, just as always used to happen when she was here, she
> goes into a trance. The god leaves our temple here in China and flies
> to Indiana to possess her. Her husband then asks all the questions
> and writes down the answers. When the possession is over, the god
> returns to our village, and the spirit medium and her husband return
> all the phone calls to report the wisdom of the god.

Perhaps the look on my face and my one raised eyebrow alerted the master to my initial skepticism. "We can feel the god leave here every time," he said. "Really. Why don't you believe that? In America you have lots of Christians who believe the Christian god can be everywhere in the world at the same time. Why can't ours?"

The more I thought about it, the more I wondered why the local god of a village in China couldn't also be in Indiana. As an anthropologist of religion, I was reminded once again that religious practices and beliefs in today's age of globalization continue to be fluid and adaptable. After all, humans are adaptable, and so are their cultural constructions. Religion is a vibrant example of this core anthropological insight.

Anthropology challenges us to understand the beliefs and practices of others from within their own cultural framework. By making the strange familiar, we may then also make the familiar strange. In other words, we may take what seems natural and normal in our own lives and see it through new eyes.

The study of religion often forces anthropologists to address personal issues of identity, belief, and objectivity in ways that many other areas of study do not. Is it possible to fully understand a religion without being a practitioner? Can researchers remain objective if they practice the religion they study? Anthropologists of religion consider these important questions when conducting fieldwork and writing about their experiences. Through any experience of intensive fieldwork, we risk challenging, transforming, and possibly shattering our own worldviews even as we risk influencing those of the people we study. These dynamics are particularly volatile in the study of religion.

Toolkit

Thinking Like an Anthropologist
Religion in the Twenty-First Century

After reading this chapter, you should have a deeper understanding of some of the approaches anthropologists take to understanding the role of religion in people's lives and in communities large and small. These insights can serve as a toolkit as you consider expressions of religion in other countries and at home in the United States.

Think again about the story of Reverend William Barber II and the Poor People's Campaign (PPC) that opened the chapter, and recall the key questions we have asked about religion:

- **What is religion?**

- **What tools do anthropologists use to understand how religion works?**

- **In what ways is religion both a system of meaning and a system of power?**

- **How is globalization changing religion?**

After reading the chapter, can you apply the writings of Durkheim, Marx, Weber, Geertz, and Asad to events in the real world? Can you see the concepts of sacred and profane, ritual, rite of passage, communitas, symbol, and power emerge in religious expressions in your own life?

Barber and the PPC have decided to use their symbolic and material power to challenge what they consider unjust policies of the state. Of particular concern are the 140 million poor and low-wealth people in the United States. Over the past five years, the PPC has worked to build a grassroots coalition that includes these people, along with religious leaders, community organizers, union workers, anti-poverty activists, and interested leaders from other intersecting social movements. One of the campaign's innovations has been the creation of a Moral Budget in collaboration with leading Washington, D.C., economic think tanks like the Institute for Policy Studies and the Economic Policy Institute. The Moral Budget attempts to provide an alternative to the U.S. government's budget, replacing it instead with a financial blueprint that reflects the religious and social values embodied by the PPC. In speaking about the U.S. budget, Barber often says that a country that can spend $850 billion dollars each year on the military can find money to make sure people have enough to eat, a place to sleep, and a job that pays a living wage. Poverty is not a result of scarcity. It is a policy choice.

The PPC seeks to address not only poverty but also what it calls other "interlocking evils": systemic racism, ecological devastation, the war economy, and the distorted moral narrative often associated with Christian nationalism. Consider how the work of Barber and the PPC reveals religion to be a system of both meaning and power. As you think about religion in your own life and in your community, nation, and world, how can your anthropological toolkit help you better understand both the personal and public role of religion?

Key Terms

Chapter 14
Health, Illness, and the Body

Learning Objectives

- Describe from an anthropological perspective the relationship of culture with health and illness.

- Explain ways that different cultural conceptions of the body affect health practices.

- Report on strategies anthropologists use to help solve health-care problems.

- Assess how the distribution of health and illness mirrors that of wealth and power.

- Summarize an anthropological approach to analyzing and addressing global health challenges, such as COVID-19.

On the morning of May 24, 2022, an eighteen-year-old former student of Robb Elementary School in Uvalde, Texas, walked into the school, entered a classroom full of third and fourth graders, and opened fire with an AR-15-style semiautomatic rifle. Nineteen children and two teachers were killed. More were wounded. Despite frantic demands from parents who had rushed to the school,

---

Families and friends of those killed and injured in the mass shooting at Robb Elementary School in Uvalde, Texas, take to the streets to protest gun violence and honor the lives of those who were lost.

law enforcement waited seventy-eight minutes before entering the classroom and killing the shooter. Just days before the shooting, Daniel Defense, one of the nation's largest privately held manufacturers of guns—including the weapon used in Uvalde—posted an image on Twitter of a young boy holding a Daniel Defense gun. The caption read: "Train up a child in the way he should go and when he is old, he will not depart from it" (NBC News 2022). Despite the horror of the events at Robb Elementary School, and at hundreds of other schools before it, the loss of young lives to gun violence has become tragically familiar in American culture.

In 2020, gun violence became the number one cause of death for children and young people between the ages of one and eighteen, surpassing motor vehicle traffic deaths. Twelve children die from guns every day. Another thirty-two are shot and injured. Since the massacre at Columbine High School in Colorado gripped the nation in 1999, shootings at 331 schools in the United States have left 185 students and teachers dead and another 369 injured. In 2020 alone, the U.S. Centers for Disease Control reported 45,222 deaths caused by firearms, including 24,292 suicides and 19,384 homicides (Johns Hopkins Center for Gun Violence 2022). Since 1968, the first year statistics were recorded, there have been 1.7 million gun-related deaths in the United States, more than have died in all the wars in U.S. history. As one student said after the 2018 shooting at Marjory Stoneman Douglas High School in Parkland, Florida, "For our generation, it's not a question of if there will be a shooting, but when."

As anthropologists, how do we understand this American epidemic of gun violence and school shootings, which is unique among the world's industrialized nations? How do we understand the roots of American gun culture and its impact on public health? Americans own an estimated 400 million firearms for a population of 330 million people, more than double the ratio per capita of any country in the world. Forty percent of households and 30 percent of individuals own guns. Nearly twice as many men as women own guns. A gun that fires a projectile designed to penetrate and rip apart flesh at a distance has taken on a cultural meaning far beyond its component parts. Owners buy guns for protection, hunting, and sport. For some men, hunting together is an outdoor tradition, an expression of their masculinity, and a social glue connecting generations of men, families, and communities. Politicians, lawyers, and judges argue whether owning a gun is an inalienable right. But the costs of that right fall disproportionately on young people, poor people, and people of color, all of whom are more likely to be victims of gun violence.

In the aftermath of the Parkland shooting in 2018, survivors and students began to organize. While many politicians offered their thoughts and prayers and the National Rifle Association mobilized to defend gun rights, Parkland students demanded legislative action on gun safety measures. They marched, organized, lobbied, and generated a mass movement on social media in favor of raising the minimum age to purchase a gun from eighteen to twenty-one, imposing a waiting period, and requiring background checks for firearms purchases. Students walked out of classes, demanding action in March for Our Lives rallies across the country. After the Uvalde shooting, the young leaders of March for Our Lives stepped up again, holding gun safety rallies in hundreds of cities across the nation on June 11, 2022.

Still, our nation grapples with its cultural confusion about guns and violence. On June 24, 2022, the U.S. Supreme Court ruled against a New York State gun safety law and expanded gun rights. The next day, the U.S. Congress passed limited but significant gun safety legislation for the first time in nearly thirty years. Which direction is the country going in addressing this epidemic?

Conventional wisdom attributes health and longevity to a combination of "good genes" and good behavioral choices: eating right, not smoking, drinking in moderation, avoiding illegal drugs, exercising, and even flossing. This advice aligns with the core American values of individualism, personal responsibility, and the benefits of hard work and clean living. But are these factors sufficient to explain health and longevity—or the lack of it? Where does the epidemic of gun violence fit into this cultural narrative about health? Getting sick is a part of life. Everyone experiences colds, fevers, cuts and bruises, perhaps a broken bone. But some people get sick more often than others. Death and dying, too, are a part of life, but some people suffer more and die sooner, while others are healthier and live longer. Anthropologists are interested in knowing why.

In this chapter, we will explore anthropologists' interest in health, illness, and the body. Although these concerns have deep roots in our discipline, the specialization of *medical anthropology* has grown immensely in recent decades. Since the 1980s, anthropology's key research strategies—intensive fieldwork, extensive participant observation in local communities, and deep immersion in the daily lives of people and their local problems and experiences—have proven profoundly effective in solving pressing public health problems.

Medical anthropologists use a variety of analytical perspectives to examine the wide range of experiences and practices that humans associate with disease, illness, health, well-being, and the body—both today and in the past. We study the spread of diseases and pathogens in the human population (known as epidemiology) through the lens of *medical ecology*: the interaction of diseases with the natural environment and human culture. Looking more broadly, medical anthropologists use an *interpretivist approach* to study health systems as systems of meaning: How do humans across cultures make sense of health and illness? How do we think, talk, and feel about illness, pain, suffering, birth, and mortality? *Critical medical anthropology* explores the impact of inequality on human health in two important ways. First, it considers how economic and political systems, race, class, gender, and sexuality create and perpetuate unequal access to health care. Second, it examines how health systems themselves are systems of power that promote health disparities by defining who is sick, who gets treated, and how treatment is provided.

Medical anthropology's holistic examination of epidemiology, meaning, and power assumes that health and illness are more than a result of germs, individual behavior, and genes. Health is also a product of our environment—our access to adequate nutrition, housing, education, and health care and the absence of poverty, violence, and warfare. This has become particularly evident since the outbreak of COVID-19 in early 2020. The COVID-19 virus presents itself in the same way to everyone, but infections, hospitalizations, and deaths have reflected age, access to health care, race, gender, class, vaccination status, and, in the United States, political affiliation. In this chapter, we will explore the following questions:

- **How does culture shape health and illness?**
- **How do different cultural conceptions of the body affect health practices?**
- **How can anthropologists help solve health-care problems?**
- **Why does the distribution of health and illness mirror that of wealth and power?**
- **How does anthropology help analyze and address global health challenges like COVID-19?**

By the end of the chapter, you will understand how anthropologists approach the study of health, illness, and the body and how these concepts vary across cultures. You will recognize how your own conceptions of health and illness have been culturally constructed. You will be able to critically analyze both the systems of power that shape access to health care and the ways in which health systems create and exacerbate inequalities within and between populations.

How Does Culture Shape Health and Illness?

Describe from an anthropological perspective the relationship of culture with health and illness.

health
The absence of disease and infirmity as well as the presence of physical, mental, and social well-being.

What does it mean to be healthy? The World Health Organization proposes that **health** includes not merely the absence of disease and infirmity but complete physical, mental, and social well-being. This is a standard that few people in the world currently attain. Perhaps it is enough to be functionally healthy—not perfectly well, but healthy enough to do what you need to do: get up in the morning, go to school, go to work, reproduce the species. What level of health do you expect, hope for, and strive for? What level of health enables your culture to thrive?

Medical anthropologists have dedicated significant effort to documenting healing practices and health systems among a diversity of communities around the globe, from Indigenous and tribal societies and urban metropolises to farming communities and groups of migrant workers. In the process, medical anthropologists have identified a vast array of ideas about the causes of health and disease, different notions of the body, and varied cultural strategies for addressing pain, treating illness, and promoting health. One key finding is that these beliefs and practices are intricately intertwined with how local cultures imagine the world works and conceive of the relationship between the body and its surroundings.

In assessing how disease and health conditions affect specific populations and how specific cultural groups diagnose, manage, and treat health-related problems, medical anthropologists have found it useful to distinguish between disease, illness, and sickness. A **disease** is a discrete, natural entity that can be clinically identified and treated by a health professional. A disease may be caused genetically or through infection by bacteria, a virus, or parasites. These bacteria, viruses, or parasites are the same regardless of location or cultural context. Illness, however, is more than the biological disease. **Illness** is an individual patient's experience of being unwell—the culturally defined understanding of disease. It includes the way the patient feels about it, talks about it, thinks about it, and experiences it within a particular cultural context. Diseases can be observed, measured, and treated as biological entities by sufferers and healers. But culture gives meaning to disease, shaping the human experience of illness, pain, suffering, dying, and death (Singer and Baer 2007).

Sickness refers to an individual's public expression of illness and disease, including social expectations about how one should behave and how others should respond. Being sick may release the sick person from social obligations like work, school, or parenting. But sickness also requires the patient to perform a certain "sick role" in order to receive the corresponding social support. In American culture, this involves showing a clear wish to get well and a willingness to cooperate with medical experts (from parents to doctors). If, for instance, you are sick enough to miss class and expect to be released from schoolwork, the social agreement about sickness suggests that you should be resting at home and following a doctor's advice.

People recognize widely different symptoms, illnesses, and causes of health challenges and, accordingly, have developed widely different strategies for achieving and maintaining health. Though the stereotypical Western images of health care often revolve around doctors in white coats, dentists' chairs, hospitals, strong medications, and advanced technology (such as X-rays, MRIs, and CT scans), medical anthropologists have found that these are not the primary points of access to health care for most people in the world. Nor are they even the first

disease

A discrete natural entity that can be clinically identified and treated by a health professional.

illness

An individual patient's experience of being unwell.

sickness

An individual's public expression of illness and disease, including social expectations about how one should behave and how others should respond.

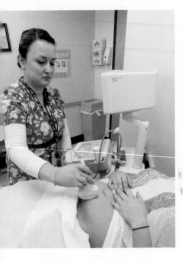

Globally, people have created a vast array of healing practices, all intricately intertwined with local cultural understandings of disease, health, illness, and the body. (*Left*) A clinical assistant performs an ultrasound on a pregnant woman. (*Right*) An Indian healer provides villagers with ayurvedic medicines.

ethnomedicine

Local systems of health and healing rooted in culturally specific norms and values.

ethnopharmacology

The documentation and description of the local use of natural substances in healing remedies and practices.

point of access for most people in Western countries. Rather, before seeking the assistance of a trained medical professional, people everywhere apply their personal medical knowledge, their own strategies—often handed down within families or communities—for dealing with disease, illness, pain, and discomfort.

ETHNOMEDICINE

Over the years, medical anthropologists have focused extensive research on **ethnomedicine**. This field involves the comparative study of local systems of health and healing rooted in culturally specific norms and values, with a focus on how local cultures create unique strategies for identifying and treating disease and conceptualizing experiences of health, illness, and the physical world.

Early research on ethnomedicine, which focused primarily on non-Western health systems, emphasized natural healing remedies such as herbs, teas, and massage; reliance on religious ritual in health practices; and the role of locally trained healers such as shamans, spirit mediums, and priests as health-care professionals. The subdiscipline of **ethnopharmacology** emerged from efforts to document and describe the local use of natural substances, such as herbs, powders, teas, and animal products, in healing remedies and practices. But today, medical anthropologists use the concept of ethnomedicine to refer to local health systems everywhere (Green 1999; Saillant and Genest 2007). Even Western biomedicine—which emphasizes science and technology in healing but also reflects a particular system of cultural meanings—is considered through the lens of ethnomedicine.

Healing Practices of Tibetan Buddhism Applied in Northern India. French anthropologist Laurent Pordié (2008) has documented one typical system of ethnomedicine—a variation of Tibetan medicine practiced in the sparsely populated Ladakh region of northern India. Roughly three times the

size of Switzerland and straddling the northwestern Himalayas, Ladakh is home to 275,000 villagers, mostly Tibetans, living primarily in remote areas at altitudes up to 5,000 meters (16,400 feet). Their only health care is provided by approximately 200 *amchis*, traditional healers whose practices are deeply rooted in Tibetan Buddhism.

Amchi medicine is based on achieving bodily and spiritual balance between the individual and the surrounding universe. *Amchis* diagnose ailments by asking questions of the patient, examining bodily wastes, and carefully taking the patient's pulse. Recommended treatments include changes in diet and behavior—both social and religious—and the use of natural medicines made from local plants and minerals. Shaped into pills, these remedies are then boiled in water and taken by the patient as an infusion, or drink. Pordié reports that *amchi* treatments are effective for the vast majority of the Ladakhis' health problems, such as respiratory difficulty from the high altitude and from smoke exposure in dwellings, hypertension from high-salt diets, and psychological stress. *Amchis* do not perform surgery. Patients who need surgery are transported, if possible, to an urban area to be treated by a doctor trained in Western biological medicine.

Amchi medicine plays a vital role in the survival of Ladakhis. But *amchis* and their healing practices are under threat from Westernization, militarization, and economic liberalization. For example, the Indian government strongly favors Western biological medicine over traditional ethnomedicine, though it is still unable to provide care to its dispersed rural population. The pervasive presence of

MAP 14.1
Ladakh

An *amchi*, a traditional healer, mixes medicines in his home pharmacy in Ladakh, India.

the Indian military due to civil unrest in the bordering Kashmir region inhibits the movement of *amchis* as they gather plants and minerals for natural medicines. In addition, urbanization and modernization have increasingly fragmented community life. In the past, *amchi* healers bartered their services for help in plowing, harvesting, and raising livestock. The *amchis* then had time to forage for medicinal plants. But with the penetration of market-oriented economics even into the rural Ladakh region, the barter system has been undermined. *Amchis* must now run their therapeutic practices more like businesses, selling medicines and charging for services rather than bartering. Their time to gather medicines has become limited. And with increasing social mobility, the intergenerational transmission of *amchi* skills has been disrupted.

To address this challenge to the *amchi* system, Pordié and a French nongovernmental organization, Nomad RSI, have been working with local *amchis* to establish a coordinated system for growing medicinal plants and distributing them among far-flung villages. *Amchis* from across Ladakh now gather annually to share diagnosis and treatment strategies, and a school has been established to train new practitioners.

Although Tibetan medicine is struggling in rural areas where it has been practiced for centuries, it is experiencing unprecedented prominence internationally. Pordié's study also considers how the local *amchi* system of healing is entering the global health arena. Over the last thirty years, as more Tibetans have migrated abroad and carried their cultural and religious practices with them, Tibetan medicine has been embraced as an "alternative medicine." The international health market, particularly in Europe and North America, has welcomed Tibetan medicine as natural, spiritual, and holistic, drawing as it does from traditional Indigenous practices, Buddhist moral values, and Tibetan ecological worldviews. *Amchis* and their practices of Tibetan medicine have become quite popular.

Medical anthropologists like Pordié have played a significant role in documenting the diverse forms of treatment and care as well as the complex medical epistemologies (ways of knowing) developed by local cultures across the globe. As we will continue to see in our discussion of Western biomedicine, all medical systems constitute a form of ethnomedicine because they develop from and are embedded in particular local cultural realities. From the perspective of medical anthropology, we might also call all healers "ethno-healers" who practice local health knowledge about disease, illness, and health—whether they are Tibetan *amchis* or American cardiovascular surgeons.

BIOMEDICINE

biomedicine

A practice, often associated with Western medicine, that seeks to apply the principles of biology and the natural sciences to the practice of diagnosing diseases and promoting healing.

Biomedicine is the approach to health that has risen to predominance in many Western cultures. **Biomedicine** seeks to apply the principles of biology and the natural sciences (such as physics and chemistry) to the practice of diagnosing diseases and promoting healing. Individual and institutional practitioners of biomedicine—whether doctors, pharmacies, hospitals, medical schools, or pharmaceutical companies—work to clinically identify discrete natural disease entities that can be diagnosed and treated by biomedically trained health professionals. The term *biomedicine* encompasses many local variations and a wide range of treatment practices. But the use of medication, surgery, and other invasive treatments is characteristic of biomedical healing practices (Baer, Singer, and Susser 2003; Saillant and Genest 2007).

Western industrialized countries employ biomedicine in different ways, as we will consider later in our discussion of the anthropology of birth. For example, British doctors are far less concerned about elevated blood pressure and cholesterol counts than their counterparts in the United States are. The German health system, which uses far fewer antibiotics than other Western health systems do, recognizes two complementary approaches: *schulmedizin* (school medicine), which focuses on typical biomedical treatments, and *naturheilkunde* (nature cure), which draws on natural remedies. Biomedicine in the United States emphasizes the most extreme treatments—psychotropic drugs, antibiotics, cholesterol and blood pressure medications, C-section births, and hysterectomies (Payer 1996).

Western biomedicine or alternative medicines? At a biotech company near Berlin, Germany, researchers develop natural remedies to complement biomedical treatments.

Because biomedicine is closely linked with Western economic and political expansion, it has taken hold well beyond its original local cultural boundaries and has increasingly gained an aura of universality, modernity, and progress. But medical anthropologists have been careful to point out the ways in which, like other ethnomedical systems, the epistemology and practice of Western biomedicine are rooted in a particular system of knowledge. This system draws heavily on European enlightenment values of rationality, individualism, and progress— values and ideas that are culturally specific and not universally held. The individual body is the focus of treatment. Diagnosis and treatment are based on rational scientific data. And there is a firm conviction that direct intervention through surgery and medications based on scientific facts will positively affect health.

ARE THERE OTHER GLOBAL HEALTH SYSTEMS?

Although Western biomedicine is intimately tied to Western culture and its values, anthropologists also acknowledge that with the spread of Western cultural influences, biomedicine has crossed beyond its original cultural and regional boundaries to become a global health system: Biomedicine is now used in a wide array of countries as well as by international health agencies that engage in health promotion globally. But are there health systems other than biomedicine that function on a global level? Earlier in this chapter, we discussed the growing popularity of Tibetan medicine, especially in Europe and North America. Now let's

What are those purple circles on Olympic swimmer Michael Phelps's shoulders? Phelps, winner of a record 23 gold medals, is one of a growing number of athletes using the Chinese healing practice of cupping, a technique that places specialized cups on the skin, which, when heated, create suction to stimulate blood flow and healing.

consider Chinese medicine as one health system with a long history; elaborate theories of health, illness, and the body; a global reach; and proven effectiveness (e.g., Farquhar 1986; Scheid 2002; Zhan 2009).

Chinese Medicine Today. In very general terms, Chinese medicine conceptualizes health as a harmonious relationship between Heaven and Earth, which are considered the major forces of the universe. An individual's *qi*—translated as "breath" or "air" and referring to an energy found in all living things—must be balanced and flowing in equilibrium with the rest of the universe for that person to be healthy. Illness occurs when the *qi* is blocked and the flow and balance are disrupted. In traditional Chinese medicine, health-care practices such as acupuncture, *tuina* (therapeutic massage), acupressure, moxibustion (the burning of herbs near the skin), and the consumption of healing herbs and teas promote health by restoring the free flow of *qi* along the body's meridians, or energy pathways (Farquhar 1986; Scheid 2002).

In her book *Other-Worldly: Making Chinese Medicine through Transnational Frames* (2009), medical anthropologist Mei Zhan challenges many of the stereotypes of Chinese medicine, including the perception that it is somehow emblematic of an ancient Chinese culture, regionally limited with fixed healing practices that are the antithesis of, or merely "alternative" to, Western biomedicine. Instead, Zhan argues that Chinese medical practices vary widely even within China. Rather than undergoing a regimented and fixed set of health-care practices, patients participate in a dynamic health-care environment. Patients and doctors carefully negotiate treatments. And no good physician ever writes the same prescription twice, because the treatment must meet the needs of each specific patient (Scheid 2002).

Zhan notes three key moments that have significantly reshaped modern Chinese medicine over the past century. First, the early-twentieth-century expansion of Western biomedicine—with its emphasis on institution building, laboratory research, clinical and teaching practices, and even insurance policies—reshaped Chinese medical thinking and practice. Today, the everyday world of Chinese medicine includes interactions with biomedical professionals. Patients move back and forth between biomedicine and Chinese medicine.

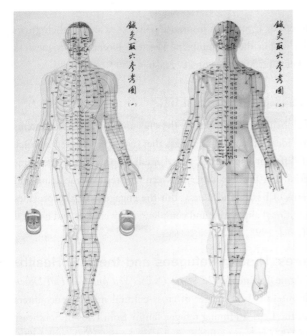

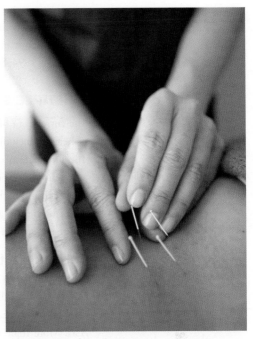

Chinese medicine is a globalized health system with its own internal logic for diagnosing disease and promoting healing. A Chinese diagram of meridians, or energy pathways (*left*), indicates potential sites of blockage that can be restored through treatment with acupuncture (*right*), massage, herbs, and teas.

Second, upon the founding of the People's Republic of China in 1949, the new Chinese government moved to institutionalize traditional Chinese medicine, subsidize research, formalize teaching, and establish a process for professional certification. The government widely promoted traditional Chinese medicine as a low-tech, low-cost approach to preventive care and trained and deployed "barefoot doctors" to promote health care in every rural Chinese community. The government also exported traditional Chinese medicine—including medicines, doctors, and health-promotion strategies—to the developing world, particularly Africa, to establish international ties of solidarity with other developing nations. This move marked a rapid expansion of Chinese medicine beyond China's national borders into the international arena.

Finally, Zhan documents the shift of Chinese medicine beginning in the 1980s from primarily a developing-world medical practice to one with established niches in developed countries. Traditional Chinese medicine has become popular with cosmopolitan consumers in China, North America, and Europe, both for preventive care and as an alternative treatment for illness when biomedicine proves ineffective. The flow of Chinese medical practitioners and Chinese medical knowledge has increased encounters with Chinese medicine, particularly along routes between Asia and Europe and across the Pacific Ocean. Throughout much of California, for example, acupuncture and Chinese herbal medicines have grown increasingly popular. They have gained a foothold in mainstream medical practices ranging from biomedical hospitals to medical schools, and they are increasingly covered by U.S. health insurance policies—a sign of their growing acceptance even within the predominant Western biomedical framework (Farquhar 1994; Scheid and MacPherson 2012; Zhan 2009).

MULTIPLE SYSTEMS OF HEALING

The current era of globalization has spurred the encounter of multiple systems of healing, including ideas of health and illness that overlap and often conflict. The intersection of different approaches, called **medical pluralism**, often creates tensions, especially in the encounter between Western biomedicine and other cultural patterns of health and illness. But the engagement also provides opportunities for additional alternative and complementary choices and medical options to emerge (Lock 1993, 2002).

medical pluralism
The intersection of multiple cultural approaches to healing.

Colliding Cultures: Hmong Refugees and the U.S. Health-Care System.

Anne Fadiman's *The Spirit Catches You and You Fall Down* (1997) captures the intensity and danger of cross-cultural medical encounters through the story of the Lees, a Hmong refugee family from Laos in Southeast Asia. More than 150,000 Hmong refugees fled Laos in the 1970s and 1980s, many of whom had fought clandestinely with the United States on the losing side of wars in Vietnam and Laos. More than 12,000 Hmong—including the Lees—eventually settled in Merced, a city of only 61,000 people in California's agricultural Central Valley.

The Lees' fourteenth child, Lia Lee, was born on July 9, 1982, apparently a healthy, happy baby. But at three months of age, her seizures began. At first, her family comforted her and cared for her at home. Her uncontrollable convulsions on October 24 led the family to Merced Community Medical Center (MCMC), a small county hospital and a teaching hospital where first-year residents from the University of California, Davis, train in family practice. The October 24 visit began a long and painful encounter—a collision—between the Lee family and the U.S. health-care system.

Unbeknownst to the doctors at MCMC, the Lees had already diagnosed Lia's illness as *qaug dab peg*, which translates into English as "epilepsy." Familiar with *qaug dab peg* in their own cultural context, the Lees were ambivalent about their daughter's illness. The seizures, they knew, could be dangerous. But among the Hmong, those suffering from *qaug dab peg* were held in high esteem. Many became powerful shamans—traditional healers and community visionaries. The Lees had come to the hospital for their daughter to be healed, but they also wondered about her potentially auspicious future.

Also unbeknownst to the MCMC doctors, the Lees knew what had caused Lia's illness and how to treat it. She suffered from soul loss. Her older sister had allowed the front door of their small home to slam, and the loud noise had

MAP 14.2
Laos

scared Lia's soul away. An elaborate ritual of soul-calling conducted by a Hmong shaman could trap the lost soul and return it to Lia's body. But her seizures on that October night were overwhelming, and her parents feared that she would die without immediate care.

By the time the Lees arrived at the hospital, the seizures had stopped. With no clear symptoms to treat, the doctors were at a loss. The hospital had no translator, and the Lees spoke no English. The resident on call misdiagnosed the remaining symptoms as an infection, prescribed medication, and sent the family home. Unfortunately, the prescription and medication instructions were written in English, which the Lees could not understand. Lia was misdiagnosed at the hospital again on November 11. Finally, on March 3, 1983, the family arrived with Lia still convulsing. A young family member who spoke some English translated. The resident on call diagnosed the cause as epilepsy. Then the child was subjected to a battery of invasive tests, including a spinal tap, a CT scan, a chest X-ray, and blood work—none of which the hospital staff could adequately explain to Lia's parents. The child had experienced five months of seizures small and large without proper diagnosis and medication, and now she endured a terrifying night at the hospital.

Between the ages of eight months and four and a half years, Lia was admitted to MCMC seventeen times and made more than a hundred outpatient visits for treatment of her seizures. Over the same period, her doctors prescribed fourteen different medications in different combinations and dosages and changed her prescription twenty-three times—all with a family unfamiliar with English, Western medical practices, or the U.S. system of weights and measures needed to determine the proper dosages.

The collision of cultures escalated when doctors decided that Lia's ongoing seizures were caused by her parents' failure to comply with the medication prescriptions. This, the lead doctor determined, qualified as child neglect and child abuse. Acting on the doctor's concerns, the county courts ordered Lia removed from her parents' custody and placed in foster care so that her medicines could be properly administered. The doctors thought they were acting to protect the child. Her parents, however, unable to understand the medical, legal, or moral logic of removing a child from her family and convinced that they were doing everything in their power to care for their daughter, could only imagine that they were being punished for some unknown reason.

The courts eventually returned Lia to her parents after nearly a year in foster care. Her condition had not improved. Her parents, in fact, felt that her cognitive abilities and social skills had deteriorated during the year away. Despite the parents' efforts to comply with Lia's drug regimen, another series of catastrophic epileptic seizures landed her in MCMC again and finally in a children's hospital in nearby Fresno. Treatment of the seizures was ultimately ineffective. Despite

Foua Yang weeps as she talks about her daughter, Lia Lee, who died on August 31, 2012, at the age of thirty after a lifelong struggle for health. A collision of two cultural approaches to healing left her severely wounded in childhood.

what hospital staff considered heroic measures, Lia was left with the dramatically reduced brain activity that doctors call a "persistent vegetative state." Doctors removed all life support and feeding tubes. She was returned to MCMC and finally to the Lees' home.

Considering her lingering fevers, the medical professionals expected her to die. But Lia's parents placed her in soothing herbal baths, fed her, carried her with them, slept with her in their bed, and continued the elaborate Hmong rituals of soul-calling to return her to health. Though her brain activity never returned, Lia did not die. Her parents were convinced that all the medicines the doctors had forced on her had left her in this condition. (Indeed, Fadiman found some evidence suggesting that Lia's massive final seizure may have been caused by a hospital-acquired infection.) They hoped that their traditional healing methods might still return her lost soul to her body.

Bridging Cultural Divides via Illness Narratives. Fadiman's interviews found that the parties in this cross-cultural health encounter held vastly different views of what had occurred. Most of the doctors criticized the parents as uncooperative. They debated whether this stemmed from cultural barriers, lack of intelligence, or character flaws that kept them from caring properly for their daughter. Many saw the parents as ungrateful for all the effort and resources that had been expended on their daughter's case. Few made any attempt to ask the Lees how they understood Lia's illness and how they would treat it. In contrast, the Lees considered most of the medical staff to be uncommunicative, arrogant, cold, and punitive; they also described the medical procedures Lia had undergone as invasive, culturally inappropriate, and ineffective. They never understood how the government could take their beloved daughter from them to be put in the care of strangers.

At the conclusion of her research, Fadiman contacted a preeminent medical anthropologist, Arthur Kleinman of Harvard University. Kleinman, a specialist in cross-cultural issues in health and illness, has been instrumental in formulating a concept of collecting illness narratives as a way to bridge cultural divides in treating illness and promoting health (Kleinman 1988). **Illness narratives** are the personal stories people tell to explain their illness. The narratives reveal the psychological, social, and cultural aspects that give illness its context and meaning. These stories can provide healers with an essential framework for developing treatment strategies that will make sense to the patient and have the greatest chance of success.

Would Lia's treatment have been effective had the MCMC medical staff asked the family to provide this illness narrative—the cultural framework through which they viewed the cause and potential treatment of her illness? Doing so might have provided an avenue for engaging the family in a cooperative treatment process. Through that process, multiple systems of healing and concepts of health and illness might have intersected to create a multifaceted approach to healing for Lia.

Encounters of distinct medical systems like that experienced by Lia and her family in the California health-care system will only increase as globalization continues to break down barriers to the flow of ideas, people, diseases, medical treatments, and health practitioners from one world region to another. These encounters will continue to challenge and expand our notions of disease, illness, and health care.

How Do Different Cultural Conceptions of the Body Affect Health Practices?

Explain ways that different cultural conceptions of the body affect health practices.

We live in our bodies. We are embodied beings. Our bodies mediate all of our experiences of living in and encountering the world. But what exactly is a body, and what does the body signify?

Anthropological research has challenged the prevalent biomedical notion of the body as an isolated, natural, and universal object. Instead, anthropologists recognize the body as a product of specific environments, cultural experiences, and historical contexts. Culture has shaped the evolution of the human body and shapes individual bodies today. Culture also shapes our experience of the world around us, including how we feel and how others feel about us. And health-care systems are a key site of contestation over the management of bodies.

BIOMEDICAL CONCEPTIONS OF THE BODY

Nancy Scheper-Hughes and Margaret Lock (1987) recount a now-famous story of a challenging case that illustrates the powerful influence of cultural values on understanding the body in biomedical healing practices. At a teaching hospital, the case of a woman suffering chronic, debilitating headaches was presented to a lecture hall of 250 medical students. When asked about her ailment, the woman recounted that her alcoholic husband beat her, that she had been virtually housebound for five years while caring for her ailing and incontinent mother-in-law, and that she worried about her teenage son, who was failing high school. Then one of the medical students raised her hand and asked, "But what is the *real* cause of her headaches?" By this the student meant, What is the real *biomedical* diagnosis—what neurochemical changes in the woman's body created the pain? In the mind of the medical student, the patient's statements were irrelevant to the task of identifying the cause of her pain or determining a treatment. The student's biomedical training, with its focus on the individual body, science, and technology, had not prepared her to recognize that social experiences might produce embodied responses.

THE HUMAN MICROBIOME

Is the typical biomedical notion of the discrete, treatable, individual body really based in science? Recent scientific research suggests that our bodies are not as independent or as self-contained as we once thought. Researchers at the Human Microbiome Project have discovered that the human body, made up of 10 trillion cells, is also host to 100 trillion microbes—microscopic organisms such as bacteria, viruses, and fungi—that live on and within our bodies. Rather than being discrete biological entities, our bodies appear to be more like complex ecosystems (think tropical rain forests), habitats for trillions of different organisms living with us. Thus, we can define the **human microbiome** as the complete collection of microorganisms in the body's ecosystem.

human microbiome
The complete collection of microorganisms in the human body's ecosystem.

These microbes are not random hitchhikers, opportunistic parasites, or dangerous outsider enemies of our bodies. They are deeply integrated into the ways our bodies work. Microbes help us digest food, synthesize vitamins, make natural antibiotics, produce natural moisturizer for our skin, guide our immune system, and spur the development of body parts (such as the intestines). Scientists suggest that we have evolved alongside these microbes as part of our personal ecosystem for promoting health and combating the pathogens that create disease in our bodies. We not only tolerate these microbes, we need them (Helmreich 2009).

Discoveries about microbes' role in our experience of health and illness open the door to rethinking one of the central tenets of Western biomedicine—the notion of the discrete individual body—and offer new pathways for the innovative treatment of both common and rare diseases (Zimmer 2010, 2011).

THE BODY AND CHILDBIRTH ACROSS CULTURES

The anthropology of childbirth provides one clear example of the cross-cultural variation of health beliefs, practices, and understandings of the body. Anthropologists consider childbirth a biosocial event. Yes, the physiology of childbirth—the biological process—is the same no matter where the birth occurs. But anthropological research shows that cultures around the world have developed unique social and cultural practices and beliefs about pregnancy, delivery, and the treatment of newborns and their mothers that shape people's understandings and experiences of childbirth. For example, a popular view of birth in the United States sees it as a medical procedure—what Robbie Davis-Floyd

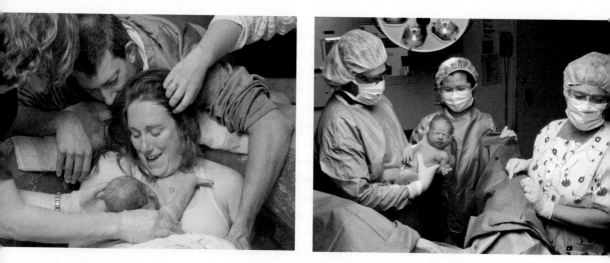

The physiological process of childbirth may be universal, but the experience of childbirth, including the approach toward pain, varies from culture to culture. (*Left*) The Dutch view birth as an entirely natural process that often takes place at home with no pain medication. (*Right*) In the United States, women become patients admitted to a delivery room for a procedure in a sterile environment with lots of equipment.

(1992) calls the "technocratic birth." In this view, people having babies become patients, seeking the assistance of a medical professional to resolve a dangerous life crisis. Melissa Cheyney and Robbie Davis-Floyd's collection *Birth in Eight Cultures* (2019) reveals that, in contrast, other cultural frameworks emphasize humanistic, holistic care in which birth is perceived as a natural, physiological process—one that is both highly fulfilling and part of normal life. These differing conceptualizations shape and justify the practices each culture uses to support, monitor, and control the birth process. Such practices include the location of the birth, the personnel who attend, the decision-making authority as the birth proceeds, and the expectations of pain and pain management.

Birth experiences in Brazil and Japan contrast sharply. In Brazil, the technocratic model of childbirth dominates. Today, most births take place in hospitals—a significant shift from the latter part of the twentieth century, when home births were most common. The move from home to hospital has successfully reduced deaths from post-partum hemorrhage and obstructed labor, but widespread use of high-tech machines and the overuse of medical interventions that are not always based on solid scientific evidence have contributed to continuing poor maternal and neonatal outcomes. Doctors with technology may intervene too much, too soon, including performing cesarean sections—a surgical procedure by which the baby is removed directly from the mother's abdomen rather than through the birth canal—before babies are finished developing. Today, 55 percent of babies born in Brazil are delivered by C-section, much higher than the global rate of approximately 20 percent, in part because C-sections have become highly sought after as a marker of class status.

Class and inequality shape Brazilian women's birth experiences by determining where births take place in the country's two-tiered health system of public and private hospitals. Government-subsidized public hospitals are intensively technocratic with high levels of medical intervention, including frequent vaginal exams, reliance on pain medication, administration of oxytocin to speed delivery, and widespread use of episiotomies—cutting the vaginal opening to widen the birth canal. Forty-five percent of births in public hospitals are by C-section, and only 5 percent of women give birth with no interventions. In contrast, 88 percent of births in private hospitals occur via C-section. Women regularly schedule birth appointments, and their labor is induced. Seventy percent of women do not go into spontaneous labor (Williamson and Matsuoka 2019).

In contrast, Japanese birth practices tend to be more humanistic. Birth is seen as a normal, natural, physiological process not to be tampered with or altered physically. A uniform stipend for all pregnant women makes class less likely to affect care. Nutrition is considered essential prenatal care for the pregnant mother, who is growing and nurturing a fetus. Hospital births are common, but so are births at home, in birth centers, and in obstetric clinics. Medical interventions during labor and childbirth are infrequent. Women freely move about, eat and drink at will, and go through labor and birth in an upright position. Midwives accompany most births, providing emotional support, encouragement, and medical advice. Japan's maternal and perinatal mortality rates are low. Most Japanese women prefer vaginal delivery, and overall, Japanese culture values childbirth's life-changing nature. Japan's C-section rate, 19 percent, is one of the lowest in the world (Williamson and Matsuoka 2019).

Can culture shape women's experience of pain during childbirth? Brigitte Jordan and Robbie Davis-Floyd (1993) have noted that some women in every culture give birth without pain, but a certain amount of pain is expected in almost all cultures. What differs from one medical system to another is how that pain is handled. Their study explored the possibility that cultural expectations of pain during childbirth shape the actual experience and display of pain by laboring mothers. In Japan, labor pain is considered a positive path to becoming a strong and empowered woman. Most Japanese women go through childbirth without a pain relief intervention, such as an epidural (Williamson and Matsuoka 2019). In the United States, in contrast, where labor and childbirth are more medicalized, women request an epidural in 71 percent of births (White 2018).

The United States' for-profit maternity care system is highly technocratic and medicalized. Prejudices within the medical profession and overall culture against home births mean that there are few choices available in birth place or provider. Ninety-eight percent of American births occur in a hospital, where they may benefit from access to sophisticated equipment and the attention of highly trained medical professionals. But humanistic approaches are changing the system rapidly. Episiotomy rates have dropped from 70 percent to 14 percent in recent decades. Midwives participate in 11 percent of births, up from

2 percent in 1980 (Cheyney et al. 2019). While global rates for C-section births have increased, U.S. rates have remained steady in recent years at 32 percent, though this is still an increase from 20.7 percent in 1996 (U.S. Centers for Disease Control and Prevention 2020).

The global variation in C-section rates raises questions about how many of these procedures are performed out of necessity and how many are influenced by cultural understandings of birth and the institutional pressures that shape health care in hospitals. Rates also vary from region to region in the United States, a reflection of regional cultural variations in the practice of medicine rather than regional variation in rates of birth complications.

The variety of cultural approaches to labor and childbirth—a common human biological activity—suggests the extent to which cultural concepts of the body, health, illness, and pain, along with social and economic inequality, may shape every aspect of a medical system.

THE BODY AND DISABILITY

Anthropology's increasing attention to the body has been accompanied by a recent expansion of work on issues of disability—the embodied experiences of people with impairments as shaped by broader forms of social inequality (Ginsburg and Rapp 2013). Significantly, anthropologists have explored the ways disability is not simply lodged in the body but is socially defined—specifically by the often painful and isolating encounters with social and material conditions that "dis-able" and impair people considered to be atypical in a particular culture. So, for instance, people restricted to wheelchairs experience their impairment— are disabled—differently by the presence or absence of accessibility ramps.

Anyone can experience impairment and disability, and most people will at some point in their lives. In fact, being "able-bodied" might be considered only a temporary condition. This is a distinctive quality of disabilities when compared to other systems of power and inequality, which may affect only certain portions of a population. Disability may include sensory impairments to hearing and sight, limited mobility, epilepsy, autism, psychiatric illness, or chronic pain or dementia related to aging. Or, disability may result from a sudden illness like a heart attack, an accident, or warfare. These disabilities may interact with other stratified systems of power to create additional vulnerabilities. Poverty, warfare, natural disasters, and unequal access to health care directly affect the experience of disability. Through groundbreaking cross-cultural ethnographic work (Friedner 2015; Ingstad and Whyte 2007; Kohrman 2005; Nakamura 2006; Phillips 2011), anthropologists have also explored how the lived experience of disability varies widely within and between cultures. (See, for instance, Kulick and Rydstrom's study on sexuality and disability in Chapter 8.)

How Can Anthropologists Help Solve Health-Care Problems?

Report on strategies anthropologists use to help solve health-care problems.

Anthropologists can apply research strategies and key theoretical concepts of our field to solve pressing public health problems, understand the spread of disease, and improve the delivery of health care. In fact, the work of an anthropologist may be just as crucial to explaining and resolving health challenges as that of a physician, epidemiologist, pathologist, or virologist. The following discussion illustrates this point through the groundbreaking efforts of anthropologists working in Haiti and Papua New Guinea.

CREATING A PUBLIC HEALTH SYSTEM IN RURAL HAITI

MAP 14.3
Cange, Haiti

When the American Paul Farmer first visited Cange, Haiti, in 1983, the remote village of one hundred families was one of the poorest places in the country. Most people in Haiti lived on $1 a day, but residents of Cange lived on less. The village also struggled with high levels of infant mortality, childhood malnutrition, typhoid, dysentery, HIV/AIDS, and tuberculosis. Many residents were water refugees, having been pushed off their land by the construction of a hydroelectric dam that flooded their valley to provide power to Haiti's cities and irrigation for large landholders and agribusinesses downstream. With the best farmland taken out of production by the dam's reservoir, the surrounding area suffered from widespread deforestation, soil erosion, and terrible health statistics (Farmer 2006).

Farmer's work in Cange, popularized in the best-selling biography *Mountains beyond Mountains* (Kidder 2003), began with the encouragement of a Haitian Anglican priest, Father Fritz Lafontant, who had been working in the area for years. In 1984, the year after Farmer's first visit to Haiti, he enrolled in Harvard's medical school and doctoral program in anthropology. He believed that anthropology would be essential to addressing the health needs of poor Haitians; the delivery of medicines and medical procedures would not be enough. Deeper questions would need answers: What made the people sick? How could they stay healthy after being treated? The basic approaches of an anthropologist—understanding the local language, norms, values, classifications of reality, and religious beliefs—would help a trained physician think about health in the broadest possible sense.

While at Harvard, Farmer immediately began to apply what he was learning—the research strategies of anthropology and the professional knowledge

of medicine—to create a public health system for Cange. Living in the community and speaking the local language, Farmer engaged in a process of listening to the residents' needs and experiences and working with them to identify and treat their public health problems. First, he recruited a few villagers to help him conduct a health census. Moving from family to family in Cange and two neighboring villages, the census takers identified the breadth of residents' health problems and established a baseline by which to measure future success. To address the community's needs, Farmer launched Partners in Health, or Zanmi Lasante in Haitian Creole, with financial support from backers in the United States.

How do you create an effective public health system? (*Left*) Patients receive direct treatment at a clinic. (*Right*) Anthropologist Paul Farmer at the opening of a new teaching and primary care hospital in Mirebalais, north of Haiti's capital.

Zanmi Lasante began to create multiple lines of defense to protect the Cange villagers' health. Clean water came first. Because they lived on Haiti's central plateau, the villagers had been climbing down an 800-foot hillside to draw water from the stagnant reservoir created by the hydroelectric dam. Using old plastic jugs and calabash gourds, they had been carrying water back up the hill to their homes, where it sometimes sat uncovered for days. Father Lafontant recruited a construction crew from an Episcopal Church diocese in South Carolina to tap into an underground river to provide fresh water to the families at the top of the hill. Thereafter, Farmer and his associates noticed that the incidence of infant deaths began to drop almost immediately.

Sanitation and hygiene came next. Father Lafontant organized the construction of latrines (outdoor toilets) to improve human waste disposal and protect the water supply. He and Farmer raised money to replace the dirt floors and thatched roofs of the residents' crude lean-to homes with tin roofs and concrete floors. An expanded village school provided a place to teach children to read and write and a place to teach the community about basic health practices. Malnourished schoolchildren received free meals with dignity. Childhood vaccinations dramatically improved health in the community.

Perhaps most significant, Zanmi Lasante trained local community members as health workers. Being familiar with the local language, social structure, values, and religious beliefs, the community health workers were able to identify emerging health-care problems, administer vaccinations, and assist people in taking medications. The newly constructed health clinic and hospital of Zanmi Lasante served those who were too sick to be cared for at home. Over time, Zanmi Lasante became one of the largest nongovernmental health-care providers in Haiti, serving an area of 1.2 million people with more than 4,000 doctors, nurses, and community health workers.

Farmer's research and work in Cange explored how anthropology could tackle the day-to-day challenges of health on the ground—nutrition, clean water, prevention of illness, and promotion of health. Public health work could be guided and greatly improved by the strategies and theoretical concerns of anthropology. However, as Farmer notes, to truly make a difference, anthropology must be used not only to analyze and scrutinize a problem but also to turn research into action (Farmer 1985).

Why Does the Distribution of Health and Illness Mirror That of Wealth and Power?

Assess how the distribution of health and illness mirrors that of wealth and power.

Writing in the late 1800s, Rudolf Virchow, a renowned pathologist considered to be one of the ancestors of medical anthropology, asked why the distribution of health and illness appeared to mirror the distribution of wealth and power. Although anthropology from its inception has focused on concerns of health and illness, in recent years, Virchow's question has become central to the critical medical anthropology approach to these areas of research. If the distribution of health and illness cannot be explained solely on the basis of genetic vulnerabilities, individual behaviors, and the random spread of pathogens through a population, then what are the root causes of health disparities (Singer and Baer 1995)?

HEALTH TRANSITION AND CRITICAL MEDICAL ANTHROPOLOGY

health transition

The significant improvements in human health made over the course of the twentieth century; they were not, however, distributed evenly across the world's population.

Over the twentieth century, much of the human population experienced dramatic improvements in health. Life expectancy rose significantly. Infectious diseases (with the exception of HIV) declined as the primary causes of death, replaced by chronic diseases such as cancer and heart disease and by syndromes such as stroke. Unfortunately, despite improvements in global health statistics, local populations have not experienced the **health transition** equally. Inequalities of health—sometimes extreme—and unequal access to health care persist both between and within local populations.

Although the global average life expectancy increased from 31 years in 1900 to 71.9 in 2019 (from 49.2 to 79.1 in the United States over the same period), extreme differences exist among countries. As Table 14.1 shows, in 2019 Hong Kong ranked first in overall life expectancy at birth at 85.2 years. Sierra Leone ranked last of 194 countries, with an overall life expectancy at birth of 56 years. The United States ranked forty-fourth at 79.1 years.

These statistics raise crucial questions about health disparities: If the United States is the richest and most technologically advanced country in the world, why is its population's average life expectancy shorter than those of forty-three other countries? Why is the average life expectancy of the population of Sierra Leone 25 percent below the global average? Questions like these are central to the concerns of critical medical anthropologists.

Critical medical anthropology examines health as a system of power. Specifically, it explores the impact of inequality on human health by examining (1) how economic and political systems, race, class, gender, and sexuality create and perpetuate unequal access to health care and (2) how health systems themselves are systems of power that generate disparities in health by defining who is sick, who gets treated, and how. Critical medical anthropologists look beyond Western biomedicine's traditional focus on individual patients' problems; instead, they analyze patterns of health and illness among entire groups. They search for the origins of health disparities, the mechanisms that perpetuate them, and strategies for overcoming them (Baer, Singer, and Susser 2003; Budrys 2010).

Patterns of inequality in a culture create patterns of inequality in health care. Health practices and policies in turn create and reinforce patterns of inequality. We might actually say that illness can have social origins in poverty, violence, fear of violence, and discrimination based on race, ethnicity, gender, sexuality, and age. Illness and disease can result from cultural patterns of inequality and the distribution of health-care resources within a population (Schulz and Mullings 2006).

critical medical anthropology

An approach to the study of health and illness that analyzes the impact of inequality and stratification within systems of power on individual and group health outcomes.

STAFF ATTITUDES AFFECT HEALTH-CARE DELIVERY IN A NEW YORK WOMEN'S CLINIC

Various systems of power—including economics, politics, race, class, gender, and sexuality—shape the distribution and accessibility of health-care resources (Chapman and Berggren 2005). In *Reproducing Race* (2011), legal scholar and anthropologist Khiara Bridges examines the ways in which race, class, and gender intersect to shape the delivery of health care in a women's health clinic at a famous trauma hospital on Manhattan's East Side. This facility provides prenatal, delivery, and postpartum checkups and services to pregnant women who are poor. The women's health clinic of Alpha Hospital (a pseudonym), which also serves as a

MAP 14.4
New York City

top-tier teaching hospital, treats an incredibly diverse population of patients, including some White people but mostly people of color. Because of their economic status, all patients qualify for the U.S. federal government's Medicaid program.

In contrast to the patient population, physicians working in Alpha's women's health clinic are predominantly White. Most medical staffers are women of color but of immigrant backgrounds. Tensions exist between these groups. During a year and a half of fieldwork, Bridges documented the stereotypes and prejudices expressed by physicians and medical staff about their patients. Bridges raises the possibility that physicians' racial attitudes may contribute to the health disparities experienced by patients who are women of color.

For example, Bridges's research documents a racist oral tradition within the medical profession that features stories and folklore about Black women's bodies. One common theme centers on the supposedly unique strength and hardiness of Black women and other women of color, who, often referred to as more "primitive" by health workers, were assumed to be able to endure more intense pain and overcome more hardship in medical procedures than other women.

Bridges presents these troubling anecdotes in relationship to statistics that show significant racial disparities in infant and maternal mortality. In the United States, Black babies are nearly two and a half times more likely than White babies to die as infants. Black women are three times more likely than White women to die from complications of pregnancy and childbirth. In New York City, they are five times more likely to do so.

Are these women and infants dying because they are poor or because they are Black? Bridges suggests that the mortality rates reflect more than poverty.

How might dynamics of race, gender, age, and class affect the medical care that patients receive in a hospital, clinic, or doctor's office?

TABLE 14.1
Global Life Expectancy by Country

Country (state/territory)	Rank	Life Expectancy at Birth (in years)
Hong Kong	1	85.2
Japan	2	85.0
Macao	3	84.6
Switzerland	4	84.2
Singapore	5	84.0
Italy	6	84.0
Spain	7	83.9
Australia	8	83.9
Channel Islands	9	83.6
Iceland	10	83.5
Canada	16	82.9
United Kingdom	29	81.7
Germany	27	81.8
United States	46	79.1
Mexico	90	75.4
China	64	77.4
Saudi Arabia	86	75.6
Egypt	118	72.5
India	136	70.4
Senegal	143	68.8
Papua New Guinea	161	65.2
Haiti	165	64.9
Sierra Leone	189	55.9

Source: Worldometer. 2022. "Life Expectancy of the World Population." https://www
.worldometers.info/demographics/life-expectancy/.

Studies consistently show that racial and ethnic minorities in the United States receive lower-quality health care. But even when ruling out variables such as insurance status, income, age, and severity of medical condition, Black women and infants have higher mortality rates than Whites with similar profiles.

Bridges notes a deep reluctance within Western medicine to invade physicians' privacy by interrogating their human frailties. Perhaps as a result, the existence of physicians' racism is never addressed in the larger medical literature. But based on the patterns of behavior she observed at Alpha Hospital's women's health clinic, Bridges argues for the need to explore the possibility that physicians' views regarding patients of color may lead to different treatment during pregnancy and childbirth, disparate health outcomes, and higher infant and maternal mortality rates (Bridges 2011; Chapman and Berggren 2005).

How Does Anthropology Help Analyze and Address Global Health Challenges Like COVID-19?

Summarize an anthropological approach to analyzing and addressing global health challenges, such as COVID-19.

Perhaps never before has the world seen a disease spread as quickly and widely as COVID-19. The Chinese city of Wuhan suddenly locked down in January 2020 in an attempt to stop the initial outbreak, but by March, skyrocketing infections and deaths in Italy, Spain, France, and the United States confirmed a global pandemic. By the end of May, nearly 24,000 residents of New York City were dead. Since then, despite lockdowns, social distancing and vaccinations, millions of people have died, hundreds of millions have been infected, and we have only begun to understand the long-term health consequences of COVID-19 infections. Throughout the pandemic, the disease has reshaped cultural practices around the world, from personal greetings to religious practices, from home to work and school.

In this era of intensifying globalization, medical anthropologists have long expressed concern about the rapid transmission of infectious diseases—from HIV/AIDS, Ebola, and Zika to influenza, measles, mumps, and now COVID-19. Elaborate and expanding road, rail, sea, and air transportation networks allow us to move within ever-thickening webs of connection. In 2019 alone, the year before the coronavirus pandemic, airlines carried 4.5 billion passengers on 38.9 million flights (International Civil Aviation Organization 2019; Statista 2022), and post-pandemic travel numbers are returning to their earlier norms. We are an increasingly connected global population. As we move, we carry many things with us, including pathogens like COVID-19.

As contagious and deadly as COVID-19 is, any pathogen—a bacteria or virus—requires the right conditions to spread. And so, as we discussed at the beginning of this chapter, medical anthropologists studying the spread of a disease or pathogen through the human population look carefully at the medical ecology surrounding it. How does the disease interact with the natural environment and with human culture?

Pathogens and their movements can be quite mysterious, even to epidemiologists. In the case of COVID-19, proximity may not lead to infection. Infection might create any number of a wide variety of symptoms and long-term complications—or none at all. Some who are infected but asymptomatic can still transfer the disease. Although scientific knowledge about COVID-19 has expanded rapidly since its inception, when pathogens and contagion are not fully understood, humans engage in constant interpretive work about their health and illness (Wynn 2020).

Within medical anthropology, interpretivist approaches consider how health systems become systems of meaning. For instance, as we will see in the case studies that follow, COVID-19 has brought a radical reorganization of our cultural concepts of care. What does it mean to care for someone, love someone, or look out for someone during a global pandemic with a highly contagious pathogen? How are these sentiments expressed on an individual and collective level? Closeness, proximity, and physical interaction are often considered central to norms and values that express caring. But in conditions where closeness is associated with the dangers of infecting oneself and others, acts of physical distancing—mask wearing, hand sanitizing, keeping six feet apart, school closings, and lockdowns—have become new expressions of care. For many, decisions about distance require complicated ethical negotiations to determine how, when, and how much to apply these new standards of care and what personal and legal implications may be involved. And in countries such as Brazil, Mexico, the United Kingdom, and the United States, mask wearing itself has become a contested behavior associated not only with public health but also with attitudes toward authority, expressions of individualism and freedom, religious beliefs, and political affiliation. In many places, as we will see in South Africa, the United States, and Qatar, the ability to comply with physical distancing guidelines and mandates is an unaffordable or even unavailable privilege (Trnka 2020).

SOUTH AFRICA: COVID LOCKDOWNS AND APARTHEID HISTORY

Critical medical anthropology explores the mutually reinforcing impacts of structural inequalities and health systems. The COVID-19 pandemic, like other pandemics before it, has powerfully exposed the correlations of health outcomes with wealth and power.

In March 2020, the government of South Africa imposed a harsh lockdown in an effort to "flatten the curve" of COVID-19 infections—that is, to reduce infections and hospitalizations until the country's perpetually underfunded health-care system could ramp up to face the crisis. Police, security guards, and armed forces were deployed to monitor and enforce compliance with school closings, work-from-home orders, curfews, limits on gatherings, and beach closures. Writing about the extreme physical distancing required, medical anthropologists Susan Levine and Lenore Manderson (2021) explore what "lockdown" means for a nation already systematically divided.

South Africa's contemporary lockdown restrictions recall the country's history of apartheid, a government-enforced system of institutionalized racism and violent controls on mobility, social engagement, and intimacy. Beginning with the Group Areas Act of 1950, the minority-White-dominated government imposed extreme spatial restrictions on the non-White population that affected their physical movement, residency, and social and political engagement. Apartheid was maintained by the state's political system and military apparatus. Physical distancing created and enforced extreme inequality within the country along lines of race and class.

Levine and Manderson note that, despite the passage of more than twenty-five years since South Africa's transition to a democratic government, economic equality has not followed political equality. As a result, social groups today live largely as they did before the end of apartheid, their life chances shaped by racism, residential segregation, and deeply embedded inequality in housing, sanitation, health care, and employment opportunities. For many in South Africa, crowded housing conditions and low-wage economic realities make distancing impossible. Distancing also reinforces the inequalities made manifest by previous and ongoing epidemics of HIV/AIDS, tuberculosis, heart disease, and gender-based violence. Restrictions on movement further widen existing health disparities along lines of race and class for those who must travel to access health services, medication, and treatment for chronic conditions. In fact, Levine and Manderson document that those already struggling for survival must ignore COVID-19 physical distancing conventions to best take care of themselves. These new protocols, which hauntingly recall South Africa's historical political system, only work for those economically privileged enough to enact them. To effectively assess their success requires viewing them through the lens of long-term patterns of inequality in divided South Africa and a divided world.

MAP 14.5

South Africa

CLASS, RACE, AND THE U.S. CORONAVIRUS RESPONSE

The uneven health impacts of the coronavirus in the United States, like those in South Africa, have aligned directly with class and race. Many professional, white-collar workers with health benefits and sick days have been able to work from home. Meanwhile, essential workers—including large numbers of immigrants and people of color working low-wage jobs as store clerks, grocery stockers, delivery workers, bus drivers, gas station attendants, farmworkers, meat-packers, and civil servants—were required to work in person, often commuting on public transportation, and without adequate protective equipment, testing, tracing, or the ability to quarantine—not to mention access to health care. These conditions dramatically increased essential workers' exposure to the coronavirus pathogen.

A look at coronavirus infections and deaths in the United States reveals the close linkage between health outcomes and race. Black and Latinx persons who contract the virus have been hospitalized more than twice as often as Whites and are almost twice as likely to die. Native Americans have been hospitalized three times as often as Whites and are more than twice as likely to die (Centers for Disease Control 2022). These disparities tie to the disproportionate exposure of essential workers of color to the coronavirus. Medical anthropologists also trace these outcomes to deeply entrenched patterns of inadequate health care, discrimination within the health-care system, and underlying health conditions created by long-standing conditions of racism and poverty.

Amid the coronavirus pandemic, the murder of George Floyd by Minneapolis police officers in early June 2020 sparked a summer of racial justice uprisings across the country demanding an end to repeated and systemic police violence against people of color. Demonstrations in solidarity with the Movement for Black Lives spread across the globe. Black Lives Matter activists called for rethinking what makes a community safe, defunding local police departments, and reinvesting those funds in programs that would make communities of color truly healthy and safe—an end to the daily violence from poverty, mass incarceration, poor housing, underfunded schools, and discriminatory health-care practices. Using an intersectional analysis, they tied structural violence and racism directly to the conditions that made the pandemic so deadly, and they linked Floyd's cry—"I can't breathe"—to the virus unequally attacking the lungs of tens of thousands of people of color across the country and world.

FIGURE 14.1
Hospitalization and Death by Race/Ethnicity

RATE RATIOS COMPARED TO WHITE, NON-HISPANIC PERSONS	AMERICAN INDIAN OR ALASKA NATIVE, NON-HISPANIC PERSONS	ASIAN, NON-HISPANIC PERSONS	BLACK OR AFRICAN AMERICAN, NON-HISPANIC PERSONS	HISPANIC OR LATINO PERSONS
Cases	1.5x	0.8x	1.1x	1.5x
Hospitalizations	3.0x	0.8x	2.3x	2.2x
Death	2.1x	0.8x	1.7x	1.8x

Source: U.S. Centers for Disease Control and Prevention. 2022. "Hospitalization and Death by Race/Ethnicity." https://www.cdc.gov/coronavirus/2019-ncov/covid-data/investigations-discovery/hospitalization-death-by-race-ethnicity.html.

QATAR'S *CORDON SANITAIRE*: PUBLIC HEALTH OR THE NATIONAL IMAGINATION

Anthropologist Natasha Iskander's research (2020) on COVID-19 policies in Qatar adopts a critical medical anthropology approach to explore how health systems and health measures, often assumed to promote the public health of the general population, can be used instead to sharpen structural inequalities that serve economic and political purposes. Qatar is a small, oil-rich country of 3 million people on the Arabian Peninsula. Ninety percent of Qatar's population is composed of foreign migrant workers from India, Nepal, Bangladesh, Sri Lanka, Pakistan, the Philippines, and Egypt. Regardless of their length of stay, these migrant workers have no ability to claim citizenship. Their right to residency is based solely on their employment.

MAP 14.6

Qatar

Early in the pandemic, Qatar developed one of the highest per capita rates of COVID-19 in the world. In response, the government imposed extensive mitigation efforts, including testing, contact tracing, social distancing, the closing of nonessential businesses. Certain neighborhoods in the capital, Doha, were completely locked down. In an extraordinary step, Qatar established a strictly enforced spatial quarantine, called the *cordon sanitaire*, around the area of Doha where migrant construction workers are housed, despite lacking evidence of elevated pandemic conditions there. Newly erected concrete barriers cordoned off the workers' barracks, factories, and warehouses from the rest of the city. Residents were not allowed to leave, even for medical care. Militarized roadblocks guarded against unauthorized movement in and out.

These restrictions had little effect on the spread of COVID-19 in Qatar. But they did create conditions for rapid spread in the crowded labor camps, where migrants shared kitchens and bathrooms, physical distancing was impossible, and protective hygiene measures like masking and hand sanitizing were impractical. Public health protocols use quarantines to remove from the general population persons who are ill or exposed to a pathogen. But Qatar's *cordon sanitaire* placed a whole population into conditions of increased risk and exposure. Ironically, workers could only leave quarantine on overcrowded government-arranged buses to work on construction sites building facilities, stadiums, and fields for the high-profile 2022 World Cup matches.

In conclusion, Iskander reflects on how Qatar's public health measures, particularly the *cordon sanitaire*, augmented existing structural inequalities, protecting some from exposure while functionally mandating increased exposure for others. Rather than responding to evidence of COVID-19 contagion, these public health measures served political goals—namely, further clarifying who was included in and excluded from the nation-state—while further advancing Qatar's economic development strategies and nation-building dreams.

ANTHROPOLOGISTS ENGAGE THE CORONAVIRUS

From the field's inception in the mid-1800s, anthropologists have sought to apply their research strategies, knowledge, and insights to practical problems facing the world. That remains true during this time of global pandemic. Early in the coronavirus health crisis, the State of Massachusetts called upon the organization Partners in Health (PIH) to set up a statewide contact tracing program. As discussed earlier in the chapter, Boston-based PIH was co-founded by anthropologist-physician Paul Farmer. It has a thirty-year record of anthropologically informed community-based health care around the world, including work on epidemics and infectious disease outbreaks in Haiti, Rwanda, Lesotho, and West Africa. Working with the Massachusetts Department of Public Health, PIH staff drew upon their expertise to recruit and train a corps of 1,900 mostly young public health workers. The program was up and running within weeks. Tracing the contacts of those infected with the coronavirus allows officials to identify and isolate asymptomatic carriers before they can infect others, thus cutting off the spread of COVID-19. By the summer of 2020, PIH tracers were able to reach 90 percent of contacts within 24 hours. Through intensive testing, contact tracing, and isolation, Massachusetts's cases fell dramatically (Partners in Health 2020).

As we have seen throughout this chapter, anthropologists bring a unique combination of analytical perspectives and research strategies to the treatment of disease and illness. In an era of globalization, as the human population surpasses 8 billion, climate change alters natural habitats, and more people live densely together in cities and move more frequently within and between countries, the anthropological toolkit has much to offer in addressing the rapid transmission of diseases and in promoting sophisticated, people-centered, and holistic approaches to the challenges of health and illness facing local communities integrated into a global economic and political system.

Toolkit

Thinking Like an Anthropologist
Health in the Individual and in the
Global Population

The human body is a spectacularly sophisticated organism. Its 10 trillion cells constitute complex cardiovascular, pulmonary, and digestive systems made up of muscles, ligaments, organs, veins, and arteries, all shaped and guided by approximately 20,000 protein-coding genes that form our DNA sequence. The body, which has evolved over millions of years, enables us to interact with one another, reproduce our species, and adapt to the remarkable variety of environments found on Earth.

When medical anthropologists consider issues of health, they think about both the individual body and the social body. As discussed in this chapter, we humans and our individual bodies do not live in isolation. Nor is our health created in isolation. We live in relation to one another as part of a social body—a collection of individuals whose health is tied to the success of the group as well (Scheper-Hughes and Lock 1987). The health and safety of the schoolchildren discussed in the chapter opener, like the health of Lia Lee, is directly related to the health of those around them, to understandings of bodies, to the availability of guns, and to the system of health care created and shared by the larger culture in which they live.

As you think more about health and illness—perhaps your own personal experiences or those of people around you—remember the big questions we have been exploring:

- **How does culture shape health and illness?**
- **How do different cultural conceptions of the body affect health practices?**
- **How can anthropologists help solve health-care problems?**
- **Why does the distribution of health and illness mirror that of wealth and power?**
- **How does anthropology help analyze and address global health challenges like COVID-19?**

After reading this chapter, are you able to apply these questions to specific situations?

As we have seen, medical anthropologists examine the diverse strategies that cultures have developed to protect and promote the health of the body. And they work to apply the methodological and analytical tools of anthropology to enhance and expand health care in the face of increasing global health inequalities. Debates about health and illness are all around us: Will all fifty U.S. states expand Medicaid eligibility for the poor, as envisioned by the 2010 Affordable Care Act? How will women access reproductive health care now that the U.S. Supreme Court has struck down the right to abortion? Will your college or university adequately fund its student health center to provide for all students' health needs? Would you consider joining or supporting an organization like Paul Farmer's Partners in Health (see pp. 442 and pp. 453) to help address the health-care needs of people in another part of the world? How will you engage these debates?

The U.S. gun violence research community, comprising emergency room doctors, psychiatrists, epidemiologists, law professors, and social policy experts, has a clear idea of what to do to reduce gun violence. Their research identifies highly effective measures to sharply reduce gun deaths: red flag laws that allow authorities to temporarily remove guns from people deemed dangerous by a court, licensing laws that require obtaining permits before buying a gun, bans on high-capacity ammunition magazines, and gun storage safety locks. But as we have seen, the debate has become about so much more than science or public health concerns.

Thinking like an anthropologist can help you better understand and address these issues, whether they present themselves as your own personal issues of health and illness, those of your friends and family, or the health of the global human population.

Key Terms

health (p. 426)

disease (p. 427)

illness (p. 427)

sickness (p. 427)

ethnomedicine (p. 428)

ethnopharmacology (p. 428)

biomedicine (p. 430)

medical pluralism (p. 434)

illness narratives (p. 436)

human microbiome (p. 438)

health transition (p. 444)

critical medical anthropology (p. 445)

Chapter 15
Art and Media

Learning Objectives

- Define art from an anthropological perspective.

- Describe the unique contributions anthropologists make to the study of art.

- Explain the relationship between art and power.

- Appraise the ways art intersects with media.

In a favela, or shantytown, set on a steep hillside above Rio de Janeiro, Brazil, a remarkable 4,000-square-foot miniature model of the city overlooks the sprawling metropolis below. Known as Morrinho (Little Hill), this virtual urban world began as a children's game in 1997 and today draws the attention of government officials, filmmakers, development agencies, and artists from around the world.

Working and playing together with other neighborhood kids, two brothers began to construct the miniature city out of discarded bricks, tiles, and mortar and borrowed masonry tools. As the game gradually grew in size and complexity, streets began to emerge, followed by homes, restaurants, stores, hospitals, and police stations. Each of the children began to inhabit the game, making avatars for themselves from Lego blocks. The streets came alive with human interactions: friendships and fights, games and business. The constructed city took on a life of its own, yet it was a life that

---

Youth in a Brazilian shantytown have constructed a miniature city where they reenact their complex urban world in an elaborate game started in 1997.

reflected and illuminated human relations and social conditions in the favela and the city of Rio.

Today, thousands of avatars placed within the miniature city engage in an elaborate dramatization of community life. They live and die, work and play, break the law and make love. Battles rage between gangs and with police. Brazilian pennies have become currency, exchanged in the game for goods and services, motorcycle rides, and bags of drugs. Each youth controls their own avatar and portion of the model.

Anthropologist Alessandro Angelini has conducted ethnographic fieldwork in this miniature world and the surrounding community since 2008. He notes the ways Morrinho has become significant as more than just an interactive model city, particularly as the youths' manipulation of miniature urban life has cast a spotlight on the intersections of poverty, class, power, kinship, identity, the state, and politics. For instance, Morrinho has drawn the attention of Brazilian political authorities. Morrinho's community—now well known in Rio and beyond—became one of the first favelas to receive state infrastructure improvements, including sewage systems, housing, road paving, lighting, pathways, and railings. It was also one of the first to be targeted with increased police presence and social programs as the government sought to pacify and eliminate any undesirable elements.

Morrinho—spanning boundaries between play, creative expression, politics, and art—has also drawn the attention of artists and activists. Tourists visit from Rio and beyond. Filmmakers document the story of the miniature city and its surrounding community in work shown at international festivals. A small group of Morrinho's originators has been invited on multiple occasions since 2004 to reproduce models of Morrinho at art festivals in cities such as Barcelona, Paris, Vienna, Munich, Venice, and Innsbruck as well as in Holland, Colombia, and East Timor. Collaborating with local underprivileged youth from South London in the

Art? Play? Politics? All are expressed in the reconstruction of Morrinho, a virtual urban world in a Brazilian favela begun as a children's game but now a national and international destination. Youth from Morrinho have even re-created their favela as art installations in cities abroad, including London, where they integrated miniatures of St. Paul's Cathedral, Big Ben, the London Eye, and the London "tube" subway.

summer of 2010, the group created an installation of Morrinho at a prominent Brazilian arts festival in the United Kingdom—while adding to their miniature city certain elements of London, such as Big Ben, prisons, and other features important to London youth. In these settings, what began as a game is admired as art, not as play (Angelini 2016).

In this chapter, we will explore the array of human creative expression and interaction that anthropologists consider when exploring the world of art. Humans express themselves creatively and interact meaningfully through the visual and written arts, movement, sound, and more. An anthropological approach to art may include attention to paintings, drawings, design, weavings, photographs, film, sculpture, architecture, dance, music, songs, games, sports, clothing, cuisine, and even virtual online design and creativity. In addition, we will consider the intersections of art and globalization, art and politics, and art and media, as technologies such as television, radio, film, and social media establish new venues for creative expression and new avenues for sharing and engaging those expressions. In particular, we will consider the following questions:

- **What is art?**
- **What is unique about how anthropologists study art?**
- **What is the relationship between art and power?**
- **How do art and media intersect?**

By the end of the chapter, you will have gained an understanding of the unique approach that anthropologists take to the study of art, the many ways art reflects and transforms culture, and the ways globalization and new forms of media are transforming art and its dissemination.

What Is Art?

Define art from an anthropological perspective.

Anthropologists define **art** broadly as all the ideas, forms, techniques, and strategies that humans employ to express themselves creatively and to communicate their creativity and inspiration to others. Art may include a vast array of music, songs, stories, paintings, plays, design, sculpture, architecture, clothing, food, and games. But art is not only meaningful for the artist.

THE ANTHROPOLOGY OF ART

Art is both created and received. Cooking and building, fashion and oratory, decorating and dressing, sewing and play—all are media through which artists

art
All ideas, forms, techniques, and strategies that humans employ to express themselves creatively and to communicate their creativity and inspiration to others.

and audiences communicate. Through these often dynamic encounters, art takes its shape not only in creation but also in perception. In the story of Morrinho, for example, the full impact of the game created by the young people of the favela emerges in the interaction of those who are creating it and those who are perceiving it, interpreting it, and making it come alive for the community—a community that stretches far beyond local boundaries.

When thinking anthropologically about art in its global context, it is helpful to first consider some of the Western tradition's common but flawed assumptions about how to evaluate what is and is not art. In particular, we will examine how the anthropology of art challenges commonplace notions of (1) a distinction between fine art and popular art, (2) the existence of a universal art aesthetic, and (3) the assumption of qualitative differences between Western art and so-called primitive art.

Fine Art versus Popular Art. In Western traditions, art has often been associated with notions of "high culture" or "fine art," especially elite representations of visual and performance arts experienced in formal venues. Paintings and sculptures displayed in museums and art galleries; operas, symphonies, and ballets performed in recital halls; musicals and plays performed in theaters; fashion shows on runways; and fine cuisine prepared in expensive restaurants fit a view of **fine art** as the province of the elite. Such art is often evaluated and portrayed in contrast to **popular art**—less refined and less sophisticated creative expressions associated with the general population—in the same way that high culture might be simplistically compared to popular culture.

fine art

Creative expression and communication often associated with cultural elites.

popular art

Creative expression and communication often associated with the general population.

What is art? Art can be expressed in various venues and through an array of media. (*Left to right*) *Giant Metal Eyes* by Louise Bourgeois at Williams College Museum of Art, Williamstown, Massachusetts; Chinese artists performing Beijing Opera at the National Theater in Algeria; and *Stingray Mola*, a fabric design of the Kuna Indians of Panama, Central America.

From a broad anthropological perspective, however, art is not the sole province of elites or professional artists: Any members of a group can create and experience art. Art is integral to all of human life. As such, it can be expressed through elaborate performances in specialized venues as well as through routine activities in mundane settings.

The significance of art cannot be underestimated as anthropologists consider the full expression of human life. All creativity expressed through cultural products such as songs, paintings, dance, architecture, clothing, games, and food carries rich deposits of information about culture as a system of meaning and a system of power. In fact, the very distinction between fine art and popular art may have more to do with political choices and hierarchies of power than with any intrinsic character of the art itself. Who decides, for instance, what will be performed in an opera house or displayed in a national museum? Who directs and who funds the selection, acquisition, and presentation of art (Thornton 2009; Werner 2006)? Can you identify other cultural dynamics of power and stratification—perhaps race, gender, class, religion, or sexuality—that might be reflected in these decisions and representations of what is fine art and what is popular art (Marcus and Myers 1995; see Perkins and Morphy 2006; Schneider and Wright 2006)?

Considering Aesthetics across Cultures. The human encounter with art entails an aesthetic experience—that is, art is largely perceived through one's senses rather than through intellect and logic. Western art traditions, specifically those in Europe and North America, have tended to focus primarily on the aesthetic value of art and on a particular concept of aesthetics associated with standards of beauty, creativity, and innovation that are presumed to represent the most refined expressions of a group's culture. But is there a universal art aesthetic found across cultures that informs what people consider to be art and not art? Is there a **universal gaze**—an intrinsic way of perceiving art—that guides how people respond to art?

The Western concept of a universal art aesthetic traces back to the German philosophers Immanuel Kant (1724–1804) and Georg W. F. Hegel (1770–1831). They suggested that nature creates a universal aesthetic in humans—particularly a sense of what is beautiful—and that it undergirds a universal gaze through which all art can be seen. Through this universal gaze, art can provide viewers with a "transcendental" aesthetic experience, lift them out of the day-to-day, and transform their vision of the world (Stoller 2003).

The presumption of a universal art aesthetic characterized much of the Western art world throughout most of the twentieth century. Western art institutions, particularly those focusing on fine art, strove to reinforce this aesthetic experience through their style of presentation. Beginning in the last half of the twentieth century, curators displayed art in a minimalist manner, perhaps accompanied only by a piece's title, date, and name of artist, in an attempt to allow the art to speak for itself. Neutral, objective presentation encouraged viewers to contemplate objects removed from their worldly context, including their social and economic conditions of production, marketing, and consumption.

Anthropologists of art have actively challenged the widespread belief in and representation of a universal art aesthetic. Not all cultures have the same aesthetic. Perceptions of beauty, imagination, skill, and style vary widely across cultures, as do approaches to artistic ideas, objects, and practices. In fact, what many people have considered to be a universal aesthetic has frequently proved to be a unique product of Western history and culture. And within the Western art world itself, the power to define the artistic aesthetic was systematically exercised without the participation of women and other members of marginalized groups (Alexander 1996; Alpers 1991; Karp and Lavine 1991; Price 1989).

Expectations of art and cultural frameworks for perceiving art may also vary from place to place and even within different cultures. Art may be viewed as beautiful and inspirational: A painting, sculpture, dance, or song may bring pleasure and joy to those who experience it. But people may perceive and respond to art in other ways. Art may also shock, terrify, horrify, or anger its audience. Like other key elements of culture, art is deeply embedded in the processes of enculturation that shape observers' perceptions, expectations, and experiences when evaluating art.

To further illustrate the vast range of possible aesthetic perspectives, consider the following simple contrasts. Whereas Western art traditions may emphasize

universal gaze

An intrinsic way of perceiving art—thought by many in the Western art world to be found across cultures—that informs what people consider to be art or not art.

How does the presentation of art—for instance, in this minimalist gallery—affect your experience and understanding of it?

innovation and originality—creating something entirely new—other traditions may celebrate improvisation on already-existing themes (Boas 1927; Price 1989; Vogel 1991). Likewise, whereas many Western cultures may idealize the artist as an individual genius—as a cultural outsider separated from mundane daily life— other cultures may prioritize engagement with the audience and interaction with the community as the highest aspects of artistic expression. In such instances, the artist may be celebrated for playing a central role in the community's life rather than for their individual behavior (Perkins and Morphy 2006).

Beyond "Primitive" Art. Western art traditions have often imposed a problematic distinction between Western art and so-called primitive art. In the nineteenth and early twentieth centuries, early anthropologists played key roles in building great ethnographic museum collections to store and display the art and lifeways of "other" cultures for a Western audience—though they often acquired these treasure troves through the colonial encounter (that is, they stole rather than purchased or borrowed them).

The Western art world became interested in what came to be known as "primitive art" in the early twentieth century. At that time, modernist European artists such as Pablo Picasso began to incorporate African and Oceanic art features and themes into their own work, though largely without reference to the art's original cultural context. In the twentieth century, museums and galleries mounted prominent displays, dioramas, and collections of "primitive" art itself (typically, the art of Africa, Oceania, and Latin America).

In contrast to the anthropological approach to world art, which seeks to understand the development and meaning of local art forms within their unique and complex cultural contexts, this tendency to draw clear distinctions between Western and "primitive" art reinforced the perception of a hierarchy of world art organized along an evolutionary trajectory from simple to complex, primitive to civilized. Displays of art from non-Western cultures without reference to the art's original context or meaning reinforced stereotypes about non-Western people and their relationship to Western civilization.

Anthropologists of art (as well as economic anthropologists and political anthropologists) reject an evolutionary framing and evaluation. These anthropologists have also encouraged an ethnographic turn toward thorough contextualization of the processes and meaning of art as it emerges—whether that means investigating art's "social life" as it moves beyond local borders or reconsidering Western art within its own Indigenous, local cultural context (Alexander 1996; Alpers 1991; Karp and Lavine 1991; Price 1989).

ART IN HUMAN HISTORY

An examination of art throughout human history provides crucial context for our deliberations as we consider what "art" is. The expanding archaeological record reveals a connection between humans and art that reaches back tens of thousands of years. Art appears to be a fundamental aspect of what it means to be human. Though the archaeological record of human artistic work expands dramatically around 40,000 years ago, clear evidence has emerged of human creative expression dating back at least 100,000 years.

MAP 15.1
South Africa

Blombos Cave, South Africa. Archaeological discoveries over the past two decades in South Africa's Blombos Cave—set high in a cliff overlooking the Indian Ocean—reveal that as early as 75,000 years ago, anatomically modern humans were crafting stone weapon points, carving tools out of animal bones, and engraving symbols on blocks of a red stone called ochre.

In 2008, Henshilwood's team uncovered what amounts to a 100,000-year-old painters' workshop in the cave: bone tools for mixing paint, stones for pounding and grinding, yellow and red ochre for color. The ochre would have been blended with fat, charcoal, and mammal-bone marrow to form a paint mixture. The bone tools retained traces of red ochre, and remnants of the reddish material were still attached to the interior of two large abalone shells used to mix the paint (Henshilwood et al. 2011; Larsen 2019).

Recent archaeological evidence suggests that our human ancestors in Africa may have become cognitively and behaviorally "modern" as early as 300,000 to 400,000 years ago. Later, the development of bone and stone tools—along with the processing and use of pigment, art, and decoration at sites across Africa and from various eras—suggests that these ancestors gradually assembled the package of modern human behaviors associated with art and eventually carried them from Africa to other regions of the world (McBrearty and Brooks 2000).

Paleolithic Cave Paintings in Europe.

Perhaps the best-known examples of early art outside Africa are the spectacular Paleolithic cave paintings that have been discovered in areas of southern France (Lascaux Cave and Chauvet-Pont-d'Arc Cave) and northern Spain (Altamira Cave). The early artists, working 32,000 to 10,000 years ago, elaborately depicted reindeer, bison, mammoth, horses, lions, and other animals prevalent in that period. Carved human figurines, jewelry, ritual objects, and bone and ivory carvings accompany elaborate burial sites found in the caves.

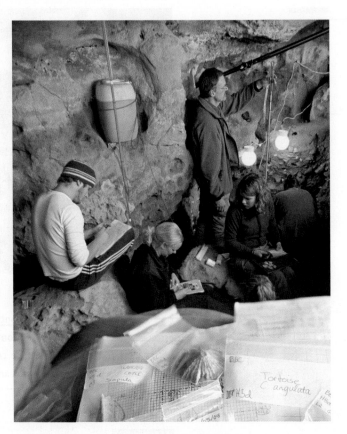

The cave art reveals highly developed artistic skills. Artists incorporated the contours of partially sculpted cave walls to provide a sense of dynamism and movement in the paintings. Analysis has revealed that the cave art was not the work of a few individuals or small groups but rather developed over a 20,000-year period through the efforts of many different artists who reused, modified, and painted over the artwork of their predecessors (Herzog 2010; Larsen 2019).

The connection between humans and art reaches back tens of thousands of years. Here, archaeologists excavate a 100,000-year-old "artists' studio" in Blombos Cave, South Africa, with artifacts in the foreground.

The purpose of the cave paintings is not clear. Our ancestors may have used them in storytelling, recordkeeping, rituals, ceremonies, or perhaps all of these. Despite their ambiguous purpose, their complexity of materials, subjects, and symbolism reveal an elaborate social life and an advanced level of cognitive development among the artists that does not fit contemporary stereotypes of "cavemen" living during the most recent ice age in Europe.

Whether through a 100,000-year-old painters' studio in southern Africa, Paleolithic cave art in southern France, or a fine art museum in a contemporary global city, we see that art is integral to all of human life. It can be expressed in elaborate displays or through simple craftwork. But by examining these events, objects, and expressions, anthropologists can gather crucial insights into people and their cultures. As we will explore in the following section,

MAP 15.2
Spain and France

This elaborate wall painting in Lascaux Cave, France, depicting horses, bison, mammoth, and lions and dating between 32,000 and 12,000 BCE, reveals the highly developed artistic skills of our immediate ancestors.

one of anthropologists' unique contributions to the study of art lies in careful ethnographic analysis and attention to the cultural production and transaction of art. This focus illuminates the complex social life of art as it is produced and exchanged between people and across geographic spaces and cultural boundaries.

What Is Unique about How Anthropologists Study Art?

Describe the unique contributions anthropologists make to the study of art.

Anthropologists' unique approach to art includes particular attention to how art is embedded in a community—how art connects to social norms and values and economic and political systems and events. Who makes it and why? What does it mean to the people who create it and to those who perceive it? What are its functional and inspirational roles? As ethnographers, anthropologists of art attend both to the form of the art itself—its designs, movements, and sounds—and to its context. We consider not only the creative production of a piece of art but also each work's unique and often complex history as it journeys through human culture. After all, as we will see, art is embedded in everyday exchanges, social networks, business negotiations, and other struggles over profit, power, and prestige.

THE ETHNOGRAPHY OF ART

Placing art in context has become more complicated and interesting in recent years. In today's era of intensifying globalization, local art is created in a global landscape. Local art practices, objects, and events intersect with global movements of people and ideas. Art is often a key juncture through which local communities engage the global economy (Kopytoff 1986). Within this global "artscape" (Appadurai 1986), the creation of local art may provide not only a means of economic activity but also a venue for demonstrating cultural skills and values and asserting local cultural identity in the face of rapid change (Perkins and Morphy 2006). As a result, contemporary anthropologists of art explore the journeys of objects across boundaries and the implications of the "traffic in culture" for both producers and consumers of art (Marcus and Myers 1995; Schneider and Wright 2006; Venbrux, Rosi, and Welsch 2006).

The Trade in West African Art. In *African Art in Transit* (1994), anthropologist Christopher Steiner explores the dynamic role of art in human culture through an ethnographic study of art traders in Abidjan, the main port city of Côte d'Ivoire in West Africa. Abidjan's art traders, mostly Muslims, serve as middlemen in the flow of African art between its creators (mostly rural villagers) and its consumers (Western tourists and international art collectors).

MAP 15.3
Abidjan

The itinerant traders circulate among upcountry villages, purchasing wooden carvings and clay figurines. They sometimes buy unique ritual items and family heirlooms directly from individuals, but generally they acquire mass-produced objects from artisan workshops that cater to the tourist and export art trade. The traders then sell to urban dealers, small and large, who resell the pieces to street hawkers, market stands, and upscale galleries. Within this milieu, Steiner investigates the intricate business practices and networks that link traders, suppliers, and consumers. And he details the elaborate production, presentation, description, alteration, authentication, and pricing of local art pieces within an increasingly globalized art market driven by tourists, Western and non-Western art dealers, and art connoisseurs.

As is true in all art markets, whether for carvings, paintings, fabrics, jewelry, or cuisine, an object's aesthetic value translates into a monetary value. Steiner examines the process by which West African art objects acquire value as they move through the art market. For example, how does a piece of carved wood become a desired object for purchase and collection? In Côte d'Ivoire, it is primarily a few Western tourists and art dealers who determine these values. For the most highly valued objects, an influential and wealthy elite of dealers, scholars, collectors, and exhibitors establishes their worth.

Key to the creation of value in this market is the perception of art objects as "authentic" or "genuine." Indeed, buyers and collectors are drawn to objects

authenticity

The perception of an object's antiquity, uniqueness, and originality within a local culture.

perceived to be of a certain origin and initial use. In turn, Côte d'Ivoire's local traders actively engage in the construction of **authenticity**—the perception of an object's antiquity, uniqueness, and originality within a local culture. Art objects are dirtied, artificially aged, stained, made to appear "primitive" to Western eyes, and altered to fit buyers' ideals. Local traders tell stories about the objects' origins, meaning, and use to enhance the impression of authenticity. For tourists, traders create stories that appeal to the buyers' aesthetic tastes and desires to acquire a genuine, authentic object. For high-end collectors, traders provide an elaborate market history—a description of each object's origins and when, where, and how it was collected. Most of these stories, Steiner finds, are fabricated to meet the tastes of Western consumers and thereby raise the object's value.

The aesthetic values of Western tourists and collectors, expressed in their consumption patterns, significantly influence the production, marketing, and display of West African art. In fact, West African art traders continually move between local and global art markets as they communicate between image creators and image consumers, artists and audiences. In this context, the production of art

What makes art "authentic"? A woodworker in West Africa makes carved figurines for market.

does not occur solely for art's sake but is part of an economic strategy that engages multiple levels of the art market. Steiner notes, "West African traders leave each negotiation with a new sense of the aesthetic sense of the Western buyers, a sense that the traders and manufacturers must be closely in tune with as they go about their business of making a living in a rapidly globalizing world and in their niche in a rapidly globalizing art market" (1995, 164). In this way, West African art traders play a sophisticated role in a global art market. They serve as cultural brokers and mediators who communicate Western desires to the native artists and who promote a particular image of African art and culture to the West (Beidelman 1994; Gell 1995; Zilberg 1996).

Think about your own perception of art. What makes a piece of art "authentic" in your eyes?

Transforming West African "Wood" and "Mud" into Global Art.

In recent years, facilitated by increased migration and enhanced global transportation and communication systems, West African art traders have extended their business networks across the Atlantic Ocean to New York and throughout the United States. As a result, the long-distance trade of West African artwork, particularly "wood" (carved statues and masks) and "mud" (terra-cotta clay figurines), documented by anthropologist Paul Stoller (2003), is leading to encounters between cultures and commerce at the intersection of two worlds.

The hub of the West African art trade in the United States is New York City—in particular, a multistory building on the west side of Midtown Manhattan called the Warehouse. The Warehouse is packed with stalls and shelves and display tables, each overflowing with "wood" and "mud." Every day, moving vans unload newly arrived shipments from West Africa, while others on-load pieces to be distributed by itinerant traders across the United States. West African traders cater to a wide array of clients: high-end art collectors, middle-class shoppers, and low-end street markets. High-end collectors search the New York galleries and art shows for what they consider fine art. At the same time, West African art traders crisscross the country delivering mass-produced art objects for sale at boutiques, street markets, flea markets, and cultural festivals. They even deliver directly to some individual clients. The traders rely on networks of "cousins" and other fictive kin who provide housing, marketing advice, cultural interpretation, and shared transport in an extension of practices developed in West African long-distance trade networks.

Global flows of people, art, and ideas have the power to shape worlds of work and worlds of meaning. The introduction of West African art pieces expands Western cultural notions of art and beauty. Simultaneously, Western notions of art affect West African patterns of production and marketing, including what traders will buy from artisans in the "mud" and "wood" workshops in towns and villages throughout West Africa.

How do wood and mud become art? Pictured here is an African art stall at the San Diego County Fair in California.

Moreover, on a practical level, these encounters at the crossroads of immigration and trade enable West African traders to meet their own social and economic obligations. They can pay off debts acquired in the immigration process and in starting up their small businesses. They can send remittances home to West Africa to support close family and extended kin groups. They can provide small amounts of start-up capital for rural and urban family enterprises. In the process of meeting these obligations, the traders themselves receive honor and respect from their home communities.

The studies by Steiner and Stoller provide ethnographic insight into the power of movement, encounter, and exchange to shape key aspects of human life, including categories such as art. By considering the production, marketing, and consumption of art within this framework, Steiner and Stoller challenge notions of ideal art types and universal standards of aesthetic beauty. They discuss how aesthetic perceptions, commonly viewed as timeless and universal, can be constructed and negotiated in encounters among humans—person to person, group to group, locally and globally.

What Is the Relationship between Art and Power?

Explain the relationship between art and power.

Anthropologists do not study art for art's sake. Instead, they inquire about the intersection of art with key systems of power such as race, ethnicity, class, gender, sexuality, politics, religion, and economics (Marcus and Myers 1995; Perkins and

Morphy 2006). Creative expressions, performances, and interactions through music, dance, song, museum displays, art events, and other art forms can be sites of dynamic engagement with these systems of power, unmasking patterns of stratification, making the unconscious conscious, and opening space for alternative visions of reality (see Downey 2005; Dunham 1969; Shannon 2006). Artistic expressions enable people to explore and perform identities outside the bounds of "normal" within the dominant culture. In some instances, as we will discuss in the case of Middle Eastern and Islamic art exhibits, they may also create and reinforce stereotypes and misunderstandings.

BLACK GIRLS' PLAYGROUND GAMES AND MUSICAL SOCIALIZATION

When we think of kids jumping rope on the sidewalk or standing in a circle on the playground calling out rhymes and clapping to keep the beat, we may not automatically think of art. But in *The Games Black Girls Play* (2006), ethnomusicologist Kyra Gaunt explores the sophisticated musical forms that are taught and learned, particularly by young Black girls, on the playground.

Gaunt, herself a gifted musician and an anthropologist trained in **ethnomusicology**—the study of music in cultural context (see Nettl 2005)—applies a unique combination of musical analysis and gender analysis in her study of games that Black girls play. According to Gaunt, the girls' hand-clapping and rope-jumping games embody a unique musical genre that combines body movement and voice to produce what she calls a **kinetic orality**. Hand clapping, foot stomping, and highly percussive singing create a musical expression deeply tied to the body—a performance that does not rely on musical instruments but only on body and voice.

ethnomusicology
The study of music in cultural context.

kinetic orality
A musical genre combining body movement and voice.

These performances may appear to be improvised on the playground or street corner or in the schoolyard. But Gaunt argues that they are learned in an elaborate process of enculturation. Through this process, complex rhythmic syncopations, chants, call-and-response vocal patterns, dances, and melodies are transferred from generation to generation as central lessons of socialization for young African American girls. Gaunt challenges the stereotypes that attribute musical patterns and bodily movement in Black children's games to biology. Instead, she traces the enculturation processes of what she calls "learned musical blackness," which begins at an early age as part of African American identity construction.

Gaunt also explores how Black girls' games and songs influence the development of commercially popular music associated with the African American community—namely, hip-hop, soul, and rhythm and blues. In particular, she details the ways the rhyming, syncopations, dancelike gestures, melodies, and lyrics of Black girls' game songs have been adopted from and borrowed by the

commercial music of Black men from the 1950s to the present. Although others have suggested that Black girls' games and songs imitate music from radio and television, borrowing from genres such as rhythm and blues and hip-hop, Gaunt documents a dynamic circular relationship. Commercial songs may indeed be adopted, modified, and played within the girls' games and songs, but their games, musical styles, and group play are also sampled, borrowed, and appropriated by the popular music industry. Moreover, this occurs with a particular gender twist, as they are incorporated into music predominantly associated with men and masculinity.

As an example of this borrowing, Gaunt documents how "Down, Down Baby," a common song in Black girls' games, was appropriated into the chorus of the hit song "Country Grammar" by Grammy award–winning rap artist Nelly. (Elements of "Down, Down Baby" appear not only in "Country Grammar" but in many other commercial music sources as well, including the 1988 Tom Hanks movie *Big*.) In "Country Grammar," Nelly incorporates significant lyrical, rhythmic, melodic, and linguistic features of the game song while revising the lyrics to fit commercial, masculine-centered, mainstream hip-hop expectations.

By examining musical performance through the lens of gender, Gaunt raises important questions about the performance of gender and the patterns of interaction between women and men that are reflected through music. As women transfer embodied music across generations as a form of socialization, men appropriate women's music for commercial purposes, often without attribution. Nelly's rewritten lyrics, complete with macho references to being "cocked ready to let it go" and cannabis culture, stand in sharp contrast to the language and tone of girls' performances on the playground. Unlike many artists who have borrowed from girls' games, Nelly has publicly acknowledged the borrowing from a chant in a popular "children's game," although he fails to acknowledge girls as the primary performers of schoolyard songs.

Gaunt's examination of kinetic orality in the games Black girls play opens a window on the dynamic process of identity construction, including the construction of racial and gender identities, that emerges at the intersection of play, performance, creative expression, and art (Jamison 2006).

SHAPESHIFTING: PERFORMANCE AS RESISTANCE

In her book *Shapeshifters: Black Girls and the Choreography of Citizenship* (2015), anthropologist Aimee Cox explores the relationship between artistic performances and resistance work. Over a period of eight years, Cox conducted fieldwork as director, volunteer, and board member at Detroit's Fresh Start homeless shelter for girls and young women ages 15–22 and as co-founder of The BlackLight Project, an arts-based social justice project that emerged from the shelter.

Cox had been dancing since she was three years old, including studying classical ballet in high school at the College Conservatory of Music at the University of Cincinnati. While at Vassar College, Cox spent a semester studying with the Dance Theatre of Harlem—the world's first Black ballet company—and then spent a semester at the Alvin Ailey School to pursue modern dance. Eventually she danced professionally with Ailey II in New York City.

In graduate school, Cox decided to give up dancing to focus on establishing her credentials as an academic and intellectual. Then she began doing fieldwork at Fresh Start. "The minute I came to the homeless shelter," Cox said, "those young women would not allow me to leave [my professional training] behind. They were dancing on their own—not trained, they were not taking classes—they were moving their bodies, choreographing for each other, making these connections across their individual stories through dance and through writing. When I saw that, I said to myself, 'I need to start dancing again. I can't act like this is not a part of me.'

"It started off for them as kind of a creative healing space. They were frustrated at the end of the day by their struggles to survive in Detroit, and they started moving and dancing. I helped turn it into an artistic medium and a community, an educative creative space where they used those art forms to connect their stories. Through dance and storytelling they began to move from feeling their frustration and anger, to in-house community building, to political commentary."

In what eventually became the BlackLight Project, these women developed community workshops, training sessions, and street theater. "They did a lot of this on the street, because if they stayed in the shelter, no one would come and see it. Let's say they were at a bus stop in Detroit. And they'd have a hat, like street performers in New York City have a hat, saying that we're trying to collect some money. They would have the hat, and it would already be full with slips of paper with facts and stories, comments about the city, about the mayor at the time.

As part of the BlackLight Project, young women used their bodies to reimagine their relationship to intersecting oppressions.

They would start performing, and as the audience grew around them, they would stop; and in order for them to continue with the performance, one of those in the audience would have to take a piece of paper, read it, and start a discussion about it. So, in a small way, that was the way that these women used performance as more than just a spectacle, but also as a way to engage in a dialogue."

Cox refers to this kind of performative resistance work as shapeshifting. Through it, these young women shift the shape of the spaces they occupy, opening room within the intersecting oppressions that they experience in their daily lives—racism, poverty, sexism—for new possibilities and new imaginations. They also shift the shape of their own lives, reimagining themselves, transforming the stereotyped narratives too often limiting their futures, and fully claiming their rights to citizenship, visibility, and self-definition. "Through this kind of embodiment," notes Cox, "something else opens up—a different space, a different way of seeing the world, a different language, and even a different sort of courage around thinking about possibilities" (Cox 2013; Hetzler 2017; Nabinett 2016).

ART EXHIBITIONS AND DISPLAYS OF POWER: PLAYING THE HUMANITY GAME

How might art exhibits, special events, and museum displays that are designed to educate, illuminate, and build bridges of understanding across cultures instead reinforce stereotypes and create and maintain narratives of difference and exclusion? After September 11, 2001, many local and national institutions, universities, and grassroots organizations in the United States organized Middle Eastern art exhibits and special events for the first time. Established art institutions increased their displays of Middle Eastern and Islamic art, and art funders including the Rockefeller, Soros, Mellon, and Flora Family foundations contributed generously to underwrite the events and exhibits. All hoped to mobilize galleries and exhibit spaces to counter growing anti-Muslim rhetoric and rising talk of an inevitable "clash of civilizations" between Islam and the West. Art, they believed, would provide a unique venue for building bridges of cross-cultural understanding and an awareness of a common humanity (Boas 1927; Buchli 2002; Kant 1790; Morgan 1877).

But did the art events achieve this goal?

Anthropologist Jessica Winegar, a scholar of Middle Eastern art and politics, suggests that in fact these art events may have had the opposite of their intended effect—that is, they may have reinforced stereotypes and dichotomies rather than built bridges of understanding (see Marcus and Myers 1995; Price 1989). Winegar had a front-row seat to observe this phenomenon as virtual gallery operator for ArteEast, a nonprofit organization promoting cultural exchange between the United States, the Middle East, and North Africa. Drawing on her fieldwork in Egypt and her ethnography *Creative Reckonings: The Politics of Art*

and Culture in Contemporary Egypt (2006), Winegar was surprised to discover that displays of Middle Eastern art in Egypt and the United States differed dramatically, with U.S. art events presenting an extremely narrow slice of the Middle Eastern art world. Three selection biases were most frequent: historical art focusing on Islam's past achievements; music and rituals of Sufism, a mystical tradition within Islam, rather than mainstream orthodox Islam; and events featuring visual art and films by Middle Eastern women.

Why, wondered Winegar, were these the only categories considered "good Middle Eastern art" and selected for exhibition? Exhibitions largely ignored works celebrating contemporary orthodox Islam, despite the success of shows of art from Buddhist, Hindu, African, and Native American religious traditions. They seldom featured art by men. Middle Eastern art such as abstract painting or sculptures with no explicit reference to Islam or the Middle East could have been shown but was not. Missing was art representing resistance to occupation, music critical of the United States or Israel, political cartoons and graffiti, graphic art from Islamic publications, and even the genre of martyr posters and videos—all representing cultural practices involving significant creativity. Winegar suggests that what the U.S. art market would bear—what would attract funders and audiences—was shaped not by some objective notion of art but rather by the post–September 11 political landscape of war in Afghanistan and Iraq and a War on Terror that had established Islam and the Middle East as the enemy.

Winegar warns that by focusing on certain limited categories of art as "good Middle Eastern art" worthy of exhibition, these events actually served to reinforce perceived differences. So, while work by Middle Eastern women artists was popular, its representation played on stereotypes of Middle Eastern women and assumptions about gender inequality in Islam. For instance, such exhibits were

How do museums choose what to exhibit? Anthropologist Jessica Winegar critiques the narrow slice of Middle Eastern art considered appropriate for display. More frequently displayed "good Middle Eastern art," like this photograph "Speechless" (*left*) from the series *Women of Allah* by Shirin Neshat, an Iranian woman artist living in New York, contrasts with less frequently displayed, controversial pieces like "Saffurya" (*right*), a display of ceramic sacks by Palestinian artist Mervat Essa that memorializes the depopulation and destruction of Al Biram, her family's village, and many other Palestinian villages in 1948 at the creation of the state of Israel.

often presented and viewed as if critiquing Middle Eastern culture, particularly gender inequalities presumed to be derived from Islam. The artists themselves were often born in the Middle East but now residing in the West. While they were frequently viewed as human bridges of understanding, they were also seen as uniquely positioned and actively engaged in critiquing the culture from which they had come. In interviews with Winegar, audience members described the art as reflecting the submission of Middle Eastern and Muslim women and the desire of those women for freedom and liberty, even if these were not the intended meanings of the artist or presenter or were clearly contradicted by the exhibition booklets or wall descriptions.

Is it possible that, by framing so-called Islamic art to make it attractive, interesting, and palatable to funders and audiences, exhibitors actually reinforced the clash of civilizations and War on Terror frameworks rather than bring clarity to a complicated situation or build bridges of understanding? In the process of trying to accentuate common humanity through art—what Winegar calls "the Humanity Game"—could curators and funders' narrow selections have reinforced assumed oppositions between freedom and oppression, understanding and ignorance, civilization and barbarism? Winegar's research reveals the narrow limits imposed on the role of art as bridge builder and suggests that art's potential to serve as an avenue for expressing and perceiving common humanity is severely limited by the political context in which art is selected, funded, marketed, and viewed (Winegar 2008).

How Do Art and Media Intersect?

Appraise the ways art intersects with media.

Historically, anthropologists have carefully analyzed visual systems and visible culture as part of their ethnographic fieldwork. Art, media, material culture, and even museums become objects of anthropological inquiry. But visual media, including photography, film, television, videos, and web-based techniques, can also become tools of anthropological inquiry, drawing attention to the imaginative and sensory in ways ethnographic writing may not and opening up new possibilities for understanding the world.

Since the late nineteenth century, anthropologists like Franz Boas have incorporated photography and recorded film footage into their research, both to document their ethnographic projects and to provide visual support for their public educational work at home. Anthropologists Margaret Mead and Gregory Bateson set new standards for integrating the visual into their work, taking

25,000 photos and 22,000 feet of film in Bali, Indonesia, between 1931 and 1938. With the technological advance of portable, synchronous sound cameras in the 1960s, ethnographic filmmaking entered a new and expansive era (Ruby and Banks 2011).

Just as globalization has intensified the worldwide movement of people, money, data, goods, and services, so it has transformed the flow of images and sounds through new media technologies (Askew and Wilk 2007). Social media provide dynamic tools for disseminating art and engaging multiple populations. The anthropologist Arjun Appadurai (1990) calls this new formation a **global mediascape**: Global cultural flows of media and visual images enable linkages and communication across boundaries of culture, language, geography, economics, and politics in ways unimaginable a hundred years ago. Faye Ginsburg and colleagues (2002) have introduced the concept of **media worlds** to reflect more textured local realities and the tensions that exist when political, economic, and visual worlds collide in the context of contemporary globalization.

Just as newspapers dominated the mediascape in the late nineteenth century, radio, audio recordings, film, television, and the Internet have shaped communication in the twentieth and twenty-first centuries. In contemporary culture, the image—whether in photograph, film, or video—has replaced written texts as the primary educator. **Social media**, including Facebook, YouTube, Twitter, Instagram, Snapchat, and TikTok, have transformed communication for many people, and computer- and Internet-based technologies serve as sources of pleasure and social engagement, not merely as tools for work (Boellstorff 2008).

Today, media reach every corner of the globe and permeate all aspects of daily life. Media are everywhere humans live and everywhere anthropologists work. In fact, it is fair to say that media are central to human life in the twenty-first century. The decentralized production and circulation of new media, facilitated by satellites, computers, and handheld communication devices, has undermined the old media empires and has challenged the state's ability to control media content and media flows. In turn, new media have facilitated opportunities for activism as Indigenous and marginalized groups use photographs, film, text, and video to mobilize movements for social change and to challenge existing power structures (Askew and Wilk 2007; Ginsburg, Abu-Lughod, and Larkin 2002; Juris and Khasnabish 2013).

VISUAL IMAGES AND CULTURAL IDENTITY

Visual anthropology explores the production, circulation, and consumption of visual images, including photographs, film, television, and new media, focusing on the power of visual representations in art, performance, museums, and the mass media to influence culture and cultural identity (Hockings 2003). As you

global mediascape

Global cultural flows of media and visual images that enable linkages and communication across boundaries in ways unimaginable a century ago.

media worlds

An ethnographic and theoretical approach to media studies that focuses on the tensions that may exist when visual worlds collide in the context of contemporary globalization.

social media

Forms of communication founded on computer- and Internet-based technologies that facilitate social engagement, work, and pleasure.

visual anthropology

A field of anthropology that explores the production, circulation, and consumption of visual images, focusing on the power of visual representation to influence culture and cultural identity.

read the following discussion, you may be surprised to discover the power that photographs have to wield such influence.

National Geographic's Photographic Gaze.
In a classic work of visual anthropology, *Reading National Geographic* (1993), anthropologists Catherine Lutz and Jane Collins examine the photographs of the popular U.S. magazine *National Geographic* to reveal the power of visual images to shape cultural perspectives and behavior. Launched in 1888, *National Geographic* has successfully blended science, art, photojournalism, and entertainment to become one of the most popular and influential U.S. sources of information about other cultures. Indeed, it collects "the world between its covers." At its peak, the reasonably priced magazine attracted more than 10 million monthly subscribers (97 percent White and middle class) and, including casual readers in classrooms, lobbies, and doctors' offices, perhaps 40 million total viewers. *National Geographic*'s beautiful photos of smiling people from around the globe have inspired world travel, scientific exploration, and even sexual fantasies for generations of U.S. readers.

National Geographic may at first glance appear to offer a straightforward presentation of evidence about human nature and the natural world. But Lutz and Collins, using the analytical frameworks of visual anthropology, ask how the particular "gaze" of *National Geographic* photographs may reflect the worldviews of those behind the lens—that is, the magazine's owners, editors, photographers, and graphic designers. This gaze, the authors suggest, can shape the understandings of the magazine's readers as they think about humanity, the natural world, and their own culture's position in the global arena.

To investigate this claim, Lutz and Collins interviewed editors and readers and analyzed photographs from the magazine's nearly 600 articles published about non-Western topics between 1950 and 1986. The researchers asked: What messages did these images convey? What was their intent?

According to the magazine's mission statement, issued in 1915, "only what is of a kindly nature is printed about any country or people; everything unpleasant or unduly critical is to be avoided" (Lutz and Collins, 1993, 27). Indeed, underlying the exquisite photos of seemingly happy people, elaborate rituals, and exotic costumes, Lutz and Collins perceive a particular editorial perspective and philosophical worldview. They draw the following conclusion: "Clearly, photographic practice at *National Geographic* is geared to a classic form of humanism, drawing readers' attention through its portrayal of difference, and then showing that under the colorful dress and skin, as it were, we are all more or less the same" (1993, 61). Even though this editorial viewpoint—expressed in the **photographic gaze**—appeared neutral, it projected a particular perspective on human nature, the natural world, history, and difference.

photographic gaze

The presumed neutral viewpoint of the camera that in fact projects the perspective of the person behind the camera onto human nature, the natural world, and history.

In projecting an almost magical sense of unity, the magazine's photographic gaze tended to overlook key aspects of human history. Photographers and editors selected and framed images to limit political and economic contexts. Conflict, inequality, poverty, and hunger were downplayed or completely avoided. In keeping with this editorial approach, photos of the period under study rarely portrayed dramatic world events of the time. Struggles for decolonization, the Cold War, the Vietnam War, or movements for civil rights, women's rights, and gay rights in the United States were left out of the magazine's photographic gaze. Lutz and Collins note that the magazine's editorial choices consistently minimized diversity and difference, especially along the lines of race and gender.

The authors suggest that during the period they studied, the gaze of *National Geographic*'s images created a cultural lens that mediated U.S. middle-class readers' experiences of the world, its diverse people, and the United States' place in it. The photographs avoided images that might disrupt readers' views. Instead, the magazine's gaze provided reassurance that (1) in essential ways the world that seems so diverse is actually quite familiar; (2) fundamentally, all is well with the world; and (3) the readers and their country play a benevolent role in world events. Here, Lutz and Collins suggest, the power of *National Geographic*'s photographs to shape the U.S. cultural worldview held deep implications for how the magazine's primarily middle-class readers engaged debates about the nation's domestic and foreign policy (Fernea 1996; Goldstein 1998).

National Geographic's photographic gaze has continued to change over the years. But the concept of the gaze, central to visual anthropology, provides an important tool for thinking about how the form and content of media are shaped by those "behind the camera." As you engage with media throughout your day— through television shows, news broadcasts, websites, tweets, YouTube channels, movies, social media—can you use the concept of the photographic gaze as a tool to analyze the intentionally and unintentionally expressed worldviews of the owners, editors, designers, videographers, and others behind the scenes?

ETHNOGRAPHIC FILMS AND THE GLOBAL MEDIASCAPE

Ethnographic filmmaking, with a long history in anthropology, has emerged in recent decades as the dominant force in visual anthropology. Classic ethnographic films, such as Robert Flaherty's silent film *Nanook of the North* (1922) shot among the Indigenous Inuit of Canada, John Marshall's many films about the Ju/'hoansi of Namibia, Napoleon Chagnon and Tim Asch's *The Ax Fight* (1975) about the Yanomami in southern Venezuela, and Robert Gardner's *Dead Birds* (1963) set in New Guinea, broke ground in promoting the use of images for the description, analysis, and interpretation of human behavior, often focusing on individuals and communities in rural, tribal, and seemingly isolated settings. More contemporary ethnographic films, like *Exit Zero* and *Leviathan* discussed in this section, strive to show local communities in their rapidly shifting, friction-filled global contexts and to illuminate the complex and changing web of relationships between humans, diverse species, and their environments (Grimshaw and Ravetz 2009; MacDougall 2005; Young 1995).

In today's interconnected global age, digital video filmmaking has taken on a key role in giving voice to the concerns of local communities through what visual anthropologists call **Indigenous media**. The power of media to overcome boundaries of time and space is increasingly harnessed by people who have experienced massive economic, political, and geographic disruption to mediate rapid change and build alternative strategies for communication, survival, and empowerment.

Indigenous media
The use of media by people who have experienced massive economic, political, and geographic disruption to build alternative strategies for communication, survival, and empowerment.

Chinese Villagers Stay Connected through Festival Videos.

For new immigrants far from home, for instance, the creation and circulation of media forms like digital video has tremendous potential to unify immigrants, help them resist dominant narratives of otherness, and reinforce their solidarity with their native communities.

In early 2007, I attended a temple festival in a small village on China's southeast coast. I had visited the village previously, but the opportunity to participate in a full two weeks of festivities at the invitation of the temple master was a unique privilege. Vivid rituals, raucous processions, solemn prayers, and bountiful banquets filled the days. But the constant presence of a small film crew documenting every element of temple life surprised me. One afternoon, the temple master asked if I would be willing to be interviewed on camera to say a few words about the festival. As a grateful guest—and an oddity as the only non-Chinese person at the festival—I readily agreed, gave an interview at the foot of a beautiful new pagoda overlooking the harbor, and thought little more about the matter.

Back in New York a few weeks later, I placed a call to a young woman from the village now living in Flushing, Queens. Her mother, still living in China, had entrusted me to deliver some baby clothes for her new granddaughter. We agreed to meet the next day on a corner of Main Street in Flushing—a meeting that, despite her assurances, I doubted would go smoothly on one of the busiest intersections in New York City.

I patiently waited the next day on the appointed corner. Much to my surprise, at the agreed-on time a car pulled up, a window rolled down, and a young woman said in Chinese, "Professor Guest, get in!" Over dumplings and tea she explained, "Everyone from the village knows you! You're in the video!" It turns out that in order to keep immigrant villagers connected to the home temple and engaged in its spiritual and financial life, the temple master regularly produced and circulated festival videos to his devotees now living in the New York metropolitan area. Video of the festival I attended had traversed the globe from a rural Chinese village to the streets of New York City, serving to build solidarity among immigrant villagers now in the United States and to strengthen connections with their kinfolk, fellow townspeople, and religious co-adherents in China.

The forces of globalization move people, money, things—and images. A Chinese village festival had now entered the global mediascape.

Can you also imagine some of the power dynamics that may be revealed by such a video production? Consider all of the players involved: funders, filmmakers, editors, an anthropologist, distributors, and recipients. How might the global exchange of media intersect and affect existing relationships of power?

Today, media is reshaping human life in every part of the world as it increasingly permeates the routines of daily life. As you think about the expanding global mediascape, can you see how your everyday actions—friendships, education, love life, job, entertainment, religion, political engagements, communications, and more—are mediated by technologies in ways unimaginable even two decades ago? The anthropology of media will continue to develop as this global mediascape expands and deepens. What will the next two decades bring? How will anthropologists use the tools of our discipline to understand the impact of these changes on people and their communities across the globe?

Toolkit

Thinking Like an Anthropologist
The Landscape of World Art

Art is everywhere in our lives. From the games we play and the songs we sing to the way we dress and the food we eat, we humans express ourselves creatively and interact with one another through creative expression. As we have seen throughout this chapter, communication between artist and audience through art objects, performances, events, and experiences is not limited to elite actors or venues but is present throughout human cultures and deeply rooted in the activities of everyday life. This chapter's opening story described the creative ways young people in a Brazilian favela have built community, challenged the political and economic assumptions of the state, and projected their concerns into a national and international dialogue. When do games take on a life of their own? How do they become political action or efforts at community building? How do they become art? How are creative expression, play, performance, and art related?

Through Morrinho, imaginative young people engage in an evolving drama that performs, imitates, and examines life. The players construct artificial scenarios and relationships through which they explore their own emotional and social worlds. By telling an untold story or history, speaking the truth of a community back to its members and the surrounding culture and political structures, the virtual world of Morrinho explores those boundaries among real life, play, and the creative expressions and engagements that anthropologists call art.

In this chapter, we have begun to consider the vast landscape of world art. Where can you find these dynamics in your own life? In what ways are you an artist? How do you use media technology to express your creativity and communicate with others through the global mediascape?

As you think more about the world of art, remember the opening questions that framed this chapter's inquiries:

- **What is art?**

- **What is unique about how anthropologists study art?**

- **What is the relationship between art and power?**

- **How do art and media intersect?**

After reading this chapter, you should be able to apply these questions to situations in which you encounter art and media and the intersections of real life, play, politics, and creative expression. Thinking like an anthropologist about the world of art can give you a more complete set of tools for comprehending this complex part of human culture, understanding your own creativity, and engaging the world around you.

Key Terms

art (p. 459)

fine art (p. 460)

popular art (p. 460)

universal gaze (p. 462)

authenticity (p. 468)

ethnomusicology (p. 471)

kinetic orality (p. 471)

global mediascape (p. 477)

media worlds (p. 477)

social media (p. 477)

visual anthropology (p. 477)

photographic gaze (p. 478)

Indigenous media (p. 480)

References

Abu-Lughod, Janet L. 1989. *Before European Hegemony: The World System* A.D. *1250–1350*. New York: Oxford University Press.

———. 2000. *Veiled Sentiments: Honor and Poetry in a Bedouin Society*. Berkeley: University of California Press.

Abu-Lughod, Lila. 2005. *Dramas of Nationhood: The Politics of Television in Egypt*. Chicago: University of Chicago Press.

Agard-Jones, Vanessa. 2013. "Bodies in the System." *Small Axe: A Caribbean Journal of Criticism* 17(3) 182–192.

Agrama, Hussein Ali. 2010. "Ethics, Tradition, Authority: Toward an Anthropology of the Fatwa." *American Ethnologist* 37(1): 2–18.

———. 2012. *Questioning Secularism: Islam, Sovereignty and the Rule of Law in Modern Egypt*. Chicago: Chicago University Press.

Ahearn, Laura M. 2012. *Living Language: An Introduction to Linguistic Anthropology*. Malden, MA: Wiley-Blackwell.

———. 2017. *Living Language: An Introduction to Linguistic Anthropology* 2nd ed.. Malden, MA: Wiley-Blackwell.

Alexander, Edward P. 1996. "What Is a Museum?" In *Museums in Motion: An Introduction to the History and Functions of Museums*, edited by Edward P. Alexander and MaryAlexander. Walnut Creek, CA: AltaMira. Published in cooperation with the American Association for State and Local History.

Alexander, J. 2001. "Islam, Archaeology, and Slavery in Africa." *World Archaeology*, 33(1): 44–60.

Alexander, Michelle. 2012. *The New Jim Crow: Mass Incarceration in the Age of Colorblindness* (rev. ed.). New York: The New Press.

Allison, Anne. 1994. *Nightwork: Sexuality, Pleasure, and Corporate Masculinity in a Tokyo Hostess Club*. Chicago: University of Chicago Press.

———. 2019. "Caravans of Martyrs: A Review." *American Ethnologist* 46 (2): 227–228.

Alpers, Svetlana. 1991. "Museums as a Way of Seeing." In *Exhibiting Cultures: The Poetics and Politics of Museum Display*, edited by Ivan Karp and Steven Lavine, 25–32. Washington, DC: Smithsonian Institution.

American Anthropological Association. 2004. "Statement on Marriage and the Family." www .aaanet.org/issues/policy-advocacy/Statement -on-Marriage-and-the-family.cfm.

———. 2019. "What Is Anthropology?" www .americananthro.org/AdvanceYourCareer /Content.aspx?ItemNumber=2150&navItem Number=740.

American Academy of Pediatrics. 2000. "Evaluation of the Newborn with Developmental Anomalies of the External Genitalia." *Pediatrics* 106(1): 138–42.

———. 2006. "Children, Adolescents, and Advertising." *Pediatrics* 118(6): 2563–69.

Anderson, Benedict. 1983. *Imagined Communities: Reflections on the Origin and Spread of Nationalism*. London: Verso.

Anderson, E. N. 2005. *Everyone Eats: Understanding Food and Culture*. New York: NYU Press.

Angelini, Alessandro. 2016. "Favela in Replica: Iterations and Itineraries of a Miniature City." *Journal of Latin American and Caribbean Anthropology* 20(3): 39-60.

Anglin, Mary K. 2002. *Women, Power, and Dissent in the Hills of Carolina*. Urbana: University of Illinois.

Antioch College Sexual Offense Prevention Policy, cited in Cameron, Deborah. 1994. "Degrees of Consent: The Antioch College Sexual Offense Policy." In *The Language and Sexuality Reader*, edited by Deborah Cameron and Don Kulick. New York: Routledge, 2006.

Appadurai, Arjun, ed. 1986. *The Social Life of Things: Commodities in Cultural Perspective*. Cambridge, UK: Cambridge University Press.

———. 1990. "Disjuncture and Difference in the Global Cultural Economy." *Public Culture* 2(2): 1–24.

Appiah, Kwame Anthony. 2006. *Cosmopolitanism: Ethics in a World of Strangers*. New York: Norton.

Archetti, Eduardo P. 1999. *Masculinities: Football, Polo and the Tango in Argentina.* Oxford, UK: Berg.

Arobba, Biagio, Robert E. McGrath, Joe Futrelle, and Alan B. Craig. 2010. *A Community-Based Social Media Approach for Preserving Endangered Languages and Culture.* www.ideals.illinois.edu /bitstream/handle/2142/17078/lat-comm-info -2-sep-2010.pdf?sequence=2.

Asad, Talal, ed. 1973. *Anthropology and the Cultural Encounter.* London: Ithaca Press.

———. 1992. *Anthropology & the Colonial Encounter.* Atlantic Highlands, NJ: Humanity Books.

———. 1993. *Genealogies of Religion: Discipline and Reasons of Power in Christianity and Islam.* Baltimore: Johns Hopkins University Press.

Asch, Timothy, and Napoleon Chagnon. 1975. *The Ax Fight.* Watertown, MA: Documentary Educational Resources.

Askew, Kelly Michelle, and Richard R. Wilk, eds. 2007. *The Anthropology of Media: A Reader.* Malden, MA: Blackwell.

Baer, Hans A., and Merrill Singer. 1995. *Critical Medical Anthropology.* Amityville, New York: Baywood Publishing Co.

Baer, Hans A., Merrill Singer, and Ida Susser. 2003. *Medical Anthropology and the World System.* Westport, CT: Praeger.

Baker, Lee D. 1995. "Racism in Professional Settings: Forms of Address as Clues to Power Relations." *Journal of Applied Behavioral Science* 31(2): 186–201.

———. 2004. "Franz Boas Out of the Ivory Tower." *Anthropological Theory* 4(1): 29–51.

Bank for International Settlements. "About Derivatives Statistcs." 2018. https://www.bis.org/publ /otc_hy1810.htm.

———. 2021. "OTC derivatives statistics at end-June 2021." https://www.bis.org/publ/otc _hy2111.htm.

Barth, Fredrik. 1959. *Political Leadership among Swat Pathans.* London: Athlone Press.

———. 1969. "Introduction." In *Ethnic Groups and Boundaries,* edited by Fredrik Barth. Boston: Little, Brown.

Basquiat, Jennifer Huss. 2004. "Embodied Mormonism: Performance, Vodou and the LDS Faith in Haiti." *Dialogue: A Journal of Mormon Thought* 37 (4): 1–34.

Beidelman, T. O. 1994. "*African Art in Transit* [Review]." *Anthropos* 89(4/6): 653–54.

Beilin, Ruth. 2011. "Conservation is our Government Now: The Politics of Ecology in Papua New Guinea: A Review." *Journal of Agricultural and Environmental Ethics* 24 (1) 75-85.

Bellah, Robert. 1980. *Varieties of Civil Religion.* San Francisco: Harper & Row.

Bellamy, Carla. 2011. *The Powerful Ephemeral: Everyday Healing in an Ambiguously Islamic Place.* Berkeley: University of California Press.

Benedict, Ruth. 1934. *Patterns of Culture.* Boston: Houghton Mifflin.

———. 1946. *The Chrysanthemum and the Sword: Patterns of Japanese Culture.* Boston: Houghton Mifflin.

Bennett, R. L., et al. 2002. "Genetic Counseling and Screening of Consanguineous Couples and Their Offspring: Recommendations of the National Society of Genetic Counselors." *Journal of Genetic Counseling* 11(2): 97–119.

Benton, Aida and Kim Yi Dionne. 2015. "International Political Economy and the 2014 West African Ebola Outbreak." *African Studies Review* 58(1): 223-236.

Berger, Peter, ed. 1999. *The Desecularization of the World: Resurgent Religion and World Politics.* Grand Rapids, MI: Wm. B. Eerdmans.

Bern, Sandra Lipsitz. 1981. "Gender Schema Theory: A Cognitive Account of Sex Typing." *Psychological Review* 88: 354–64.

———. 1983. "Gender Schema Theory and Its Implications for Child Development: Raising Gender-Aschematic Children in a Gender-Schematic Society." *Signs: Journal of Women in Culture and Society* 8: 598–616.

Bernal, Victoria. 2014. *Nation as Network: Diaspora, Cyberspace and Citizenship.* Chicago and London: The University of Chicago Press.

Besteman, Catherine L. ed. 2002. *Violence: A Reader.* New York: New York University Press.

Besteman, Catherine L., and Lee V. Cassanelli. 1996. *The Struggle for Land in Southern Somalia: The War Behind the War.* Boulder, CO: Westview Press.

Bestor, Theodore C. 2001. "Supply-Side Sushi: Commodity, Market, and the Global City." *American Anthropologist* 102(1): 76–95.

———. 2004. *Tsukiji: The Fish Market at the Center of the World.* Berkeley: University of California Press.

Bickford, Andrew. 2011. *Fallen Elites: The Military Other in Post-unification Germany.* Stanford, CA: Stanford University Press.

Blackless, Melanie et al. 2000."How Sexually Dimorphic are We? Review and Synthesis." *American Journal of Human Biology* (12) 2.

Board of Governors of the Federal Reserve System. 2016. "Changes in U.S. Family Finances from 2013 to 2016: Evidence from the Survey of Consumer Finances." https://www.federalreserve.gov/publications/files/scf17.pdf.

Boas, Franz. 1912. "Changes in the Bodily Form of Descendants of Immigrants." *American Anthropologist* 14(3).

———. 1927. *Primitive Art.* New York: Dover.

———. 1966. *Kwakiutl Ethnography* (Classics of Anthropology). edited by Helen F. Codere. Chicago: University of Chicago Press.

Boehm, Christopher. 1999. *Hierarchy in the Forest: The Evolution of Egalitarian Behavior.* Cambridge, MA: Harvard University Press.

Boellstorff, Tom. 2007. "Queer Studies in the House of Anthropology." *Annual Review of Anthropology* 36: 17–35.

Boellstorff, Tom, and Cymene Howe. 2015. "Queer Futures." http://culanth.org/fieldsights/709-queer-futures.

Bohannan, Laura. 1966. "Shakespeare in the Bush: An American Anthropologist Set Out to Study the Tiv of West Africa and Was Taught the True Meaning of *Hamlet*." *Natural History* 75: 28–33.

Bolin, Anne. 1992. "Families We Choose: Lesbians, Gays, Kinship [Review]." *American Anthropologist* 94(4): 947–48.

Bonilla-Silva, Eduardo. 2010. *Racism without Racists: Color-Blind Racism and Racial Inequality in Contemporary America* (3rd ed.). New York: Rowan and Littlefield.

Bonvillain, Nancy. 2007. *Women and Men: Cultural Constructions of Gender* (4th ed.). Upper Saddle River, NJ: Prentice Hall.

Bourdieu, Pierre. 1982. *Ce que parler veut dire*. Paris: Fayard.

———. 1984. *Distinction: A Social Critique of the Judgment of Taste*. Translated by R. Nice. Cambridge, MA: Harvard University Press.

Bourdieu, Pierre, with Jean-Claude Passeron. (1970) 1990. *Reproduction in Education, Society and Culture* (2nd ed.) (Theory, Culture, and Society Series vol. 4). Translated by Lois Wacquant. New York: Sage.

Bourgois, Philippe. 2003. *In Search of Self-Respect: Selling Crack in El Barrio* (2nd ed.). Cambridge, UK: Cambridge University Press.

Bowen, John R. 2006. *Why the French Don't Like Headscarves: Islam, the State, and Public Space.* Princeton, NJ: Princeton University Press.

Bowie, Fiona. 2006. *The Anthropology of Religion: An Introduction* (2nd ed.). Malden, MA: Blackwell.

Brash, Julian. 2011. *Bloomberg's New York: Class and Governance in the Luxury City*. Athens: University of Georgia.

Braudel, Fernand. (1979) 1992. *Civilization and Capitalism, 15th to 18th Centuries*, vol. 3, *The Perspective of the World*. Translated by Siân Reynolds. Berkeley: University of California Press.

Brettell, Caroline B., and C. F. Sargent, eds. 2009. *Gender in Cross-Cultural Perspective* (5th ed.). Upper Saddle River, NJ: Pearson/Prentice Hall.

Bridges, Khiara M. 2011. *Reproducing Race: An Ethnography of Pregnancy as a Site of Racialization.* Berkeley: University of California Press.

Bridges, Tristan S. 2007. "Dude You're a Fag: Masculinity and Sexuality in High School [Review]." *Gender and Society* 21(5): 776–78.

Bringa, Tone. 1995. *Being Muslim the Bosnian Way: Identity and Community in a Central Bosnian Village.* Princeton, NJ: Princeton University Press.

Bringa, Tone, and Peter Loizos. 2002. *Returning Home: Revival of a Bosnian Village.* Sage Film and Video (Sarajevo).

Brodkin, Karen. 1998. *How Jews Became White Folks and What That Says About Race in America.* New Brunswick: Rutgers University Press.

———. 2007. "Foreword." In *The Gender of Globalization: Women Navigating Cultural and Economic Marginalities*, edited by Nandini Gunewardena and Ann Kingsolver. Santa Fe, NM: School for Advanced Research Press.

Brown, Jacqueline Nassy. 2007. "Suriname, Sweet Suriname [Review]." *GLQ: A Journal of Lesbian and Gay Studies* 13(2–3): 406–8.

Brown, Lester R. 2011a. "When the Nile Runs Dry." *New York Times*, June 1.

———. 2011b. *World on the Edge: How to Prevent Environmental and Economic Collapse.* New York: Norton.

Brubaker, Rogers. 2004. *Ethnicity without Groups.* Cambridge, MA: Harvard University Press.

Brundage, W. Fitzhugh. 1993. *Lynching in the New South: Georgia and Virginia, 1880–1930.* Chicago: University of Illinois Press.

Buchli, Victor, ed. 2002. *The Material Culture Reader.* Oxford, UK: Berg.

Buck, Pem Davidson. 2001. *Worked to the Bone: Race, Class, Power, and Privilege in Kentucky.* New York: Monthly Review Press.

———. 2009. *In/equality: An Alternative Anthropology.* Redding, CA: CAT Publishing.

Budrys, Grace. 2010. *Unequal Health: How Inequality Contributes to Health or Illness.* Lanham, MD: Rowman & Littlefield.

Buss, David M. 2016 [1994]. *The Evolution of Desire: Strategies of Human Mating, Revised.* New York, NY: Basic Books.

Butler, Judith. 1990. *Gender Trouble: Feminism and the Subversion of Identity.* New York: Routledge.

Calderwood, Brent. 2008. "Be Butch or Be Bashed." *Gay and Lesbian Review* 155(1): 38–39.

Cameron, Deborah. 2007. *The Myth of Mars and Venus.* Oxford, UK: Oxford University Press.

Cameron, Deborah, and Don Kulick, eds. 2006. *The Language and Sexuality Reader.* New York: Routledge.

Cardoso, Fernando Henrique, and Enzo Faletto. 1969. *Dependencia y desarrollo en American Latina: ensayo de interpretación sociologica.* Mexico City, México: Siglo Veintiuno Editores.

Carneiro, Robert. 1978. "Political Expansion as an Expression of the Principle of Competitive Exclusion." In *Origins of the State*, edited by Ronald Cohn and Elman Service. Philadelphia: Institute for the Study of Human Issues.

———. 1981. "The Chiefdom: Precursor of the State." In *The Transition to Statehood in the New World*, edited by Grant Jones and Robert Kautz, 37–79. Cambridge, UK: Cambridge University Press.

Carrillo, Héctor. 2018. *Pathways of Desire: The Sexual Migration of Mexican Gay Men.* Chicago: The University of Chicago Press.

Carrington, Damian. 2018. "'Our leaders are like children,' school strike founder tells climate summit." *The Guardian.* https://www.theguardian.com/environment/2018/dec/04/leaders-like-children-school-strike-founder-greta-thunberg-tells-un-climate-summit.

Caroll, Patrick. 2016. "Beyond the Big Ditch: Politics, Ecology, and Infrastructure at the Panama Canal: A Review." *Technology and Culture* 57 (2) 467–469.

Carroll, John B., ed. 1956. *Language, Thought, and Reality: Selected Writings of Benjamin Lee Whorf.* Cambridge, MA: MIT Press.

Carse, Ashley. 2014. *Beyond the Big Ditch: Politics, Ecology and Infrastructure at the Panama Canal.* Cambridge: The Massachusetts Institute of Technology Press.

Carsten, Janet. 1997. *The Heat of the Hearth: The Process of Kinship in a Malay Fishing Community.* Oxford, UK: Clarendon Press.

———. 2004. *After Kinship.* Cambridge, UK: Cambridge University Press.

Casanova, Jose. 1994. *Public Religions in the Modern World.* Chicago: University of Chicago Press.

Cawthon Lang, Kristina. 2005. "Primate Factsheets: Gorilla Taxonomy, Morphology, & Ecology." Primate Info Net. http://pin.primate.wisc.edu/factsheets/entry/gorilla/taxon.

Cazenave, Noel A. 2011. *The Urban Racial State: Managing Race Relations in American Cities.* Lanham, MD: Rowan and Littlefield.

Ceraldi, Sara. 2018. "Can Cryptocurrency Revolutionize the Rituals of Money?" *Sapiens*, August 3. https://www.sapiens.org/culture/cryptocurrency-money-ritual/.

Césaire, Aimé Fernand David. 1955. *Discourse on Colonialism.* Paris: Preĭsence africaine.

Cha, Ariana Eunjung, 2018. "44 Siblings and Counting." *Washington Post.*

Chagnon, Napoleon A. 1968. *Yąnomamö: The Fierce People.* New York: Holt, Rinehart and Winston.

Chan, Kai M.A. and Terre Satterfield. 2007. "Conservation is our Government Now: The Politics of Ecology in Papua New Guinea: A Review." *Conservation Biology* 21 1380-1382.

Chan, Selina Ching. 2006. "Love and Jewelry: Patriarchal Control, Conjugal Ties, and Changing Identities." In *Modern Loves: The Anthropology of Romantic Courtship and Companionate Marriage*, edited by Jennifer S. Hirsch and Holly Wardlow, 35–50. Ann Arbor: University of Michigan Press.

Chang, Liu. 2017. "What China's Migrant Numbers Say About Labor Discrimination." *Sixth Tone.* https://www.sixthtone.com/news/2066/what-chinas-migrant-numbers-say-about-labor-discrimination.

Chapman, Gary. 2010. *The 5 Love Languages: The Secret to Love That Lasts.* Chicago: Northfield Publishing.

Chapman, Rachel R., and Jean R. Berggren. 2005. "Radical Contextualization: Contributions to an Anthropology of Racial/Ethnic Health Disparities." *Health* 9(2): 145–67.

Checker, Melissa. 2005. *Polluted Promises: Environmental Racism and the Search for Justice in a Southern Town.* New York: New York University Press.

Cheyney, Melissa, Bahareh Goodarzi, Therese Wiegers, Robbie Davis-Floyd, and Saraswathi Vedam. 2019. "Giving Birth in the United States and the Netherlands: Midwifery Care as Integrated Option or Contested Privilege?" In *Birth in Eight Cultures.* 2019. Davis-Floyd, Robbie and Melissa Cheyney, eds. Long Grove, IL: Waveland Press.

Chio, Jenny. 2014. *A Landscape of Travel: The Work of Tourism in Rural Ethnic China.* Seattle: University of Washington Press.

Chodorow, Nancy. 1974. "Strategies, Cooperation and Conflict among Women in Domestic Groups." In *Woman, Culture and Society*, edited by Michelle Z. Rosaldo and Louise Lamphere, 97–113. Stanford, CA: Stanford University Press.

Claeys, Priscilla and Marc Edelman. 2020. "Grassroots Voices: The United Nations Declaration on the Rights of Peasants and Other People Working in Rural Areas." *Journal of Peasant Studies* 47(1): 1–68.

Coe, Cati. 2013. *The Scattered Family: Parenting, African Migrants, and Global Inequality. Chicago:* University of Chicago Press.

———. 2019. *Changes in Care: Aging, Migration, and Social Class in West Africa.* New Brunswick, NJ: Rutgers University Press.

Cohen, Yehudi A. 1974. *Man in Adaptation: The Cultural Present.* Chicago: Aldine.

Coleman, Simon. 2021. *Powers of Pilgrimage: Religion in a World of Movement.* New York: New York University Press.

Coles, Kimberly. 2007. *Democratic Designs: International Intervention and Electoral Practices in Postwar Bosnia-Herzegovina.* Ann Arbor: University of Michigan Press.

Comaroff, John L., and Jean Comaroff. 2009. *Ethnicity, Inc.* Chicago: University of Chicago Press.

Contessa, Damien. 2013. "Swamplife: People, Gators, and Mangroves Entangled in the Everglades: A Review." *Journal of Ecological Anthropology* 16 (1) 104-107.

Coontz, Stephanie. 1988. *The Social Origins of Private Life: A History of American Families 1600–1900.* New York: Verso.

———. 1992. *The Way We Never Were: American Families and the Nostalgia Trap.* New York: Basic Books.

Cowen, M. P., and R. W. Shenton. 1996. *Doctrines of Development.* London: Routledge.

Cox, Aimee Meredith. 2013. Personal interview with Kenneth J. Guest.

———. 2015. *Shapeshifters: Black Girls and the Choreography of Citizenship.* Durham, NC: Duke University Press.

Cronon, William. 1995. "The Trouble with Wilderness; or, Getting Back to the Wrong Nature." In *Uncommon Ground: Rethinking the Human Place in Nature*, Cronon, William ed., New York: W. W. Norton & Co.

Cruikshank, Julie. 2005. *Do Glaciers Listen? Local Knowledge, Colonial Encounters, and Social Imagination.* Vancouver: The University of British Columbia Press.

Curtis, Debra A. 1996. "Review of *Nightwork: Sexuality, Pleasure, and Corporate Masculinity in a Tokyo Hostess Club.*" *Gender and Society* 10(2): 215–16.

———. 2009. *Pleasures and Perils: Girls' Sexuality in a Caribbean Consumer Culture.* New Brunswick, NJ: Rutgers University Press.

Dahlberg, Frances, ed. 1981. *Woman the Gatherer.* New Haven, CT: Yale University Press.

Darwin, Helana. 2017. "Doing Gender Beyond the Binary: A Virtual Ethnography." *Symbolic Interaction* 40(3), 317-334.

Davidov, Veronica. 2013. *Ecotourism and Cultural Production: An Anthropology of Equal Spaces in Ecuador.* New York: Palgrave MacMillan.

Davidson, Julia O'Connell. 1997. "Review of *Nightwork: Sexuality, Pleasure, and Corporate Masculinity in a Tokyo Hostess Club.*" *Signs* 22(3): 759–61.

Davies, James B., Susanna Sandstrom, Anthony Shorrocks, and Edward N. Wolff. 2009. *The Level and Distribution of Global Household Wealth.* Helsinki: UNU-WIDER.

Davis, Frederick R. 2012. "Swamplife: People, Gators, and Mangroves Entangled in the Everglades." *Environmental History* 17 (2) 443-445.

Davis, Georgiann. 2015. *Contesting Intersex: The Dubious Diagnosis.* New York: NYU Press.

Davis-Floyd, Robbie. 1992. *Birth as an American Rite of Passage.* Berkeley: University of California Press.

Davis-Floyd, Robbie, and Joseph Dumit, eds. 1997. *Cyborg Babies: From Techno-Sex to Techno-Tots.* London: Routledge.

Davis-Floyd, Robbie and Melissa Cheyney, eds. (2019). *Birth in Eight Cultures.* Long Grove, IL: Waveland Press, Inc.

Deloria, Vine, Jr. 1969. *Custer Died for Your Sins: An Indian Manifesto.* New York: Macmillan.

D'Emilio, John, and Estelle B. Freedman. 1998. *Intimate Matters: A History of Sexuality in America* (2nd ed.). Chicago: University of Chicago Press.

de Waal, Frans. 2002. "Primate Behavior and Human Aggression." In *Must We Fight?: From the Battlefield to the Schoolyard, a New Perspective on Violent Conflict and Its Prevention*, edited by William L. Ury, 13–25. San Francisco: Jossey-Bass.

———. 2014. *The Bonobo and the Atheist: In Search of Humanism Among the Primates.* New York: W.W. Norton.

Dhillon, Jaskiran. 2018. "Indigenous Resurgence, Decolonization and Movements for Environmental Justice." *Environment and Society: Advances in Research* 9 (1): 1-5.

Diamond, Jared. 1997. "The Animal with the Weirdest Sex Life." In *Constructing Sexualities: Readings in Sexuality, Gender and Culture*, edited by Suzanne LaFont. Upper Saddle River, NJ: Prentice Hall, 2002.

Dill, Bonnie Thornton. 1983. "Race, Class and Gender: Prospects for an All-Inclusive Sisterhood." *Feminist Studies* 9: 131–50.

Dolan, Kerry A., and Luisa Kroll. 2019. "Forbes 2019 Billionaires: The Richest People in the World." *Forbes*, March 5, 2019. https://www.forbes.com/billionaires/#75aac7f6251c

Domhoff, G. William. 2019. *Who Rules America?* https://whorulesamerica.usc.edu/.Dorow, Sara. 2006. *Transnational Adoption: A Cultural Economy of Race, Gender, and Kinship.* New York: New York University Press.

Downey, Greg. 2005. *Learning Capoeira: Lessons in Cunning from an Afro-Brazilian Art.* New York: Oxford University Press.

Dunbar-Ortiz, Roxanne. 2015. *An Indigenous Peoples' History of the United States.* Boston: Beacon Hill Press.

Dunham, Katherine. 1969. *Island Possessed.* Garden City, NY: Doubleday.

Duranti, Alessandro, ed. 2009. *Linguistic Anthropology: A Reader* (second edition). Malden, MA: Blackwell Publishing.

Durkheim, Émile. (1912) 1965. *The Elementary Forms of Religious Life.* New York: Free Press.

Durrenberger, E. Paul, and Suzan Erem. 2010. *Anthropology Unbound: A Field Guide to the 21st Century* (2nd ed.). Boulder, CO: Paradigm.

Edelman, Marc. 1999. *Peasants against Globalization: Rural Social Movements in Costa Rica.* Stanford, CA: Stanford University Press.

———. 2001. "Social Movements: Changing Paradigms and Forms of Politics." *Annual Review of Anthropology* 30: 285–317.

———. 2014. "Linking the Rights of Peasants to the Right to Food in the United Nations." *Law, Culture and the Humanities* 10 (2) 196-211.

Edelman, Marc, and Angelique Haugerud. 2005. *The Anthropology of Development and Globalization: From Classical Political Economy to Contemporary Neoliberalism.* Malden, MA: Blackwell.

Edwards, David B. 2017. *Caravan of Martyrs: Sacrifice and Suicide Bombing in Afghanistan.* Oakland: University of California Press.

Ehrenreich, Barbara, and Arlie Russell Hochschild, eds. 2004. *Global Woman: Nannies, Maids, and Sex Workers in the New Economy.* New York: Holt Paperbacks.

Eller, Jack David. 1999. *From Culture to Ethnicity to Conflict: An Anthropological Perspective on Ethnic Conflict.* Ann Arbor: University of Michigan Press.

England, Sarah. 2002. "The Production and Consumption of Pink-Collar Identities in the Caribbean." *Current Anthropology* 43(3): 522–23.

Englund, Harri. 1999. "A Different Kind of War Story [Review]." *Journal of the Royal Anthropological Institute* 5(1): 141–42.

Ericksen, Thomas Hylland. 2010. *Ethnicity and Nationalism* (3rd ed.). Boulder, CO: Pluto Press.

Estes, Nick. 2019. *Our History Is the Future: Standing Rock Versus the Dakota Access Pipeline, and the Long Tradition of Indigenous Resistance.* New York: Verso.

Estes, Nick and Jaskiran Dhillon. 2019. *Standing with Standing Rock: Voices from the #NoDAPL.* Minneapolis: Minnesota University Press.

Evans-Pritchard, E. E. 1937. *Witchcraft, Oracles and Magic among the Azande.* Oxford, UK: Clarendon Press.

———. 1940. *The Nuer: A Description of the Modes of Livelihood and Political Institutions of a Nilotic People.* Oxford, UK: Clarendon Press.

———. 1951. *Kinship and Marriage among the Nuer.* Oxford, UK: Clarendon Press.

Fadiman, Anne. 1997. *The Spirit Catches You and You Fall Down: A Hmong Child, Her American Doctors, and the Collision of Two Cultures.* New York: Farrar, Straus, and Giroux.

Falk, R. 1993. "The Making of Global Citizenship." In *Global Visions: Beyond the New World Order*, edited by Jeremy Brecher, John B. Childs, and Jill Cutler, 39–50. Boston: South End.

Fanon, Frantz. 1961. *The Wretched of the Earth.* Paris: F. Maspero.

Farmer, Paul. 1985. "The Anthropologist Within." *Harvard Medical Alumni Bulletin* 59(1): 23–28.

———. 2003. *Pathologies of Power: Health, Human Rights and the New War on the Poor.* Berkeley: University of California Press.

———. 2006. *AIDS and Accusation: Haiti and the Geography of Blame.* Berkeley: University of California Press.

Farquhar, Judith Brooke. 1986. "Knowledge and Practice in Chinese Medicine." PhD dissertation, University of Chicago, Department of Anthropology.

Fausto-Sterling, Anne. 1993. "The Five Sexes: Why Male and Female Are Not Enough." *The Sciences* May/April: 20–24.

———. 2000. "The Five Sexes, Revisited." *The Sciences* (July/August), 18-23.

———. 2012. *Sex/Gender: Biology in a Social World.* New York, NY: Routledge.

Feagin, Joe R., and Clairece Booher Feagin. 2011. *Racial and Ethnic Relations* (9th ed.). New York: Pearson.

Feagin, Joe R., and Melvin P. Sikes. 1994. *Living with Racism: The Black Middle-Class Experience.* Boston: Beacon Press.

Fedigan, Linda. 1982. *Primate Paradigms: Sex Roles and Social Bonds.* Montreal: Eden Press.

———. 1986. "The Changing Role of Women in Models of Human Evolution." *Annual Reviews of Anthropology* 15: 25–66.

Feldman, Jeffrey D. 2001. "Reproducing Jews: A Cultural Account of Assisted Conception in Israel [Review]." *American Ethnologist* 28(4): 924–25.

Ferguson, Brian. 2002. "The History of War: Fact vs. Fiction." In *Must We Fight?: From the Battlefield to the Schoolyard, a New Perspective on Violent Conflict and Its Prevention*, edited by William L. Ury, 26–37. San Francisco: Jossey-Bass.

———. 2011. "Tribal Warfare." In *Encyclopedia of War*, 1–13. Malden, MA: Blackwell.

Ferguson, James, and Akhil Gupta. 2002. "Spatializing States: Toward an Ethnography of Neoliberal Governmentality." *American Ethnologist* 29(4): 981–1002.

Finkler, Kaja. 2002. "Reproducing Jews: A Cultural Account of Assisted Conception in Israel [Review]." *Journal of Anthropological Research* 58(2): 299–301.

Finnstrom, Sverker. 2005. "Shadows of War: Violence, Power and International Profiteering in the Twenty-First Century [Review]." *Anthropological Quarterly* 78(2): 491–96.

Fisher, Bonnie, Leah E. Daigle, and Francis T. Cullen. 2010. *Unsafe in the Ivory Tower: The Sexual Victimization of College Women.* Los Angeles: Sage Publications.

Fisher, Helen. 2004. *Why We Love: The Nature and Chemistry of Romantic Love.* New York: Henry Holt.

Floyd, Charlene J. 1996. "A Theology of Insurrection? Religion and Politics in Mexico." *Journal of International Affairs* 50(1): 142–65.

Flueckiger, Joyce. 2006. *In Amma's Healing Room: Gender and Vernacular Islam in South India.* Bloomington: Indiana University Press.

Fluehr-Lobban, Carolyn. 2019. *Race and Racism: An Introduction*, 2nd. ed. Lanham, MD: Altamira Press.

Fortes, Meyer. 1949. "Time and Social Structure: An Ashanti Case Study." In *Social Structure: Studies Presented to A. R. Radcliffe-Brown*, edited by Meyer Fortes. Oxford, UK: Clarendon Press.

Foucault, Michel. (1976) 1990. *The History of Sexuality*, vol. 1: *An Introduction.* New York: Vintage Books.

———. 1977. *Discipline and Punish: The Birth of the Prison.* New York: Pantheon.

———. 1978. *The History of Sexuality.* New York: Pantheon.

Fouts, Roger. 1997. *Next of Kin: What Chimpanzees Have Taught Me about Who We Are.* New York: William Morrow.

Frank, Andre Gunder. 1969. *Latin America: Underdevelopment or Revolution: Essays on the Development of Underdevelopment and the Immediate Enemy.* New York: Monthly Review Press.

———. 1998. *ReORIENT: Global Economy in the Asian Age.* Berkeley: University of California Press.

Franklin, Sarah. 1997. *Embodied Progress: A Cultural Account of Assisted Conception*. London: Routledge.

Frazer, James George. 1890. *The Golden Bough: A Study in Comparative Religion*. New York: Macmillan.

Freeman, Carla. 2000. *High Tech and High Heels in the Global Economy*. Durham, NC: Duke University Press.

Freud, Sigmund. 1952. *Totem and Taboo: Some Points of Agreement between the Mental Lives of Savages and Neurotics*. New York: Norton.

Freyre, Gilberto. (1933) 1944. *The Masters and the Slaves: A Study in the Development of Brazilian Civilization*. New York: Knopf.

Friedman, Jaclyn, and Jessica Valenti. 2008. *Yes Means Yes! Visions of Female Sexual Power and a World without Rape*. Berkeley, CA: Seal Press.

Friedner, Michele. 2015. *Valuing Deaf Worlds in Urban India*. Rutgers, NJ: Rutgers University Press.

Fuentes, Augustin. 2013. "Blurring the Biological and Social in Human Becomings." In *Biosocial Becomings: Integrating Social and Biological Anthropology*, edited by Tim Ingold and Gisli Palsson, 42–58. New York: Cambridge University Press.

García-Colón, Ismael. 2020. *Colonial Migrants at the Heart of Empire: Puerto Rican Workers on U.S. Farms*. Berkeley: University of California Press.

Gardner, R. Allen, Beatrix T. Gardner, and Thomas E. Van Cantfort, eds. 1989. *Teaching Sign Language to Chimpanzees*. Albany: State University of New York Press.

Gaunt, Kyra Danielle. 2006. *The Games Black Girls Play: Learning the Ropes from Double-Dutch to Hip-Hop*. New York: New York University Press.

Geertz, Clifford. 1973a. "Deep Play: Notes on a Balinese Cockfight." In *The Interpretation of Cultures*. New York: Basic Books.

———. 1973b. "Religion as a Cultural System." In *The Interpretation of Cultures*. New York: Basic Books.

———. 1973c. "Thick Description: Toward an Interpretive Theory of Culture." In *The Interpretation of Cultures*. New York: Basic Books.

Gell, A. F. 1995. "*African Art in Transit* [Review]." *Journal of the Royal Anthropological Institute* 1(4): 841–42.

Gellner, Ernest. 1983. *Nations and Nationalism*. Ithaca, NY: Cornell University Press.

Geyer, Michael. 1989. "The Militarization of Europe, 1914–1945." In *The Militarization of the Western World*, edited by John Gillis, 65–102. New Brunswick, NJ: Rutgers University Press.

Gibson, Jane. 1996. "The Social Construction of Whiteness in Shellcracker Haven, Florida." *Human Organization* 55(4): 379–89.

Giddens, Anthony. 1985. *The Nation-State and Violence*. Cambridge, UK: Polity.

Ginsburg, Faye D., Lila Abu-Lughod, and Brian Larkin, eds. 2002. *Media Worlds: Anthropology on New Terrain*. Berkeley: University of California Press.

Ginsburg, Faye and Rayna Rapp. 2013. "Disability Worlds." In *Annual Review of Anthropology* 42: 53-68.

Glazer, Nathan, and Daniel Patrick Moynihan. 1970. *Beyond the Melting Pot* (2nd ed.). Cambridge, MA: MIT Press.

Gledhill, John. 2000. *Power and Its Disguises: Anthropological Perspectives on Politics*. London: Pluto.

Global Footprint Network. 2022. https://www.footprintnetwork.org/.

Gluckman, Max. 1954. *Rituals of Rebellion in South-East Africa*. Manchester, UK: Manchester University Press.

Gmelch, George. 1992. "Superstition and Ritual in American Baseball." *Elysian Fields Quarterly* 11(3): 25–36.

Goldstein, Daniel M. 2016. *Owners of the Sidewalk: Security and Survival in the Informal City*. Durham, NC: Duke University Press.

Goldstein, Donna M. 2003. *Laughter out of Place: Race, Class, Violence, and Sexuality in a Rio Shantytown*. Berkeley: University of California Press.

Goldstein, Judith L. 1998. "Reading *National Geographic* [Review]." *American Ethnologist* 25(1): 9–10.

Goldstein, Melvyn. 1987. "When Brothers Share a Wife." *Natural History* 96(3): 39–48.

Goode, Judith, and Jeff Maskovsky, eds. 2001. *The New Poverty Studies: The Ethnography of Power, Politics, and Impoverished People in the United States*. New York: New York University Press.

Gough, Kathleen. 1971. "Nuer Kinship: A Reexamination." In *The Translation of Culture: Essays to E. E. Evans-Pritchard*, edited by Thomas O. Beidelman, 79–121. London: Tavistock Publications.

Graeber, David. 2011. *Debt: The First Five Thousand Years*. Brooklyn, NY: Melville House.

Gramsci, Antonio. 1971. *Selections from the Prison Notebooks*. Quintin Hoare and Geoffrey Nowell Smith, translators and editors. New York: International Publishers.

Gray, John. 2004. *Men Are from Mars, Women Are from Venus: The Classic Guide to Understanding the Opposite Sex*. New York: HarperCollins Quill.

Green, Edward C. 1999. *Indigenous Theories of Contagious Disease*. Walnut Creek, CA: AltaMira.

Green, Erica, Katie Benner and Robert Pear. 2018. 'Transgender' Could Be Defined Out of Existence Under Trump Administration." *New York Times*, October 21.

Green, L. J. 2002. *African American English: A Linguistic Introduction*. Cambridge, MA: Cambridge University Press.

Gregg, Jessica L. 2003. *Virtually Virgins: Sexual Strategies and Cervical Cancer in Recife, Brazil*. Stanford, CA: Stanford University Press.

Gregory, Steven. 1998. *Black Corona: Race and the Politics of Place in an Urban Community*. Princeton, NJ: Princeton University Press.

Gregory, Steven, and Roger Sanjek, eds. 1994. *Race*. New Brunswick, NJ: Rutgers University Press.

Grimshaw, Ana, and Amanda Ravetz. 2009. *Observational Cinema: Anthropology, Film, and the Exploration of Social Life*. Bloomington: Indiana University Press.

Guarasci, Bridget, Amelia Moore and Sarah E. Vaughn. 2018. "Citation Matters: An Updated Reading List for Progressive Environmental Anthropology." *Society for Cultural Anthropology*. https://culanth.org/fieldsights/citation-matters-an-updated-reading-list-for-a-progressive-environmental-anthropology.

Gudmundson, Lowell. 2001. "Peasants against Globalization: Rural Social Movement in Costa Rica [Review]." *Agricultural History* 75(4): 504–6.

Guest, Kenneth J. 2003. *God in Chinatown: Religion and Survival in New York's Evolving Immigrant Community*. New York: New York University Press.

———. 2009. "All You Can Eat Buffets and Chicken With Broccoli to Go." *Anthropology Now* 1(1): 21-28.

———. 2011. "From Mott Street to East Broadway: Fuzhounese Immigrants and the Revitalization of New York's Chinatown." *Journal of Chinese Overseas* 7(1): 24–44.

Guest, Kenneth J., and Peter Kwong. 2000. "Ethnic Enclaves and Cultural Diversity." In *Cultural Diversity in the United States: A Critical Reader*, edited by Ida Susser and Thomas C. Patterson, 39–50. Malden, MA: Blackwell.

Gusterson, Hugh. 1996. *Nuclear Rites: A Weapons Laboratory at the End of the Cold War*. Berkeley: University of California Press.

———. 1997. "Studying Up Revisited." *Political and Legal Anthropology Review* 20(1): 114–19.

———. 2004. *People of the Bomb: Portraits of America's Nuclear Complex*. Minneapolis: University of Minnesota Press.

———. 2008. "When Professors Go to War: Why the Ivory Tower and the Pentagon Don't Mix." *Foreign Policy*, July 21.

Gutmann, Matthew C. 2007. *The Meanings of Macho: Being a Man in Mexico City*. Berkeley: University of California Press. Originally published in 1996.

Hamilton-Smith, Elery. 2007. "Conservation is our Government Now: The Politics of Ecology in Papua New Guinea: A Review." *Electronic Green Journal* 25 1-1.

Hannerz, Ulf. 1996. *Transnational Connections: Culture, People, Places*. London: Routledge.

Haraway, Donna. 2016. *Staying with the Trouble: Making Kin in the Chthulucene*. Durham: Duke University Press.

Harding, Jennifer. 1998. "Investigating Sex: Essentialism and Constructionism." In *Sex Acts*, 8–22. London: Sage Publications.

Hargrove, Melissa D. 2009. "Mapping the 'Social Field of Whiteness': White Racism as Habitus in the City Where History Lives." *Transforming Anthropology* 17(2): 93–104.

Harris, Marvin. 1964. *Patterns of Race in the Americas*. New York: Walker.

———. 1970. "Referential Ambiguity in the Calculus of Brazilian Racial Identity." *Southwestern Journal of Anthropology* 21(1): 1–14.

———. 1974. *Cows, Pigs, Wars, & Witches: The Riddles of Culture*. New York: Random House.

Harrison, Faye V. 1998. "Introduction: Expanding the Discourse on 'Race.'" *American Anthropologist* 100(3): 609–31.

———. 2002a. "Subverting the Cultural Logics of Marked and Unmarked Racisms in the Global Era." In *Discrimination and Tolerations*, edited by K. Hastrup and G. Ulrich, 97–125. London: Kluwer Law International.

———. 2002b. "Unraveling 'Race' for the 21st Century." In *Exotic No More: Anthropology on the Front Lines*, edited by Jeremy MacClancy. Chicago: University of Chicago Press.

Harrison, K. David. 2007. *When Languages Die: The Extinction of the World's Languages and the Erosion of Human Knowledge.* New York: Oxford University Press.

Hartigan, John Jr. 1999. *Racial Situations: Class Predicaments of Whiteness in Detroit.* Princeton, NJ: Princeton University Press.

———. 2005. *Odd Tribes: Toward a Cultural Analysis of White People.* Durham, NC: Duke University Press.

Harvey, David. 1990. *The Condition of Postmodernity: An Enquiry into the Origins of Cultural Change.* Malden, MA: Blackwell.

———. 1996. *Justice, Nature and the Geography of Difference.* Oxford: Blackwell.

———. 2003. *The New Imperialism.* Oxford: Oxford University Press.

Hattori, Anne Perez. 2016. "Consuming Ocean Island: Stories of People and Phosphate from Banaba: A Review." *The Contemporary Pacific* 28(2) 492-494.

Haugerud, Angelique. 1998. "Purity and Exile: A Book Review." *International Journal of African Historical Studies* 31(1): 214–16.

Haugerud, Angelique, Margaret Priscilla Stone, and Peter D. Little. 2000. *Commodities and Globalization: Anthropological Perspectives.* Lanham, MD: Rowman & Littlefield.

Hearn, Jonathan. 2006. *Rethinking Nationalism: A Critical Introduction.* New York: Palgrave Macmillan.

Helmreich, Stefan. 2009. *Alien Ocean: Anthropological Voyages in Microbial Seas.* Berkeley: University of California Press.

Henshilwood, Christopher S., et al. 2011. "A 100,000-Year-Old Ochre-Processing Workshop at Blombos Cave, South Africa." *Science* 334(6053): 219–22.

Herdt, Gilbert. 1981. *Guardians of the Flutes.* Chicago: Chicago University Press.

———. 1987. *The Sambia: Ritual and Gender in New Guinea.* Belmont, CA: Wadsworth, Cengage Learning.

Herzog, Werner (director). *Cave of Forgotten Dreams.* 2010. IFC Films.

Hetzler, Olivia. 2017. "Shapeshifters: Black Girls and the Choreography of Citizenship, A Review." *Gender and Society* 31 (1): 124–5.

Higgenbotham, Evelyn Brooks. 1992. "African-American Women's History and the Metalanguage of Race." *Signs: Journal of Women in Culture and Society* 17: 251–74.

Hirsch, Jennifer. 2007. "'Love Makes a Family': Globalization, Companionate Marriage, and the Modernization of Gender Equality." In *Love and Globalization: Transformations of Intimacy in the Contemporary World*, edited by Mark Padilla, Jennifer Hirsch, Miguel Munoz-Laboy, Richard Sember, and Richard Parker, 93–106. Nashville, TN: Vanderbilt University Press.

Hirsch, Jennifer S., and Shamus Khan. 2020. *Sexual Citizens: A Landmark Study of Sex, Power, and Assault on Campus.* New York: W. W. Norton.

Hitchner, Sarah. 2008. "Conservation is Our Government Now: The Politics of Ecology in Papua New Guinea: A Review." *American Ethnologist* 35 (1) 1050-1052.

Ho, Karen. 2009. *Liquidated: An Ethnography of Wall Street.* Durham, NC: Duke University Press.

Hobhouse, L. T. 1915. *Morals in Evolution; A Study in Comparative Ethics.* New York: Holt.

Hobsbawm, Eric, and Terence Ranger. 1983. *Invented Traditions.* Cambridge, UK: Cambridge University Press.

Hockings, Paul Edward, ed. 2003. *Principles of Visual Anthropology* (3rd ed.). Berlin: Mouton De Gruyter.

Holland, Dorothy and Jean Lave. 2001. *History in Person: Enduring Struggles, Contentious Practice, Intimate Identities.* Santa Fe, NM: School of American Research Press.

Holmes, Janet. 1998. "Women's Talk: The Question of Sociolinguistic Universals." In *Language and Gender: A Reader*, edited by Jennifer Coates, 461–83. Oxford, UK: Blackwell.

Hondagneu-Sotelo, Pierrette. 2001. *Domestica: Immigrant Workers Cleaning and Caring in the Shadows of Affluence.* Berkeley: University of California Press.

Honwana, Alcinda. 1999. "A Different Kind of War Story [Review]." *American Ethnologist* 26(2): 504–5.

Hubbard, Ruth. 1990. "The Social Construction of Sexuality." In *The Politics of Women's Biology.* New Brunswick, NJ: Rutgers University Press.

Hurston, Zora Neale. 1935. *Mules and Men.* Philadelphia: Lippincott.

———. 1938. *Tell My Horse.* Philadelphia: Lippincott.

Hutchinson, Sharon. 1996. *Nuer Dilemmas: Coping with Money, War and the State.* Berkeley: University of California Press.

Ignatiev, Noel. 1995. *How the Irish Became White.* New York: Routledge Press.

Inda, Jonathan Xavier, and Renato Rosaldo. 2002. *The Anthropology of Globalization: A Reader.* Malden, MA: Blackwell.

Ingold, Tim. 2013. "Prospect. P." In *Biosocial Becomings: Integrating Social and Biological Anthropology,* edited by Tim Ingold and Gisli Palsson, 1–21. New York: Cambridge University Press.

Ingraham, Chrys. 2008. *White Weddings: Romancing Heterosexuality in Popular Culture,* (rev. ed.). New York: Routledge. First published in 1999.

Ingstad, Benedicte, and Susan R Whyte, eds. 2007. *Disability in Local and Global Worlds.* Berkeley: University of California Press.

Inhorn, Marcia. 1996. *Infertility and Patriarchy: The Cultural Politics of Gender and Family Life in Egypt.* Philadelphia: University of Pennsylvania Press.

Intergovernmental Panel on Climate Change. 2010. https://www.ipcc.ch/.

———. 2022. "IPCC Sixth Assessment Report: Mitigation of Climate Change." https://www.ipcc.ch/report/ar6/wg3/.

Internal Displacement Monitoring Center. 2012. "Internal Displacement Global Overview 2011: People Internally Displaced by Conflict and Violence." www.internal-displacement.org/publications/global-overview.

International Civil Aviation Organization. 2019. "The World of Air Transport in 2019." https://www.icao.int/annual-report-2019/Pages/the-world-of-air-transport-in-2019.aspx.

International Monetary Fund. 2019. "World Economic Outlook Database." https://www.imf.org/external/datamapper/NGDPD@WEO/OEMDC/ADVEC/WEOWORLD.

International Organization for Migration. 2022. "World Migration Report 2022." https://publications.iom.int/books/world-migration-report-2022.International Telecommunication Union. 2018. "Statistics." www.itu.int/en/ITU-D/Statistics/Pages/stat/default.aspx.

Iskander, Natasha. 2020. "Qatar, the Coronavirus, and Cordons Sanitaires: Migrant Workers and the Use of Public Health Measures to Define the Nation." *Medical Anthropology Quarterly* 34 (4): 561–77.

Ivana, Greti-Julia. 2015. "Nation as Network: A Book Review." *Information, Communication and Society* 18(12): 1481–83.

Jacobs, A. J. 2005. "Tsukiji: The Fish Market at the Center of the World [Review]." *Contemporary Sociology* 34(4): 373–75.

Jacobs, Sue-Ellen, ed. 1997. *Two-Spirit People: Native American Gender Identity, Sexuality, and Spirituality.* Champaign: University of Illinois Press.

Jamison, Sandra L. 2006. "The Games Black Girls Play [Review]." *Black Issues Book Review,* Vol. 8 Issue 3, 43–44.

Jaynes, Gregory. 1982. "A Louisiana Lawsuit Asks What It Means to Be Black, White, or 'Colored' in America." *Providence Sunday Journal,* October 14, A-19.

Jenkins, Richard. 1996. *Social Identity.* New York: Routledge.

———. 2008. *Rethinking Ethnicity* (2nd ed.). Thousand Oaks, CA: Sage.

The Johns Hopkins Center for Gun Violence Solutions. 2022. "A Year in Review: 2020 Gun Deaths in the U.S." https://publichealth.jhu.edu/sites/default/files/2022-05/2020-gun-deaths-in-the-us-4-28-2022-b.pdf.

Jolaosho, Omatayo. 2015. "Political Aesthetics and Embodiment: Sung Protest in Post-Apartheid South Africa." *Journal of Material Culture* 20 (4): 443–58.

———. 2022. *You Can't Go to War without Song: Performance and Community Mobilization in South Africa.* Bloomington: Indiana University Press.

Jones, Bradley. 2022. "The Changing Political Geography of COVID-19 Over the Last Two Years." Pew Research Center, March 3. https://www.pewresearch.org/politics/2022/03/03/the-changing-political-geography-of-COVID-19-over-the-last-two-years/.

Jones, Camara Phyllis. 2000. "Levels of Racism: A Theoretic Framework and a Gardener's Tale." *American Journal of Public Health* 90(8): 1212–15.

Jones, Jeffrey M. 2022. "Belief in God in U.S. Dips to 81%, a New Low." Gallup. https://news.gallup.com/poll/393737/belief-god-dips-new-low.aspx.

Jones, Ryan Tucker. 2016. "Consuming Ocean Island: Stories of People and Phosphate from Banaba: A Review." *The American Historical Review* 121 (1) 227–228.

Jordan, Brigitte. 1993. *Birth in Four Cultures: A Cross-cultural Investigation of Childbirth in Yucatan, Holland, Sweden, and the United States.* Rev. and expanded by Robbie Davis-Floyd. Prospect Heights, IL: Waveland Press.

Jordan, Miriam. 2010. "Arizona Grades Teachers on Fluency: State Pushes School Districts to Reassign Instructors with Heavy Accents or Other Shortcomings in Their English." *Wall Street Journal*, April 30.

Juris, Jeffrey S. 2012. "Reflections on #Occupy Everywhere: Social Media, Public Space, and Emerging Logics of Aggregation." *American Ethnologist* 39(2): 259–79.

Juris, Jeffrey S. and Alex Khasnabish. 2013. *Insurgent Encounters: Transnational Activism, Ethnography, and the Political.* Durham, NC: Duke University Press.

Kahn, Susan Martha. 2000. *Reproducing Jews: A Cultural Account of Assisted Conception in Israel.* Durham, NC: Duke University Press.

Kant, Immanuel. 1790. *Critique of Judgement.* Translated by J. H. Bernard. London: Collier Macmillan.

Karp, Ivan, and Steven Lavine. 1991. *Exhibiting Cultures: The Poetics and Politics of Museum Display.* Washington, DC: Smithsonian Institution.

Katz, Jonathan Ned. 2007. *The Invention of Heterosexuality*, with a new preface. Chicago: University of Chicago Press. First published in 1995.

Kearney, M. 1995. "The Local and the Global: The Anthropology of Globalization and Transnationalism." *Annual Review of Anthropology* 24: 547–65.

Keynes, John Maynard. (1936) 2007. *The General Theory of Employment Interest and Money.* Houndmills, UK: Palgrave Macmillan.

Kidder, Tracy. 2003. *Mountains beyond Mountains: The Quest of Dr. Paul Farmer, A Man Who Would Cure the World.* New York: Random House.

Kinsey, Alfred C. 1953. *Sexual Behavior in the Human Female.* Philadelphia: W. B. Saunders.

Kinsey, Alfred C., Wardell Baxter Pomeroy, and Clyde E. Martin. 1948. *Sexual Behavior in the Human Male.* Philadelphia: W. B. Saunders.

Kleinman, Arthur. 1988. *The Illness Narratives: Suffering, Healing, and the Human Condition.* New York: Basic Books.

Kohn, Eduardo. 2013. *How Forests Think: Toward an Anthropology beyond the Human.* Berkeley: University of California Press.

Kohrman, Matthew. 2005. *Bodies of Difference: Experiences of Disability and Institutional Advocacy in the Making of Modern China.* Berkeley: University of California Press

Kopnina, Helen and Eleanor Shoreman-Ouimet. 2017. "An Introduction to Environmental Anthropology" in Kopnina, Helen and Eleanor Shoreman-Ouimet, *Routledge Handbook of Environmental Anthropology.* New York: Routledge.

Kopytoff, Igor. 1986. "The Cultural Biography of Things: Commoditization as Process." In *The Social Life of Things: Commodities in Cultural Perspective*, edited by Arjun Appadurai, 64–91. Cambridge, UK: Cambridge University Press.

Korten, David C. 2001. *When Corporations Rule the World.* San Francisco: Berrett-Koehler.

———. 2015. *Change the Story, Change the Future.* Oakland, CA: Berrett-Koehler.

Kottak, Conrad P. 2006. *Assault on Paradise: The Globalization of a Little Community in Brazil* (4th ed.). New York: McGraw-Hill.

Koven, Michele. 2007. *Selves of Two Languages: Bilinguals' Verbal Enactments of Identity in French and Portuguese.* Amsterdam: John Benjamins Publishing Company.

Kromidas, Maria. 2004. "Learning War/Learning Race: Fourth-Grade Students in the Aftermath of September 11th in New York City." *Critique of Anthropology* 24(1).

Krugman, Paul R. 2015. "Ending Greece's Bleeding." *New York Times*, July 5.

Kulick, Don, and Jens Rydstrom. 2015. *Loneliness and Its Opposite: Sex, Disability, and the Ethics of Engagement.* Durham, NC: Duke University Press.

Kuper, Adam. 1983. *Anthropology and Anthropologists: The Modern British School.* London: Routledge & Kegan Paul.

Kurtz, Donald V. 2001. *Political Anthropology: Power and Paradigms.* Boulder, CO: Westview Press.

Kusimba, Sibel. 2021. *Reimagining Money: Kenya in the Digital Finance Revolution.* Stanford, CA: Stanford University Press.

Kuzawa, Christopher, et al. 2009. "Fatherhood, Pair-Bonding, and Testosterone in the Philippines." *Hormones and Behavior* 56(4): 429–35.

Labov, William. 1972. *Language in the Inner City: Studies in the Black English Vernacular.* Philadelphia: University of Pennsylvania Press.

Lakoff, Robin T. 2004. *Language and Woman's Place: Text and Commentaries*, edited by Mary Bucholtz. New York: Oxford University Press.

Lan, Pei-Chia. 2006. *Global Cinderellas: Migrant Domestics and Newly Rich Employers in Taiwan*. Durham, NC: Duke University Press.

Lancaster, Roger N. 1994. *Life Is Hard: Machismo, Danger, and the Intimacy of Power in Nicaragua*. Berkeley: University of California Press.

Landers, Melissa A., and Gary Alan Fine. 1996. "Learning Life's Lessons in Tee Ball: The Reinforcement of Gender and Status in Kindergarten Sport." *Sociology of Sport Journal* 13(1).

Larrain, Jorge, 1989. *Theories of Development: Capitalism, Colonialism and Dependency*. London: Polity Press.

Larsen, Clark Spencer. 2014. *Our Origins: Discovering Physical Anthropology* (3rd ed.). New York: Norton.

———. 2018. *Essentials of Biological Anthropology*. New York: W.W. Norton & Co.

Lappan, Susan 2014. "Mating in the Presence of a Competitor: Audience Effect May Promote Male Social Tolerance in Polyandrous Siamang (symphalangus syndactylus) groups." *Behavior* 151(7) 1067-89.

Latham, Andrew. 2022. "Consumer Debt Growing at the Fastest Pace in 20 Years." https://www.supermoney.com/credit-debt-increased-by-23-4-billion-in-march/.

Latour, Bruno. 2014. "Anthropology at the Time of the Anthropocene—a personal view of what is to be studied." Lecture at the American Association of Anthropologists.

Leach, Edmund. 1954. *Political Systems of Highland Burma: A Study of Kachin Social Structure*. Cambridge, MA: Harvard University Press.

Leacock, Eleanor Burke. 1971. *The Culture of Poverty: A Critique*. New York: Simon & Schuster.

———. 1981. *Myths of Male Dominance: Collected Articles on Women Cross-Culturally*. New York: Monthly Review Press.

Lee, Richard B. 1984. *The Dobe !Kung*. New York: Holt, Rinehart and Winston.

———. 2003. *The Dobe JuHoansi* (3rd ed.) (Case Studies in Cultural Anthropology). Belmont, CA: Wadsworth Publishing.

Lee, Richard B., and Irven Devore, eds. 1968. *Man the Hunter: The First Intensive Survey of a Single Crucial Stage of Human Development—Man's Once Universal Hunting Way of Life*. New York: The Wenner-Gren Foundation for Anthropological Research.

Lessinger, Johanna. 1995. *From the Ganges to the Hudson: Indian Immigrants in New York City*. Boston: Allyn & Bacon.

Lewellen, Ted C. 2002. *The Anthropology of Globalization: Cultural Anthropology Enters the 21st Century*. Westport, CT: Praeger.

———. 2003. *Political Anthropology: An Introduction*. Westport, CT: Praeger.

Lewin, Ellen. 1992. "Families We Choose: Lesbians, Gays, Kinship [Review]." *American Ethnologist* 19(4): 825–26.

———. 1995. "Life Is Hard [Review]." *American Ethnologist* 22(2): 441–42.

———.1998. *Recognizing Ourselves: Ceremonies of Lesbian and Gay Commitments*. New York: Columbia University Press.

Lewis, Oscar. 1959. *Five Families: Mexican Case Studies in the Culture of Poverty*. New York: Basic Books.

———. 1966. *La Vida: A Puerto Rican Family in the Culture of Poverty—San Juan and New York*. New York: Random House.

Leys, Colin. 1996. *The Rise and Fall of Development Theory*. Oxford, UK: James Currey.

Liang, Zai. 2012. "Recent Migration Trends in China: Geographic and Demographic Aspects of Development Implications." Presentation for UN Expert Group Meeting on New Trends in Migration: Demographic Aspects, New York, December 3. www.un.org/esa/population/meetings/EGM_MigrationTrends/UN_presentation_Dec_2012_FINAL_SH.pdf.

Liang, Zai, Zhen Li, Zhongdang Ma. 2014. Changing Patterns of the Floating Population in China, 2000–2010. *Population and Development Review* 40(4): 695–716.

Limon, Jose E. 1997. "The Meanings of Macho: Being a Man in Mexico City [Review]." *American Anthropologist* 99(1): 185.

Lipset, David. 2013. "Swamplife: People, Gators, and Mangroves Entangled in the Everglades." *Environment & Society* 4, 177-178.

LiPuma, Edward, and Benjamin Lee, 2004. *Financial Derivatives and the Globalization of Risk*. Duke University Press.

Lock, Margaret M. 1993. *Encounters with Aging: Mythologies of Menopause in Japan and North America*. Berkeley: University of California Press.

———. 2002. *Twice Dead: Organ Transplants and the Reinvention of Death*. Berkeley: University of California Press.

Lopez, Ian Haney. 2006. *White by Law: The Legal Construction of Race* (2nd ed.). New York: New York University Press.

Lorber, Judith. 1994. *Paradoxes of Gender*. New Haven, CT: Yale University Press.

Lorimer, Jamie. 2013. "Swamplife: People, Gators, and Mangroves Entangled in the Everglades: A Review." *Social & Cultural Geography Journal*. 14 (3) 363-364.

Latham, Andrew. 2019. "Consumer Debt Growing at the Fastest Page in 20 Years." www.supermoney .com/2018/4/credit-card-industry-report/.

Levine, Susan, and Lenore Manderson. 2021. "Proxemics, COVID-19, and the Ethics of Care in South Africa." *Cultural Anthropology* 36 (3): 391–99.

Low, Setha, and Sally Engle Merry. 2010. "Engaged Anthropology: Diversity and Dilemmas: An Introduction to Supplement 2." *Current Anthropology* 51 (S2): 203–26.

Lowie, Robert Harry. 1920. *Primitive Society*. New York: Harper & Brothers.

Lutz, Catherine. 2001. *Homefront: A Military City and the American Twentieth Century*. Boston: Beacon.

———. 2004. "Militarization." In *A Companion to the Anthropology of Politics*, edited by David Nugent and Joan Vincent, 318–31. Malden, MA: Blackwell.

Lutz, Catherine, and Jane L. Collins. 1993. *Reading National Geographic*. Chicago: University of Chicago Press.

MacDougall, David. 2005. *Film, Ethnography, and the Senses: The Corporeal Image*. Princeton, NJ: Princeton University Press.

Malinowski, Bronislaw. (1922) 2002. *Argonauts of the Western Pacific*. Reprint, London: Routledge.

———. 1927. *Sex and Repression in Savage Society*. London: Kegan Paul, Trench, Trübner & Co.

———. 1929. *The Sexual Life of Savages in North Western Melanesia: An Ethnographic Account of Courtship, Marriage and Family Life among the Natives of the Trobriand Islands, British New Guinea*. London: Kegan Paul, Trench, Trübner & Co.

———. 1930. "Parenthood—The Basis of Social Structure." In *The New Generation: The Intimate Problems of Modern Parents and Children*, edited by Victor F. Calverton and Samuel D. Schmalhausen. London: George Allen & Unwin.

Malkasian, Carter. 2017. "Caravan of Martyrs: A Review." *Journal of Military History* 81 (4): 1242.

Malkki, Liisa. 1995. *Purity and Exile: Violence, Memory, and National Cosmology Among Hutu Refugees in Tanzania*. Chicago: University of Chicago Press.

Mallory, J. P., and D. Q. Adams. 2006. *The Oxford Introduction to Proto-Indo-European and the Proto-Indo-European World*. Oxford, UK: Oxford University Press.

Mamdani, Mahmood. 2002. *When Victims Become Killers: Colonialism, Nativism, and the Genocide in Rwanda*. Princeton, NJ: Princeton University Press.

Marable, Manning. 2000. *The Great Wells of Democracy: The Meaning of Race in American Life*. New York: Perseus.

———. 2002. "Whither Whiteness." *Souls: A Critical Journal of Black Politics, Culture and Society* 4(4): 45–73.

Marcus, George E., and Fred R. Myers. 1995. *The Traffic in Culture: Refiguring Art and Anthropology*. Berkeley: University of California Press.

Mardi Gras: Made in China. 2005. Directed by David Redmon. Carnivalesque Films.

Martin, Emily. 1991. "The Egg and the Sperm: How Science Has Constructed a Romance Based on Stereotypical Male-Female Roles." *Signs: Journal of Women in Culture and Society* 16(3): 485–501.

Martin, Joann. 1999. "Women and Social Movements in Latin America: Power from Below [Review]." *American Ethnologist* 26(2): 482–83.

Marx, Karl. 1867. *Capital: Critique of Political Economy*. Reprint, London: Penguin, 1986.

Marx, Karl, and Friedrich Engels. 1848. *The Communist Manifesto*. Reprint, London: Penguin, 1967.

———. 1957. *On Religion*. Moscow: Foreign Languages Publishing House.

Mascia-Lees, Frances E. 2009. *Gender and Difference in a Globalizing World: Twenty-First Century Anthropology*. Prospect Heights, IL: Waveland Press.

Massey, Douglas S., Joaquin Arango, Graeme Hugo, Ali Kouaouci, Adela Pellegrino, and J. Edward Taylor. 2005. *Worlds in Motion: Understanding the International Migration at the End of the Millennium*. New York: Oxford University Press.

Maurer, Bill. 2015. *How Would You Like to Pay? How Technology Is Changing the Future of Money*. Durham, NC: Duke University Press.

Mauss, Marcel. 1979. "Body Techniques." In *Sociology and Psychology: Essays by Marcel Mauss*. Translated by Ben Brewster. London: Routledge and Kegan Paul.

Maybury-Lewis, David. 2002. *Indigenous Peoples, Ethnic Groups and the State*. Boston: Allyn and Bacon.

McAdam, Doug, John D. McCarthy, and Mayer N. Zald. 1996. *Comparative Perspectives on Social Movements: Political Opportunities, Mobilizing Structures, and Cultural Framings*. Cambridge, UK: Cambridge University Press.

McAdoo, Harriette Pipes. 2000. "All Our Kin: Strategies for Survival in a Black Community [Review]." *Journal of Marriage and Family* 62(3): 864–65.

McBrearty, Sally, and Alison S. Brooks. 2000. "The Revolution That Wasn't: A New Interpretation of the Origin of Modern Human Behaviour." *Journal of Human Evolution* 39(5): 453–563.

McClaurin, Irma. 2007. "Finding Zora." www.research.ufl.edu/publications/explore/v07n1/zora.htm.

McCracken, Grant. 1991. *Culture and Consumption: New Approaches to the Symbolic Character of Consumer Goods and Activities*. Bloomington: Indiana University Press.

———. 2005. *Culture and Consumption II: Markets, Meaning, and Brand Management*. Bloomington: Indiana University Press.

McFate, Montgomery. 2005. "Anthropology and Counterinsurgency: The Strange Story of Their Curious Relationship." *Military Review* (March–April): 24–38.

McIntosh, Peggy. 1989. "White Privilege: Unpacking the Invisible Knapsack." *Peace and Freedom* (July–August): 10–12.

McKibben, William. 2010. *Earth: Making a Life on a Tough New Planet*. New York: Henry Holt.

———. 2012. "Global Warming's Terrifying New Math." *Rolling Stone*, July 19.

McKinnon, Susan, and Sydel Silverman, eds. 2005. *Complexities: Beyond Nature and Nurture*. Chicago: University of Chicago Press.

McWhorter, John H. 2001. *The Power of Babel: A Natural History of Language*. New York: HarperCollins.

Mead, Margaret. 1928. *Coming of Age in Samoa: A Psychological Study of Primitive Youth for Western Civilization*. New York: William Morrow.

———. 1935. *Sex and Temperament in Three Primitive Societies*. New York: William Morrow.

———. 1940. "Warfare Is Only an Invention—Not a Biological Necessity." In *Approaches to Peace: A Reader in Peace Studies*, edited by David P. Barash, 19–22. New York: Oxford University Press, 2000.

Medeiros, Melanie A. 2014. "The Other End of the Bargain: The Socioeconomics of Marital Dissolution in Rural Northeast Brazil." *Transforming Anthropology* 22(2): 105–20.

Melillo, Edward. 2017. *Consuming Ocean Island: Stories of People and Phosphate from Banaba*: [A Review]. *The Journal of Pacific History*, 52(1) 116–117.

Miles, H. Lyn White. 1993. "Language and the Orangutan: The Old 'Person of the Forest.'" In *The Great Ape Project*, edited by Paola Cavalieri and Peter Singer, 45–50. New York: St. Martin's Press.

Milkie, Melissa A. 2000. "White Weddings [Review]." *Gender and Society* 14(6): 824–26.

Miller, Raegen, and Diana Epstein. 2011. "There Still Be Dragons: Racial Disparity in School Funding Is No Myth." Center for American Progress. www.americanprogress.org/issues/education/report/2011/07/05/9943/there-still-be-dragons/.

Mills, Mary Beth. 2003. "Gender and Inequality in the Global Labor Force." *Annual Review of Anthropology* 32: 41–62.

Miner, Horace. 1956. "Body Ritual among the Nacirema." *American Anthropologist* 58(3): 503–7.

Mintz, Sidney W. 1985. *Sweetness and Power: The Place of Sugar in Modern History*. New York: Viking Penguin.

Mitchell, Timothy. 2011. *Carbon Democracy: Political Power in the Age of Oil*. New York: Verso Press.

Molyneux, Maxine. 1999. "Women and Social Movements in Latin America: Power from Below [Review]." *Journal of Latin American Studies* 31(2): 535–37.

Monnier, Oliver. 2013. "Agribusiness: Smoothing Out the Bumps in Côte d'Ivoire." *The Africa Report*. July 25. www.theafricareport.com/West-Africa/agribusiness-smoothing-out-the-bumps-in-Cote-divoire.html.

Moore, Mignon R. 2011. *Invisible Families: Gay Identities, Relationships, and Motherhood among Black Women*. Berkeley: University of California Press.

———. 2012. "Intersectionality and the Study of Black, Sexual Minority Women." *Gender and Society* 26: 33–39.

Morgan, Lewis Henry. (1877) 1964. *Ancient Society*. Cambridge, MA: Belknap Press.

Morrell, Virginia. 2008. "Inside Animal Minds: Birds, Apes, Dolphins and a Dog with a World-Class Vocabulary." *National Geographic*, March.

Mukhopadhyay, Carol C., Rosemary Henze, and Yolanda T. Moses. 2007. *How Real Is Race? A Sourcebook on Race, Culture, and Biology*. Lanham, MD: Rowman & Littlefield.

Muller, Martin N. et al., 2009. "Testosterone and Paternal Care in East African Foragers and Pastoralists." *Proceeding of the Royal Society: Biological Sciences 276*: 347–354.

Mullings, Leith. 2005a. "Interrogating Racism: Toward an Anti-Racist Anthropology." *Annual Review of Anthropology* 34: 667–93.

———. 2005b. "Resistance and Resilience: The Sojourner Syndrome and the Social Context of Reproduction in Central Harlem." *Transforming Anthropology* 13(2): 79–91.

Mullings, Leith, and Alaka Wali. 2001. *Stress and Resilience: The Social Context of Reproduction in Central Harlem*. New York: Kluwer Academic/ Plenum Publishers.

Murray, David A. B. 2015. *Real Queer? Sexual Orientation and Gender Identity Refugees in the Canadian Refugee Apparatus*. New York: Rowman & Littlefield.

Myerhoff, Barbara G. 1974. *Peyote Hunt: The Sacred Journey of the Huichol Indians*. Ithaca, NY: Cornell University Press.

———. 1978. *Number Our Days*. New York: Dutton.

Nabinett, Denice. 2016. "Shapeshifters: Black Girls and the Choreography of Citizenship, A Review." *Journal of Negro Education* 85 (3): 395–7.

Nader, Laura. 1972. "Up the Anthropologist: Perspectives Gained from Studying Up." In *Reinventing Anthropology*, edited by Dell H. Hymes, 284–311. New York: Pantheon.

Nahman, Michal Rachel. 2002. "Reproducing Jews: A Cultural Account of Assisted Conception in Israel [Review]." *Canadian Review of Sociology and Anthropology* 39(3): 359–61.

Nakamura, Karen. 2006. *Deaf in Japan: Signing and Politics of Identity*. Ithaca, NY: Cornell University Press.

Nanda, Serena. 1998. *Neither Man nor Woman: The Hijras of India* (2nd ed.). Florence, KY: Wadsworth.

Nash, June C., ed. 2005. *Social Movements: An Anthropological Reader*. Malden, MA: Blackwell.

National Aeronautics and Space Administration. 2015. "The Consequences of Climate Change." http://climate.nasa.gov/effects/.

Nelson, Diane M. 1999. *A Finger in the Wound: Body Politics in Quincentennial Guatemala*. Berkeley: University of California Press.

Nettl, Bruno. 2005. *The Study of Ethnomusicology: Thirty-One Issues and Concepts*. Urbana: University of Illinois Press.

Neubeck, Kenneth J., and Noel A. Cazenave. 2001. *Welfare Racism: Playing the Race Card against America's Poor*. New York: Routledge.

Nixon, Rob. 2011. *Slow Violence and Environmentalism of the Poor*. Cambridge: First Harvard University Press.

Nordstrom, Carolyn. 1997. *A Different Kind of War Story*. Philadelphia: University of Pennsylvania Press.

———. 2004. *Shadows of War: Violence, Power, and International Profiteering in the Twenty-First Century*. Berkeley: University of California Press.

North, James. 2011. "The Roots of the Côte d'Ivoire Crisis: How the Demand for Chocolate—Yes, Chocolate!—Helped Fuel the Country's Civil War." *The Nation,* April 25, 2011.

Norton, M. I., and D. Ariely. 2011. "Building a Better America—One Wealth Quintile at a Time." *Perspectives on Psychological Science* 6(1): 9–12.

Nugent, David, and Joan Vincent, eds. 2004. *A Companion to the Anthropology of Politics*. Malden, MA: Blackwell.

Ogasawara, Yuko. 1995. "Review of *Nightwork: Sexuality, Pleasure, and Corporate Masculinity in a Tokyo Hostess Club*." *American Journal of Sociology* 100(4): 1071–73.

Ogden, Cynthia L., Cheryl D. Fryar, Margaret D. Carroll, and Katherine M. Flegal. 2004. "Mean Body Weight, Height, and Body Mass Index, United States 1960–2002." *Advance Data from Vital and Health Statistics* 347(October 27).

Ogden, Laura A. 2011. *Swamplife: People, Gators and Mangroves Entangled in the Everglades*. Minneapolis: University of Minnesota Press.

Ogden, Laura A., Billy Hall, and Kamiko Tanita. 2013. "Animals, Plants, People, and Things: A Review of Multispecies Ethnography."

Environment and Society: Advances in Research. 4 (1): 5-24.

Omi, Michael, and Howard Winant. 1994. *Racial Formation in the United States from the 1960s to the 1990s* (2nd ed.). New York: Routledge.

Ore, Tracy. 2010. *The Social Construction of Difference and Inequality: Race, Class, Gender, and Sexuality.* New York: McGraw-Hill.

Ortner, Sherri. 1974. "Is Female to Male as Nature Is to Culture?" In *Woman, Culture and Society,* edited by Michelle Z. Rosaldo and Louise Lamphere. Stanford, CA: Stanford University Press.

Ossorio, Pilar, and Troy Duster. 2005. "Race and Genetics: Controversies in Biomedical, Behavioral, and Forensic Sciences." *American Psychologist* 60 (1): 115–28.

Palsson, Gisli. 2013. "Ensembles of Biosocial Relations." In *Biosocial Becomings: Integrating Social and Biological Anthropology,* edited by Tim Ingold and Gisli Palsson, 23–41. New York: Cambridge University Press.

Parker, Richard. 1999. "The Meanings of Macho [Review]." *American Ethnologist* 26(2): 497–98.

Parsons, Talcott. 1964. *Theory of Social and Economic Organization.* New York: Simon & Schuster.

Pascoe, C. J. 2007. *Dude, You're a Fag: Masculinity and Sexuality in High School.* Berkeley: University of California Press.

Passariello, Phyllis. 2015. "Ecotourism and Cultural Production: An Anthropology of Indigenous Spaces in Ecuador: A Review." *American Anthropologist* 117(4) 824-825.

Partners in Health. 2020. "Massachusetts Response." https://www.pih.org/ma-response.

Pârvulescu, Radu Andrei. 2017. *Consuming Ocean Island: Stories of People and Phosphate from Banaba:* [A Review]. International Sociology 32 (5) 644–646.

Patterson, Francine. 1978. "Conversations with a Gorilla." *National Geographic,* October, 438–65.

Payer, Lynn. 1996. *Medicine and Culture: Varieties of Treatment in the United States, England, West Germany, and France.* New York: Henry Holt.

PayScale. 2015. www.payscale.com.

Peletz, Michael G. 1999. "The Heat of the Hearth [Review]." *American Ethnologist* 26(1): 251–52.

Pérez-Alemán, Paola. 1994. "Life Is Hard [Review]." *American Journal of Sociology* 99(5): 1393–95.

Perkins, Morgan, and Howard Morphy, eds. 2006. *The Anthropology of Art: A Reader.* Malden, MA: Blackwell.

Petersen, Glenn. 2015. "American Anthropology's 'Thailand Controversy': An Object Lesson in Professional Responsibility." *SOJOURN: Journal of Social Issues in Southeast Asia* 30(2): 528–49.

Peterson, Kristin. 2015. *Speculative Markets: Drug Circuits and Derivative Life in Nigeria.* Durham, NC: Duke University Press.

Pew Forum on Religion & Public Life. 2015. "America's Changing Religious Landscape." www.pewforum.org/2015/05/12/americas-changing-religious-landscape.

———. 2013. "Second Generation Americans: A Portrait of the Adult Children of Immigrants." www.pewsocialtrends.org/2013/02/07/second-generation-americans/

Phillips, Sarah. 2011. *Disability and Mobile Citizenship in Postsocialist Ukraine.* Bloomington: Indiana University Press.

Polanyi, Karl. (1944) 2001. *The Great Transformation.* Boston: Beacon.

Portes, Alejandro, Patricia Fernández-Kelly, and William Haller. 2009. "The Adaptation of the Immigrant Second Generation in America: Theoretical Overview and Recent Evidence." *Journal of Ethnic and Migration Studies* 35(7): 1077–1104.

Portes, Alejandro, and Rubén G. Rumbaut. 2014. *Immigrant America: A Portrait, Updated, and Expanded.* Oakland, CA: University of California Press.

Price, David. 2004. *Threatening Anthropology.* Durham, NC: Duke University Press.

———. 2011. *Weaponizing Anthropology: Social Science in Service of the Militarized State.* Oakland, CA: AK Distribution.

Price, Sally. 1989. *Primitive Art in Civilized Places.* Chicago: University of Chicago Press.

Quinn, Naomi. 1977. "Anthropological Studies on Women's Status." *Annual Review of Anthropology* 6: 181–222.

Radcliffe-Brown, A. R. 1922. *The Andaman Islanders: A Study in Social Anthropology.* Cambridge, UK: Cambridge University Press.

Ralph, Laurence. 2014. *Renegade Dreams: Living through Injury in Gangland Chicago.* Chicago: University of Chicago Press.

Rebhun, L.A. 1999. *The Heart Is Unknown Country: Love in the Changing Econmy of Northeast Brazil.* Stanford, CA: Stanford University Press.

Redfield, Robert. 1941. *The Folk Culture of the Yucatan.* Chicago: University of Chicago Press.

Reynolds, Terry S. 2015. "Beyond the Big Ditch: Politics, Ecology and Infrastructure at the Panama Canal: A Review." *Choice Journal*. 52(10).

Richards, Audrey. 1956. *Chisungu: A Girl's Initiation Ceremony among the Bemba of Northern Rhodesia*. London: Faber.

Richards, Paul. 1999. "A Different Kind of War Story [Review]." *American Anthropologist* 101(1): 214–15.

Richman, Karen. 2001. "High Tech and High Heels in the Global Economy [Review]." *American Ethnologist* 28(4): 954–55.

Rickford, John R., and Russell J. Rickford. 2000. *Spoken Soul: The Story of Black English*. New York: Wiley.

Robbins, Richard H. 2013. *Global Problems and the Culture of Capitalism* (6th ed.). Boston: Pearson.

Robbins, Richard H. and Rachel A. Dowty. 2019. *Global Problems and the Culture of Capitalism* 7th ed. Boston: Pearson.

Roberts, Elizabeth F. S., and Nancy Scheper-Hughes. 2011. "Introduction: Medical Migrations." *Body and Society* 17(2–3): 1–30.

Rodriguez, Clara. 2000. *Changing Race: Latinos, the Census, and the History of Ethnicity*. New York: New York University Press.

Rodseth, L., R. W. Wrangham, A. M. Harrigan, and B. Smuts. 1991. "The Human Community as a Primate Society." *Current Anthropology* 32: 221–54.

Roediger, David. 1992. *The Wages of Whiteness: Race and the Making of the American Working Class*. New York: Verso.

Rosaldo, Michelle Z. 1974. "Women, Culture and Society: A Theoretical Overview." In *Woman, Culture and Society*, edited by Michelle Z. Rosaldo and Louise Lamphere. Stanford, CA: Stanford University Press.

———. 1980. "The Use and Abuse of Anthropology: Reflections on Feminism and Cross-Cultural Understanding." *Signs: Journal of Women in Culture and Society* 5(3): 389–417.

Roscoe, Will. 1991. *The Zuni Man-Woman*. Albuquerque: University of New Mexico Press.

Roseberry, William. 1997. "Review Essay: On Historical Consciousness." *Current Anthropology*, 38(5): 926–32.

Roth-Gordon, Jennifer. 2016. *Race and the Brazilian Body: Blackness, Whiteness and Everyday Life in Rio de Janeiro*. New York: Macmillan.

Rouse, Roger. 1994. "Life Is Hard [Review]." *Contemporary Sociology* 23(1): 57–9.

Rubin, Gayle. 1975. "The Traffic in Women: Notes on the 'Political Economy' of Sex." In *Toward an Anthropology of Women*, edited by Rayna Reiter. New York: Monthly Review Press.

Ruby, Jay, and Marcus Banks. 2011. *Made to Be Seen: Historical Perspectives on Visual Anthropology*. Chicago: University of Chicago Press.

Rumbaut, Ruben G., and Alejandro Portes, eds. 2001. *Ethnicities: Children of Immigrants in America*. Berkeley: University of California Press.

Sachs, Jeffrey. 2005. *The End of Poverty: Economic Possibilities for Our Time*. New York: Penguin.

Sahlins, Marshall D. 1971. *Social Stratification in Polynesia*. Seattle: University of Washington Press.

———. (1974) 2004. *Stone Age Economics*. New York: Routledge.

Saillant, Francine, and Serge Genest, eds. 2007. *Medical Anthropology: Regional Perspectives and Shared Concerns*. Malden, MA: Blackwell.

Salas, Erick Burgueño. 2022. "Global air traffic – number of flights 2004–2022." Statista. https://www.statista.com/statistics/564769/airline-industry-number-of-flights.

Sanday, Peggy. 1990. *Fraternity Gang Rape: Sex, Brotherhood, and Privilege on Campus*. New York: New York University Press.

Sanders, Stephanie A., and June Machover Reinisch. 2006. "Would You Say You 'Had Sex' If . . .?" In *The Language and Sexuality Reader*, edited by Deborah Cameron and Don Kulick. New York: Routledge.

Sanjek, Roger. 1994. "The Enduring Inequalities of Race." In *Race*, edited by Steven Gregory and Roger Sanjek, 1–17. New Brunswick, NJ: Rutgers University Press.

Sapir, Edward, and Morris Swadesh. 1946. "Word 2." In *American Indian Grammatical Categories*, 103–12. Reedited for Dell Hymes in *Language in Culture and Society*, 100–7. New York: Harper & Row, 1964.

Saria, Vaibhav. 2021. *Hijras, Lovers, Brothers: Surviving Sex and Poverty in Rural India*. New York: Fordham University Press.

Sassen, Saskia. 1988. *The Mobility of Labor and Capital: A Study in International Investment and Labor Flow*. New York: Cambridge University Press.

———. 2016. "A Massive Loss of Habitat: New Drivers for Migration." *Sociology of Development* 2 (2): 204–233.

Schapiro, Rich. 2022. "Maker of Rifle Used by Texas Gunman Draws Fury for 'Incendiary' Ads." NBC News, May 26. https://www.nbcnews.com/news/crime-courts/maker-gun-used-uvalde-shooting-long-known-incendiary-ads-rcna30631.

Scheid, Volker. 2002. *Chinese Medicine in Contemporary China: Plurality and Synthesis.* Durham, NC: Duke University Press.

Scheid, Volker and Hugh MacPherson. 2012. *Integrating East Asian Medicine into Contemporary Healthcare.* London: Churchill Livingstone.

Scheper-Hughes, Nancy. 1989. "Death without Weeping: Has Poverty Ravaged Mother Love in the Shantytowns of Brazil?" *Natural History* 98(10): 8–16.

———. 1992. *Death without Weeping: The Violence of Everyday Life in Brazil.* Berkeley: University of California Press.

———. 1995. "The Primacy of the Ethical: Propositions for a Militant Anthropology." *Current Anthropology* 36(3): 409–20.

———. 2002. "Min(d)ing the Body: On the Trail of Organ-Stealing Rumors." In *Exotic No More: Anthropology on the Front Lines,* edited by Jeremy MacClancy, 33–63. Chicago: University of Chicago Press.

———. 2013. "No More Angel Babies on the Alto do Cruzeiro: A Dispatch from Brazil's Revolution in Child Survival." *Natural History.* www.naturalhistorymag.com/features/282558/no-more-angel-babies-on-the-alto-do-cruzeiro.

Scheper-Hughes, Nancy, and Margaret M. Lock. 1987. "The Mindful Body: A Prolegomenon to Future Work in Medical Anthropology." *Medical Anthropology Quarterly* 1(1): 6–41.

Scheper-Hughes, Nancy, and Philippe Bourgois. 2004. *Violence in War and Peace: An Anthology.* New York: Wiley.

Schneider, Arnd, and Christopher Wright. 2006. *Contemporary Art and Anthropology.* Oxford, UK: Berg.

Schneider, David M. 1980. *American Kinship: A Cultural Account* (2nd ed.). Chicago: University of Chicago Press.

Schneider, Harold. 1979. *Livestock and Equality in East Africa: The Economic Bases for Social Structure.* Bloomington: Indiana University Press.

Schneider, Jane. 1977. "Was There a Pre-Capitalist World System?" *Peasant Studies* 6(1): 20–29.

Schoendorf, Kenneth C., Carol J. R. Hogue, and Joel C. Kleinman. 1992. "Mortality among Infants of Blacks as Compared to White College-Educated Parents." *New England Journal of Medicine* 326(23): 1522–26.

Schulz, Amy J., and Leith Mullings. 2006. *Gender, Race, Class, and Health: Intersectional Approaches.* San Francisco: Jossey-Bass.

Scott, A. O. 2013. "Or Would You Rather Be a Fish?" *New York Times,* February 28.

Scott, James C. 1985. *Weapons of the Weak: Everyday Forms of Peasant Resistance.* New Haven, CT: Yale University Press.

Sebeok, Thomas A., and Donna J. Umiker-Sebeok, eds. 1980. *Speaking of Apes: A Critical Anthology of Two-Way Communication with Man.* New York: Plenum Press.

Service, Elman R. 1962. *Primitive Social Organization; An Evolutionary Perspective.* New York: Random House.

———. 1966. *The Hunters.* Englewood Cliffs, NJ: Prentice Hall.

Severson, Kim. 2011. "Race-Based Names Dot the Landscape." *New York Times,* October 6.

Shankar, Shalini. 2015. *Advertising Diversity: AdAgencies and the Creation of Asian American Consumers.* Durham: Duke University Press.

Shanklin, Eugenia. 1998. "The Profession of the Color Blind: Sociocultural Anthropology and Racism in the 21st Century." *American Anthropologist* 100(3): 669–79.

Shannon, Jonathan Holt. 2006. *Among the Jasmine Trees: Music and Modernity in Contemporary Syria.* Middletown, CT: Wesleyan University Press.

Sharma, Aradhana, and Akhil Gupta, eds. 2006. *The Anthropology of the State: A Reader.* Malden, MA: Blackwell.

Shaw, Stephanie. 1996. *What a Woman Ought to Be and to Do: Black Professional Women Workers during the Jim Crow Era.* Chicago: University of Chicago Press.

Shepler, Susan. 2014. *Childhood Deployed: Remaking Child Soldiers in Sierra Leone.* New York: New York University Press.

Siebel, Catherine. 2000. "White Weddings [Review]." *Teaching Sociology* 28(2): 175–76.

Simons, Gary F. 2022. *Ethnologue: Languages of the World*, Twenty-fifth edition. Dallas, TX: SIL International. Online version: https://www.ethnologue.com/.

Singer, Merrill, and Hans A. Baer. 2007. *Introducing Medical Anthropology: A Discipline in Action*. Lanham, MD: AltaMira.

Smedley, Audrey. 1993. *Race in North America: Origins and Evolution of a Worldview*. Boulder, CO: Westview Press.

Smith, Adam. 1776. *Wealth of Nations*. Reprint, New York: Simon & Brown, 2010.

Smith, Christen. 2016. *Afro-Paradise: Blackness, Violence and Performance in Brazil*. Champaign: University of Illinois Press.

Smith, Neil. 2010. *Uneven Development: Nature, Capital, and the Production of Space*. London: Verso.

Smith, Robert C. 2006. *Mexican New York: Transnational Lives of New Immigrants*. Berkeley: University of California Press.

Smith, Roberta. 2014. "In a Mattress, a Lever for Art and Political Protest." *New York Times*, September 21.

Snow, Dean R. 1994. *The Iroquois*. Cambridge, MA: Blackwell.

Speed, Shannon. 2006. "At the Crossroads of Human Rights and Anthropology: Toward a Critically Engaged Activist Research." *American Anthropologist* 108(1): 66–76.

———. 2007. *Rights in Rebellion: Indigenous Struggle and Human Rights in Chiapas*. Stanford, CA: Stanford University Press.

Spence, Jonathan D. 2013. *The Search for Modern China* (3rd ed.). New York: Norton.

Spice, Anne. 2018. "Fighting Invasive Infrastructures Indigenous Relations Against Pipelines." *Environment and Society: Advances in Research* 9 (1) 40-56.

Stack, Carol B. 1974. *All Our Kin: Strategies for Survival in a Black Community*. New York: Harper & Row.

Stange, Mary Zeiss. 1997. *Woman the Hunter*. Boston: Beacon Press.

Stark, Rodney, and William Sims Bainbridge. 1985. *The Future of Religion: Secularization, Revival, and Cult Formation*. Berkeley: University of California Press.

Steiner, Christopher Burghard. 1994. *African Art in Transit*. Cambridge, UK: Cambridge University Press.

———. 1995. "The Art of the Trade: On the Creation of Authenticity in the African Art Market." In *The Traffic in Culture*, edited by George E. Marcus and Fred R. Myers, 151–66. Berkeley: University of California Press.

Stephen, Lynn. 1995. "Women's Rights Are Human Rights: The Merging of Feminine and Feminist Interests among El Salvador's Mothers of the Disappeared (CO-MADRES)." *American Ethnologist* 22(4): 807–27.

Sterk, Claire E. 2000. *Tricking and Tripping: Prostitution in the Era of AIDS*. Putnam Valley, NY: Social Change.

Stevens, Carolyn S. 2005. "Tsukiji: The Fish Market at the Center of the World [Review]." *Journal of Asian Studies*, 64(4): 1022–23.

Steward, Julian H. 1956. *The People of Puerto Rico: A Study in Social Anthropology*. Urbana: University of Illinois Press.

Stiglitz, Joseph E. 2010. *Freefall: America, Free Markets, and the Sinking of the World Economy*. New York: Norton.

———. 2012. *The Price of Inequality: How Today's Divided Society Endangers Our Future*. New York: Norton.

Stocking, George W. Jr. 1968. *Race, Culture and Evolution: Essays in the History of Anthropology*. Chicago: University of Chicago Press.

———. 1983. *Observers Observed: Essays on Ethnographic Fieldwork*. Madison: University of Wisconsin Press.

———, ed. 1989. *A Franz Boas Reader: The Shaping of American Anthropology, 1883–1911*. Chicago: University of Chicago Press.

Stoller, Paul. 2003. "Circuits of African Art/Paths of Wood: Exploring an Anthropological Trail." *Anthropological Quarterly* 76(2): 207–34.

Stoller, Paul, and Cheryl Olkes. 1987. *In Sorcery's Shadow: A Memoir of Apprenticeship among the Songhay of Niger*. Chicago: University of Chicago Press.

Stone, Amy L. 2007. "Sexuality and Social Change: Sexual Relations in a Capitalist System." *American Anthropologist* 109(4): 753–55.

Stone, Linda. 2009. *Kinship and Gender: An Introduction* (4th ed.). Boulder, CO: Westview Press.

Sue, Derald Wing. 2010. *Microaggressions in Everyday Life: Race, Gender, and Sexual Orientation*. Hoboken, NJ: Wiley.

———. *Race Talk and the Conspiracy of Silence: Understanding and Facilitating Difficult Dialogues on Race*. Hoboken: Wiley.

Tannen, Deborah. 2001. *You Just Don't Understand: Women and Men in Conversation* (2nd ed.). New York: Ballantine.

Tax Policy Center. 2019. "Tax Facts." https://www.taxpolicycenter.org/statistics?term_node_tid_filter=All&field_effective_date_value2%5Bvalue%5D%5Byear%5D=2019.

Taylor, Robert Joseph. 2000. "All Our Kin: Strategies for Survival in a Black Community [Review]." *Journal of Marriage and Family* 62(3): 865–67.

Teaiwa, Katerina Martina. 2014. *Consuming Ocean Island: Stories of People and Phosphate from Banaba*. Bloomington: Indiana University Press.

Terrace, Herbert S., L. A. Petitto, R. J. Sanders, and T. G. Bever. 1979. "Can an Ape Create a Sentence?" *Science* 206(4421): 891–902.

Tett, Gillian. 2009. *Fool's Gold: The Inside Story of J. P. Morgan and How Wall Street Greed Corrupted Its Bold Dream and Created a Financial Catastrophe*. New York: Free Press.

Thayer, Zeneta M., and Amy L. Non. 2015. "Anthropology Meets Epigenetics: Current and Future Directions." *American Anthropologist* 117(4): 722–35.

Thornton, Sarah. 2009. *Seven Days in the Art World*. New York: Norton.

Tierney, Patrick. 2000. *Darkness in El Dorado: How Scientists and Journalists Devastated the Amazon*. New York: Norton.

Tilly, Charles. "Reflections on the History of European State-Making." In *The Formation of National States in Western Europe*, edited by Charles Tilly. Princeton, NJ: Princeton University Press.

Townsend, Patricia K. 2018. *Environmental Anthropology: From Pigs to Policies*. Long Grove: Waveland Press Inc.

Trinkaus, Erik, and Pat Shipman. 1994. *The Neandertals: Of Skeletons, Scientists, and Scandal*. New York: Vintage.

Trnka, Susanna. 2021. "Be Kind: Negotiating Ethical Proximities in Aotearoa/New Zealand during COVID-19." *Cultural Anthropology* 36 (3): 368–80.

Trouillot, Michel-Rolph. 1994. "Culture, Color, and Politics in Haiti." In *Race*, edited by Steven Gregory and Roger Sanjek, 146–74. New Brunswick, NJ: Rutgers University Press.

———. 2003. *Global Transformations: Anthropology and the Modern World*. New York: Palgrave Macmillan.

Turnbull, Colin M. (1961) 2010. *The Forest People*. New York: Simon & Schuster.

Turner, Victor. 1957. *Schism and Continuity in an African Society: A Study of Ndembu Village Life*. Manchester, UK: Manchester University Press.

———. 1969. *The Ritual Process: Structure and Anti-Structure*. Chicago: Aldine.

Tylor, Edward. 1920 [1871]. *Primitive Culture*. New York: J. P. Putnam's Sons.

United Nations Department of Economic and Social Affairs, Population Division. 2017. "Population Facts." http://esa.un.org/unmigration/documents/The_number_of_international_migrants.pdf.

———. 2020. "International Migration 2020 Highlights." https://www.un.org/en/desa/international-migration-2020-highlights.

United Nations Department of Economic and Social Affairs. 2017. "International Migration 2017." www.un.org/en/development/desa/population/migration/publications/wallchart/docs/MigrationWallChart2017.pdf.

———. 2015b. "Sustainable Development Goals: 17 Goals to Transform our World." www.un.org/sustainabledevelopment/development-agenda/.

———. 2015c. "World Population Prospects: The 2015 Revision, Key Findings and Advance Tables." Working Paper No. ESA/P/WP.241.

———. 2019. "Total International Migrant Stock." https://www.un.org/en/development/desa/population/migration/data/estimates2/estimates19.asp.

United Nations High Commissioner on Refugees. 2018. "UNHCR Global Trends: Forced Displacement in 2017." http://unhcr.org/556725e69.html.

———. 2022. "Refugee Data Finder." https://www.unhcr.org/refugee-statistics/.

United Nations International Migration Report. 2017. "International Migration Report 2017." www.un.org/en/development/desa/population/migration/publications/migrationreport/docs/MigrationReport2017_Highlights.pdf.

United Nations Refugee Agency. 2018. "Internally Displaced People." www.unhcr.org/internally-displaced-people.html.

United Nations Women. 2020. "Facts and figures: Women's leadership and political participation." https://www.unwomen.org/en/what-we-do/leadership-and-political-participation/facts-and-figures#_edn7.

Urciuoli, Bonnie. 1996. *Exposing Prejudice: Puerto Rican Experiences of Language, Race, and Class.* Boulder, CO: Westview Press.

Ury, William, ed. 2002. *Must We Fight? From the Battlefield to the Schoolyard—A New Perspective on Violent Conflict and Its Prevention.* San Francisco: Jossey-Bass.

U.S. Census Bureau. 2010. "America's Families and Living Arrangements: 2010," Table FG3. www.census.gov/hhes/families/files/cps2010/tabFG4-all.xls.

———. 2014. "Families and Living Arrangements." www.census.gov/hhes/families/data/families.html.

———. 2015. "Detailed Languages Spoken at Home and Ability to Speak English for the Population 5 Years and Over: 2009-2013." https://www.census.gov/data/tables/2013/demo/2009-2013-lang-tables.html.

———. 2016. "Examining Change in the Percent of Married-Couple Households that are Interracial and Interethnic: 2000 to 2012–2016." https://www.census.gov/content/dam/Census/library/working-papers/2018/demo/SEHSD-WP2018-11.pdf.

———. 2017. "Facts for Features: Hispanic Heritage Month, 2017." https://www.census.gov/newsroom/facts-for-features/2017/hispanic-heritage.html.

———. 2018. "Income and Poverty in the United States: 2017." https://www.census.gov/library/publications/2018/demo/p60-263.html.

———. 2021. Historical Household Tables. https://www.census.gov/data/tables/time-series/demo/families/households.html.

———. 2021. "QuickFacts: New Orleans city, Louisiana." https://www.census.gov/quickfacts/neworleanscitylouisiana.

U.S. Centers for Disease Control and Prevention. 2020. "Cesarean Delivery Rate by State." https://www.cdc.gov/nchs/pressroom/sosmap/cesarean_births/cesareans.htm.

———. 2022. "Risk for COVID-19 Infection, Hospitalization, and Death By Race/Ethnicity." https://www.cdc.gov/coronavirus/2019-ncov/covid-data/investigations-discovery/hospitalization-death-by-race-ethnicity.html.

U.S. Customs and Border Protection. 2019. "Southwest Border Migration FY 2019." https://www.cbp.gov/newsroom/stats/sw-border-migration.

U.S. Department of Agriculture. 2020. "Household Food Security in the United States in 2020." https://www.ers.usda.gov/publications/pub-details/?pubid=102075.

Valentine, David. (2007). *Imagining Transgender: An Ethnography of a Category.* Durham, NC: Duke University Press.

Van Gennep, Arnold. (1908) 1960. *The Rites of Passage.* Chicago: University of Chicago Press.

Venbrux, Eric, Pamela Sheffield Rosi, and Robert L. Welsch. 2006. *Exploring World Art.* Long Grove, IL: Waveland Press.

Victoria, Aaron G. 2018. "Beyond the Big Ditch: Politics, Ecology, and Infrastructure at the Panama Canal: A Review." *The Journal of Transport History* 39 (1) 123–124.

Vitelli, Romeo. 2013. "Television, Commercials, and Your Child." *Psychology Today*, July 22.

Vogel, Susan Mullin. 1991. *Africa Explores: 20th Century African Art.* New York: Center for African Art.

Volsche, Shelly. 2019. *Voluntarily Childfree: Identity and Kinship in the United States.* Lanham, MD: Rowman & Littlefield.

Wade, Lisa, and Myra Marx Ferree. 2015. *Gender: Ideas, Interactions, Institutions.* New York: Norton.

Wakin, Eric. 1992. *Anthropology Goes to War: Professional Ethics & Counterinsurgency in Thailand.* Madison: University of Wisconsin, Center for Southeast Asian Studies.

Walker, Sheila S. 2002. "Africanity vs. Blackness: Race, Class and Culture in Brazil." *NACLA Report on the Americas* 35(6): 16–20.

Wallace, Anthony F. C. 1957. "Political Organization and Land Tenure among the Northwestern Indians, 1600–1830." *Southwest Journal of Anthropology* 13: 301–21.

Wallerstein, Immanuel Maurice. 1974. *World-Systems Analysis: An Introduction.* Durham, NC: Duke University Press.

Walsh, Andrew. 2007. "Conservation is our Government Now: The Politics of Ecology in Papua New Guinea: A Review." *Journal of Anthropological Research.* 63 (3) 426 –428.

Wardhaugh, Ronald. 2009. *An Introduction to Socio-linguistics* (6th ed.). London: Blackwell.

Wardlow, Holly. 2006. *Wayward Women: Sexuality and Agency in a New Guinea Society.* Berkeley: University of California Press.

Warriner, Christina, and Cecil M. Lewis Jr. 2015. "Microbiome and Health in Past and Present Human Populations." *American Anthropologist* 117(4): 740–41.

Waterston, Alisse. 2009. *An Anthropology of War: Views from War Zones.* New York: Berghahn.

Watson, James L., ed. 1998. *Golden Arches East: McDonald's in East Asia.* Stanford, CA: Stanford University Press.

Weber, Eugen. 1976. *Peasants into Frenchmen: The Modernization of Rural France, 1870–1914.* Stanford, CA: Stanford University Press.

Weber, Max. 1905. *The Protestant Ethic and the Spirit of Capitalism.* London: Routledge, 2002.

———. 1919. *Politics as a Vocation.* Philadelphia: Fortress, 1965.

———. (1920) 1946. "Class, Status and Party." In *From Max Weber: Essays in Sociology*, edited and translated by Hans Gerth and C. Wright Mills. New York: Free Press.

———. 1920. *Sociology of Religion.* Boston: Beacon Press, 1993.

Wedding Stats. 2022. "Average Cost of a Wedding 2022." https://www.weddingstats.org/average-cost-of-a-wedding/

Weiner, Annette. 1976. *Women of Value, Men of Renown: New Perspectives in Trobriand Exchange.* Austin: University of Texas Press.

———. 1988. *The Trobrianders of Papua New Guinea.* New York: Holt, Rinehart and Winston.

Weiss, Margot. 2011. "The Epistemology of Ethnography: Method in Queen Anthropology." *GLQ: A Journal of Lesbian and Gay Studies* 17(4): 649–664.

Wekker, Gloria. 1999. "What's Identity Got to Do with It? Rethinking Identity in Light of the Mati Work in Suriname." In *Female Desires: Same-Sex and Transgender Practices across Cultures*, edited by Evelyn Blackwood and Saskia E. Wieringa, 119–38. New York: Columbia University Press.

———. 2006. *The Politics of Passion: Women's Sexual Culture in Afro-Surinamese Diaspora.* New York: Columbia University Press.

Welch, Cliff. 2001. "Peasants against Globalization: Rural Social Movement in Costa Rica [Review]." *Latin American Politics and Society* 43(4): 166–68.

Werner, Paul. 2006. *Museum Inc.: Inside the Global Art World.* Chicago: Prickly Paradigm Press.

West, Paige. 2006. *Conservation Is Our Government Now: The Politics of Ecology in Papua New Guinea.* Durham: Duke University Press.

———. 2016. *Dispossession and the Environment: Rhetoric and Inequality in Papua New Guinea.* New York: Columbia University Press.

West, Candace and Don H. Zimmerman. 1987. "Doing Gender." *Gender and Society* 1(2), 125-151.

———. 2009. "Accounting for Doing Gender." *Gender and Society* 23(1), 112-122.

West, Candace. 1998. "When the Doctor Is a 'Lady': Power, Status and Gender in Physician-Patient Encounters." In *Language and Gender: A Reader*, edited by Jennifer Coates, 396–412. London: Blackwell.

Weston, Kath. 1991. *Families We Choose: Lesbians, Gays, Kinship.* New York: Columbia University Press.

———. 1993. "Lesbian/Gay Studies in the House of Anthropology." *Annual Review of Anthropology* 22: 339–67.

White, Tracie. 2018. "Epidurals Increase in Popularity, Stanford Study Finds." Stanford Medicine Scope Blog. https://scopeblog.stanford.edu/2018/06/26/epidurals-increase-in-popularity-stanford-study-finds/

Whitehouse, Bruce. 2012. *Migrants and Strangers in an African City: Exile, Dignity, Belonging.* Bloomington: Indiana University Press.

Wittfogel, Karl. 1957. *Oriental Despotism: A Comparative Study of Total Power.* New Haven, CT: Yale University Press.

Wilkins, Amy C. 2008. "Dude You're a Fag: Masculinity and Sexuality in High School [Review]." *Contemporary Sociology* 37(3): 242–43.

Williams, Brackette F. 1995. "The Public I/Eye: Conducting Fieldwork to Do Homework on Homelessness and Begging in Two U.S. Cities." *Current Anthropology* 36(1): 25–51.

Williams, Walter. 1992. *The Spirit and the Flesh: Sexual Diversity in American Indian Cultures* (2nd ed.). Boston: Beacon Press.

Williamson, K. Eliza and Etsuko Matsuoka. 2019. "Comparing Childbirth in Brazil and Japan: Social Hierarchies, Cultural Values, and the Meaning of Place." In *Birth in Eight Cultures.* 2019. Davis-Floyd, Robbie and Melissa Cheyney, eds. Long Grove, IL: Waveland Press, Inc.

Wilson, William Julius. 1987. *The Truly Disadvantaged: The Inner City, the Underclass, and Public Policy.* Chicago: University of Chicago Press.

Winegar, Jessica. 2006. *Creative Reckonings: The Politics of Art and Culture in Contemporary Egypt.* Stanford, CA: Stanford University Press.

———. 2008. "The Humanity Game: Art, Islam and the War on Terror." *Anthropological Quarterly* 81(3), 651–81.

Wolcott, Victoria W. 2001. *Remaking Respectability: African American Women in Interwar Detroit.* Chapel Hill: University of North Carolina Press.

Wolf, Eric R. 1966. *Peasants.* Englewood Cliffs, NJ: Prentice-Hall.

———. 1982. *Europe and the People without History.* Berkeley: University of California Press.

———. 1990. "Distinguished Lecture: Facing Power—Old Insights, New Questions." *American Anthropologist* 92: 586–96.

———. 1999. *Envisioning Power: Ideologies of Dominance and Crisis.* Berkeley: University of California Press.

———. 2001. "Ethnicity and Nationhood." In *Pathways of Power: Building an Anthropology of the Modern World.* Berkeley: University of California Press.

Wolf, Eric, and Joseph Jorgensen. 1970. "Anthropology on the Warpath in Thailand." *New York Review of Books,* November 19.

Woolard, Kathryn. 1989. *Double Talk: Bilingualism and the Politics of Ethnicity in Catalonia.* Stanford, CA: Stanford University Press.

World Bank. 2018. "Record High Remittances to Low-and Middle-income Countries in 2017." https://www.worldbank.org/en/news/press-release/2018/04/23/record-high-remittances-to-low-and-middle-income-countries-in-2017.

———. 2018. "Nearly Half the World Lives on Less than $5.50 a Day." https://www.worldbank.org/en/news/press-release/2018/10/17/nearly-half-the-world-lives-on-less-than-550-a-day.

———. 2018. "School Enrollment, Primary (% net)." https://data.worldbank.org/indicator/se.prm.nenr?end=2018&start=1970.

———. 2019. "Poverty and Shared Prosperity." www.worldbank.org/en/publication/poverty-and-shared-prosperity.

———. 2020. "GDP (current US$)." https://data.worldbank.org/indicator/NY.GDP.MKTP.CD.

———. 2020. "Poverty and Shared Prosperity 2020: Reversals of Fortune." https://www.worldbank.org/en/publication/poverty-and-shared-prosperity#a.

———. 2022. "Life expectancy at birth, total (years)." https://data.worldbank.org/indicator/SP.DYN.LE00.IN.

———. 2022. "Mortality rate, infant (per 1,000 live births)." https://data.worldbank.org/indicator/SP.DYN.IMRT.IN?end=2020&start=1960.

World Economic Forum, 2018. "The Inclusive Development Index 2018: Summary and Data Highlights." http://www3.weforum.org/docs/WEF_Forum_IncGrwth_2018.pdf.

World Health Organization. 2018. "Drinking-water: Fact sheet." https://www.who.int/news-room/fact-sheets/detail/drinking-water.

———. 2015b. "Life expectancy." http://who.int/gho/mortality_burden_disease/life_tables/en/

———. 2019a. "Infant Mortality." https://www.who.int/gho/child_health/mortality/neonatal_infant_text/en/.

———. 2019b. "Life Expectancy." https://www.who.int/gho/mortality_burden_disease/life_tables/en/.

———. 2020. "Children: improving survival and well-being." September 3. https://www.who.int/news-room/fact-sheets/detail/children-reducing-mortality.

Worldometer. 2022. "Energy used today in the world." https://www.worldometers.info/energy/.

———. 2022. "Life Expectancy of the World Population." https://www.worldometers.info/demographics/life-expectancy/.

World Wildlife Fund. 2015. "Living Blue Planet Report." http://assets.worldwildlife.org/publications/817/files/original/Living_Blue_Planet_Report_2015_Final_LR.pdf?1442242821&_ga=1.106224195.1712001709.1442418559.

World Population Review. 2018. http://world populationreview.com/

Worldwatch Institute. 2015. *State of the World 2015: Confronting Hidden Threats to Sustainability.* Washington, DC: Island Press/Center for Resource Economics.

Wynn, L. L. 2021. "The Pandemic Imaginerie: Infectious Bodies and Military-Police Theater in Australia." *Cultural Anthropology* 36 (3): 350–59.

Yan, Yunxiang. 2003. *Private Life under Socialism: Love, Intimacy, and Family Change in a Chinese Village, 1949–1999*. Stanford, CA: Stanford University Press.

———. 2004. "Of Hamburgers and Social Space: Consuming McDonalds in Beijing." In *The Cultural Politics of Food and Eating: A Reader*, edited by James L. Watson and Melissa L. Caldwell. New York: Wiley.

Young, Colin. 1995. "Observational Cinema." In *Principles of Visual Anthropology*. edited by Paul Hockings, 99–113. Berlin: Mouton de Gruyter.

Zaloom, Caitlin. 2006. *Out of the Pits: Traders and Technology from Chicago to London*. University of Chicago Press.

Zhan, Mei. 2009. *Other-Worldly: Making Chinese Medicine through Transnational Frames*. Durham, NC: Duke University Press.

Zhang, Phoebe. 2019. "Wanted: Sperm Donor for Single Chinese Woman in Video Appeal, as Unmarried Parents Still Face Barriers." *South China Morning Post*, January 23. https://www.scmp.com/news/china/society/article/2183298/wanted-sperm-donor-single-chinese-woman-video-appeal-unmarried.

Zilberg, Jonathan. 1996. "African Art in Transit [Review]." *International Journal of African Historical Studies* 29(1): 147–49.

Zimmer, Carl. 2010. "How Microbes Defend and Define Us." *New York Times*, July 13.

———. 2011. "Bacterial Ecosystems Divide People into 3 Groups, Scientists Say." *New York Times*, April 20.

Zinn, Howard. 2005. *A People's History of the United States: 1492–Present* (rev. ed.). New York: Harper Perennial.

Credits

Archives of Florida; **p. 339:** World History Archive/ Alamy Stock Photo; **p. 341:** Jean-Michel Andre/ AFP/Getty Images; **p. 345 left:** Julio Etchart/Ullstein Bild via Getty Images; **p. 345 right:** Adventure Tours Australia/Intrepid Group and Tree Hugger Travel; **p. 352:** AP Photo/J. Scott Applewhite.

CHAPTER 12

PHOTOS: Page 356: ZUMA Press, Inc./Alamy Stock Photo; **p. 360:** SOPA Images Limited/ Alamy Stock Photo; **p. 361:** Louise Murray/Alamy Stock Photo; **p. 366 left:** Xinhua/Alamy Stock Photo; **p. 366 center:** ZUMA Press, Inc./Alamy Stock Photo; **p. 367 left:** Stringer/Mexico/Reuters/ Newscom; **p. 367 right:** Robert Mora/Alamy Stock Photo; **p. 370:** Jason Redmond/REUTERS/Alamy Stock Photo; **p. 372:** © Frans Lanting/lanting.com; **p. 376 top left:** Todd Heisler/The New York Times/ Redux; **p. 376 bottom left:** Xinhua/Lu Zhe/ eyevine/ Redux; **p. 376 right:** Ali Hashisho/Reuters/Newscom; **p. 377 top:** Muhammad Hamed/RReuters/Newscom; **p. 377 bottom left:** Roger Hutchings/Alamy Stock Photo; **p. 377 bottom right:** Paul Hackett/Reuters/ Newscom; **p. 379:** Navesh Chitrakar/Reuters/ Newscom; **p. 382:** Julian Guadalupe/Alamy Stock Photo; **p. 384:** Fatih Pinar/Anzenberger/Redux.

CHAPTER 13

PHOTOS: Page 388: Jemal Countess/Getty Images for Repairers Of The Breach; **p. 393:** © Ed Kashi; **p. 395:** François-Olivier Dommergues/Alamy Stock Photo; **p. 397:** Pictorial Press Ltd/Alamy Stock Photo; **p. 398:** Copyright: 2021 from Chisungu : A Girl's Initiation Ceremony Among the Bemba of Zambia by Audrey Richards. Reproduced by permission of Taylor and Francis Group, LLC, a division of Informa plc.; **p. 400:** Ahmad Faizal Yahya/ Alamy Stock Photo; **p. 401:** Glasshouse Images/ Alamy Stock Photo; **p. 402:** Paul Springett C/Alamy Stock Photo ; **p. 403:** Hulton Archive/Getty Images; **p. 405 left:** CBW/Alamy Stock Photo; **p. 405 right:**

Frances M. Roberts/Newscom; **p. 407:** Images & Stories/Alamy Stock Photo; **p. 409 left:** Keith Torrie/ NY Daily News Archive via Getty Images; **p. 409 right:** Scott Halleran/Getty Images; **p. 411:** Baz Ratner/Reuters/Newscom; **p. 413:** AP Photo/Pascual Gorriz; **p. 415:** Haroon Sabawoon/Anadolu Agency/ Getty Images.

CHAPTER 14

PHOTOS: Page 422: AP Photo/Eric Gay; **p. 428 left:** © Erich Schlegel; **p. 428 right:** Eye Ubiquitous/ Newscom; **p. 429:** Earl & Nazima Kowall/Corbis Documentary/Getty Images; **p. 431:** Siewert Falko/picture-alliance/dpa/AP Photo; **p. 432:** Ian MacNicol/Getty Images; **p. 433 left:** Courtesy Everett Collection/agefotostock; **p. 433 right:** Fuse/ Getty Images; **p. 436:** Manny Crisostomo /MCT/ ZUMAPRESS.com; **p. 439 left:** Ginger Horsburgh/ Earthside Birth Photography; **p. 439 right:** Mira/ Alamy Stock Photo; **p. 443 left:** Wallace, Daniel/ St. Petersburg Times/PSG/Newscom; **p. 443 right:** AP Photo/Dieu Nalio Chery; **p. 446:** AP Photo/Eric Gay; **p. 453:** Pete Pattisson.

CHAPTER 15

PHOTOS: Page 456: Bjanka Kadic/Alamy Stock Photo; **p. 458:** Mike Booth/Alamy Stock Photo; **p. 460 left:** Sandra Foyt/Alamy Stock Photo; **p. 460 right:** Xinhua/Mohamed Kadri/eyevine/ Redux; **p. 461:** Kevin Schafer/Alamy Stock Photo; **p. 463:** Mario Fourmy/Redux; **p. 465:** John Reader/ Science Source; **p. 466:** JM Labat/Science Source; **p. 468:** Cindy Hopkins/Alamy Stock Photo; **p. 470:** Michelle V. Agins/The New York Times/Redux; **p. 472 left:** Tom Williams/Roll Call/Getty Images; **p. 472 right:** Ethan Miller/Reuters/Newscom; **p. 474:** Courtesy of Amiee Cox; **p. 475 left:** Agencia el Universal/El Universal de Mexico/Newscom; **p. 475 right:** Courtesy of Station Museum of Contemporary Art, photography by Michael Stravato.

Glossary/Index

AAA, *See* American Anthropological Association

AAE, *See* African American English

Abidjan, Côte d'Ivoire, 282, 283, *467*, *467*–68

Abu-Lughod, Lila, 60–61

acculturation, 43

Aceh province, Indonesia, *15*

acupuncture, *433*

Adelso Island, *103*

ADM (Archer Daniels Midland), 282

Admiralty Islands, *75*

advertising, 56–57

Advertising Diversity (Shankar), 147, 148

aesthetics across cultures, in art, 461–63

affinal relationship, 260–61 A kinship relationship established through marriage and/or alliance, not through biology or common descent.

affirmative consent policy, 220

Afghanistan

    child labor in, *42*

    religion, politics, and suicide bombing in, *414*, 414–16, *415*

Africa; *See also specific countries*

    agriculture in, *286*

    art in, *464*, 464–65, *465*, *467*, 467–69, *468*

    magic in, 405–7, *406*, *407*

    migration within, *323*, 323–24, *324*

    slaves from, 290–92

    trade with, *289*, 289–92

African American English (AAE), 109–10, *110*, *111*

African Americans, *See* Blacks

African Art in Transit (Steiner), 467–69

Agard-Jones, Vanessa, 341–42

agency, 51–52, 379 The potential power of individuals and groups to contest cultural norms,

values, mental maps of reality, symbols, institutions, and structures of power.

aging, 273–75, *274*

Agrama, Hussein Ali, 383–85

agriculture, 174–76, 285–87, *286* An intensive farming strategy for food production involving permanently cultivated land.

ahimsa (nonviolence toward living things), 410

Ahmadpour, Saeid, *322*

air *(qi)*, 432

Al Azhar Fatwa Council, 383–85, *384*

Algeria, anti-colonial struggles in, 292, *293*

Alien Ocean (Helmreich), 338–39

Aliyah Senior Citizens' Center, *78*, 78–79

Allison, Anne, 227, 229–30

All Our Kin (Stack), 267

Alto do Cruzeiro, Brazil, *64*, 65–66, *66*, 85, 91–93

Amazon rain forest

    ecotourism in, 344–46, *345*

    multispecies ethnography of, 338, *338*

ambilineal (cognatic; bilateral) descent groups, 254, 258

Amchi medicine, 428–30, *429*

American Academy of Pediatrics, 198

American Anthropological Association (AAA), 88–89, 273

American Museum of Natural History, 45, 72

American Sign Language, 100, 103

Americas; *See also specific countries*

    anti-colonial struggles in, 293

    trade with Europe and Africa, 290–92

Amsterdam, Netherlands, *40*

anal penetration, 222

Andaman Islands, 47

Anderson, Benedict, 178–79, 268

Angelini, Alessandro, 458

Angola, agriculture in, *286*

animals, language and, 99, 100, *100*

"The Animal with the Weirdest Sex Life"
      (Diamond), 223–24

anomie, 398

anonymity, 90 Protecting the identities of
the people involved in a study by changing
or omitting their names or other identifying
characteristics.

Anthropocene, 26, 332–36 The current historical era in which human activity is reshaping the
planet in permanent ways.
    construction of Panama Canal, *334,* 334–36
    mining in Banaba Island, *333,* 333–34

anthropologist's toolkit, 80 The tools needed
to conduct fieldwork, including information, perspectives, strategies and even equipment.

anthropology, 5–29 The study of the full scope
of human diversity, past and present, and the
application of that knowledge to help people
of different backgrounds better understand one
another.
    applied, 10
    approach of, 11–15
        focus on local level, 12–13
        global scope, 12, *13*
        people and power structures, 14
        shared connections, 14–15
    of art, 459–64
    challenge of, 7–9
    changes in, 24
        communities, 25
        environment, 25–27
        research strategies, 27–29
    defined, 9
    environmental, 331–32
    four-field approach of, 15–16
        archaeology, *18,* 18–19

biological anthropology, *15,* 16–18, *17*
    cultural anthropology, 20
    linguistic anthropology, 19–20
  globalization and, 21–24
  health and illness and, 442–44
  historical background of, 9–10
  overview of, 9
anti-apartheid movement, 135

anti-colonialism, 181, 292–93, *293*

anti-gay violence, 243

Antioch College, 220

Anti-Privatisation Forum (APF), 380

anti-racist liberation movements, 135

apartheid, 38, 135, 380, 449–50

APF (Anti-Privatisation Forum), 380

Appadurai, Arjun, 304, 477

applied anthropology, 10

Archaea, 338–39, *339*

archaeology, *18,* 18–19 The investigation of the
human past by means of excavating and analyzing artifacts.

Archer Daniels Midland (ADM), 282

arctic drilling, *370*

Argentina
    gender-neutral terms in, 115
    same-sex marriage in, 264

Argonauts of the Western Pacific (Malinowski), 46,
        72–73

Aristotle, 359

Arizona, immigration and language in, *97,*
    97–98

arms sales, global, 378

arranged marriage, 261 Marriage orchestrated
by the families of the involved parties.

art All ideas, forms, techniques, and strategies
that humans employ to express
themselves creatively and to
communicate their creativity and
inspiration to others.
    aesthetics in, 461–63
    anthropology of, 459–64

authenticity of, 467–68
community versus individualism in, 462
defined, 459
ethnography of, 467–70
fine, 460–61, *461*
in human history, 464–66
media's intersection with, 476–81
  ethnographic film and Indigenous media,
    479–81
  visual images and cultural identity, 477–79
Middle Eastern, 474–76, *475*
miniature city model, *457*, 457–59, *458*
popular, 460–61, *461*
post-9/11, 474
power and, 461, 470–76, *475*
  art exhibitions and, 474–76
  gender identity and, 471–73, *472*
  resistance and, 473–74, *474*
"primitive," 463–64
style of presentation, 462
West African, *467*, 467–68, *468*, *470*
Western cultures and, 46–464
women and, *472*, 472–73, 474
artificial insemination, 268–70, *269*
Asad, Talal, 410
Asch, Tim, 479
Asia; *See also specific countries*
  anti-colonial struggles in, 293
  trade routes through, 289, *289*
Asian Americans, 147–48, 152

assimilation, 43, 176–78 The process through
which minorities accept the patterns and norms
of the dominant culture and cease to exist as separate groups.

assisted reproductive technologies
  in China, 249, 250
  impact of, on family, 271–72
  for Jews in Israel, *269*
  in for Jews in Israel, 269–70
asylum seekers, with SOGIESC claims,
    201–3
athleticism, *See* sports and athleticism
Augusta, Georgia, 352

Australia
  ecotourism in, *345*
  life expectancy in, *447*
  same-sex marriage in, 264
  structural functionalist studies of, 47
Austria, same-sex marriage in, 265

authenticity, 467–68 The perception of an
object's antiquity, uniqueness, and originality
within a local culture.

authorizing process, 410 The complex historical and social developments through which symbols are given power and meaning.

The Ax Fight (Asch), 479
Aymara people, 106
ayurvedic medicines, *428*
Azande, South Sudan, magic in, 405–7, *406*

Bahuchara Mata, 199
Bakken Oil Fields, 347
balanced reciprocity, 287–88
Bali, cockfights in, 47–48, *48*, *49*
Banaba Island, *333*, 333–34

band, 362–63 A small kinship-based group of
foragers who hunt and gather for a living over a
particular territory.

Bangalore, India, *393*
Bangladesh
  child labor in, *42*
  coast of, 27
  Rohingya refugees in, *160*, 161–63, *162*, 166
Bankoe, Ghana, *274*
Barbados, *212*
  languages in, 109
  women in labor force, 212–13, *213*
Barber, William, *389*, 390–91
Barrios, Steven, *200*
Barry Callebaut (company), 282
barter, 287
Barth, Fredrik, 165
Bateson, Gregory, 476–77

The Battle of Algiers (film), 293

Beggs, Mack, 188

Being Muslim the Bosnian Way (Bringa), 172

Belgium

in ethnic conflict in Rwanda, 170

same-sex marriage in, 264

Bemba people, 10, *398*

Benedict, Ruth, 46, *46*

Bernal, Victoria, 179, 180

Bestor, Theodore, 304–5

Beyond the Big Ditch (Carse), 334–35

Beyond the Melting Pot (Glazer and Moynihan), 177

bifurcate collateral kinship systems, 254

bifurcate merging kinship systems, 254

bin Laden, Osama, 414

biological anthropology, *15*, 16–18, *17* The study of humans from a biological perspective, particularly how they have evolved over time and adapted to their environments. *See also* biology and genetics; evolution.

biology and genetics

consanguineous unions, 264

culture versus, 52–53

culture and behavior, 55

human evolution and life span development, 54

nature versus nurture, 53–54

epigenetics, 54

fairy tale of the egg and sperm, 205–6

generational kinship systems, 255–57

integrated gene pool, 132–33

intersection of sexuality and, 223–26

language and, 100

race, biological assumptions about, 131–34

integrated gene pool, 132–33

linking phenotype to genotype, 133–34

overview, 131–32

sexual dimorphism, 190–91

biomedicine, 430–31 A practice, often associated with Western medicine, that seeks to apply the principles of biology and the natural sciences to the practice of diagnosing disease and promoting healing.

biomedical conceptions of body, 437–38

defined, 430

biopower, 198

Birth in Eight Cultures (Cheyney and Davis-Floyd), 439

Bitcoin, 301, 302

BlackLight Project, 473–74, *474*

#BlackLivesMatter movement, 128

and COVID-19 pandemic response, 451

and #OurLivesMatter, 314

in Palestine, *126*

as social movement, 381–83

Blacks

Black gay women, 236–37

in #BlackLivesMatter movement, 128, 381–83

COVID-19 response for, 451

fieldwork on folk culture of, 75–77

gender identity and games played by girls, 471–73, *472*

Hurricane Katrina's impact on, 340

intersectionality for, 154–55

kinship networks of, *267*, 267–68

language habits of, 109–10, *110*, *111*

marginalization of Black students, 313–14

performance as resistance for, 473–74

protests of police violence targeting, *37*

racism against, in medical profession, 446–48

resilience amid injury for, 156–57

blockchain, 301

Blombos Cave, South Africa, art in, *464*, 464–65, *465*

Bloomberg, Michael, 351

blue-collar workers, 307

Boas, Franz, 10, 45–46, 72, *72*, 75, 76, 79, 84, 104

"Body Ritual among the Nacirema" (Miner), 11–12

Boehm, Christopher, 363

Bohannan, Laura, 105

Bolivia

language usage in, 106

street vendors in, *315*, 315–16

Bolsonaro, Jair, *32*, 33

Bonilla, Yarimar, 91, 382

Bonilla-Silva, Eduardo, 153

bonobos

aggressiveness in, 372, *372*

sexuality in, 224, *224*

Bosnia, ethnic conflict in, *172*, 172–73, *173*

Civil Rights Act (1964), 188
civil rights movement, 135, 390–91

civil society organization, 370–71 A local
nongovernmental organization that challenges
state policies and uneven development, and advocates for resources and opportunities for members
of its local communities.

clan, 253–54 A type of descent group based on
a claim to a founding ancestor but lacking genealogical documentation.

class A system of power based on wealth,
income, and status that creates an unequal distribution of a society's resources.
    in Brazil, 136–38
    COVID-19 response and, 450–51
    defined, 305
    distribution of health and illness and, 445–48
    and global economy, 305–17, *316*
        economic statistics, 310–12
        globalization and inequality, 314–15
        inequality in United States, 309–10
        roots of poverty, 312–14
        street vendors, 315–17
    race and, 313–14
    sustainable cities and, 351–52
    theories of, 305–9

clay figurines, West African, 469–70, *470*

climate change Changes to Earth's climate,
including global warming produced primarily by
increasing concentrations of greenhouse gases
created by the burning of fossil fuels.
    defined, 27
    in Maldives, *328,* 329–30
    student strikes in Sweden on, 330, *331*

clines, 132
Clinton, Bill, 222
CMWMA (Crater Mountain Wildlife
    Management Area), 343–44
Cochabamba, Bolivia, *315,* 315–17

cockfighting, 47–48, *49*
cocoa, as example in global economy, *280,*
    282–83

code switching, 108 Switching back and
forth between one linguistic variant and another
depending on the cultural context.

Coe, Cati, 273–75
Cohen, Yehudi, 284, 285
college students
    credit cards and debt, 58
    culture, 37
    sexual assault against, 219–20, 237–38
    sleep for, 53
Collins, Jane, 478–79
Colombia, same-sex marriage in, 264

colonialism, 290 The practice by which a
nation-state extends political, economic, and
military power beyond its own borders over an
extended period of time to secure access to raw
materials, cheap labor, and markets in other
countries or regions.
    anthropology and, 9–10, 71, 77, *88,* 88–89
    defined, 135, 290
    in ethnic conflict in Rwanda, 169–70
    language and, 109
    race and, 135–38
        in Brazil, 136–38
        overview, 135–36
    settler, 348

Colonial Migrants at the Heart of Empire (García-
    Colón), 174–76
color blindness, 153–54
Colt Defense factory, *376*
Columbine High School shooting, 424
Columbus, Christopher, 290
CO-MADRES, 209–11, *211*
Coming of Age in Samoa (Mead), 46, 74–75
commitment ceremonies, lesbian and gay, 234–35

commodity, 303 A good that can be bought,
sold, or exchanged in a market.

cultural appropriation, 43–44 The unwanted taking of cultural practices or knowledge from one group by another, more dominant group.

cultural capital, 308–09 The knowledge, habits, and tastes learned from parents and family that individuals can use to gain access to scarce and valuable resources in society.

cultural construction of gender, 192–95 The ways humans learn to behave as a man or woman and to recognize behaviors as masculine or feminine within their cultural context.

cultural materialism, 401 A theory that argues that material conditions, including technology, determine patterns of social organization, including religious principles.

cultural relativism, 72, 84 Understanding a group's beliefs and practices within their own cultural context, without making judgments.

Cultural Revolution, 259

culture, 33–61 A system of knowledge, beliefs, patterns of behavior, artifacts, and institutions that are created, learned, shared, and contested by a group of people.
    biology versus, 52–53
        culture and behavior, 55
        human evolution and life span development, 54
        nature versus nurture, 53–54
    common core of, 38–43
        mental maps of reality, 41–43
        norms, 38–39
        symbols, 40–41
        values, 39–40
    contested, 37–38
    creation of, 55–58
    defined, 36
    development of concept, 44
        evolutionary frameworks, 44–45
        historical particularism, 45–46

        interpretivist approach, 47–48
        structural functionalism, 46–47
    gender and, 192–95
    globalization and, 25, 58
        cosmopolitanism, 60–61
        homogenization versus diversification, 58–59
        migration, 60
    influences on ideas of health and illness, 426–37
        body concepts, 437–41
        ethnomedicine, 428–30
    overview of, 35–36
    power and, 48–49
        cultural institutions, 49–50
        hegemony, 51
        human agency, 51–52
    process of learning, *36*, 36–37
    sexuality and, 114, 225–26
    shared, 37–38

"culture of poverty," 312
culture shock, 69
Custer Died for Your Sins (Deloria), *165*

Dai Minority Park, Yunnan Province, China, *174*
Dakota Access Pipeline (DAP), *347*, 347–49
Daniel Defense, 424
dargah (Muslim saint shrine), *395*, 395–96
Darkness in El Dorado (Tierney), 89
Darwin, Charles, 44–45
Davidov, Veronica, 344–46
Davis-Floyd, Robbie, 438–39, 440
Death without Weeping (Scheper-Hughes), 65
Declaration on the Rights of Peasants and Other People Working in Rural Areas, 347
"Deep Play" (Geertz), 47–48
deep sea volcanic vents, microbes in, 338–39, *339*
Deloria, Vine, Jr., *165*
Democratic Republic of Congo
    migration to, *323*, 323–24, *324*
    refugees from, 22
Denmark, *239*
    same-sex marriage in, 264
    sexuality of people with disabilities in, 239–41

dependency theory, 294–95 A critique of modernization theory arguing that despite the end of colonialism, the underlying economic relations of the modern world economic system had not changed.

descent group, 252–60, *253* A kinship group in which primary relationships are traced through certain consanguineous ("blood") relatives.
    ambilineal, 254, 258
    defined, 252
    matrilineal, 254
    for Nuer people, 254, *255*
    patrilineal, 254, 258–60
    reconstructing, in Fuzhou, China, 258–60
    systems of kinship classification, 254–58, *256–57*
    unilineal, 254

descriptive linguistics, 102 The study of the sounds, symbols, and gestures of a language, and their combination into forms that communicate meaning.

descriptive linguists, 19–20 Those who analyze languages and their component parts.

development, 294 Post-World War II strategy of wealthy nations to spur global economic growth, alleviate poverty, and raise living standards through strategic investment in national economies of former colonies.
Dhillon, Jaskiran, 348

dialect, 107–8 A nonstandard variation of a language.

Diamond, Jared, 223–24

diaspora, 180 A group of people living outside their ancestral homeland yet maintaining emotional and material ties to home.

Dick, Ramona, *120*
difference model, 113
A Different Kind of War Story (Nordstrom), 375–76

diffusion, 43
digital ethnography, 91
Dinka people, 258
disability, 441
disability rights, sexuality and, 239–41
Discipline and Punish (Foucault), 51
discrimination, 151, *187*, 187–88

disease, 317, 427 A discrete natural entity that can be clinically identified and treated by a health professional.

distancing mandates, for COVID-19, 448–53
distribution and exchange, 287–88
diversification, 58–59
diversity, human, 17–18
dividend, 311
division of labor, 191–92, 203–4, 206–8, *207*, 296
DNA, biological anthropology and, 16
dogs, communication and, 99, *100*
dolphins
    communication between, 99
    sexuality in, 224, *224*
dominance model, 112–14
"do no harm" mandate, 88–89
dopamine, 225
"Down, Down Baby" (song), 472
Down Syndrome, sexuality of individuals with, *240*

dowry, 265 The gift of goods or money from the bride's family to the groom's family as part of the marriage process.

Dramas of Nationhood (Abu-Lughod), 60–61
Dude, You're a Fag (Pascoe), 195
Durkheim, Émile, 396–98, *397*, 415

Ebonics, 110, *111*
ecological overshoot, 349–50
economic base, 307
economic liberalism, 299
economics; *See also* global economy
    consumerism, 56–58
    economic independence and martial
        dissolution, 262

Kula ring system, 72
money as symbol, *40*, 41
role of women in, 77–78, 204–5, *205*

economy A cultural adaptation to the environment that enables a group of humans to use the available land, resources, and labor to satisfy their needs and to thrive. *See also* global economy.
defined, 284
informal, *315*, 315–16

ecotourism, 344–46, *345* Tours of remote natural environments designed to support local communities and their conservation efforts.

Ecotourism and Cultural Production (Davidov), 344–45
Ecuador
ecotourism in, 344–46, *345*
multispecies ethnography in, 338, *338*
same-sex marriage in, 265
Edelman, Marc, 347
education and schools
code switching in, 108–9
debate over Muslim head coverings in, 50
Ebonics in, 110
enculturation in, *36*, 36–37, 195
in France, 179
race and racism and, 151–53
school shootings, *423*, 423–25
sex education class, *226*, 239
Spanish and Inverted Spanglish in, 111–12
Edwards, David B., 414–16
egg, gender stereotypes and, 205–6, *206*
Egypt, *61*
archaeology in, 8
brother-sister marriage in, 263
hieroglyphs, *103*
Islamic Fatwa Councils in, 383–85
LGBTQ rights support in, *202*
life expectancy in, *447*
McDonald's menu adaptations for, 59
protests in, *52*
television in, 60–61, *61*
Elementary Forms of Religious Life (Durkheim), 397

El Salvador
CO-MADRES in, *209*, 209–11, *211*
cryptocurrency in, 301–2
Emancipation Proclamation, 141

emic, 85 An approach to gathering data that investigates how local people think and how they understand the world.

emoticons and emoji, 104, *104*
employment and labor
child labor, *42*
sweatshop factories, *84*
for women, 212–13, *213*

enculturation, 36, 36–37, 193–95, *194* The process of learning culture.

endogamy, 39, 264 Marriage to someone within the kinship group.

energy consumption, by country, *350*
Energy Transfer Partners, 347

engaged anthropology, 79 Applying the research strategies and analytical perspectives of anthropology to address concrete challenges facing local communities and the world at large.

Engels, Friedrich, 307, 400

entrepreneurial immigrants, 322 Persons who move to a new location to conduct trade and establish a business.

environment, 25–27, 329–53
Anthropocene era, 332–36, *333–34*
construction of Panama Canal, *334*, 334–36
mining in Banaba Island, *333*, 333–34
climate change, 27
economic system sustainability, 349–53, *350*, *352*
globalization and, 342–49, *343*, *345*, 347 *343*, *324*
conservation, 343–44

Dakota Access Pipeline, *347, 347*–49
ecotourism, 344–46, *345*
  human rights for peasant farm workers,
    346–47
human shaping of natural world,
    26–27
multispecies ethnography, 336–39,
    337–39
shaped by power, 339–42, *340, 341*

environmental anthropology, 331–32 The
study of the relations between humans and the
environment.

environmental justice, 351–52

epigenetics, 54 An area of study in the field
of genetics exploring how environmental factors
directly affect the expression of genes in ways that
may be inherited between generations.

epilepsy *(qaug dab peg)*, 434–36
Eritrea, transnational citizenship in, *179*,
    179–80
Essa, Mervat, *448*
ethics, 88, *88*
  anonymity, 90
  "do no harm" mandate, 88–89
  informed consent, 89–90

ethnic boundary marker, 166 A practice or
belief, such as food, clothing, language, shared
name, or religion, used to signify who is in a
group and who is not.

ethnic cleansing, 173 Efforts by representatives of one ethnic or religious group to remove or
destroy another group in a particular geographic
area.

ethnic groups, *See* tribes
ethnic identity, 165–68
  creating, 165–68
  Indian identity in U.S., 167–68
  Rwandan identity cards, *171*

ethnicity, 161–83 A sense of historical,
cultural, and sometimes ancestral connection to a
group of people who are imagined to be distinct
from those outside the group.
  defined, 164
  identity and, 164–68
  relationship to nation, 178–83
    anti-colonialism, 181–83
    imagined communities and invented
      traditions, 178–80
  as source of conflict, 169–73
    in former Yugoslavia, 172–73
    Hutu refugees in Tanzania, 171–72
    in Rwanda, 169–71
  as source of opportunity, 173–76
  in U.S., 176–78

Ethnicity without Groups (Brubaker), 169

ethnocentrism, 11, 69, 71 The belief that one's
own culture or way of life is normal and natural;
using one's own culture to evaluate and judge the
practices and ideals of others.

ethnographic authority, 87

ethnographic fieldwork, 13, 65–93 A primary
research strategy in cultural anthropology typically involving living and interacting with a community of people over an extended period to better understand their lives.
  as art, 69
  defined, 13, 68
  development of
    colonialism, 71
    early accounts of encounters, 70
    engaged anthropology, 79
    professionalization, 71–79
  effects of, on anthropologists, 68–69
  focus on people, 68
  globalization and, 90
    content changes, 91–93
    digital ethnography, 91
    process changes, 90–91
  as informing daily life, 70

moral and ethical concerns, 88
  anonymity, 90
  "do no harm" mandate, 88–89
  informed consent, 89–90
as social science, 69
techniques in, 80
  analysis, 85
  mapping, 82–83
  preparation, 80
  skills and perspectives, 83–85
  strategies, 81–82
ethnographic film, 479–81
ethnographic writing, 86
  ethnographic authority, 87
  moral and ethical concerns, 88–90
  polyvocality, 86–87
  reflexivity, 87
ethnography
  digital, 91
  multi-sited, 27–29, *28*
  multispecies, *316*, 336–39, *337–39*
  salvage, 72, 76
Ethnologue (SIL), 119

ethnology, 20, 85 The analysis and comparison of ethnographic data across cultures.

ethnomedicine, 428–30 Local systems of health and healing rooted in culturally specific norms and values.

ethnomusicology, 471 The study of music in cultural context.

ethnopharmacology, 428 The documentation and description of the local use of natural substances in healing remedies and practices.

etic, 85 Description of local behavior and beliefs from the anthropologist's perspective in ways that can be compared across cultures.

Eurocentrism, 71
Europe
  Industrial Revolution in, 292

Paleolithic cave paintings in, *465,* 465–66, *466*
trade routes through, 289, *289*
trade with Africa and Americas, 290–92
Europe and the People Without History (Wolf), 77
Evans-Pritchard, E. E., 46, 73–74, *74,* 78, 87, 106, 254, 258, 331, 405–7
Everglades, *337,* 337–38
evolution, 16, 25–26
  development of concept of culture, 44
  human becomings, 54
  influence of culture, 54
  language and, 100–101
  unilineal cultural, 45

exogamy, 39, 254, 264 Marriage to someone outside the kinship group.

facial expressions, *See* gestures and facial expressions
factory assembly line, 296
Fadiman, Anne, 434, 436
Families We Choose (Weston), 271
family, *See* kinship

family of orientation, 270 The family group in which one is born, grows up, and develops life skills.

family of procreation, 270 The family group created when one reproduces and within which one rears children.

Farmer, Paul, 442–44, *443*
Farm Labor Program, 175
farm workers, 346–47
Fatwa Councils, 383–85, *384*
Fausto-Sterling, Anne, 197
favela, model of, 457–59, *458*

femininity, 193, 196 The ideas and practices associated with womanhood.

feminism, 77–78
Ferguson, J., 367–68
"#Ferguson" (Bonilla and Rosa), 382

Ferron, Zoe, 235–36
festival videos, 480–81
fictive kin, 267–68

field notes, 82 The anthropologist's written observations and reflections on places, practices, events, and interviews.

fieldwork, *See* **ethnographic fieldwork**

"Fighting Invasive Infrastructures" (Spice), 348
figurines, clay, West African, 469–70, *470*
Fiji, 333–34
film, ethnographic, 479–81
financial services, 57–58
Fine, G. A., 193–94

fine art, 460–61, *461* Creative expression and communication often associated with cultural elites.

Finland, same-sex marriage in, 264
first cousins, 263
Fisher, Helen, 224–25
The 5 Love Languages (Chapman), 112
"The Five Sexes" (Fausto-Sterling), 197
flags, 40–41
Flaherty, Robert, 479

flexible accumulation, 23, 297–98 The increasingly flexible strategies that corporations use to accumulate profits in an era of globalization, enabled by innovative communication and transportation technologies.

Florida, *149*
   Everglades, *337,* 337–38
   intersections of race and class in, 149
Florida Fish and Wildlife Conversation Commission, 337
Floyd, Charlene, 412
Floyd, George, *126,* 127–28, 131, 381, 451
folk religions, world distribution of, *394*
food and nutrition
   agriculture, 285–86

culture and, 53
foraging for, 284–85, *285, 361*
horticulture, 285
hunter-gatherer stereotypes, 206–8
McDonald's menu adaptations, 59, *59*
pastoralism, 285

food foragers, 284–85 Humans who subsist by hunting, fishing, and gathering plants to eat.

food insecurity, 6–7, 346
football, American, kneeling to protest police violence, *37*
foraging, 284–85, *285, 361*
Ford, Henry, 296

Fordism, 296–97 The dominant model of industrial production for much of the twentieth century, based on a social compact between labor, corporations, and government.

Ford Motor Company, 296–97
Fort Laramie, Treaty of, 347
Foucault, Michel, 51, 198, 235

four-field approach, 15–20, 72 The use of four interrelated disciplines to study humanity: physical anthropology, archaeology, linguistic anthropology, and cultural anthropology.
   archaeology, *18,* 18–19
   biological anthropology, *15,* 16–18, *17*
   cultural anthropology, 20
   defined, 15
   linguistic anthropology, 19–20

Fourteenth Amendment, U.S. Constitution, 140
FOXP2 gene, 100

framing process, 381–83 The creation of shared meanings and definitions that motivate and justify collective action by social movements.

France, *179*
   arms sales by, 378
   in Côte d'Ivoire conflict, 282–83

gender ideology, 205–8 A set of cultural ideas, usually stereotypical, about the essential character of different genders that functions to promote and justify gender stratification.

    challenging, 208–11

    defined, 205

    fairy tale of the egg and the sperm, 205–6, *206*

    hunter-gatherer stereotype, 206–8, *207*

gender-neutral terms, 114–15

gender performance, 195–97 The way gender identity is expressed through action.

gender stereotypes, 205–8, *206, 207* Widely held preconceived notions about the attributes of, differences between, and proper roles for men and women in a culture.

gender stratification, 205–8 An unequal distribution of power in which gender shapes who has access to a group's resources, opportunities, rights, and privileges.

    challenging, 200–203

    defined, 205

    globalization and, 211–14

gender studies, 189 Research into masculinity and femininity as flexible, complex, and historically and culturally constructed categories.

Genealogies of Religion (Asad), 410

generalized reciprocity, 287

generational kinship systems, 254

genetics, *See* biology and genetics

Gennep, Arnold van, 398

genocide, 169 The deliberate and systematic destruction of an ethnic or religious group.

genotype, 133–34 The inherited genetic factors that provide the framework for an organism's physical form.

geographic information system (GIS) devices and data, 83

Germany

    arms sales by, 378

    health system in, 431

    life expectancy in, *447*

    McDonald's menu adaptations in, 59

    Nuremburg Laws, 38

    same-sex marriage in, 264

gesture–call system, 103

gestures and facial expressions

    kinesics, 103

    winking, 47

Ghana, migration, kin care, and aging in, 273–75, *274*

Giant Metal Eyes (sculpture), *461*

GI Bill of Rights, 144–45

Gibson, Jane, 149

Gimi people, 343–44

Ginsberg, Faye, 477

GIS (geographic information system) devices and data, 83

gladesmen, *337*, 337–38

Glazer, Nathan, 177

GLBTQ Legal Advocates and Defenders, 188

global economy, 281–325; *See also* globalization

    arms sales, 378

    class and inequality, 305–17, *316*

        economic statistics, 310–12

        globalization, 314–15

        poverty, 312–14

        street vendors, 315–17

        theories of class, 305–9

        in United States, 309–10

    distribution and exchange in, 287–88

    food production, 284–87

    linking workers with consumers, 303–5

    migration and, 317–25

        bridges and barriers, 318–21

        patterns of, 321, *321*

        pushes and pulls, 318

        types of immigrants, 322–25

    modern economic system, 294–98

        conflicting theories, 294–95

        core and periphery, 295–96

        flexible accumulation, 297–98

        Fordism, 296–97

        sustainability, 349–53, *350, 352*

global mediascape, 477 Global cultural flows
of media and visual images that enable linkages
and communication across boundaries in ways
unimaginable a century ago.

grammar, 102 The combined set of observations
about the rules governing the formation of morphemes and syntax that guide language use.

Gutmann, Matthew, 196–97
Guyana, 109

habitus, 308 Bourdieu's term to describe the self-perceptions, sensibilities, and tastes developed in response to external influences over a lifetime that shape one's conceptions of the world and where one fits in it.

Haiti
    independence of, 293
    life expectancy in, *447*
    public health care system in, 442–44, *443*
half-siblings, 263
Han (ethnic group), *174*
haptics, 103
Haraway, Donna, 336
Harlem Birth Right Project, 154–55
Harold, Eli, *37*
Harris, Kamala, 143
Harris, Marvin, 401–2
Harris, Neil Patrick, 272
Harry Potter series (Rowling), *405*
Harvey, David, 297
hashtag activism, 91
Hawaii
    brother-sister marriage in, 263
    kinship classification in, 255, *256*
healing
    multiple systems of, 434–37
    remedies, 428–30, *429*

health The absence of disease and infirmity, as well as the presence of physical, mental, and social well-being.
    anthropologists and, 442–44
    COVID-19 pandemic, 426, 448–53
        digital ethnography in, 91
        disparities in vaccine administration in, 317
        food insecurity/hunger in, *4*, 6, *6*, 7, 24
        mask wearing and, *32*, 33–35
        outsourcing after, 298
        Qatar's response to, 452, *452*
        South Africa's response to, 449–50, *450*
        spread of disease, 5–6, 8, 34

United States response to, 450–51, *451*
        values in, 40
    cultural influences on body concepts,
        437–41
        biomedical conceptions of body, 437–38
        childbirth, 438–41
        disability, 441
        human microbiome, 438
    cultural influences on ideas of, 426–37
        biomedicine, 430–31
        Chinese medicine, 432–34
        ethnomedicine, 428–30
    defined, 426
    distribution of, 444–48
        critical medical anthropology and, 445
        health transition, 444–45
        race, class, and gender, 445–48
    multiple systems of healing, 434–37

health-care professionals, migration to U.S., 322

health transition, 444–45 The significant improvements in human health made over the course of the twentieth century that were not, however, distributed evenly across the world's population.

Hegazi, Sarah, *202*
Hegel, Georg W. F., 462

hegemony, 51, 368–69 The ability of a dominant group to create consent and agreement within a population without the use or threat of force.

Helmreich, Stefan, 338–39
Henshilwood, Christopher, 464
Herodotus, 70

heterosexuality, 231–32 Attraction to and sexual relations between individuals of the opposite sex.

Hidalgo y Costilla, Miguel, 412
Hierarchy in the Forest (Boehm), 363

High Tech and High Heels in the Global Economy
(Freeman), 212–13

hijras, 199

Hillcrest neighborhood, San Diego, Mexican gay men in, *242, 243–44*

Hinduism

alternative gender constructions in, 199, *199*

cow as symbol in, 410

world distribution of, *394*

hip-hop music, 471–72

Hirsch, Jennifer, 237–39

Hispanics, *See* Latinx people

historical linguistics, 101 The study of the development of language over time, including its changes and variations.

historical particularism, 45–46 The idea, attributed to Franz Boas, that cultures develop in specific ways because of their unique histories.

historic archaeology, 19 The exploration of the more recent past through an examination of physical remains and artifacts as well as written or oral records.

historic linguists, 20 Those who study how language changes over time within a culture and how languages travel across cultures.

Hite, Shere, 231

HIV/AIDS, 203, 317

Hmong refugees, U.S. health-care and, *434, 434–36*

Hobsbawm, Eric, 179

Hogan, Nick, *240*

holidays, 56, *57, 84*

holism, 16 The anthropological commitment to look at the whole picture of human life-culture, biology, history, and language-across space and time.

Holocene period, 332

Homefront (Lutz), 373–74

homelessness, 70

homogenization, 58–59

Homo sapiens, 16

homosexuality, 231 Attraction to and sexual relations between individuals of the same sex.; *See also* gays and lesbians

Hong Kong

COVID-19 pandemic in, 34

life expectancy in, 445, *447*

Hopi people, 105

hormones, sex, 224–25

horticulture, 285 The cultivation of plants for subsistence through nonintensive use of land and labor.

How Forests Think (Kohn), 338, 344

How the Jews Became White Folks (Brodkin), 144

Huckman, Sarah Rose, *186,* 187–88

Huichol people, 78

human becomings, 54

human microbiome, 54, 438 The complete collection of microorganisms in the human body's ecosystem.

human rights, for peasant farm workers, 346–47

Human Terrain Systems program, *88,* 89

humor, as coping strategy, 137–38

hunger, 6–7, 317

hunter-gather bands, 362–63

Hurricane Katrina, 340

Hurston, Zora Neale, 75–77, *76,* 331

Husain Tekri shrine, *395,* 395–96

Hussein, Saddam, 181, 182

Hutus, 169–72

hypodescent, 136, 142–43 Sometimes called the "one drop of blood rule"; the assignment of children of racially "mixed" unions to the subordinate group.

Iceland
  historic archaeology in, 19
  life expectancy in, *447*
  same-sex marriage in, 264

identity entrepreneurs, 169 Political, military, or religious leaders who promote a worldview through the lens of ethnicity and use war, propaganda, and state power to mobilize people against those whom they perceive as a danger.

ideological superstructure, of society, 307
Idrisi, Muhammad al-, *289*

illness, 427 The individual patient's experience of being unwell.; *See also* health

illness narratives, 436 The personal stories that people tell to explain their illnesses.
images, cultural identity and, 477–79

Imagined Communities (Anderson), 268

imagined community, 178–80 The invented sense of connection and shared traditions that underlies identification with a particular ethnic group or nation whose members likely will never all meet.

IMF (International Monetary Fund), 299–300
immigration and immigrants, *See* migration
Immigration and Refugee Board (IRB), 201–3
Inca people, 263
incense, chunks of *(loban), 395,* 396

incest taboo, 262–63 Cultural rules that forbid sexual relations with certain close relatives.

income, 311, *311, 316* What people earn from work, plus dividends and interest on investments, along with rents and royalties.

income tax, 297

increasing migration, 23–24 The accelerated movement of people within and between countries.

indentured workers, 139
India, *167*
  Buddhist healing practices in, 428–30, *429*
  cousin marriage in, 263
  COVID-19 pandemic in, 34
  cryptocurrency investments in, 302
  dowries in, 265
  healing practices in, 395–96
  hijras in, 199
  Indian identity in U.S., 167–68
  life expectancy in, *447*
  outsourcing to, 23
  polyandry in, 262
  sex of unborn children in, identifying, 272
India Day Parade, *167,* 168

Indigenous media, 480 The use of media by people who have experienced massive economic, political and geographic disruption to build alternative strategies for communication, survival, and empowerment.

Indigenous people; *See also* Native Americans
  ecotourism revenue for, 344–46
  identity-building strategies of, 364
  media use by, 479–81
individualism, art and, 462

individual racism, 150–51 Personal prejudiced beliefs and discriminatory actions based on race.

Indonesia, migration of women from, *213,* 213–15

industrial agriculture, 286–87 Intensive farming practices involving mechanization and mass production of foodstuffs

industrial mass production, 296

Industrial Revolution, 292 The eighteenth- and nineteenth-century shift from agriculture and artisanal skill craft to machine-based manufacturing.

inequality
    economic statistics on, 310–12
    globalization, 314–15
    roots of poverty, 312–14
    street vendors, 315–17
    in United States, 309–10
infant mortality, mothers' perception of, *66*,
    66–67
infopolitics, 180
informal economy, *315*, 315–16
informatics, 212–13

informed consent, 89–90 A key strategy for
protecting those being studied by ensuring that
they are fully informed of the goals of the project and have clearly indicated their consent to
participate.

infrastructure projects, France, 179
Ingraham, Chrys, 232–34
In Sorcery's Shadow (Stoller), 407–8

institutional racism, 151–53 Patterns by which
racial inequality is structured through key cultural
institutions, policies, and systems.

InterACT: Advocates for Intersex Youth, 198
interbreeding, 132
InterConnect, 198
interest, 311
internally displaced persons, 323
International Monetary Fund (IMF), 299–300
International Phonetic Alphabet, 102
International Youth Climate Strike, *352*
Internet
    digital ethnography, 91
    in least-developed countries, 23
    time-space compression and, 22–23

interpretivist approach, 47–48 A conceptual
framework that sees culture primarily as a symbolic system of deep meaning.

interracial marriage
    in Brazil, 136
    in United States, 38–39, 51, 140, 264–65, *265*

intersectionality An analytic framework for
assessing how factors such as race, gender, and
class interact to shape individual life chances and
societal patterns of stratification.
    of class and race, 148–49
    defined, 131
    of race and sexuality for Black gay women, 236–37
    for San Francisco students, 313–14

intersex, 198 The state of being born with a
combination of male and female genitalia, gonads,
and/or chromosomes.

Intersex Society of North America, 198
interviews, 81
Inuit people, *72*
Inverted Spanglish, 111–12
Invisible Families (Moore), 236–37
iPhone, 23, *296*
Iraq, 50, *181*, 181–83
IRB (Immigration and Refugee Board), 201–3
Ireland
    migration to U.S. from, 143–45
    same-sex marriage in, 264
Iroquois people, kinship classification, 255, *257*
Iskander, Natasha, 452
Islam, *See* Muslims and Islam
Israel, *269*
    artificial insemination and kinship in, 268–70,
    269
    McDonald's menu adaptations in, 59
Italian language, 101, 107–8
Italy, life expectancy in, *447*

Jamaica, 109
Japan
    childbirth in, 440
    life expectancy in, *447*
    McDonald's menu adaptations in, 59
    race in, 42
    sexuality in, 229–30
Jesus Christ, 403, 410
Jews and Judaism
    artificial insemination and kinship, 268–70
    fieldwork at senior center, *78*, 78–79
    migration of, 144

Torah scroll as symbol, 409, *411*
world distribution of, *394*
Jiaen fertility hospital, *248*

Jim Crow, 141, 310, 312 Laws implemented after the U.S. Civil War to legally enforce segregation, particularly in the South, after the end of slavery.

John, Elton, 272
Johnson, Lyndon B., 390
Johnson, Virginia, 231, *232*
Jolaosho, Omotayo, 380–81
Jordan, Brigitte, 440
Judaism, *See* Jews and Judaism
Julian calendar, 42
Juris, Jeffrey, 382

Kaepernick, Colin, *37*
Kahn, Susan, 268–69
Kant, Immanuel, 462
Katz, Jonathan, 231
kayakctivists, *370*
Kentucky, *309*, 309–10
Kenya, *302*
mobile-based payment systems in, 302–3
same-sex marriage in, 264
Kepone, 341–42

key informant, 81 A community member who advises the anthropologist on community issues, provides feedback, and warns against cultural miscues. Also called *cultural consultant.*

Keynes, John M., 299
Keynesian economics, 299
Khan, Shamus, 237–39
Kichwa people, 344–46
kin care, in Ghana, 273–75, *274*
kindred exogamy, 264

kinesics, 103 The study of the relationship between body movements and communication.

kinetic orality, 471 A musical genre combining body movement and voice.

King, Martin Luther, Jr., 390, 391
Kinsey, Alfred C., 231

kinship, 249–75 The system of meaning and power that cultures create to determine who is related to whom and to define their mutual expectations, rights, and responsibilities.
classification system, *256, 257*
defined, 250
ethnicity as version of, 164
globalization and, 270–75
assisted reproductive technologies, 271–72
chosen families, 271, *272*
families of same-sex partners, 272–73
in Ghana, 273–75
nuclear family, 270–71
global perspective, 266–68
Black networks in Chicago, 267–68
Langkawi of Malaysia, 266–67, *267*
interracial marriage and, 38–39, 51
nation-states and, 268–70
overview, 251–52
as poverty survival strategy, 267–68
relationship organization, 252–65
descent group, *253, 255*
descent groups, 252–60
marriage and affinal ties, 260–65

kinship analysis, 81 A fieldwork strategy of examining interlocking relationships of power built on marriage and family ties.

kissing, 222
Kleinman, Arthur, 436
Kohn, Eduardo, 338, 344
Krafft-Ebing, Richard von, 231
Kromidas, Maria, 145–47
Ku Klux Klan, 141
Kula ring, 72
Kulick, Don, 114, 239–41
!Kung San people, *285*
Kurds, 181–83

Kusimba, Sibel, 302, 303
Kwakiutl people, 45, 72

labor, *See* employment and labor

labor immigrants, 322 Persons who move in search of a low-skill and low-wage job, often filling an economic niche that native-born workers will not fill.

Labov, W., 109
Ladakh, India, Buddhist healing practices in, 428–30, *429*
Lafontant, Fritz, 442, 443
laissez-faire capitalism, 299
Lakoff, Robin, 106
Lakota people, 120–21
Lan, Pei-chia, 213–15
Lancaster, Roger, 227, 229
Landers, M. A., 193–94
Langkawi people, kinship for, *266, 266–67, 267*

language continuum, 101 The idea that variation in languages appears gradually over distance so that groups of people who live near one another speak in a way that is mutually intelligible.

language ideology, 107–9 Beliefs and conceptions about language that often serve to rationalize and justify patterns of stratification and inequality.
    defined, 109
    and Latinx identity, 111–12

language loss, 118–19 The extinction of languages that have very few speakers.

language(s), 97–121 A system of communication organized by rules that uses symbols such as words, sounds, and gestures to convey information.
    adaptability of, 101–2
    defined, 99
    descriptive linguistics, 102

gender enculturation, 195
globalization and, 116
    diminishing diversity, 116, *117, 118*
    language loss, 118–19, *120*
    preserving endangered languages,
        120, 120–21
    revitalizing languages, 119–21
linguistic anthropology, 19–20
nonverbal communication, 103–4
number of by country, *117*
origins of, 100–101
power systems and, 106–7
    dialects and ideologies, 107–9
    gender, 112–15, *115*
    race, 109–12, *110*
prestige, 107, 108
thinking and, 104
    adaptability, 105–6
    culture, 104–5
top twenty, *118*

Laos
    Hmong refugees, *434*
    life expectancy in, *447*
Lascaux Cave, France, paintings in, *466*
Latin language, 101
Latinx people, 139
    gender-neutral designation, 115
    language ideologies and identity for,
        111–12
    racism targeting, 152
Latour, Bruno, 336
Lattimore, Owen, 331
Laughter Out of Place (Goldstein), 137–38
lay teachers *(catequistas)*, 413–14
League of Nations, 182
Lee, Lia, 434–36, *436*
lesbians, *See* gays and lesbians
Lessinger, Johanna, 167
Levine, Susan, 450
Lewin, Ellen, 234–35
Lewinsky, Monica, 222

lexicon, 106 All the words for names, ideas, and events that make up a language's dictionary.

LGBTQ rights, 201–3
Liberia, 374

life chances, 307 An individual's opportunities to improve quality of life and realize life goals.

life expectancy, 317, 445, *447*

life history, 81 A form of interview that traces the biography of a person over time, examining changes in the person's life and illuminating the interlocking network of relationships in the community.

Life Is Hard (Lancaster), 229
life span, 43, 317

liminality, 399 One stage in a rite of passage during which a ritual participant experiences a period of outsiderhood, set apart from normal society, that is key to achieving a new perspective on the past, future, and current community.

Lincoln, Abraham, 141

lineage, 253 A type of descent group that traces genealogical connection through generations by linking persons to a founding ancestor.

lineal kinship systems, 254

linguistic anthropology, 19–20 The study of human language in the past and the present.

linguistic relativity, 104 The notion that all languages will develop the distinctive categories necessary for those who speak them to deal with the realities around them.

linguistics, 19–20; *See also* language
Linnaeus, Carolus, 41
listening skills, 84
literature review, 80
"Little Hill" (Morrinho), Rio de Janeiro, Brazil, *457, 457–59, 458*
LiveAndTell, 120–21

loban (chunks of incense), *395,* 396
Lock, Margaret, 37
Loneliness and Its Opposite (Kulick and Rydstrom), 239–41
long-distance trade routes, 289–90
Looking Like a Language, Sounding Like a Race (Rosa), 111–12
Lord of the Rings trilogy (Tolkien), 405
Louisiana, 340
Loving, Mildred, 39, *265*
Loving, Richard, 39, *265*
Loving v. Virginia, 39, *265*
Lutz, Catherine, 373–74, 478–79
Luxembourg, same-sex marriage in, 264

Macao, life expectancy in, *447*
machismo, 196, 196–97, 229

magic, 405–8, 417–19 The use of spells, incantations, words, and actions in an attempt to compel supernatural forces to act in certain ways, whether for good or for evil.

Maginhawa community pantry, *4,* 6–7
malaria, 317
Malaysia, *266,* 266–67, *267*
    kinship in, *266,* 266–67, *267*
    McDonald's menu adaptations in, 59
    protests in, *52*
Maldives, *328,* 329–30
Malendoski, Savanna E., *192*
Mali
    migration from, *323,* 323–24, *324*
    Mopti port of, *8*
    trade routes in, *14*
Malinowski, Bronisław, 45, 46, 72–73, *73,* 77, 78, 80, 204–5, 221, 263, 331
Malkki, Liisa, 171
Malta, same-sex marriage in, 264
Maman (Bourgeois), *461*
Managua, Nicaragua, sexuality in, 229
Manderson, Lenore, 450
mangrove forests, *337,* 337–38
Manila, Philippines, 6–7, *8, 59*
Mapa, Alec, 272

mapping, 82–83 The analysis of the physical and/or geographic space where fieldwork is being conducted.

March for Our Lives, 425
Mardi Gras, *84*
Marjory Stoneman Douglas High School shooting, 424–25
market exchange, 287
Marks, Jonathan, 134

marriage, 260–66 A socially recognized relationship that may involve physical and emotional intimacy as well as legal rights to property and inheritance.
    arranged, 261
    companionate, 261–62
    defined, 261
    endogamy, 264
    exchange of gifts with, 265
    exogamy, 264
    incest taboos, 263–64
    interracial, 38–39, 51, 136, 140, 264–65, *265*
    monogamy, 262–63
    norms regarding, 38–39
    polyandry, 262–63
    polygyny, 262–63
    same-sex, 263–65, 272–73

Marseille, France, 7
Marshall, John, 479
Martin, Emily, 205–6, 208
Martin, Ricky, 272
Martin, Trayvon, 381
Martinique, *340*, 340–42

martyr, 395 A person who sacrifices his or her life for the sake of his or her religion.

Marx, Karl, 305–7, 396–97, 400–401, *401*, 403
Marxism
    religion and, 401–2
    as theory of class, 305–7

masculinity The ideas and practices associated with manhood.; *See also machismo*
    corporate, in Japan, 229–30
    defined, 193
    performance of gender, 195–97

Maskovsky, Jeff, 312–13
masks
    in COVID-19 pandemic, *32*, 33–35
    West African, 469–70, *470*
Massachusetts, 60, 453
mass production, industrial, 296
Masters, William, 231, *232*
masturbation, 231
material power, 51
mati work, 227–28
matrilineal descent groups, 254
McDonald's, 59, *59*
McIntosh, Peggy, 147–48
MCMC (Merced Community Medical Center), 434–36
Mead, Margaret, 46, 74–75, *75*, 79, 189, 221, 359, 476–77
meaning, in religion, 408–16

means of production, 306 The factories, machines, tools, raw materials, land, and financial capital needed to make things.

measles, 317
Medeiros, Melanie, 262
media, 476–81
    ethnographic film and Indigenous media, 479–81
    media worlds, 477
    visual images and cultural identity, 477–79

media worlds, 477 An ethnographic and theoretical approach to media studies that focuses on the tensions that may exist when visual worlds collide in the context of contemporary globalization.

Medicaid patients, 446
medical anthropology, 423–53

medical pluralism, 434 The intersection of multiple cultural approaches to healing.

Medicine, Beatrice, 79

melting pot, 177 A metaphor used to describe the process of immigrant assimilation into U.S. dominant culture.

Men Are from Mars, Women Are from Venus (Gray), 112

mental maps of reality, 41–43 Cultural classifications of what kinds of people and things exist, and the assignment of meaning to those classifications.

Merced Community Medical Center (MCMC), 434–36
meritocracy, 153–54
Mesopotamia, 182
#MeToo movement, 220
Metropolitan Community Church, 243
Mexican New York (Smith), 60
Mexico, 60, *197*
   archaeology in, 18
   life expectancy in, *447*
   machismo in, *196*, 196–97
   McDonald's menu adaptations in, 59
   migration of gay men from, 242–44
   religion and revolution in, 412–14
Mexico City, Mexico, *197*
Michaels, Jillian, 272

microaggressions, 151 Common, everyday verbal or behavioral indignities and slights that communicate hostile, derogatory, and negative messages about someone's race, gender, sexual orientation, or religion.

microbes, 338–39, *339*, 438
middle class, 307
Middle East
   art exhibits and events originating from, *448*, 474–76
   immigrants from, 145–47
   trade routes through, 289, *289*
Midway Atoll, *26*

Migrants and Strangers in an African City (Whitehouse), 323
migration, 317–25
   anti-immigrant cartoon, *142*
   bridges and barriers, 318–21
   COVID-19 responses and, 452, *453*
   effects of culture on, 45–46, 60
   in Ghana, 273–75
   increasing, 23–24
   kinship connections and, 259–60, 273–75
   language and, *97*, 97–98, 108
   of Mexican gay men, 242–44
   multi-sited ethnography on, 27–29, *28*
   patterns of, 321, *321*
   of Puerto Rican farmworkers, 174–76
   pushes and pulls, 318
   race and, 143–48
      Chinese, 143–45
      Irish, 143–45
      Middle Easterners, 145–47
      overview, 143
   religion and, 416–19
   types of immigrants, 322–25
   by women, 213–15

militarization, 373–74 The contested social process through which a civil society organizes for the production of military violence.

military
   anthropology and, *88*, 89
   women in, 192, *192*
Miner, Horace, 11–12
Minerva Initiative, 89
miniature city model, *457*, 457–59, *458*
mining
   on Banaba Island, *333*, 333–34
   in Kentucky, *309*, 310
Minneapolis Police Department, 127–28
Mintz, Sydney, 77

miscegenation, 136 A demeaning historical term for interracial marriage.

mobile phone-based payment systems, 302–3

modernization theories, 294 Post-World War II economic theories that predicted that with the end of colonialism, less-developed countries would follow the same trajectory toward modernization as the industrialized countries.

modern world economic system, 294–98
   conflicting theories, 294–95
   core and periphery, 295–96
   flexible accumulation, 297–98
   Fordism, 296–97
   sustainability, 349–53, *350, 352*
money, *See* economics; global economy

monogamy, 262–63 A relationship between only two partners.

Moore, Mignon, 236–37
Mopti, Mali, *8*
Moral Mondays campaign, 390
Morgan, Louis Henry, 44, 45, 71
Morocco, McDonald's menu adaptations
   in, 59

morphemes, 102 The smallest units of sound that carry meaning on their own.

morphology, 102 The study of patterns and rules of how sounds combine to make morphemes.

Morrinho ("Little Hill"), Rio de Janeiro, Brazil,
   457, 457–59, 458
Mountains beyond Mountains (Kidder), 442
Movement for Black Lives, 381–83, *382,* 451
Moynihan, Daniel P., 177, 267–68
Mozambique, war in, 375–76, 378
M–Pesa, 302–3
muftis, 384–85
Muhammad, 394
Mulatto race category, 138
Mules and Men (Hurston), 76
Mullings, Leith, 154–55, 314

multiculturalism, 176–78 A pattern of ethnic relations in which new immigrants and their

children enculturate into the dominant national culture and yet retain an ethnic culture.

multiple systems of healing, 434–37
multi-sited ethnography, 27–29, *28*

multispecies ethnography, 316, 336–39, 337–339 Ethnographic research designed to consider the interactions of all species living on the planet and see the world from a more than human perspective.

Murray, David, 201–3
music
   freedom songs, 380–81
   gender identity and, 471–72, *472*
Muslims and Islam, 395–96
   384, 364
   art exhibits and events of, 474–76
   in Bosnia, 172–73, *173*
   Fatwa Councils, 383–85
   religious law, 383–85, 411
   religious symbols, 50, *50*
   Rohingya refugees, *160,* 161–63, *162,* 166
   sacrifice and martyrdom in, 415
   saint shrines, *395,* 395–96
   world distribution of, *394*

mutual transformation, 69, 84–85 The potential for both the anthropologist and the members of the community being studied to be transformed by the interactions of fieldwork.

Myanmar, Rohingya refugees from, *160,* 161–63,
   162, 166
Myerhoff, Barbara, *78,* 78–79
mythico-histories, 171–72

"Nacirema" people, *11,* 11–12
Nanda, Serena, 199
Nandi people, 264
Nanook of the North (Flaherty), 479
Naples, Italy, *202*
Nash, Niecy, 272
Nasheed, Mohamed, *328,* 329–30

nation, 178 A term once used to describe a group of people who shared a place of origin; now used interchangeably with *nation-state*.

National Football League, *37*, 43–44
National Geographic magazine, photographs in, 478–79

nationalism, 178, 181, 268 The desire of an ethnic community to create and/or maintain a nation-state.

nationality, 178 The identification with a group of people thought to share a place of origin.
National Rifle Association, 424

Nation as Network (Bernal), 179, 180

nation-state, 178, 268–70 A political entity, located within a geographic territory with enforced borders, where the population shares a sense of culture, ancestry, and destiny as a people.

Native Americans, *120*; *See also* Indigenous people
COVID-19 responses and, 451
cultural appropriation targeting, 43–44
displacement of, 348–49
engaged anthropology with, 79
identity-building strategies of, 364
languages of, 108, 120–21
transgender, 200, *200*

nativism, 143 The favoring of certain long-term inhabitants, namely whites, over new immigrants.

natural disasters, 340
natural healing remedies, 428–30
naturheilkunde (natural cure), 431
Nazism, Nuremburg Laws, 38
Neandertals, language and, 101
Neel, James, 89
negative reciprocity, 288
"The Negro Family" (Moynihan), 267–68
Neither Man nor Woman (Nanda), 199
Nelly, 472, *472*

neocolonialism, 294 A continued pattern of unequal economic relations despite the formal end of colonial political and military control.

neoliberalism, 298–300, 369–70 An economic and political worldview that sees the free market as the main mechanism for ensuring economic growth, with a severely restricted role for government.

Nepal, polygyny and polyandry in, 262
Neshat, Shirin, *448*
Netherlands
    life expectancy in, *447*
    mati work in, 227–28
    same-sex marriage in, 264
    stock exchange of, *40*
New Hampshire House Bill 1319, *186*, 188
New Hampshire Interscholastic Athletic Association (NHIAA), 187, 188
New Hampshire Legislative Youth Advisory Council, 188
New Orleans, Louisiana
    Hurricane Katrina in, 340
    Mardi Gras beads used in, *84*
New York Chinese School, *36*
New York City, *27*, *70*, *83*, *167*
    COVID-19 pandemic in, 34
    diverse communities in, *13*
    green urban revitalization in, 351–52
    Harlem Birth Right Project, 154–55
    homeland connections for immigrants in, 27–29, 60
    homelessness and begging in, 70
    kindergartners learning Mandarin in, *36*
    migration from Fuzhou, China to, 318–21
    multi-sited ethnography in, 27–29
    school funding in, 152–53
    West African art sold via, 469–70
New Zealand, same-sex marriage in, 264
NGOs, *See* nongovernmental organizations
NHIAA, *See* New Hampshire Interscholastic Athletic Association
Nicaragua, sexuality in, 229, *229*
Niger, magic in, 407–8

Nigeria, 105, *105*, *447*
Nightwork (Allison), 229–30
"no," in sexual relations, 114
Nomad RSI, 430
Non, Ana Patricia, *4*, 6–7
nongovernmental organizations (NGOs), 370, 374–75
nonviolence toward living things *(ahimsa)*, 410
Nordstrom, Carolyn, 373, 375–76, 378
norepinephrine, 225

norms, 38–39 Ideas or rules about how people should behave in particular situations or toward certain other people.

North America, fur trade in, 291–92; *See also*
       specific countries
North Atlantic Biocultural Organisation, 19
North Dakota, *347*, 347–49
Norway, same-sex marriage in, 264

nuclear family, 251, 270–71 The kinship unit of mother, father, and children.

The Nuer (Evans-Pritchard), 46, 73–74
Nuer people, *73*, *254*
   kinship and descent for, 254, *255*, 258
   language of, 106
   polygyny for, 262
   reflexivity in fieldwork with, 78
   same-sex marriage in, 264
   social anthropological studies of, *72*, 73–74
Number Our Days (Myerhoff), 78–79
nutrition, *See* food and nutrition
Nyar people, 262
Nyimba people, 262

Oakland Unified School District, *111*
Obama, Barack, 143
Obergefell, Jim, *226*
offshoring, 23, 297–98
Ogden, Laura, 337–38
oil industry
   in Amazon jungle, 345–46
   Dakota Access Pipeline, *347*, 347–49
Oliveto, Karen, 272

Olkes, Cherl, 407
Omaha people, 255, *257*
one child policy, in China, 249–50
open-mindedness, 83–84
oral sex, 222
Orange is the New Black (television show), 199
orangutans, language and, 100
Organs Watch, 93
organ trafficking, *92*, 92–93
orientation, family of, 270

origin myth, 166 A story told about the founding and history of a particular group to reinforce a sense of common identity.

Ortner, Sherri, 203
Other-Worldly (Zhan), 432–33
Ottoman Empire, 182
Ouattara, Alassane, 282–83
#OurLivesMatter demonstration, 313–14
outsourcing, 23, 297, *298*
Ovsyannikova, Marina, *356*, 358
ovum, gender stereotypes and, 205–6, *206*
oxytocin, 225

Pacific Ocean, plastic pollution in, *26*, 26–27
paintings, in caves, *465*, 465–66, *466*

paleoanthropology, *15*, 16 The study of the history of human evolution through the fossil record.

Paleolithic cave paintings, *465*, 465–66, *466*
Palestine, *126*
Panama, *334*
Panama Canal, *334*, 334–36
Papua New Guinea, *324*; *See also* Trobriand Islands
   conservation in, 343–44
   life expectancy in, *447*

paralanguage, 103–4 An extensive set of noises (such as laughs, cries, sighs, and yells) and tones of voice that convey significant information about the speaker.

parallel cousins, 263

Paramaribo, Suriname, 227–28, *228*
Parkland, Florida, school shooting, 424–25

participant observation, 20, 73 A key anthropological research strategy involving both participation in and observation of the daily life of the people being studied.

Partners in Health (PIH), 443–44, 453
Pascoe, C. J., 195

pastoralism, 285 A strategy for food production involving the domestication of animals.

Pathways of Desire (Carrillo), 242–44
patience, 84

patrilineal descent group, 254, 258–60 A kinship group in which membership passes from the next generation from father to son.

Patterns of Culture (Benedict), 46
Patterson, Francine, *100*
peasant farm workers, rights of, 346–47
Pediatrics (journal), 198
people of color, racism targeting, 152,
    446–48
The People of Puerto Rico (Steward), 77
A People's History of the United States (Zinn),
    166
performance, as resistance, 473–74, *474*

periphery countries, 295, 296 The least-developed and least-powerful nations; often exploited by the core countries as sources of raw materials, cheap labor, and markets.

Personal Status courts, in Egypt, 383–85
Peru, brother-sister marriage in, 263
pesticides, *340*, 340–42, *341*
petroglyphs, 207
petting, 222
Peyote Hunt (Myerhoff), 78
Pham, Xuyen, *253*
Phelps, Michael, *432*

phenotype, 133–34 The way genes are expressed in an organism's physical form as a result of genotype interaction with environmental factors.

Philadelphia, Pennsylvania, COVID-19 pandemic
    in, 7
Philippines, *213*
    community pantry movement in, 6–7
    McDonald's menu adaptations in, 59, *59*
    migration of women from, 213–15
    organ trafficking in, *92*
    outsourcing to, 23, *298*
    pointing in, 103
Phipps, Susie, 142–43

phonemes, 102 The smallest units of sound that can make a difference in meaning.

phonology, 102 The study of what sounds exist and which ones are important in a particular language.

phosphate mining, *333*, 333–34

photographic gaze, 478 The presumed neutral viewpoint of the camera that in fact projects the perspective of the person behind the camera onto human nature, the natural world, and history.

physical anthropology, *See* biological anthropology
Picasso, Pablo, 463
PIH, *See* Partners in Health

pilgrimage, 399 A religious journey to a sacred place as a sign of devotion and in search of transformation and enlightenment.

plantation economy, in Caribbean and South
    America, 290–91
PlaNYC, 351
Plessy v. Ferguson, 152
police violence, protests against, *37*
political anthropology, 361–62
political systems
    bands, 362–63

prestige language, 107, 108 A particular language variation or way of speaking that is associated with wealth, success, education, and power.

primates, 16–17
    aggressiveness in, *372, 372–73*
    language and, 100
    sexuality in, 224, *224*

primatology, 16–17 The study of living nonhuman primates as well as primate fossils to better understand human evolution and early human behavior.

"primitive" art, 463–64
Primitive Culture (Tylor), 44
procreation, family of, 270

profane, 397 Anything that is considered unholy.

professional immigrants, 322 Highly trained individuals who move to fill economic niches in a middle-class profession often marked by shortages in the receiving country.

Progressive Dystopia (Shange), 313–14

proletariat, 306–7 Marxist term for the class of laborers who own only their labor.

pronouns, gender-neutral, 115
The Protestant Ethic and the Spirit of Capitalism (Weber), 403
Protestantism, secularization and, 403–4
protests and resistance
    anti-mask, *32,* 33–34
    art and, 473–74, *474*
    CO-MADRES of El Salvador, 208–11, *211*
    against dominant power relationships and structures, 52, *52*
    Emma Sulkowicz, *218,* 219–20
    gun violence, *156,* 424–25
    mask wearing in Brazil, *33,* 34–35
    Moral Mondays campaign, 390

Movement for Black Lives, 381–83
Muslim headscarf bans in France, 50, *50*
Poor People's Campaign: A National Call for Moral Revival, 389–91
of Russian invasion of Ukraine, *356,* 358, *360*
against suspicion based on language, *97*
proto-Germanic language, 101
proxemics, 103
Psychopathia Sexualis (Krafft-Ebing), 231
public health care system, in Haiti, 442–44
Puerto Rico
    ethnographic fieldwork in, 77
    farmworkers from, 174–76
Purity and Exile (Malkki), 171

pushes and pulls, 318 The forces that spur migration from the country of origin and draw immigrants to a particular new destination country.

Putin, Vladimir, 357

Qatar, COVID-19 response in, 452, *452*
qaug dab peg (epilepsy), 434–36
qi (breath or air), 432

qualitative data, 81 Descriptive data drawn from nonstatistical sources, including personal stories, interviews, life histories, and participant observation.

quantitative data, 81 Statistical information about a community that can be measured and compared.

Rabi Island, Fiji, 333–34

race A flawed system of classification, with no biological basis, that uses certain physical characteristics to divide the human population into supposedly discrete groups.
    biological assumptions, 131–34
        integrated gene pool, 132–33
        linking phenotype to genotype, 133–34
        overview, 131–32

classifications of, lack of biological basis for, 17–18, 42
colonialism and, 135–38
  in Brazil, 136–38
  overview, 135–36
concepts of, 42
COVID-19 and, 449–51, *451*
defined, 130
distribution of health and illness and, 445–48
general discussion, 129–31
intersections with
  class, 313–14
  sexuality, 236–37
language and, 109–12, *110*
in U.S. culture, 138–49
  census, 138–39
  constructing Whiteness, 139–41
  current concept of Whiteness, 148–49
  hypodescent, 142–43
  immigration, 143–48
  overview, 138
wealth inequality and, 312

racial democracy thesis, Brazil, 137

racial ideology, 153–54 A set of popular ideas about race that allows the discriminatory behaviors of individuals and institutions to seem reasonable, rational, and normal.

racialization, 147 The process of categorizing, differentiating, and attributing a particular racial character to a person or group of people.

racism Individuals' thoughts and actions and institutional patterns and policies that create or reproduce unequal access to power, privilege, resources, and opportunities based on imagined differences among groups.
  defined, 130
  environmental justice and, 351–52
  general discussion, 129–31
  in medical profession, 446–48
  resilience amid injury of, 156–57
  types of, 150–56

  individual racism, 150–51
  institutional racism, 151–53
  intersections of race and power systems, 154–55
  racial ideology, 153–54
  Whiteness and, 148–49

Racism without Racists (Bonilla-Silva), 153
Radcliffe-Brown, Alfred, 47
rain forests, 338, *338*
Rakhine State (Myanmar), *160*, 161–63, 166
Ralph, Laurence, 156–57
Ranger, Terence, 179
rape, 210, *218*, 219–20, 237–38

rapport, 81 Relationships of trust and familiarity that an anthropologist

develops with members of the community under study.
RCF, *See* Research and Conservation Foundation
Reading National Geographic (Lutz and Collins), 478–79
Real Queer? (Murray), 201–3

reciprocity, 287–88 The exchange of resources, goods, and services among people of relatively equal status; meant to create and reinforce social ties.

Recognizing Ourselves (Lewin), 234–35

redistribution, 288 A form of exchange in which accumulated wealth is collected from the members of the group and reallocated in a different pattern.

reflexivity, 78, 87 A critical self-examination of the role the anthropologist plays and an awareness that one's identity affects one's fieldwork and theoretical analyses.

refugees Persons who have been forced to move beyond their national borders because of political or religious persecution, armed conflict, or disasters.

same-sex marriage, 263–65, *272*, 272–73

Samoa, *74*

    gender roles in, 74–75

    sexual freedom and experimentation in, 46

San Antonio Food Bank, *6*

San Diego, California, gay Mexican immigrants in, *242*, 243–44

San Francisco, California, class and race in, *313*, 313–14

São Paulo, Brazil, anti-mask protests in, *32*, 33–34

Sapir, Edward, 105

Sapir–Whorf hypothesis, 105 The idea that different languages create different ways of thinking.

Saudi Arabia, life expectancy in, *447*

The Scattered Family (Coe), 273

Scheper-Hughes, Nancy, 37, 65–67, 79, 81, 85, 90–93

Schneider, David, 270

schools, *See* education and schools

schulmedizin (school medicine), 431

Scott, James, 52, 385

sea-level rise, 27, 329–30

secular, 403 Without religious or spiritual basis.

segregation, in U.S., 141, *141*, *152*

semiperiphery countries, *295*, 296 Nations ranking in between core and periphery countries, with some attributes of the core countries but with less of a central role in the global economy.

Senegal, life expectancy in, *447*

senses, art and, 461–62

September 11, 2001 terrorist attacks, 50

serial monogamy, 263

Seri people, *120*

serotonin, 225

Service, Elman, 363, 364

settler colonialism, 348 Displacement and pacification of indigenous people and expropriation of their lands and resources.

sex characteristics, asylum claims based on, 201–3

sex education class, 239

sex(es) The observable physical differences between male and female, especially biological differences related to human reproduction.

    alternate, 199–200

    defined, 190

    theory of five sexes, 197–98

sex hormones, 224–25

sexology, 231–32

sexual assault, on college campuses, *218*, 219–20, 237–38

Sexual Citizens (Hirsch and Khan), 238–39

sexual citizenship, 237–39

sexual dimorphism, 190–91 The phenotypic differences between males and females of the same species.

sexual geographics, 238

sexuality, 219–45 The complex range of desires, beliefs, and behaviors that are related to erotic physical contact and the cultural arena within which people debate about what kinds of physical desires and behaviors are right, appropriate, and natural.

    in advertising, *222*, 226

    asylum seekers with SOGIESC claims, 201–3

    cross-cultural variations, 46

    culture and, 225–26

    defined, 223

    ethnocartography of, 230

    globalization and, 241–44

    global perspective, 227–30

        Japan, 229–30

        Nicaragua, 229

        Suriname, 227–28

    intersection of biology and, 223–26

    Mardi Gras beads and nudity, *84*

    in Martinique, *340*, 340–42, *341*

    overview, 222–23

    power and, 235–41

shaman, 404–5 Part-time religious practitioners with special abilities to connect individuals with supernatural powers or beings.

sickness, 427 An individual's public expression of illness and disease, including social expectations about how one should behave and how others will respond.; *See also* health

situational negotiation of identity, 166 An individual's self-identification with a particular group that can shift according to social location.

social media, 477 New forms of communication based on computer- and Internet-based technologies that facilitate social engagement, work, and pleasure.

social mobility, 308 The movement of one's class position, upward or downward, in stratified societies.

social movement, 379–81 Collective group actions that seek to build institutional networks to transform cultural patterns and government policies.

social network analysis, 82 A method for examining relationships in a community, often conducted by identifying whom people turn to in times of need.

social reproduction, 308 The phenomenon whereby social and class relations of prestige or lack of prestige are passed from one generation to the next.

society, 46 The focus of early British anthropological research whose structure and function could be isolated and studied scientifically.

sociolinguistics, 107 The study of the ways culture shapes language and language shapes culture, particularly the intersection of language with cultural categories and systems of power such as age, race, ethnicity, sexuality, gender, and class.

sociolinguists, 20 Those who study language in its social and cultural contexts.

speech community, 102 A group of people who come to share certain norms of language use through living and communicating together.

state, 365–69 An autonomous regional structure of political, economic, and military rule with a central government authorized to make laws and use force to maintain order and defend its territory.

stratification, 49, 305 The uneven distribution of resources and privileges among participants in a group or culture.; *See also* **gender stratification**

structural functionalism, 46–47 A conceptual framework positing that each element of society serves a particular function to keep the entire system in equilibrium.

Tolkien, J. R. R., *405*
Torah scroll, as symbol in Judaism, 409, *411*
trade routes, *289*

transgender, 191 A gender identity or performance that does not fit with cultural norms related to one's assigned sex at birth.

transgender people
  engaged anthropology with, 79
  in Hinduism, 199
  in Native American cultures, 200, *200*
  rights of, *186*, 187–88, *200*
transnational citizenship, in Eritrea,
    179–80
Transparent (television show), 199
Treaty of Fort Laramie, 347

triangle trade, 290–92, *291* The extensive exchange of slaves, sugar, cotton, and furs between Europe, Africa, and the Americas that transformed economic, political, and social life on both sides of the Atlantic.

tribe, 363–64 Originally viewed as a culturally distinct, multiband population that imagined itself as one people descended from a common ancestor; currently used to describe an indigenous group with its own set of loyalties and leaders living to some extent outside the control of a centralized authoritative state.

Trinidad, 109
Trobriand Islands, 46, *73*, 204
  exchange system in, *72*
  women in economy of, 77–78, *204*, 204–5
Trouillot, Michel-Rolph, 342
Trump, Donald J., 97
Truth, Sojourner, 155
Tsukiji Fish Market, *304*, 304–5
Tucson, Arizona, 70, *70*
tuna trade, *304*, 304–5
Turner, Victor, 46, 79, 398–99
Tutsis, 169–72
Two-Spirits, 200, *200*

Tylor, Edward B., 44, 45, *45*, 71

Ukraine, Russian invasion of, 357–59, *360*
UN, *See* United Nations

underdevelopment, 295 The term used to suggest that poor countries are poor as a result of their relationship to an unbalanced global economic system.

uneven development, 24 The unequal distribution of the benefits of globalization.

unilineal cultural evolution, 45 The theory proposed by nineteenth-century anthropologists that all cultures naturally evolve through the same sequence of stages from simple to complex.

unilineal descent groups, 254
United Kingdom; *See also* Great Britain
  life expectancy in, *447*
  same-sex marriage in, 264
United Methodist Church, 272
United Nations (UN)
  child soldiers defined by, 374
  in Côte d'Ivoire conflict, 282
  Declaration on the Rights of Peasants and
      Other People Working in Rural Areas, 347
  High Commissioner for Refugees, *377*
  sustainable development goals of, 350
United States
  advertising in, 57
  agriculture in, 174–76
  arms sales by, 378
  consumerism in, 56, 57, *57*
  COVID-19 pandemic in, 34, 450–51, *451*
  cultural worldview of, 37, 478–79
  debt in, 57
  ethnicity in, 174–78
  exogamy, 264
  fieldwork in American South, 75–77
  financial recession of 2008 in, 300–301
  fossil fuel production, 347–49
  gender in, 191, 193–95, *194*, 205–8
  Gregorian calendar, 42

universal gaze, 462 An intrinsic way of perceiving art-thought by many in the Western art world to be found across cultures-that informs what people consider to be art or not art.

values, 39–40 Fundamental beliefs about what is important, what makes a good life, and what is true, right, and beautiful.

visual anthropology, 477 A field of anthropology that explores the production, circulation, and consumption of visual images, focusing on the power of visual representation to influence culture and cultural identity.

power and, 359
Russian invasion of Ukraine, 357–59, *360*
state and, 373–75
Warehouse, in New York City, 469–70
"Warfare Is Only an Invention—Not a Biological
   Necessity" (Mead), 359
Washington Commanders, 43–44
Washoe (chimpanzee), 100
Washoe people, *120*
water resources, stress of human activity on, 26–27
Watson, James, 59

wealth, 303, 311–12 The total value of what
someone owns, minus any debt.

The Wealth of Nations (Smith), 299
Weapons of the Weak (Scott), 52
Weber, Max, 307–8, 368, 396–97, 403, *403*, 405, 409, 410
wedding culture and industry, 232–34, *233*
   constructing heterosexuality, 233–34
   inequality and unequal access, 234
Weiner, Annette, 77–78, 204–5
Weinreich, Max, 107
Wekker, Gloria, 227–28
Wendell, Turk, *409*
West, Paige, 343–44
West Africa
   art from, *467*, 467–69, *468*, *470*
   magic in, 407–8
   migration from, *323*, 323–24, *324*
Western cultures
   art and, 46–464
   development model of, 294
   health care and, 427, 430–31
   homosexual identity in, 228
   religion in, 403–4, 410
   state model, 366–68
Weston, Kath, 230, 271
whales, communication and, 99
white-collar workers, 307
Whitehouse, Bruce, 323

Whiteness A culturally constructed concept
originating in 1691 Virginia designed to establish
clear boundaries of who is white and who is not,

a process central to the formation of U.S. racial
stratification.
   constructing in U.S. culture, 139–41
   current concept of, 148–49
   defined, 140
   poverty and, 149
   in rural Kentucky, 309–10
   "unmarked" category, *150*

White privilege, 140–41, 147–49
"White Privilege" (McIntosh), 147–48

White supremacy, 140, 141 The belief that
whites are biologically different from and superior
to people of other races.

White Weddings (Ingraham), 232–34
Whorf, Benjamin L., 105
Why We Love (Fisher), 224–25
Williams, Brackette, 70
wine, as symbol in Christianity, 410
Winegar, Jessica, 474–76
Wiradyana, Ketut, *15*
witchcraft, 405–7
Witchcraft, Oracles, and Magic among the Azande
   (Evans-Pritchard), 405–7
Wolf, Eric, 48, 77, 85
women; *See also* gender
   art and, *472*, 472–74
   economic independence and martial dissolu-
      tion for, 262
   economic role of, 77–78, 204–5, *205*
   engaged anthropology with, 79
   HIV/AIDS for, 203
   hunter-gatherer stereotype for, 206–8, *207*
   in labor force, 212–13, *213*
   language use by, 112–14, *115*
   migration by, 213–15, 321
   in military, 192, *192*
   perception of color by, 106
   in politics, 203
   poverty for, 203
   pregnancy for, *66*, 66–67, 203
Women of Value, Men of Renown (Weiner), 204
Worked to the Bone (Buck), 140–41, 309–10

zeros, 84 Elements of a story or a picture that are not told or seen and yet offer key insights into issues that might be too sensitive to discuss or display publicly.